D0334175

Product Strategy and Management

MICHAEL BAKER

AND

SUSAN HART

PRENTICE HALL

LONDON • NEW YORK • TORONTO • SYDNEY • TOKYO

SINGAPORE • MADRID • MEXICO CITY • MUNICH • PARIS

First published 1988 by
Prentice Hall
A Pearson Education company
Edinburgh Gate, Harlow
Essex CM20 2JE, England

© Prentice Hall 1999

Typeset in 9.75/12pt Galliard
by Acorn Bookwork, Salisbury, Wiltshire.

Printed and bound in Great Britain by
Redwood Books, Wilts.

Library of Congress Cataloging-in-Publication Data

Baker, Michael John
    Product strategy and management / Michael Baker and Susan Hart.
        p.   cm.
    Includes bibliographical references and index.
    ISBN 0-13-065368-3
    1. Product management.   2. New products—Management—Case studies.
    I. Hart, Susan J.   II. Title.
    HF5415. 15.B353   1998
    658.5′6—DC20
                                                    96-25428
                                                      CIP
                                                      Rev.

British Library Cataloguing in Publication Data

A catalogue record for this book is available from
the British Library

ISBN 0-13-065368-3

2   3   4   5   03   02   01   00   99

Contents

chapter 1

....

Product strategy and management

Introduction
....

Few, if any, would challenge the view that specialization enhances efficiency, increases productivity and adds value. Indeed, it is the principle of specialization which has been the main driver of human progress and improved standards of living since time immemorial. However, for specialization to succeed as a strategy certain conditions need to be satisfied. Of these the most important is a mechanism for effecting exchanges of the goods and services created which also has the ability to balance the supply of the different goods and services with the demand for them. Markets and price satisfy these conditions and are central to the functions of production and consumption.

Of these two functions – production and consumption – the former is the more important because, ultimately, it determines what *can* be made available to be consumed. Obviously, the value added by production will be optimized when it reflects consumption needs and it is for this reason that, in the second half of this century, the emphasis has tended to be on the customer and the market whereas, previously, it was on the producer and the factory. This change in emphasis, occasioned by continuous and rapid improvements on the production or supply side, has resulted in the current preoccupation with competition and marketing and a tendency to overlook or play down production. This tendency is to be avoided if for no other reason than that production is concerned with the creation of *products* (and services) and it is these which form the whole *raison d'être* for exchange. Without them there would be no markets, no customers, no competition and certainly no marketing. Yet, while product strategy and management are at the very heart of the exchange process there are relatively few books on the subject.

In most marketing texts the product is regarded as only one of the four P's or elements which go to make up the marketing mix, and frequently the space given to it is less than that given to selling and promotion. Further, those books which do deal with product strategy and management in any detail tend to dwell largely on the process of new product development and neglect all other aspects. In the field of medicine this would be equivalent to training doctors in gynaecology and obstetrics but ignoring all other branches of health care! This book seeks to address this imbalance.

Perspective
....

As hinted in the Introduction our *objective* in writing this book is to offer a holistic discussion and explanation of product strategy and management. Our *perspective* is that in

1

commerce, as in life, our primary and basic objective is to survive. In a volatile and turbulent environment survival will only be achieved by the fittest and most flexible organizations able to adapt to the changes confronting them. To survive one must compete, and the *purpose* of this book is to show why product strategy is fundamental to a firm's competitiveness and why and how product management can help achieve and sustain this.

In our view, product strategy lies at the very heart of the firm's overall strategy and must occupy a dominant, if not *the* dominant, position in the firm's thoughts and actions. As such, knowledge and understanding of the nature and practice of product strategy and management is a necessary element in the development and formation of the professional manager. Indeed, issues related to product strategy and management (PSM) are among the few which are common to the curricula of both engineers and business students. Similarly, the manufacture and sale of specific products is the usual training ground for new entrants to industry so that an understanding of PSM provides an invaluable foundation on which to build. This book has been developed particularly to meet this need and is based on the authors' experience of teaching final-year undergraduate and postgraduate students in both the engineering and business faculties of two leading 'technological' universities.

While we are conscious of the danger of omnibus claims which suggest that books intended to support formal courses of study are equally relevant for practising managers, we believe the latter may also derive benefit from parts of the text. As we explain in the next section, the book falls naturally into four major parts, the first of which explores the theoretical underpinnings of the subject, while the remaining three deal with practical management issues and contain specific advice on techniques and methods of direct value to practitioners. Thus, while the book has been conceived as a holistic treatment of the subject, individual chapters or sections of them may serve equally well to underpin the focused discussion of specific issues.

Structure

As mentioned above, the book is divided into four major parts:

Part 1: The Theoretical Foundations
Part 2: New Product Development
Part 3: Product Management
Part 4: Product Elimination.

The first part, *The Theoretical Foundations*, comprises five chapters. Chapter 2, *Competition and Product Strategy*, traces briefly the factors which underlie the present preoccupation with 'competitiveness' and of what we term the 'rediscovery' of marketing as a major source of sustainable competitive advantage (SCA). It is from this review and analysis that we conclude that product strategy lies at the very heart of the firm's overall strategy and so must occupy a dominant position in its thinking and actions.

In Chapter 3, *The Product in Theory and Practice*, we open with a discussion of the precise nature of products as artefacts or objects which are conceived and developed to satisfy customer needs. This leads naturally into consideration of how customer needs are converted into *demand* and the factors which influence it. While the primary function of a product is determined by its attributes and performance characteristics, the salience and perception of these will vary considerably between different potential users. This observation prompts analysis of the role of objective and subjective factors as determinants of demand, and of the role of branding as a technique which enables both buyers and sellers to 'chunk' large amounts of information and develop preferences for highly specific products. The chapter concludes with an examination of the nature and influence of novelty in buying decisions and an assessment of whether services, or intangible products, merit separate treatment.

Any attempt to describe and define the product in theory and practice leads to the inevitable conclusion that this depends very largely on the individual buyer's perceptions and behaviour. Accordingly, Chapter 4, *Buyer Behaviour*, is an in-depth evaluation of this topic. Following consideration of some of the many different models of buyer behaviour and of the importance of perception as a mediating variable, we propose a simple, composite model of our own which seeks to integrate the key factors involved in the buying decision process. Analysis indicates that much consumption is habitual and the repetition of past learned behaviour. Changing this behaviour is often difficult and subject to resistance, representing a major challenge to sellers in both established and emerging markets. The chapter concludes with an examination of how innovation, or new product development, may be used to precipitate such change.

Chapter 5, *The Product Life Cycle in Theory and Practice*, develops the theme that while change may be difficult to initiate it is both inevitable and the wellspring of human progress. Central to the chapter is an extended discussion of the concept of the product life cycle (PLC) which posits that, like biological organisms, all products pass through a series of stages starting with gestation and culminating in elimination. As will be seen, this concept and analogy is not without its critics, but we will argue strongly that it provides a powerful analytical framework with which to organize all our thinking about product strategy and management.

Chapter 6, *Product Portfolios*, is a logical development of the more theoretical content of the preceding chapter as it addresses the issues and problems actually involved in managing products at various stages of their life cycles. The central theme and organizing principle for the chapter is that if products do have life cycles then the continued existence of the firm will depend upon its having more than one product. Indeed, we will argue that successful firms need a portfolio of products at different stages of their respective life cycles which mutually reinforce and support one another. This chapter rounds out the theoretical discussion and paves the way for the more practical issues comprising the remainder of the book.

Part 2, *New Product Development* (NPD), contains seven chapters dealing with different aspects of the process by which ideas and market opportunities are brought together so as to enable new companies to enter or create markets and established companies to protect and enhance their competitive position. As mentioned before, this topic is the focus of most books which purport to deal with product strategy and management. Many of them contain more detail than is possible in a comprehensive book like this and reference will be made to them where appropriate. That said, it is necessary to remember that, important as NPD is, it represents only one aspect of the firm's business and is highly dependent on the successful management of existing products (Parts 3 and 4) for its funding.

The first chapter in this part (Chapter 7) deals with the process of new product development, or what is sometimes called 'The Normative Theory'. In the social sciences, of which business and management is one, most theory is derived from empirical observation of what managers actually do, which leads to conclusions about the most effective way of doing things. In other words, we are dealing with a normative theory which can be learned by others, so avoiding the potentially negative outcomes of learning from experience. The process of NPD has been the subject of a great deal of observation and research, and there is now widespread agreement about the stages involved and the sequence in which the process develops.

In this chapter we begin with a review of the literature concerning success and failure in new product development. Here the paradox is that while NPD is regarded as essential to continuing corporate success, a high proportion of new products fail, representing a loss to their developers. Obviously anything which can improve the 'strike rate' is to be pursued assiduously and we identify what are generally regarded to be the success and failure factors.

To a very large degree success and failure depend upon organization and management of the new product development process, and we give these topics and models of the process itself extended treatment.

Given an understanding of the process and various approaches to its structuring and management, Chapter 8 deals with *New Product Strategy*. Specifically, we consider the need for an explicit new product innovation strategy and then explore in detail the essential components of such a strategy.

Chapters 9 to 13 deal with the key stages of the NPD process in depth. Chapter 9 addresses the question of *Idea Management for New Product Development* and provides a detailed discussion of what is involved in stimulating creativity and of the many sources of ideas available both internally and externally.

Once a pool of ideas has been generated, it is necessary to evaluate these in order to select those which offer the greatest market opportunity and will make greatest use of the firm's skills and competencies. Chapter 10, *Screening New Product Ideas*, describes precisely how to do this.

Chapter 11, *Concept Development and Testing*, recognizes that while members of the NPD team may be happy with their short list of ideas which have survived the screening process, they may not have the same appeal to others – especially the intended customer. Accordingly, this chapter discusses the objectives and purposes of concept testing and then describes a variety of techniques which may be used to articulate and test product concepts.

Assuming that a *prima facie* case is established that the concept is both meaningful and attractive to the intended market, as well as the members of the firm who make up the internal market, then the concept should be subjected to formal *Business Analysis*, the subject of Chapter 12. This is a particularly critical and important stage. Up to this point the firm will need to commit very little other than thinking time to the process. To undertake a business analysis, assumptions about market size and production and distribution costs will need to be firmed up. The marketers may well have to undertake formal market research while the development engineers and production managers develop prototypes to establish the costs of manufacturing the new product. It is these topics which are the subject of this chapter.

Chapter 13, *Product Testing*, marks the transition from a largely paper-based exercise into the physical creation and testing of the product. Capital investment will be required and this may be large where a radically new product is proposed. It is at this stage that design and production engineers bring the product to life and ensure that it meets the agreed specifications in terms of cost and performance. The chapter discusses the decisions involved in constructing valid product tests and the methods employed in executing them. If successful the product is now ready for commercialization and the start of its life cycle. The remainder of the book is concerned with the management of this life cycle.

As stated earlier, a distinguishing feature of this book is that it takes a *holistic* approach. Thus, while many authors and texts see commercialization as the final step in the NPD process (which it is), we prefer to regard it as the first step of a management process which will only end when the product is dropped or eliminated from the firm's product portfolio. Conventionally, the PLC is seen as having four basic phases – Introduction, Growth, Maturity and Decline. We prefer a 'stretched' variant of this basic concept which conceives of a period of *gestation* preceding the launch or introduction of a new product (the subject of Part 2 of this book). Product introduction or *Commercialization* is the subject of Chapter 14, while Chapter 15 deals with *Managing Growth* and Chapter 16 with *Managing the Mature Product* (we identify two phases in maturity – maturity and *saturation*).

Again, conventionally, the final phase of the PLC was seen as one of decline. Given that products in decline were generally regarded as having reduced or no profitability, little attention was given to this phase. A distinctive feature of this book is that while it recognizes that declining products will eventually have to be withdrawn from the marketplace it also perceives the potential for managing the process in a profitable way. In light of this belief we have clustered Chapters 14, 15 and 16 into Part 3, *Product Management*, and have developed three separate chapters for Part 4, *Product Elimination*, i.e. Chapter 17, *Controlling the Product Line*; Chapter 18, *Reaching the Decision to Delete a Product*; and Chapter 19, *Implementing the Deletion Decision*.

All of the chapters in Parts 3 and 4 take a managerial perspective and describe and discuss not only *what* needs to be done and *why* but perhaps more importantly *how*. It is this combination of theory and practice which we believe differentiates this book from others in its field and makes it suitable both as a core text and as a source of reference and advice for practitioners.

As a core text we have incorporated a number of features which we hope will improve the book's accessibility to the reader and also reinforce the learning process. Each chapter is preceded by a set of learning objectives. These are reinforced by the use of subheadings to signpost the major themes and topics. There is a short summary to every chapter to remind the reader what has been covered as well as questions to test memory and understanding. To reinforce learning still further, a short case study accompanies most of the chapters so that the reader may evaluate the application of the knowledge content to the solution of a relevant problem.

Finally, the book ends with a *Reprise* in which we summarize the key points which have been covered in the preceding chapters.

part 1

The Theoretical Foundations

chapter 2

Competition and product strategy

LEARNING OBJECTIVES

1. To describe the emergence of global competition.
2. To define the contribution of marketing to competitive success.
3. To establish the importance and impact of environmental change.
4. To describe the nature and relevance of life cycles to the process of evolutionary change.
5. To define the nature of competition and the basic forces which shape it.
6. To identify the basic alternative strategies open to the firm.
7. To establish the nature and importance of product strategy and management.

On completion of this chapter you will:

1. Understand the forces which have given rise to intense, global competition.
2. Be able to explain why marketing is an important source of competitive success.
3. Appreciate and be able to account for the process of evolutionary change and the life cycle phenomenon.
4. Be able to define the nature of competition, the forces which drive it and the two basic strategies of cost leadership and differentiation.
5. Understand and be able to explain the importance of product strategy and management.

Introduction

In commerce, as in life, the primary and basic objective is to survive. In a volatile and turbulent environment survival will only be achieved by the fittest and most flexible organizations able to adapt to the changes confronting them. To survive one must compete, and the purpose of this book is to show why product strategy is fundamental to a firm's competitiveness and how product strategy and management can achieve this.

In this chapter we trace briefly the factors which have resulted in the current preoccupation with the 'rediscovery' of marketing which has been presented as a major source of competitiveness. To define competitiveness it is necessary first to define competition, and we review current thinking on this subject, drawing, *inter alia*, on the writings of Ansoff, Drucker and Porter. Based upon this review it will be argued that, fundamentally, product strategy lies at the very heart of the firm's overall strategy and so must occupy a dominant position in the firm's thinking and actions.

The emergence of global competition

Competition is the process by which the 'invisible hand' of the market seeks to solve the basic economic problem of maximizing satisfaction from the consumption of scarce resources. Since the beginning of recorded time the greatest challenge facing humanity has been the management of scarcity – the ability to exercise a degree of control over an often hostile environment and so secure physical survival. Through organizational innovation (task specialization and the division of labour), social innovation (the establishment of markets and exchange) and technological innovation (the harnessing of energy, creation of tools, etc.) history is an almost continuous record of progress to the achievement of this ultimate goal – the elimination of want.

Paradoxically, however, the solution to the problem of improving the quality of life has delayed its actual achievement. With every improvement in people's control over their environment the chances of survival were improved thus stimulating an increased demand from an enlarged population. Thus, it was not until this century that, in any significant way (i.e the level of a national economy), supply creation was able to meet, let alone exceed, demand. Of course, there have been occasions in the past when an excess supply has existed on a limited and local basis, but it is only recently that there has developed any real prospect of these conditions prevailing into the foreseeable future.

Perhaps the first manifestation of the problems which accompany excess supply (or a lack of demand) was the world-wide depression of the 1920s and 1930s. Then, as now, numerous solutions, fiscal and economic, were proposed to alleviate the problem but, in retrospect, it was rearmament and the outbreak of war which solved the problem of unemployment and under-utilized manufacturing capacity. Following the war, reconstruction and the satisfaction of deferred consumer demand was sufficient to keep the major industrial economies fully occupied, at least until around the middle 1950s. About this time the US economy again began to exhibit signs that supply was beginning to run ahead of demand, with an increased emphasis upon high-pressure selling and vigorous promotion to help boost flagging sales. Although such efforts can only help alleviate the symptoms in the short term, they led to widespread criticism of the dangers of materialism (Galbraith, Packard) and the search for an alternative paradigm to the prevailing view that much consumption was the consequence of unscrupulous salesmen foisting unwanted goods on gullible and unsuspecting consumers. It was consideration of the roles of buyer and seller which led Peter Drucker (1954) to pronounce that 'Marketing is the distinguishing, the unique function of the business'.

Marketing had been rediscovered!

What links competitiveness, marketing and product strategy?

Forty years on, however, there is still much controversy and debate about the nature and scope of marketing and its role in contributing to the survival of the firm. The essence or concept of marketing is concerned with 'mutually satisfying exchange relationships' – the idea that two parties can freely enter into an exchange of objects (or services) of commercial value in such a way that it will enhance the value for both of them. Indeed, if this were not the case the exchange would not occur as there would be no purpose or logic to it. But, while mutual satisfaction is the objective, the interests of one party must determine the courses of action open to the other. Ever since Adam Smith (1776) asserted that 'The sole end and purpose of production is consumption', the interests of the consumer have been recognized as being dominant. If this is so then it follows that decisions about what to produce, where, in what quantities, etc. must be determined by reference to consumer demand. It is for this reason that phrases like 'customer oriented' and 'market driven' have become clichés in the current business vocabulary – all are agreed that such an emphasis is a necessary condition for success. What has changed significantly in the past 30 to 40 years has been the emergence of global competition which, in many cases, has turned the original concept of comparative advantage on its head.

According to Ricardo's original conceptualization, economic efficiency would be optimized when nations based their production decisions on the creation of those goods or services where they enjoyed a natural advantage over other potential producers and then engaged in international exchange to the mutual benefit of both importer and exporter. The problem with such an objectively attractive proposition is that it makes no allowance for the subjective aspirations of the people constituting the various nation states of the world. Whether it be a matter of national pride or national security few, if any, countries are prepared to concentrate solely on those activities in which they enjoy some comparative advantage if it results in their becoming dependent upon some other nation for goods or services considered essential to an adequate standard of living.

More recently Michael Porter has developed the ideas introduced in *Competitive Strategy* (1980) and *Competitive Advantage* (1985) into an analysis of *The Competitive Advantage of Nations* (1990) in which he challenges the views of classical economists who attribute national prosperity to a country's natural endowment of land, labour and capital. As Baker (1992) points out, Porter asserts that prosperity is *created*, not inherited, and depends upon the capacity of a country's industry to innovate and upgrade. Porter (1990) comments:

> A nation's endowment of factors clearly plays a role in the competitive advantage of a nation's firms, as the rapid growth of manufacturing in low-wage countries such as Hong Kong, Taiwan, and more recently, Thailand attests. But the role of factors is far more complex than is often understood. The factors most important to competitive advantage in most industries, especially the growth in advanced economies, are not inherited but created within a nation, through processes that differ widely across nations and among industries. Thus, the stock of factors at any particular time is less important than the rate at which they are created, upgraded and made more specialised in particular industries. (p. 74)

This assertion builds on his earlier (p. 45) statement that:

> 'Firms create competitive advantage by perceiving or discovering new and better ways to compete in an industry and bringing them to market, which is ultimately an act of innovation. *Innovation* is here defined broadly, to include both improvements in technology and better methods of doing things. It can be manifested in product changes, process changes, new approaches to marketing, new forms of distribution, and new conceptions of scope.'

What Porter, essentially an economist, terms innovation is what business people, and especially marketers, refer to as *new product and process development* (NPPD) which constitutes the major theme of this book, the balance being concerned with the successful management of new products and processes through the remainder of their life cycle following their first introduction.

As noted elsewhere (Baker, 1992):

> 'Frequently, innovation occurs when firms identify a new market opportunity or a segment of a market which has been neglected by those serving the market as they understand it. Thus the Japanese success in world auto markets (both cars and motor cycles) was based upon the production of small, high quality, high-performance machines when the prevailing fashion was for large, comparatively low-performance machines. By definition innovation consists of *doing something new* and so must overcome the inertia of the old, established and hitherto successful way of doing things. It is for this reason that innovation is often precipitated by an "outsider" or a "newcomer" who is unaware of the thousand and one reasons why the existing way of doing things cannot be changed.
>
> Basically, however, humans possess only a limited range of needs (see Maslow's needs hierarchy) so that innovation represents an improved way of serving an existing and known need. It was for this reason that in "Marketing myopia" [*Harvard Business Review*, 1960] Ted Levitt exhorted suppliers to define markets in terms of the need served such as transportation, entertainment, "fast food", convenience, etc. rather than in terms of the current products through which these needs were served. Thus the vast majority of innovations are substitute products which offer a more satisfying way of meeting a consumer need. Given that consumers are motivated more by self-interest than by supplier loyalty it is unsurprising that innovations will displace existing products or ideas if they offer enhanced satisfaction.
>
> It follows that a necessary condition for competitive success is that one's own product is at least equivalent to that of one's competitors. Thus the ultimate goal of competition is usually seen as having a "better" product than one's competitors. Indeed, it is a truism that no company can survive unless a sufficient number of customers hold that view so as to ensure that it can achieve a profitable sales volume. Overall "better" reflects a combination of both objective and subjective factors as implied by Rogers' (1962) definition of "relative advantage". In most cases the objective characteristics of a product are a *sine qua non* of the intending consumers' willingness even to consider it – if you want to buy a washing machine you don't look in a car showroom! However, the value attached to particular objective features of a product will vary significantly according to the intending users' attitudes, knowledge, discretionary purchasing power, etc. In other words, they are *situation specific*. They also *change over time*.'

If one accepts this diagnosis then it becomes clear that while the prevailing preference is to avoid or resist change – because change implies risk and uncertainty, of having to learn new ways and modify old habits – in the real world one can only improve one's position by encouraging and accepting change. For producers this means that they must continuously develop new products and processes, because otherwise any competitive advantage they possess will be eroded by other organizations which seek new and improved ways of satisfying the customers' needs. While this has always been true, it is only in the second half of this century that competition has become truly global in nature, and a brief survey of major changes in this period is necessary to help understand the current competitive position and why marketing and NPPD have come to assume such a central role in determining competitive success.

Marketing and competitive success

In the period following the conclusion of the Second World War there was a significant acceleration in the scope and intensity of international competition. During the late 1940s and 1950s much economic effort was devoted to making good the losses occasioned by the war so that the emphasis was upon the restoration of national domestic economies. In parallel with the post-war reconstruction taking place in Europe and Japan a number of developing countries sought to improve their economic performance through industrialization leading to the establishment of a new group of NICs (newly industrializing countries).

Initially much of the increased output of countries like West Germany, Japan, Hong Kong, Singapore, Taiwan, etc. was consumed domestically. But, as growth slowed, these countries began to look to international markets in order to sustain economic growth. Thus, the 1960s and early 1970s witnessed the steady growth of international trade and a marked change in the standing of traditional trading countries such as the USA and the UK. From the mid-1970s onwards the 'threat' of this increasing competition resulted in more and more attention being given to the sources of competitive advantage and the nature of competitive success.

The nature of the threat and the appropriate response are to be found documented in two seminal publications. The first, 'Managing our way to economic decline' by Bob Hayes and Bill Abernathy, appeared in the July/August 1980 issue of the *Harvard Business Review*. In drawing attention to the USA's decline in competitiveness in international markets and the import penetration of domestic markets, such as automobiles and electronics, which it had 'invented', Hayes and Abernathy pointed out that even the UK had outperformed the USA in terms of economic growth over the past two decades. The diagnosis was an over-emphasis upon a financial/sales orientation, the key features of which may be summarized as:

- The emphasis tends to be upon short-range profit at the expense of growth and longer-range profit. Budgeting and forecasting frequently pre-empt business planning.
- Efficiency may out-rank effectiveness as a management criterion.
- Pricing, cost, credit, service and other policies may be based on false economy influences and lack of marketplace realism.

- The business focus is not on the customer and market but on internal considerations and numbers.

The other seminal publication which could be seen as a response to Hayes and Abernathy's concern was the best-selling *In Search of Excellence* (1982) by Thomas Peters and Robert Waterman.

The subtitle of Peters and Waterman's book – *Lessons from America's best run companies* – helps to explain how it captured the imagination of American managers. This was the real thing, an insight into how eminently successful and widely admired corporations managed their affairs. As Baker and Hart (1989) note, the success of *In Search of Excellence* and other such best-sellers is that they themselves conform with a formula for success, namely:

- They assert the superiority of American management and systems.
- They stress entrepreneurial values and the money-making ethic which had been so strongly challenged by the consumerist movement in the 1960s and 1970s.
- They are based upon the analysis of the practice and procedure of firms or people who are leaders in their field and manifestly successful.
- They reduce the ingredients of success to simple catechisms or formulae.
- They emphasize that the essential catalyst and hero of the piece is the manager himself.

But the managerial best-sellers were not without their critics. Based upon an extensive review of the literature, Baker and Hart (Chapter 1) came to a number of conclusions concerning a real understanding of the possible relationship between marketing and competitive performance:

1. While a number of suggestions have been made regarding the *practical* nature of a 'marketing orientation', the majority of writers have been content with a broad and general statement that a marketing orientation enhances success.
2. There is a tendency for many authors to focus solely on the organizational dimensions of marketing: the *trappings* rather than the *substance*.
3. Empirical work has often been concerned with only one or two factors and their effect on corporate success. This means that having carried out a literature review, a broad view is gained of how important the variable under consideration is to the success of the company, but no indication is obtained of the *relative importance* of each variable in the total number of factors. A more comparative investigation of the variables would greatly improve knowledge in the area.
4. Empirical studies, where they have been undertaken, have often been confined to *one industry*, which limits the findings to the industry under investigation.
5. A large number of authors write *normatively*, and this widens the gulf between theory and practice. That theorists and practitioners do not see some managerial issues in the same way is an indication of the work that needs to be done by researchers.

6. The various articles dealing with this subject have been written in different countries at different times and pertain to the economic and social environments which existed *at the time the study was executed*. Such environments, in many cases, are no longer applicable to marketing in the 1990s and beyond.

7. A number of key empirical studies have identified the characteristics of successful companies, etc., without attempting to verify if such characteristics are also present in *less successful* companies. Some progress towards defining what is *exclusive* to successful firms would consolidate findings which would otherwise remain uncontested and invalidated.

It was against this background that Baker and Hart undertook a survey with a rigorous design to try and remedy the weaknesses noted in earlier work, Readers requiring the full detail of this study should refer to Baker and Hart's original book. However, it will be helpful here to present the multi-factor model which guided both a consideration of other work and the survey of actual practice. In Figure 2.1 it can be seen that five sets of factors – environmental, strategic, marketing, organizational and managerial – are generally invoked in seeking to explain business performance. All but managerial factors are the subject of more extended discussion in this book. Based upon extensive qualitative research involving depth

Figure 2.1 ● Factors influencing competitive success (*source*: Baker and Hart, 1989)

interviews with industry leaders, government officials, management writers and other academics, a formal questionnaire was developed for administration to a representative sample of companies with the overall objective of measuring the contribution of marketing factors to competitive success.

In order to avoid the criticisms levelled against earlier studies, it was decided to sample both growth and mature or declining industries (sunrise and sunset). Within these industries respondents were selected who were successful or less successful within the industry by comparison with three performance indicators – sales growth, average profit margin, and average return on capital employed. The details of the final sample composition and the findings of the survey are contained in Baker and Hart's Chapters 5 and 6. Based on our analysis the overriding conclusion was that, contrary to the impression gained from many earlier commentators, 'unsuccessful' companies deserve more credit than they are usually given. Given that the data were collected following a major recession in the late 1970s and early 1980s, all of the respondents satisfied the minimum criterion of success which was that they had survived. Further, our analysis confirmed that knowledge and use of modern management ideas and techniques were widely diffused and accepted in the 'less successful' companies. Specifically, we found that at the structural level the existence of a particular department's or board's titles is as much related to size as to any other factors. In other words, it is fruitless to look at obvious indicators of commitment to marketing. It is therefore necessary to look at more subtle factors, at both a strategic and tactical level.

At the *strategic* level, the studies identified a few factors that seem to distinguish between above- and below-average companies: a long-term approach, specific strategic objectives, linking strategic plans closely with changes in markets, and a continuous commitment to new product development are all activities apparent in *more* successful companies rather than *less* successful ones.

At the *tactical* level, market research, market segmentation, and certain promotional techniques are more common in successful companies.

Overall, it is possible to say that relatively few of the factors studied actually accounted for differences in performance. However, the fact that these tightly controlled studies failed to find more factors which distinguish the successful from the less successful is, in itself, very important. Both studies covered a wide range of issues, from the McKinsey 7S Framework and the simultaneous loose–tight structures of Peters and Waterman (1982) to the managerial style reported as being important by Wong, Saunders and Doyle (1992).

Clearly, in order to sustain and improve their competitive edge managers seek information and advice on best practice and try to incorporate it in their planning and execution. Ultimately, it is clear that it is the quality of implementation that differentiates most between more and less successful competitors. But it is important to emphasize that the quality of implementation will become determinant only provided that the *initial analysis and planning* is of equivalent quality. It is only when one has taken full advantage of the analytical procedures and techniques described in the managerial literature that the quality of implementation will become important. Otherwise, an excellent plan executed by average management will always out-perform a below-average or non-existent plan executed by above-average managers.

As noted, a continuous commitment to new product development was present in all the more successful companies irrespective of whether they were members of sunrise or sunset industries, and it is for this reason that we believe product strategy to lie at the heart of overall competitiveness. But even more important is the commitment to innovation.

At the 1992 International Strategic Management Society Conference, Stanford Professor Richard Pascale reminded the delegates that only five years after the publication of *In Search of Excellence*, 'all but 14 of its 43 excellent companies had either grown weaker or were really on the slide, in spite of the best efforts of their bosses to improve things' (*Financial Times*, 23 October 1992). While Pascale would claim that 'this shows we don't know what we're doing' and Tom Peters was to open his next best-seller *Thriving on Chaos* (1987) with the assertion 'There are no excellent companies', we would disagree. Indeed the purpose of this book is to demonstrate that a commitment to continuous innovation through new product and process development is the source of sustainable competitive advantage (SCA). This view is strongly supported by the evidence published by the UK Select Committee on Science and Technology's Report *Innovation in Manufacturing Industry* (1995) which stated:

> 'Innovation is crucial to the competitiveness of manufacturing industry. Without it, United Kingdom companies cannot increase their share of world markets. The introduction of new or improved products, which meet the needs of the customer, quickly, reliably and at a competitive price, gives a company an edge over its competitors. As Lord Weinstock, Managing Director of the General Electric Company Ltd said, "Innovation is indispensable in maintaining a successful business ... If you do not change as the times, the markets and products require, you are dead".' (paragraphs 1 and 2)

Environmental change

While it has become almost a cliché to speak of turbulence in the environment, accelerating technological change and global competition, many observers 'throw away' these phrases without offering any evidence to support their claim, nor any explanation of what underlies these changes. In this section we seek to avoid these failings.

In 1967 the Club of Rome published a highly influential report in which it claimed that if current trends continued the world would soon run out of many non-renewable resources, such as oil and copper; that population growth would exceed the potential of both renewable and non-renewable resources; and that, in the process, mankind would destroy the world in which he lived. Such forecasts are not new. Nostradamus predicted similar outcomes in the Middle Ages as did Malthus in the late eighteenth century. So far none of the predictions has come to pass, although this is not the same as saying they will not. Indeed if one accepts the underlying assumptions of such predictions then, ultimately and inevitably, they will come to fruition.

Essentially the underlying assumptions behind such predictions are that supply is fixed but demand will continue to grow, often exponentially. There is considerable support for both these assumptions, until we allow for the impact of innovation and technological change.

Consider, for example, the Club of Rome's prediction that given the known reserves of oil in the early 1960s, and the rising trend in consumption, then all the known oil would be consumed before the end of the century. This clearly has not occurred – indeed the known reserves of oil in 1995 exceeded those in 1965, and while consumption has increased in overall terms it has declined in per capita terms. The reasons are not hard to find.

Concern about the growing scarcity of oil sensitized Gulf oil producers to the power they could exercise if they were to form a cartel (OPEC) and control the supply. This they did with the effect which any economist could have predicted – price soared from around $2 a barrel to over $40 a barrel. Now at $40 a barrel it really becomes worth your while to bring on stream hitherto marginal fields and also to look for more oil in highly inaccessible and hostile environments like the Arctic and the North Sea. Result – the known reserves now exceed those of 1965. Of course, ultimately, the reserves of oil are finite but it would be a foolish person who tried to predict what exactly they are. But the impact of increased prices not only affected an increase in the 'supply' of oil; it also had at least two other major effects. First, it encouraged the more economical use of oil, and a great deal of product and process innovation has been directed to this end with the result that today's cars, for example, are at least twice as efficient in fuel consumption terms as those of the early 1960s when oil was cheap. Second, the increased price of oil as an energy source makes it more attractive to undertake research into alternative, substitute sources of energy and so accelerates the prospect that long before oil runs out it will have become as obsolete as the stagecoach in Europe and North America.

The above example helps us understand why predictions such as the Club of Rome's are fundamentally flawed. Their underlying assumptions are that demand will increase exponentially while supply will not grow as fast or, if we are dealing with a non-renewable resource, will not grow at all. The reality is almost the opposite. All demand is ultimately driven by population and, in the past, population has tended to grow exponentially – until it catches up with or overtakes the available supply when the Malthusian controls of famine, disease and war restore the equilibrium. In less-developed countries the absence of population control frequently results in the Malthusian checks coming about. Elsewhere, social and political influence has broken the exponential growth cycle and population growth has slowed or stabilized.

By contrast the creation of supply through technological innovation is an exponential process, and we currently appear to be on an upward swing so that the acceleration implicit in such processes has become easily discernible. Two examples from the field of electronics – a major area for innovation – will help make the point.

In a book entitled *The Mighty Micro* published in 1979, Christopher Evans posed the question what would have happened in the field of automobile engineering if development had matched that in electronics over the preceding 25 years since 1955. Taking three frequently used performance indicators – price, efficiency and size – Evans concluded that if the pace of change had been the same it would have been possible to buy a Rolls-Royce for 35p (50 cents), drive it right round the world on half a cup of petrol, and park six of them on the head of a pin. Since 1979 the rate of change has accelerated even more. The PC on my desk, purchased for £1500 in 1996, has the same computing power as the University's mainframe computer had in 1974. It cost £2 million!

More to the point, however, is that every advance in computer hardware and software greatly increases our ability to innovate in other areas, especially in manufacturing industry on which we depend for physical products and the greater part of our service infrastructure – buildings, transport, communication. Indeed the impact of the microelectronics revolution has prompted the view that we are moving or have moved from an industrial era into an *information* era in which the following trends may be discerned:

Standardization	⟶	Customization
Centralization	⟶	Decentralization
Dependence	⟶	Self-help
Transportation	⟶	Communication
Autocracy	⟶	Participation
Hierarchy	⟶	Network
Information scarcity	⟶	Information overload

At this juncture it will be helpful to introduce the concept of life cycles and, specifically, product life cycles, a subject to which we return in much greater detail in Chapter 5.

Life cycle analysis

Historical analysis lends considerable support to the view that human progress has proceeded in a series of evolutionary cycles. Each of these cycles appears to have been initiated by some kind of social or technological innovation which gave impetus to a significant step forward in people's control over their environment and general standard of living. The development of stone tools, the discovery of bronze, the domestication of cattle and the development of agriculture were all innovations which led a marked improvement in the human condition. Similarly, task specialization, exchange and the evolution of markets (and marketing!) gave impetus to the process.

In and of itself, however, each successful innovation appears to share some common characteristics whose existence has prompted the analogy with the biological life cycle. At birth an innovation's prospects of survival are slim (many if not most new products fail) and the progress or growth of the innovation is hardly perceptible. If, however, the innovation survives infancy then it is likely to experience a period of rapid growth until it approaches its full potential. As this occurs growth slows down and a period of maturity sets in. Inevitably, maturity will move into decline, slowly at first but then with gathering momentum until the innovation 'dies' or ceases to exist in any meaningful way. If we plot these phases then a curve similar to that in Figure 2.2 will be seen – a skewed version of the *normal distribution*.

In Figure 2.3 we have superimposed labels or descriptors on the curve to delineate the phases described earlier, while in Figure 2.4 we have modified these to use the descriptors commonly used for physical or product innovations in the so-called product life cycle.

The value of the life cycle concept is the insight it offers into the *process* of evolutionary change. Its weakness is that the misguided seek to use it as a predictive

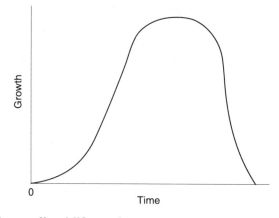

Figure 2.2 ● Generalized life cycle curve

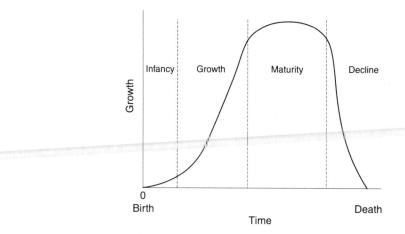

Figure 2.3 ● Stages in the life cycle

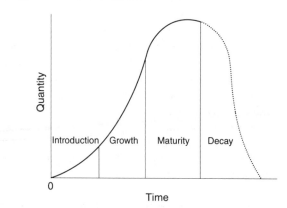

Figure 2.4 ● The product life cycle

device when, by definition, one can only establish the length of each phase of the life cycle after the event – *a posteriori*. In the case of individual members of the same species – fruit flies, humans or elephants – we can generalize about the length of each of the phases. Fruit flies complete the cycle in 24 hours, humans in 70–80 years, and elephants in 80–100 years. The problem with seeking to apply the concept of predictability to innovations is, of course, that if an innovation is genuinely new, and not a clone of an existing species, then we cannot know *a priori* how long each of the phases will be, although we can generalize about the characteristics of the process. Herein lies the value of the concept of the life cycle of species or genuine innovations.

In an article entitled 'The origin of strategy' (*Harvard Business Review*, Nov.–Dec. 1989) Bruce Henderson demonstrates why the concept of evolution and life cycles is helpful to an understanding of the nature of competition – and also why the analogy should not be taken too far. Henderson cites Gause's *Principles of Competitive Exclusion* to explain why only differentiated organisms can survive. According to this principle, 'No two species can co-exist that make their living in an identical way'. This principle can be demonstrated by putting two simple organisms into a controlled environment with an ample supply of food. If the organisms are of the same species then only one will survive. However, if one regards Earth as a controlled environment (remember the Club of Rome) then we can see that over time more than a million distinct species have evolved. Henderson comments:

> 'What explains this abundance? *Variety*. The richer the environment the greater the number
> of potentially significant variables that can give each species a unique advantage. But, also,
> the richer the environment, the greater the potential number of competitors – and the
> more severe the competition.'

However, business is distinguished from natural Darwinian and gradual evolutionary change by the application of imagination and logic to the development of strategy which incorporates an understanding of the nature of competition. But, before looking at the nature of competition in a little more detail, it is important to underline the most important insight which the process of evolution and the nature of life cycles has to offer. In very simple terms evolution based on natural selection is about the survival of the fittest. New species displace old species because they are better adapted to the prevailing environmental conditions. Ultimately, however, the world is a finite environment so that new species can only come into existence if they can displace existing species which dominate the environment at a given time. The fundamental reason which determines the shape of the biological life cycle is that initially one has to struggle to establish a foothold against an already established species. As Gause's *Principles* demonstrate, one will survive, one will decline – the new is substituted for the old, and the reason for the almost symmetrical life cycle curve for a species is that it mirrors a substitution effect. (The reason it is asymmetrical is that many innovations generate new growth so that the growth phase of the new thing is longer than the decline phase of the old thing it displaces.)

Biological life cycles also offer an insight into the fact that competition from something new or an apparent limit to growth does not automatically lead to decline. As a

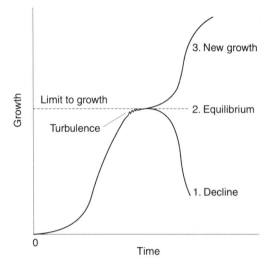

Figure 2.5 ● Life cycles and limits to growth

phenomenon (new product, new species) approaches a limit to growth it begins to exhibit what has been described as hunting behaviour as it seeks to find a way round the barrier. This hunting behaviour creates turbulence – a familiar word in the description of competition! Three possible outcomes are possible:

1. The phenomenon cannot find a way round the barrier and goes into decline.
2. The phenomenon adjusts to the barrier and establishes an equilibrium (extended maturity).
3. The phenomenon finds a way forward and initiates a new growth phase.

Figure 2.5 illustrates these alternatives.

Taking products (services) as the phenomenon under investigation this book seeks to show how the application of knowledge, imagination and logic may be used to develop successful product strategies. Our emphasis will be mainly on new product development (innovation) as this is essential to develop new market opportunities, to sustain equilibrium in mature markets and to initiate new growth when apparent limits to growth emerge. Decline is invariably the result of an absence of innovation but, in recent years, it has come to be appreciated that managing decline is as important to the long-term welfare of the organization as growth. Accordingly we accord it more attention than is to be found in most texts dealing with product strategy.

Managing mature products is, of course, the subject of mainstream texts on the subject of marketing and brand management and the manipulation of the marketing mix. Given the extent of the advice available, we simply summarize some of the key issues which are discussed at length elsewhere.

To provide perspective to these issues a brief overview of the nature of competition and competitive strategy follows.

Managing competition: product strategy is central

The nature of competition

In *Marketing Strategy and Management* (1992) Baker comments:

'From 1776, and the publication of Adam Smith's *Wealth of Nations*, to 1960, and Ted Levitt's "Marketing myopia", the formal study of the nature of competition remained the province of the professional economist. As a consequence, and in common with many other professions, much of the substance of the body of knowledge which distinguished the field of study was poorly communicated to others who might have benefited considerably from the insights it was able to offer to the solution of real world problems. Indeed, few managers appreciate that the essence of Michael Porter's influential writings on competition and competitive advantage is derived directly from the sub-field of economics known as "industrial organisation" or "industrial economics".' (p. 17)

Porter's (1980) analysis of the forces that shape competition are probably more widely accepted than his later analysis of *The Competitive Advantage of Nations* (1990), although this is not to say the former enjoy universal support. Nonetheless, Porter's interpretation of the applied economist's view of competition is believed to provide a sound basis for an understanding of the phenomenon and is summarized below.

One of the crucial decisions which faces the industry analyst is precisely where to draw the boundaries which define an 'industry'. As we shall see, similar difficulties exist in terms of defining a 'market' and the parameters which one uses will have a major bearing upon the applicability of most, if not all, of the tools and techniques which have been developed to aid management. In particular, therefore, the firm's definition of its industry and its market will be critical to the formulation of its own competitive strategy and the success or otherwise of that strategy. In general, however, and as a prerequisite to such specific definition, it is useful to assume that the industry has been defined so that attention can be concentrated upon the determinants of competition.

Porter uses the economists' concept of substitutability when he offers a working definition of an industry as 'the group of firms producing products that are close substitutes for each other'. In order to define the interaction or state of competition between these firms, economists have developed definitions of a continuum of competitive states ranging from zero (monopoly) to absolute ('perfect'). While the theoretical implications of these states are conceptually important, it will suffice here if we appreciate that the nature of competition is to ensure that the marginal rate of return on capital will be the same everywhere. Thus the forces of competition work to ensure that capital will flow from less efficient firms in an industry to more efficient firms, and from less efficient industries to more efficient industries. The ultimate aim of every strategist should therefore be to have the *most effective firm in the most efficient industry*.

In 'How competitive forces shape strategy' Michael Porter (1979) distinguishes five basic forces which govern competition in an industry – the threat of new entrants, the threat of substitution, the bargaining power of suppliers, the bargaining power of customers, and rivalry between current competitors – and depicts their interaction as in Figure 2.6. Porter describes the key features of these five forces along the following lines.

Threat
of new
entrants

Bargaining
power of
suppliers

The industry
Jockeying for
position among
current competitors

Bargaining
power of
customers

Threat of
substitute
products or
services

Figure 2.6 ● Forces governing competition in an industry (*source:* Porter, 1979)

The threat of new entrants

Freedom of entry to an industry is widely regarded as a key indicator of an industry's competitiveness such that, in the case of a monopoly, by definition no other firm can enter, while in the case of 'perfect competition' there are no barriers to entry. From the firm's viewpoint the greater the barriers to entry the less the threat from new competitors and the more secure its own position.

Seven major barriers to entry are proposed by Porter:

1. Economies of scale.
2. Product differentiation.
3. Capital requirements.
4. Switching costs.
5. Access to distribution channels.
6. Cost disadvantages independent of scale.
7. Government policy.

A full discussion of these factors is to be found in Porter, and at this juncture we wish only to underline a point to which we will return many times: namely, that product differentiation has become *the* key competitive factor. Simplistically, the reason why this should be so is that if one owns a product which is perceived as differentiated by users then one has a monopoly and so is not exposed to competition for as long as one can maintain this position of the perceived difference. As we shall see in Chapter 4 on 'Buyer Behaviour', perception is a subjective state and one which can be influenced significantly by marketing activities, thus explaining the current importance attached to the subject.

The threat of substitution

As Porter notes: 'Identifying substitute products is a matter of searching for other products that can perform the same *function* as the product of the industry', a point which underlines our assertion that if your product is sufficiently differentiated to be perceived as unique by a sufficient number of users to comprise an economically viable market then the threat of competition is latent rather than active. Given such a position the danger lies in complacency, for change is inevitable, if only because the act of consumption will *change the consumers* and so make them susceptible to improved products.

The bargaining power of suppliers

According to Porter a supplier group is powerful if the following apply:

- It is dominated by a few companies and is more concentrated than the industry it sells to.
- It is not obliged to contend with other substitute products for sale to the industry.
- The industry is not an important customer of the supplier group.
- The supplier's product is an important input to the buyer's business.
- The supplier group's products are differentiated or it has built up switching costs.
- The supplier group poses a credible threat of forward integration.

Porter also makes the important point that 'labour must be recognized as a supplier as well, and one that exerts great power in many industries' – a point even more true of the UK economy than that of the USA, albeit of diminishing importance in recent years.

The bargaining power of customers

Many of the factors which apply here are corollaries of those cited as applying to the power of suppliers. Eight specific conditions are proposed by Porter where a buying group will exercise power:

- The buyer group is concentrated or purchases large volumes relative to seller sales, e.g. Marks & Spencer *vis-à-vis* its suppliers, or the multiple grocery chains like Tesco or Sainsburys.
- The products it purchases from the industry represent a significant fraction of the buyer's costs or purchases.
- The products it purchases from the industry are standard or undifferentiated, e.g. basic chemicals, steel, aluminium, etc.
- It faces few switching costs.

- It earns low profits, i.e. it will be active in seeking cost reductions in bought-in supplies.
- Buyers pose a credible threat of backward integration.
- The industry's product is unimportant to the quality of the buyers' products or services, e.g. most packaging materials.
- The buyer has full information.

Rivalry between current competitors

'Jockeying for position' is the phrase which Porter uses to describe the tactical moves employed by firms to seek an advantage over their competitors. Clearly the greater the degree of skirmishing between the rivals the more active and volatile is the competitive state. The intensity of this rivalry is a function of numerous factors, of which Porter distinguishes eight:

1. Numerous or equally balanced competitors (a basic condition for a state of 'perfect' competition).
2. Slow industry growth, e.g. retail food sales.
3. High fixed or storage costs. On this point Porter makes the important observation that 'The significant characteristic of costs is fixed costs *relative to value added* [emphasis ours], and not fixed costs as a proportion of total costs'.
4. Lack of differentiation or switching costs.
5. Capacity augmented in large increments, e.g. steel, shipbuilding.
6. Diverse competitors – particularly international rivals.
7. High strategic stakes.
8. High exit barriers, e.g. specialized assets with low liquidation values, redundancy costs, social implications, etc.

Porter comments:

> 'When exit barriers are high, excess capacity does not leave the industry, and companies that lose the competitive battle do not give up. Rather, they grimly hang on and, because of their weakness, have to resort to extreme tactics. The profitability of the entire industry can be persistently low as a result, *cf.* the world automobile and steel industries.'

From this brief summary of the forces which influence competition, it is clear that differentiation is a major source of competitive advantage. Indeed, for the vast majority of all firms in all industries it is the only basis for survival in the long run – a point to which we will return later. Before doing so, however, it will be helpful to summarize the basic alternative strategies open to the firm.

Strategic options

One of the earlier and most influential writers on the subject of corporate strategy was Igor Ansoff whose seminal work *Corporate Strategy* was first published in 1965. In this

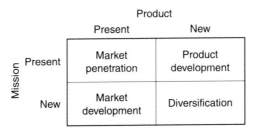

Figure 2.7 ● Growth vector matrix

book Ansoff introduced the idea of the growth vector matrix as shown in Figure 2.7. As can be seen from this diagram, the vertical axis is labelled Mission and the horizontal axis Product, and only two states – Present and New – are recognized for each dimension or axis. From this simple 2 × 2 matrix four possible strategies are identified.

In fact Ansoff's growth vector matrix was first described in his article in the *Harvard Business Review* (Sept.–Oct. 1957) entitled 'Strategies for diversification' in which he defined the alternative strategies as follows:

1. Market penetration: the company seeks increased sales for its present products in its present markets through more aggressive promotion and distribution.
2. Market development: the company seeks increased sales by taking its present products into new markets.
3. Product development: the company seeks increased sales by developing improved products for its present markets.
4. Diversification: the company seeks increased sales by developing new products for new markets.

Clearly, the latter two strategies depend directly on product innovation and the former two on marketing (or process) innovation.

In effect Ansoff's growth vectors are determined by the two basic forces of supply and demand, or technology and customers, so that it is possible to reconfigure his matrix with these, possibly more meaningful, labels as in Figure 2.8. The strategic alternatives remain the same.

In our earlier study *Marketing and Competitive Success* (1989) we discovered that one

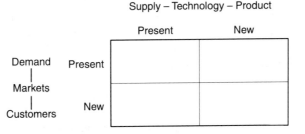

Figure 2.8 ● Extended growth vector matrix

of the features which distinguished more successful from less successful firms was the fact that rather than regarding these alternative strategies as being mutually exclusive the successful companies were pursuing strategies of penetration, market and product development simultaneously. Further, as a consequence of developing both new products and markets, the successful firms were also diversifying.

Irrespective of what strategy or strategies a firm is pursuing, its basic aim is the same – to create and maintain a sustainable differential or competitive advantage (SDA or SCA). In essence SDA or SCA exists where a firm has developed a unique position which distinguishes it from its competitors as a result of which it has created a franchise with a group of customers who will regard it as the preferred source of supply for the product or service in question. This group of customers, or market segment, will be sufficient to ensure the firm's continuing profitability and provide a basis for future growth.

As a competitive advantage is a benefit perceived by a customer there is an infinite variety of sources. However, for the purposes of analysis it is useful to regard competitive advantage as arising from one or other of two basic sources – *cost leadership* or *differentiation*. Economic rationality dictates that if two objects are perceived as identical in every respect by an intending purchaser then they will select that with the lower price as it represents better value for money. But if an intending purchaser perceives meaningful differences (either tangible or intangible, objective or subjective) between two objects this will influence their perception of value such that they may well prefer the higher priced object.

In markets for undifferentiated products (usually commodities with a precise specification) the market price will be determined by the interaction of supply and demand. Under these circumstances it is clear that the supplier with the lowest costs will enjoy the highest margins and so may be regarded as the most successful supplier. Cost leadership is the strategy which seeks to achieve this position and is usually founded on economies of scale and experience curve effects reinforced by more efficient and effective management. Traditionally economies of scale were associated with the size of the producing unit, but with the advent of information technology and the development of techniques such as CAD–CAM and flexible manufacturing systems (FMS) many production-scale economies have been eroded or eliminated. However, this is not the case with economies of scale attributable to marketing, and many marketing mix functions such as selling, distribution, advertising and promotion still enjoy economies of scale and confer cost advantages on the larger suppliers.

This latter point is of particular importance. *Economies of scale are only available to the largest suppliers.* In most industries the Pareto Principle applies: 20% of the suppliers will account for 80% of the total output with the obvious corollary that the great majority of suppliers (80%) account collectively for only a small (20%) share of the market. It follows that, for the great majority of firms, cost leadership is *not* a viable strategy and these firms must necessarily compete on the basis of differentiation.

Differentiation may take many forms. As suggested earlier, an objective and tangible difference intrinsic to the product itself is easiest to define and demonstrate and this is why we regard product development as the *key* competitive strategy. In today's competitive environment the achievement and maintenance of objective differences is becoming increasingly difficult to sustain. It has been estimated that any new technology will be fully understood within 18 months of its first appearance so that competitors will be able to benchmark the new product and establish the basis of its technological advantage. Further, given the nature of international competition, the protection of intellectual property rights through patents has become increasingly difficult and copying has become commonplace.

This situation is not new, of course – it is only new to complex products incorporating high technology. For most products which depend on low and well understood technologies – food processing, soap manufacturing, etc. – suppliers have appreciated for decades, if not centuries, that other approaches than purely technological differentiation are necessary if their output is to be seen as differentiated by intending purchasers. It is for this reason that marketing has assumed such importance in saturated and highly competitive markets, for it is only through branding, positioning, the provision of service and availability through location and distribution advantages that the great majority of firms can differentiate themselves and survive. It is for this reason that the great majority of all firms will follow a differentiation strategy based upon a combination of product features reinforced by a distinctive marketing mix which will enable them to establish a franchise with a sufficient number of customers to enable them to survive and grow.

We have already suggested that cost leadership is a strategy only available to the largest firms. Size of firm is also an important determinant of the kind of differentiation strategy available to a supplier. Michael Porter distinguishes between firms with a range of products, which may or may not be complementary but are differentiated from one another and the competitive offerings of others, and firms with a single product which, in absolute terms, account for the majority of supplier firms. Firms with a single product can, by definition, only appeal to a single segment and so are deemed to pursue a strategy of *focus*. While it is possible that a firm pursuing a focused strategy may 'own' the largest segment in a market, the more usual case is that it will appeal only to a small segment of the market and often one which is not sufficiently attractive to merit the attentions of the larger competitors. Such small segments are often defined as niches and, like all other market segments, call for a distinctive marketing mix.

In passing it may be noted that marketers recognized these three distinctive marketing approaches before Porter gave them the labels by which they are now generally known. In earlier marketing textbooks and writings cost leadership is recognized as an *undifferentiated* strategy, differentiation as *differentiated* and focus as a *concentrated* strategy. Recommendations as to the appropriate marketing mix remain the same and are summarized in Table 2.1.

From the foregoing discussion it is clear that the size of a firm is an important factor determining the strategic options available to it. Large firms have the option of following an undifferentiated, differentiated or concentrated strategy; medium-sized firms have the option of a differentiated or concentrated strategy; but the small, single product firm can only pursue a concentrated or niche strategy.

In common with most textbooks a comprehensive treatment requires that we deal with all three strategic options and, in the succeeding chapters, much of the discussion may well give the impression that the insights and advice offered (the normative

Table 2.1 ● Marketing mix strategies

Strategy	Product	Price	Distribution	Promotion
Undifferentiated (cost leadership)	Standardized	Low	Intensive	Mass
Differentiated	Different for each market segment	What the market will bear	Extensive	Targeted by segment
Concentrated (focus)	Customized	Premium	Highly selective	Direct

theory) are only applicable to larger companies. This is not the case as most of the processes, procedures and techniques are equally appropriate to smaller companies. It is important to stress, however, that while there are some single product companies which have survived for generations they are the exception rather than the rule. Their survival is usually attributable to their adaptability and flexibility which has enabled them to anticipate and keep pace with the changing needs of their customers – indeed, most successful single product firms practise a policy of incremental innovation which, over a period of years, may lead to a radical change in the product they sell. (Consider, for example, Mulliners who transformed their skills as coach builders into the production of highly distinctive automobile bodies for Rolls-Royce and Bentley.) But for the majority of single product firms the inevitability of the product life cycle means that unless they develop new products they will eventually decline and die, so that the best advice to such firms must be to develop a portfolio of products to spread the risk of failure. We return to this proposal in detail in Chapter 5.

Irrespective of size or which strategy a firm chooses to follow, it should now be clear that innovation or new product and process development is central to them all. As President and CEO of the Arthur D Little Company observed:

'In the 21st century .... comparative advantage will be man-made. The effective management of technology – whether in identifying market risks and opportunities, accelerating organizational planning and product development, streamlining service delivery, or extending the organization's influence out into its customers and suppliers – will determine which companies thrive and grow. It will also determine both the wealth of nations and the health of the planet.'

Product strategy and management

'Product diversification is currently the center of widespread executive interest as a means of market adjustment. Product development and innovation have always been major facets of competitive rivalry, but the present dynamic quality of the economy is particularly characterized by an expanding frontier of new products, acquisitions, and mergers.

Management today must be unusually alert in finding effective strategy adjustments to keep pace with fluctuations in the business cycle, changes in demand, and an ever-increasing rate of technological development. These conditions have been manifested in an accelerated rate of product displacement and less resistance to change on the part of consumers and industrial purchasers. Product diversification has consequently been called upon successfully by many executives to meet the challenge of a changing industrial environment. This article is a discussion of some aspects of the planning, analysis, and methods useful to management in programming diversification.'

So what is this article and when was it written? In fact, the article, 'Program for product diversification', was written by Thomas A. Staudt and appeared in the *Harvard Business Review* for Nov./Dec. 1954. *Plus ça change, plus c'est la même chose.* Thomas Staudt could well have been writing in 1994. Indeed, there is great merit in returning to the classic contributions of the early writers on marketing who were publishing in the 1950s and 1960s, for it was they who first spelled out some of the basic principles which still underlie the successful practice of marketing. Indeed, a cynic might be moved to observe that much of the writing which has built upon these early seminal contributions has tended to obscure rather than clarify the original insights which they contain. In *Product Strategy and Management* we will attempt to avoid the trap of considering only the most recent contributions as being relevant. Of course, this does not mean that we will ignore the current literature where it is appropriate, but the reader should not be surprised if we also draw heavily upon some of the early contributions to marketing thinking from the formative years of the 1950s and 1960s.

Reconsideration of these marketing classics often leads to rediscovery. For example, in the early 1990s the authors proposed adoption of a technique which they termed multiple convergent processing. As will be seen in Chapter 7, the choice of title for this model was deliberate in order to emphasize the need for participants in a new product development process to agree on specific decision points. Thus, while they might work simultaneously or in parallel (both favoured adjectives of the 1990s), it is our view that formal efforts have to be made to co-ordinate and integrate these efforts at certain critical points in the process. And therein lies the clue to rediscovery. 'Critical path analysis for new product planning' was the title of an article in the *Journal of Marketing* published in October 1964 by Yung Wong. The technique was also advocated strongly in Booz, Allen and Hamilton's *Management of New Products* (1968) in which they talked about 'a programme for new product evolution'. At that time the company claimed:

'"New product evolution" is the phrase originated for the first edition because business language had no word that described this management process in which "development" is only one stage, in which R & D is only one department. The term "new product evolution" now has rather widespread acceptance and usage.'

Manifestly this has not been the case and the term has not caught on, although for the reasons set out by Booz, Allen and Hamilton it is a more apt description of the process than the much more favoured 'new product development'.

In 'Program for product diversification', Staudt examines the reasons why companies seek to diversify their product range and offers a blueprint for company management to

follow in arriving at policy decisions on diversification. To begin with, Staudt addresses
the question why companies diversify, and suggests that this is usually attributable to
one or more of six major reasons which he identifies as:

- Survival
- Stability
- Productive utilization of resources
- Adaptation to changing customer needs
- Growth
- Miscellaneous.

In all he identifies 43 specific factors which may prompt the company to diversify its
product lines. Having identified a need to do so from one or other of these reasons,
Staudt argues forcefully for the adoption of an organized and systematic approach to
product development. In his words the basic elements of a sound programme for
product diversification consist of five steps:

1. A clear definition of objectives.
2. An analysis of the diversification situation in the light of present operations.
3. An audit of the tangible and intangible corporate resources for diversification.
4. Establishment of specific criteria for new products in line with the three preceding
   points.
5. A comprehensive search for products and their evaluation against the criteria.

It will be noted that like Kline (1955) Staudt is proposing that we start inside the
organization and work outwards. Indeed, he asserts that 'the clue to successful formulation of objectives is to think in terms of what the company can *accomplish* through use
of its resources rather than in terms of what products it may happen to find. Here the
concept of convergence can be very useful.'

In introducing the concept of convergence Staudt is anticipating the model subsequently proposed by Igor Ansoff which proposes that one can pursue a policy of
market development by emphasizing current marketing experience, or of product development by emphasizing current product experience. Full diversification implies modifying both product and market together. Clearly, this is a more dangerous strategy as it
takes the company into uncharted territory. By building upon existing expertise in
either production (technology) or marketing (customer franchise) it may well be able
to move into a full diversification but without the inherent risks of doing this directly.
(In his analysis Staudt classifies product and market development as convergent diversification and what Ansoff terms diversification as divergent diversification.)

The prescience of Staudt's final comment on diversification is particularly revealing:
'in sum, a diversification appears most likely to be successful when it capitalizes on the
unique know-how or special qualities which provide the firm with lasting distinctiveness as against perishable distinctiveness. In this respect, final judgment should weigh

heavily the human capabilities available for the venture.' As Porter's *The Competitive Advantage of Nations* (1990) shows, this is clearly the case.

It is these issues with which this book is concerned. However, before turning to them in more detail it will be useful to look at the conclusions of J.-P. Deschamps and P.R. Nayak, two Arthur D Little consultants, on 'Lessons from product juggernauts' (*Prism*, Second Quarter, 1993). In their view, 'When the shouting is over, one factor is clear: what differentiates perennially great companies from others is the products they sell' (p. 5).

Based upon visits to a number of leading companies, Deschamps and Nayak take the view that such companies succeed competitively because they believe there is no such thing as a 'commodity' product. Even in basic industries such as minerals, chemicals and agribusiness, 'Suppliers can always find ways to differentiate their products from those of their competitors' (p. 5). The corollary is that if one fails to differentiate the only basis for competition is cost and price.

Deschamps and Nayak propose five basic strategies for competing through products, which they designate:

- Competing through product proliferation
- Competing through value
- Competing through design
- Competing through innovation
- Competing through service.

Competing through product proliferation

This strategy was pioneered by General Motors in the 1920s and 1930s in its battle with Ford. Once thought to be the preserve of large, rich companies, it is now recognized as reflecting a company's development effectiveness and seen as one of the most effective strategies for all companies in the 1990s.

Japanese companies are seen as being particularly adept at a proliferation strategy in which they take 'a scattershot approach to the marketplace' (p. 7) which is contrasted with Western companies which have a 'rifle mentality'. Thus Japanese firms will launch many new products simultaneously or in close succession and use market response to determine which to support and which to withdraw – what, elsewhere, we have called 'trial and error marketing'. By contrast, Western firms seek to define their single shot and its target much more precisely with the result that if they miss they have to repeat the procedure again.

Key exponents of a proliferation strategy are Honda in motorcycles who overwhelmed Yamaha's challenge in the early 1980s with new models and 113 product alterations against Yamaha's 34 and 37 in an 18-month period; Sony whose Walkman technology could not be protected so that 80% of the market went to competitors until Sony introduced 150 new models in the period 1981–9 and regained pre-eminence with over 50% market share; and Procter & Gamble who introduced numerous variants of its Pampers brand to fight off competition.

Competing through value

Offering high quality at low cost is seen by some to be the ultimate strategy. To quote Deschamps and Nayak, 'In the hands of daring entrepreneurs such as Henry Ford, this strategy spurred the great consumer revolution of the 20th century' (p. 9). They identify two discrete approaches: *continuous improvement* and *radical restructuring*. 'Many companies in traditional industries operate instinctively within a relatively simple quality/cost trade-off model. In this way of thinking there is a single, fixed, direct relationship between quality and cost. Any significant improvement in the product, whether in design, features, or even quality "feel", necessitates a proportional increase in costs' (p. 10). BMW and Mercedes-Benz are seen to support this view.

By contrast Toyota has 'a mental model of multiple and moveable trade-off curves. This alternative view allows for the systematic planning and introduction of process improvements that dramatically shift any given quality/cost curve' (p. 10). Shifting from one quality/cost curve to another is achieved by a number of complementary approaches, including process efficiencies in development and manufacturing, systematic design improvements and 'a persistent tracking of inefficiencies and waste at all levels'.

The merits of these alternative approaches are readily seen in Toyota's success and Mercedes' difficulties!

The approach of radical restructuring is typified by IKEA which 'has revolutionised furniture design, manufacturing, and retailing by re-thinking the entire business system of its industry from product concept to distribution' (p. 11). By offering excellent design and product quality backed up by strong customer service and a liberal return policy for its range of self-assembly furniture, IKEA offers superior value when compared to conventional furniture manufacturers/retailers.

Competing through design

For manufacturers who compete through design excellence like IBM, Sony, Harley-Davidson and Olivetti, '...design is not a cosmetic add-on but a means of expressing their corporate identity in the marketplace and establishing their products as synonymous with quality' (p. 12). This is achieved 'by designing products that are:

- Aesthetically appealing
- Safe and pleasing to touch and use
- Immediately intelligible and easy to operate
- Easy to install, handle, store, clean, and maintain
- Easy and economical to manufacture' (p. 13).

Success in design calls for a combination of engineering design (from the inside out) with aesthetic design (from the outside in).

Competing through innovation

Few companies compete consistently through innovation. Those that do include Black & Decker, Canon, Dupont, 3M, Merck, Philips and Sony. Because of the risks of innovation fast-followers often reap the rewards lost by the true innovator. 'However, fast-followers usually succeed only when the original innovator lacks the market position or financial strength to fully exploit its innovation. Few fast-followers succeed against a healthy, well-positioned innovator' (p. 15).

Innovation strategies may be incremental or breakthrough and may be either top-down or bottom-up in their origins and process.

Radical (breakthrough) innovations may be the result of a conscious policy. But, according to Deschamps and Nayak, 'Top-down breakthroughs happen only when these are all in place:

- A top management with a strong vision of where and how to innovate and the capability to communicate and mobilize people to make it happen.
- A strong technological culture and world-class capability to develop innovation – enabling technologies and new proprietary product concepts.
- A very clear sense of the customer (through a combination of research and intuition) and the ability to translate product concepts into attractive, saleable products.
- An ability to combine mutually reinforcing innovations (for example in product and in manufacturing process)' (p. 16).

That said, bottom-up breakthroughs probably predominate (if for no other reason that there are many more of them). However, incremental innovation is more commonplace, particularly in a top-down mode where formal R & D policies exist. For bottom-up incremental innovation to occur the right culture has to exist which establishes a climate which encourages innovations and provides mechanisms for facilitating them.

Competing through service

While customers regard product and service as 'two faces of the same coin', most manufacturers give greater emphasis to the product and see services as adding costs rather than value. This perception is being rapidly eroded with the growing recognition of the importance of customer service.

Deschamps and Nayak conclude: 'Underlying all these diverse ways to compete is the realization that products are created through a *process*' (original emphasis, p. 21). Two Exhibits summarize their conceptualization of this process.

Summary
....
In this chapter we have explored a wide range of issues in order to explain and justify our claim that product strategy and management lie at the very heart of business strategy and are critical to survival and competitive success.

To begin with, we reviewed the forces which have led to the emergence of global competition. Essentially, we attribute this to the fact that, in order to overcome supply deficiencies and optimize output, firms and countries pursue the principle of comparative advantage. For specialization to succeed exchange is essential. It follows that producers will compete with each other, both directly and indirectly, for the patronage of customers. So long as demand exceeds supply competition will be limited and the balance of power will lie with the producer. However, in this century accelerating technological change has greatly enhanced productivity and output while demand has stabilized in the more advanced and affluent countries due to the absence of population growth. As a result of these environmental changes international competition has intensified and the balance of power has moved to the customer. Marketing – defined as the creation and maintenance of mutually satisfying exchange relationships – has been rediscovered and is now accepted as a critical factor in achieving competitive success.

A central theme of this book is that change is evolutionary and proceeds in cycles. Each cycle is initiated by the introduction of an innovation or new product which is believed to offer greater benefits to users compared with the existing product which it seeks to replace. In essence innovation is a process of substitution. To begin with, innovations make slow progress as most consumers buy from habit and are the victims of inertia. For them change represents risk. However, if an innovation does offer real benefits people will switch to it in increased numbers, resulting in rapid growth until all persons with the need which the innovation satisfies have converted to it. This state of saturation or maturity will prevail until the next cycle of innovation occurs when sales of the new product will erode those of the existing product, leading to decline and eventual withdrawal. It is this cycle of change which provides the structure for this book.

Most markets comprise many suppliers and customers with the result that suppliers must compete with each other to secure the customers' patronage. If customers perceive suppliers' offerings as undifferentiated then they will buy from the firm asking the lowest price. Obviously you can only survive offering a lower price than your competitors if you have lower costs. Such a strategy of *cost leadership* is dependent on the economies of scope and scale which accrue to the most efficient producers and marketers. But, by definition, only a few suppliers can achieve the size which triggers these economies. The majority of smaller producers can only survive through a strategy of *differentiation* so that customers will be willing to pay higher prices for what they see as additional benefits. Innovation or new product development is seen as central to this process and accounts for the product (or service) being regarded as at the very heart of every successful competitive strategy.

In the next chapter, 'The Product in Theory and Practice', we develop this theme in detail.

QUESTIONS

1. Summarize the factors which have given rise to the growth of global competition.
2. Explain the notion of *comparative advantage*.
3. Discuss the contribution of marketing to competitive success.
4. Why was the Club of Rome's 1967 prediction of environmental collapse flawed?

5. Describe the process of evolutionary change and explain the concept of life cycles associated with such change.

6. Identify Porter's 'Five Forces' and show how they govern competition in an industry.

7. Portray Ansoff's 'growth vector matrix' and summarize the nature of the strategic options defined by it.

8. Discuss the proposition that there are only two basic sources of competitive advantage – cost leadership and differentiation.

9. Why is product strategy central to business performance and success?

Mini-case ● Pepys & Company Limited

Located in London's East End, Pepys & Company Limited is a medium-sized family-owned business which specializes in the production and sale of diaries. The company was founded in 1946 when Bill Pepys was demobilized from the army just after the end of the Second World War. A printer by trade, Bill decided to use his gratuity to set up a small jobbing print shop. Fifty years on in 1996 the company has grown significantly and now employs 350 people and has a turnover approaching £10 million per annum.

Soon after setting up in business Bill Pepys was asked if he could make up a line of diaries to be used as Christmas gifts by a local garage. These proved to be a great success and word got around the Junior Chamber of Commerce and Rotary Club, leading to a number of other orders the following year. As the company's reputation spread by word-of-mouth recommendation Bill invested more in specialized production equipment and began to advertise his range of diaries in the trade press and the London Yellow Pages. In 1964 Bill's son Jim began to attend the local technical college to study for an HND in Business Studies. On registering for his course he was given a diary by the Students' Association, which ran from September to August, and he quickly recognized that here was a market opportunity which would help offset the extreme seasonality of the diary business. On completing his course, Jim joined the family business and quickly built up a customer base of local schools and colleges for whom the firm developed a specialized line of customized diaries.

By now Pepys & Company were depending on diaries for more than 70% of their business, and in 1975 when Bill retired his son took over and decided to drop the jobbing work and concentrate solely on diaries. Over the years the range was extended and a number of products were developed for sale to the general public. At first these were sold via jobbers and wholesalers, but gradually this was extended to direct mail and then direct sale to key accounts such as W.H. Smith and John Menzies. By the end of the 1980s Pepys & Company was one of the largest specialist diary producers in the UK, with 80% of its turnover coming from 100 standard designs, 10% from a range of 12 academic designs, and 10% from a newly introduced line of novelties. (The latter had been introduced following Jim's attendance at a marketing seminar, when he had been advised his company should become customer driven and develop products suggested by his customers. Unfortunately, these diaries took up a lot of time with special bindings, etc., and had yet to earn a profit.)

In 1994 Jim died of a heart attack and his wife took over the firm temporarily so that their son, Bill junior, could complete his MBA at City University Business School. On 1 September 1996 Bill junior took over the reins and decided that his first task should be to undertake a marketing audit to determine just what were the company's strengths and weaknesses, and what threats and opportunities faced it in the marketplace. To begin with, however, he needed to define the firm's business.

At Business School one of the lectures he remembered best had been based on an article by Ted Levitt in the *Harvard Business Review* called 'Marketing myopia'. In this article Levitt argued that while the consumers' basic needs are fairly limited there is an almost infinite way of satisfying them. Further, because of competition and innovation, new and better ways of satisfying these basic needs evolved with new products (and industries) replacing the old. With all this talk of IT (information technology), the Internet and the paperless society, perhaps the future wasn't very bright for a company making diaries. On the other hand, all Pepys & Company's assets and skills were geared to the manufacture and sale of this product. Clearly, in the short term the company's business must be defined by the product, but how could this be defined to take account of the threat (and opportunity) of a micro-electronic revolution? Just what is a diary?

chapter 3

The product in theory and practice

LEARNING OBJECTIVES

1. To define the nature of demand and the factors which influence it.

2. To develop a classification of different kinds of products.

3. To identify possible differences between services and physical products.

4. To introduce the concept of branding.

5. To suggest approaches to classifying new products.

6. To present the Buygrid as a framework for analyzing buyer behaviour.

On completion of this chapter you will:

1. Understand the difference between effective, latent and potential demand and the factors which shape and influence them.

2. Be familiar with different approaches to the classification of products and the criteria used.

3. Have been introduced to the concept of branding.

4. Appreciate some of the features used to distinguish physical products from services.

5. Know Everett Rogers' scheme for classifying new products.

6. Be familiar with the Buygrid approach to analyzing buying decisions.

Introduction

In everyday life we use the word 'product' freely as a noun which describes 'a thing or substance produced by natural process or manufacture' (*Concise Oxford Dictionary*) with its associated connotations of 'artefact, good(s), produce, commodity, output, merchandise, offering, work' (*Oxford Thesaurus*). Through common usage 'product' has come to embrace all kinds of offering including services despite the fact that services possess a number of distinctive features which often discriminate strongly between physical products and non-physical services, especially in terms of their marketing. For all practical purposes, however, we would argue that the similarities between products and services are such that it will be much more fruitful to treat them as the *same*, and only dwell upon differences where this will be helpful in developing specific strategies for more effective marketing. Accordingly, throughout this text 'product' should be understood to embrace the word 'service' unless merit is seen in distinguishing between them.

What is a product?

Basically, the product is the object of the exchange process, the thing which the producer or supplier offers to a potential customer in exchange for something else which the supplier perceives as equivalent or greater value. Conventionally, this 'something else' is money or a title to money which is freely exchangeable as a known and understood store of value. In the absence of money, or similar medium of exchange, we must resort to barter or counter trade where the two parties agree between themselves how many pounds of meat are worth a yard of cloth or how many barrels of oil are worth a ton of grain. It follows that for an exchange to occur someone must have a *demand* for the object in question and be willing to exchange other assets or objects, which are seen as possessing value. Where this demand is widely held it represents an opportunity for producers to create supplies of the object in question and for markets to develop where those with a demand can meet those with a supply and negotiate a mutually satisfying exchange relationship (our preferred definition of 'marketing').

In less developed economies markets are invariably physical places where sellers (those with a supply) and prospective buyers (those with a potential demand) can meet. This is also true of more advanced economies where local markets, flea markets and car boot sales have enjoyed a resurgence of popularity. Otherwise it is unusual for buyers and producers to come into direct physical contact, and elaborate channels of distribution have been created to facilitate the exchange of goods. (This is less true of services and especially *personal services* where the essence of the exchange is an act performed by a seller specifically for the purchaser.)

Irrespective of the degree of contact between producer and consumer, the activities of a producer possess value only to the extent that consumers are willing to exchange. It is for this reason that supply has always been subservient to demand, though in times of scarcity it may appear to be the other way round. Thus the 'rediscovery' of marketing in the second half of the twentieth century reflects the potential for excess supply in most markets for goods and services in the more affluent industrialized economies where population growth has stabilized and technological advances result in continuing productivity gains. Because of this potential to create an excess supply – which will probably lead to a reduction in the perceived value of the total supply and to what cannot be consumed becoming worthless – producers have become far less certain about the demand for their products. Defining and quantifying demand for specific products has become a major preoccupation and it is with the nature of demand that we should start our enquiry into the question 'What is a product?'.

Demand

As with the noun 'product' so too does the noun 'demand' have many meanings, most of which are inconsequential in everyday usage. It is only when we get down to the serious business of seeking to define demand as a business opportunity that precision in definition becomes important.

To begin with it will be useful to recognize three broad categories of demand:

- effective
- potential
- latent.

Effective demand is the kind of demand in which economists are primarily interested and may be defined as 'demand backed up by purchasing power'. As explained in *Marketing* (6th edition) (Baker, 1996):

> 'Latent demand may also be thought of as a vague want in the sense that the consumer feels a need for a product, or service, to fill a particular function but is unable to locate anything suitable. It is clear that latent demand constitutes an important consideration in management planning. In the case of a demand which is latent due to lack of purchasing power a manufacturer may be able to change a consumer's preference through his marketing and promotional activities. Alternatively, if there is a trend towards increasing disposable income, then the producer may be able to project how such increases in purchasing power will enable consumers to translate their latent demand into an effective demand. Given such a forecast he will be able to plan increased production, distribution and sale to keep pace with rising disposable incomes.
>
> In the case of a demand which is latent because the consumer is unaware of the existence of a product or service which would satisfy his ill-defined want, then clearly if the manufacturer produces a product which he feels should satisfy the need, he will wish to bring it to the attention of those with latent demand for it. Alternatively, if a manufacturer does not produce a product which should satisfy a known latent demand but is able to specify what the characteristics of such a product would be, then the latent demand becomes a marketing opportunity which he may wish to exploit.
>
> Potential demand may be said to exist where a consumer possesses purchasing power but is not currently buying. Thus, where a marketer has identified a latent demand and developed a new product to satisfy it, the potential demand consists of all those who can back up their latent want with purchasing power. In another context potential demand may be thought of as that part of the total market or effective demand for an existing product which a firm might anticipate securing through the introduction of a new competitive product.'

Two particularly important ideas have been introduced in this discussion of demand – preference and substitutability. Preference defines the extent to which a consumer will favour one product over another, while substitutability reflects how well one object may take the place of another, either directly or indirectly. (The latter qualification is particularly important for marketers. If I am a sugar manufacturer then clearly Aspartame is a direct substitute for my product. If I manufacture dishwashers or carpets it may not be so obvious that I am competing with two weeks in Lanzarote on a package tour as a substitute!)

In theory (and the realms of economic analysis) every individual has a schedule of preferences which rank-orders all consumption goods for which they have an effective demand. At the top of most people's preference schedules are those objects necessary for survival – food, clothing, shelter, etc. – followed by social goods which display our self-concept of our status. Of course, depending on our wealth an almost infinite variety of individual products will meet our needs and these preferred 'wants' make up a consumer's personal preference schedule. In practice most of us give very little explicit consideration to our overall preference schedule. Indeed we are remarkably skilled at adjusting this with little or no conscious thought according to changing times and circumstances. While this is less true of organizational markets than those for consumer goods, it has important implications for the seller's ability to predict or forecast demand. There is, however, one very useful generalization about preference which is sufficiently robust to have become accepted as a 'law' – the law of diminishing marginal utility. Simply put, this law observes that beyond a certain point the acquisition of additional units of anything will decline in value progressively *vis-à-vis* the perceived utility or value of other objects. This is even true of money as is apparent from the fact that people will forego opportunities to increase their earnings at the expense of their leisure time.

This latter example reinforces our earlier point about the indirect substitution effect and hints at the difficulty of predicting the demand for specific goods and services. In general the effective demand will represent the basic level of demand or sales at a given point in time. In mature markets this demand is likely to be fairly stable and move up and down with the prevailing economic climate. In such markets competition may be thought of as a zero-sum game in which one seller's gain is counterbalanced by another's loss with no change in overall sales. Total demand in such mature markets is particularly vulnerable to the threat of direct substitutes from new and improved products. For example, a new process for making smooth floor coverings from vinyl largely replaced the manufacture of linoleum which had been the preferred product for many years. In this particular case the major manufacturers of linoleum – Armstrong Cork and Congoleum Nairn – switched to the new process and survived the competitive threat. Frequently, however, existing suppliers to a market are not so fortunate, which is one of the reasons why product strategy and management are so important to the firm's overall corporate strategy.

The introduction of new products, whether they are substitutes (like vinyl for linoleum) or completely new in the sense that they release a hitherto unsatisfied latent demand, e.g. TV and the demand for in-home entertainment, offers the opportunity for the firm to increase its sales and so enhances both its competitive standing and potential for survival. Through the creation of new products firms stimulate customers to re-evaluate their existing preference schedule and, when successful, create completely new markets as well as diverting expenditure away from other existing markets which may go into decline as a result. The importance of new product development in creating and sustaining competitive advantage is reflected in the space given to it in this book. Fundamentally, however, success in new product development depends upon producers' ability to define, anticipate and measure demand. In the next section we review some of the factors which influence demand in general before introducing some of the elements that affect it in particular.

General demand influencers

In his book *Product Planning* (1976) Merlin Stone distinguished six factors which have a general influence on demand:

- Price
- Income
- Tastes
- Population
- Stocks
- Distribution.

We will look briefly at each of these but in our preferred ordering of Population, Tastes, Income, Price, Distribution and Stocks.

We prefer to discuss population first because, ultimately, demand reflects the aggregated needs and wants of individuals. It follows that if the population is growing so will demand and vice versa. This is true of all goods and services whether the demand is *direct*, i.e. for consumption by individuals and households, or *derived* as is the case with all other goods and services, such as power stations, transportation systems, steel mills, retail outlets, financial services organizations, etc., employed in creating final consumption goods. Effective demand is determined first by population, and population forecasting is comparatively simple compared with forecasting tastes or economic cycles.

Given that we can now predict life expectancy at birth with a fair degree of accuracy and we can also predict stages in the human life cycle, we should be able to predict demand for social services, like health, education and welfare. More prosaically we should also be able to predict the demands for different kinds of consumer and consumer durable goods and from these forecasts derive others for the raw materials and producer goods needed to create the required supply of consumer goods. In broad, aggregate terms, we should be able to predict broad kinds of aggregate demand 50, 60 or even 70 years into the future.

The reality is that past experience shows that even in advanced and sophisticated economies two things are apparent. First, attempts to forecast population, and particularly the birth rate, have been largely unsuccessful and often highly inaccurate. Second, even when we have the data we are very poor at using this to develop basic forecasts. For example, if we know the retirement age is 65 then from 1995 onwards we should be able to state quite accurately (barring some unforeseen cataclysmic event) how many people will retire every year up to 2060. Furthermore, as each year passes and we know the number of live births we can update our forecast for a further year into the future. Closer at hand we should be able to predict accurately how many pre-school places we need four years ahead, primary places five years ahead, secondary education places 11 years ahead, tertiary education places 18 years ahead and so on. Even a cursory examination of recent economic history shows that governments have been singularly unsuccessful in getting such forecasts right. Hopefully, professional marketers will be more successful as the basic information is readily to hand for establishing at least the latent demand for all kinds of goods and services.

For latent demand to become effective demand, the other five factors must come into play, most of which are much less easy to predict. While broadly based taxonomies like Maslow's Hierarchy of Human Needs will be useful in giving a basic understanding of 'tastes', and Engels' Laws provide guidance on how people's expenditure will change as their income rises, neither concept is of much practical use in forecasting demand for specific goods and services. We need detailed knowledge of consumer behaviour, both in theory and in practice. We need to establish how people are behaving now before we can speculate on how they may behave in future. And, when we seek to forecast future behaviour, we quickly become aware that while we can make some useful generalizations about human needs (transportation, energy, entertainment) it is much more difficult to predict specific wants (cars, solar power, satellite TV) because we cannot predict accurately technological innovation nor how people will react to it.

The remaining three factors which influence demand – price, distribution and stocks – really have more to do with achieving some kind of equilibrium between demand and supply than in shaping long-term demand changes. Price, in theory, reflects the value consumers place upon securing a supply of the good in question such that the market price will settle at a point where no supplier is willing to offer an additional unit for sale below that price and no consumer is willing to offer more to secure an additional unit for consumption. If the market or going price is seen as too low by potential producers then they will use their resources to make something else with greater added value. Alternatively, if the going price offers a better return than can be made in producing other products, producers will seek to switch from producing those goods or services. Stocks and the distribution channel serve to ensure that suppliers are available where and when they are wanted and to buffer fluctuations on both the supply and demand sides.

This brief discussion of factors which influence demand indicates that while it should be possible to develop long-term predictions about population changes, and indeed it may be possible to forecast technological change, these macro-environmental changes are likely to be of limited use to producers seeking to secure the greatest possible return on the resources under their control in the short to medium term. To do this we must get much closer to the consumer and seek to determine what it is that is shaping his or her needs and wants and the relative importance or preference which is attached to them. In other words we need to look at specific products and markets and to do so must return to our opening question 'What is a product?'.

Product classification

As a first step towards refining our consideration of demand it will be helpful to develop some kind of classificatory system for products as this should enable us to make useful generalizations about particular categories or kinds of products. In fact a possible classificatory system exists in our references to consumer goods and consumer durable goods and in distinguishing these from producer goods. This dichotomy between producer and consumer goods is reflected in industrial marketing and consumer marketing – a distinction which has proved very useful in developing specific recommendations for marketing strategy and marketing mix decisions.

As we have seen, the demand for industrial goods is derived from that for consumer goods. This being so, we should establish first how consumer goods are perceived, bought and consumed before explaining how this affects the demand for industrial goods. One of the earliest and most influential contributions to the classification of consumer goods was that made by Melvin T. Copeland in 1923 ('Relation of consumers' buying habits to marketing methods', *Harvard Business Review*, 1: 282–9) in which he proposed that consumer goods could be classified as shopping goods, convenience goods and specialty goods. These were defined formally by the American Marketing Association's Committee on Definitions (1948) as follows:

- **Convenience goods**: Those consumer goods which the customer purchases frequently, immediately, and with the minimum of effort, e.g. chocolate, pens, shoe repairs.
- **Shopping goods**: Those consumer goods which the customer in the process of selection and purchase characteristically compares on such bases as suitability, quality, price and style, e.g. cosmetics, TVs, PCs, hairstyle.
- **Specialty goods**: Those consumer goods on which a significant group of buyers are habitually willing to make a special purchasing effort, e.g. house, car, holiday.

Copeland's schema has been subject to much comment and criticism since it first appeared, but, as Bucklin (1963, 1973) makes clear, it remains a remarkably robust conceptualization which has been found to be operationally useful. In his earlier (1963) article, 'Retail strategy and the classification of consumer goods' (*Journal of Marketing*), Bucklin seeks to synthesize some of the criticisms of Copeland by introducing the notion that consumer buying behaviour is a form of problem solving which enables one to distinguish two broad categories, shopping goods and non-shopping goods. 'Shopping goods are those for which the consumer *regularly* formulates a new solution to his need each time it is aroused. They are goods whose suitability is determined through search before the consumer commits himself to each purchase'. By contrast non-shopping goods are those 'products for which the consumer is both willing and able to use stored solutions to the problem of finding a product to answer a need.... non-shopping goods have purchase determinants which do not change, or are perceived as changing inconsequentially, between purchases.'

Bucklin continues to propose that non-shopping goods may be divided into either convenience or specialty goods depending on whether the consumer is indifferent (as between a number of close substitutes) or has a decided preference for one particular product. Given this classification it becomes possible to develop a categorization of patronage motives and, from this, a product patronage matrix containing nine possible cells as indicated in Figure 3.1. Some of the possible combinations may not be appropriate for certain products/markets, but by using the matrix it becomes possible both to select a preferred segment and to devise a differentiated marketing strategy for it.

In both the original article and his retrospective comment on it (1973) Bucklin emphasizes that the underlying objective of the attempt to classify goods in terms of consumer buying behaviour is the development of marketing strategies, with specific advice as to which strategy should be used under what circumstances. However,

Store type

	Convenience	Shopping	Specialty
Convenience			
Shopping			
Specialty			

Good type

Figure 3.1 ● The product–patronage matrix

Bucklin also points to 'manifold barriers that lie in the way of attempting to validate any classification of goods theory' which probably accounts for the limited attention the theory has received in marketing literature. Despite the lack of theoretical validation, and in common with many other current marketing ideas and techniques, the theory is widely referred to in writings intended 'to instruct practitioners in the profession'. Bucklin explains why: 'The reason is that qualitative as it is, the classification theory provides a broad and essential integration of much material in marketing. It provides a framework for the analysis of marketing problems, at least at rudimentary level, and suggests where students might look to devise answers to marketing strategy problems. It provides a logic which can be readily understood and appreciated.'

On the other hand it is important to recognize that product classification may be the *consequence* of marketing strategies as well as *a priori* classifications suggesting preferred strategies. This apparent paradox is clarified by Hume Winzar in his 1992 paper 'Product classification and marketing strategy' (*Journal of Marketing Management*, 8: 259–68) the abstract for which reads as follows:

> 'Marketers have often attempted to use product classification schemes to provide a "cookery book" for marketing strategy. This so-called commodity school of thought is argued, in this paper, to be less than fruitful in providing such a cookery book. Product classifications are shown to be contingent upon marketing mix elements and assumptions about consumer response. These lead to four specific problems:
>
> ● *Ex post* definitions and circular logic: Products are classified *ex post* and classification theory gives no hint about how to classify new products or how to change existing products.
>
> ● The problem of induction: Experiences with similar or existing products give few guides to appropriate or optimum strategy.
>
> ● Fuzzy sets: Product classification of the same product differs according to the nature of the consumer and at different times for the same consumer.
>
> ● Generalizability of scheme: Application of a classification scheme requires the specification of all physical, market and social contexts.'

Winzar makes a detailed and convincing case to support the above arguments but, in doing so, misses the point that theoreticians develop definitions and theoretical constructs to provide a frame of reference for examining states of nature or reality. Thus the ideas of perfect competition and pure monopoly are rarely encountered in the real world but, by being defined, provide a basis for describing and defining all the myriad cases which lie between them. In the same way by classifying goods in terms of the buying behaviour they elicit we can easily see that all new or improved products are by definition shopping goods; the innovator is left to decide whether he wishes to position them as convenience, shopping or speciality purchases. By defining products *a priori* as to how we want them to be perceived *ex post* we can then select the strategy/marketing mix which we think will achieve this. Only if we are successful will the logic be circular! In other words by classifying existing products as belonging to particular categories and identifying the strategies which have contributed to this outcome we have a useful managerial tool for plotting future action.

Objective versus subjective selection criteria

If products and services are defined in terms of the buyer's behaviour towards them, it will be useful here to consider the factors that determine that behaviour. Most models of buyer behaviour implicitly recognize two kinds of factors – objective and subjective. Objective factors may or may not be tangible but they must be quantifiable and measurable and are present in the object itself. By contrast subjective factors are intangible and are influenced by attitudes, belief, experience and associations which the decision maker holds towards the object and feels to be relevant in forming a judgment about the level of satisfaction to be gained from its consumption. In economic theory it is the objective factors which settle the decision and form the basis of economic 'rationality'. In the behavioural sciences it is accepted that objective criteria are subject to subjective interpretation and so are not as hard and fast as the rational decision-making school would have us believe. In addition behavioural scientists recognize that it is possible to discriminate between objectively similar objects – perfect substitutes in the language of the economist – and hold a firm preference for one substitute product over another.

Of course, to prefer one substitute product over another it is necessary first to be able to judge that they are objectively similar, i.e. we need a set of *criteria* on which to form this judgement. Next we need to be able to discriminate between the objectively similar products in terms of other, to us, meaningful criteria. Objective criteria are sometimes termed 'performance factors' and, for some technical products, may be summarized in a performance specification so that only objects which conform with the specification would be considered as belonging to the product category under consideration, e.g. chemicals, fabricated materials like steel, plastic or aluminium, microprocessors, electrical generating equipment, etc. In *Marketing and Competitive Success* (1989) Baker and Hart identified 16 performance factors commonly used by buyers in assessing a product. As can be seen from the list in Table 3.1, some of these performance factors are intrinsic properties of the product itself while other factors are associated with availability and use. An alternative list of objective product characteristics is to be found in *Marketing Strategy and Management* (Baker, 1992) which comprises both technical and economic factors with the latter divided between price and non-price factors (see Table 3.2).

Organizations which produce things which are seen as objectively similar are usually regarded as belonging to the same industry and so as being in direct competition with

Table 3.1 ● Critical success factors: product factors influencing competitiveness (in rank order)

1.	Performance in operation
2.	Reliability
3.	Sale price
4.	Efficient delivery
5.	Technical sophistication
6.	Quality of after-sales service
7.	Durability
8.	Ease of use
9.	Safety in use
10.	Ease of maintenance
11.	Parts availability and cost
12.	Attractive appearance/shape
13.	Flexibility and adaptability in use
14.	Advertising and promotion
15.	Operator comfort
16.	Design

Source: Baker and Hart (1989).

Table 3.2 ● Product characteristics

Technical	Non-price	Price
Size	Servicing costs	List price
Shape	Availability of parts and	Sale price
Weight	service	Net price after trade-in
Consistency	Running costs	allowance
Materials used in	Breakdown costs	Financing or leasing
construction	Depreciation	arrangements
Complexity	User training facilities	Discounts
Power source	Instructions	Sale or return
Power output	Delivery	Special offers
Speed/production rate		
Reliability		
Flexibility/adaptability		
Ease of use		
Ease of maintenance		
Safety		
Appearance/design features		
Smell		
Taste		

Source: Rothwell *et al.* (1983), Evans and Berman (1982).

one another. Indeed product characteristics form the basis for classifying industries and their products in schemas such as the United States Standard Industrial Classification (SIC). The Standard Industrial Classification Manual was first published in 1945 in the USA and was concerned solely with manufacturing and non-manufacturing industries.

The SIC is a numerical system set up by the Federal Government to classify the total economy into different industry segments. Primarily, the system categorizes all business activities into broad industrial divisions and then sub divides each into major groups, sub groups, and into detailed four digit sub-sub groups. For example, the two digit number "28" refers to "Chemicals and Allied Products"; the three digit number "283" refers to "Drugs"; and four digit "2834" refers to "Pharmaceutical Preparations". Figure 3.2 illustrates the principle.

While four-digit SIC codes are quite precise this precision is significantly enhanced by the addition of further distinguishing digits to form five, six and even seven figure codes with the latter defining individual products and services that are truly perfect substitutes for one another. SIC codes are not confined to the USA but are part of an International SIC system, making it possible to make very precise comparisons between products and services between all countries subscribing to the code.

Once it is agreed that things are objectively similar (i.e. they share the same SIC code) then the question becomes: how can consumers discriminate between homogeneous products and services? The answer is, of course, that they can only do so if some other information is provided which identifies individual units of output as belonging to individual suppliers. This identification is made possible by the practice of *branding* whereby the supplier provides some distinguishing feature – name, symbol, trademark, packaging etc. – which enables the consumer to exercise differentiation between the objectively similar offerings of competing suppliers. In addition to providing some physical means of identification, suppliers also seek to develop images or associations with their own particular offerings which will enhance their attractiveness in the eyes of prospective purchasers. This is the function of the promotion and, to some extent, place elements of the marketing mix.

Branding

'A successful brand is a name, symbol, design, or some combination which identifies the "product" of a particular organisation as having a sustainable differential advantage' (Doyle in Baker (1992)).

Several important points are contained within this definition:

● Brands can take many forms and are not just names.

● Brands are not restricted to physical products. A brand can just as easily be a service, an organization or even an aspiration.

● Most importantly, successful brands confer a sustainable competitive advantage – the corollary being that unsuccessful brands have precisely the opposite effect.

Doyle defines 'sustainable' as an advantage that is not easily copied by competitors and so represents a barrier to entry in the markets in which the brand competes, while

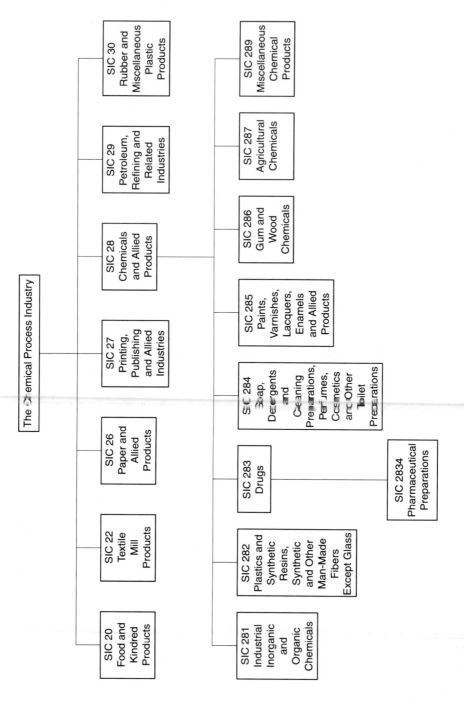

Figure 3.2 ● US Standard Industrial Classification (SIC) for the chemical process industry

'differential' means an advantage that is important to at least some consumers such that they will use it as a basis for discriminating between suppliers of similar products.

As noted elsewhere (Baker, 1992) the importance of brands for consumers is that they help simplify decision-making. The brand is a form of mental shorthand that neatly summarizes all the factors to be taken into account in making a decision to purchase. Once we have identified a brand which possesses the desired attributes and delivers the desired satisfactions, then we can use that brand as a summary statement of our wants for a given category of object and select it on future occasions when the need it satisfied arises.

Such a state of 'brand loyalty' is the one to which all producers aspire. Once it exists then the object has the status of a specialty good, for consumers will expend special effort to acquire it and will not easily accept a substitute. In most situations brand loyalty confers a status equivalent to shopping goods – we will make an effort to acquire the preferred brand but, if it is unavailable, will be willing to consider substitutes on the basis of a careful evaluation of their properties *vis-à-vis* our preferred brand. From this it follows that convenience goods are those for which no supplier has been able to create a sustainable differential advantage and brand loyalty is non-existent.

Paradoxically many of the strongest and best-known brands are products where it is difficult to differentiate one supplier's output from another using physical or objective criteria. Thus in blind usage tests people find it difficult or impossible to discriminate between cola drinks, breakfast cereals, instant coffees, soaps, detergents and so on. Only when the product is clothed in its packaging and linked with the familiar brand and its promotional support do strongly held preferences have any real meaning; it is clear that brands are essentially subjective by nature. That said, many of the world's best-known brands are companies rather than specific products. Indeed eight out of the top 10 in 1990 were companies rather than specific products, as can be seen from Figure 3.3.

This trend – to brand the organization – has considerable benefits, especially in markets whose product differentiation is strong and often the major basis for competition. Thus Sony, Kodak and IBM use technological innovation as their major source of sustainable differential advantage. In these markets, where change is rapid and often of a revolutionary rather than evolutionary nature, it is the customers' confidence in the organization to deliver the promised benefits that overcomes the natural resistance to radical change that makes it difficult for unknown innovators to pioneer new markets. Thus the corporate identity or brand acts as an 'umbrella' for all of its outputs and activities and a source of sustainable differential advantage.

Branding is, of course, a subject in its own right. Reverting to our basic theme – the definition and classification of products – we turn now to consider a schema developed by Everett Rogers specifically for classifying new products.

Classifying new products

From the preceding discussion on branding it is clear that firms are seeking to achieve a sustainable competitive advantage, and also that customers will seek to differentiate between competitive offerings in terms of their objective performance factors, but that, faced with two or more objectively similar products or services, they will look for other

Figure 3.3 ● The global top ten brand names (*source*: Landor Associates, 1990)

subjective factors to help them discriminate and make a final choice. From the producer/supplier point of view, objective benefits are to be preferred, hence the emphasis on innovation and new product development. Of course, innovation is not without its risks – if the new thing is not sufficiently different from the old (incremental innovation) customers may see little benefit in changing a currently satisfactory form of behaviour. Conversely, if the new thing is radically different from the intended users' past experience, then they may perceive considerable risk in trying it and defer a purchase decision until they have more and better information.

Based upon an extensive review of the characteristics of new products Rogers (1983) developed a very useful framework which classifies characteristics under five headings:

● Relative advantage
● Compatibility
● Complexity
● Divisibility
● Communicability.

The first characteristic, *relative advantage*, seeks to measure the economic benefit conferred upon or available to the adopter of an innovation adjusted to take cognisance of the adopter's present situation. Thus, for example, if a manufacturer has brought out three models of a machine, the first with a rated output of 1000 units per hour, the second with 1200 units per hour and the third with 1500 units per hour, then the introduction of model 3 offers a 50% improvement to owners of model 1, but only 25% to owners of model 2. Clearly the absolute performance is the same, but a 25% improvement may not be sufficient relative advantage for the model 2 owner to trade in or scrap his machine in favour of the new one, whereas 50% is sufficient incentive for the model 1 owner to do so. Thus, a planned replacement policy related to the age of the existing stock of machines would suggest model 1 owners as better targets for replacement than model 2 owners.

Compatibility and complexity are both dimensions of the degree of novelty associated with an innovation, but tend to be inversely related to each other. The more compatible a new product is with the existing system, the more likely it is to be readily accepted. Of course, beyond a certain point the new product may so resemble what it seeks to replace that it is insufficiently distinguishable to prompt users to change. For example, a survey by McGraw-Hill indicated that many industrial purchasing agents were unwilling to switch from a currently satisfactory source of supply unless the change offered a saving equivalent to a reduction of 8%–10% of the current price.

While *complexity*, defined as the degree of difficulty associated with full understanding of the application of an innovation, does not automatically increase with novelty, this is often the case. It certainly is true that the less compatible an innovation is with the existing way of doing things, the more complex it is likely to seem to be.

Divisibility measures the extent to which it is possible to try an innovation before coming to a final adoption/rejection decision and it can have a significant influence upon attitudes towards a new product. Where there is a high degree of uncertainty about an innovation and trial is only possible by firms or individuals for whom the economic risks are small, then most potential users will prefer to wait and see. In other words, for them trial is vicarious and based upon the reactions of the early adopters. Two points are worth noting in this context.

First, it is an established fact that many early buyers in industrial markets are the largest firms in the industry. However, experience suggests that many large firms which buy during the launch phase do so only on a trial basis and without any commitment to large-scale or continued use. In some cases early trial may even be used as a delaying tactic, and it would be a mistake to concentrate all one's launch efforts on the biggest potential users. Equally, one should not ignore the opportunity to sell to 'trialists', for, in addition to generating much-needed revenue, they also provide feedback on problems which only become apparent when the new product is put into 'normal' use.

The second point to make is that sellers can do a great deal to minimize risk during the launch phase by providing a trial period or its equivalent. For example, one can supply goods on sale or return terms, provide additional guarantees to early adopters or lease the product rather than sell it outright. Endorsement by an authority figure can also help reduce risk.

The final characteristic, *communicability*, is heavily influenced by the preceding four factors, for it reflects the degree of difficulty associated with communicating the benefits of an innovation to prospective users, which, in turn, is a function of its relative advantage, compatibility, complexity and divisibility. Communication is a vital activity throughout the new product purchase decision process, with impersonal or media communications being most important in creating initial awareness, both impersonal and personal sources influencing interest, personal sources becoming dominant as the buyer moves towards a decision, and impersonal sources assuming the primary role of reassurance after the decision has been made.

All these factors can be measured objectively, but as we have noted on a number of occasions, such objective measurement is of secondary importance. It is the way prospective users perceive and interpret the factors which is important. In turn, it would seem reasonable to infer that early adopters do perceive 'the facts' differently from followers and laggards – that is, the selling proposition must seem more attractive and/or less risky to them, and marketers have expended a great deal of effort in attempts to determine what the distinguishing features are.

The above discussion of the characteristics of new products provides an opportunity to link a number of ideas introduced in the chapter with a model of buyer behaviour developed for industrial products but of equal relevance to consumer buying decisions.

The Buygrid Analytic Framework
· ·

The Buygrid Analytic Framework is shown in Figure 3.4. As can be seen, the Buygrid uses two sets of variables distinguished as Buy Phases (Steps 1–8 on the vertical axis) and Buy Classes which are defined as follows:

1. **New task**: The recognition of a purchasing problem which has not been encountered previously. The buyer will face considerable uncertainty and will seek to

Buy phase		Buy classes		
		New task	Modified rebuy	Straight rebuy
1.	Anticipation or recognition of a problem (need) and a general solution			
2.	Determination of characteristics and quality of needed item			
3.	Description of characteristics and quantity of needed item			
4.	Search for and qualification of potential sources			
5.	Acquisition and analysis of proposals			
6.	Evaluation of proposals and selection of supplier(s)			
7.	Selection of an order routine			
8.	Performance feedback and evaluation			

Figure 3.4 ● The Buygrid Analytic Framework for industrial buying situations (source: Robinson et al., 1967)

reduce this through the acquisition of as much information as possible from both personal and impersonal sources. All the Buy Phases are likely to receive careful and explicit attention.

2. **Modified rebuy**: The buyer has prior experience of the purchase problem but has reason to re-evaluate this in light of some new information or stimulus. Some of the Buy Phases may be truncated or omitted.

3. **Straight rebuy**: The buyer is satisfied with an existing source of supply and sees no reason to change. Phases 4–7 are likely to be omitted altogether and only cursory attention given to the others, i.e. purchase has become habitual and routinized.

In the case of consumer goods purchased by individuals it is unlikely that the Buy Phases will be specified quite as formally as they are in the Buygrid. Nonetheless, the same procedure and sequence would seem to be applicable to both industrial and consumer buying situations, just as the notion of New Task corresponds closely to the idea of Extended Problem Solving, and Modified Rebuy to Limited Problem Solving, in the consumer behaviour literature. Similarly, Straight Rebuy is clearly the same as Routinized Response Behaviour, and the concept of novelty provides a common thread for linking individual and organizational buyer behaviour through the characteristics of products. It now remains to return to the question of whether services are sufficiently different from products to merit separate treatment.

Are services different?

In the 6th edition of *Marketing: An Introductory Text* (Baker, 1996) Chapter 23 is concerned exclusively with the marketing of services. Only a brief resume of the key points will be attempted here.

The first point to be made is that there are at least three schools of thought concerning the existence of a separate sub-field of service marketing (just as there are with most other sub-fields of marketing – industrial, not-for-profit, etc.). The first school of thought maintains that products and services are but two faces of the same coin and that the principles and practices of marketing are equally applicable to both. The second school refutes this and claims that there are important and significant differences between products and services such that they require a quite different marketing approach. The third school (to which we subscribe) argues that the basic principles apply to both but that the distinctive nature of services calls for an extended marketing mix comprising seven elements with process, physical evidence and people being added to McCarthy's familiar four P's of Product, Price, Place and Promotion.

Most arguments about the distinctiveness of services centre on the fact that services possess certain characteristics which set them apart from conventional 'products'. This is true of *intangibility* and *inseparability* but less so of *heterogeneity* and *perishability and fluctuating demand*.

As noted in *Marketing*, 'Intangibility is probably the single most important factor in distinguishing services from goods. While it is possible to describe the nature and performance of physical products using objective criteria, this is only possible to a limited

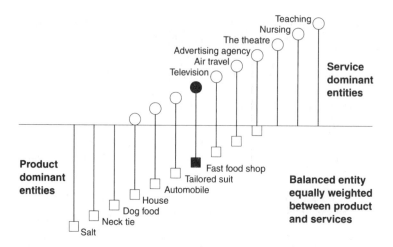

Figure 3.5 ● Scale of elemental dominance (*source*: Shostack, 1982)

extent in the case of services'. But if services are purely ideas and experiences, how are potential users to evaluate them and how are potential suppliers able to distinguish themselves and develop customer loyalty? One answer is of course to make at least some aspects of the service tangible, e.g. impressive bank and insurance buildings to reassure us about their solid values, security and stability. By the same token, as we have seen earlier, when it becomes impossible to discriminate between products on purely objective or tangible factors suppliers invest them with subjective factors (intangible associations and services) to help customers distinguish. Increasingly, it is accepted that because buyers are concerned with benefits or satisfactions this is a combination of *both* tangible and intangible 'products' and 'services'. Shostack (1982) illustrates this in her conceptualization of a continuum from product dominant entities such as salt, and service dominant entities such as teaching, as illustrated in Figure 3.5.

This idea is encapsulated neatly in the concept of the augmented product (illustrated in Figure 3.6) at the heart of which is a physical entity but where distinctiveness depends very much on the layers of subjective and service factors which surround it.

The other major characteristic which distinguishes products and services is that the provision of the service is inseparable from the provider and requires the involvement of the customer for the service to be created and consumed. This characteristic also makes it often difficult to standardize a service: they are heterogeneous rather than homogeneous, although as Ted Levitt showed in his famous article 'The industrialization of service' (1976a), the success of McDonalds is largely one of standardization of service. Similarly, as the creation of a service requires customer involvement, if there is no customer then the potential to create and consume that service, e.g. a seat on an aeroplane or hotel room, is gone (hence 'perishability and fluctuating demand').

So much for the characteristics which help distinguish products from services. How about the proposal that they call for an extended marketing mix comprising process, physical evidence and people in addition to the conventional four P's? First, what are

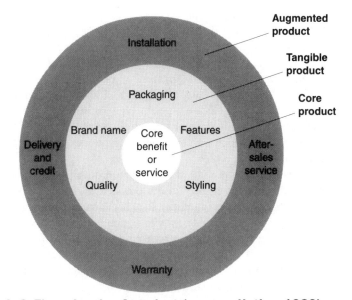

Figure 3.6 ● Three levels of product (*source*: Kotler, 1989)

they? Process is concerned with the way in which the service is delivered to the custo-mer; physical evidence consists of those tangible clues which the consumer may receive which verify either the existence or completion of a service, e.g. a cheque book, ticket, policy document, etc.; finally, people embraces all the members of the service organiza-tion, whether or not they have any direct contact with customers.

It requires little more than a moment's reflection to realize that all three factors are important in marketing physical products too and so are a poor basis for distinguishing between goods and services. As we have seen, as it becomes more difficult to distin-guish between physical objects, the idea of the augmented product as a bundle of satis-faction or benefits combining both tangible and intangible elements has displaced the earlier, more 'economic', representation featuring only performance and price. Similarly, concepts like total quality management and internal marketing recognize that all members of a supplier organization are responsible for the quality of its relationships with customers and so influence the perceived value of these relationships.

To sum up, the distinction between products and services will be helpful if it is used to develop enhanced marketing mixes for both; it will be harmful if it hinders the trans-fer of ideas and practices between marketers whose outputs lie at different ends of the continuum between product dominant and service dominant entities.

Summary
In this section we have reviewed some of the factors which should be taken into account when considering the nature of the product or services in order to be able to answer the question 'What is a product?'.

It has been shown that there is value in seeking to classify products as this requires us to consider carefully precisely what is the basis of exchange between producer and consumer. Such consideration makes it clear that for a successful exchange to occur both parties must be satisfied: it is a win–win outcome. If it is a win–lose outcome it cannot satisfy our definition of the purpose of marketing as establishing 'mutually satisfying exchange relationships'. Our review has also made it clear that it is the prospective buyers' perception of benefit or satisfaction which is determinant and they are best able to define what mix of benefits – objective or subjective, tangible or intangible, 'product' or 'service' – will best match their want. The consumers' wants and their buying behaviour define the market.

We have also established that the classification of products helps determine which suppliers offer direct substitutes for each other's products and so may be regarded as being in direct competition with one another. The characteristics of the product define the nature of the industry and so provide us with the ability to identify our immediate competitors and devise strategies for outmanoeuvring and outperforming them. In addition we have been reminded that as well as direct competition we must also be concerned with indirect competition whereby a preference for quite different products may deflect or reduce demand in a given market. This is a theme to which we will return in Chapter 11, on testing product (and service) concepts.

As the focus of the exchange relationship the product must occupy centre stage in the suppliers' strategic thinking. It is the medium through which producers communicate with prospective customers and the means by which they establish long-lasting and profitable relationships with them. Ultimately it is the only source of a sustainable competitive advantage. The creation and maintenance of such an advantage is the subject of the remainder of this book.

QUESTIONS

1. What is a 'product'?
2. Distinguish and define three broad categories of demand.
3. What is preference and how is it affected by the law of diminishing marginal utility?
4. Discuss the factors which may influence demand.
5. Suggest and explain a system for classifying products.
6. Why has branding become so important in increasingly competitive markets?
7. Discuss the five characteristics used by Rogers for classifying new products.
8. Describe the Buygrid and discuss its implications for analyzing buyer behaviour.
9. Are services different?

Mini-case ● New Coke

One of the largest and most dynamic global markets is that for Cola-flavoured carbonated beverages. Internationally this market is dominated by two brands – Coca-Cola and Pepsi-Cola – and recent years have seen a continuous battle between the two brands as Pepsi seeks to wrest supremacy from Coke.

By the mid-1970s Coca-Cola had become an American institution and, despite the efforts of its arch-rival Pepsi, outsold them by 2 to 1. But, as Levitt demonstrated so vividly in his 'Marketing myopia' (1960), success can breed complacency and inertia, and between 1976 and 1979 Coca-Cola's annual growth rate dropped from an average 13% to only 2%. Much of this lost momentum was due to the inroads made by Pepsi in what subsequently came to be known as 'the Cola wars'.

As is the case in many highly competitive markets there was little objective difference between the products of Coca-Cola and Pepsi-Cola. Such differences as were seen to exist between the two products depended very much upon marketing and particularly on distribution and promotion. Thus, much of Coca-Cola's difficulties in the late 1970s can be explained by the particularly effective advertising campaign which Pepsi targeted at the idealism and youth of the baby-boomers which they identified with as 'the Pepsi generation'.

The success of 'the Pepsi generation' which linked the image of Pepsi strongly with youth and vitality was strongly reinforced by Pepsi featuring comparative taste tests in its advertising which showed that in blind taste tests more consumers chose Pepsi than Coca-Cola. As a result of the Pepsi challenge Pepsi's market share increased from 6% to 14% of the total US soft drink market. In addition to its more effective advertising Pepsi had also chosen to attack Coca-Cola in the grocery store market where Coke was at its weakest. By 1984 Pepsi had reduced Coca-Cola's overall lead in market share to only 2.9% whilst in the grocery store market it led Coke by 1.7%.

It was in light of the erosion of its market share and the confirmation from its own blind taste tests that, indeed, consumers did prefer Pepsi that Coca-Cola was prompted to launch a new product.

In April 1985 Robert Goizueta, Chairman of Coca-Cola, announced 'The best has been made even better'. After offering the same formulation for 99 years New Coke had been developed with a sweeter and softer taste much closer to that of Pepsi, which their own blind taste tests had proved to be the most preferred offering.

Contrary to expectations the launch of New Coke created an immediate backlash from existing customers. Over 5000 calls a day from dissatisfied customers were registered on the company's free phone number whilst consumers demonstrated in the streets of Atlanta calling for the return of the original Coca-Cola brand. Seventy-nine days after its launch New Coke was withdrawn from the market and disappeared for ever.

Having spent two years and $4 million on market research one would have imagined that Coca-Cola might reasonably have expected New Coke to be a success. With the benefit of hindsight a re-examination of the market research shows that it concentrated mainly on objective factors and comparative taste testing and overlooked the symbolic and emotional values associated with the brand. As noted, Coca-Cola's formulation had not been changed in 99 years and its bottle shape had remained the same since 1916. Generations of Americans had been brought up with Coke and it had become an integral part of the American psyche. More than that, world-wide Coca-Cola is perceived as a drink that symbolizes many American values – dynamism, ambition, drive, modernity, entrepreneurship and a product which unifies the country as it targets the whole population regardless of nationality, age or social class. By withdrawing the original product and introducing a replacement the company was seen to be destroying a national institution.

In face of the enormous groundswell of public opinion Coca-Cola was forced to bring 'Old Coke' back under the name 'Coca-Cola Classic'. As a result of the relaunch of the original product Coca-Cola enjoyed the biggest one-year rise in sales ever so that, despite the failure of New Coke, at the end of the year Coca-Cola had once again restored its supremacy over Pepsi-Cola.

Of the many lessons which can be learned from the failure of New Coke, perhaps the most important is that people's perception of a brand and their attitude towards it are based upon a combination of both objective and subjective factors. In the case of the original Coke it had a century of tradition behind it and had become an integral part of a national culture. In an era of continuing flux and change, constancy and tradition are important values. In hindsight, to claim that 'Coke is the Real Thing' and then change it was not a particularly enlightened move, although in the the final analysis the relaunch of classic Coke allowed the company to increase its dominance of the market.

chapter 4

....

Buyer behaviour

LEARNING OBJECTIVES
....

1. To introduce some of the better known models of buyer behaviour.

2. To define and explain the nature of perception.

3. To present a composite model of buyer behaviour and explain its essential elements and their interaction with each other.

4. To examine the process by which new products are adopted and diffuse through a population.

5. To illustrate by means of a case study how an understanding of buyer behaviour is critical when introducing new products into a market.

On completion of this chapter you will:

1. Be aware of various different models of buyer behaviour.

2. Understand how perception influences the interpretation of phenomena.

3. Be familiar with a composite model of buyer behaviour which integrates both objective and subjective factors.

4. Comprehend the process by which innovations spread through populations of adopters.

Introduction
....
A major objective of this book is to provide a framework, together with practical advice, concerning the role of product strategy and management in enhancing competitive performance. In doing so, however, it is important always to remember that marketing, including product development, is not something sellers do *to* buyers but something they do *for* them. This simple distinction, which is at the very heart of the marketing concept, has been in danger of being overlooked in the marketing management model which dominated both academic and practitioner approaches between 1960 and 1990, especially in the USA which many regard as the homeland of modern marketing.

The marketing management model focuses on the way in which organizations manipulate inputs and transform them into goods and services which they can sell profitably to buyers. Such an approach usually concentrates on the management of the four

P's – product, price, place and promotion – and the transaction, i.e. the sale itself. As the recognition of relationship marketing, particularly in the USA (Webster, 1992), has served to remind us, marketing is all about customers and the sellers' efforts to establish mutually satisfying exchange relationships with them. An article by Shiv Mathur entitled 'Talking straight about competitive strategy' in the *Journal of Marketing Management* (1992) serves to underline this point. Mathur argues that the offering – what customers choose to buy – should be the primary focus of competitive strategy. In his view:

> 'To be meaningful, marketing must start with competitive offerings. Its focus must be on outputs and their competitive positioning in markets, not on inputs. Yet even the corner-stones of marketing's vocabulary, the terms – service, systems, product and commodity – usually describe the characteristics of *what* a business sells rather than on *how* it positions its offering; they are input, not output terms. They are centred on the seller, not the choosing customer. Customer orientation would become automatic if our terminology centred on the customer's viewpoint rather than on the things that are sold; if we adopted an output- or buyer-centred language, not an input- or supplier-centred one.'

Now this book is primarily concerned with the product – an output. But, in this chapter, we wish to affirm our support that throughout our ultimate concern is the customer and our recognition that customers decide what will succeed in the marketplace. To quote Mathur again:

> 'Those benefits and drawbacks that influence customers when making buying decisions are the outputs. By contrast, inputs are all those attributes to which customers are not sensitive when making their choice; for example, the costs, culture, resources and skills, that go to make up what the seller offers, but which are usually invisible to the choosing customer. Market positions are determined solely by outputs. Customers' buying decisions rest entirely on them and it is for favourable buying decisions that sellers compete. Inputs are immensely important in achieving a market position, but they are not the position itself, only the means to it.'

It follows that while the product or service is the embodiment of all the firms' inputs its relevance and success will be determined entirely by the customers' buying behaviour and this is the subject of the present chapter.

The chapter opens with a general introduction to some of the better known and accepted models of buyer behaviour before considering two key determinants of choice – risk and perception. Recognizing the importance of perception in influencing buyer behaviour, we propose a composite model which incorporates this phenomenon and use this as background to a discussion of the adoption and diffusion of new products. A detailed case study – Aluminium Sleeve Bearings – is used to highlight the importance of conducting research into buyer behaviour and the chapter concludes with a brief discussion of this topic.

Models of buyer behaviour

A decision to buy is usually the outcome of a sequential process, and a large number of models of varying degrees of complexity seek to encapsulate the essence of this process. Before considering some of these models, two points need to be made. Firstly, while some models claim to represent industrial or organizational buying behaviour, which implicitly infers that this somehow differs from the behaviour of ultimate consumers, we do not find the distinction helpful. In fact, such a distinction may be positively harmful, for it can lead sellers to underestimate the ultimate consumer's ability to make judgments based on objective criteria, while in the case of industrial purchase decisions, undue emphasis upon 'the facts' can lead to a neglect of the subjective dimensions which are often critical when the buyer is seeking to choose between two or more evenly matched alternatives. Secondly, the models describe a decision to buy *de novo*. Once a buyer has been through the process once, they may well omit several of the stages, in which case purchase becomes a form of learned behaviour and it may take considerable effort to make a consumer 'unlearn' this behaviour – precisely the problem facing the seller of a new product.

Perhaps the simplest, most basic and best-known model of buyer behaviour is that summarized by the salesmen's mnemonic AIDA, standing for Awareness, Interest, Desire and Action. To have any hope of making a sale, you must first get your customer's attention, which may be seen as no easy task once it is appreciated that it has been estimated that every individual is exposed to something like 1500 selling messages a day and recognizes only five or six. As soon as you have awareness, it is necessary to convert this into interest – to get the customer actively to consider the selling proposition – and then to convert this into desire. Getting a prospect to want your product, however, is not enough, for the nearer one comes to the decision, the greater the risk of making a wrong decision and the greater the resistance – you must 'close the sale' and get action.

Since Strong first proposed this basic model in 1914, a large number of variants have been offered, the best known of which are summarized in Table 4.1. Such models are sometimes referred to as 'hierarchy of effects' models, on the grounds that one proceeds through a series of steps to attain the given outcome. They are closely related to the psychologists' so-called CAC model, standing for Cognitive (the realm of thought), Affective (the realm of emotion) and Conative (the realm of motivation). Elaboration of these models is to be found in most texts on consumer behaviour and is beyond the scope of this book. For our purposes, we shall use Rogers' five-step model for, while it closely resembles the others, it is distinctive in its inclusion of a trial phase and our own research suggests this is often of critical importance.

Without doubt, the possibility of trial helps to reduce risk for the new buyer, but, since it does not signify final commitment, it may also give the seller a misleading impression of the level of acceptance he is achieving. Conversely, where trial is not possible, as is often the case with capital goods and consumer durables, there would seem to be only a very small proportion of firms or individuals who are prepared to act as guinea pigs for the rest. As we shall see in this chapter, the potential pay-off from being able to identify these innovative customers prior to or during the market launch phase is considerable.

Topics which depend on the identification of innovative customers are central to new product concept testing, the subject of Chapter 11.

Table 4.1 ● Models of stages of buyer behaviour

Lavidge and Steiner (1961)	Rogers (1962)	Robinson et al. (1967)	Engel et al. (1968)
Unawareness Awareness Knowledge	Awareness	Problem recognition Determination of characteristics and quantity needed. Description of characteristics and quantity needed	Problem recognition
Liking	Interest	Search for and qualification of source	
Preference	Evaluation	Requisition and analysis of proposals. Evaluation of proposals and selection of supplier	Evaluation and search
Conviction	Trial	Selection of order routine. Performance feedback and evaluation	Purchase processes
No purchase	Adoption		

Influences on the decision process

So much for the process. What actually influences the manner in which people perform buying activities? Kotler suggests that the social sciences offer four models which underlie and direct the process:

1. The Marshallian economic model.
2. The Pavlovian learning model.
3. The Freudian psychoanalytic model.
4. The Veblenian social–psychological model.

The key features of these four models are as follows.

The *Marshallian economic model* postulates that buying decisions are the result of 'rational' and conscious economic calculations designed to maximize the buyer's utility or satisfaction. Industrial buying behaviour is usually believed to be of this type.

Pavlov's learning model contains four central concepts: drive, cue, response and re-inforcement. Drives may be inherited or learned – hunger is a basic physiological drive, for example, while ambition is learned – but they are usually latent or passive until stimulated by a cue. In the case of hunger, this may be internal (being physiologically hungry) or external (the sight or smell of food), but either way a response is called for.

In Rogers' model, this response is 'trial', for only if the outcome is satisfactory will re-inforcement occur and the new learned behaviour become habitual, or, as Pavlov would have termed it, a conditioned response.

The *Freudian psychoanalytic model* is concerned with the subconscious motivations which direct and condition behaviour. Motivation research enjoyed a vogue in the 1950s with the work of Ernest Dichter, which was mainly concerned with consumer goods. However, this approach was brought into disrepute with the publication of Vance Packard's *Hidden Persuaders* (1957) and it enjoys only limited currency today.

Finally, the *Veblenian model* proposes that people's attitudes and behaviour are conditioned by the norms of the social groupings to which they belong: culture, subculture, social class, reference groups and family affiliations.

Each of these models, however, provides only a partial explanation and the real-world buying decision would seem to be a composite of conscious and subconscious reactions to a variety of stimuli – some objective, measurable and 'rational'. In turn, the reactions or responses will be the product of a host of socio-cultural influences reflecting the decision maker's background, upbringing and current affiliations, their values, beliefs and attitudes.

Novelty

The relative importance of all these influences will vary considerably, depending upon the novelty of the situation to the buyer and the degree of risk associated with the decision.

The degree of novelty must be assessed from the prospective buyer's point of view and not judged in terms of the actual age of the innovation, e.g. the first robots were marketed in the 1950s, but their application and use would have been entirely novel to the great majority of manufacturing organizations which had never considered buying one. While novelty exists on a continuum, it is helpful to classify it into discrete stages and the most useful schema is that proposed by Robinson, Faris and Wind (1967) of 'new task', 'modified rebuy' and 'straight rebuy', introduced in the previous chapter.

Although Robinson *et al.* were concerned with industrial buying, and this is reflected in their definitions of the three states, the classification is felt to be equally appropriate to consumer purchasing, as follows:

New task

1. Need for the product has not arisen previously.
2. Little or no past buying experience is available to assist in the purchasing decision.
3. Members of the buying unit require a great deal of information.
4. Alternative ways of meeting the need are likely to be under review.
5. The situation occurs infrequently, but the decisions taken may set a pattern for more routine purchases subsequently.

6. Opportunities exist at an early stage in the decision process for external (marketing) inputs to have an influence on the final decision made.

Modified rebuy

1. A regular requirement for the type of product exists.

2. The buying alternatives are known, but sufficient change has occurred to require some alteration to the normal supply procedure.

3. Change may be stimulated by external events, e.g. inputs from supplying companies.

4. Change may be stimulated by internal events, e.g. new buying influences, value analysis, reorganization.

Straight rebuy

1. Routine purchasing procedures exist.

2. The buying alternatives are known, and a formal or informal list of 'approved' suppliers is available.

3. No supplier not on the list is considered.

4. Decision on each separate transaction is made by the purchasing department.

5. Buyers have relevant buying experience and require little new information.

From these definitions, it is obvious that the degree of risk felt by the prospective purchaser is likely to be very high in the case of new buy situations and negligible for straight rebuys. Some discussion of the role of risk and perception in the buying decision is called for.

Risk and perception

Strictly speaking, it is not risk which bothers decision makers, it is uncertainty. One can assess risk objectively and express it in terms of the likelihood of a given outcome: the odds against the outsider beating the favourite are clearly stated by bookmakers; life insurance premiums are assessed in terms of average life expectancies; and the insurance on your car may be reduced by a no-claims bonus which reflects the insurer's knowledge of your past driving record. By contrast, uncertainty cannot be assessed in objective terms, although Bayesian analysts such as Raiffa and Schleiffer at the Harvard Business School have demonstrated how one can use subjective expectations to assess the value to the decision maker of uncertain alternative courses of action.

On the other hand, very few buyers are familiar with Bayesian analysis and so do not use their subjective perceptions of uncertainty in a logical and structured manner. Faced with uncertainty, most buyers prefer to stand by the tried and trusted supplier – the phenomenon of source or brand loyalty – rather than chance the possibility of even greater satisfaction by switching to something new. It follows that some very strong stimulus, cue or 'precipitating circumstance' will be necessary to prompt even consideration of an alternative for something which is already judged to be acceptable.

Given that such circumstances do occur, then it is useful to recognize perceived risk as comprising two components: the actual uncertainty surrounding the outcome of the decision and the consequences associated with alternative decisions. Sweeney *et al.* suggested that industrial buyers engage in four categories of action to handle these two dimensions:

1. External uncertainty reduction, e.g. visit supplier's plant.
2. Internal uncertainty reduction, e.g. consult other buyers.
3. External consequence reduction, e.g. buy from several suppliers.
4. Internal consequence reduction, e.g. consult with company's top management.

Again, it requires little imagination to see how the first three risk reduction strategies are used by individual consumers, and the fourth is quite characteristic of household buying behaviour when husbands and wives make joint decisions on big-ticket purchases in order to spread the risk. In other words, involvement in the decision is more important than any expertise which the other party may bring to the situation. From these comments it is obvious that any stratagem the seller can use to reduce the risk experienced by prospective buyers will help to accelerate acceptance.

Unfortunately, it is not easy to make this advice operational, for uncertainty, like success and failure, is a subjective state particular to the individual firm or person, and it is a dynamic state which varies over time. For this reason, the marketing concept, which exhorts suppliers to put themselves in their prospective customers' shoes and look at the selling proposition from their point of view, holds out the greatest prospect of success to sellers in competitive markets. It is also the reason why emphasis has been placed upon subjective factors in decision making – not to the exclusion of objective and measurable facts, but as influences which moderate and even distort these facts. To understand why this occurs, it is necessary to understand the phenomenon of perception, an exposition of which is to be found in any basic psychology text. The following, greatly simplified, review is taken from Baker (1991).

A fundamental aspect of perception is that it represents the reviewer's effort to organize received stimuli into a meaningful structure. In doing so two major groups of factors are involved – stimulus factors and functional factors. Stimulus factors are neutral in the sense that they are intrinsic to the stimulus and so will be received in exactly the same way by all receivers with normal sensory capabilities. On receipt the brain organizes the incoming stimuli into patterns following four basic tendencies: similarity, proximity, continuity and context.

By similarity we understand the tendency of the receiver to group similar things together, while proximity results in the perception that things which are close to one another belong together. In marketing practice similarity is to be seen in the concept of segmentation, while proximity is employed in the use of prominent people to endorse particular products, in the use of generic brands like St Michael, and so on. The need to impose a meaningful structure on stimuli is particularly noticeable in the case of continuity, which is closely associated with closure. The phenomenon of continuity is well illustrated with the use of a simple diagram like that below:

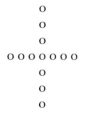

In this one sees the dots as straight lines rather than as separate dots, and as two continuous lines rather than four short ones. Closure occurs when one completes an otherwise incomplete diagram, picture, sentence, etc. For example, we all know what 'Beanz meanz'.

Finally, context, or the setting in which a stimulus is received, will have a marked effect upon perception (see any basic book for marketing illustrations of the context influencing perception). In this sense context can have a similar 'halo' influence to proximity and is frequently used by marketers when seeking to develop an image of a product by using media or a setting which conveys the overall impression they wish to create, e.g. use of the Sunday colour supplements to convey a feeling of quality allied to value for money, or young people in leisure situations to promote Coca-Cola.

As noted, stimulus factors are neutral and create sensations which are then interpreted in light of what are generically termed functional factors. Thus individuals have an ability to screen out stimuli which they do not understand or do not wish to recognize, just as they also have an ability to modify stimuli to make them acceptable to us — a phenomenon sometimes termed 'selective perception'.

The classic example of selective perception is that reported by Hastorf and Cantril (1954) of the perceptions of supporters of two American football teams, Dartmouth and Princeton. The match contained a number of incidents which led to players being injured and penalties being imposed. While most uninvolved viewers felt these were the joint responsibility of both teams, supporters of the two sides were almost unanimous in their view that all the trouble was the fault of the other team.

This tendency to perceive what one wants to 'see' can be traced to several factors. First, there is our ability to screen out or ignore a very large number of stimuli and so enable us to give our full attention to those which have some particular relevance or which strike a discordant note because of the contrast they make with other stimuli. Research has shown that we screen out the vast majority of advertisements to which we are exposed and, in fact, perceive less than 1% of all those we come into contact with. Thus in order to secure our attention advertisers must use contrast, e.g. a colour advertisement in a black-and-white medium, loud noise (or silence) in broadcast media, luxury yacht advertisements in *The Economist*, etc. By the same token we possess perceptual defences which block out stimuli which are offensive, or are otherwise in conflict with our values or attitudes.

The issue of relevance is also important, for clearly we will be more likely to perceive stimuli which cater to our needs, both psychological and emotional, than those which do not. On occasion physical and emotional needs may generate a conflict (termed 'cognitive dissonance') such that acquisition of a physical object to satisfy a need (a car for transportation) may generate uncertainty as to the wisdom of that choice. Under these circumstances it has been shown that purchasers of objects pay more attention to advertising or other stimuli relating to the object than do intending purchasers.

Another perceptual phenomenon of importance to the marketer is that of preparatory set, which, put simply, means that people tend to perceive objects in terms of their own expectations (cf. closure, discussed above). A well-known marketing manifestation of the influence of preparatory set is the use of branding and price labelling. Hence, while consumers are unable to distinguish between unbranded products they have no such difficulty when brand names are given. Similarly, Gabor and Grainger, Shapiro and others have clearly demonstrated that we use price as an indicator of quality and will select products with a higher price as 'better' when no differences exist with those carrying a lower price, and even when the higher-priced items are objectively inferior.

A composite model of buying behaviour

While it may be argued that all models of buyer behaviour are inadequate in that they are seen as pre-scientific in the sense that they are untestable, our own practical experience has shown that models can be made operational in practice. For example, discussion of Baker's (1975) composite model with senior executives suggests that it provides a useful framework for organizing their own thinking. This last qualification is particularly important, for it would be unrealistic to expect any model to capture completely the complexity and dynamic nature of the buying process. Accordingly, the Baker model seeks to synthesize the key elements discussed in the preceding pages, but to make the model work one must add an essential ingredient: the specialized knowledge and experience of persons familiar with the specific product–market interface in question. The model has been modified several times, the better to capture a very elusive process.

The current version of the model may be expressed notationally as follows:

$$P = f\,[SP, (PC, EC, IS, PF, CB)\ BR]$$

where

P = purchase
f = a function (unspecified) of:
SP = selective perception
PC = precipitating circumstances
EC = enabling conditions
IS = information search
PF = performance factors
CB = cost benefit
BR = behavioural response

The first point to be made is that this is a sequential process model: PC is equivalent to *awareness*, EC to *interest*, IS, PF and CB represent *evaluation*, and BR indicates the action taken, which, of course, is not always to purchase but may be to reject the proposition or to defer judgment. Neither of these is precluded by the model, which is concerned solely with positive purchase outcomes.

Secondly, the precise nature of the function is not specified for the simple reason that it is not known and that it is unlikely, to say the least, that any single functional form could capture the interaction between the other variables in the model.

SP or selective perception is a new variable in the model. In earlier versions, the influence of this factor was subsumed within BR, which occurs at the end of the process. By placing SP at the beginning as a factor mediating the other variables, it is possible to communicate that this is a process model and that selective perception will determine whether or not one will even become aware of a purchase opportunity (EC) besides conditioning the information selected for evaluation and the interpretation placed upon it.

Finally, the behavioural response (BR) may be almost automatic, as, for example, when the preceding evaluation indicates that one option is clearly to be preferred. Alternatively, it may be an extremely difficult and protracted stage when the preceding analysis has failed to suggest one choice before all others – a common occurrence in many markets.

Having described the general model, some elaboration of the variables will indicate what sort of factors one would need to take into account to use it.

When discussing the Pavlovian learning model of buyer behaviour earlier, reference was made to the need for some cue or stimulus to activate a drive and initiate action. In our model, this factor is termed a precipitating circumstance (PC) – what would make a buyer consider a change in the *status quo*? Clearly, dissatisfaction with existing alternatives constitutes a marketing opportunity, and is one type of precipitating factor. The need to replace or renew a piece of capital equipment or consumer durable is another opportunity, whether the need is caused by breakdown, loss, destruction or a planned replacement policy. Knowing which customers might be in this state would enable the firm to focus its marketing effort to much greater effect, in terms of both the information to be conveyed and the means of conveying it. Similarly, being able to satisfy a known need – we have a faster computer, a more economical car, and so forth – is a claim likely to precipitate active consideration of a new purchase.

Enabling conditions (EC) embraces all those factors which make it possible for a prospec-tive purchaser to benefit from the new product. A television is no use if you have no electricity, nor a gas oven if you have no gas. In the same way, many manufacturers try to avoid mixing materials such as steel, aluminium and plastics, since each requires different skills and techniques in use and increases the investment necessary in both plant and labour. In other words, a new product must be compatible with the user's current status and, in many cases, also with their self-image. In the absence of such enabling conditions, interest is likely to be short lived and unlikely to proceed further to an evaluation.

Information search (IS) reflects the fact that the prospective buyer has moved from passive awareness to an active interest and so is looking for additional information to establish whether or not they should seek satisfaction.

Technology or performance and the economics or cost–benefit of a purchase are at

Table 4.2 ● Features for effective selling in machine tool markets

Q. Reviewing the last five years, what factors or reasons appear to discriminate most between success and failure with new products?

	Total	F & D	Others
Product quality	33(53%)	22(65%)	11(39%)
Uniqueness of product	27(44%)	14(41%)	13(47%)
Level of trade acceptance	24(39%)	15(44%)	9(32%)
Level of advertising investment	22(36%)	12(35%)	10(36%)
Level of distribution achieved	20(32%)	12(35%)	8(29%)
Price	19(31%)	13(38%)	6(21%)
Company commitment	15(24%)	8(24%)	7(25%)
Sales force motivation	14(23%)	10(29%)	4(14%)
Total	62(100%)	34(100%)	28(100%)

Note: The sample comprises '62 major UK manufacturers'.
Source: Derived from Artingstall (1980).

the very heart of the Marshallian and 'rational' schools of buying behaviour's models – PF, CB in our model.

Some broad guidelines as to the relative importance of different features which go to make up an effective selling proposition in industrial markets generally are shown for machine tools in particular in Table 4.2 and more generally in Figure 4.1. But, while these offer an indication of the relative importance of groups of features, it must always be remembered that the majority of buying decisions turn on highly specific characteristics – another reason why a general model cannot possibly accommodate all conceivable sets of circumstances.

We have already stipulated that the importance of behavioural response will depend

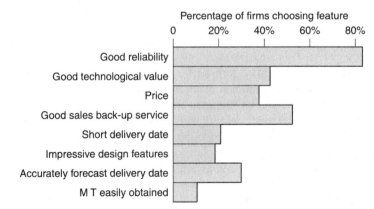

Figure 4.1 ● Features of a machine tool considered one of the three most important (*source: Machine Tool Review*)

heavily upon the objective evaluation of the available facts (albeit that these are perceived subjectively), and 'build a better product at an equivalent price or an equivalent product at a lower price' is clearly the best advice to management. But, in most competitive markets, there is often little to choose objectively between alternative offerings, and the buyer will have to make deliberate recourse to subjective value judgments to assist in distinguishing between the various items available. Because people do this daily when preferring Persil to Ariel, Nescafé to Maxwell House. etc., they are often characterized as choosing irrationally. Nothing could be further from the truth. The important objective decisions about a shopping basket relate to its overall mix and composition *vis-à-vis* the available budget – the choice decision is which detergent, which coffee, and so on. It would be a fatal mistake to imagine that the industrial buyer doesn't have just the same problems when deciding between Scania, Mercedes or Leyland for lorries, or Cincinnati, Kearney and Trecker for machine tools.

At the outset it must be recognized that in no way does the model contradict the normative approach to market research and market segmentation which is described fully in almost every basic marketing text. Rather it should be seen as reinforcing and amplifying standardized techniques for the identification and measurement of potential demand. Indeed, it would not be too extravagant to assert that our analytical framework seeks to emphasize the marketing dimensions of marketing research as it attempts to address the problem from the perspective of prospective buyers rather than from the standpoint of the seller. That said, it should be clear from our brief statement of the nature of enabling conditions (EC) that this factor seeks to establish a prima facie case of primary demand such that EC will describe the maximum potential market for any new product. Thus the existence of EC will define all those individuals or organizations which could conceivably have a use for our new product, more often than not by a process of exclusion rather than of inclusion. Thus, for example, our primary demand specification for baby products would be likely to use the birth rate as a basic parameter in establishing potential market size – being or having a baby constituting a basic qualifying criterion for the existence of EC. (Of course, as we all now know from the example of Johnson & Johnson, to confine the use of baby products to babies actually constrains the potential market since items such as powder and shampoo are widely used by adults. But, if one is launching a new baby product such as nappy liners, it would seem sensible, at least until the product has become established, to regard mothers as the primary demand for the product.)

Thus EC is a necessary but not sufficient condition for defining the potential market for a product and constitutes the first crude cut at isolating a group of potential users for a more detailed analysis – for example, the use of two-digit SIC codes. Yet as we have argued earlier, such a basic definition of a target market leaves a great deal to be desired, for it lacks focus and would undoubtedly lead to the dissipation and waste of a great deal of marketing effort. The whole thrust of our approach is to try and identify the most receptive sub-set or segment within the potential market as the target for our initial marketing development work.

To provide a more selective focus, we suggest that one should seek to isolate some cue or stimulus which would have the effect of converting an essentially latent primary demand into an active recognition of the possible means of satisfying a felt need. For firms already operating in a market, for whom a new product frequently represents a product line extension, such identification of a precipitating circumstance (PC) should present much less difficulty than is the case with a firm which has no previous experience of, or contact with, a potential market. Nonetheless there is considerable evidence to suggest that sellers frequently make inadequate or no use of information available to them through their continuing relationship with present customers, and/or frequently misinterpret information available to them – the age of the existing stock or holding of a product, for example, which the innovation seeks to replace or substitute for. This point will be made again in Chapter 7. Perhaps the most obvious yet most frequently committed error, however, is to concentrate early marketing efforts upon the largest potential customers, presumably following the logic that they have most to gain and that by securing orders from them one will stand the best chance of achieving one's initial sales targets. There is considerable evidence to suggest that the alternative hypothesis, that small companies are most likely to adopt first, has much to commend it.

On the assumption that any new product which aspires to success must possess advantages over the one it seeks to replace, it seems to us that this advantage is potentially of much greater significance to the small rather than the large user. For the large firm, the incentive to increase its share of market is limited. First, there is the possibility that an increase in market share might attract the unwelcome attentions of the Monopolies Commission, Federal Trade Commission or its foreign equivalent. Second, as any marked increase in market share must be at the expense of major competitors, there is a strong likelihood that any effort to achieve such an increase would result in aggressive retaliation by these competitors, probably to the detriment of all concerned. Third, there may be strong grounds for adopting a 'wait and see' attitude ('anticipatory retardation' in Fellner's terminology), owing to the belief that the present innovation may itself soon be made obsolete by further improvements. Fourth, there is a marked trend to pursue the 'strategy of the fast second' as described, *inter alia*, by Levitt in his 'Innovative imitation' (see Levitt, 1976b). For these reasons alone, many large firms may well adopt a 'don't rock the boat' attitude towards those markets in which they already have a major share, on the grounds that, by disturbing the existing equilibrium, they are much more likely to lose than gain.

For the small firm, with a market share measured as a fraction of 1%, the situation is very different. Assume that such a firm were offered a new raw material with superior properties and a lower or equivalent cost to one of its major inputs. By adopting this new material, the small firm could, in turn, offer end users a superior product at a lower or equivalent price to the inferior substitute which it seeks to replace. Other things being equal, economic rationality predicates that end users will prefer the new product and transfer their demand to its supplier, thereby increasing the latter's market share. If it is assumed that the small firm originally had 0.25% of the total market share, then it is clear that, even were it to increase this fourfold to 1%, it could only reduce a major supplier's share by a maximum of 0.75% of the total market. The significance of such a reduction would vary depending upon the loser's prior market share as indicated in Table 4.3. Of course, the smaller the large firm's present market share, the less likely it becomes that the small firm's gain would be entirely at its expense.

Table 4.3 ● Impact of loss of 0.75% of total market share on various levels of existing market share

Present market share (%)	Reduction in sales volume occasioned by loss of 0.75% of total market
10	−7.50
15	−5.00
20	−3.75
25	−3.00
30	−2.50

If the foregoing assumptions are correct, then it follows that the small firm has a much greater incentive to adopt than does the large firm. Ignoring for the present the question of variation between small firms in terms of their receptivity to innovation, it is accepted that time to first adoption is a critical determinant of the speed and extent of the overall diffusion process. Once an innovator has secured a successful first adoption, he may use it to substantiate his claims as to the value of the innovation in a far more convincing manner than is possible with purely theoretical or 'trial' data. Even though the small firm's increased share of the market may be insufficient to stimulate the market leaders to adopt the innovation, it may nonetheless be impressive enough to encourage other small firms to emulate its achievement, giving rise to the so-called 'bandwagon' or 'contagion' effect which underlies exponential growth. Clearly, if this occurs, the cumulative effect of several small firms securing an increased share of market will eventually result in the market leaders suffering a sufficient loss to prompt retaliatory action, and so accelerate adoption even further.

Of course, in most markets one is still faced with large numbers of prospective customers, and it is here that the evaluation of the perceived benefits of adoption (the technical and economic performance and cost benefit) will lay considerable weight upon careful and thorough analysis of both the status and needs of likely users. Any standard text on market research will provide a comprehensive review of the techniques available to accomplish this, and only two comments seem appropriate here.

The first is to emphasize yet again that the important, indeed critical thing is to try and look at the 'facts' from the standpoint of the possible buyer; and the second is to underline the value of actually asking the prospective customer for their views. Many sellers appear to be reluctant to attempt a direct approach to customers under the misguided impression that they will not co-operate. Our own experience in sales, market research and consultancy is directly contrary to this view since we have always found that people and companies which have considered purchasing a new product and rejected the idea are very willing to tell you why, and are usually much more objective than are actual purchasers seeking to rationalize their behaviour in terms of what they think you want to hear. The message is quite clear: a direct, personal approach to potential customers is likely to pay handsome dividends in defining precisely what they want.

Finally, we return to the influence of behavioural response, which may best be described as conscious selective perception, for whereas selective perception will have conditioned the prospective buyer's view of all the preceding variables, factual or not, its influence will have been largely subconscious. Behavioural response (BR) only assumes any importance when an 'objective' techno-economic analysis still leaves more than one alternative from which to choose. In these circumstances, the would-be buyer recognizes that subjective and qualitative factors have a contribution to make and consciously invokes them. It is for this reason that we argue that marketing has a double role to play, for not only can it influence perception in terms of creating attention, stimulating interest and helping to determine what 'facts' are evaluated, but, in a multiple choice situation, it can prove to be the determinant factor which results in a decision to buy rather than reject or defer purchase.

Ways in which marketing can achieve this discriminating role are manifold and often highly situation-specific, but a few examples will help make the point.

Consider the husband and wife trying to select a consumer durable such as a cooker, fridge or video recorder – the retail outlet has a wide variety on offer and those of comparable size/performance tend to have very similar prices. It is here that personal influence can help to tip the balance, but how many manufacturers offer to help train retail store assistants or otherwise influence them to put their weight behind their particular product? Similarly, how many manufacturers provide an adequate after-sales service to ensure satisfaction and predispose the buyer to repeat purchase when the need comes to replace a durable? Equally important, how many try to communicate that, while you shouldn't need service and hope not to collect on your fire or health insurance, if you do it will be forthcoming willingly, speedily and without hassle?

In industrial markets, as we have already suggested, small firms are more often quicker to adopt than large, and, because such innovation decisions are proportionately more important to them than is a similar decision in a large firm, where a first purchase may be no more than a trial, they are also more likely to commit themselves fully to making the innovation succeed. But for many small firms cash and technical expertise contribute major barriers to innovation, and it would seem reasonable to propose that sellers should seek to 'normalize' the financial implications by offering a package which makes it possible for the small customer to invest in innovation – after all, if it is going to improve his performance as significantly as you claim, should you not be willing to defer or spread payment until these cash flows are forthcoming? Similarly, technical advice both prior to sale and after installation will enable the seller to ensure that his product is used as intended, will provide information on performance in normal working environments (as opposed to prototypes in laboratories) which may be used for modification and improvement, and give the necessary reassurance to the buyer who might otherwise be put off by the sophistication of the technology. Training operatives also helps to reduce or 'eliminate' key factors in the decision process.

Marketing is essentially a dynamic and creative activity, and it is for these reasons that it is often difficult to prescribe appropriate courses of action. Each situation calls for its own analysis and for an original solution, albeit that the latter may be heavily influenced by either direct or vicarious (reading a book?) experience. It is in this spirit that the model is offered as a framework for structuring one's own analysis and decision making. As the case studies published in *Market Development* (Baker, 1983b) demonstrated, the model is robust and has practical utility.

The adoption and diffusion of new products

The generalized or composite model of buyer behaviour discussed in the preceding pages is primarily concerned with the sequence or process through which an individual or organization passes in deciding whether or not to buy a product or service. As was made clear when introducing the Robinson *et al.* Buygrid, intending buyers are only likely to pass through all eight Buy phases in the case of a New Task situation. Where they are faced with a Modified or Straight Rebuy they may well skip some or several stages in the process. The extent to which they may do this will also be influenced by the buyer's perception of whether the purchase is high or low involvement.

The question of whether a purchase is high or low involvement depends in part on the novelty of the purchase for the buyer and the extent of the risk they perceive associated with a wrong decision. The degree of novelty is greatly influenced by Rogers' five factors – Relative Advantage, Complexity, Compatibility, Divisibility and Communicability – introduced in Chapter 3, and is, obviously, particular to the intending buyer. This is also the case with perceived risk which also involves a measure of potential financial loss. In addition to novelty and perceived risk, the issue of whether a product or service is considered high or low involvement will also depend upon its psycho-social importance for the buyer. Thus, as we saw in Chapter 3, a given product may be regarded as a convenience good or routine purchase as a shopping good involving problem solving, or as a specialty good calling for extended problem solving. Thus some shoppers may agonize at length over the vineyard and vintage of a wine while others will gladly buy a variety such as Cabernet Sauvignon, Shiraz or Chardonnay with little or no regard for either of these criteria.

The question of high or low involvement is also important when the purchase price, and so the perceived risk, is low. When this is the case, which it is with many low-priced fast-moving consumer goods (FMCG), the simplest way to establish whether one should 'buy' a product or not is to try it and defer the decision as to commitment and possible repurchase until after the test. Observation of consumers buying such low involvement products with little or no apparent evaluation is sometimes cited as evidence of irrational buying behaviour. In reality, it is the opposite, as the opportunity cost of a full evaluation is greater than the financial outlay. (If a supermarket stocks 24 000 different items, which it may well do, then to consider each item in the assortment for only 10 seconds would take up 67 hours!) It is for this reason that we prefer Rogers' five-step model – Awareness, Interest, Desire, Trial, Action – to the simpler AIDA model which does not provide for explicit trial. Indeed 'trial' is central to the notions of concept and product testing, the subjects of Chapters 11 and 12 respectively.

We are also indebted to Everett Rogers for popularizing the concepts of diffusion and adopter categories in his seminal study *Diffusion of Innovations* (subsequently republished in collaboration with Floyd Shoemaker as *The Communication of Innovation* in 1971).

Table 4.4 ● Hierarchy-of-effects models

	Strong (AIDA) (1912)	Lavidge and Steiner (1961)	Rogers (1962)	Engel et al. (1968)
Conative (motive)	Action	Purchase Conviction	Adoption Trial	Purchase processes
Affective (emotion)	Desire	Preference	Evaluation and interest	Evaluation Search
Cognitive (thought)	Interest Awareness	Liking Knowledge Awareness	Awareness	Problem recognition
		Unawareness		

Adoption

Adoption is generally defined as the decision to use a product or service in preference to alternative or substitute goods which might be used to satisfy the same need. Adoption is the outcome of a decision-making process in which the individual or firm is moved from a state of unawareness about the existence of the product or service to a conscious decision to prefer it to alternative or substitute products. The stages through which the decision-maker may move are reflected in what have been termed 'hierarchy of effects models', as illustrated by Table 4.4. All the models share the common feature that they indicate that the decision to act in a particular way is the consequence of a process which starts with recognition of a stimulus, evaluation of it and then a decision as to how to act upon the information. (cf Table 4.1 p. 64)

As indicated in Table 4.4 Rogers' model comprises five steps from awareness through interest to evaluation, trial and adoption. These stages have been defined as follows:

1. *Awareness*
   The individual is exposed to the innovation but lacks complete information about it. The individual is aware of the innovation but is not yet motivated to seek further information.

2. *Interest*
   The individual becomes interested in the new idea and seeks additional information about it. Innovation is favoured in a general way but it is not yet judged in terms of its utility to a specific situation.

3. *Evaluation*
   The individual mentally applies the innovation to his or her present and anticipated future situation and then decides whether or not to try it.

4. *Trial*
   The individual uses the innovation on a small scale in order to determine its utility in his or her own situation.

5. *Adoption*
   The individual decides to continue the full use of the innovation.

   Clearly, one must go through all the stages to achieve adoption but there are many instances where the individual will break off the decision-making process before reaching its ultimate conclusion of adoption. It is also important to recognize that the length and complexity of any or all of the stages will vary considerably depending upon the nature of the decision to be taken. Thus, with low involvement goods with a low unit price that are very similar to other existing products or brands with which the consumer is familiar, one may move immediately through an impulse purchase to the trial stage, deferring the decision to adopt until one's own experience confirms or otherwise the acceptability of the new thing. Conversely, with high involvement products which may call upon the user to radically change their current behaviour and/or contain high perceived risk, the decision process may be particularly complex and drawn out.

Diffusion

In Chapter 3, when referring to the product life cycle (PLC), it was noted that the concept is firmly founded in the biological sciences and that there is a great deal of data to support the view that it is an accurate representation of the way in which products develop, prosper, mature, decline and die. Studies in the field of rural sociology confirm that new methods and techniques exhibit this pattern, as do studies in the field of education concerning the spread of ideas about curriculum development, new approaches to teaching and the like. In the realm of medicine, studies of the way in which new drugs are adopted by doctors exhibit the familiar S-shaped diffusion curve, as do large numbers of studies of specific, individual innovations in fields as diverse as man-made fibres, plastics, nuclear power, computers, and electronically controlled machine tools. Taken together, these findings point inexorably to the existence of an underlying natural process. In essence this may be summarized as a substitution effect in which new things are substituted for and displace the old. Diffusion is the general term for this process.

   The adoption of an innovation gives rise to a process known as diffusion. Rogers (1962) identified four elements as critical to the diffusion process:

1. The innovation.

2. Its communication from one individual to another.

3. The relevant social system of which these individuals are a part.

4. Time.

   As we have seen in discussing the attributes of an innovation, novelty is both an objective and a subjective state. Objectively we can measure novelty by establishing the time of the first introduction of a product. Subjectively, however, an object which has been available for months or even years may still be seen as new by an individual who has no prior knowledge or experience of it. Further, the degree of novelty implicit in an innovation may be capable of being measured objectively but will usually be judged subjectively depending upon the prospective adopter's knowledge and status. In turn,

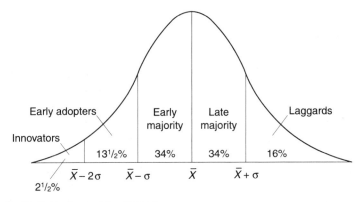

Figure 4.2 ● Adopter categories

this will have a significant influence on the speed with which the innovation diffuses through a population until reaching full adoption.

When the cumulative sales which give rise to the familiar S-shaped curve are plotted in terms of actual sales per period of time over the life of the product, the result is a normal distribution. By using the parameters of such a distribution – the mean and standard deviation – a useful classificatory system has been developed as depicted in Figure 4.2.

As we shall see, the identification and classification of adopter categories has important implications for marketing strategies and marketing mix development. We return to this in more detail in Chapter 5 when dealing with the PLC.

Clearly, product development has a central role to play in product strategy. Much of the literature places a particular emphasis upon *new* product development and then implies that all NPD is concerned with totally new products. This is obviously not the case as many 'new' products are modifications or extensions of already existing products. While this book also describes the development of a new product, from idea generation through concept testing to physical product development and commercialization, it will be helpful here to distinguish what we mean by 'innovation' or 'new' as this will prepare the ground for the idea of product line extensions which are so important to increase growth (Chapter 14) and extend maturity (Chapter 15).

One of the best-known typologies of innovation was proposed by Robertson (1971) in which he distinguished innovation as being *discontinuous, dynamically continuous*, or *continuous*.

A discontinuous innovation is one which involves a major radical technological advance, creating new products that require new patterns of behaviour. The steam engine, motor car, television, microchip, personal computer, cellular telephone, plastics, etc. are all examples of discontinuous innovations. By contrast a dynamically continuous innovation represents further development of a known technology but does not call for a change in behaviour patterns – colour TV, compact discs, laptop computers, etc., are examples. As for continuous innovations these generally represent minor modifications of existing products, usually but not always, with minor changes in technology, e.g. enzymes in detergents, squeezy bottles for ketchup and washing-up liquid.

By far the majority of innovations are extensions or derivatives of known technology; very few are the result of major technological breakthroughs or discontinuous innovations. That said, the acid test of perceived novelty is the intended user's reaction to the new product, summarized in Rogers' five attributes as the greater the perceived novelty the greater the likely resistance to change, and the slower the take-up or diffusion of that product. Interestingly, ultimate consumers are often more willing to adopt radical technological change more easily than are intermediaries who are more knowledgeable about it. While this may be a case of fools rushing in where angels fear to tread, the job of the marketers is not to challenge observed behaviour but to try and harness it to their advantage. Thus, end consumers tend to evaluate new products in terms of the benefits they offer rather than in terms of the means whereby these benefits are created and/or the changes in the manufacturer's production system which may be required to switch to a new technology. As reflected in a famous case, described by E. Raymond Corey of the Harvard Business School (Corey, 1956), acceptance of this fact (as well as a knowledge of the composite model of buyer behaviour) could have greatly accelerated the development by the Aluminum Company of America (Alcoa) of aluminium sleeve bearings.

Case study: aluminium sleeve bearings

A recurring theme of this book is that an ability to pre-identify likely early adopters of an innovation will greatly enhance the possibility of early market penetration, and thereby the overall likelihood of success. In advance of market launch, many companies believe that they have this ability, but as the case described by Corey concerning the market introduction of aluminium sleeve bearings demonstrates, such confidence is often misplaced.

Product development

The Aluminum Company of America's interest in the development of an alloy suitable for use in sleeve bearings was prompted by information that both the British and the Germans were using aluminium sleeve bearings in the manufacture of aircraft engines. Laboratory work was initiated in 1936, and within a year a suitable alloy, designated Alcoa Alloy 750, had been developed. Alloy 750 consists of 91½% pure aluminium by weight, 6½% tin, 1% copper and 1% nickel, and experimental bearings made of this alloy were made available in 1937 for test purposes. In the first instance, Alcoa restricted the test programme, conducted in conjunction with a manufacturer of large diesel engines, since it was recognized that faulty bearings could cause extensive damage to the engine if they failed. On the basis of the limited test programme proposed, it was estimated that sufficient test data on the performance characteristics of such bearings would take between two and six years to accumulate.

Further development of the bearings was prevented by shortages of tin during the Second World War, but by 1944 sufficient tin had become available to permit commercialization. As the test data had conclusively proved the suitability of aluminium in this application, the diesel engine builder who had participated in the trials ordered aluminium bearings for all his diesel engines from a bearing manufacturer.

In the first instance, Alcoa concentrated its marketing effort upon the manufacturers of large engines, mainly on the grounds that small engines called for thin-walled bearings and aluminium had to be used in a bearing that had a ratio of wall thickness to diameter that was greater than could be accommodated in smaller engines. In this application, solid aluminium bearings were claimed to possess at least five advantages:

1. Better corrosion resistance.
2. Better heat dispersion characteristics, which prevented bearings freezing on the shaft.
3. Longer life and no evidence of fatigue failure.
4. If failure were to occur, the bearing would not damage the shaft.
5. Aluminium bearings were cheaper than existing bearings.

The lower price of aluminium bearings was largely a result of the much simpler manufacturing process which they required. Basically, this consisted of machining a cylindrical casting on an automatic lathe and then finishing it in a boring machine. By contrast, conventional bearings required much more skill and tooling since they called for the bonding of a bearing surface such as copper, lead or tin onto a fabricated steel base.

On the basis of the five factors cited, it would seem clear that aluminium bearings offered significantly better performance and cost–benefit characteristics than the conventional bearings which they sought to replace.

Market development

For a variety of reasons, Alcoa decided to market bearing castings itself rather than sell the alloy in ingot form for fabrication by others. Alcoa was motivated in part by a concern for quality control and after-sales service and in part by anticipation of larger profits through higher added value following forward integration into fabrication.

In 1945, Alcoa launched their product with a national advertising campaign designed to generate customer enquiries. In response to the request for information, Alcoa sent lists of the largest bearing manufacturers and suggested that the engine builder approach these. Although the bearing manufacturers showed great interest in this development, orders were not forthcoming and enquiries showed that the bearing manufacturers' salesmen were following up the Alcoa leads but were frequently recommending their own bearings rather than aluminium.

Corey details at considerable length Alcoa's efforts at selling its new product during the period 1946–54. By the latter date, however, annual sales were only a small fraction of the estimated market potential for aluminium bearings and the great bulk of sales were being made to diesel engine builders who fabricated their own bearings. Only one large bearing manufacturer accounted for any significant sales of aluminium bearings, and this was attributable to the fact that he had firm specifications to supply these from one of his customers. Corey observes, 'as in this case, inability to predict market reception of the product may leave a company no other alternative than to try a variety of approaches until one is successful.' Clearly, one's ability to follow such advice assumes that one's top management understands that the introductory phase may be protracted and is willing to regard market development as an investment against future sales success. Even so, close consideration of Alcoa's initial marketing effort does enable us to speculate, with the benefit of hindsight, on some of the causes of resistance of an innovation which was objectively superior in terms of both performance and cost characteristics to the products which it sought to replace.

In his book, Corey identifies four distinct market groups which might be regarded as having a potential interest in aluminium bearings – large bearing manufacturers, small bearing manufacturing concerns, diesel engine builders, and diesel engine users – and offers suggestions as to why each of these groups may have reacted differently to Alcoa's basic selling proposition.

Resistance shown by large bearing manufacturers echoes the reaction of the linoleum manufacturers to vinyl flooring. Given that aluminium sleeve bearings would be a direct substitute for their present output, there was no strong incentive to promote aluminium *per se*. Furthermore, as aluminium bearings had to be fabricated in a different manner from conventional bearings, new investment would have been required, the two production processes not being compatible. Another perceived risk on the part of the bearing manufacturers was that, as aluminium bearings were much simpler to make, much of the mystique currently accorded to them would be lost and so lessen their hold over their customers. Indeed, it might be anticipated that more engine manufacturers would choose to make their own aluminium bearings rather than be dependent upon bearing manufacturers. Added to this uncertainty, it was always possible that Alcoa might integrate further forward still and get into the bearing manufacturing business itself. Under all the circumstances, it was hardly surprising if the large bearing manufacturers did not choose to commit what they may well have viewed as commercial suicide.

In the case of small bearing manufacturers who had expressed considerable interest in aluminium bearings early on, Alcoa had decided that, since such small manufacturers were not currently supplying large diesel engine makers, this would be an inappropriate way to approach the market. Corey offers the opinion that the relationship between bearing manufacturers and engine builder was particularly strong, and states:

> 'Unless there were compelling reasons for making changes, the engine builder could be expected to rely, then, on his regular bearing suppliers for bearings and for technical service and technical advice. As long as a diesel engine, and the bearings in it, perform satisfactorily for the user, there would be no impetus for change even though aluminum bearings had superior performance characteristics.'

In our terminology, Corey is suggesting that there was an absence of any precipitating circumstance which would persuade the engine builder to change from a known and satisfactory source of supply to active consideration of a material not recommended by their friendly bearing manufacturer.

The third market grouping identified by Corey is the diesel engine builder. Within this group two distinct segments may be identified: builders with their own bearing manufacturing facilities and those who bought in from specialist bearing suppliers. In the case of the former group, adopting aluminium castings offered economies in producing finished bearings, as they would then get the direct benefit of the savings made. In the case of engine manufacturers buying in bearings, the situation is very different, for, as we noted when discussing the bearing suppliers, in the absence of any precipitating circumstance there was no particular reason why the engine builders should take the risk of trying a new and to them unproven bearing, which probably represented only a very small part of the total value of their end product.

Finally, in the case of engine users, the situation was very different. Corey notes:

> 'With the development of diesel engines with high power output and with the increased use of engine lubricating oil additives, engine users began to encounter difficulties with the use of conventional bearings. Their interest in aluminum bearings therefore sprang from a recognized need to find a type of bearing that would require less frequent replacement and would not cause engine maintenance problems.'

Clearly, engine users were faced with strong precipitating circumstances and as Corey observes:

> 'If engine users could be identified as that group of customers having both the greatest incentive to adopt the new product and the least resistance to it, initial efforts to introduce aluminum bearings might logically have been expected to be most successful in this segment of the market.'

With the benefit of hindsight, the lesson seems clear, but, before dismissing Alcoa's initial marketing efforts as inept, one has to give some consideration of the problems facing a materials supplier who sets out to bypass his normal customer in order to reach the ultimate end user. Clearly, this is a matter of judgment, but as Corey points out, once Alcoa were committed to selling to bearing manufacturers and then through engine builders it became virtually impossible for them to sell aluminium against conventional bearings. In the case of Delaware Floor Products, who pioneered the sale of vinyl flooring, they were not inhibited by such niceties and so were able to stress the competitive advantages of vinyl against linoleum to the full.

Finally, in assessing this case study, Corey points to the added dangers which attend a protracted market introduction, as it gives a market and the current suppliers to it an opportunity to develop additional resistance to the innovation – a fact which also lends weight to the desirability of early market penetration.

This case study reinforces the advice that one must adopt a marketing approach and seek to evaluate how the new product will be perceived by potential users and how this perception will condition their reaction. Thus the market segment selected by Alcoa as having the best sales potential in terms of its present activities (large bearing manufacturers) in reality had the least cause to change, since to do so not only would require them to disinvest in their present skills and equipment, but would sensitize their customer – the engine manufacturers – to the possibility of fabricating their own bearings. As noted, this failure to look at the proposition from the user's point of view resulted in Alcoa's failure to detect the absence of precipitating circumstances for an innovation with almost overwhelming advantages.

The message from this case study is clear – one must research opportunities thoroughly and on a continuous basis if one is to succeed in new product development. That said, the implementation of consumer/user research during the development of major innovations is not without its difficulties, as we discuss in the next section.

Researching the market for major innovations

As stated earlier, major or discontinuous innovations require buyers to change their behaviour patterns. As Ortt *et al.* (1993) have pointed out, such research faces significant problems compared with product line extensions where there are existing data on consumers and their behaviour. Three major difficulties are:

1. The problem of the selection of respondents.
2. The problem of the understanding of major innovations.
3. Problems concerning time and group aspects.

To overcome the problem of selecting appropriate respondents it is proposed that one should concentrate on need assessment research to establish the problem which consumers experience as they are likely to be more closely related with their behaviour than expressed needs and wants: 'Confronted with a radically new technology, consumers may not understand what needs the technology can satisfy. The reason for this, is that consumers are not able to link physical product characteristics with the consequence of the innovation.' Since the consequences or benefits perceived by the consumer determine their receptivity, it is important to establish what these are. Research has shown that experts are better able to infer benefits from perceived attributes than those with less product knowledge. Accordingly, one should undertake research with such experts or proxy experts (persons knowledgeable of other product fields) when determining how to position the innovation.

While the take-up of an innovation is strongly influenced by word of mouth recommendation (it is a social process) most consumer research concentrates on the individual rather than interactions between them. Similarly, adoption is the consequence of a multi-stage process over time, yet most research is cross-sectional rather than longitudinal. It follows that effective consumer research should seek to address both these issues – the problem, of course, being the time and expense involved.

Ortt *et al.* discuss research undertaken on the introduction of video telephones in the consumer market and the possible introduction of telematic information services in an industrial market using methods designed to overcome the problems identified.

Recent developments in coding and compressing data signals have made it possible to combine speech and moving images using ordinary telephone cables. The innovation is clearly one of technology push, and the question is how consumers might react to it and how these reactions might be incorporated in the development of the product. To answer this question Ortt *et al.* avoided exploration of consumers' general reaction to the concept and concentrated on particular usage situations or 'behavioural domains'. Specifically the use of video phones in distant education, tele-work and tele-care was investigated: 'In distant education, it was presumed that the video telephone would be beneficial in the communication between the students and teachers. In tele-work it was presumed that the video phone would be beneficial in the communication between someone working at home and his office. In tele-care, it was presumed that the video phone could be used by people who are ill or are not able to leave their home and therefore need extra attention.'

As well as selecting specific behavioural domains, the researchers also followed their own advice on addressing problems of undertaking research of this kind. Thus, the research focused on communication problems within specific behavioural domains which were then used to establish whether they might be solved by use of a video phone and, if so, whether this would be the best solution, e.g. might an ordinary phone and fax be better? Focus groups of five to seven respondents with experience of the specific behavioural domain and more than average experience with advanced communication appliances and services were used.

In the case of distance education it soon became apparent that it has developed to overcome problems of direct contact between teacher and student. As video phones would require both participants to be available at the same time, this would be a constraint, and other forms of communication such as e-mail and fax were preferred. In cases of difficulty where personal contact was considered essential then the video telephone was perceived as 'an inadequate surrogate of [sic] face-to-face contact'.

'In tele-work only a few communication problems seem to exist.' Ironically most people work at home because they don't want to be disturbed and so wish to avoid contact! While the video telephone would permit contact when required, its advantages over an ordinary phone, fax, or personal computer with a modem were not particularly apparent.

In the case of tele-care the video telephone was again seen as a surrogate for face-to-face contact which might be useful when distance made this difficult. On balance, however, physical contact was to be preferred.

Based on these findings it is clear that the video phone will not solve the perceived communication problems. In addition, nearly all the focus groups perceived the general problem with video phones in that their use requires mutual approval and that failure to activate one's video could be considered an insult.

Innovators will not be surprised by these findings. The very first people to take up radical technological change are often considered as deviant by the population at large. The challenge for those seeking to launch radically different new products is to identify the deviants who will make the product known to a larger audience. It would be a foolhardy product manager who took this research as indicating there is no market for a video phone!

The second piece of research was concerned with the potential for providing telematic information services to market gardeners in the horticultural glass-house industry in the Netherlands. In this case the opportunity arose from the replacement of a copper cable used to control electricity supply with a glass-fiber network with a much higher information flow capacity. To examine the potential of this technological innovation the researchers undertook a market investigation designed to establish the present problems and unfilled information needs of the market gardeners and the ways in which telematic information services might meet these.

The sample chosen was the innovative sub-group which specializes in the cultivation of flowers and vegetables who have invested heavily in advanced, and often totally computerized climate systems and robotized handling of the crop. Interviews were conducted with 55 market gardeners in which the researchers asked them to describe the main information flows between the respondents and those with whom they interacted.

These contacts were then classified by sub-group, e.g. suppliers, customers, professional services like accountancy, etc., to develop an information map. For each group the communication form (personal, telephonic, written) and the content and intensity of the contact were established by direct questioning. Respondents were also asked to indicate which telematic information services, e.g. telebanking, they thought might be helpful to them in their own business.

The research indicated that in the market gardening business there is often daily face-to-face contact between buyers and sellers associated with delivery/collection of the products. While the telephone was used to confirm orders made, face-to-face non-verbal contacts rarely occurred. Overall, 'the information flow between the market gardeners and their business environment can be summarized as an informal, direct verbal information flow'. Apart from databases and specialized weather reports, neither of which needed the glass-fiber network, the farmers could think of no other telematic information services that they required.

As with the video telephone it would be a mistake to take these findings at face value and assume there is no demand for additional information services. What the research by Ortt *et al.* clearly shows is that people often have great difficulty in identifying unfilled needs and often suffer from what we might term the Pangloss syndrome (we live in the best possible world). Indeed, in the case of both the telephone and climate control in greenhouses it is not hard to conceive of earlier generations being satisfied with the extant solution. For example, prior to the invention and widespread adoption of the telephone, mail services were far superior to what they are today. Similarly, the rapid take-up of the fax has confirmed that the requirement for two parties to be present to hold a telephone conversation means that this can be both an intrusive and an inconvenient means of communication.

Summary
....
As noted in the case of the video telephone, research of the kind proposed by Ortt *et al.* is an essential part of the NPD process. What it highlights is that pre-identifying the benefits/appeals of a radical innovation requires one to have a sound understanding of current consumer behaviour towards the product or process which is to be complemented or replaced. Given this knowledge and understanding one is better placed to segment the market and determine who the innovators might be. This interest in pre-identifying the innovators/early adopters which underpinned *Marketing New Industrial Products* (Baker, 1975) and *Market Development* (Baker, 1983b) is a theme we return to later.

QUESTIONS

1. Explain AIDA.
2. Identify the four social science models of buyer behaviour and describe their salient features.
3. What is risk and how does it influence buyer behaviour?

4. Discuss the nature of perception and the role it plays in the buyer decision process.

5. Describe and critique Baker's composite model of buyer behaviour.

6. Why do subjective factors play an important role in determining the buyer's decision?

7. Why may small firms be more receptive to innovation?

8. Define adoption and diffusion. What value do these concepts have for the practising marketer?

9. What are the main lessons to be learned from the case study of aluminium sleeve bearings?

10. Discuss the problems involved in introducing radical (discontinuous) innovations to the marketplace and suggest ways of overcoming these.

Mini-case ● Yorkie

Introduction

While the events described in this case occurred over 20 years ago it remains a classic example of innovative marketing based upon a superior understanding of buyer behaviour. Two comments will help the reader appreciate the significance of this case.

First, in confectionery markets many products are sold at a price point. To protect this price point – often associated with views about children's 'pocket-money' – manufacturers are forced to reduce size/quantity to maintain margins as costs rise due to inflation. In the 1970s, while manufacturers retained the surface size of a chocolate bar, they progressively reduced its thickness, reducing consumers' satisfaction with the product. Yorkie reversed this trend.

Second, in addition to transforming competition in this segment of the market Rowntree Mackintosh became brand leader. It was this leadership, combined with a portfolio of other strong brands like KitKat, Fruit Pastilles, etc., that prompted Nestlé, the Swiss multinational corporation, to buy the company for five times its stock market valuation of around £500 million – a compelling reason for any seller to want to gain a better understanding of buyer behaviour!

The launch of the Yorkie bar

The apparently unassailable giants in the highly competitive UK chocolate bar market, Cadbury and Mars, were given a nasty jolt when an unexpected rival appeared on the scene and snatched a startling 20% share of sales only two years after its launch. That product was Rowntree's Yorkie, and the result was a pitched battle between the major manufacturers that has culminated in massive promotional budgets, in the region of £1.5 million per year, being spent by each contestant to protect its brand. Yorkie is Rowntree Mackintosh's attempt to strengthen its hitherto comparatively weak position in the chocolate blocks sector of the confectionery market. The launch was a marketing classic, and it won a well-deserved first place in Category One of the Institute of Marketing's Annual Awards.

The repercussions of this meticulously planned marketing coup are reverberating in the marketplace still. Rowntree Mackintosh has assumed lead position in the total UK confectionery market (worth an estimated £1250 million in 1977) over the former leader, Cadbury-Schweppes. The introduction of Yorkie played a major role in increasing the company's share of the solid chocolate block market from 6% in 1976 to 20% in 1977. Sales of the brand have risen from £3 million in 1976, when it was launched in test in the London area, to some £18 million last year [1977] when it was made available nationally. Sales of £8 million were achieved in the first quarter of 1978 alone.

Over the past two years, the market for moulded milk chocolate has expanded in volume terms by some 20% and in value terms by 30%, say experts. This is a direct result of the vicious competition stimulated by Yorkie. This included a relaunch in October 1977 of the brand leader, Cadbury's Dairy Milk, with a complete change of marketing strategy in response to the Yorkie challenge.

Sales of CDM had been steadily declining since the early 1970s. The rising price of cocoa had forced the company to make its bars thinner in order to maintain the size of the surface of the bar, while keeping the price stable. In this way, it hoped that consumers' perception of value for money would not be affected. Gareth Hughes, Marketing Director of Cadbury's, admits that the thinning process went too far, causing sales to fall. Consumers prefer thick chunky chocolate as the success of Yorkie clearly demonstrates. Cadbury's retaliatory action therefore included a thickening of its CDM blocks.

At the same time, Cadbury reintroduced the famous 'glass and a half of full cream milk in every half pound' advertising theme. Research showed that it had a high level of consumer awareness – even after a ten year absence from television screens. Then, in March this year, the brand label was redesigned to incorporate a picture of the glass and a half of milk.

CDM still maintains brand leader position, which it has held for over 70 years, with a 40% share of sales of solid block milk chocolate. Yorkie is a good second with a 20% share and Hughes is full of admiration for its clever positioning in the marketplace. 'Yorkie has done a marvellous job', he says. 'It has taken sales as much from countlines as it has from the strict milk chocolate blocks market. It is a hybrid product that embraces both sectors of the market.' Traditionally Cadbury's strength has been in moulded bars, like CDM and Fruit and Nut; Mars has been big in countlines, as Rowntree has dominated the boxed chocolate market. Now Yorkie has performed the unprecedented feat of threatening sales in two product areas.

Aggressive strategy pays

The feat is all the more remarkable when seen against a background of fierce competition, hitherto impregnable brand leaders, and the rare new product successes in the market. It clearly demonstrates the wisdom of Rowntree Mackintosh's aggressive new product strategy, in which the aim is to add continually to its range of major advertised brands. To Rowntree the two most important criteria for selecting new products are the size of the market and the company's present share. That is why, in the early years of the 1970s, Rowntree found particular interest in the chocolate blocks sector of the market. At that time the sector was big, about 70 000 tonnes, and the company's share was relatively small.

The company spent several years carefully researching the market opportunities. There was already a good deal of information available on the products, their sales volumes and the main market trends. Consumer attitudes to existing brands and advertising claims, reasons for switching, perceptions of differences between brands and products and usage of different pack sizes were also well documented. Nevertheless, Rowntree augmented the existing data with further qualitative research in order to obtain a clear understanding of consumer motivation, tastes, needs and satisfactions.

Five concepts tested

As a result of this research, five possible new product concepts were devised by the company and its agency, J Walter Thompson. Each one was designed to meet a different consumer taste, and each was subjected to further consumer research. They were presented to four groups of consumers, who tasted and discussed them in the presence of the market research team. Four out of the five were discounted, but one particular bar showed a great deal of potential. It was called Rations and was designed as a thick, sustaining bar, and was associated, in its presentation, with open-air activity. The advertising would have suggested that it should be eaten 'when you've got to keep going' with, for example, pictures of mountaineers taking a rest and eating nourishing Rations. Consumer interest in the chunky block was seen against a background of falling sales of the thinner bars of CDM. A gap in the market was thus identified for a solid, thick block of chocolate.

However, during the research, consumers criticized the connotations of wartime austerity invoked by the rations image. The presentation, as it stood, suggested mere utility without enough implication of enjoyment. So, more ideas were developed, based on the same Rations theme, but with a more attractive presentation. The moulds used on what was to become the Yorkie prototype were the same as those used to make iron rations for commandos, which says a lot about the sort of products Rowntree was aiming for. Eventually the mould was refined, as was the entire image of the brand. A whole series of new names and wrapper designs were invented and underwent rigorous consumer tests, and Yorkie proved to be the most popular.

Imitation fear ruled out testing

The launch strategy was just as carefully planned and implemented as the design of the product itself. The company recognized that Yorkie chould be quickly and easily imitated. For this reason, the idea of localized test marketing was discounted, and the decision was taken to launch to a substantial proportion of the country (about 25%), and use the experience gained there to assess necessary production rates and stock holding in order to be able to extend rapidly to national distribution. So Yorkie was introduced in the London TV area and made available nationally a year later.

Another reason for choosing a large test area was the need to convince large national chain customers that Rowntree Mackintosh was determined to achieve national distribution in the face of the competition, and large customer listings (permission for branches to purchase a line) were essential.

Before selling began, Rowntree's national account managers and sales managers attended a conference at which they were carefully briefed about the product. In this way the entire sales team could be prepared and motivated to promote Yorkie, ready for the mammoth selling task ahead. This was so successful that the selling effort to major customers achieved the best listings ever achieved for a new confectionery line. In other words, every major customer accepted Yorkie.

At a separate national sales conference, the company's field salesmen were given the full information on market analysis, objectives and research that backed the Yorkie launch. At the same time, they were supplied with a full range of selling aids.

It was vital to achieve high distribution quickly to take maximum advantage of the television advertising that accompanied the launch. The company therefore conducted what it called a 'commando-like' exercise in which a number of teams and relief salesmen placed supplies of Yorkie in retail outlets normally only visited by its salesmen in the later part of their six-week visiting cycle. As a result, some 20 weeks after the launch, distribution had been achieved in over 90% of all retail confectionery outlets.

Salesmen were asked to report their success stories back to head office and these were published to the entire sales force to maintain high sales-force enthusiasm.

Value for money crucial

The specific consumer demand met by Yorkie was for something satisfying and sustaining to eat. It was therefore crucial that it should offer competitive value for money in terms of the amount of chocolate per penny. Because it is so thick, its surface area is considerably smaller than that of its competitors. But it is also heavier than most of its competitors, and though it is slightly higher in price (CDM costs 9p for 48 grammes: Yorkie costs 11p for 66 grammes) it weighs considerably more.

Distributors were encouraged to eat samples of Yorkie themselves, which convinced them that it was good value and so further stimulated sales. Since the launch, according to Rowntree, a 'deliberately aggressive pricing policy has maintained Yorkie as equal or better value than competitors' blocks'. But the main problem for the chocolate manufacturers today is that both production and raw materials costs are rising, and chocolate is becoming extremely expensive for the consumer to buy. It costs over 50p to buy a 200 gramme bar – which is less than half a pound. This means that the aggressive marketing evident over the past two or three years must continue in the near future at least, in order to persuade consumers to continue to buy chocolate – whatever the brand.

Difficulty of remaining competitive

The problem of escalating production costs, and the difficulty of remaining competitive and profitable in this market, is clearly reflected in Rowntree Mackintosh's recent disappointing half-year results. By its competitors' standards its six months' profits are fair, with a 4% increase last year. But bearing in mind the success of Yorkie and the company's knack of raising earnings by nearly a third each year in the recent past, the results are not brilliant. Company deputy chairman Kenneth Dixon predicts no quick return to the rate of profits growth of the last four years.

Nevertheless, the Yorkie launch demonstrates the brilliant use of clever marketing to challenge the supposed unassailable leaders in a market and carve out a substantial slice of sales. And in spite of the problems of the confectionery market at present, in the words of the television advertisement, Yorkie 'keeps moving on' towards greater sales.

(Reproduced from *Marketing*, November 1978, with permission)

chapter 5

The product life cycle in theory and practice

LEARNING OBJECTIVES

1. To introduce the concept of the product life cycle (PLC).

2. To explain its use as an analytical framework.

3. To identify criticisms of the PLC concept.

4. To suggest how the PLC may be operationalized and put into practice.

5. To present deviant variations of the classic PLC.

On completion of this chapter you will:

1. Be able to explain the nature of PLCs and the stages associated with them.

2. Understand the managerial applications of the PLC concept.

3. Be familiar with the criticisms made of the PLC concept.

4. Know how to use the PLC concept in practice.

5. Be aware of and be able to explain variants of the classic life cycle.

Introduction

According to Scheuing (1974), until the 1960s the initiative for and control of new product programmes traditionally resided with engineering and production personnel 'who were far removed from the final consumer and had nothing to do with the marketing of the resulting products. The outcome was necessarily a hit-and-miss proposition since technological aspects were likely to take priority over marketing considerations' (p. ix). With the rediscovery of the marketing concept and the switch to a buyer's market following the post-war boom, the importance of new product development became critical to survival and success. In consequence new product management became 'accepted and institutionalized as an integral and essential part of a firm's marketing effort, receiving extensive top management attention and support' (p. ix).

As a result of these changes the topics of product policy and management have become a distinct sub-field within the disciplines of marketing and have spawned a large literature dealing specifically with the subject. Scheuing was among the first to develop a specialist text based upon the proposition that 'the principal guiding force of all new product management efforts should be a thorough understanding of consumer behavior' (p. ix) – a direct consequence of the marketing concept. Much of Scheuing's book is familiar reading to students and practitioners in the 1990s, dealing as it does with the job of product management, the evolution of new products and the introductory marketing programme. In part this is true of his discussion of the diffusion of innovations, but what makes his book of particular interest to the present authors is the final part which is devoted to the product life cycle.

During the 1960s the Product Life Cycle (PLC) concept was the subject of considerable research, especially at the Harvard Business School and, through it, at the Marketing Science Institute. Among the leading researchers in the field was Robert D. Buzzell whose definition of the product life cycle is still widely cited, viz: 'a generalized model of the sales trend for a product class or category over a period of time, and of related changes in competitive behaviour' (Buzzell, 1966). This definition underpins the use of the PLC concept as the organizing principle for the present book as it is believed that the basic model provides a sound foundation for the development of a normative theory of product policy and management.

In adopting this definition and the basic model which describes it (see below) the authors are conscious that PLC, concept and theory, have been widely challenged by many and rejected by some. If we look back to the 1960s it is possible to see how this disparity has arisen.

In the particular case of the PLC, once the generalized model had been articulated the search began for more refined versions, especially where they could be used predictively. Among the researchers who took up this challenge were Victor Cook and Rolando Polli with the assistance of the Marketing Science Institute (MSI). Scheuing refers to their work in suggesting that while Buzzell's definition 'is principally correct, a few qualifications are in order' (p. 269). Two main qualifications are proposed. First, there are extraneous influences which may distort the picture and Scheuing cites the three singled out by Cook and Polli (1969) – population growth (one assumes a declining population would also affect demand), change in the level of personal consumption, and price changes. Second, it is necessary to be clear on the level of aggregation with which one is concerned – product, product line or product category. Unfortunately, there are no universally agreed definitions to ensure these descriptors are used consistently.

In essence the product is the lowest common denominator and may be distinguished in some way from other very similar products. Thus, a number 8, 1-inch screw may be made of steel, stainless steel, brass or plated, have a countersunk or round head with a straight, Phillips or Pozidrive slot and may be self-tapping or not: 48 product permutations for number 8 alone. In the case of consumer goods (and some industrial products too) otherwise near-perfect substitute products will be distinguished by their brand name – Coke and Pepsi, Camel and Marlboro, Daz and Surf, M & Ms and Smarties, etc.

A product line consists of a number of related products which are close substitutes for one another but sufficiently distinctive to form a sub-group within the product category which defines all those objects satisfying the same basic needs. Thus, within the product category 'carbonated beverages' the major producers have a variety of flavours – cola, orange, lemon, etc. – which compete head-on with each other at the brand or product level and less directly at the product line level which includes all the different brands.

For predictive and tactical purposes the major interest is at the brand or product level where the action is. But for strategic and planning purposes it is the product category which is important. Product categories are based upon distinctive technologies and manufacturing operations and frequently develop specialized channels of distribution and after-sales service. Producers of goods within a product category compete directly with one another and constitute what is commonly referred to as an 'industry'. In this book we are concerned with both strategy and tactics and our primary focus will be on the firm and the actions it needs to take to ensure its continuing success. We believe the PLC concept provides an excellent framework for both analyzing and planning the firm's competitive strategy through the management of its product mix, but we shall be concentrating on courses of action and their implementation rather than detailed predictions of brand marketing. It is against this background that we introduce the concept of the product life cycle as the organizing and analytical framework for the book.

The product life cycle

Conventionally, and as represented in Figure 5.1, the product life cycle (PLC) is conceived of as having four stages – *Introduction, Growth, Maturity* and *Decline*. In this book we shall be concerned with a 'stretched' PLC consisting of seven stages by adding *'Gestation'* before the Introduction stage; by including *Saturation* as a stage between Maturity and Decline; and by adding a final stage of *Elimination*. The stretched PLC is shown in Figure 5.2.

In terms of emphasis we stress the Gestation or *New Product Development* phase, the Introduction or *Launch* phase, and the Elimination phase. The reason for this emphasis is that not only does it reflect the research interests of the authors but it acknowledges the fact that most marketing management books concentrate on the Growth/Maturity

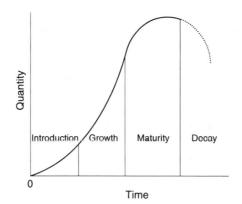

Figure 5.1 ● The product life cycle

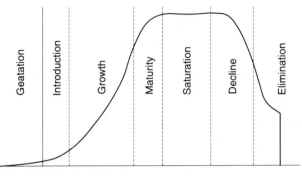

Figure 5.2 ● The 'stretched' PLC

phases as these represent the areas where most marketing activity occurs, i.e. the source of most revenue and profit.

The case for the existence of product life cycles rests fundamentally on the fact that if one examines the sales trend for products, especially those which have passed through most if not all the stages, then it is possible to discern a distinct pattern similar to that shown in Figures 5.1 and 5.2. Further, the phases or stages of the product's developmental cycle correspond closely to the phases observed for the life cycles of living organisms and suggest that the analogy with biological life cycles may be helpful in providing insight and understanding into the reasons why PLCs behave as they do. In *Market Development* Baker (1983b) described the analogy as follows.

The analogy of a product life cycle is firmly founded in the biological sciences and the observation that living organisms pass through an inevitable cycle from conception through gestation to growth leading to maturity. In turn, the mature organism begins to decay progressively until its life is terminated in death. This progression is the inescapable sequence through which normal organisms will pass. That said, it would be a foolhardy bioscientist who would attempt to generalize about the expectations of a particular organism without first establishing its genus, species and sub-species, and even then they would only speculate about any distinct organism in terms of some form of probabilistic statement concerning expected outcomes.

The validity of this assertion is easily demonstrated by reference to ourselves – human beings. An inspection of life expectancies quickly reveals major disparities between the inhabitants of advanced, affluent economies and their less fortunate brothers and sisters in the developing countries. Thus, while the average British male can look forward to a life span of 72 years, an Indian has a life expectancy of only 51 years. However, if we were to compare a Briton and an Indian aged 30 years, the discrepancy in their respective life expectancies would be relatively small. The problem is a familiar one in the field of descriptive statistics; means or averages are largely meaningless unless we also possess some measure of dispersion about the mean.

In the case of Indians, infant mortality is very high and the age distribution at death is heavily skewed towards young persons. On the other hand, if a child in India survives the dangers of childhood, the probability of a reasonably long life is quite high. A broadly similar pattern also applies to Britons, in that infants and young children are more susceptible to disease and death by accident or genetic defect than are teenagers and adults. On the other hand, by enabling weak specimens to survive childhood one increases the probability of death in middle life, with the result that life expectancies for mature adults are very similar between advanced and developing countries.

Actuaries understand this perfectly and base life insurance premiums upon average probabilities. The impression that your policy is written specifically for you is illusory, for no actuary would presume to predict your personal life expectancy. The irony is that while all of this is entirely commonplace and acceptable to us as insurance risks, as managers we expect analogous models to possess a level of predictive ability which cannot be achieved with very large populations of essentially homogeneous units.

The level of information which we are likely to possess about a product group such as detergents or industrial fasteners is minuscule by comparison with the demographic data available upon people in general or nationalities in particular. But, despite this, we try to make a generalized statement about the sales history of a successful (unspecified) product into a highly specific predictive device. In fact, PLCs can be used as forecasting tools, but only when one has a considerable amount of information about the product, or one analogous to it, and the market into which the product is to be introduced. In the present context, however, the relevance of the PLC is that it is a constant reminder of the inevitability of change and does mirror the stages through which all successful products pass. These stages and the titles given to them are represented in Figure 5.2.

The seven stages of the product life cycle

Stage one: Gestation (new product development)

As a consequence of accelerating technological change and increased competition, firms have found it necessary to introduce more and more new products in an effort to distinguish themselves from their competitors and gain a competitive edge. Two consequences follow almost automatically – many new products are stillborn or survive for only a short period, and the average product life cycle is shortening as successful new products displace the old. This, in turn, has two main effects on marketing management. First, there is the need to accelerate the actual time taken to develop the new product – the so-called 'Time *to* Market' issue which we discuss at some length in Chapter 14. Second, there is the need to get it right first time through a process of Total Quality Management (TQM).

Of the two issues, research by McKinsey in the early 1990s would seem to suggest that time *to* market is the more important. Based on three assumptions – a PLC of five years, annual growth of 15% and price erosion of 12% per annum – they concluded that a firm bringing a new product to market on budget but six months late would forfeit up to 50% of its profit potential. By contrast, a product brought to market on time but 50% over budget would forfeit only 4% of its profit potential.

Of course, the ideal is to be on time and on budget with a product which precisely meets the intended customer's needs: the goal of the processes, procedures and techniques suggested in later chapters. But, having said that, it has to be recognized that few if any managers are blessed with perfect foresight and there is no known market research technique which can guarantee 100% accuracy in predicting how an intended market will actually respond to a new product. It follows that the firm which launches a less than perfect product, but which has the capability to respond quickly and effectively to customer reactions and feedback, may well outperform the 'perfectionist' organization which takes much longer to get to the market. These issues and the trade-offs involved will be dealt with in greater depth in Chapter 14.

Stage two: Introduction (launch)

One of the seminal contributions which laid the foundations for the rediscovery of marketing was Ted Levitt's 'Marketing myopia' (*Harvard Business Review*, July–August 1960). In essence the thesis of Levitt's analysis was that change is inevitable on the grounds that consumers will continuously search for new and better ways of satisfying their needs. In turn, this prompts producers to innovate and introduce new products to the marketplace in order to secure their survival and growth. Based on this diagnosis Levitt argued that success will accrue to the organizations which best understand customers' needs – what 20 years later Peters and Waterman (1982) were to term 'close to the customer'. Indeed, there is much recent evidence to support the view that products developed from customers' ideas and/or with their collaboration are much more likely to succeed than products which lack such inputs.

But, with or without customer collaboration, there can be no doubt that the introduction or launch phase of a new product is the most critical in its life for, if it can survive infancy, its prospects of a reasonable life and an acceptable return on investment are quite high. It is also true to say that the more radical the new product, i.e. the more it differs from the current, accepted solution to a need, the greater the resistance it will meet and the longer it will take to be taken up or diffuse.

Scheuing (1974) cites Buzzell's (1966) explanation of some of the reasons why take-up may be slow in the introductory phase, namely:

'**1.** Delays in the expansion of production capacity;
2. Technical problems i.e. . . . . "working out the bugs";
3. Delays in making the product available to customers, especially in obtaining adequate distribution through retail outlets; and
4. Customer inertia, arising primarily from reluctance to change established behavior patterns . . .'.

Clearly, these reflect issues and problems on the supply side as well as the demand side.

Stage three: Growth

The growth phase of a new product marks its successful survival of the trials and tribulations of infancy and promises the prospects of profitability. As hinted in the last paragraph, growth is usually a consequence of changes on both the demand and supply sides of the market and on what is often referred to as 'pull' and 'push'.

On the pull or demand side the contagion model mentioned earlier is obviously at work. The owners of new products like to display them, and discussing them with others is a well-known device for helping to justify purchase to oneself and so reduces post-purchase dissonance. As visibility and word-of-mouth recommendation gather momentum so resistance falls and more customers seek supplies of the new product. These swings in consumer attitudes certainly won't go undetected by potential suppliers who have not yet entered the market, usually because they don't want to cannibalize existing sales. But, faced with the threat of a loss in market share, new suppliers will enter the market offering their variant of the new product in substitution for part of their old supply. The bandwagon has started to roll!

The growth period is one of particular dynamism because it offers the opportunity for new entrants to take on the established suppliers and win market share. This stimulates incremental innovation and product improvement which may well lead to real growth in demand for the product category and their acceptance and use by a much larger number of consumers than hitherto. Managing growth presents its own particular problems, not least that mistakes are easy to make which may not affect the market growth but could be fatal to the unlucky firm that makes them, and the issues are elaborated on fully in Chapter 6. As noted earlier, however, the growth and maturity phases are the primary preoccupation of marketing management texts and we shall confine ourselves to the product-related issues.

Stage four: Maturity

Maturity occurs when the new product has successfully displaced the product(s) for which it was a substitute such that all the suppliers of the former product have now switched to its replacement or else quit the market. By the maturity stage the product form will have achieved a state in which it is capable of little if any further physical development. The proliferation of variants so typical of the growth stage will cease. In maturity the customer knows what he wants and the physical attributes of the product are well known and understood. Further, market segmentation on the basis of physical differences and usage becomes difficult if not impossible.

As a result suppliers to the market must look to other forms of differentiation as the basis for building and retaining market share. Thus, it is in the maturity stage that the professional marketer is most heavily engaged in developing and delivering an effective marketing mix. Competition becomes much more intense and focused as growth slows down and sellers struggle to avoid price concessions in an increasingly difficult market. Non-price competition based upon promotion, distribution and service – both pre-sales and after-sales – dominate as supplier firms jockey for position. This phase is covered more fully in Chapter 16.

Stage five: Saturation

Saturation is the advanced stage of maturity. By now the market has settled down, usually with three or four major players serving the mass market and a constellation of small firms meeting the specialist needs of the minority. The 80/20 or Pareto principle will usually obtain with a small number of large firms accounting for 80% of sales and a large number of small firms accounting for the remaining 20%.

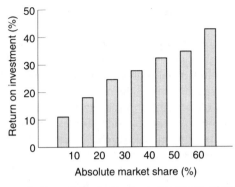

Figure 5.3 ● The relationship between market share and profitability (*source*: Buzzell and Gale, 1987)

In the case of the mass market, competition will be intense as suppliers seek to defend or possibly build market share for, as the PIMS study (Buzzell and Gale, 1987) has clearly shown, there is a very strong correlation between market share and profitability. As can be seen from Figure 5.3 profitability doubles for every 15% increase in market share.

Wherever possible, however, the major firms will seek to avoid direct price competition with the largest player setting the industry norm (administered pricing in the economist's analysis of oligopolistic pricing). This is not to say that firms will not use price directly as a short-term promotional device through discounts, couponing etc., or indirectly by offering more for less ($13\frac{1}{2}$% extra in the standard beer can, eight for the price of six for carbonated beverages, etc.). Overall, however, price levels will remain fairly stable in the mass market. For the rest the niche players will tend to cater either for the price-conscious buyer who regards the product as a commodity and so will patronize the lowest-cost source with little or no expectation of sophisticated packaging, promotional devices or service, or for the small number of buyers for whom the product has a special significance and who are willing to pay a price premium, for a variant of the product which caters precisely to their specific needs.

Saturation is the stage of greatest reward and greatest danger. Having successfully established one's place in the mature market, now is the time to reap the rewards for one's efforts. True, one will still need to deploy a considerable marketing effort to protect one's position but, at worst, competition consists of armed neutrality or, at best, peaceful co-existence as the established barriers to entry deter all but the foolhardy from seeking to join an established, no-growth industry. Not only are the suppliers entrenched and secure in their positions but the customers are generally content with their lot and resistant to change.

The product is now in its most advanced form, with little scope for further improvement, is well known and understood by users, many of whom will have developed strong preferences for particular suppliers, and, thanks to competition, is probably available at a lower price in real terms than in earlier stages in the life cycle. Small wonder that the complacency, against which Levitt (1960) warns us, sets in. 'Every (declining) industry was once a growth industry' – you have to succeed before anyone will notice you have failed.

Looking back to the problems of gestation and launch it is understandable that those who have succeeded in creating new products and markets should be reluctant willingly to risk all this by trying to repeat the process. This is particularly the case for basic products (especially consumer goods) where the mature phase of the life cycle is very long and where it is difficult to conceive of a major technological change which will revolutionize the industry structure on the supply side. Constant attention to the performance of the product across multiple criteria is required. This is the subject of Chapter 17.

It is also important to recognize that until the mid-1950s in the USA, and somewhat later in Europe, the impact of a growing population and the post-war boom had resulted in continuous growth in the markets for consumer goods (on which, ultimately, all demand depends). It was only the depressions of the mid-1950s in the USA which led to recognition that markets could not be expected to grow forever as a result of population growth and so raised the spectre of widespread stagnation in growth and prosperity. Indeed, it was this very recognition which was to lead first to the rediscovery of the marketing concept, and its emphasis upon customer satisfaction as the basis of competitive advantage, and second to environmentalism and the recognition that there are 'limits to growth' (Meadows et al., 1972).

For the established firm the challenge is to sustain its market position for as long as possible; for the new firm the challenge is to disturb equilibrium and initiate a new cycle of change. Invariably it is a technological breakthrough which provides the opportunity to do this, leading to the next stage in the life cycle, decline.

Stage six: Decline

As innovators and entrepreneurs conceive of alternative ways of satisfying customer needs, they will bring their ideas to the marketplace and challenge the status quo. For all the reasons discussed earlier the initial impact of innovation may be small, and the more radical the innovation, the greater the resistance to its establishment. Inevitably some innovations will succeed and, as they win market share from a saturated market, so the fortunes of the existing players will move into decline. However, while industry sales may begin to decline the big players will usually be the last to feel the effects of this.

By definition big players cater for the majority, and the majority are much more likely to be resistant to change than are those customers who have special interests in the core product. Thus, the first persons to switch from LP records or tape to compact disks were those who perceived a sufficient benefit in the sound quality offered to be willing to invest in the cost of new equipment and the higher unit cost of each recording. In time, if the claims for CDs are substantiated, increasing demand will result in their becoming more widely available and the cost of both CD players and disks will start to fall. Contagion and bandwagon effects will begin to occur as the big players detect accelerating losses in market share and have to decide on their next competitive move.

There are basically two options available. Either you resist totally the change, with the risk of extinction, or you consider voluntary elimination. These issues, together with related ways of dealing with them, are the subject of Chapter 18.

Stage seven: Elimination

This new stage of the life cycle has been added to recognize that while change is inevitable and most, if not all, products have finite lives, evolution is about the survival of the fittest and the role of management is to ensure the survival of the species. In this analogy, of course, the species is the firm and only if it is a single-product firm will survival of firm and product be the same thing. Usually it is not, for, implicitly or explicitly, firms recognize and understand the implications of the PLC and so seek to develop a portfolio of products each at different stages of their individual life cycle. We shall return to the concept of the Product Portfolio or, as it is often known, the 'Boston Box' later. Meantime it is sufficient to recognize that the elimination/withdrawal of a product requires to be just as much a conscious and considered decision as was its introduction and launch. Comparatively little attention has been given to this phase, however, so we deal with it at some length in Chapter 17.

In the previous pages we have described briefly the general concept of product life cycles. Using a biological analogy we have exposed some of the underlying forces which appear to account for the rise and fall of species/products and we have described briefly some of the salient characteristics of the seven phases of the PLC which provide the framework for this book. In the next section we review the managerial application of the PLC concept in practice.

Managerial applications of the PLC concept

Some five years after the publication of his seminal 'Marketing myopia' Ted Levitt (1965) published another major article in the *Harvard Business Review* in which he urged practitioners 'To convert a tantalising concept into a managerial instrument of competitive power – "EXPLOIT the Product Life Cycle"!'. He opened this article with the following observation:

> 'Most alert and thoughtful senior marketing executives are by now familiar with the concept of the product life cycle. Even a handful of uniquely cosmopolitan and up-to-date corporate presidents have familiarized themselves with this tantalizing concept. Yet a recent survey I took of such executives found none who used the concept in any strategic way whatever, and pitifully few who used it in any kind of tactical way. It has remained – as have so many fascinating theories in economics, physics and sex – a remarkably durable but almost totally unemployed and seemingly unemployable piece of professional baggage whose presence in the rhetoric of professional discussion adds a much coveted but apparently unattainable legitimacy to the idea that marketing management is somehow a profession. There is, furthermore, a persistent feeling that the life cycle concept adds luster and believability to the insistent claim in certain circles that marketing is close to being some sort of science.
>
> The concept of the product life cycle is today at about the stage that the Copernican view of the universe was 300 years ago: a lot of people know about it, but hardly anybody seemed to use it in any effective or productive way.'

In his article Levitt first described the concept to ensure a common background to a discussion of 'ways of using the concept effectively and of turning the knowledge of its existence into a managerial instrument of competitive power'. Twenty-five years later, Laurie Wood ('The end of the product life cycle', *Journal of Marketing Management*, Vol. 6, No. 2, Autumn 1990) seems to have come to the same conclusion, although she suggests that the concept has outlived its usefulness and, in accordance with its own tenets, should be allowed to die – a theme we return to in the next section.

In his analysis Levitt describes the simplified four-stage model comprising Market Development, Market Growth, Market Maturity and Market Decline. More importantly, he focuses on the key operating questions which the claimed existence of a PLC should prompt in the minds of alert executives, namely:

- 'Given a proposed new product or service, how and to what extent can the shape and duration of each stage be predicted?'
- 'Given an existing product, how can one determine what stage it is in?'
- 'Given all this knowledge, how can it be effectively used?'

Only the most naive would expect hard and fast answers to such questions but, unfortunately, that is precisely what the majority seem to want. As Levitt himself remarks,

> 'As with so many things in business, and perhaps uniquely in marketing, it is almost impossible to make universally useful suggestions regarding how to manage one's affairs. It is certainly particularly difficult to provide widely useful advice on how to foresee or predict the slope and duration of a product's life. Indeed, it is precisely because so little specific day-to-day guidance is possible in anything, and because no checklist has ever by itself been very useful to anybody for very long, that business management will probably never be a science – always an art – and will pay exceptional rewards to managers with rare talent, enormous energy, iron nerve, great capacity for assuming responsibility and bearing accountability.'

That said, Levitt still firmly believes that benefits will accrue by attempting to answer the questions he posed. In doing so he is very much in the same vein as Eisenhower who claimed that 'planning is all, the plan is nothing'. What is important is that we seek to identify the issues and events which will bear upon the process and devise strategies and tactics to deal with them. As we shall see later, a great deal of effort has been directed at defining and seeking to measure the factors which influence consumers' choice behaviour, whether it be to adopt a new product, remain loyal to an existing product, or switch their loyalty to something new.

For all the reasons set out by Levitt it will be impossible to come up with a universal prescription to suit all diagnoses; more often than not the maxim 'physician heal thyself' will apply. Given the unique and complex nature of the context, only those directly involved will be able to develop a sufficiently detailed diagnosis to enable prescription to be possible. What is needed, therefore, is instruction in diagnostic skills and analytical procedures within some over-arching analytical framework. It is this which the product life cycle concept provides.

Among the proponents of the product life cycle (PLC) is George F. MacKenzie who stated that 'In reality this concept may well be the potentially most productive day-to-day marketing and planning tool available to business management' ('On marketing's missing link – the product life cycle concept', *Industrial Marketing*, April 1971).

MacKenzie's enthusiasm for the PLC concept is founded on the belief that its value consists in the development of a simple but vital attitude: 'The required attitude is simply the act of recognizing that a manufacturer or service company should base its entire business operation on the actual requirements and timing of its potential markets in terms of products which they must have and will purchase at a price sufficient to yield a significant profit.' In other words, a firm's primary business is to solve problems rather than sell products.

In MacKenzie's view the components of the PLC 'are empirically self-defining.' Consequently, and contrary to managerial opinion which regards 'estimating and forecasting the timing factor associated with a product's present and future development' as impractical, it is possible to define the phases of the PLC and take appropriate action. For example:

1. The market development of an important new product will end with the entry of a significant new competitor. This will herald the onset of the rapid growth phase.

2. The end of high growth is usually signalled by the entry of a cluster of new competitors, increased price competition and intensified promotional activity.

3. Decline is heralded by an observed decline in overall market size (volume and/or value).

However, MacKenzie's assertion that it is possible to use the PLC as an operational planning tool inevitably has to recognize that its use will depend heavily on management's diagnostic and predictive powers, and nothing other than the benefits of experience is proposed to accomplish this.

The issue of predictability of PLCs was the subject of an article by Chester R. Wasson ('How predictable are fashion and other product life cycles?', *Journal of Marketing*, Vol. 32, July 1968). According to Wasson:

'Market planning needs a fundamental explanatory theory of the fashion cycle which would explain the clearly observable, ceaseless fluctuations and their subsequent course. The explanation can be sound only if based on known tendencies of human behaviour and on the way human motives, both innate and socially conditioned, cause people to react to the kind of stimulus called a new product. To be useful the theory also must indicate at the minimum the general direction of the next fluctuation and detect the timing of at least the first signs of a new swing.'

Wasson argues that a framework exists for such a theory, that it can be drawn from the documented results of product acceptance research interpreted in light of the social psychology of perception and motivation, and that it can be tested, for at least some kinds of products, in unpublished proprietary research. Its existence (the fashion life cycle) is clearly antithetical to the notion that fashion is a 'synthetic creation of the seller'.

Wasson considers the acceptance cycle of a fashion as similar to the theoretical course of the normal life cycle. This is distinguished from a fad by having an initially slow rise to popularity, a plateau of continuing popularity and a low rather than abrupt decline. But, as many have observed, 'such an empirical after-the-fact basis for distinction deprives any theory of most of its potential utility'. What is needed is a theory which can distinguish fads from other new products in advance. Wasson considers that such a theory must be based on known tendencies of individual and social behaviour and help explain:

1. Why and how new products gain acceptance as well as why others fail.
2. Why some new products grow rapidly while others develop slowly.
3. Why some products become 'standards' while others fluctuate in popularity, and why the popularity of fads collapses at their sales peak.
4. How and why classics exist in a fashion environment.

Wasson sees choice as a trade-off or compromise between conflicting motives and aspirations which are dynamic and change over time. He also recognizes the paradox implicit in our own maxim 'The act of consumption changes the consumer' when he writes:

> 'The oscillation (in fashion) will tend to be polar, swinging from one extreme to the opposite, because the satisfaction-yield span of any one design will extinguish the very drives which led to its adoption and bring to the fore those drives least well fulfilled by the design.'

Because the 'desire-set' varies so much between individuals, Wasson considers that an additional element is required to account for the rapidity and completeness of most new-fashion adoption. This element is social approval – a factor which leads inevitably to 'over-adoption' by persons who do not actually benefit from the new product (replacing a $300 a month clerk with a $3000 per month computer which was less efficient!). It is this over-adoption which precipitates an avoidance reaction and so triggers the decline from the peak.

Wasson claims that 'The three principles of product acceptance – inherent purchase, compromise, the changing hierarchy of motivation, and the tendency toward over-adoption – furnish a necessary and sufficient explanation of the swings of fashion.' But they don't explain 'the classic'! Wasson regards classics as 'midpoint compromises' which satisfy core function attributes and are least likely to become 'unfashionable'. Paradoxically, this means the classic customer is least likely to respond to a fad but might be among the first to respond to a radical innovation if it were perceived as meeting the core function attributes best.

Apparent anomalies of this kind are abundant in marketing. For example, Wasson cites the following:

> 'Soluble coffee existed for over a generation before World War II; and even when wartime developments brought its price down, six years were needed to develop the market potential. Frozen orange juice, another wartime beneficiary, rose from scratch to peak market in three years, as fast as facilities could be developed. The astonishing benefits of hybrid corn yields were not sufficient to get more than 6 per cent of the farmers interested during the

first six years on the market, although little else is planted today. However, another farm improvement, 2-4-D and related insecticides, were so avidly sought by farmers upon their release after the war that they became a real threat to health.'

The explanation given is that the product is but one element in a use-system 'which is the real source of satisfaction of the desire-set. Products deliver their potential satisfactions only in the context of some established set of procedural habits organized around their use. Seed corn yields the sought-after crop only when procured, planted, cultivated, harvested and stored in a carefully-planned and well-learned system of habitual practices.'

Habit or experience is often hard-earned and not to be lightly discarded. Indeed, consistent with the pleasure–pain principles, we usually adopt patterns of behaviour (habits) because they give us pleasure. Subsequently, the degree of pleasure or satisfaction may decline but research suggests we will only discard existing habits if they lead to actual dissatisfaction (pain) or we receive a cue or stimulus which promises greater satisfaction. In Rogers and Shoemaker's terminology the more compatible the new thing with our existing behavioural pattern the more likely we are to adopt it. Thus, new orange juice and insecticides fitted easily into existing procedures, whereas hybrid seed corn and instant coffee called for learning new habits and behaviour.

Wasson suggests that any new offering may pose problems of one or more of three kinds of learning:

'**1.** Learning new sequence of motor habits...

2. Learning to perceive new benefits as valuable and thus worth paying for...

3. Learning to perceive one's role in the use of the product as of less importance (as in the acceptance of an automatic transmission).'

Thus, the speed of adoption is seen as contingent upon the degree of learning necessary to understand and use the new product.

Wasson claims that his model is valid on the basis of three kinds of evidence. First, 'known proprietary research clearly demonstrates that taste and fashion are predictable ahead of promotion and sales, and even in advance of design, on the basis of analysis of consumer reaction'. Second, 'it is possible to cite at least a few examples of situations in which a simple learning-content analysis would have greatly improved otherwise extensive research on product acceptance'. And third, 'some limited observation and research has proved successful in prediction of a fashion cycle'.

Examples are offered to support his claims but, as he notes, in the early 1960s the subject of 'innovation' did not enjoy the popularity it had gained by the late 1960s so examples were few and far between. Since then a growing body of research findings has lent considerable support to his findings, so much so that most marketing management texts contain prescriptive models as to the most appropriate marketing tactics and mix to use at each stage of the PLC. Table 5.1 is a classic example of such a summary of some key characteristics and actions to be taken at different stages in the life cycle.

We return to the issue of operationalizing the PLC in the final section of this chapter. However, before we do so it is important to recognize that PLC theory and, particularly, its application have not been without their critics.

Table 5.1 ● Characteristics of life cycle stages

Product life-cycle	Introduction	Growth	Maturity	Decline
Characteristics				
Sales	Low	Fast	Slow to decline	Declining
Profits	Negligible	Peak levels	Begin to decline	Declining to zero
Cash flow	Negative	Moderate	High	Low
Customers	Early adopters	Mass market	Mass market	Laggards
Competitors	Few	Growing	Many 'me too' rivals	Taking market
Key actions				
Strategy	Expand market	Market penetration	Defend share	Productivity
Marketing costs	High	High (declining %)	Falling	Low
Marketing emphasis	Product awareness	Brand preference	Brand loyalty	Image maintenance
Pricing	High	Maintain	Maintain/increase	Rising
Distribution	Patchy	Intensive	Intensive	Selective
Product	Basic	Improved	Broaden position Product development Resegment	Rationalize

→→→ Brand life →→→ Generic life →→→

Source: Doyle (1976).

Criticisms of the PLC

As Thomas (1994) reminds us, 'Forget the product life cycle' was the command made in a now famous article (Dhalla and Yuspeh, 1976). Thomas continues:

'Their command was based upon conceptual and operational arguments. The conceptual arguments were that:

- Products are not living things, hence the biological metaphor is entirely misleading.
- The life cycle of a product is the dependent variable, being a function of the way in which the product is managed over time. It is certainly not an independent variable.
- The product life cycle cannot be valid for product class, product form and for brands – indeed, an important function of a brand name is to create a franchise that has value over time, permitting changes to take place in the product formulation.
- Trying to fit product life-cycle curves into empirical sales data is a sterile exercise in taxonomy.

The main operative arguments include:

- The four phases or states in the life cycle are not clearly definable.

- It is impossible to determine at any moment in time exactly where a product is in its life cycle hence:
- The concept cannot be used as a planning tool.
- There is evidence that companies who have tried to use the product life cycle as a planning tool have made costly errors and passed up promising opportunities.'

In the face of such trenchant criticism it is surprising that the PLC was not dropped immediately from the marketing repertoire! But, 14 years later Laurie Wood (1990) was still predicting 'The end of the product life cycle' in the *Journal of Marketing Management* (Vol. 6, No. 2). In her paper Wood 'seeks to provide a critical appraisal of PLC theory, and to examine the value of this pervasive concept in educating our future marketing managers into the next century'. She concludes that the PLC has outlived its own life cycle and so should be discarded as a useful marketing theory.

Wood begins by pointing to the analogy between the PLC and biological life cycles (Tellis, 1981), the physical sciences and the periodic table of elements (Smallwood, 1973) but believes its origins are rooted in economic theory (Schumpeter, 1934).

'This combination of scientific rationale – derived from biology, chemistry and economics – served to enhance the legitimacy of marketing as a profession (Levitt, 1965) and has endowed the concept with its enduring appeal.'

Wood then proceeds to describe the classic S-shaped curve and its four or five stages as defined *inter alia* by Rogers (1962), Levitt (1965) and Kotler (1967).

Although widely accepted as a concept the PLC has been little used as a marketing tool. Attempts to validate or refute the life cycle concept empirically have been constrained by two factors:

'(a) the lack of definition as to which "life" we are actually investigating and,
(b) the complications of empirical research – in that by tracking sales trends over time, we inevitably observe the effects of management strategies on the life cycle itself.'

With regard to the former it is clear that different authors have adopted widely different definitions, from the *industry* life cycle of economics, through the *market* life cycle of authors like Levitt, through *brand* life cycles to *Product Class* and *Product Form* concepts. Given this range of definitions, it is unsurprising that 'no comparable and satisfac-tory empirical validation of the "classical" product life cycle concept exists'.

As to the impact of management strategies, the work of Cox (1967) established at least six patterns of life cycle curve, while Polli and Cook (1969) found that only 17% of product classes and 20% of product forms for over 100 consumer products conformed with the classic S-shaped curve of PLC theory. In large measure these variations were attributed to management taking action to modify market behaviour through promotional and sales activity.

Wood concludes: 'Variations in the PLC are inevitable if we accept Levitt's original premise that the main utility of the concept lies in the fact that the life cycle can be managed. The life cycle itself must be a dependent variable, if it can be shaped by marketing action.'

This view that the PLC is the consequence rather than the cause of marketing strategy decisions is seen by us as the fundamental misunderstanding which seeks to use the

PLC as a marketing tool rather than accepting it as reflecting an inevitable deterministic process for 'surviving' products in the absence of any managerial or other intervention. In other words the PLC defines the underlying process of growth and decay and so permits the isolation and possible use of factors which may accelerate or slow down the process. A more sophisticated understanding of the analogies is needed.

If one is to use the PLC as a basis for developing mix strategies, then one needs to know the answers to three key questions:

1. Given a proposed new product or service, how and to what extent can the shape and duration of each stage be predicted?

2. Given an existing product, how can one predict which stage it is in?

3. Given all this knowledge, how can it be effectively used?

Wood argues that, as Kotler's (1989) study showed, the problem with answering these questions is the lack of the necessary information on the performance, in the marketplace, of products (both one's own and those of one's competitors).

Wood cites Day's (1981) conclusion that the PLC 'represents the outcome or summary of numerous forces for change in the relevant product-market, each force acting in concert with others to facilitate or inhibit the rate of product sales growth or decline'. Wood argues that this means one needs to revert to basic marketing principles in developing marketing strategies and to avoid the 'dangerous "short-circuitry" of the PLC and "formula" marketing' if managers are to develop a practical understanding of product management.

Wood proceeds to argue that there have been significant changes in emphasis in marketing from the 1950s and 1960s, in which support for the PLC first developed, and that these changes point up the weakness of the theory as a marketing tool. Thus writers like Levitt and Kotler in the 1960s argued for the PLC's use as a forecasting and planning device. More recently Kotler (1989), in a much extended discussion of the PLC, sees its use as a forecasting tool as severely limited and stresses its application in reviewing historical sales patterns and performance for planning and control.

Wood concludes that the PLC concept has reached the end of its useful life cycle and that it should be eliminated from the marketer's toolkit lest it mislead the next generation of marketing practitioners.

This view is clearly not shared by Doyle (1995) in his definitive entry on 'Product life cycle management' in the *Companion Encyclopedia of Marketing*. As Doyle points out, part of the problem is that 'product' does not enjoy a single, accepted definition. Doyle suggests that one should start with the needs of customers and then look successively at demand, current technology, product, product forms and brands, as illustrated in Table 5.2. Brands may have an indefinite life as their producers 'change the technological, design and service content of the offer while still retaining the brand values'.

Given these definitions it is possible to see that even if demand is declining, specific product forms may be enjoying spectacular growth, e.g. tea, instant and herbal teas.

Doyle cites six reasons why the PLC is not of much use to marketing strategy:

1. *Undefined concept* (see Table 5.2).

Table 5.2 ● Doyle's product life cycle factors

Concept	Definition	Typical length	Examples
Need	Basic underlying requirement	Indefinite	Transportation, calculating
Demand	Specific solution to a need	Very long	Car, computer
Technology	Current state-of-the-art	Short	Composite engine, 16-bit computer
Product	Product with specific technology	Shorter	4-wheel drive car, 16-bit PC
Product form	Variant of product	Very short	Open-top-4-wheel drive, 16-bit notepad PC
Brand	Manufacturer's offer	Long	Honda Civic, IBM PC

Source: Doyle (1995).

2. *No common shape* – if for no other reason that 'actual sales development is shaped by both outside events and by the strategies of competition'.

3. *Unpredictable turning points.*

4. *Unclear implications*, e.g. rapid growth may not lead to high profits in fiercely competitive markets like electronics whereas when there is little competition the decline stage can be very profitable, e.g. foundry supplies business.

5. *Not exogenous*, i.e. the PLC is often the result of management actions rather than outside events, particularly if management accept that change is inevitable and implement the tactics/strategy appropriate to the next stage. When one does this the PLC becomes a self-fulfilling concept.

6. *Product oriented* – the PLC 'is a production rather than a marketing oriented concept'. 'The fortunes of the company are not tied to its products but to five other primary forces which determine its ability to maintain a competitive advantage. These forces are:

● The changing requirements of customers.

● The objectives and strategies of competitors.

● The attractiveness of the market to new competitors.

● The emergence of new technologies which can replace existing solutions.

● The performance and power of those companies supplying resources, raw materials and components to the business.

These are the drivers which obsolete the product.'

According to Doyle it follows that 'it is better to tune managers into concentrating on the causes of change rather than the consequences of it'. Doyle concludes that 'just as there is no uniform, predictable product life cycle, so there is no standard pattern of market evolution', but there are common processes which shape markets. It is by ana-lyzing these processes that managers can anticipate how markets and competition will develop and so devise appropriate competitive strategies. Doyle then proceeds to discuss market dynamics in terms of the five principal actors – customers, competition, new entrants, substitute product and technologies, and supply relationships – in other words the five forces popularized by Porter. Changes which may be anticipated in the market in the actions and behaviour of these five factors are discussed at some length.

Doyle believes that the five key components of the market are affected by evolution-ary forces and suggests that these developments may be divided into four phases:

● The Emerging Market
● The High Growth Phase
● The Mature Phase
● The Decline Phase

Doyle describes the conditions and changes associated with each of these phases in some detail, and makes the point that whereas the Boston Consulting Group (BCG) and other portfolio approaches advise divestment and exit in the 'decline' phase, this is not very practical advice as more and more firms find themselves in such industries/markets.

In effect, Doyle is proposing the more sophisticated application of the PLC which we have long advocated – a concept which provides insight into the forces which shape market opportunity and competitive action which need to be consciously addressed by management to ensure the continued survival and success of their organization. It is to these issues that we turn in the next section.

Operationalizing the PLC

Throughout our discussion of the PLC we have emphasized its value as an analytical framework rather than a predictive device. At the level of Grand Strategy or Policy For-mulation even the most successful managers need to be reminded regularly of the inevi-table fate of the organization (or species) which fails to adapt to its changing environment. As the biological analogy makes clear, evolution has been a continuing process of adaptation to change in order to survive. If one understands this, one can develop systems to monitor the environment continuously and use this feedback to adjust policies and practices in response to change. Given sudden and catastrophic change, even the dinosaur may be rendered extinct but, in most cases, evolution may be seen as a gradual adaptive process in which species (products) compete with one another for scarce resources (customers) such that some will succeed and flourish while others will fail and disappear.

Such disappointment as has been expressed with the PLC usually originates at the opposite end of the managerial spectrum – that concerned with local tactics related to day-to-day brand management. Because of the seductive consistence of the S-shaped logistic growth curve there is an expectation that this can be converted into a precise formula which will predict accurately the behaviour of individual brands in a market.

This ingenuous belief persists despite the fact that the PLC is a generalization about a successful product which survives all the phases.

The seven phases of the PLC, like Shakespeare's seven ages of man, only apply if nothing interferes with the 'normal' course of events. The real challenge for the Brand Manager is to do everything necessary to ensure that the product has the best possible chance of achieving the norm. For example, infant mortality in the UK declined from 142 per 1000 in 1902 to 6 per 1000 in 1996. In India it was 139 per 1000 in 1972 falling to 105 per 1000 in 1982 and 74 per 1000 in 1995. Further, as noted earlier, the average life expectancy for a Briton at birth is 72 years; for an Indian it is only 51 years.

Clearly, medical science is more advanced than marketing science for we know generally what accounts for the differences in human life cycles described above and take steps to ensure the expectation becomes reality. The problem with seeking to use the PLC as a forecasting/predictive device is that it can only work if we take all the prophylactic measures necessary to ensure proper ante-natal care, safe delivery and constant attention in the formative years until a sufficient degree of respect for the environment, self-monitoring and self-care have been achieved.

As to the length of the various phases, our best guide must be past observation and experience. For some products (species) and particularly those which are only marginally different from the product they seek to displace, the introductory phase is likely to be very short. Intended customers will be able to discern quickly and easily if the new variant offers sufficient advantages over the old to justify the switching costs.

If the perceived benefits of the new product exceed the anticipated switching costs then a decision is easily made and the new product will enter a rapid growth phase and soon reach maturity. Usually, however, products which represent only a limited improvement on the status quo are likely to be easily displaced themselves by another incremental innovation. As a result the life cycles of such new products may well assume the shape of the classic life cycle but the length of each of the stages will differ significantly from those of a more radical innovation.

As another generalization, the longest life cycles will be associated with the distinctiveness of the core technology underlying a product, associated with the useful life of the infrastructure necessary to support that technology. For example, in the case of a major manufacturing industry like steel the scale of investment required to enter the industry or to adopt its technology has been very high. As a result, existing producers have a vested interest in maintaining the old technology for as long as possible in order to recoup their original investment. Only if a technological breakthrough occurs which reduces the entry costs to the point that new competitors will emerge will existing producers consider switching to that new technology. Thus, the traditional steel producers in the USA and Western Europe were slow to recognize the benefits of direct reduction and continuous casting which eliminated several costly steps from the traditional processes of blast furnace, transfer of molten iron to steel furnace, casting ingots, reheating ingots and slabbing. Only when new international competition emerged (e.g. Japan) which incorporated these new technologies were the old suppliers forced to upgrade their plant to compete – a process accelerated by the emergence of mini-mills using electric smelting of scrap as a means of avoiding the enormous front-end costs associated with the conversion of ore into steel.

From this discussion it is clear that while the PLC is broadly applicable to all products (we will discuss some well-recognized 'deviants' later) its particular application requires much more detailed knowledge and experience of specific products and industries. At least two possible scenarios suggest themselves. First, we are responsible for the launch of a new product and are required to develop a clear operational plan for the launch as part of a much longer-term strategic plan which aims to plot our expectations well into the future. Second, we have been given responsibility for the management of an existing brand or products. As the second case is more frequently encountered in a marketer's career we will deal with it first.

If the product/brand manager is to use the PLC operationally, the first need is to establish what the PLC for a particular product may look like and what stage it has reached on that PLC. Scheuing (1974) suggests that to do this one must analyze simultaneously three complementary indicators – sales volume, the rate of change of sales volume, and the profit–loss curve. Provided that basic trends are being observed rather than short-term fluctuations, these three complementary measures provide an accurate measurement of the life cycle stage as indicated in Figure 5.4.

From this figure the comparative evolution of the three curves over the life cycle is clear. As soon as sales commence we will generate revenue, and both volume and revenue will grow rapidly after the slow introductory phase. On the other hand the cash flow during the introductory phase is invariably negative owing to the high launch costs so that profit will only begin to be earned with the onset of growth. Of course, the point at which the product will begin to break even is an arbitrary one which will depend upon the firm's own internal accounting procedures. Provided the original sales forecast/budget have been developed in expectation of exponential rather than linear growth, a useful discipline is to set one's cost recovery so that the onset of growth, which marks the end of the launch or introductory phase, marks the break-even point between total revenue and cost for the product.

More important, however, is to compare the relationship between our three measures and especially between sales volume and the rate of change in sales volume, for this is the critical measure of what is happening in the marketplace, rather than the firm's internal costing procedures. As the graph and our model show, growth in the introductory phase is slow as the new product seeks to establish itself against strong resistance. But 'The rate of growth is increasing faster than the sales volume itself as the latter is very low and every added dollar will represent a higher growth percentage than at any later stage of the cycle' (Scheuing, op. cit.). During growth all three indicators move ahead rapidly, but note that the *rate* of growth in sales will achieve its highest level around the middle of the actual growth phase. Similarly, profits are likely to peak around here too, as by this time competitors will have seen the success of the new product and begun to climb on to the bandwagon. As they do so competition will intensify and margins will be eroded as sellers seek to build market share through active use of the marketing mix.

The onset of a negative growth rate in sales volume marks the peak of maturity, and from now on it is downhill all the way. Unit profit is still declining, but for the successful survivors with large market shares there will still be a large positive cash flow. Inevitably, the loss of sales volume to new competitive products will accelerate as decline sets

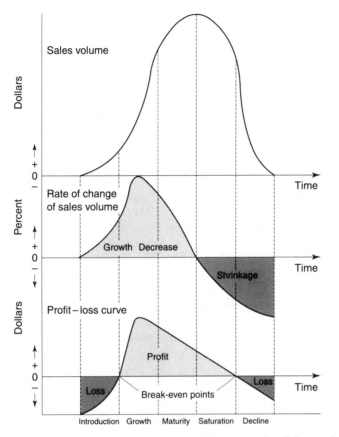

Figure 5.4 ● Determining a product's position on the life cycle (*source*: Scheuing, 1974)

in. Whether this will lead to a loss on unit sales as the figure suggests will again depend upon internal accounting policies. That said, management must accept that with rising costs due to smaller quantities, products in the decline phase call for very careful evaluation to determine whether they are profitable or not.

As Scheuing points out it is the underlying trends which are important and one must seek to smooth out temporary fluctuations around them. It is the changes in inflection which are important as these represent the decision points. Particularly this is true of the rate of change curve. When this goes into reverse, sales are still accelerating and it can take a brave manager to counsel the need to start thinking of a replacement product at this juncture!

As to the second scenario, developing a strategic plan for a completely new product, then the issues involved remain much the same with the salient difference that one will not have any sales or cost data for the actual product from which to determine the parameters of the PLC curve. At least two things appear to be vital if we are to operationalize the PLC under these circumstances. First, we need to convince our colleagues that, other things being equal, the actual sales pattern for the new product will follow the trajectory of a PLC. Second, we need to estimate what the length of the phases might be.

For reasons which are hard to discern the great majority of managers prefer linear forecasts. As one of us has explained elsewhere (*Market Development*, 1983) such linear projections can have serious implications for the perceived performance of the product if it does follow a classic PLC with a slow start-up followed by accelerating growth. Now, if a firm is to make a judgment about the success or failure of a new product, it must have some predetermined sales target against which it can measure this, and given the shape of the PLC, it would seem reasonable to expect that such sales targets would exhibit an exponential progression with very slow initial headway succeeded by rapid growth until the market is saturated. In reality, however, it is believed that many firms use linear forecasts, although my evidence for this is largely anecdotal and based on only a small number of actual cases of which I have direct experience.

The danger of using linear extrapolations for sales targets is clearly demonstrated in Figure 5.5, from which it can be seen that such an approach greatly over-estimates the speed with which a new product can penetrate a market or develop a new one. As a consequence, the new product consistently under-performs its target and so is likely to attract the attention of top management, concerned that it is going to be a failure. Worse still, the position deteriorates progressively at first as forecast and reality get further and further apart.

Faced with such a picture, the question is how long can one continue to accept a failure to meet sales targets before deciding to cut one's losses and withdraw the product, thereby acknowledging it as a failure? Much, of course, will depend upon the product itself and management's previous experience with launching new products. For minor product improvements in frequently purchased items of low unit value, one would expect fairly early indications as to the acceptability of the new product, but in the case of radical innovations, one would anticipate a fairly protracted introductory phase, possibly extending over several years.

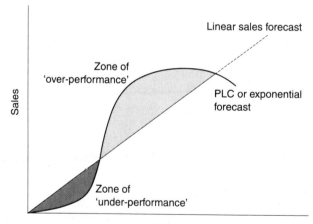

Figure 5.5 ● Linear vs exponential sales forecasts

It therefore seems reasonable to assume that some proportion of commercial new product 'failures' might indeed have been potential successes, but, because of management's unwillingness to allow sufficient time for market penetration and/or their setting of unrealistic sales targets for the introduction phase, they are withdrawn prematurely. Figure 5.5 also suggests that had such managers persevered until the sales of the new product 'took off', they could have looked forward to a period of over-performance by comparison with their linearly extrapolated expectations, and that such over-performance would more than compensate for the early under-performance.

Superficially, the remedy seems obvious: persuade those responsible for setting sales targets for new products to use exponential rather than linear forecasting models. While this may help, there is no certainty that it will alleviate the number of new product failures – indeed, it might have just the opposite effect and encourage managers to hang on to the products whose sales are stagnant or growing very slowly, not because they are experiencing a long gestation, but because only a very small number of customers are interested in the product, that is, it is a *genuine* failure.

With the exception of the deviant cases (which we have yet to discuss) it is our firm conviction that the PLC curve offers the best representation of reality available to us for purposes of strategic planning. It is clear we must convince our colleagues of this and eschew any other underlying assumption *unless and until* someone can come up with a more convincing alternative, i.e. the PLC is the null hypothesis. Acceptance of an S-shaped growth curve is likely to be confirmed (or, possibly, rejected) when the planner(s) draw upon past experience and knowledge of the market, of customers, of the prevailing environmental conditions and of the performance of other similar products in order to estimate the anticipated length of the stages of the life cycle.

The more closely the proposed new product corresponds to existing products the more quickly it will be accepted or rejected and the shorter its overall life cycle will be. Conversely, with radical innovations the introduction phase may last for many years and prediction will have to depend on analogies with earlier innovations of similar magnitude. As another broad generalization, life cycles are shortening as are the lags between invention and commercial use, as indicated by Table 5.3.

Table 5.3 ● Elapsed time, from invention to commercial development, of a number of familiar products

Product	Time from invention to commercial exploitation
Electric motor	65 years
TV	52 years
Vacuum tube	33 years
Zip-fastener	30 years
X-ray tube	18 yeras
Frozen foods	15 years
Nuclear reactors	10 years
Radar	5 years
Solar batteries	3 years

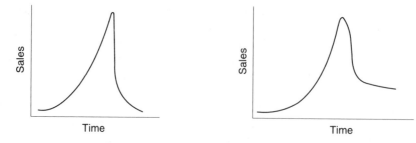

Figure 5.6 ● The classic fashion-good PLC

Figure 5.7 ● The fad PLC

Deviant cases – fads and fashions

As mentioned at a number of places previously, *all* life cycles do not conform to the classic S-shaped curve or U-shaped distribution. It is these 'deviant' cases which are usually invoked as evidence of the non-applicability of the PLC concept. The best-known exceptions to the PLC rule are fads and fashions.

From the practitioners' point of view, PLCs are increasingly likely to take on a distorted version of the classic, inverted-U-shaped curve. Indeed, this has probably always been the case with specific brands which represent only one variant of the generic product. Thus in a 1967 study of 258 ethical drug products, William Cox Jr identified six different kinds of life cycle curve of which only 28.3% followed the classic pattern. The life cycle of fashion products, for example, follows a curve shaped as in Figure 5.6, whereas a fad product which refuses to die will have a life cycle curve like that shown in Figure 5.7.

Two features of the fad/fashion curve which are particularly noteworthy are the near absence of an introductory phase and the meteoric fall in sales once market saturation has been reached. In the case of the second curve, Figure 5.7, a residual demand saves the product from extinction and results in what might be considered a delayed maturity. In fact, while textbooks usually do not discriminate between fads and fashions, it seems likely that Figure 5.6 represents a fashion PLC and Figure 5.7 a fad PLC for some or all of the following reasons.

Fashion life cycles are usually supply-led by firms which substitute a new product for an existing product – hence no introductory phase – and then withdraw the 'new' product at a sales peak to make way for yet another product. Thus, by constantly changing the 'fashion' the firm prevents its competitors from benchmarking or copy-catting its products as well as developing a reputation as an industry leader rather than a follower. The following example of Stoddard-Sekers International in the highly competitive carpet market provides a classic example of a company which has avoided price competition through the use of design and a fashion-led or design-led competitive strategy. Further detail is given in the mini-case study at the end of Chapter 6.

Stoddard-Sekers International plc is a major UK carpet manufacturer best known for its Stoddard Templeton range of domestic carpets. Like many other markets for household goods, the demand for floor coverings is primarily a replacement market with very little new business arising from population growth. Carpet sales also suffer from the severe disadvantage that purchase is deferrable. When the washing machine or TV breaks down, immediate repair or replacement becomes a priority, but one can always make the carpet last a little longer. In such a market it is clearly important that manufacturers stimulate interest among potential buyers by offering them new and improved products whose added value will overcome the natural tendency to defer purchase against other more pressing priorities.

It follows that to succeed in this marketplace one must have distinctive competencies in both design and construction and a clearly defined product policy for managing existing stock ranges as well as new product development. In Stoddards, all existing stock ranges require an annual refurbishment of 20–25% of the range, while new range development averages between 5–20% of the total product portfolio every year. Given the seasonal nature of the market, most new product changes are planned for launch onto the market during a period between April and September, with the design studio normally working six to nine months ahead of these launch dates.

A major element in Stoddard's product planning is the preparation of a colour prediction board. This board is prepared by the group design team under the leadership of Bill Naysmith, the group director responsible for design and development. Its purpose is to predict trends in colour fashions and it is compiled from a variety of materials and sources. In addition, imagery for design direction related to colour areas is also considered and gathered. Amongst the numerous sources used are trade fairs, related exhibitions, galleries, shops, fashion magazines and fibre/yarn producers, including ICI, DuPont and Allied, each of whom prepares their own colour predictions considered on a world-wide basis. Fabric cuttings and architectural materials also form part of the completed collage board.

The completed colour prediction board provides an important visual aid for the group designers and is closely compared with sales by range and colour for the previous year. The board is presented to the group design team during January each year, following the major international trade exhibitions, and is also presented to the group board for information and discussion. It is on the basis of this consultation that decisions are taken as to what colours are to be in demand in the following year and this dictates the whole production planning process.

According to Bill Naysmith, in the carpet industry there are basically two colour-wheels depicting colour trends – an inner wheel and an outer wheel. The inner wheel reflects colours which are always in demand and consists largely of colours that are easily used in the average interior design scheme. They tend to be mid-tone in colour value, with more saturated colours in the leisure and contract market. Thus, this wheel would contain neutrals, beige, green, terracotta and blue. However, the actual tone of each colour group is influenced by the other colour wheel which reflects colour trends. For example, if blue were fashionable, its influence would also be felt in other colour areas. Green would move on to the blue side of the spectrum into the jade green category.

For the leisure and contract markets the inner wheel reflects colours which are always in demand and known to be conducive to eating and drinking habits. Rust and red colours dominate in this sector. As noted, the outer colour wheel reflects the colour cycle of what might be termed fashionable colours. Experience suggests that in the carpet industry it normally takes between 20 and 25 years for a colour to complete the cycle and re-emerge as fashionable again. For example, the last time grey was popular was during 1985–90, prior to which it was 1965–70. Gold, now re-emerging as a popular colour, was last fashionable in the late sixties and early seventies. By contrast to the inner circle colours which remain fairly constant over time, the fashion colours tend to have a cycle lasting for a period of approximately five years. In the main they tend to be used to accent colour values rather than ground shades or else are used in modern designs rather than traditional ones.

Colour values and strengths are also dependent on design trends and to some extent on economic influences. Thus, lighter colours sell better during more affluent times, while the recessionary period of the late 1980s and early 1990s saw a greater emphasis upon darker, more practical colours. Similarly, the return to traditional and classical styles and values in building and furniture in the early 1990s is reflected in the use of colour and design in carpets and fabrics.

The Stoddard example clearly illustrates that it is the designer/manufacturer who dictates what colours will be available in the marketplace. It follows that, through a process of natural selection, only those companies which are successful in anticipating colours that will be acceptable to intending buyers will sell their products. In other words, those who are successful at predicting and anticipating changing consumer tastes will achieve most success in stimulating sales and winning market share.

A similar strategy to that of Stoddard-Sekers may also be seen in the cut-throat consumer electronics market. Figure 5.8 summarizes the lives of portable hi-fi systems for the period 1980–89 and shows a dramatic decline even in the case of top of the-line brand Sony. On the other hand, Figure 5.9 plots the frequency of product introductions for the same period, from which Sony emerges as the clear leader followed by all except Toshiba who have adopted a quite different strategy.

Sony set the pace with all but one of the improvements to its Walkman resulting directly from monitoring consumer reactions. Virtually every Sony innovation has been imitated by competitors thus increasing further the pressure to introduce still more

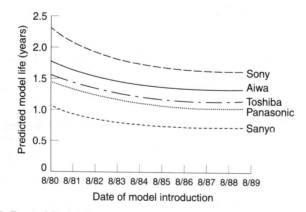

Figure 5.8 ● Portable hi-fi systems' model life decline

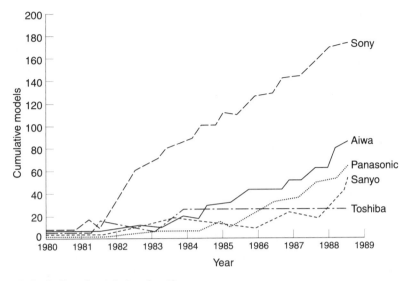

Figure 5.9 ● Product introductions

improvements – and make room for them by withdrawing old models. As the examples illustrate, fashion products are clearly controlled by suppliers who decide when to introduce and withdraw the product and so dictate precisely its life cycle. This is a quite different scenario from the concept of the PLC which implies an evolutionary sequence that probably applies to technologies but not specific products.

In an increasingly competitive environment it seems highly likely that the most successful firms will be those which take control over the PLC and manage it to their advantage.

As for fad products, it would seem these are the product of firms which have no clear idea of precisely what the market wants and so practise what might be termed trial and error marketing, i.e. make it available for sale and see if anyone wants it. Occasionally one of the myriad new products launched in this way will strike a receptive chord and sales will grow as fast as suppliers can cash in on the craze – hula hoops, Rubik cubes, skateboards. Then the next new craze appears and sales stop almost overnight as the followers of fashion switch their allegiance. However, the original product still retains some appeal and a residual market emerges, albeit at a much more modest level. The message here is that the market is in control and it is a matter of luck as to whether your exciting new product will be perceived as such by the intended customer. The real message when developing products is that success comes from satisfying customer needs. But you need to define these closely if you are to stand out in an increasingly crowded and dynamic marketplace.

Summary

In the introduction to this chapter we defined the product life cycle as 'a generalized model of the sales trend for a product class or category over a period of time, and of related changes in competitive behaviour' (Buzzell), and indicated that the PLC concept provides the organizing principle for this book. Our reason for adopting the PLC as a basic model rests on the belief that it provides a sound foundation for the development of a normative theory of product policy and management. The content of this chapter has sought to explain and support this belief.

To begin with we described the basic model of the PLC and its four stages of *Introduction*, *Growth*, *Maturity* and *Decline* which are analogous to the phases of the biological life cycle from which the concept is derived. We then suggested that it would be helpful to 'stretch' the four-stage model to include an initial phase of *gestation*, a period of *saturation* between maturity and decline, and a final phase of *elimination* to mark the withdrawal of a product from the market. Each of these seven phases was described in some detail.

Having established the nature of the product life cycle we then looked more closely at its managerial application. The dominant theme was that the PLC is essentially an analytical and planning tool. It is not a technique for forecasting. This distinction is vitally important, for misguided attempts to use the PLC as a forecasting device have given rise to many of the criticisms of the PLC which were reviewed in some detail.

Based on this review we concluded that the importance of the PLC is that it reflects an inevitable cycle of change and the substitution of new ways of doing things for old. As such the PLC defines the underlying process of growth and decay and so permits the isolation and possible use of factors which may accelerate or slow down different phases of the process. In other words it provides us with a diagnostic and analytical framework that offers the opportunity to influence the cycle through managerial intervention.

The chapter then looked at ways of operationalizing the PLC and putting it into practice and discussed possible deviant cases which do not conform with the general theory.

Irrespective of whether a product has a normal or deviant life cycle, it is clear that eventually this will come to an end, leading to the death of the industry responsible for its creation. But, while technologies may be superseded and replaced, firms strive to survive. To do so it is necessary to anticipate and manage change and this means avoiding putting all your eggs in one basket. To survive the firm needs to innovate and develop a sequence of new products at different stages in their individual life cycles. It is this which we turn to in the next chapter.

QUESTIONS

1. What are the four 'traditional' stages in the PLC? What other stages are suggested in the text? Why?

2. Why is it unreasonable to try and use PLC's for predicting specific outcomes?

3. What are the major managerial implications and applications of the PLC concept?

4. What were Dhalla and Yuspeh's (1976) major criticisms of the PLC concept?

5. What other criticisms have been suggested?

6. Explain why the PLC is a useful tool for helping managers organize their thinking about product strategy and management.

7. What are fads and fashions? Why do their life cycles deviate from the classic pattern?

8. Does the existence of fads and fashions invalidate the PLC concept?

Mini-case ● cK One

The company

Calvin Klein Cosmetics Company was born in 1985 with Obsession, the first perfume of the American designer Calvin Klein. In 1989, the company was purchased by the Anglo-Dutch Unilever Group, but the Calvin Klein brands continued to be run autonomously. This was to give the American perfumer a world-wide scope.

Executive headquarters oversees the world-wide business of Calvin Klein fragrances in New York City. It continuously strives to access international markets with affiliated companies now operating in Canada, the United Kingdom, Germany, Italy and France, which shows the company's commitment to global expansion. In 1996, Calvin Klein fragrances were distributed throughout the world via a network of affiliated distributors and non-affiliated distributors.

Calvin Klein Cosmetics Company operates in the market of premium male and female fragrances. Its range has been extended to include three major brands: Escape, Eternity and Obsession – all of which are available in both female and male variants. Though the French perfumes Chanel No. 5 and Lancôme's Trésor had the lion's share with a turnover above £126 million each in 1995, Eternity was ranked third, ahead of successful perfumes such as Beautiful from Estée Lauder, Dune from Christian Dior, Opium from Yves-Saint-Laurent and Anais-Anais from Cacharel. Calvin Klein Cosmetics' Obsession, Obsession for men, Eternity, Eternity for men, Escape, and Escape for men fragrances recorded world-wide sales of £262 million in 1994 and £298 million in 1995. Over the past five years, these have kept growing by an average of at least 10% per year and have led to a gradual increase in market share to above 5%. On the other hand, the profit margin has decreased over the past five years from more than 15% and tends to level off to around 10% due to increasing promotional expenditure required to support existing perfumes and to stimulate the launch of cK One, the latest perfume from Calvin Klein.

The industry and the market

The market for premium fragrances was worth £5.56 billion in 1995. Calvin Klein, together with Unilever's other brands Elizabeth Arden, Karl Lagerfeld, Chloe, Nino Cerruti, Valentino and Liz Taylor, had a turnover of £707 million, which accounts for 10.7% of the premium fragrances market. Their major competitors are, in declining order, Estée Lauder (Beautiful, Spellbound, Youth Dew...), the world-wide leader with a turnover of £808 million, L'Oréal (Lancôme, Ralph Lauren, Cacharel...), LVMH (Christian Dior, Guerlain, Givenchy, Kenzo...), Elf Aquitaine (Yves-Saint-Laurent, Nina Ricci...) and lastly Chanel, Procter & Gamble and Shiseido. Each of these groups has a turnover of above

£100 million in the prestige fragrances market. The number of brands and the move towards more and more launches makes the market very fragmented and competitive.

Despite a world-wide growth of 5% consumer demand is more and more sluggish in the mature markets of North America and Western Europe: whereas one woman out of 10 used a perfume in 1975, today eight out of 10 do so with a higher level of use. However, the boundaries between mass fine fragrances get blurred due to increasing promotions and discounting, which maintains a pressure on prices; thus, the opportunities for market development get much smaller and a slower growth may be expected in the future. The faster growing markets of Latin America and south-east Asia are too small to compensate and the competition between the brands in the market keeps growing. As a result of acquisitions and the involvement of major consumer product manufacturers like Procter & Gamble and Unilever costs have spiralled. These spiralling costs have obliged perfumers to aim at world-wide success by appealing to mass markets while, at the same time, maintaining an exclusive up-market image. Continuous new product development is essential to sustain product portfolios as brands progress through their life cycles.

The technology when making a perfume

Three ingredients make a perfume: the name, the bottle and the scent. Their specific combination will support the differentiation of the product, on which the competition in the market for premium fragrances is based. Thus, the role of most perfumers in the conception of the product consists essentially of defining the requirements of the scent, the bottle and the name.

Perfumers usually resort to olfactory specialists, the so-called 'nez' in France, to create a specific scent from natural oil and products of synthesis from the chemicals industry to a smaller extent. The use of synthetic products may increase if their olfactory quality can be improved as natural oils remain very expensive. Thus, technological progress of the chemical industry, which is in a growth stage, may drastically change the perfume sectors.

The perfumer also employs specialized designers who design new bottles using computers. Bottle makers are then required to perform miracles with glass to satisfy the perfumers and achieve the differentiation expected from the design of the bottle. Thus, the perfume sector also relies a lot on the technical skills of bottle makers and innovations in glass technology. However, the creation of a perfume depends mainly on human skills, creativity, olfactory, and manual, to make the bottle.

cK One: the latest innovation of Calvin Klein

All these ingredients have been useful to Calvin Klein Company in developing cK one, its latest innovation to join Calvin Klein's existing lines of Obsession, Eternity and Escape. The new scent differentiates itself through a refreshing and light blend of musk and fruity notes with a woodsy base; it is close to eau de cologne. The product is packed in glass and aluminium containers which can be recycled; they look like a chemist's syrup flask, without artifice. The name, cK One, is also very simple and direct. This new scent, its packing and brand is the core of a new product. However, it is not there where the real innovation of cK One lies but in its marketing strategy.

The great novelty of this perfume is that it can be used by both men and women; it is a unisex fragrance. According to designer Calvin Klein, 'cK One fragrance can be shared by couples, by lovers, and by friends and that is really what is modern'. A second trick which is also new is that cK One is targeting a generation – the 15–30 year olds – a previously neglected group within the fragrance market. In this context, cK One is positioned as a light, refreshing scent to be worn 'lavishly' by men and women, clean, pure and contemporary.

The fragrance was first launched in the United States and Canada in autumn of 1994, and a year later in Europe, Latin America and south-east Asia. The launch was supported by a large advertising campaign through TV and press in the United States and mainly through press everywhere else. The media were chosen in order to reach young consumers. This has been a multi-million switched-on advertising campaign, 'Portraits of a generation', by celebrity photographer Steven Meisel. The cK One ads have featured a group of young people, partially clad, in which you can recognize some young stars such as the distracted model Kate Moss or the musician Donovan Leitch. It takes some time to distinguish the men from the women, and the interaction of young people with one another enhances the impression that they are only one with no particular sexual orientation. This backs the argument for women and men to use the same fragrance. Thus, the ads invite you to be part of the gang by using cK One.

Speciality outlets such as music stores, which are unconventional in the premium fragrance sector, and department stores are the main distribution channels of cK One. In the United States, Calvin Klein's new perfume has been available in Tower Records' 85 stores as well as 2200 department stores since September 1994. The 'relaxed, hip and youthful atmosphere' of Tower makes this chain suitable according to Calvin Klein.

Calvin Klein Company has also adopted an innovative approach in pricing cK One. It has chosen a tactically low price of $35 for a 100 ml bottle of cK One eau de toilette against $50 for Obsession.

Unilever is thought to have spent considerably more than the now usual £25 million on cK one to introduce it world-wide.

The performance of cK One

This effort has been rewarded by the specially bright performance of the new Calvin Klein fragrances for both men and women. cK One, introduced in September 1994, was the best-selling fragrance during the 1994 holiday season; it emerged as the star of the prestige fragrance business during Christmas 1994 and its sales kept growing in 1995. American stores say that the sales of cK One are out of control. Though figures are not disclosed, one may suspect that cK One's sales account for at least £110 million in 1995 and its performance in 1996 was expected to be even greater putting it alongside the sales of the leaders, Trésor from Lancôme and Chanel No. 5. With this latest success, Calvin Klein's fragrances (Eternity, Obsession, Escape) have entered the very closed circle of brands at more than £315 million of turnover.

The price of the success is the number of duplications of cK One introduced in 1995, which revitalized the discount fragrance business. The counterfeiting industry accounted for more than £150 million in 1995 in the US. There you can get a copy of a Calvin Klein brand for only £3 which may undermine the brand's premium positioning.

A recipe for success?

Firstly, cK One has offered an obvious advantage against the cluster of fragrances within the market: it allows men and women to share the same fragrance, which can be seen as more practical, or which may be a way of stating a sense of community.

Secondly, the image of cK One seems in tune with the times. cK one points to the blurring of sexual identity which would reflect the need for men and women to use and share the same products while, for years, perfumers have linked their products with sexual role playing, seduction and enhancement of the differences between men and women. cK One may in fact match the value of sharing, by making men and women use the same perfume, the value of belonging to a group without difference by giving a specific and uniform image of cK One and its users. This level of compatibility is enhanced by the chosen target, a generation whose way of life is uniform throughout the world. Furthermore, cK One reflects the environmentally aware nineties as it is packaged in recyclable containers. The external packaging is minimized and the container is protected during transportation by 100% recycled cardboard cartons. Moreover, the distribution in music stores enhances the fashion associated with buying cK one.

Thirdly, the purchase of cK One does not require a long evaluation as its benefits are very specific and its use is for any circumstance as its image is associated with simplicity. Fourthly, as cK one is displayed in free-standing wire racks, shoppers can freely look at the packaging and test it.

Lastly, the image of cK one and its users has been built with so much backing that it is very easy for a user to identify with this image or to form their own impressions by referring to the promoted image when talking about it. As a result, word of mouth has been a key success factor.

Conclusion

Surviving in the highly competitive market for prestige fragrances requires continuous launches of new products from perfumers, though failure rates amount to 90% and launching costs are continuously increasing. This flow of new products contributes to shorter product life cycles, and thus becomes more crucial. Nevertheless, the prestige fragrance market is marked by the popularity of a few classical brands which are useful in funding the world-wide introduction of a new product.

Calvin Klein Company has the support necessary to launch new products since it was purchased by Unilever; furthermore, it has been able to use it successfully. It has especially managed to identify a previously neglected segment whose way of life tends to get closer and closer, to understand it, and then to develop an appropriate product with its scent, its bottle and its name, and an appropriate marketing strategy to support the new product. The broad lines of the marketing strategy came before the creation of the scent. Thus, the high-powered brand marketing seems more important than the product itself: cK one is indeed much more than a clean scent close to eau de toilette in a plain screw-top bottle. Its unconventional marketing approach has built the new product, cK one, and its image. Therefore, a new product in the fragrance industry cannot be confined to a product itself but includes its marketing; it may even derive exclusively from an innovative marketing approach which creates a very new image. In fact, cK One could have targeted either men or women but this would have reduced both its novelty and its appeal. When people are tested blind, they overlap the fragrances designated male and those designated female. This shows that marketing in the past required us to make choices between male and female scents. Calvin Klein did exactly the opposite!

Furthermore, this case shows that a new concept which fails once can be used successfully later as it may be defined and applied more appropriately and as consumers change. Unisex failed in the seventies when fashion designers tried to encourage consumers to sport the same haircuts, wear the same jeans and use the same toiletries. The success of Calvin Klein's shared fragrance seems to show that consumers are now ready to share the same fragrance. Continued heavy and well-managed support of cK one may assure the new product a place among the strong classical brands in the future.

Bibliography

Key Notes (1995) *Cosmetics and Fragrances*.

Kotler, P. (1994) *Marketing Management: Analysis, Planning, Implementation and Control*, 8th edition, Prentice Hall, p. 350.

Mintel (1994) *Women's Fragrances*, May.

Mintel (1995) *Men's Toiletries*, March.

Villard, N. (1995) 'Combat de titans dans les parfums', *Capital*, September, 58–73.

This case was prepared from published sources by Elisabeth Geneau de Lamarlière under the supervision of Michael J Baker.

chapter 6

. . . .

Product portfolios

LEARNING OBJECTIVES
. . . .

1. To introduce and explain the concept of Product Portfolios.

2. To propose measures for assessing the contribution of individual products to the portfolio.

3. To describe and explain the Boston Consulting Group's growth-share matrix (the Boston Box).

4. To review criticisms of portfolio analysis.

5. To examine Shell's Directional Policy Matrix as an alternative approach for developing product strategy.

On completion of this chapter you will:

1. Understand the nature and importance of Product Portfolios.

2. Be familiar with methods for evaluating products in the portfolio.

3. Appreciate the value of the Boston Box as an analytical framework and its weakness as an operational tool.

4. Know the main criticisms of portfolio analysis.

5. Understand the nature and use of Shell's Directional Policy Matrix.

Introduction
. . . .

While most textbooks tend to be written from the perspective of the professional manager employed by a multinational, multi-divisional firm, the reality is that the great majority of people work for small organizations. In both the UK and Australia, for example, 96% of all people work for firms with less than 200 employees, and the same pattern is probably true of most other countries too. Thus most firms do not consist of several distinct strategic business units (SBUs) selling quite different products into distinctive end-use markets. Indeed the opposite is the case and the great majority of firms are highly focused, selling a narrow range, or even a single product, into a single or limited number of geographically distinct markets. Under these circumstances the marketing strategy and corporate strategy are one and the same. What then is the role of product policy in the small firm with only a single or small range of products? In this chapter we address this issue and suggest that even the smallest company needs to pay careful attention to the creation of a portfolio of products to ensure its continued survival.

To begin with we define and describe the concept of the product portfolio. Next we look at the factors to be used in determining the size and nature of the portfolio as a basis for examining some of the better-known portfolio models. In turn this leads to a consideration of the development of models tailored to the needs of the individual firm and the issues to be taken into account when developing such a model.

The concept of the product portfolio

The desirability of a portfolio or range of different products is implicit in the concept of the product life cycle which emphasizes that, ultimately, all products and the technologies which underlie them will change. Thus human progress and economic growth are the consequence of new and improved ways of doing things being substituted for old methods and approaches. It follows that as a result of technological innovation even the most successful of products will become obsolescent and displaced by new and better ways of serving a particular need. For example, for centuries passenger transport by sea was the only available option for persons wishing to travel between Europe and North America. It is now almost impossible to arrange a transatlantic sea crossing and such as are available are hardly likely to meet the convenience or cost needs of persons wishing to travel.

And so it is with most other products and technologies. Indeed, as we have seen in earlier chapters, given that both generic strategies of cost leadership and differentiation depend on innovation, new product and process development have become the basis for competitive activity in all kinds of markets. In turn this has led to an acceleration in the substitution of new products for old and a shortening of product life cycles.

Faced with such a scenario it is clear that the firm must take active steps to ensure that it does not become a victim of market myopia. In Chapter 3 we introduced Ansoff's Growth Vector Matrix as a simple summary statement of the strategic options available. In order to survive, let alone grow, the firm needs to pursue simultaneously the strategies of market penetration (selling more of the existing product to existing users), market development (finding new customers in new geographic regions with similar needs to one's existing customers) and product development (improving and changing the product both to keep up with the changing wants of one's existing customers and to attract new customers whose needs were not satisfied by the original product).

The fourth option of diversification was considered to be risky in that, unlike the other options, it involves changing both product and market together, whereas the other three options retained contact with one or both of the key dimensions of the exchange process – products and/or customers. That said, it was noted that a product development could also result in a market development by attracting new customers, while market development might suggest new opportunities for product development. Thus both kinds of development might lead to diversification – new products in new markets – but by a less risky route.

The key lesson to be learned is that in order to survive firms need to be constantly looking for new products and new customers. However, there is a working rule of thumb in marketing which states that it costs five to six times as much money to create a customer as it does to keep one. It is for this reason that in recent years the emphasis in marketing has moved away from the transaction to the relationship. The tendency for customers – individual and organizational – to prefer to repeat purchase from a known and proven source of supply may amount to satisficing behaviour but that is the way most of us behave. In the absence of any compelling evidence to the contrary, why would one want to change one's behaviour provided it yields satisfactory results? It is also a well-known fact that many of the best ideas for new products are generated by customers who identify means of improving or changing existing products so that they will perform better.

Given these facts it seems reasonable to assert that the first priority is to maintain and grow one's customer franchise. From this it follows that one must accept that, ulti-mately, one's customers' first loyalty is to themselves, their families and organizations so that if someone else can offer them better value for money (greater satisfaction) then they will switch to the new source of supply. To avoid this one must anticipate the cus-tomers' needs and to do so requires that one develop a range or portfolio of products designed to match changing needs and situations.

The idea of the product portfolio is, of course, borrowed from that of investment management, where the investor seeks to acquire a selection of stocks and shares which will meet his or her needs. Usually these needs will embrace a desire for current income balanced by a desire for capital growth. In turn, investment management theory is derived from the broader field of economics in which the portfolio may comprise any kind of asset and the purpose of portfolio analysis is to determine the composition of the ideal or optimum portfolio taking into account basic preferences for fixed or vari-able yields, short or long term returns, etc. It follows that the construction of a product portfolio will depend very much upon the overall objectives of an organization and its attitude towards the basic trade-off between risk and return. Once these have been established it becomes possible to determine what kinds of product are needed to achieve the desired balance.

One of the earlier contributions to the idea of developing a portfolio of products was Peter Drucker's *Harvard Business Review* article 'Managing for business effectiveness' (Vol. 42, May–June, 1963) in which he proposed that products could be classified as falling into one of six categories:

- 'breadwinners' – today's, tomorrow's and yesterday's
- also-rans
- failures
- in-betweens (those capable of becoming successful given appropriate action).

Drucker's classification was based on the contribution of the product to overall profitability. Once diagnosed, the prescription was simple – support today's and tomorrow's breadwinners, 'milk' yesterday's breadwinners, make up your mind on the in-betweens, and drop the also-rans and failures. Given that one is able to measure the criterion value (others use profitability, growth, market share, etc. as criteria), this classification is relatively simple. The difficult decision is balancing the portfolio to achieve the overall objective(s). Wind (1982, p. 110) suggests that the following questions need to be answered to make this decision:

1. What dimensions should be used in constructing a product portfolio?
2. What are the current approaches to portfolio management, and how do they differ from each other?
3. How can the portfolio management approach be used to develop guidelines to product marketing decisions?

However, before seeking to answer these questions Wind suggests that one must first decide the desired level of business analysis, the level of the market and the time dimension of analysis.

The level of business analysis will depend very much upon the extent of the firm's existing portfolio. For many small organizations there will be only a single line, though there may be variants within it at different stages of their life cycle conforming with Drucker's six-way classification. Larger firms may have two or more distinct lines while the largest strategic business units will have multiple product lines. Irrespective of the number of product lines, the individual product line constitutes the basic unit of analysis and a clear understanding of each is fundamental to any higher-order level of comparative strategic analysis.

With regard to the 'level' of market Wind has in mind the degree of aggregation or, rather, disaggregation to be used in analysis. Given that it is users' perceptions which underlie consumption behaviour, the advice here is that one should disaggregate the market into profitable segments and then analyze the characteristics of the customers who comprise the distinct segments. However, it is also important to bear in mind that even brand-loyal customers may switch to competing brands from time to time and also that their choice is often influenced by a wider product assortment. Thus, in addition to analyzing micro-segmentation variables one should also keep in mind macro-segmentation factors and even different markets which may be more attractive than existing markets but accessible to the firm, given its assets and resources, e.g. a packaging manufacturer specializing in metal containers could use its customer franchise to move into say plastic or glass packaging.

As to the time factor Wind observes that most analyses of products relate to their current rather than their future position. Given the implications of the PLC, it is obvious that one should also take into account future trends and try to forecast the direction in which the product is moving – up, stable, or down – as this will have a major bearing on one's strategy and planning.

Factors influencing the product portfolio

As noted the purpose behind developing a product portfolio is to allocate the firm's resources so as to optimize its long-term growth and profitability. It follows that to do this effectively one must select measures for assessing the actual or potential contribution of individual products to the portfolio. Such measures may be objective, such as sales, profitability or market share, or they may be more subjective, such as competitive strength, perceived risk or stage in the product life cycle. As will be seen when discussing some of the standardized approaches to portfolio analysis, such as those developed by the Boston Consulting Group (BCG) or Shell, it has become conventional to plot the performance of individual products on a two-dimensional matrix; one or both measures may act as a summary or surrogate for others. However, before reviewing some of the standardized approaches which have been developed, it will be useful first to examine the measures available.

Perhaps the most obvious and most frequently used measure is sales, if for no other reason than that actual or potential sales determine the firm's revenue and it is the timing and volume of revenue related to expenditure which determines whether the firm will succeed or fail. Measures of sales are also involved in computing profitability and/or market share, either of which may be used as a surrogate for actual sales when constructing a portfolio matrix.

For purposes of analysis several distinct sales measures are required. Obviously the firm will know its actual sales at any given point in time but this information will be of limited value unless it can be compared with the total sales of the product class and those of other major competitors. Such information is essential to calculate market share, but this information will also be of limited value unless it summarizes past sales trends and projects these into the future. In other words one needs to establish whether sales of the product class are growing, stable or declining and how one's own product is performing when measured against these industry trends. By plotting both industry and firm's sales it should be possible to establish the stage of both the industry life cycle and that of the firm's own offering and, from this, project future sales for both.

Conventionally sales are recorded in terms of volume, or units sold, and value. Ideally both should be measured as this will enable the analyst to form a view about the shape of the demand curve and price elasticity, both of which are important inputs when devising a competitive strategy or planning new product developments. When measuring sales it is necessary to ensure one is comparing like with like and avoid mixing manufacturer's, wholesalers' and retailers' prices, as well as making sure that data cover the same time period.

Comparative sales data are an essential input to the computation of market share which is one of the primary dimensions of the Boston Consulting Group's growth–share matrix (see below). Market share is widely cited as an important measure of competitive performance, particularly since the publication of the PIMS (Profit Implications of Market Strategy) study in which it was found that there was a strong association between market share and profitability. However, one must be careful not to exaggerate the importance of market share comparisons if for no other reason than that they are difficult to compute on a consistent and meaningful basis, added to which market share may be a meaningless statistic for the great majority of competitors in a market.

Difficulty in accurately calculating a market share largely arises from problems of definition. One extreme view is that every firm has 100% market share whatever the value of its sales. This perspective is based on the proposition that a firm's customers must regard its product as distinctive in some way, otherwise they would not prefer it to other close substitutes. The more conventional view is that we can define markets for a class or product, like carbonated beverages, detergents, petrol, etc. calculate the total sales value of these products and then derive the individual seller's market share by dividing their sales by total sales to obtain a percentage.

Calculations of this kind for a product class may disguise significant variations in the performance of individual brands within a firm's product line in terms of, say, colas versus fruit flavours, diet and non-diet versions and so on. In the case of major markets of this kind, with significant and distinctive segments, it is likely that major suppliers will analyze market share at both the product class (industry) and brand level. On the other hand, such calculations would be meaningless for a small producer of a given product serving a local market; it might be meaningful to calculate the small firm's penetration or market share of its narrowly defined geographical market area provided that the value of knowing this statistic was greater than the cost of establishing it.

This is not a trivial issue for, as we have pointed out earlier, the great majority of firms are small and the cost of performing analyses which may be useful or even necessary for large firms may greatly exceed any tangible benefit. As Wind (1982, p. 114) notes, defining a brand's market share 'requires the explication of several concepts: the unit of measurement, the product definition, the boundaries of the market and competitors; the time horizon involved, and the nature of the denominator in the share calculation'. Wind then devotes four pages to a discussion of these factors. It is doubtful if such an exercise in definition and measurement would be worthwhile for most small firms, for whom a more subjective, judgmental approach would seem more appropriate. Whether such mainly judgmental methods constitute a product portfolio analysis or a more broadly based strategic overview is a matter of opinion.

In *Marketing Strategy and Management* (1992) Baker confines his discussion of portfolio analysis to the BCG growth–share matrix and classifies other similar analytical frameworks such as Shell's Directional Policy Matrix (Shell, 1975) as a 'strategic overview'. This distinction is made on the basis that obtaining the kind of objective data necessary for portfolio analysis can be both difficult and costly, in addition to which there are many other factors top management might wish to consider when developing a strategy which are subjective and qualitative. However, other authors (notably Wind, 1982) lump all these techniques together. For the sake of completeness we will do the same while still taking the view that, strictly, the BCG approach is concerned with *product portfolios* while the other techniques take a wider, strategic perspective.

The BCG growth-share matrix

The Boston Consulting Group (BCG) growth–share matrix was developed by Bruce Henderson, founder of BCG, in the late 1960s and dominated thinking about strategy for over a decade. It still commands substantial support and is invariably included in texts, courses and seminars concerned with the development of marketing strategy. However, as we shall see, it has also been the subject of considerable criticism – especially following the fragmentation of markets which has arisen with increased international competition, the acceleration of technological change and the impact of information technology. As a result, its continuing value is more as an analytical framework, which encourages structured analysis of the implications of the product life cycle (PLC) for competitive strategy, than as a planning technique in its own right.

The matrix was developed from Henderson's earlier work with experience curve effects which he applied as a purchasing agent at Westinghouse to help explain the link between increased experience and lower manufacturing costs. Although the phenomenon was not new, it was Henderson who brought it to real prominence and demonstrated how it could be harnessed for strategic planning. In essence the experience curve – or learning curve as it was more widely known prior to Henderson's publication of *Perspectives on Experience* in 1968 – has been known for centuries. As Winfred B. Hirschmann pointed out in 'Profit from the learning curve' (*Harvard Business Review*, January–February 1964, pp. 125–39), it is encapsulated by the well-known aphorism 'practice makes perfect'. With experience we learn how to perform tasks more efficiently and effectively, giving rise to significant improvements in productivity. Of course, such gains are not automatic nor will they necessarily lead to cost reduction unless these are consciously and assiduously pursued. When Henry Ford set out to make an affordable car his original ambition was to produce one for $500 – less than half the prevailing price in the early twentieth century. In 1918, not 10 years after starting production at Baton Rouge, he had got the cost down to $258, a cost which no one else could hope to equal unless they were able to achieve the same economies of sourcing, production, selling and distribution as were enjoyed by Ford.

But experience effects are not just the product of scale economies or learning effects. For example, scale effects are independent of time. As one increases the scale of a project the cost of additional capacity or output will usually not grow proportionately with the increase in scale, but this relationship is not dependent upon time. Experience is. Similarly, learning effects are, strictly, concerned with the notion that productivity will grow with familiarity and repetition as a worker learns a job. By contrast, the idea of experience embraces a number of other dimensions. Schnaars (1991) summarizes these as:

- The learning curve
- Specialization of labour
- Process innovations
- New materials
- Product standardization
- Product redesign.

Clearly, these dimensions are closely related to one another. With experience one discovers new and more efficient ways of completing the task in hand, including both product and process innovation.

In Henderson's *Perspectives on Experience* (1968) the BCG proposed two idealized experience curves in which total units produced are plotted against cost or price per unit. On a linear scale the result is a smooth curve similar to that in Figure 6.1(a). However, when plotted using double logarithmic scales the result is a straight line similar to that in Figure 6.1(b). The latter is claimed to be the more useful as it demonstrates 'the unique property of showing percentage change as a

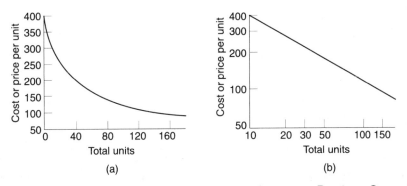

Figure 6.1 ● Idealized experience curve (*source*: Boston Consulting Group, 1968, p. 13)

When prices or costs are plotted against cumulative volume, the resulting graph characteristically takes the form of a curve on a linear scale (a). Although the smoothness of the curve suggests the regularity of the relationship, some of the particular aspects are obscured. As a result, it is more useful to plot C/V or P/V slopes on double logarithmic scales (b).

Plots on a log-log scale have the unique property of showing percentage change as a constant distance, along either axis at any position on the grid. A straight line on log-log paper means, then, that a given percentage change in one factor results in a corresponding percentage change in the other, the nature of that relationship corresponding to the slope of the line, which can be read right off a log-log grid.

In the case of cost–volume or price–volume slopes, the plotting of observed data about costs or prices and accumulated experience for a product on log-log paper has always produced straight lines, reflecting a consistent relationship between experience and prices, and experience and costs.

constant distance, along either axis at any position on the grid' which can be read straight from the plot.

That said, it is the linear plot which demonstrates the properties of the experience most clearly – costs per unit decline as the volume produced increases but increasingly slowly. The nature of the relationship varies by industry but the usual range is a fall in costs of 10–30% for each doubling of output, with 20% considered average. Perversely, however, experience curves are described in the *opposite* way so that a 90% experience curve implies that costs will fall by 10% for each doubling of output, 80% represents a 20% fall in costs, and so on. It is important to emphasize that the experience curve measures the relationship between costs and volume. The firm's fortunes will depend on the *prices* it can obtain in the marketplace. The BCG analysis pays close attention to this and suggests that the relationship between price and cost will vary depending upon the overall competitive situation.

Irrespective of whether conditions are stable or unstable, costs tend to exceed prices when a product is first introduced into a market. With increasing experience costs fall

Figure 6.2 ● The growth–share matrix

below prices and two distinct patterns emerge. In stable markets increasing cost effi-ciencies are paralleled by price reductions. But in unstable markets demand outstrips supply in the growth phase and sellers are able to command higher margins as it is not necessary to pass on cost efficiencies as price cuts. The result is much as economic theory would predict. The opportunity to earn above-average profits attracts new investment and an increase in supply. However, if demand continues to grow more quickly than supply, costs will tend to fall more quickly than prices. Inevitably, demand will cease to grow as the market approaches saturation and a shake-out will occur as suppliers cut prices to hold on to their share of the market. Only the fittest (most effi-cient) will survive but, once excess capacity has been removed, stability will return to the mature market and the remaining players will tend to avoid using price as a compe-titive weapon.

Given that the opportunity to earn above-average returns is greatest in unstable markets exhibiting rapid growth in demand, it is unsurprising that these are intrinsically more attractive to capitalists and entrepreneurs. It is also clear, however, that if one is to succeed in such a market then one must be able to survive the shake-out when it comes; as competition will be based mainly on price in this stage, one will only be able to compete if one's costs are similar to those of other major competitors. In turn, it follows that this will only be the case if one is producing a similar volume of output and has a comparable experience function. Expressed another way: sales volume = market share. Hence the fascination with market share and the evolution of the BCG growth–share matrix.

With only one product the growth–share matrix is only of academic interest. But if one has a number of products or businesses then it is a powerful tool in helping to diag-nose how these products compare with one another and in determining the most effec-tive strategy for their joint management. In its basic format the growth–share matrix comprises a 2 × 2 rectangular array as shown in Figure 6.2 with the two dimensions representing market growth and market share, each dichotomized into high and low.

Each of the quadrants summarizes a position in the life cycle of a successful product to which the BCG attaches a label.

Quadrant 1 represents a product being introduced into a market which is perceived to have high growth potential. But as it has yet to perform successfully and has only a low market share it is regarded as a *question mark*.

Quadrant 2 represents a successful product with a high market share in a rapidly growing market. It is undoubtedly a *star*.

Quadrant 3 represents an established player in a mature market. It has survived the shake-out and is now benefiting from experience effects in a stable and not particularly aggressive market. It has become a *cash cow*.

Quadrant 4 defines the product in the decline phase. There is little or no market growth and the product's low share means that it lacks the cost advantages enjoyed by cash cows. In the BCG nomenclature it is a *dog*. (The British regard dogs as pets and cherish them. In the USA this is true too but, in this context, American usage denotes something useless to be disposed of.) How to dispose of these types of products is dealt with in Chapter 19.

Another important aspect of the matrix is that it indicates likely cash flows associated with each quadrant/stage of the life cycle. As noted earlier, new products in both stable and unstable markets tend to have a negative cash flow (costs exceed revenue) due to the high costs of promotion and distribution and the absence of any significant experience effects. In the rapid growth phase successful firms tend to plough their profits back into the business to both grow and protect their position. As a result cash flow tends to be marginally negative or neutral. In maturity the benefits of experience and stability accrue and cash flow is invariably positive and provides funding to support new products in the earlier stages of their life cycle. Finally, products in declining markets are usually portrayed as being in balance or negative in terms of cash flow. If negative then the conventional wisdom is that they should be eliminated. However, as we shall see (particularly in Chapters 17 to 19), in recent years more attention has been given to managing products in the decline phase of the life cycle, leading to the conclusion that dog products may also be cash positive if properly managed. The resultant term is the cash-dog.

So far, so good. The matrix offers a useful analytical tool which allows the planner to plot the position of all his products in an easily understood way. More than that, having classified where our products are in their life cycle we can identify the strategic options available by reference to a checklist such as that provided in Chapter 5. However, the BCG growth–share matrix depends upon the concept of relative market share and it is determining this which creates problems. In some markets comparative data are available so that one can establish which firm has the largest market share in order to express one's own and other competitors' market shares as a proportion of this. It follows that if one firm has a larger share than any other (say 30%) then it will be classified as high (either a star or cash cow), whereas another large firm with a 25% share (0.83 relative market share) would be classified as low and considered either a question mark or dog!

Numerous refinements have been proposed for both plotting and diagnosing the matrix. Size of market may be incorporated by plotting circles whose size reflects the importance of the product to the firm's overall sales or profits. Similarly, following a methodology proposed by George S. Day ('Diagnosing the product portfolio', *Journal of Marketing*, April 1977), one can plot the direction in which products are expected (or intended) to move in the future, thus introducing dynamism into an otherwise static analysis.

Based upon their original analysis the Boston Consulting Group developed a number of strategic implications from the growth–share matrix which, in turn, underpin the evolution of explicit market-share strategies. Simplistically, the message of the Boston

Box is that because of the inevitable progression of product life cycles one needs a continuing stream of new products, with the surpluses from cash cows being reinvested in question marks and stars to ensure their future success. In other words, one needs a balanced portfolio and appropriate strategies for managing products at different stages of their life cycle. In addition, it is important to recognize that particular advantages may accrue to first movers – they start to acquire experience first – and to those with the largest market shares as they are likely to have the lowest cost base and so be best placed to resist price competition and/or earn above-average margins.

Most texts devote a chapter or chapters to market share strategies with advice on *gaining* and *holding* share, i.e. the management of question marks and stars respectively, to *harvesting* cash cows and *divestment* of dog products in the decline stage (see Schnaars, Chapter 4). The reader should consult one or more of these sources for advice on *managing* the product portfolio, a subject which is also dealt with in some detail in later chapters of this book. At this juncture we will conclude this section by reviewing some of the criticisms levelled against the Boston Box approach with its emphasis on market share.

As we have observed at several places already, the weakness of the market share approach to developing a successful marketing strategy is that, ultimately, only one or a very small number of evenly matched competitors can prosper from adopting such an approach. The logic of the experience curve is that the firm with the largest share will always enjoy a cost advantage over smaller competitors. Whether it chooses to use this to build more share by pursuing a price leadership policy over extended periods reflects the weakness of management in exploiting this advantage itself. As the evidence shows, some firms are better than others at defending a leadership position, with the result that those seeking to displace them by building their own market share have often failed because their costs are higher and they run out of cash before they can achieve the same market share as the leader and eliminate its cost advantage.

It is for this reason that most firms, and especially those with low market shares, seek to compete through a strategy of differentiation. Differentiation leads to the fragmentation of markets and reduces the economies of scope and scale that comprise a major element in the experience effects which yield cost advantages in undifferentiated markets. This is not to say that cost and price are not important elements in determining competitive advantage in fragmented markets. They are, but the source of cost savings is more likely to arise from innovation, managerial efficiency and implementation than from the size of the firm's market share.

Schnaars cites 13 sources of criticism which have been levelled against the growth–share matrix (pp. 85–90). In our view they are all related to the fundamental distinction between strategies of cost leadership and differentiation and the fact that for the great majority of firms the latter is the only realistic option. That said, we believe the growth–share matrix is both valuable and important because:

1. It reinforces the inevitability of change implicit in the PLC concept.
2. It underlines the importance of having a portfolio of products at different stages of development.
3. It requires formal consideration of the competition and their relative standing.

4. It is intuitively appealing and simple to implement conceptually despite the difficulty of operationalizing it in practice.

Much the same advantages are seen to attach to other similar approaches and a brief review of these follows.

Shell's directional policy matrix

As noted earlier, we do not consider the Directional Policy Matrix (DPM), developed by corporate planners at Shell, strictly as a portfolio planning model. However, many other authors do, so in the interests of completeness it will be described here as representative of a number of similar models designed to inform strategic product/market decisions, such as General Electric's stoplight strategy.

Shell's DPM is based upon two key parameters – the Company's Competitive Capabilities and the Prospects for Sector Profitability – each of which is divided into three categories as shown in Figure 6.3.

The basic matrix may be used to plot the position of products in the company's portfolio or it could be used for competitor analysis by plotting the position of all competitors in a particular business sector. In their original conceptualization Shell (1975) suggest a hypothetical portfolio of products for a chemical company as shown in Figure 6.4.

In order to use the DPM it is necessary to develop measures of the two parameters Business Sector Prospects and Company's Competitive Capabilities. In the context of a petroleum-based chemical business like Shell four main criteria are suggested:

- Market growth rate
- Market quality
- Industry feedback situation
- Environmental aspects.

Obviously, these may vary by industry, although the first two will usually apply to any industry. Similarly, the precise values for assessing growth rate will vary by both

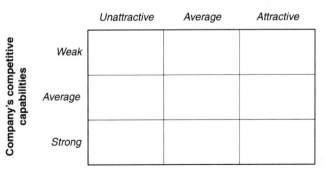

Figure 6.3 ● The Directional Policy Matrix (*source: Shell, 1975*)

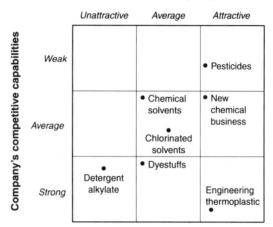

Figure 6.4 ● Positions of business sectors in a hypothetical company's portfolio

product/industry and stage of the life cycle, and the intention should be to establish an average growth rate – say 5–7% – so that greater or lesser rates may be classified as such in relation to the average.

With regard to market quality, Shell acknowledges that these are difficult to quantify but suggest that some of the more important questions to be answered might be:

1. Has the sector a record of high, stable profitability?
2. Can margins be maintained when manufacturing capacity exceeds demand?
3. Is the product resistant to commodity pricing behaviour?
4. Is the technology of production freely available or is it restricted to those who developed it?
5. Is the market supplied by relatively few producers?
6. Is the market free from domination by a small group of powerful customers?
7. Has the product high added-value when converted by the customer?
8. In the case of a new product, is the market destined to remain small enough not to attract too many producers?
9. Is the product one where the customer has to change his formulation or even his machinery if he changes supplier?
10. Is the product free from the risk of substitution by an alternative synthetic or natural product?

While these specific questions relate to an industrial chemicals company it is clear that they embrace competitive forces, such as barriers to entry and exit, contained in Porter's Five Forces model.

With regard to a company's competitive capabilities three basic criteria are identified:

● Market position
● Production capability
● Product research and development.

Market position is measured in terms of market share, and the firm (or firms) is classified according to whether it is a leader with a pre-eminent position, a major producer (one of several evenly matched competitors), and so on. Production capability is a composite factor designed to encapsulate issues such as process economies, manufacturing capacity, sources of raw materials, etc., while product R & D embraces product range, product quality, record of successful NPD, service capability, and so on.

Shell recommend that once the definitions of factors and measurement criteria have been developed, ratings should be secured from a combination of functional specialists and non-specialists to provide both expertise and a degree of detachment. It is further suggested that while individual ratings should be encouraged initially these should provide the basis for a group discussion to evolve a consensus view. Failing this, some form of averaging may prove necessary. However, a process involving the participants likely to be affected by the outcome is seen to be preferable to more 'objective' methods based on sampling and computerized analysis. Once a 'score' has been agreed, this may be weighted to reflect the factor's relative importance to the company. The outcome is then plotted on the matrix as shown earlier in Figure 6.4.

For diagnostic purposes specific strategies are recommended for each position on the matrix as shown in Figure 6.5.

It should be stressed that the regularity implied in the rectangular format of a matrix rarely exists in real life, and the boundaries between one position and another are likely to be decidedly 'fuzzy' and call for considerable judgment in their interpretation. It should also be recognized that the 'recommended' strategy may be infeasible or inap-

Prospects for sector profitability

		Unattractive	Average	Attractive
Company's competitive capabilities	*Weak*	Disinvest 9	Phased withdrawal 6 Custodial	Double or quit 3
	Average	Phased withdrawal 8	Custodial 5 Growth	Try harder 2
	Strong	Cash generation 7	Growth 4 Leader	Leader 1

Figure 6.5 ● The Directional Policy Matrix completed (*source*: Shell, 1975)

propriate. For example, a version of the DPM was used to analyze the perceived standing and attractiveness of various subjects in a university. According to the analysis, Physics and Mathematics were located in the *Unattractive* column and performance defined as *Weak* to *Average*. According to the proposed strategies the university should have started to get out of these subjects!

Such a diagnosis was unacceptable: Physics and Mathematics are core disciplines which underpin many others. In a university renowned for its Engineering faculty quite the opposite strategy was necessary – at the very least Physics and Maths needed to be moved into the *Strong* category as subjects in their own right, through focused investment. Alternatively, if Physics and Maths were seen as essential components in subjects like Electronic Engineering and Computer Science they needed classifying under the *Attractive* column. As the example makes clear, models of this kind are useful as analytical frameworks – they can be useless, or positively dangerous, if regarded as prescriptive planning devices.

Before leaving the DPM one final comment is called for. Both the DPM and BCG growth–share matrix have been reported here as originally described by their 'inventors'. What would happen if we were to relabel the DPM as below?

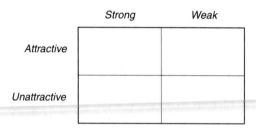

	Strong	Weak
Attractive		
Unattractive		

If we were to do this and incorporate the diagnosis from both GSM and DPM we would find:

	Strong	Weak
Attractive	Star	Question mark
	Leader	Double or quit
Unattractive	Cash cow	Dog
	Cash generation	Disinvest

Much the same similarities are to be found in other strategic overview/portfolio planning models. While this may not be immediately obvious it is unsurprising, given that all such models seek to capture the product or firm's standing *vis-à-vis* its rivals and the status/nature of competition which, in turn, is largely determined by the stage of the product/industry life cycle. As Wensley (1981) has pointed out, a salient difference between the growth–share matrix and other 'box classifications' is that the former is based upon univariate dimensions while the DPM, A D Little and GE/McKinsey schemes are based on composite dimensions involving the subjective weighting of a number of factors The issue, therefore, is which approach is to be preferred.

This issue was addressed by Wensley (1981) in his critical review 'strategic marketing: betas, boxes, or basics'. We can do no better than quote his conclusions:

> 'In undertaking strategic marketing analysis of any particular investment option it is important to avoid the use of classificatory systems that deflect the analysis from the critical issue of why there is a potential sustainable competitive advantage for the corporation. The market growth/share portfolio approach advocated by BCG encourages the use of general rather than specific criteria as well as implying assumptions about mechanisms of corporate financing and market behaviour that are either unnecessary or false. The DPM approach, on the other hand, appears to add little to a more specific project based form of analysis.'

Both classificatory schemes would be positively harmful if used to justify some form of cash budgeting, since it is essential that any major project is assessed independently of its box classification. The financial basis of such an assessment should be an evaluation of the project's benefits against the appropriate discount rate related to the project's systematic risk or Beta. It is critical, however, that the financial analysis should not dominate a thorough evaluation of the competitive market assumptions upon which the project is based. Such a project-based evaluation must focus not only on direct cost experience effects but also on the degree to which the project can be effectively imitated by others if successful, the extent to which progress will be adequately monitored and suitable changes implemented at a later date, and the particular ways in which the project (beyond its direct substantive benefits) will also enhance the firm's ability to exploit further opportunities at a later stage.

Summary

'Boxes' are a useful aid to analysis; to be operationalized they need to be associated with a rigorous financial analysis, but, in doing so, one must not lose sight of the competitive assumptions on which this is based and of future changes in these assumptions. In the cases of all the portfolios reviewed in this chapter, the important application relies on scrutiny of assumptions and specific adjustment.

QUESTIONS

1. Why should firms seek to develop a portfolio of products?
2. How does the idea of a product portfolio relate to that of an investment portfolio? Is the analogy useful?
3. What is involved in developing a balanced portfolio?
4. What is market share? What problems might you encounter in defining and measuring it?
5. What is the experience effect? What implications has it for managerial practice?
6. Describe the Boston Box.

7. Review the main criticism levelled against portfolio analysis.

8. Describe and explain Shell's Directional Policy Matrix.

9. Compare Ansoff's growth-vector matrix with other 'box' classifications. Which is to be preferred? Why?

Mini-case ● Stoddard-Sekers

Introduction

The marketing environment in which Stoddard-Sekers operates is dynamic in terms of competition, technology and market trends. To date the directors of the company have kept ahead of trends successfully, but mindful of the risk of complacency, they decided to engage in a strategic analysis, the results of which are outlined below.

The UK carpet industry (external analysis)

Carpet making is a traditional and highly fragmented industry in the UK. No single company or group dominates the carpet market in the UK. The traditional British weaving methods of Axminster and Wilton still form an important part of UK carpet output but account for only the upper end of the market. Tufted carpets now account for 58% of the value of UK manufacturers' sales and for about 76% of the volume of carpet output (Table 6.1).

Table 6.1 ● UK manufacturers' sales of carpets

Type	By volume	By value
Tufted	76%	58%
Woven	10%	28%
Needlepunch	12%	7%
Bonded	2%	5%
Others	–	2%

Purchase motivations and selection criteria

The British have a high household penetration for carpets and one of the world's biggest carpet markets per head of population. Recent research by KeyNote suggests that:

● 63% of purchasers spent less than £500

● 18% of purchasers spent £500–£800

● 6% of purchasers spent £800–£1000

● 8% of purchasers spent £1000–£3000.

The main reasons for purchase in the replacement market are to replace worn-out carpets (37%), redecoration (31%) and after a house move (32%).

The most important criteria for selecting carpets according to the place of use are as follows:

- durability
- type of fiber
- density
- thermal and noise insulation
- price
- colour
- design
- ease of maintenance
- environmental friendliness
- comfort.

Environmental friendliness is becoming an increasingly important factor in the selection process for carpets.

From the external analysis, it is important to note several threats and opportunities:

1. There will be growth, but only in certain markets, namely leisure, private hospitals and recreational buildings. The problems about emissions and negative health can only increase consumers' reticence, therefore a 100% 'green', safe, recycled and recyclable carpet would be an attraction.
2. North America is heading for a few super-manufacturers. This will drive down prices and raise the competition. Since 60% of the world's carpet comes from the USA, Europe must go the same way – few producers who have high technology, economies of scale and enormous market shares. It is imperative to gain and retain market share.
3. The competitors are seriously pushing recycling.
4. Design and colour will become more important as designers put their names to carpet designs.

Internal analysis

The main business is home furnishing and carpets, but with the recent entry into the contract market and the technical textile subsector the competitive position has been strengthened. The strengths and weaknesses listed in Table 6.2 have been identified.

In the product portfolio carpets and home furnishing represent the company's cash providers, while its products in the contract market and the technical textile industries are still requiring important resources in order to gain market share. However, by investing in these segments, which have a high growth rate, the company should be able to develop potential 'stars' for its future business.

In comparison with the most important competitors in the UK carpet and home furnishing industries, the company's distinctive competence is thought to lie in:

Table 6.2 ● Strengths and weaknesses of Stoddard-Sekers in the carpet market

Strengths	Weaknesses
● Advanced design technology ● Good customer service ● High speed of delivery due to short throughput time ● 150 years of experience ● Synergies between operating activities ● Diversified range of products ● Strong brand name in the sector of tufted market (Lyle Carpet) ● Well-established distribution channels ● Good reputation by being a carpet supplier to the Royal Family ● Recognized by national awards ● Competitive wool buying ● Development and introduction of technical complex yarns (Douglas Reyburn & Co.) ● Success in contract initiatives to supply the hospital and automotive markets (Sekers Fabrics) ● Relatively stable share price since 1990	● Depressed activities in traditionally strong carpet market ● Low quick ratio which may cause problems in repaying short-term debt ● Low price policy creating problems for future profitability (Stoddard Carpets) ● Reduction of staff: demotivating and worrying for the remaining workforce ● Problems in taking full advantage of the BMK acquisition ● Falling return on capital employed ● Negative growth rate in turnover and pre-tax profits over the last five years

● Flexible and advanced design technology

● Speed of delivery

● Product quality

● National recognition.

These are all key players in the future home furnishing and carpet industries, but in order to remain competitive and take market share in the contract and the technical textile subsector it is felt important to be at the industry front of innovation and new product development.

Synthesis diagram

A recent brainstorming session at a senior level produced the 'map' of the strategic issues shown in Figure 6.6.

Innovation and new product development (NPD)

In response to maturing markets, shorter product life cycles, an increasing level of competition and technological improvements, companies in the industry frequently seek to maintain their competitiveness by innovation and NPD. Owing to continuous improvements in technologies, flexible manufacturing systems, computer-aided design and computer aided manufacturing, capital-intensive, highly automated carpet production

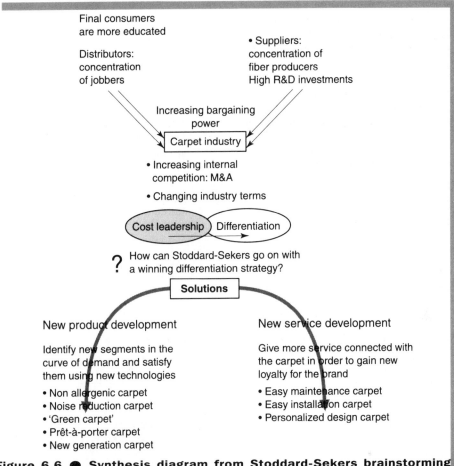

Figure 6.6 ● **Synthesis diagram from Stoddard-Sekers brainstorming session**

processes are getting increasingly flexible. Today product differentiation has therefore become a major strategy in the industry, replacing the strategy of cost leadership which was traditionally used in this phase of the industry life cycle. Thus, there has been a shift in emphasis from innovation for technical improvements to lower the costs to innovation for improved customer satisfaction. Figure 6.7 summarizes the new products and markets.

In order for Stoddard-Sekers to improve its competitive standing and performance it must choose a strategy to exploit the opportunities and overcome the threats that exist in the market.

Strategy

A strategy of innovation and NPD is necessary in order to satisfy increasingly demanding and sophisticated customers. However, it is also considered worthwhile to take advantage

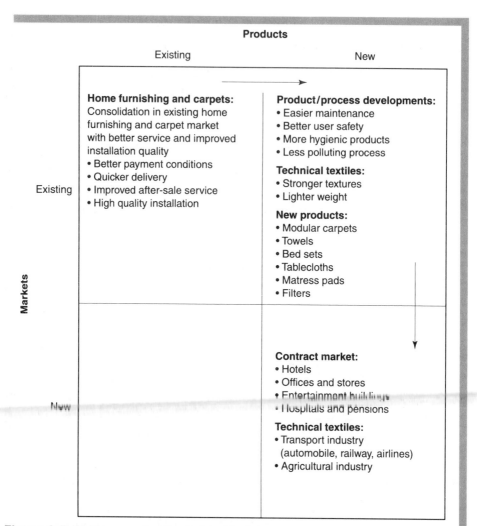

Figure 6.7 ● New products and markets

of growth in the technical textiles subsector. In other words, the company's managers see growth coming from market penetration, product development and diversification. This requires:

● Consolidation of existing markets with improved service and better installation techniques

● Developing new products that are close substitutes, but with improved performance characteristics

● Developing more efficient and less polluting production processes

● Finding new uses for existing or slightly modified products

● Entering into new markets with the new and more competitive products

Table 6.3 shows how these options have been justified.

Table 6.3 ● **Trends in new product development in the carpet market**

Environmental trends	Consequences	Key success factors
Greater product choice	Need for differentiation	Requires innovation and NPD
Increasing worldwide tourism	Need for more hotels	Requires flexible design and easy maintenance
Ageing population	Need for more hospitals and pensions	Requires safety and more hygienic products
Increasing mobility	Need for more transportation	Requires stronger and lighter textiles
Green issues	Need for more environmentally friendly processes and products	Requires less waste disposal and more durable products

Conclusion

Since Stoddard-Sekers is operating in a mature industry with intensifying competition, new technologies and changing needs of customers, it should seek to improve its performance level and exploit the opportunities that exist in the marketplace. The amount invested in R & D and innovation that is necessary to achieve international competitiveness varies from sector to sector, but the key factor is to keep up with the 'going rate' for a particular technology. Thus, despite the risk of product failure and more choosy customers, the company includes innovation and NPD in its corporate strategy. However, managers are considering forming a partnership to share the costs of R & D and to increase the chance of success. The suggestion is to concentrate on two important subsectors, namely the contract market and the technical textile niche, and to improve the key elements that affect product performance (design, texture, fibre, colour, pile weight–density and installation techniques). In order to exploit synergies and reduce the risk of innovation it is important to have a fit between existing products or technology and the NPD. To be successful a plan is needed capitalizing on the company's strengths and enhancing understanding of the customers' needs.

This case was compiled from public and private sources with the help of:
Merethe Aas, Marco Boeri, Andy Smith and Karin Schweighofer.

part 2

New Product Development

chapter 7

· ·

The importance, nature and management of the new product development process

LEARNING OBJECTIVES
· ·

This chapter is concerned with how New Product Development (NPD) can be managed within companies to create successful, profitable products. Its specific objectives are:

1. To describe and contrast the models commonly used to guide new product success.

2. To reflect upon whether or not models can and do act as a useful managerial guide.

3. To review the research literature which tries to distinguish factors leading to successful and unsuccessful new products.

4. To discuss newer models which attempt to integrate the key success factors into their prescriptions for the process.

5. To consider the kinds of organizational structures which are best suited to the new product processes that are successful.

On completion of this chapter you will:

1. Understand the various approaches to modelling the development of new products.

2. Be able to explain their usefulness and limitations as managerial tools.

3. Appreciate the more recent developments in thinking about how to model new product development.

4. Understand the major factors contributing to success and failure of new product development.

5. Appreciate the importance of managing the steps in the process and the people who carry out the steps.

6. Be able to present a plan for the organization of people involved in the development of a new product.

Introduction

The chapter, concerned with the organization and management of New Product Development, is split into three sections. The first outlines NPD models in order to paint a picture of what activities are managed; the second provides a brief résumé of what has become a vast area of academic and practitioner research, namely, the factors associated with success and failure in developing new products; the third discusses ways in which the models might be developed to reflect the lessons to be learned from studies of success and failure and provides an overview of the organizational structures which might be best suited to managing these processes.

New product development models

New product development (NPD) models are usually templates or maps which can be used to describe and guide those activities required to bring a new product from an idea or opportunity, through to a successful market launch. NPD models take numerous forms; in order to make sense of them, Saren's (1984) categorization provides an excellent starting point. He identified departmental-stage models, activity-stage models, decision-stage models, conversion process models and response models. These categories provide a useful starting point for discussion.

Departmental-stage models

These describe the NPD process by focusing on the departments or functions that hold responsibility for various tasks carried out. In an industrial context, the ideas are often assumed to arise in the R&D department; design of the new product is then carried out by the design department; the engineering function will then 'make' the prototype, after which production will become involved to work on the manufacturing problems. Finally, marketing will become involved to plan and carry out the launch. These representations are rather outmoded. It is now accepted that the 'pass-the-parcel' or 'relay' approach to NPD from one department to the next is not only unnecessarily time-consuming, but does nothing to foster ownership of, or strategic responsibility for, new products, and there is nothing in the way of market feedback, since marketing is presented with the product to market. These models have been largely abandoned by the literature which examines NPD and by major companies such as Land Rover. During the development of their successful *Discovery*, 'everything happened simultaneously'.

Activity-stage models

This type of model improves on the departmental-stage models through its focus on actual activities carried out, which include various iterations of product development and market testing. However, they too have been criticized for still promoting a pass-the-parcel approach to NPD since the activities are still seen to be the responsibility of separate departments or functions (Takeuchi and Nonaka, 1986). However, some refinements to the activity-stage models in order to counter this problem have been proposed, namely parallel processing and simultaneous engineering, as in the Land Rover example quoted above, to which we will return later in the chapter.

Decision-stage models

These are known under a number of different names, depending on their origin: Phased Review process, Stage-gate process, PACE, to name but a few. These processes consist of stages of activity, followed by review points, or gates, where the decision to continue (or not) with the development is made. This approach clarifies the reality and importance of feedback loops, which although not impossible within the framework of the simpler activity-stage models, are usually not highlighted either. With the decision-stage models, each stage is viewed in terms of its potential output.

Conversion process models

These provide little insight into the NPD process, since they view it as a 'black box' in an attempt to get away from the imposed rationality of departmental-, activity- and decision-based models. The alternative conversion process is a collection of unspecified tasks which may or may not be carried out, depending on the nature of the innovation. Essentially, a series of inputs is envisaged, which may be composed of information on customer needs, a design drawing or an alternative manufacturing procedure. Over time, depending on a multiplicity of factors, including human, organizational and resource-related, this input is converted into an output.

Response models

These take change at the beginning of the NPD as their focus, based on the work of Becker and Whistler (1967). These models focus on the individual's or organization's response to change, such as a new product idea, or R&D project proposals in terms of acceptance or rejection of the idea or project. A number of factors influencing the decision to accept or reject the proposal are helpful to the extent that they provide a new angle on what might otherwise be called the screening stage of the NPD process.

Of the various representations described above, the two that have been most widely used in and validated by research are the decision- and activity-stage models. In addition, as Biemans (1992) points out, the decision-stage model is really an extension of the activity-stage model and can be adapted to incorporate input from third parties, making it potentially useful as a means of integrating players in the NPD process, such as suppliers, which are increasingly important (Tzokas and Saren, 1991).

One of the most recognized activity-stage models is that developed by the American consultants Booz, Allen and Hamilton (BAH) (1968, 1982). This model is shown in Figure 7.1. Each of the stages is described below in turn.

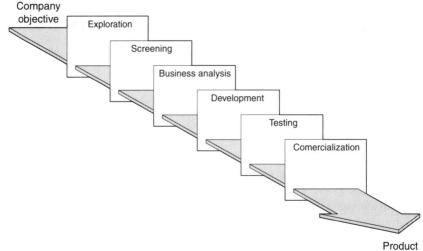

Figure 7.1 ● The Booz, Allen and Hamilton model of new product development

Overview of the stages of the new product development process
···

Strategy

In an article in *Industry Week* (16 December 1996, p. 45) a director of a large electronics consulting firm, Pittiglio Rabin Todd and McGrath (PRTM), described how many of the innovative projects being carried out in companies are actually *unknown* to top management. Worse still, some projects that had been previously 'cancelled' were alive. In addition, he finds people working on projects that don't match the company's product strategy. The ramifications of practices like these include working on projects that are unlikely to make money, overloading R&D people, not meeting schedules and increasing the chances of failure. Setting a clear strategy for new product development, on the other hand, not only provides guidelines for resource allocation, but also sets up the key criteria against which all projects can be managed through to the market launch. New product strategy, which has also been called the Product Innovation Charter (Crawford 1984) and Protocol (Cooper, 1993), is the subject of Chapter 8.

Idea generation

This is a misleading term, because, in many companies, ideas do not have to be 'generated'. They do, however, need to be managed. This involves identifying sources of ideas and developing means by which these sources can be activated. The aim of this stage in the process is to develop a bank of ideas that fall within the parameters set by 'new product strategy'. Sources of new product ideas exist both within and outside the firm.

Inside the company, technical departments such as research and development, design and engineering work on developing applications and technologies which will be translated into new product ideas. Equally, commercial functions such as sales and marketing will be exposed to ideas from customers and competitors. Otherwise, many company employees may have useful ideas: service mechanics, customer relations, manufacturing and warehouse employees are continually exposed to 'product problems' which can be translated into new product ideas. Outside the company, competitors, customers, distributors, inventors and universities are fertile repositories of information from which new product ideas come. Both sources, however, may have to be organized in such a way as to extract ideas. In short, the sources have to be *activated*. A myriad of techniques may be used to activate sources of new ideas. This topic will be the focus of Chapter 9.

Screening

The next stage in the product development process involves an initial assessment of the extent of demand for the ideas generated and of the capability the company has to make the product. At this, the first of several evaluative stages, only a rough assessment can be made of an idea, which will not yet be expressed in terms of design, materials, features or price. Internal company opinion will be canvassed from R & D, sales, marketing, finance and production, to assess whether the idea has potential, is practical, would fit a market demand and could be produced by existing plant, and to estimate the payback period. The net result of this stage is a body of ideas which are acceptable for further development. Several checklists and forms have been devised to facilitate this process and are discussed in Chapter 10.

Concept development and testing

Once screened, an idea is turned into a more clearly specified concept and testing this concept begins for its fit with company capability and its fulfilment of customer expectations. Developing the concept from the idea requires that a decision be made on the content and form of the idea. For example, a food company which has generated the idea of a low-calorie spread as a sandwich filler will decide on the *type* of spread: a low-calorie peanut butter, fish or meat paté or a mayonnaise-based concoction. All these concept variations may be specified and then subjected to concept tests. Internally, the development team needs to know which varieties are most compatible with current production plant, which require plant acquisition and which require new supplies, and this needs to be matched externally, in relation to which versions are more attractive to customers. The latter involves direct customer research to identify the appeal of the product concept, or alternative concepts to the customer. Concept testing is worth spending time and effort on, collecting sufficient data to provide adequate information upon which the full business analysis will be made. It is discussed in Chapter 11.

Business analysis

At this stage, the major 'go–no go' decision will be made. The company needs to be sure that the venture is potentially worthwhile, as expenditure will increase dramatically after this stage. The analysis is based on the fullest information available to the company thus far. It encompasses:

1. A market analysis detailing potential total market, estimated market share within specific time horizon, competing products, likely price, break-even volume, identification of early adopters and specific market segments.

2. Explicit statement of technical aspects, costs, production implications, supplier management and further R&D.

3. Explanation of how the project fits with corporate objectives.

The sources of information for this stage are both internal and external, incorporating any market or technical research carried out thus far. The output of this stage will be a development plan with budget and an initial marketing plan. These issues are discussed in Chapter 12.

Product development and testing

This is the stage where prototypes are physically made. Several tasks are related to this development. First, the finished product will be assessed regarding its level of functional performance. Until now, the product has only existed in theoretical form or mock-up. It is only when component parts are brought together in a functional form that the validity of the theoretical product can be definitively established. Second, it is the first physical step in the manufacturing chain. Whilst manufacturing considerations have entered into previous deliberations, it is not until the prototype is developed that alterations to the specification or to manufacturing configurations can be designed and put into place. Third, the product has to be tested with potential customers to assess the overall impression of the test product. Some categories of product are more amenable to customer testing than others. Capital equipment, for example, is difficult to have assessed by potential customers in the same way as a chocolate bar can be taste-tested, or a dishwasher evaluated by an in-house trial. One evolving technique in industrial marketing, however, is called 'Beta-testing', practised informally by many industrial product developers. This is explored more fully in Chapter 13.

Test marketing

The penultimate phase in the development cycle, test marketing, consists of small-scale tests with customers. Until now, the idea, the concept and the product have been 'tested' or 'evaluated' in a somewhat artificial context. Although several of these evaluations may well have compared the new product to competitive offering, other elements of the marketing mix have not been tested, nor has the likely marketing reaction by competitors. At this stage the appeal of the product is tested amidst the mix of activities comprising the market launch: salesmanship, advertising, sales promotion, distributor incentives and public relations.

Test marketing is not always feasible, or desirable. Management must decide whether the costs of test marketing can be justified by the additional information that will be gathered. Further, not all products are suitable for a small-scale launch: passenger cars, for example, have market testing complete before the launch, while other products, once launched on a small scale, cannot be withdrawn, as with personal insurance. Finally, the delay involved in getting a new product to market may be advantageous to the competition, who can use the opportunity to be 'first-to-market'. Competitors may also wait until a company's test market results are known and use the information to help their own launch, or can distort the test results using their own tactics.

Problems such as these have encouraged the development and use of computer-based market simulation models, which use basic models of consumer buying as inputs. Information on consumer awareness, trial and repeat purchases, collected via limited surveys or store data, are used to predict adoption of the new product. For a fuller explanation, see Hauser, Urban and Roberts (1990) and Shocker and Hall (1986).

Commercialization or launch

This the final stage of the initial development process and is very costly. Decisions such as when to launch the product, where to launch it, how and to whom to launch it will be based on information collected throughout the development process. With regard to timing, important considerations include:

● Seasonality of the product

● Whether the launch should fit any trade or commercial event

● Whether the new product is a replacement for the old one.

Location will, for large companies, describe the number of countries into which the product will be launched and whether national launches will be simultaneous or roll out from one country to another. For smaller companies the decision will be restricted to a narrower geographical region. The factors upon which such decisions will be based depend upon the required lead-times for product to reach all the distributive outlets and the relative power and influence of channel members.

Launch strategy encompasses any advertising and trade promotions necessary. Space must be booked, copy and visual material prepared, both for the launch proper and for the pre-sales into the distribution pipeline. The sales force may require extra training in order to sell the new product effectively.

The final target segments should not, at this stage, be a major decision for companies who have developed a product with the market in mind and who have executed the various testing stages. Attention should be more focused on identifying the likely early adopters of the product and on focusing communications on them. In industrial markets, early adopters tend to be innovators in their own markets. The major concern of the launch should be the development of a strong, unified message to promote to the market. Once accepted by the market, the company will elicit feedback to continue the improvement and redevelopment of the product. Both test marketing and launch are discussed in Chapter 14.

The usefulness of the process model

The usefulness of the process models, such as that by BAH, lies in the way in which they provide an indication of the 'total' number of tasks that might be required in order to develop and launch a new product. In fact, recent research by Page (1993) showed that a majority of American companies' studies do carry out these main activity-stages. This is not surprising. The process of developing a new product is inherently risky, plagued as it is by uncertainty at every stage. Over the process, the uncertainty is reduced – be it regarding technology, makeability or potential customer response. The whole procedure has been described as one of information processing (de Meyer, 1985; Allen, 1985), so it is of value if those executing the task of developing new products are given guidance regarding what information is required, where it might reside and to what use it might be put. Table 7.1 analyzes the BAH process model, to clarify its implications for information search, source and use.

Table 7.1 ● Analysis of the NPD process based on Booz, Allen and Hamilton (1982)

Stage of development	Information needed for stage; nature of information	Sources of information	Likely output of stage in light of information
1. Explicit statement of new product strategy, budget allocation	Preliminary market and technical analysis; company objectives	Generated as part of continuous MIS and corporate planning	Identification of *market* (N.B. not product) opportunities to be exploited by new products
2. Idea generation (or gathering)	Customer needs and technical developments in *previously* identified markets	Inside company: salespeople, technical functions. Outside company: customers, competitors, inventors, etc.	Body of initially acceptable ideas
3. Screening ideas: finding those with most potential	Assessment of whether there is a *market* for this type of product, and whether the company can make it. Assessment of financial implications: market potential and costs. Knowledge of company goals and assessment of fit	Main internal functions: – R&D – Sales – Marketing – Finance – Production	Ideas which are acceptable for further development
4. Concept development: turning an idea into a recognizable product concept, with	*Explicit* assessment of customer needs to appraise market potential. *Explicit* assessment of	Initial research with customer(s). Input from marketing and technical functions	Identification of key attributes that need to be incorporated in the product, major technical costs,

attributed and market position identified	technical requirements		target markets and potential
5. Business analysis: full analysis of the proposal in terms of its business potential	Fullest information thus far: – detailed market analysis – explicit technical feasibility and costs – production implications – corporate objectives	Main internal functions Customers	Major go–no go decision: company needs to be sure the venture is worthwhile as expenditure dramatically increases after this stage. Initial marketing plan. Development plan and budget specification
6. Product development: crystallizing the product into semi-finalized shape	Customer research with product. Production information to check 'makeability'	Customers Production	Explicit marketing plans
7. Test marketing: small-scale tests with customers	Profile of new product performance in light of competition, promotion and marketing mix variables	Market research; production, sales, marketing, technical people	Final go–no go for launch
8. Commercialization	Test market results and report	As for test market	Incremental changes to test launch Full-scale launch

Criticisms of process models

Despite its apparent usefulness, the BAH model, and, by implication, its derivatives have been criticized on a number of counts.

Idiosyncrasy

The NPD process is idiosyncratic to each individual firm and to the new product project in question. Its shape and sequence depend on the type of new product being developed and its relationship with the firm's current activities (Cooper, 1988; Johne and Snelson, 1988). In addition to the need to adapt the process to individual instances, it should be stated that in real situations there is no clear beginning, middle and end to the NPD process.

For example, from one idea, several product concept variants may be developed, each of which might be pursued. Also, as an idea crystallizes, the developers may assess the nature of the market need more easily and the technical and production costs become more readily identified and evaluated.

Iteration

The iterative nature of the NPD process results from the fact that each stage or phase of development can produce numerous outputs which implicate both previous development work and future development progress. Using the model provided by Booz, Allen and Hamilton, if a new product concept fails the concept test, then there is no guidance as to what might happen next. In reality, a number of outcomes may result from a failed concept test, and these are described below.

A new idea

It is possible that although the original concept is faulty, a better one is found through the concept tests; it would then re-enter the development process at the screening stage.

A new customer

Alternatively, a new customer may be identified through the concept testing stage, since the objective of concept testing is to be alert to customer needs when formulating a new product. Any new customers would then feed into the idea generation and screening process. Figure 7.2 shows these and other possibilities and illustrates how, viewed as linear or sequential, the BAH model is inadequate, particularly regarding up-front activities.

Related strands of development

A further point in relation to the sequencing of product development tasks is the existence of related strands of development. These related strands of development refer to marketing, technical (design) and production tasks or decisions that occur as the process unwinds. Each strand of development gives rise to problems and opportunities within the other two. For example, if, at the product development stage, production people have a problem which pushes production costs up, this could affect market

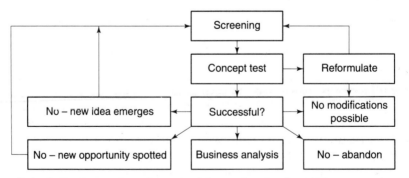

Figure 7.2 ● Horizontal and vertical iteration in the NPD process

potential. The marketing and technical assumptions need to be reworked in the light of this new information. A new design may be considered, or a new approach to the marketplace may be attempted. Whatever the nature of the final solution, it has to be based on the interplay of technical, marketing and manufacturing development issues, meaning that product development activity is iterative, not only between stages, but also within stages. These interplays are illustrated in Figure 7.3, using the example of the development of variable ratio steering columns for passenger cars. The crucial issue here is that the activity- and decision-stage models do not adequately communicate the horizontal dimensions of the NPD process.

This shortcoming has resulted in the advancement of the idea of 'parallel processing', which acknowledges the iterations between and within stages, categorizing them along functional configurations. The idea of parallel processing is highly prescriptive: it advises that major functions should be involved from the early stages of the NPD process to its conclusion. This, it is claimed, allows problems to be detected and solved much earlier than in the classic task-by-task, function-by function models. In turn, the entire process is much speedier, which is now recognized to be an important element in new product success. It should be mentioned that a substantial amount of what has been written about the concept of parallel processing is in the engineering domain.

Although greater integration through parallel processing has been attempted by various technical disciplines, for example manufacturing and engineering, the market perspective still appears to be 'tacked on' in the technical and engineering literature. True multi-disciplinary integration, embracing technical and commercial functions, is seen as crucial to the outcome of new products and will be considered later in the chapter. The example of the development of Land Rover's Discovery gives an insight into how these theories are being translated into successful practice. In addition to managing the related strands of development simultaneously, 'outside' parties such as suppliers were brought in at an early stage. Similarly, Intel's development of Pentium departed from its traditional models of development and involved both major customers and software suppliers in the design of the new product (*Management Today*, 1994). That said, the management of the NPD process is more than simply the number and sequencing of its activities. The next section of the chapter looks at this body of literature – albeit briefly – in order to decipher those 'other' factors which have an impact on new product success and of which managers should therefore take cognisance, in the management of their own NPD process.

Factors affecting success and failure of new product development

Major themes in the NPD success literature

NPD is a thriving activity. In 1996 in the US, marketers launched almost 26,000 new products in food and beverages, health and beauty and household and pet products. This was an increase of 23% on the previous year (*Grocer*, 18 January 1997, p. 15). But a success rate of less than 10% must mean a lot of effort goes to waste. In this section, attention is given to factors affecting success and failure.

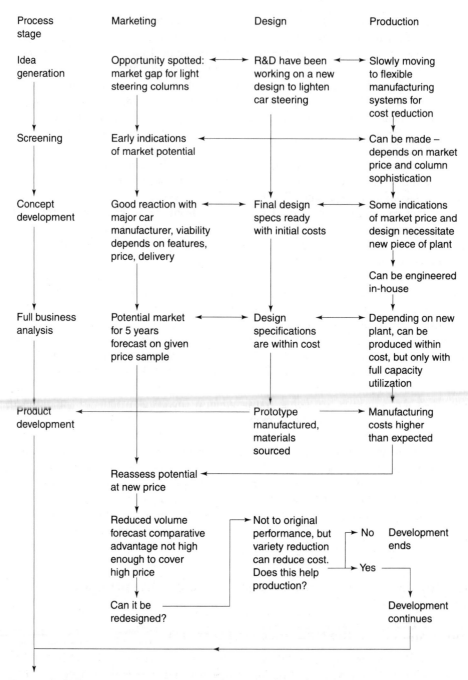

Figure 7.3 ● An example of the impact of individual interrelated strands of development

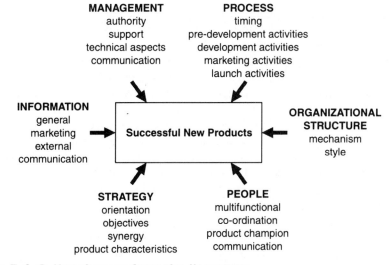

Figure 7.4 ● Key themes from the literature

A previous review of the literature (Craig and Hart, 1992) has, using content analysis, identified key themes in the NPD literature as being crucial to the success of NPD activities. Figure 7.4 presents these themes, which are briefly discussed in this section.

These themes are not directly comparable, as they relate to different levels in a company. At one level the way in which an organization is managed overall, its top managers' styles, the overall structure and strategy have a vital contribution in setting the scene for new product development and can and do have a profound effect on the outcomes of development programmes. At a second level, any one particular project may be successful or fail, depending upon how it is handled. This brief review, therefore, summarizes findings depending on whether they pertain to the managerial or 'strategic' level of a company, or whether they relate to the operational management of a given product development programme.

Strategic issues

Corporate strategy

The strategy of a company dictates how it will operate internally, and how it will approach the outside world. To be successful, NPD must be guided by, that is be derived from, the corporate goals of the company, and therefore there is a need to set clearly defined objectives for new product development projects. A new product strategy ensures that product innovations become a central facet of corporate strategies (Cooper, 1984), that objectives are set and that the 'right' areas of business are developed (Cooper, 1987). Thus, a critical success factor for NPD is the extent to which a specific strategy is set for guiding NPD efforts. While it is often argued that new product development should be guided by a new product strategy, it is important that the strategy is not so prescriptive as to restrict, or stifle, the creativity necessary for

NPD. Getting the balance right is not straightforward. The success of Tudor Dairies gives a useful example of how top management has defined the strategic direction, operationalized in terms of new product development, but in so doing has also allowed leverage for more, and possibly very different, NPD projects. Based on an analysis of the UK ice-cream market, the company identified a large untapped market for quality, but low-price, ice-cream. Given the rigorous market development being undertaken by Mars and Hägen Daas UK consumers were receptive to the idea of ice-cream as more than a 'cone in the summer', but, given the UK recession, were less inclined to pay £3 per litre as charged by the premium brands. Tudor's strategy pursued the mass market, two-litre option, positioning itself squarely in the family market, and avoiding anything with a short life cycle. Other redeveloped products include 'Raspberry ripple' and a luxury version, called Henley. In less than six months the management converted an operating loss to a profit of £500,000.

This strategic focus during development has clarified priorities for new products being developed. The way in which the strategic focus is formed can be seen as a function of technology and marketing inputs, product differentiation, synergy and risk acceptance.

Technology and marketing One of the most prevalent themes running throughout the contributions on strategic orientations is the merging of the technical and marketing strategic thrust. The emphasis on a balance between the technological and the marketing orientations in the strategy literature reflects an overall trend away from arguing the benefits of one orientation above the other, towards an acceptance that there should be a *fusion* between technology-led and market-led innovations at the strategic level (Johne and Snelson, 1988; Dougherty, 1992). An example here is that of Texaco's Clean System 3 Petrol, which is the result of the company's commitment to developing products at the forefront of fuel technology with a view to delivering value for money to customers.

Product differentiation Thirdly, the literature refers to new product strategies which emphasize the search for a differential advantage, through the product itself (Cooper, 1984). Product advantage is of course a subjective and multi-faceted term, but may be seen as comprising the following elements: technical superiority, product quality, product uniqueness and novelty (Cooper, 1979), product attractiveness (Link, 1987) and high performance to cost ratio (Maidique and Zirger, 1984). The recent 'war' between Lever Brothers' Persil Power and Ariel Future shows how these companies are competing, strategically, on a platform of technologically based product differentiation.

Synergy A fourth consideration for those developing new product strategies, identified in the literature, is the relationship between the NPD and existing activities, known as the synergy with existing activities. High levels of synergy are typically less risky, because a company will have more experience and expertise, although perhaps this contradicts the notion of pursuing product differentiation.

Risk acceptance Finally, the creation of an internal orientation or climate which accepts risk is highlighted as a major role for the new product strategy. Although synergy might help avoid risk associated with lack of knowledge, the pursuit of product differentiation and advantage must entail acceptance that some projects will fail. An atmosphere that refuses to recognize this tends to stifle activity and the willingness to pursue something new. Eaton Corporation has used several techniques to enhance its new product strategy. Among them is that every new product project includes technical, market and competitive-risk assessment, so that risk can be managed, not simply avoided (*Industry Week*, 16 December 1996, p. 73). Equally, Zeneca, a company with a strong reputation in drug discovery, distinguishes 'failures' from 'successes' and 'triumphs'. Failures occur because of incompetence: experiments not being properly carried out, for example. Successes may not be *commercial* successes (the triumph) but have given solutions to the questions asked of the research. Thus, the non-commercial project is not branded 'failure' which might be a disincentive for future scientists to run risks.

Strategic management

Some research attention has focused on the role of top management in the eventual success of NPD. While Maidique and Zirger (1984) found new product successes to be characterized by a high level of top management support, Cooper and Kleinschmidt (1987) found less proof of top management influence, discovering new product failures to often have as much top management support.

Hart and Service (1988) report on the attitudes and opinions of company managers to product design, and identify the managerial orientations which are most consistent with successful performance. A 'balanced' managerial orientation which combines technical commitment with marketing inputs is found to be most closely associated with superior competitive performance.

One of the most important roles which top management have to fill is that of climate setting by signalling the nature of the corporate culture to the rest of the organization (McDonough, 1986; Gupta, Raj and Wilemon, 1986; Gupta and Wilemon, 1988; Goltz, 1986). In some cases it is necessary for the firm to change its philosophy on NPD, in turn causing a change in the whole culture. Nike's NPD process has changed dramatically over the last 10 years. Previously they believed that every new product started in the lab and the product was the most important thing. Now they believe it is the consumer who leads innovation and the specific reason for innovation comes from the marketplace. The reason for this change is the fierce competition that has developed in recent years within the athletic shoe industry so that product innovation no longer led to sustained competitive advantage; manufacturers could no longer presume, therefore, that if Mike Jordan chooses a certain shoe everyone else in America will follow. More emphasis was then put on marketing research and targeting smaller groups of individual customers, with the emphasis changing from push to pull NPD.

Important cultural factors to encourage NPD

In general an entrepreneurial culture is most effective in achieving successful NPD. According to Peter Senge (1990), a management expert at MIT, several factors must be present in the culture to encourage 'generative learning' as he calls NPD.

1. *Encourage experimentation*.   Raytheon, an American defence and electronics group, has a New Products Center which differs from most new product teams by concentrating solely on the untested ideas of entrepreneurial employees.

2. *Make specialists generalists.* If firms want to be creative they need to pool the knowledge of their employees and this is hard to do if researchers, stuck in their labs, fail to understand the need for the customer. Honda have their R & D recruits spend training experience in all the different parts of the company to see how the whole organization works and help them come up with new ideas.

3. *Break down hierarchies.* Fredrick Taylor told Harvard students in 1909: 'your job is to find out what your boss wants and give it to him exactly as he wants'. This is why fresh ideas are much harder to push up through hierarchical structures than flat ones.

4. *Unstick information.* Encouraging the freeflow of information between different employees can be difficult. Instead Japanese firms use *Waigaya*, a technique where brainstorming groups of employees push ideas round the firm.

5. *Make time to think.* Often managers try to force-fit solutions to day-to-day problems blocking their paths, which means they can lose their sense of direction. If managers spend some time playing with computer models of the firm and market, reactive learning can be discouraged.

All these strategies concentrate on process rather than product – if organizations are set up to create rather than react, new products should follow.

Closely aligned to the notion of climate creation is the responsibility which top management has for the overall organizational structure, which is a research theme in its own right and will be discussed in the next section.

Organizational structure

In this section the overall or strategic structures of an organization are of concern, rather than the specific team structures that might be put in place for a given programme of new product development. In fact, this is a huge area of management research, with seminal inputs from Burns and Stalker (1961), Lawrence and Lorsch (1967) and Allen (1985) who discuss the difference between mechanistic and organic structures.[1]

Bentley (1990) presents the findings of an empirical study which is based on the hypothesis that the structure and style which a company adopts is closely related to its ability to connect with its market and, since proximity to the market is a determinant of new product success, the organizational structure and style is an important issue. Bentley advocates a flexible structure and style which supports the ability of individuals to behave innovatively, thus echoing, in terms of organization structure, the issues raised by the section on strategic orientation. Similarly, in considering organizational styles, Rothwell and Whiston (1990) lean toward flexibility, advocating an organic style of organization which:

● is free from rigid rules

● is participative and informal

● has many views aired and considered

● has face-to-face communication: little 'red tape'

- has interdisciplinary teams: breaking down departmental barriers
- puts emphasis on creative interaction and aims
- is outward looking: willing to take on external ideas
- has flexibility with respect to changing needs, threats and opportunities
- is non-hierarchical
- has information flowing downwards as well as upwards.

An oft-cited example of these types of structures is Sony. The Sony Corporation is one of the world's largest and most successful electronics companies. Sony is responsible for bringing to market many new innovations, including Walkman (the first portable stereo player), Discman (the first portable compact disc player), and Disc camera (the first filmless camera). The company's success has largely been attributed to its ability to miniaturize existing products.

Sony's objective is to be the electronic industry's foremost innovator. The cultural influences that allow Sony to pursue this objective can be examined in two contexts: internal influences and external influences (see Table 7.2). The main influence on Sony's culture is that the company is a product-led organization as opposed to market-led; Sony decide on the product that they want to create and then they establish how they are going to make it. Sony believe in leading the public with new products rather than asking them what kind of products they want ('the public doesn't know what is possible, but we do').

'Instead of doing a lot of market research we refine our thinking on a product and its use and try to create a market for it by educating and communicating with the public'. However, Sony have not detached themselves from the market. In order to maximize the chance of new product success, Sony maintain close contact with the

---

Table 7.2 ● Sony's internal and external influences

Internal
- Founders' vision
  - to be the electronic industry's foremost innovator
- Core beliefs:
  - Product-led, *not* market-led
  - Innovation encouraged by empowering employees
  - Sony family – friendly open management style with frequent management–employee talks; all employees wear the same uniform
  - Product quality
- Symbols:
  - Sony name and logo
  - Brand name

External:
- Japanese culture and history
- Operating environment – decreasing product life cycles and product lead times

market so that they are aware of fashionable appearances and the latest promotional techniques.

In order to maximize the company's innovative efforts, the company has established a scheme whereby an innovator will 'champion' a product from idea through to launch. This approach, combined with Sony's employee empowerment policies, encourages innovation.

Sony has eight product divisions, each division being responsible for developing new products in their particular area, such as the audio or video division. Development Project Teams from each division then research and develop products. Every month the teams meet and discuss topics such as theme, budget, expenditure, time scheduling, and real-time development. Throughout this process the Development Project Teams are in constant communication with other organizational functions. Indeed, Sony are aware that communication between R & D and all other business functions is essential as their input is required in order to assess the potential of new products.

Having looked at the three strategic influencers of success in NPD, we now turn to those influencers which operate at the level of the specific development.

Project (task) related issues

The brief review of strategic issues above shows how the way in which the whole organization functions can have an effect on the success or failure of new products. However, the way in which any one specific project is executed, the people involved and the role of information are instrumental in its outcome.

NPD process

The process of new product development involves the activities described above. A number of studies have identified the efficient execution of the development process, or particular activities within the development process, as critical to new product success (Cooper, 1979, 1980; Cooper and Kleinschmidt, 1987; Maidique and Zirger, 1984; National Industrial Conference Board, 1964; Rothwell et al., 1972, 1974).

The models of new product development processes tend to be idealized and for this reason may be quite far removed from reality. A number of authors have researched to what extent the prescriptive activities of the NPD process take place. In 1986, Cooper and Kleinschmidt used a 'skeleton' of the process taken from a variety of normative and empirically based prescriptive processes developed by other authors and found that there is a greater probability of commercial success if all of the process activities are completed. This finding is confirmed in another study which replicates the investigation in Australian companies (Dwyer and Mellor, 1990).

While it may be desirable to have a complete process of NPD, each additional activity extends the overall development time and may lead to late market introduction. There can be a price to pay for late market introduction. For example, Evans (1990) has quantified the consequence of extending the development time: delaying launch by six months can equal a loss of 33% in profits over five years. Therefore a trade-off has to be made between completing all the suggested activities in the NPD process and the time which these activities take.

In recognition of the time pressures facing those developing new products Cooper (1988, p. 246) suggests that there should be *'parallel processing'*, as discussed above.

Benefits of the parallel approach are the reduction of time to market (Cooper, 1988), a smoother transition between phases and therefore avoidance of the bottlenecks which often occur in a sequential process (Takeuchi and Nonaka, 1986), and a number of 'soft' advantages relating to those involved, such as shared responsibility, co-operation, involvement, commitment, sharpened problem-solving focus, initiative, diversified skills and heightened sensitivity toward market conditions.

A number of studies emphasize the importance of the marketing activities within the NPD process. As the result of their research findings Johne and Snelson (1988) advise companies to be novel in their market research approaches as well as to seek emerging new product opportunities and to offer more applications advice to customers so that they can create different ways of using products. Wind and Mahajan (1987) present a conceptual argument in which they identify a key role for marketing in what they call 'marketing hype'; this is a pre-launch activity encompassing concept testing, product testing and new product forecasting models.

The importance of the market research activities in the NPD process is again highlighted by Cooper and Kleinschmidt (1986, 1987, 1990). Hill (1988) argues that market appraisals are crucial to a clear understanding of the market. Much of the extensive research of the Design Innovation Group has concentrated on the importance of good market research (Bruce, 1992). An opposing view cites the well-known example of the Sony Walkman product development in which the company entrepreneurs doggedly ignored the limiting factor of current demand patterns (Morita et al., 1987). In the case of true innovations the role of traditional marketing and market research may be less useful. This does not, however, remove the importance of marketing's role in NPD. Despite these well-known examples, many others confirm the importance given to market research by practising product developers. Land Rover spends £1 million per annum on market research, compared to £20,000 five years previously (Gabb, 1991). Phileas Fogg, in launching new size bags of its Tortilla Chips, based the decision on market research (*Marketing*, 1994). Even where formal market research is not used, companies such as Boeing, Hewlett-Packard and Motorola all involve customers directly in their innovation programmes (Nauman and Shannon, 1992).

The above discussion relates to the research which focuses on the particular *activities* of the development process, but the extent to which the activities can or cannot be effectively carried out demands attention to the *people*, or *functions*, within the process. It is to these issues that we now turn our attention.

People

People involved in the NPD process and the way in which these people are organized are critical factors in the outcome of new product developments. The Stanford Innovation Project (Maidique and Zirger, 1984) identified functional co-ordination as a critical factor contributing to the development of *successful* new products. Support for the importance of functional co-ordination is to be found in numerous studies, including Pinto and Pinto (1990), who found that the higher the level of cross-functional co-operation, the more successful the outcome of new product development. The close relationship between functional co-ordination and an integrated set of NPD activities has already been emphasized, including the reduction of the development cycle time, cost savings and closer communication so that potential problems are detected very early on in the process (Larson, 1988). Although integration of all the relevant functional specialisms into the NPD process is necessary, one particular interface has been given more attention in research studies: the R&D/Marketing Interface.

A host of issues are mentioned in the literature which relate to the integration of the R&D and Marketing functions. These include the organizational climate (Gupta, Raj and Wilemon, 1986); the need for R&D and Marketing personnel to be more adaptive to each other (Lucas and Bush, 1988) for which 'role swapping' may play an important part (Souder, 1988). The key notion within all of the methods of achieving R&D/Marketing integration is that R&D and Marketing managers must work together to solve the disharmony in their relations. An interesting contribution from Souder (1988) presents seven ways in which the managers should try to achieve integration. In Souder's words they should:

- make personnel aware that interface problems naturally occur
- make personnel sensitive to the characteristics of disharmony
- give equal praise to both functions
- continuously reinforce their desire for R&D and Marketing collaboration
- use teams of R&D and Marketing personnel at every opportunity
- solve personality clashes A.S.A.P.
- avoid complacency — too much harmony is a bad thing

The literature has shown that the people who are involved in the NPD process from a variety of functions must work together, if developments are to be successful. However, achieving functional integration (especially of the R&D and marketing functions) is a difficult issue to resolve. Given its importance as a critical success factor, we will return to this later in the chapter. The sharing of information, organization of development teams and effective leadership have been suggested as ways in which this problem could be resolved.

Information

The role which information can play in facilitating an efficient NPD *process* and achieving *functional co-ordination* is implicit in the literature on success in NPD. This is the last factor from Figure 7.4 which emerges as crucial to successful NPD projects.

The notion of reducing uncertainty as the main objective of the project development activities is reiterated throughout the literature: project activities 'can be considered as discrete information processing activities aimed at reducing uncertainty.' (Moenaert and Souder, 1990, p. 92). These activities include gathering and disseminating information and making decisions based upon this information, which must include evaluations of *both the market and technical aspects* of the development project. Indeed, it is ultimately this information which is evaluated during the NPD process review through the 'gates'.

In order to reduce uncertainty, it is not sufficient that information be processed; it also has to be transferred between different functions (Bonnet, 1986; Moenaert and Souder, 1990). In this way the uncertainty perceived by particular functions can be reduced. At the same time the efficient transfer of quality information between different functions encourages their co-ordination (Moenaert and Souder, 1990).

As well as reducing uncertainty, the transfer of information between the two functions is perceived by both sides to be a key area for establishing *credibility* as a necessary input to the integration described in the previous section. The research by Workman (1993) showed, for example, that in Zytech, lack of credibility between functions inhibited integration.

Information, therefore, is a base currency of the NPD process; evaluative information is crucial and must be efficiently disseminated to facilitate communication. An example of the information elements implied by the numerous studies into success and failure is given in Table 7.3.

This review of research into the correlates of success and failure in NPD does not claim to be exhaustive, but it does give a flavour of the variety of issues and disciplines central to furthering our understanding of the processes of innovation and new product development. Nearly all contributions to the literature on NPD, irrespective of the 'base discipline' of the author, will touch on aspects of either the process of development, or the people responsible for carrying out the process. These two, therefore, might be fruitfully used as a 'common currency' across disciplinary borders. The next section reviews some recent trends in thinking about how to manage the process and structure the people involved in the process.

Implications of the success and failure literature for the process: focusing on the process and the people

Why the process and the people involved are crucial

As mentioned above, both are related to three of the most commonly cited critical success factors in NPD:

1. *The need for interdisciplinary inputs.* In order to combine technical and marketing expertise, a number of company functions have to be involved: R&D, manufacturing, engineering, marketing and sales. As the development of a new product may be the only purpose for which these people meet professionally, it is important that the NPD process adopted ensures that they work well and effectively together. Linked to this is also the need for the voice of the customer to be heard, as well as that of suppliers, where changes to supply may be required or advantageous.

2. *The need to develop product advantage.* Technical and market information, which are building blocks of NPD, have to be both accurate and timely, and must be constantly reworked in the light of changing circumstances during the course of the development, to ensure that the product under development does have competitive advantage in the eyes of the customer. Therefore the *people* must deliver the information to inform the *process*.

Table 7.3 ● The role of marketing information in achieving critical success factors: some preliminary thoughts

Success factor	Studies citing importance	Operationalization of success factors	Expected market information elements
		Strategic success factors	
Product advantage	Cooper, 1979; Cooper and Kleinschmidt, 1986, 1991	Excellent relative product quality in comparison to competitive offerings; good value for money (perceived by the customer); excellence in meeting customer needs, inclusion of benefits perceived by the customer as useful; benefits which are obvious to the customer; superior price/performance characteristics; unique attributes	Customer perceptions of competitive offerings; technological dimensions of competitive offerings; customer perceptions of new product's attributes and benefits; feedback from customers after trial; feedback on customer understanding of the message; perceptual maps based on customer data; technical specifications; product design information; attributes and features specifications
Well-specified protocol	As above; Rothwell, 1977; Rothwell et al., 1974; Rubenstein et al., 1976	Firm's knowledge and understanding, prior to development, of the target market, customer needs, wants, preferences; the product concept; product specifications and requirements	Research information detailing market demographics/psychographics; customer needs, wants and preferences; technical specifications, product design information, attributes and features specifications (prior to development)
Market attractiveness	Maidique and Zirger, 1984; de Brentani, 1989	High growth rates, high market need for product type; stability of demand; relative price insensitivity; high trial of new products	Economic market data; economic trends; level of employment; income levels; inflation rates
Top management support	Ramanujam and Mensch, 1985; McDonough and Leifer, 1986	Levels of risk aversion; aspects of corporate culture	Risk involved; identification of product champions; power and influence distribution among managers
Synergy/familiarity	Maidique and Zirger, 1984; Rothwell et al., 1974	Knowledge of technology; relevance to other projects; access to scientific institutes and laboratories	Extent of new knowledge involved; technology centres where knowledge resides; key scientists; technological networks of firms

		Development process issues	
Proficiency of pre-development activities	Cooper & Cooper and Kleinschmidt as above; Rubenstein et al., 1976; Voss, 1985	Proficiency of concept screening; preliminary market and technical assessment; preliminary business analysis; preliminary technical assessment	Research on customer perceptions, gap analysis, needs analysis, concept tests; market size potential, market segments; technical feasibility, preliminary costs; market size, likely price, profit, break-even, etc.
Proficiency of marketing activities	Roberts and Burke, 1974; Rothwell et al., 1974; Cooper, 1979, 1988; Maidique and Zirger, 1984; Link, 1987	Proficiency of concept, product and market tests, service, advertising, distribution and elements of market launch	Market information for the acceptance of alternative product concepts or designs; customer preference data; market profile information; information concerning the distribution channels of interest
Proficiency of technological activities	Rothwell et al., 1974; Maidique and Zirger, 1984	Proficiency in physical product development; in-house and in-use test iterations; trial production runs; technology acquisition	Technical solutions to functional and marketing problems; technical information on test performance; information on production costs and problems; information on suppliers' developments and adjacent technologies
Integration of R&D and Marketing	Maidique and Zirger, 1984; Takeuchi and Nonaka, 1986; Rubenstein et al., 1976; Gupta and Wilemon, 1990; Rochford and Rudelius, 1992	Amount of information shared; agreement on decision-making authority; functional involvement at each stage	Relevance, novelty, credibility, comprehensibility of information; timeousness of information provision
Speed in development	Takeuchi and Nonaka, 1986; Dumaine, 1991; Cooper and Kleinschmidt, 1994	Time-to-market; product launched on schedule; number of competitors on market at time of launch	Timeousness of information exchange; competitive information

Source: Hart et al. (1997).

3. *The need for speed in the process.* The NPD process has to be managed in such a way as to be quick enough to capitalize on the new product opportunity before competitors do. The extent to which *people* work together enhances the speed of the *process*. Heinz has restructured its marketing department in order to attempt to reduce time-to-market (*Marketing*, 31 March 1994).

Another reason for their importance is that they are inextricably linked: the process cannot unfold without the appropriate people, nor can the process be organized to facilitate cross-functional inputs without reference to the people involved. Although so apparent as to appear something of a truism, the linkage between the process (its tasks and decisions) and people (their skills and organization) has been widely ignored by researchers in most of the single disciplinary research.

A final reason for their importance is that they encapsulate other central themes. We have already discussed the role of information in promoting cross-functional integration, sharing a link between the themes of 'people' and 'information'. In addition, 'people' as a theme are clearly implicated by 'organizational structure and style' as a theme. Similarly, the theme of the 'process' is related to that of 'information', since the NPD process can be viewed as one of information processing; it is also related to top management and strategy, as these two set the context for the nature of the process itself. If these linkages are accepted, focusing on 'process' and 'people' allows access to many of the other salient variables in NPD research. Unfortunately, few representations of the NPD process make explicit provision for the major functions involved. Next, we describe two representations which do attempt to account for multi-disciplinary inputs.

The multiple convergent approach

In suggesting a way forward in NPD research which takes account of the lessons to be learned from the success literature and the importance of networks in NPD, and which attempts to break down research discipline boundaries, an alternative *process* model has been forwarded, which has direct and explicit consequences for *people*, namely the 'multiple convergent process'. This model is conceptually derived from the idea of parallel processing, and is shown in Figure 7.5.

Dictionary definitions of 'parallel' refer to 'separated by an equal distance at every point' or 'never touching or intersecting', and while there are references to simultaneity, it is a somewhat troublesome notion that suggests functional separation, when all the performance indicators in NPD point to the need for functional integration. On the other hand, 'to converge' is defined as 'to move or cause to move towards the same point' or to 'tend towards a common conclusion or result', and is therefore, a more precise indicator of what is required of NPD management.

Realizing, however, that there are still functionally distinct tasks which must be carried out at specific points throughout the NPD process, it is clear that the tasks will be carried out simultaneously at some juncture and that the results must *converge*. Due to the iterations in the process, this convergence is likely to happen several times, culminating at the time of product launch. As previously mentioned,

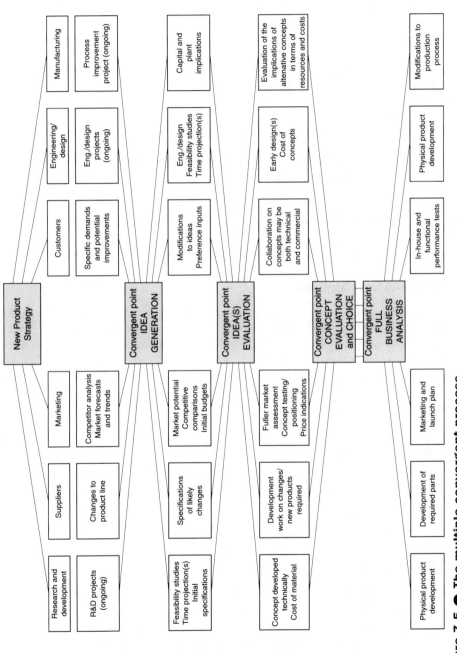

Figure 7.5 ● The multiple convergent process

the process is a series of information gathering and evaluating activities, and as the new product develops from idea to concept to prototype and so on, the information gathered becomes more precise and reliable and the decisions are made with greater certainty.

Therefore as the development project progresses, there are a number of natural points of evaluation and a number of types of evaluation (market, functional) which need to be carried out in an integrated fashion. Hence, there are multiple convergent points which link this form of activity-stage models to the decision-stage models, as the convergent points can be set around decision outputs required to further the process.

The advantages of viewing the process this way are as follows:

1. Iterations among participants within stages are allowed for.

2. The framework can easily accommodate third parties.

3. Mechanisms for integration throughout the process among different functions are set in the convergent points.

4. The model can fit into the most appropriate NPD structures for the company.

Iterations within stages

As the relevant functions are viewed in terms of their contribution to each stage in the process by their specialist contribution, the cross-functional linkages between stages are incorporated. The extent of involvement of different bodies or outside parties will be determined by the specific needs of each development in each firm. Thus, within-stage iteration can benefit from both task specialization which will increase the quality of inputs and integration of functions via information sharing and decision making.

Accommodation of third parties

Several studies have shown the importance of involving users in the NPD process to increase success rates (von Hippel, 1988; Biemans, 1992). Equally, there is growing interest in the need for supplier involvement, in order to benefit from the advantages of supplier innovation and just-in-time (JIT) policies (Tzokas and Saren, 1991).

Mechanisms for integration

Although the success literature points to the need for integration, there is some evidence to suggest that, in practice, this is not always easy to achieve. In Biemans' study, most of the companies showed an understanding of the need to integrate R&D and marketing activities, although the desirability of this is not considered to be automatic, based on the evidence of the companies surveyed. In several studies (Gupta, Raj and Wilemon, 1986; Gupta and Wilemon, 1988), it is also stressed that the appropriate level of integration must be decided upon, and that this level is dependent upon organizational strategies, environmental uncertainty, organizational factors and individual factors. As outlined earlier in the chapter, the key element in integration is the amount of information sharing, and the multiple convergent process offers the opportunity for information sharing which is neglected by other models. Clearly, a host of other factors are likely to influence the amount of cross-functional information sharing, including organizational climate and structure. This said, the multiple convergent model carries within it the impetus for information sharing through the convergent points that can be located liberally throughout the process.

Quality function deployment

The second approach to promoting integration which avoids a sequential vision of the NPD process includes Quality Function Deployment (QFD) shown in Figure 7.6 (Griffin, 1992; Hauser and Clausing, 1988).

Simply put, Quality Function Deployment uses four 'houses' to focus multi-disciplinary information inputs on the development programme. It aims, therefore, to facilitate

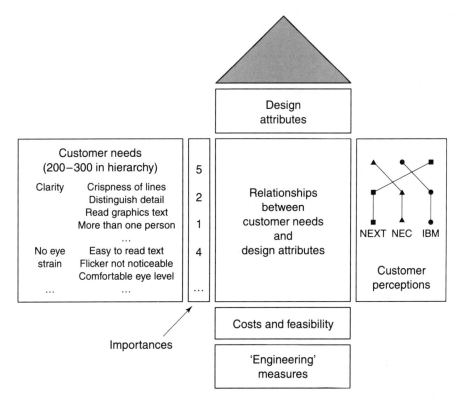

Figure 7.6 ● The House of Quality, the first house of Quality Function Deployment (QFD)

interfunctional integration, enhance design, and decrease design time and costs. The first 'house', shown in Figure 7.6, is called 'The House of Quality'. It links customer need to design attributes or 'engineering measures' of a product. Therefore, right at the outset, the process is based on the requirement to match needs with features. The second house focuses on the translation of these design attributes into the necessary action the development team needs to take. The third house details how the actions can be implemented by focusing on decisions such as the appropriate manufacturing system needed. The fourth house translates the various implementation decisions into the final production planning.

The first house is concerned with identifying customer needs, structuring those needs into a hierarchy and prioritizing them, and finally comparing customer perceptions of how well the company's and competitive products fulfil their needs. This information and analysis are used to guide product design. The other aspects of this first house relate to the search for engineering measures, or design attributes, which fulfil those customer needs. The team charged with this responsibility will also compare competitive products' design attributes. This part of the process is revisited in Chapter 10, in more detail. Much has been written about QFD, which has received detailed attention by academic and practitioner writing alike. For more information, see Clausing (1986), Griffin (1989), Hauser and Clausing (1988) and Inwood and Hammond (1993). The strengths of QFD as a holistic NPD methodology relate to the extent to which it encapsulates many of the 'new product success correlates', particularly at the project level described above. Its use, however, is difficult to assess. Emanating from Japan, adopted by several major US and European engineering firms, there is little evidence of widespread diffusion into new product development practice.

Managing the people in NPD

Our understanding of what makes products successful suggests that developing product advantage is crucial. Product advantage is achieved not merely by technological progress, but by making technologies relevant to user needs. Therefore, if new product development were a task carried out with expertise in marketing only, it might not work properly, whereas if the task were carried out by R&D only, the resultant product might not meet user needs in any way. It follows, then, that it is critically important for firms to have structures which allow not only for professional specialism and expertise, but also for sharing information across disciplinary boundaries to ensure the development is fulfilling both sides of the success mandate: technological competence and market relevance. The structures discussed in the body of literature refer to the need for 'co-ordination' and 'integration' of the perspectives of different disciplines.

The literature, however, is confusing, not only because of the variety of aspects of functional co-ordination which have been investigated, but also because of the variety of terms used to refer to what this article calls 'functional co-ordination'. Pinto and Pinto (p. 203) make an informative summary of the different terms which have been used. This summary is reproduced in part here (as Table 7.4) and has been supplemented with a number of other terms and definitions which different writers employ.

Table 7.4 ● Terms and definitions for 'functional co-ordination'

Source	Term	Definition
Argote (*Pinto and Pinto*)	Co-ordination	Fitting together the activities of the organization's members
Van de Van et al. (*Pinto and Pinto*)	Co-ordination	Integrating or linking together different parts of the organization to accomplish a collective set of tasks
Trist (*Pinto and Pinto*)	Collaboration	Willingness to align one's own purpose with those of diverse others . . . rather than trying to coerce and dominate in order to get one's own way . . . and to negotiate mutually acceptable compromises
Schermerhorn (*Pinto and Pinto*)	Inter-organizational co-operation	Deliberate relations between otherwise autonomous organizations for the joint accomplishment of individual goals
Johnson (*Pinto and Pinto*)	Co-operation	The co-ordination of behaviours among individuals to achieve mutual goals
Lawrence and Lorsch (1967) (*Pinto and Pinto*)	Integration	The quality or state of collaboration that exists among departments that are to achieve unity of effort in the accomplishment of the organization's tasks
Pinto and Pinto (1990)	Cross-functional co-ordination	The quality of task and interpersonal relations when different functional areas work together to accomplish organizational tasks
Rothwell and Whiston (1990)	Functional integration	Integration and task sharing between diverse functions
Maidique and Zirger (1984)	Functional co-ordination	The create, make and market functions are well interfaced and co-ordinated
Moenaert and Souder (1990)	Integration	Symbiotic inter-relating of two or more entities that results in the production of new benefits to them
Gupta and Wilemon (1988)	R&D Marketing integration	Information sharing and decision agreement

Whatever the precise definition, it is important for companies to institute processes and design structures which promote integration and co-ordination, at the same time as preserving the efficiencies within functional speciality. A recent article by Olsen, Walker and Ruekert (1995) identified seven types of new product structure, or co-ordination mechanisms, which they describe in terms of four structural attributes: complexity, distribution of authority, formalization and unit autonomy (Table 7.5). These are discussed below, briefly.

Table 7.5 ● Attributes of interfunctional co-ordination mechanisms

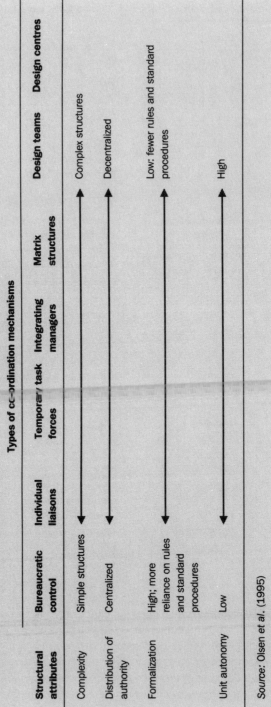

Structural attributes	Types of co-ordination mechanisms						
	Bureaucratic control	Individual liaisons	Temporary task forces	Integrating managers	Matrix structures	Design teams	Design centres
Complexity	Simple structures	→					Complex structures
Distribution of authority	Centralized	→					Decentralized
Formalization	High; more reliance on rules and standard procedures	→					Low: fewer rules and standard procedures
Unit autonomy	Low	→					High

Source: Olsen et al. (1995)

Bureaucratic control

This is the most formalized and centralized and the least participative mechanism, where a high-level general manager co-ordinates activities across functions and is the arbiter of conflicts among functions. Each functional development operates with relative autonomy within the constraints imposed by hierarchical directives, and therefore most information flows vertically within each department. In such a mechanism, the different functional activities work sequentially on the developing product.

Individual liaisons

Individuals within one functional department have to communicate directly with their counterparts in other departments. Therefore they supplement the vertical communication found in bureaucracies.

Integrating managers

In this co-ordination structure, an additional manager is added to the functional structure, responsible for co-ordinating the efforts of the different functional departments, but without the authority to impose decisions on those departments. Thus, such integrating managers have to rely on persuasion and on their ability to encourage group decision making and compromise to achieve successful results.

Matrix structures

Whereas all the previous mechanisms maintain the primacy of the functional departmental structure, a matrix organization structures activities not only according to product or market focus, but also by function. Thus, individuals are responsible to both a functional manager and a new product manager.

Beside these, two newer structural forms have appeared in order to improve the timeliness and the effectiveness of the product development efforts within rapidly changing environments. These forms are design teams and design centres.

Design teams

Like the matrix structure, design teams are composed of a set of functional specialists who work together on a specific NPD product. The difference is that such teams tend to be more self-governing and have greater authority to choose their own internal leader(s) who have more autonomy to establish their own operating procedures and to resolve internal conflicts.

Design centres

These centres have many of the same characteristics as a design team. However, such a centre is a permanent addition to an organization's structure, and members of the centre are involved in multiple development projects over time.

As one moves from bureaucratic control towards more organic and participative structures, the structural complexity of the mechanisms increases. Authority becomes more decentralized, rules and procedures less formalized and less rigidly enforced, and the individual units tend to have more autonomy. Consequently, members of relatively organic structures are more likely to share information across functional boundaries and to undertake interdependent tasks concurrently rather than sequentially.

In other words, as we move from left to right, structures become less 'mechanistic' and more 'organic' (Burns and Stalker, 1961). Relatively organic mechanisms such as design teams have some important potential advantages for co-ordinating product development. Indeed, the participative decision making, consensual conflict resolution and open communication processes of such a structure can help reduce barriers between individuals and functional groups. Such participative structures can also create an atmosphere where innovative ideas are proposed, criticized and refined with a minimum of financial and social risk. Besides, by facilitating the open exchange of creative ideas across multiple functions, the likelihood of producing innovative products that successfully address the market desires as well as technical and operational requirements is increased.

Finally, reduced functional barriers help ensure that unanticipated problems that appear during the development process can be tackled directly by the people concerned. This reduces the possibility that vital information may be delayed, lost or altered.

On the other hand, more participative structures have also some potential disadvantages, especially in terms of costs and temporal efficiency. Creating and supporting several development teams can lead to overabundance in personnel and facilities. The main reason for this is that employees have less relevant experience when developing innovative product concepts and then depend more heavily on other functional specialists for the expertise, information and other resources needed to achieve a creative and successful product. And these flows of information and resources are facilitated by less formal participative co-ordination structures. Thus, there is potential for stagnation in the process if the focus of control is unclear.

In the light of this discussion, let us now look at what kinds of structures are used for NPD.

Structures used by industry

Many studies of innovation and product development give evidence of the 'structures' used to organize the process. Hart and Service (1988) found a number of mechanisms, shown in Figure 7.7.

Their findings are similar to those of Mahajan and Wind (1992) shown in Table 7.6, while Figure 7.8 summarizes the results with respect to organizational mechanisms, found in the research of 'Best Practices' among US product developers.

These studies suggest that structures may exist either within or outside what might be termed 'existing line functions', although this is not made explicit. For example, Page's research (Page, 1993, Table 5) shows that the most common mechanism used for NPD is that of a 'multi-disciplinary team', but this was used in combination with other mechanisms, such as product manager, new product manager and new product

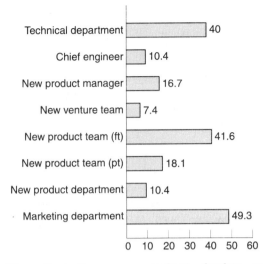

Figure 7.7 ● Managing the new product design and development process

departments. At the risk of over-simplification, we can classify venture teams and new product departments as existing completely outside the normal functional lines, such as marketing, R&D or engineering.

Venture teams tend to be a permanent 'maverick' group, with high status and separate budgets, reporting to the MD. Their responsibilities can vary, but include opportunity identification and feasibility studies through to management of the new product development. The advantages are that, freed from the 'humdrum' of current business, creativity can be encouraged, and the development has high level support. On the other side, they can turn into acquisition hunters, may be prone to get into unrelated areas and can be seen as a waste of time if they acquire such information from inside the company, which might occur if they get involved with the development of existing

Table 7.6 ● Organization of the new product process

Organization	Percentage of companies (N = 69)
Part of the planning department	3
Combination	4
Task force venture team	9
Part of R&D department	14
Separate corporate or NPD group	17
New product department at SBU level	21
Marketing department	27

Source: Mahajan and Wind (1992).

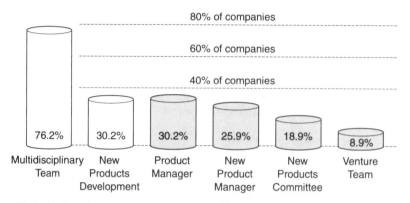

Figure 7.8 ● Best practices among US product developers – organizational mechanisms (source: Page, 1993)

products. Guinness set up a dedicated new business unit to develop products in 'non traditional areas'. The unit is named 'Guinness Ventures' and will focus at a global level, outside the usual boundaries of the company's R&D activity (*Marketing*, 13 October 1994).

New product departments or divisions have the same status as functional divisions and are essentially outside the 'mainstream' of business. They are usually staffed by a combination of factors. They may be used in different ways: as idea hunters, where ideas are passed to the 'mainstream' for development, or as developers, who manage the new product from idea through to the market launch. In the latter instance, the 'handover' of the product will take place at the launch, which may engender feelings of 'not invented here'. However, the rationale for the complete segregation of new product activity is to encourage new ideas for products not contaminated by the vested interests of those managing the amount business. If, however, new product activity does need to draw on experience of current technologies in current markets, then some linkage with those managing the current business is clearly beneficial.

Multi-disciplinary teams, new products' committees, new product teams, product managers and new product managers are all limited – some more directly than others – to the existing line structures. Indeed Page's study showed that the line functions most involved in new product development were marketing, R&D and engineering. The various teams, committees or individuals may be given 'part-time' responsibility for NPD.

There is an inevitable tension between the need for integration and existing authority and responsibility lines. Due to this tension, many firms will locate responsibility for NPD in one function, and bring others in as and when required. This, of course, raises problems in that development work may be in conflict with the management of current business. This would be manifested in time pressures, whereby development work is squeezed by existing product management, and in stifled creativity, owing to procedures already being in place for existing products; finally, fresh business perspectives may be lacking in people who are expert in managing the current business.

Alternatively, a post of new products manager may be created in marketing or technical departments. The part-time option can suffer from time pressures and conflict of roles as besets much matrix structures and, worse, NPD can become something of a secondary goal. In addition, the individual new product manager tends not to be inter-disciplinary, which forces negotiation with other departments, as opposed to collaboration. As a result, there tends to be a 'pass the parcel' approach to the development project, which gets shunted around from one department to the next. Finally, this mechanism tends to be low level with little leverage for important resource decisions, leading to an incremental approach to NPD and a new product committee. This is made up of senior managers from salient functions, and has the purpose of encouraging cross-functional co-operation at the appropriate senior level. However, these mechanisms may suffer from a remote perspective, as the line managers are not really carrying out the task.

Location of new product activity inside or outside existing functions requires a trade-off. Since autonomous structures are designed to allow the unfettered development of new ideas with greater levels of advantage, without much reliance on the existing business, it follows logically that this type of development is precisely what they should carry out.

Once these autonomous units become involved with what Johne and Snelson call 'old product development', their inevitable reliance on those within the line function may cause a conflict. In any case, perhaps the efficiency of an autonomous unit to redevelop current lines is questionable. Indeed, the research by Olsen, Walker and Ruekert (1995) showed that 'organic, decentralised participative co-ordination mechanisms *are* associated with better development performance... *but only* when used on projects involving innovative or new to the world concepts with which the company has little experience on which to draw' (p. 61).

A number of companies' recent stories highlight this finding in practice. Guinness' new business unit and the development of Chrysler's Neon, a 'sub-compact' car, used what they call 'platform teams', which are autonomous groups consisting of all the professionals required to design and produce a new car, or 'platform' (*Fortune*, January 1994).

This section has introduced some of the complexities involved in designing mechanisms which provide the appropriate balance between creativity and innovation on the one hand, and building on the expertise accumulated with regard to technologies and markets on the other. Although the success literature points to the need for cross-functional teams, the extent to which these should be autonomous will depend, among other things, on the type of new product development being pursued.

Summary

As an introduction to the section on New Product Development, this chapter has outlined the evolution of NPD models and described the main tasks involved in the process of developing new products. Research on success and failure in new product development was then reviewed in order to point out those critical issues which developers of new products must manage actively if their efforts are to be successful. It has highlighted two 'newer' attempts to remodel the process in such a way as to incorporate the lessons of research into success and failure, namely the Multiple Convergent Process and Quality Function Deployment. The former is normative in its derivation, the latter developed by engineers. Finally, the chapter discussed some of the key structures used to organize NPD activities.

The remainder of this section of the book, Chapters 8 to 13, on New Product Development, follows the steps in the process as described by Booz Allen Hamilton. The next chapter examines the strategic aspects of new product development.

QUESTIONS

1. Summarize the evolution of new product development models. What factors have encouraged this evolution?

2. What was the distinguishing feature of the Booz Allen Hamilton process, reported in 1982?

3. Argue the case that new product development models are useless as guides for new product development managers.

4. Summarize the success factors in NPD and choose and justify those you feel are most important.

5. What lessons from the success factors need to be taken account of when designing new product processes within a company?

6. What lessons from the success factors need to be taken account of when organizing for new product development?

Mini-case ● Braun's Supervolume

The firm

Braun UK is part of Braun AG, Germany, a holding company for most of the European subsidiaries of Braun, which in turn is part of the Gillette Co. Inc., USA, a large multinational corporation. Although Braun covers a world-wide base there appears to be a degree of autonomy as far as new product development (NPD) is concerned. At the same time there appears to be a great deal of integration within the company world-wide as the research and development arm within Germany and the production unit in Ireland are both involved.

In the years previous to the launch, Braun UK had been losing market share although they still retained their number 2 position (see Table 7.7).

Gillette Co. Inc. has a history of NPD and their company accounts emphasize the fact that 37% of their 1993 sales came from products developed in the last five years, with the figure growing to 45% in 1994. They also had 17 new products launched in 1992/93 and 20 launched in 1993/94 with a constant geographical roll-out of products through-

Table 7.7 ● Hairdryers: market share, percentage value 1991–93

Manufacturer	1991	1992	1993
Clairol	25	27	27
Braun	24	22	20
Babybliss	12	16	10
Boots	12	11	10
Carmen	9	8	8
Phillips	5	3	8
Hair Design	2	2	1
Morphy Richards	3	4	4
Others	8	7	12

Source: Datamonitor (1994).

out the year. Braun appear to have taken this a stage further as they estimate that 66% of sales came from products developed in the last five years.

However, the Profit and Loss accounts for Braun UK (Table 7.8) are not quite as impressive reading, with both sales and profit fluctuating over the past five years.

Table 7.8 ● Braun UK profit and loss (£000)

	1993	1992	1991	1990	1989
Turnover	44,374	47,350	47,511	53,858	45,057
Pre-tax profit (loss)	737	(367)	(1,177)	902	(740)

The industry

The market that Braun operate in is small electrical appliances for personal care/grooming; this covers a number of diverse products (see Table 7.9).

Table 7.9 ● Personal care appliances competitive structure, 1993

Product	Top threee total percent share	Relative share of no. 1
Hair styling appliances	73	1.91
Hair dryers	57	1.35
Electric toothbrushes	98	1.39
Male shavers	81	2.07
Female shavers	85	3.08
Electric blankets	97	1.42

Source: Datamonitor (1994).

The product concerned was situated in the hair dryer segment which has a total market of 2.63 million units worth £42m in the UK. This is a highly competitive market with a large number of competitors, both national (Boots) and multinational (Clairol, Phillips). Another indicator of the competitiveness of the segment is the market share of the top three companies (57% – see Table 7.7); this indicates how hard it was to gain and hold a significant part of the market. This was also evident from Babybliss, a new entrant to the UK market, which had rapidly gained market share. The market has reached the mature stage with a decline from years' 1991/92 and weak growth forecast (Datamonitor). One could say the market has reached saturation point as most producers see their products as replacements rather than new sales. The market in the US is similar, some analysts viewing hair dryers as commodities with price the only factor influencing buyer decisions.

Dependent on the firm concerned and which end of the market they focused on, the basis for competition was either size/power, price or product innovation. Most firms had a range of products which included compacts, differing wattage motors or some innovation such as Phillips Touch'n Dry which turns on/off when it is picked up or put down.

The launch

The basic technology on which the product is based is centred round three parts, namely the motor, the heating element and the casing and controls. Given the simple nature of the product and that there is no significant advantage in altering any of the parts, the product life cycle has reached a very mature stage. To reinforce this aspect, toiletry companies had actually picked up on this fact and were introducing products such as styling gel and mousse that altered the need for hair dryers. The only other 'new' idea was the introduction of diffusers in the late 1980s, which were suitable for curly or permed hair. Apart from that, most changes were cosmetic.

The innovation was a direct result of a brainstorming session involving Braun personnel and hairdressers which identified a need for a hair dryer which would give volume to straight hair. After identifying the niche, further research was done and significantly Braun realized that half the population (those with straight hair) did not have a hair dryer designed specifically for them.

Braun is committed to NPD as a company strategy. Their 'Supervolume' dryer took 12–18 months from idea to successful launch. The innovation was reinforced across the marketing mix. They brought in the German R&D to ensure the product was first class, and other internal design teams also modified the functional and cosmetic aspects. They moved away from the traditional packaging into pastels and into the 'beauty' area.

The dryer was originally priced at £22.99 compared to a conventional dryer at £15.00, which totally changed the industry's pricing structure for an average hair dryer product. Placing it in the highly competitive UK market first and then rolling it out throughout Europe, shook up their competitors and gave them the 'first to market' advantage. Braun also have excellent department store relations which gives them advantage over other producers.

Consumer promotion was focused on TV ads and promotions in hairdressers in the run-up to Christmas, and ended up so successful they had to pull their adverts, as the production facilities could not keep pace.

The result

Considering the competitiveness of the market the Supervolume was an outstanding success, gaining 9.7% of the overall market. Braun have also rolled out the product throughout Europe and have been able to repeat the ad campaign twice, which is unusual for any product. The product has also been released in the US and has taken that market and its competitors by storm. The US market had stagnated and competition was on a purely price basis, which has all been changed by the Supervolume introduction.

Discussion questions

1. What features of the new product development process would be identified with the success factors in product development?

2. Given the maturity of the market, what are the implications for the competitive pressure faced by Braun, during the development and launch of Supervolume?

3. What do you consider to be the most important element in the success of this new product, and why?

This case was compiled from public sources.

Note

1. A full discussion of this strand of research into structures for new product development is beyond the scope of this book. For an interesting review, see Brown and Eisenhardt (1995).

chapter 8

New product strategy

Introduction

In Chapter 6, one of the major sets of factors influencing the success of new products was described under the heading of 'strategic issues'. These issues encompass the direction and objectives set for new product development, which should reinforce the overall competitive strategy of a firm. The need for overall strategy, and the implied role for product development were discussed in Chapters 2 and 6. To recap briefly, unless firms respond to the changing business environment by constant development of their product mix, the inevitability of the product life cycle means they will die. Therefore, at the heart of corporate strategy is the continual development of products. However, there is enormous scope as to the direction, nature and objectives of this development. Chapter 1 has outlined some of the options – development of differentiated or cost-reduced products. Chapters 2 and 6 looked at models of strategic development which imply direction at each stage of a life cycle and in relation to market growth. This chapter looks at the way in which new product development – one component only of product management – is tied in with overall corporate strategy.

The need for product innovation strategy

The benefits of articulating new product strategy detailed by Booz, Allen and Hamilton in 1982 can be shown to have direct links to several of the success factors for NPD outlined in Chapter 7. In this chapter we explore the components of new product strategy, which essentially comprise a view of where a new programme of development sits in relation to the technologies that are employed and to the markets which these technologies will serve. The next section sets the need for new product strategy in the context of risk, and the remainder of the chapter deals with the components of the choices in technology and markets, and with the various combinations which make up the skeleton of new product strategy.

While innovation is necessary, it is both expensive and risky, and a majority of new products and services are not entirely new. The New York based Marketing Intelligence Service revealed that only 7.2% of the new products launched in 1996 were 'innovative' (*Grocer*, 18 January 1997, p. 15).

So, how do companies decide how innovative they want to be and why is this important? To answer this question we return to the seminal work of Booz, Allen and Hamilton (1968, 1982). In their 1968 study, an average of 58 new product ideas were required to produce one successful new product. By 1982, a new study showed this ratio had been reduced to seven to one. The reason forwarded for this change was the addition of a preliminary stage to the now-familiar six-step NPD process: idea generation → screening and evaluation → business and analysis → development → testing → commercialization. The preliminary stage was the development of an explicit, new product strategy that identified the strategic business requirements new products should satisfy. Effective benchmarks were set up so that ideas and concepts were generated to meet strategic objectives. Of the companies studied, 77% had initiated this procedure with remarkable success (see Figure 8.1; for discussion of the significance of curve types A, B and C see Chapter 10).

The basic requirements prescribed, in line with strategic objectives, encouraged an extremely effective 'elimination' of ideas which in the past cluttered and protracted the NPD process. Mike Anthony, a consultant with Pittiglio Rabin Todd and McGrath (PRTM), described a company manning 22 projects when it had capacity for only nine; typically it would turn out only three new products which would make money. Clearly an agenda – a strategy – for cutting down on the effort going into 22 projects would give rise to the opportunity to increase the resources channelled into the remaining projects (*Industry Week*, 16 December 1996, p. 45).

As discussed earlier, the judgment as to whether or not a new product has been a success rests largely on whether or not predetermined sales targets are met. Specifically, problems facing the many firms believed to use linear extrapolations for sales targets were introduced via the idea of the 'zone of underperformance' (see Figure 5.5).

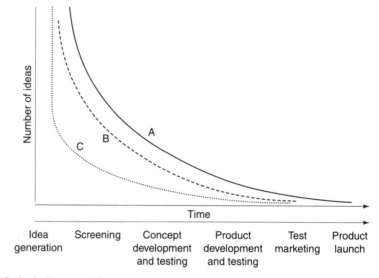

Figure 8.1 ● **Three different mortality curves of new product ideas**

Further, life cycles of new products are becoming shorter, which entails clear implications for corporate strategy and the new product decision alike. Strategic analyses of the environment must accommodate this development, while the ensuing strategy must give clear guidelines for the timely introduction of these fast-evolving products. In addition, it is crucial to precipitate the identification of likely failures *early* in the process. This can be explained by the increase of expenditure from the beginning to the end of the process (see Figure 8.2).

Total expenditure rises very sharply at the commercialization stage, representing considerable financial and psychological commitment, which would also have to be written off or 'redirected'. Therefore, it is crucial to set clear benchmarks of these early stages in NPD, due to the cumulative nature of expenditure and the 'creeping commitment' this implies. Since, as we will explore in future chapters, the problems of estimating specific market demand levels are difficult in the early stages, it is invaluable to have the benchmarks driven by strategic direction and the input to the strategic planning process. These benchmarks for product development should delineate *which markets* will be pursued by which new products (or technologies); such a definition has five important consequences:

1. It specifies the markets of potential.

2. It specifies the source of competitive advantages the development seeks to achieve in those markets with technologies.

3. It specifies the balance between 1 and 2, namely the relative orientation?? technology and market leadership.

4. By the specification in 1, 2 and 3 above, the differential advantage of the development can be set.

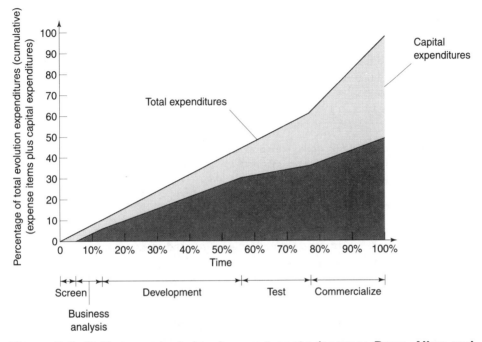

Figure 8.2 ● New product development costs (source: Booz, Allen and Hamilton, Inc., in Baker, 1983b)

5. The level of risk acceptance is set.

These specifications are vital, not only because studies have shown them to be directly related to success and failure, but also because they have implications for other issues which have an impact on the success of new products. First, setting new product strategy requires top management commitment and action. In considering how a programme of product development will contribute to overall company objectives, managers have to articulate where they see potential and what level and type of resources are required to realize that potential. This therefore underpins top management *commitment* to new product development efforts, for example. Guinness, in recognition of the marketing environment changes that are reshaping the alcoholic beverages industry, have in recent years invested in a new business unit to pursue new product development in new markets (Nicholas, 1994).

Second, having set the general direction, the area of effort required by the development team is also defined. By definition, development teams may have a multitude of potential products among which to defray their efforts, but the requirements of shorter life cycles and faster development time require them to be focused on specific tasks. Setting a clear strategy for new product development allows the team quickly to focus on those projects which fall within the boundaries of strategy, and the benchmarks for which of these should be taken further are also set. When the Glasgow-based company Alcan decided to adopt the Japanese principle of 'kaizen' – continued improvement – as their basis of innovation, the focus of teams was clearly set, causing the formation of mini-companies to handle product portfolios based around customer needs.

Third, the strategy set helps bring about the necessary levels of integration. As stated in Chapter 7, the fusion between technology and market-led innovation at a strategic level is an important variable in success. The recent turnaround in Nike's fortune from making losses around 1985, diminishing sales and redundancies in 1987, to regaining 29% of the US market in 1991, was based on a strategic refocusing of product development (Willigan, 1992). As the chief executive Phil Knight explains:

'We used to think that everything started in the lab. Now we realize that everything spins off the consumer. And while technology is still important, the consumer has to lead innovation . . . we do a lot of work at the grass root level. We go to amateur sports events and spend time at gyms and tennis courts talking to people . . . We have people who tell us what colours are going to be in. . .'. p. 94.

Nike have not abandoned innovation and technological development, but they have adjusted the balance between technical innovation and the customers' perceptions, which previously were marginalized.

Finally, the articulation of new product strategy allows the appropriate organizational mechanism to be set in place – again, important success factors. These issues were discussed in greater detail in Chapter 7. For an illustration of the link between product development strategy and the appropriate organizational mechanisms, Hewlett-Packard (HP) serves as a good example. As noted by Pascale (1993) developments in information technology used by consumers, greater familiarization and a higher level of expectation regarding computability among the components of a PC or PG network system could not be adequately exploited by HP, who traditionally used separate divisions for different product types.

Realization of the need to develop integrated IT solutions has triggered the establishment of a more centralized organizational outlook which fosters increasing co-ordination between entrepreneurial decisions.

The components of new product strategy: technologies and markets

In making choices about which technologies and markets are implicated by product development, it is the level of *newness* which, essentially, forms the decision to be made on each dimension. Returning to basic concepts of strategic choice raised in Chapter 2, new product strategies may be focused on existing markets, new markets, existing technologies and new technologies, or varying degrees of newness within these two dimensions. We will discuss the issues of both technological and market newness before constituting combinations of these.

Technological newness

In considering the concepts of technological newness, it is helpful to distinguish between invention and innovation, although they are often used in tandem. An invention is a technical phenomenon involving the discovery of some new principle, unlike an innovation which is an economic phenomenon involving the commercial use of new products or processes. It follows that for an invention to become an innovation, it must have some market value, that is, a value that someone is willing to pay for. Thus, right at the outset, 'technological innovation' is linked with the market. This said, the significance of the conceptual difference between invention and innovation lies in the following observations:

1. An invention is merely *one element*, albeit an essential one, in the realization of an innovation. Therefore the management of innovation goes beyond the discovery of new principles, goes beyond the laboratory and requires a *conversion process* to turn inventions into innovations.

2. There is considerable importance attached to the nature and direction of the conversion process. One invention may lead to one or more innovations.

3. The conversion process – more accurately, processes – may be quite separate from the invention. Inventions, therefore, will be converted by different people at different times to different degrees and across different industrial settings.

If, to these three observations, we add that inventions themselves may be of varying degrees of novelty, then the technological base from which a company has to choose its strategy is indeed complex. Figure 8.3 shows the various routes an 'invention' may take to innovation.

For example, the development of Teflon, a non-stick coating for metal, was a major technological breakthrough: the development of a new substance. However, the management of the conversion from invention to innovation was manifested in different ways. One way, for example, was the application of the substance to cooking pots and pans, resulting in 'non-stick cookware'. Yet another conversion of the invention came in the form of a coating for men's razors, resulting in a smoother, less hazardous shave. Both the cookware and razor industries applied the invention to their own products, creating innovations, which in their product markets might well be regarded as radical. Another example of new technologies bringing about innovations in industries

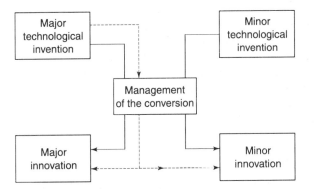

Figure 8.3 ● Technology routes from invention to innovation

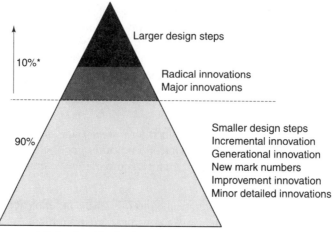

* Rothwell and Gardiner's estimates

Figure 8.4 ● The pyramid of technical change (*source*: Rothwell and Gardiner, 1988)

removed from their development is the digital printer. The importance of this idea is that it seems to reinforce the multi-faceted nature of technological newness.

An invention – or technological change – which may be major in its host industry may lead to major or minor innovations in other, unrelated industries. Similarly, minor technological changes in one industry may equally change the rules of engagement in another. This in turn means that each factor, each potential area of technology, has to be monitored in order to keep a firm aware of changes which might affect its business in the future. The enormity of this task is offset by two observations. First, it is intrinsically impossible to devise mechanisms to capture every possible technological eventuality, so it is necessary for strategic vision to delineate some boundaries for technology development and conversion. Second, radical and incremental innovation are often related, since technological change, in the main, tends to be iterative rather than a one-off event. This idea is explained by Rothwell and Gardiner (1988), in their discussions of invention, innovation and re-innovation. Figure 8.4 shows how, over time, original innovations might be worked through to spawn inventions, innovations and re-innovations, which far outweigh, in numeric terms, the original breakthrough.

Thus, companies may adopt innovations from within or outside their own industries at any point along a continuum, shown in Figure 8.5.

Of course, companies who exploit this continuum are expert in what these authors call 'robust design'. That is, in the original 'new product' there is sufficient flexibility to allow the evolution of a large number of variants. Examples of this include the Ford Cortina, with four generations and the Capri spin-off, and the Boeing 747, which is continually evolving. There is a point, however, at which companies must consider departure from even these 'robust' designs, as have both Ford and Boeing. At that point, they too must look to the breakthroughs of the future, both in their own and in other industries.

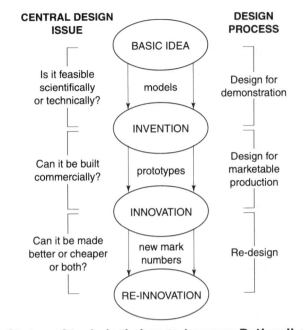

Figure 8.5 ● States of technical change (*source*: Rothwell and Gardiner, 1988)

Linking the ideas about technological change to the need to remain competitive, the necessity of integrating technology into company strategy becomes something of a truism. Truism or not, the strategic integration of technology is vital, because technological innovation has the power to propel one company into success, often at the expense of another. Eastman-Kodak, for example, ignored the first opportunities of working with Haloid, which left the stage open for a company which came to represent photocopying: Rank Xerox. Similarly, however, Canon deprived Xerox of their prime position, not exclusively through technology development, but through market development, a point to which we will return later.

A study by Harris *et al.* (1984) reported that a majority of the Fortune 1000 companies' top management acknowledged the central role of technology in competitive strategy. However, the same top management also agreed that technology was difficult to manage, and, for the most part, technology decisions were the responsibility of lower-level executives in R&D or engineering departments. Thus, technology in the Fortune 1000 companies participating in the survey is not managed in a strategic sense. Similar results to these were found by Booz, Allen and Hamilton (1982) in a study of European firms. The UK is notoriously weak in this regard. UK capital investment (as a percentage of GDP) is half that of Japan, whilst the risk-to-return ratio in UK manufacturing is unattractive to UK investors. This tends to reinforce the UK's position (and UK companies) as that of low-cost operators rather than value-adding innovators (Kruse and Berry, 1997). In short, there is a lack of technology management.

The literature on technology management is in itself copious and varied; it is beyond the scope of this book to capture anything but its basic concepts. This said, the preceding paragraphs underline the need for companies to integrate technology into their strategic context to guide the development of new products. The key roles for managing changing technology are technological forecasting, on the one hand, and the management of R&D on the other. Attention is given to each of these in turn, below.

Technology forecasting

Much of the perceived difficulty in strategic technology management centres on the question of the pace and nature of the evolution of a given technology. In short, forecasting the direction and scope of a given technology is a crucial element in technology management. A host of methods for technology forecasting exist: econometric models, expert opinions and mathematical extrapolations, to mention a few. While the detail of such techniques is not of central concern here (interested readers may refer to Wheelwright and Madrikatis (1985) for a review of forecasting methods), it is worth stating that the objective of the techniques is to predict future facets of the technology, such as its development along relevant performance measures.

The methods by which the techniques of technology forecasting seek to achieve their objectives are often based on the extrapolation of past or present trends, which is their shared weakness given the rate of technological change and the tendency towards discontinuation in technological development. Even more qualitative techniques using expert opinion are often based on observing what has occurred in the past. Indeed, there is a large body of evidence and anecdotes which bear witness to the inaccuracies of technology forecasting. For example, in the 1960s, the predictions were that AT + T's 'picture phone' would gain rapid global acceptance. The company invested heavily in the technology, believing predictions that by 1985, the market value would be around $15bn. When Xerox participated in the development of photocopying technology, 'expert opinion' predicted a total maximum annual sale of 1000 units (Schnaars, 1989)! The difficulties in technology forecasting relate to four 'grey areas':

- the difficulty in predicting a breakthrough
- the time lag between invention and innovation
- the inter-relationships among technologies which activate development
- the uncertainties regarding the diffusion of new technologies.

Predicting breakthroughs is almost an oxymoron in a practical sense. Some 'breakthroughs' are the result of a programme of technological research, such as the decade of research into antibodies that destroy fat cells in animals which has resulted in the 'injection' which can 'kill' fat (*The Times*, 16 May 1995, p. 7). On the other hand, many breakthroughs are well-known 'accidents', such as penicillin, or perhaps more prosaically, Post-It notes!

The *time lag between invention and innovation* is generally acknowledged to be shortening, but what evidence there is to support the claim is conflicting. Some studies, such as that of Giarni and Loverberge (in Twiss, 1987), suggest a pattern of shortening time lags, but results are often confounded by subjective estimates of when an invention or discovery actually took place. In Chapter 4, examples were given of times from invention to commercial exploitation of a number of products. The importance, here, however, is that in a competitive situation, a company has little guidance in deciding how quickly a discovery or invention will convert into an innovation which complicates the decisions regarding how to react strategically to the discovery. Returning to the discovery of the 'fat-killing injections', how quickly, if at all, should diet food companies react?

Cook and Morrison (1961) suggest that the time lag is shorter, the more intensely the need is felt by the potential user. Certainly, the 'need' for diet-free solutions to obesity might be most intensely felt by overfed Western populations. As we shall see in Chapters 11 and 13, however, analyzing need is no simple task.

The *interrelationships among technologies* mean that, for some discoveries or inventions to bear fruit, other related technological developments must occur. Examples include the jet engine's dependence on advances in metallurgy and, even earlier, the steam engine's need for cheap, high quality steel. Again, these distorting factors mean that the prediction of one technology's future is dependent upon a different technology. Finally, the *diffusion of new technologies*, as covered in Chapter 3, is difficult to chart, other than with the benefit of 20:20 hindsight. Again here, there may be a relationship between the need felt by the potential customer base and the diffusion of the innovation, but the need may only be satisfied given certain levels of price, which at the time of the initial invention may be prohibitive. The picture emerging thus far is that, despite the central importance of technology to the strategic direction of the firm, one of the key ways of integrating technology, namely technology forecasting, is fraught with difficulty. A variation on the theme of technology forecasting is technology spanning, which, in considering strategic development, captures many of the issues involved in dealing with technological newness.

Suggested here three core questions for technology scanning:

- What are the technologies used by our competitors?

- What technologies used in other businesses could be transferred to our business?

- What are the innovations likely to have applications in the businesses we operate in?

These questions require the coverage of a wide range of potential sources, many of which are not central to the firm's areas of business. These authors, drawing on previous research note that Japanese firms spend an average of 1.5% of sales on technology-scanning activity, which is considerably more than their US or European competitors. The investment allows them to take more immediate advantage of discovery and invention, thereby 'managing' technological change by interpreting it. To sum up on the role of technology forecasting, then, we consider this view:

> 'To raise technology to the level of strategic concern, a technologically literate and supportive top management regime is needed which views technology as a competitive weapon and regularly seeks answers to questions'

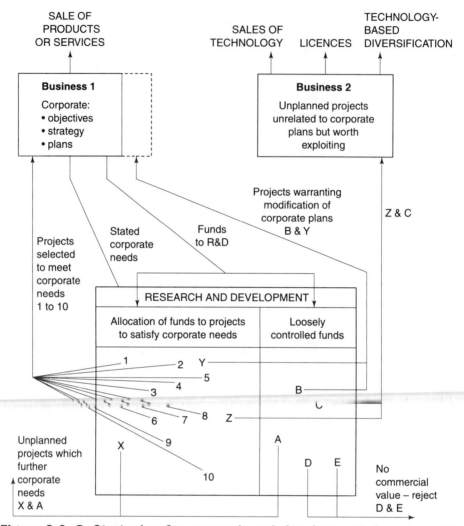

Figure 8.6 ● Strategies for research and development: investment in R&D supports two business activities

Without such an approach, even the basic decisions regarding what products to develop, let alone for which markets, can only be dealt with in a haphazard manner.

The second major issue in the management of technology focuses on how companies can actively manage discontinuities by creating them via their own R&D. The management of R&D is the subject of the next section.

Managing R&D

The way in which a firm manages research and development touches and is touched by a myriad of processes and structures: its strategic planning, organizational structure, resource allocation and development of human resources, to mention a few. The management of R&D also impinges upon a company's relationship with numerous external forces: suppliers, competitors, customers, government bodies and universities, for example. As Twiss (1990) notes, one of the central issues in R&D management is maintaining the creative flow at the same time as guiding talented R&D personnel towards corporate goals. He reconciles these somewhat opposing forces by seeing the technological company as being involved in two sets of businesses. The first (shown in Figure 8.6) is directed and defined by corporate objectives, and usually towards identified areas of market potential.

Most financial resources are set aside for these purposes (1–10 in the figure). Some projects, however, will evolve as logical extensions of these projects, or, indeed, through serendipity (X, Y, Z). In addition, some financial resource should be set aside for research of personal interest to R&D personnel (A, B, C, D, E). Without this latitude, he argues, they lose interest. All 18 projects can still be evaluated in the 'normal' way, but the important point of the figure is that the ten projects which are conceived as a result of the search to meet corporate objectives are not sidelined; they form the tenets of the company's technology strategy. 3M, a highly innovative company where over 30% of sales come from products launched within the previous four years, allows all its scientists to spend 15% of their time on projects of their own (*Management Today*, April 1997, pp. 70–2). Linking this discussion back to Chapter 1, where the relationship between products (technologies) and competitive advantage was outlined, it is important to draw the conclusion that the way in which a firm manages its R&D will have a serious impact on its competitive advantage and positioning. Outlined below are seven directions which the technology strategy might take.

- Offensive: high risk, high pay-off, develop entirely new technology
- Defensive: develop low cost base to respond to competitor innovation
- License: buy in technological know-how
- Interstition: seek the weak spot in competitors' armoury
- Create a market: increase the awareness of a new way to satisfy a need or want
- Maverick: capitalize on competitors' committed resources
- Acquisition: buy companies, their technologies or their technologists.

Arthur D Little's technology and product development division recommends that companies pursue R&D projects at four different stages of development (*Industry Week*, 16 December 1996, p. 65). Specifically the four technologies are:

- Emerging: at the earliest research stages
- Pacing: pursued by a few key competitors in a market, these give a closer indication of how they might impact on a company's business
- Key: these are held by one or two companies and dramatically differentiate products in a market
- Base: these are held by all competitors in a market and are necessary to do business.

If a company develops this mix, which represents technologies at different stages of development, then, as Taninecz (1996) claims, they plot to an S-curve over time. This allows for investment in emerging and pacing technologies, which are often abandoned before they bear fruitful new products.

The foregoing paragraphs have given the briefest of overviews into one dimension of new product strategy, namely, the technological dimension. This has been approached from the perspective of identifying the elements of technological newness. Before a company can embark upon setting a strategy for new product development, it must delineate the technological boundaries it wishes to recognize, which in turn depend on its awareness of technology forecasting and scanning and its systems for managing R&D. However, in answering the fundamental strategic question of 'what business are we in?' the technological dimension is only one element. The markets served by these technologies also need to be examined.

Market newness

With respect to newness, markets can be viewed in two ways: in relation to technologies and needs, and in relation to the firm. Although the first of these may sound similar in direction to the preceding paragraphs, it is not. It is itself linked to one of the fundamental principles of marketing, that companies should not manufacture products (a bundle of technologies) but satisfy needs. Underlying this principle is that while specific bundles of technologies might change, the needs they satisfy remain constant. Adopting this perspective allows us to view technologies as possible new ways to satisfy needs. For a technology to be accepted, it must satisfy needs, either more effectively, or as effectively, but more cheaply than its predecessor. This concept is important because it allows firms to assess the possible outcomes of alternative R&D projects. Simply put, does the technology create a 'new' market because of its qualities in satisfying needs? Take, for example, a relatively 'new market' in consumer durables: the microwave oven. Was this a new market that was created? Or was the need, or more accurately one aspect of the need (speed), better and more effectively satisfied by microwave technology?

A further point to raise in relation to the newness of markets is that, as a new technology creates a 'new market' by satisfying a need more effectively or cheaply, the initial growth rates begin to increase, leading to the increasing adoption of the new technology through the market, as covered in Chapter 5. The issue of new market growth is incorporated into the classification of new product development, which forms the basis of new product strategies covered later in this chapter. Market newness in relation to the firm describes the extent of experience a firm has with a particular market. Many products have applications across different market sectors, all or some of which might be familiar to a company. For example, electro-mechanical components such as microswitches are used in a variety of industries, and while they may be rather basic and certainly low-technology products, manufacturers of microswitches are often more familiar with sale end markets than with others. It follows, then, that there are markets – even within the definition of a product category – that are 'new' or 'unknown' to the firm. Serving these markets with a new or modified technology entails large levels of uncertainty, and therefore risk. One example of this is a small

Dutch manufacturer of radiator valves. These valves are sold by the firm, currently through building contractors, central heating installers and wholesale distributors. However, this restricts the sales potential of their products, as important market segments are being missed, including the DIY market, served through retailers. To address this market, which would be a 'new market' for the company, entails risk, not only in respect of the unknown market but also in respect of the reaction of the current market. Central to product development strategy, then, is a view of the newness to be pursued not only in technological terms, but also in market terms. Such a strategy should be drafted in order to provide direction for creativity, and to provide a rough-cut evaluation procedure which allows managers to choose among the many new product ideas that may be produced. However, it is important that markets and technologies are considered together, since they are both dynamic and influence each other. A number of useful classification schemes have been put forward, to combine these two perspectives. One of the earliest, by Johnson and Jones (1957), is reproduced in Table 8.1.

A number of more recent variations on this theme have been put forward, one of which is that by Johne and Snelson (1988), shown in Table 8.2.

The benefit of the classification of Johnson and Jones is its explicit consideration of what we can transform into statements of new product strategy. The least disruption is caused by pursuing a strategy of 'reformulation' (improving the cost/quality of existing products) while the most is caused by 'adding to classes of customers by developing new technical knowledge'. Mars is a company well known to deploy many of these strategies for new product development. Its 1995 relaunch of the 58-year-old brand 'Milky

Table 8.1 ● An early market–technology classification

	No technological change	Improved technology	New technology
No market change		*Reformulation* Usually improved cost/quality of existing products	*Replacement* Better product formulations using different technology
Strengthened market (market exploitation)	*Remerchandising* Increase sales penetration of existing markets	*Improved products extension* Provide improved product attributes to existing customers	*Product line* Applying new technology to broaden line of products offered to present customers
New market	*New use* Find new classes of customers that can utilize	*Market extension* To reach new customers by modifying present products	*Diversification* To add to the classes of customers by developing new technical knowledge

Source: Johnson and Jones (1957).

Table 8.2 ● Product development options with basis of risk and nominal risk scores

		Present technology, i.e. that used by the firm		New technology, i.e. that not yet used by the firm	
		Existing product line	New product line[+]	Existing product line[+]	New product line[++]
Present marketing, i.e. that practised by the firm	Existing customer segments	OPD	NPD[+]	OPD[+]	NPD[++]
	New customer segments[+]	OPD[+]	NPD[++]	OPD[++]	NPD[+++]
New marketing, i.e. that not yet practised by the firm	Existing customer segments[+]	OPD[+]	NPD[++]	OPD[++]	NPD[+++]
	New customer segments[++]	OPD[++]	NPD[+++]	OPD[+++]	NPD[++++]

OPD = Old product development, NPD = New product development.
[+] = Added nominal degree of risk; [++], [+++], [++++] = increasing degrees of risk.

Way' follows the 'improved products extension', by targeting a sales level designed to replace Nestlé's Smarties as the market leader in children's confectionery. As well as increased advertising the 'technology' of the product has been changed and improved: creamier chocolate on the coating and 50% more milk in the filling to make it white. Similar extensions include Mars Dark and Mars Miniatures. Moving down the uncertainty line, Milky Way Crispy Rolls represent a new configuration of technology aimed at both current and new markets (*Marketing Week*, 6 December 1996, p. 8). At the more uncertain end of the classification, adding to classes of customers by developing new technical knowledge, Mars has introduced ice-cream versions of all its major chocolate bars, and Mars drinks, and is considering adding yet more classes of customers by developing 'spreading' technology to produce chocolate spread for bread, biscuits and so on.

The classification by Johne and Snelson (1988) is useful for the way in which it articulates the varying degrees of risk in the various strategies for directing new product development. They add an extra 'layer' to technology-market newness by introducing the intermediaries of products and segments. This allows us to see that, for example, the addition of a new product line, using new technology, is every bit as risky as attracting new segments to an old product using technology the company is already familiar with. An example of the former is the move by Budweiser into the jeans market. Although the company insists that the move into quality clothing is a natural brand extension in terms of positioning in the 18–28 age group, it will have to face unfamiliar problems in quality maintenance and distribution, for example (*Marketing Week*, 7 February 1997, p. 19.) Many writers have subdivided the categories favoured by Johnson and Jones, usually without much benefit in clarity or explanatory power.

In addition to providing insights to the amount of risk involved in particular strategic directions for new product development, these classifications also indicate the comparative level of investment required. Where the technologies and markets are newer, the level of uncertainty is higher and lack of experience means that greater amounts of financial resource are required. Similarly, as a company considers the strategic new product options, from the 'top left' to the 'bottom right' of these matrices, so the level of knowledge, expertise and information required from outside the company increases. Further, the amount of co-ordination between technical (R&D) and commercial (marketing) disciplines is increased from the options in the top left of the matrix to the bottom right. Finally, newer types of product development also require more radical mechanisms, as we shall see in Chapter 8. Thus, as strategic options are considered, the classifications shed light on the scale of the operation, from finance, information and organizational perspectives.

Summary

The purpose of this chapter is to describe the variety of options available for new product development, based on the inputs of technologies and markets, which might be familiar, completely new, or somewhere in between. The degrees of newness are central to a firm's chosen strategy for product development. Technological newness has several sources and forms, all of which must be harnessed for survival, competitive advantage and, ultimately, growth.

In a similar fashion, market newness can be understood in terms of new ways to satisfy need and the familiarity of certain markets to the firm, both of which need to be understood to plan the strategic direction of new product development.

When combined, these two types of newness form the basis of the strategic chances for new product development and suggest the magnitude of the endeavour as well as the organizational issues which may be implied.

Having set out some of the key issues in new product strategy, the next chapter examines the next 'stage' in the NPP process: idea generation.

QUESTIONS

1. Why is strategy important in NPD?
2. Is invention a prerequisite for innovation? Justify your answer.
3. Is technology forecasting worth the effort, given its shortcomings?
4. Can technology be managed when it is moving so quickly in many sectors of industry and commerce?
5. Can new technology create new needs? Can it create new markets? What is the difference, if any?

6. What might be the attraction in targeting markets already served by the company with new products?

7. What might be the attraction in targeting completely new markets with new products?

Mini-case ● Microswitch International

Introduction

Microswitch International (MI) is a UK-based, medium-sized, manufacturer of industrial components, mostly microswitches, to the Heating, Ventilation and Air Conditioning market. Although the company has a solid reputation for product improvement, its longer-term survival is thought to be at risk as a majority of the functions of the micro-switch can be performed more reliably by electronic products. Although MI has the strate-gic intention and engineering skills to develop these newer technologies for a market they know well, the MD, Mr Jon Irvine, has been frequently frustrated by an apparent paralysis regarding the implementation of this strategic intention. Why is the move into this field proving difficult?

The industry market

Microswitches are bought by a variety of end customers who require customized products for their boilers, air heating/cooling units and industrial valves. Recent research carried out by MI suggests that the key buying criteria for the microswitches are the temperature rating, the sensitivity of the switch and the reliability of performance. On all counts MI rates among the top three manufacturers world-wide.

Independent industry research shows that there are three types of buying company: those who see growth in electromechanical switches; those who see the market (and their requirements) as static, and those who see the technology to be in terminal decline. The three categories of customer comprise 60%, 25% and 15% of the total market respectively.

Product development at MI

At present there are four product-market managers, each responsible for a range of microswitches to one of three markets: air conditioning, gas heating (domestic and industrial) and valve manufacturers; and one manager is responsible for new product development. Although the status of each of these managers is equal, the new product manager reports directly to the engineering director, while the other three report to the marketing director. The product-market managers are responsible for sales and profits of their products in the market, for gathering and co-ordinating market intelligence, dis-seminating this to the engineering director and liaising with the new product manager. The latter is responsible for authorization of microswitches for certain important custo-mers, as negotiated by the product market managers, and for a programme of continu-ous improvement across the range of microswitches and applications. On special projects, the marketing and engineering directors will appoint an *ad hoc* team, led by the new product manager, made up by line staff of the most appropriate product-market manager.

Development of electronic devices

Two years ago, a special 'solid state' team was set up, headed by the new product manager and further staffed by three engineers, one from each product-market area. Much of their work to date has been focused on the assessment of potential demand for electronic devices. To date, the findings suggest that:

● The function performed by the electronic–mechanical switch is simple – electronic devices may be too sensitive

● Extra precision is not often required, so the switch to electronic devices is of little benefit

● Electronics are too expensive

● Electronic replacements have been found to have problems in application

● Servicing the equipment is currently undertaken by people who are not familiar with electronic technology.

These reasons have been forwarded by the project team as reasons for taking the development slowly. However, Jon Irvine is still warned by independent market reports that emphasize the future as being electronic. In addition, it is clear from these independent sources that buyers of electromechanical switches do not see their current suppliers (including MI) as having the expertise to design and deliver reliable electronic replacements. Where electronic components are used, they are sourced in Japan, Italy and France.

Discussion questions

1. How would you react to the findings of the project team, in Jon Irvine's shoes?

2. What effect, if any, does the team structure have on MI's ability to develop improved and new products?

The information for this case was compiled from authors' private sources. Names are changed to preserve confidentiality.

chapter 9

Idea management for new product development

LEARNING OBJECTIVES

1. To introduce the concept of idea management, rather than idea generation.

2. To describe sources of new ideas.

3. To describe methods of activating sources of ideas.

4. To introduce the notion of creativity in idea management.

5. To describe some approaches to exploiting creativity.

On completion of this chapter you will:

1. Be able to collate the internal sources of new product ideas available to a company.

2. Understand how to make these sources work to produce a stream of new product ideas for the company.

3. Be able to apply numerous techniques associated with idea generation for new product development.

4. Appreciate the role of creativity in idea generation for new product development.

5. Widen your view of how to nurture and exploit creativity in the search for new product ideas.

Introduction

This chapter is the second dealing with the tasks involved in the NPD process. In Chapter 7, it was stated that the process is rarely linear, as portrayed by many of the models. It follows, therefore, that idea generation, the 'first task' in the process of bringing a new product to the market, is rarely a true beginning, set on a blank page. Before the 'first task', new product strategy and objectives have been set, all within the context of a company's strategic plan, which itself is based upon its operating, competitive and market environment. So, idea generation will be inevitably imbued with opportunities and constraints that define what can realistically be achieved. A simple example is that, without an active and resourced R&D department, radical ideas will rarely develop, nor will a company have the know-how to realize any ideas which do come to the fore. Furthermore, the results of strategic tasks of environmental scanning and market intelligence gathering should provide a fertile source of new ideas which underpins the 'idea generation' process.

As well as having no 'discrete beginning', idea generation does not stop as the NPD process unfolds. As we saw in Chapter 7, the NPD process is highly iterative. New ideas, better ideas reformulated may fall out of every stage. They do not conveniently appear in the idea generation stage only.

Ideas are not always of the same degree of newness, nor do they always apply to the product itself. To illustrate the various degrees of newness, we can look towards electronic personal organizers, where a new product may be specified as having more memory and an added feature, such as an alarm to warn of appointments. In other words the new product is a modification, as discussed in Chapter 8. Only a few years ago, however, these were new-to-the-world products! Newness affected the generation of ideas. To illustrate how ideas may not relate to the product itself, but to the process of its manufacture, let's look at food. The new ideas in irradiation for food preservation led to new food products, which may in the future challenge the traditional ways of preserving food, with sugar, salt or refrigeration. Often, ideas relating to processes of manufacture lead to the most innovative new products.

A final point in this introduction is that 'ideas' do not always have to be 'generated'. The whole process of selling corporate and new product strategies sets out ideas for development. Technologists and scientists working in research laboratories are working with ideas constantly, designers are at the creative – idea generation – heart of the organization, sales and marketing personnel are in constant contact with new ideas both from competitors and from customers. This means that, far from being 'generated', as if they do not already exist, many ideas really have to be *managed*. This chapter is about managing new ideas.

Managing new ideas involves two central themes: locating sources of new ideas and activating those sources. The chapter will review the sources of new product ideas and will examine how new product developers can activate those sources to deliver new product ideas which can be taken on to the next stage in the process.

The objective of idea generation

It is clear from previous chapters that the new product development process is fraught with risk. Failure rates among new product launches are high, but the actual number of launches emanating from new product activities is itself low, as Table 9.1 shows, based on a survey of 69 British companies carried out by the authors.

The phenomenon whereby ideas are 'killed' before ever reaching the launch phase was introduced in Chapter 8 as the 'Mortality' of new product ideas. The curves in Figure 8.1 show how many ideas are available at the start of the process, which can be subjected to evaluation, further development and further evaluation, from a variety of perspectives, including marketing, design, manufacturing, purchasing and customers. If only a few ideas begin their journey along the NPD process, then companies run the risk of killing all the new ideas because of finding them unsuitable, or, worse, letting some ideas be developed and launched which have limited market potential. On the other hand, the production of a random and indiscriminate list of ideas will absorb

Table 9.1 ● Frequency of projects and launches

Activity-based	Mean	Standard deviation
Number of R&D projects	22.6	28.6
Number of new product launches	13.4	20.6
Percentage of successful launches	72%	

much time later, as each one would be considered at the 'screening' stage. The task, therefore, of the idea generation phase is to put forward a body of *initially acceptable* ideas which can be taken on to further development and evaluation. The guidelines for deciding which ideas are initially acceptable come from the 'New Product Strategy', as we have seen in Chapter 8. The new product, in specifying new product objectives, allows developers to make judgments as to the likely potential contribution of ideas: growth, profits, gaining experience of a new technology, getting a foothold in a new market and so on. After a body of initially acceptable ideas has been produced, they will be subject to closer scrutiny at the screening stage. The link between 'idea generation', new product strategy and 'screening' is shown in Figure 9.1.

What is a new product idea?

A new product idea is, at this first stage in the process, a hypothetical suggestion which links a potential bundle of attributes with a potential market. Throughout the process these potential attributes will become more clearly specified and designed to a point where the potential of the market can be realized into sales and profits. Thus ideas, from the outset, must relate to the eventual benefits they will deliver to a set of specified potential customers. Looking back at some new products of recent years (Table 9.2) gives examples of how bundles of attributes can be matched with potential target markets.

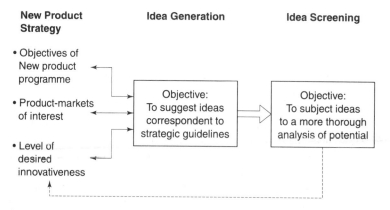

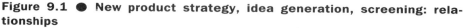

Figure 9.1 ● New product strategy, idea generation, screening: rela-tionships

Table 9.2 ● New products of the 1990s

Product idea	Attributes	Markets
Okidata.Doc.IT: Desktop fax, printer copier and document scanner	Multiple document functions Small desktop unit	Home office Small businesses
Timex Indiglo Night-Light: A watch which can be used in complete darkness	Miniature electroluminescence Non-toxic gleam Everlasting gleam	Consumers who need to clock-watch in the dark
Compaq Presario 425: Ail-in-one computer, telephone answer machine and fax modem	Multiple functions Installed WP packages Colour monitor	Home offices Business PC market

Each of the products has been successful. The Okidata.Doc, a first-to-the-market product which costs less than the sum of individual pieces, won several product-of-the-year awards. The Timex Indiglo Night-Light, a product whose glow-in-the-dark quality replicates the radium watches of the 1920s and 1930s without the lethal side-effects, was the result of a ten-year investment in miniaturizing electroluminescent technology. The new product has increased Timex revenues by 30%. The Compaq Presario was developed to be competitively priced while offering a higher level of functions. It broke industry records by selling 100,000 units in the two months following the launch. Each of these ideas represents different kinds of new product ideas. The Okidata.Doc and the Compaq Presario 425 are similar in that they combine a number of functions into a 'new' product. The former does so within the broad parameters of document creation, copying, transferring and printing, the latter within the parameters of data creation. The Timex Indiglo, on the other hand, makes use of a new, safe technology, to recapture product attributes of the past which were abandoned due to a health hazard.

All three product ideas have delivered benefits to a group or groups of customers. In other words, they are more than combinations of different or new technologies and features; those technologies and features can be translated into benefits for special customer groups. Of course, good ideas may not be developed in such a way as to deliver benefits, depending upon many factors at play throughout the development process. This said, an idea not related in any way to customer benefits is likely to face a much tougher journey towards a successful launch. Thus, the Dahon, a fold-away bicycle idea from the Hon Machinery company of Taiwan, may never be transformed into a commercially viable new product, unless its bundle of attributes (folding/unfolding quickly, comfort, strength, etc.) can be related to a market or markets which will derive benefits. This constant balancing of technologies or attributes to customer or market benefits is the *leitmotiv* of the product development process. At the idea generation stage, the balance may be swayed, depending on the source of the idea. The next section deals with the various sources of ideas.

Sources of information for new product ideas

A multiplicity of sources of information for new product ideas exist. These can be broken down into those inside and outside the company. The task facing organizations searching for new product ideas is to identify these sources, and to organize them so that they activate the flow of ideas in such a way as to direct ideas to those people charged with the responsibility for developing them into new product launches. In the next sections we will look firstly at internal, then at external sources of information. We then examine techniques for organizing and activating these sources of information, which comprise the 'techniques' of idea generation. We conclude the chapter with a more general discussion of how internal and external information can be integrated in order to manage creativity.

Internal sources of information

All major functions of the organization are potential sources of information, including research and development, design, marketing and sales, production and engineering, and technical and customer services. These are examined below.

Research and development

Many organizations employ researchers whose function is to develop, improve or integrate technologies specifically for new products. These researchers may be located in a Research and Development (R&D) unit, in an engineering or engineering design unit, or within a more general department, such as technical services. The precise definition of the unit, department or section is not of primary importance; the function of the individuals therein is to initiate (and develop) new products.

The scale of diversity in firms' R&D operations is enormous. Donprint Product Identification, a small UK manufacturer of systems and materials for identification of original equipment and components, employs a small team of chemists, whose remit is to develop ink and adhesive chemicals to a 'world-class standard' to maintain their market-leading status with international clients such as IBM, Electrolux and Digital. Dancion PLC, founded in 1978 on the basis of its founder's development of the continuous ink-jet printer, continues to build its product portfolio by employing a team of chemical engineers to develop inks in a variety of colours, edible inks, and inks visible only under ultraviolet light in readiness for expanding applications. The example of the Timex Indiglo, cited above, was based on R&D developments aimed at delivering electroluminescent solutions to light fighter–bomber cockpits. Canon's R&D centre houses 300 researchers working on leading edge technologies such as opto-electronics, super-precision controls and electron beam applications. In addition, Canon have some R&D facilities in Europe. For example, Canon Audio has established an R&D group in England, based on an innovation in what has now been termed 'wide-image stereo'. This breakthrough delivers a true stereophonic effect, without the requirement that listeners position themselves equidistant from each speaker. Canon continue to support research into this technology, which is expected to result in a range of follow-on products, such as public address systems. Such teams, departments or sections are large reservoirs of information for new products. However, it does not always follow that information residing in these reservoirs is put to profitable use, at least not immediately. IBM's drive to reassert its former dominance is being led by the development of systems which are much faster than traditional designs such as microprocessors. However, the concept behind these systems – reduced instruction set computing (RISC) – was incubated in IBM's research labs in the 1970s. IBM's failure to exploit the concept commercially gave both Sun Microsystems and Hewlett-Packard the opportunity to develop their own RISC workstations. This example emphasizes a key point of the chapter: generating ideas is not enough; companies need to organize ideas to enable them to be incorporated into new product concepts.

Marketing and sales

Since marketing and sales staff are in touch with the customer, they are an important source of information, particularly for product improvements and line extensions. For example, the launch of a range of frozen savoury pasties by Bird's Eye Walls resulted from ideas developed in the light of the growth in demand for convenient light meals, a trend monitored constantly by marketing personnel (*Marketing*, 17 March 1994, p. 5). The British retailer Marks & Spencer is testing an in-store computer, which will allow shoppers to create menus for dinner parties. The interactive terminal asks shoppers to specify the number of guests and courses, creates a menu and guides them to the right products for each recipe. Also, building on consumer trends, the company is piloting a home-delivery service. Johne (1992) describes the idea generating processes of Japanese companies such as Sony, Toyota and NEC:

> 'In these businesses, teams of specialists are engaged in studying markets in the minutest detail. The information is then fed back to see how corporate strengths can best be harnessed to the requirements of product development.' (p. 74)

A major element of Marketing's job in companies is to keep abreast of market development with a view to developing new products. For example, as the mobile phone market continues to grow, Motorola's managers intend to capitalize on growth by launching 'branded phones' with designer names and even by bringing out novelty shaped phones (*Marketing Week*, 6 December 1996, p. 6).

Where large multinational companies produce and sell in one part of the world, the ideas can be 'launched' elsewhere, as with the European roll-out by Procter & Gamble of Bounty, their top-selling US brand of kitchen towel (*Marketing Week*, 10 April 1997, p. 6).

These examples show that ideas, while they may *reside* in marketing departments, have to be organized and activated to have the chance of producing new product ideas. Thus, whilst Raleigh, the UK manufacturer of bicycles, failed to act quickly upon the growing demands for recreational cycles, US and Far Eastern suppliers were ploughing ahead with developments which could actually shape the nature of demand.

Of course, responsibility for new product ideas and their development often resides within marketing departments whose role is to monitor market trends constantly, feeding in information to new product activity. While this mode of operation is most suited to large companies with the resources necessary to meet these information collection needs, Johne (1992) contends that 'in relatively few big UK companies has responsibility for innovation been devolved upon people who are in close touch with the market' (p. 73). The way in which marketing activity searches for new product ideas is dealt with in the section on external sources of information for new product ideas.

Production and engineering

In recent years, there has been an upsurge in attention being paid to the role of manufacturing in competitiveness. With shortening product life cycles, increasing sophistication in customer tastes and needs, changing technologies and intensifying competition, it has become vital for companies to involve manufacturing in the product development process. This involvement has been regarded as necessary to speed up development cycles, to provide the capability to produce larger varieties of new products and to launch new products that are competitively priced, and reliable right from the introductory stages of their life cycles. Wheelwright and Clark (1992) describe the way in which manufacturing developments in the production of medical devices, designed to improve reliability and lower costs, also resulted in new applications of the devices and thus the treatment of a more diverse set of clinical problems and patients. Similarly, Myers and Marquis (1969) reported studies which showed that 20% of successful new products came from ideas from production. Developments in manufacturing, such as the reduction in variety of components, may well have the primary objective of rendering the production process more efficient, but may also open up opportunities for product improvement, if these ideas can be organized and activated effectively.

Customer and technical services

Potentially, ideas for new products could arise from anywhere within an organization. Purchasing and supply personnel are often privy to information about new products and technologies which can produce useful ideas for new products. Bonaccorsi and Lipparini (1994) describe the way in which the integration of suppliers into the NPD process had reduced development costs and times in a leading Italian company manufacturing machinery for food processing and packaging. Customer and technical services personnel are frequently involved with the actual use of the product, *in situ*, and are therefore exposed to problems and opportunities which might be solved or exploited by new or modified products. Potentially, any employee within the company may develop ideas, so it is important that their knowledge and suggestions be incorporated into the initial search for new ideas. At the Amoco Chemical Company, where a new ideas process has operated since 1988, a majority (49%) of 393 ideas were generated by scientists and engineers. This said, a substantial number also came from technicians and operators (22%), supervisors (12%), management (9%) and administrative staff (8%).

External sources of information

Internal sources of information for new products frequently rely on interfaces with the environment external to the company, such as customers, suppliers and technological developments. However, companies seeking to develop competitive new products will not rely solely on individuals with an interest in particular external sources of information. They will identify and monitor these sources in a proactive way. This section reviews sources of external information which can be grouped into one of the following categories:

- information from customers
- information from competitors
- information from the scientific/technological world.

Information from customers

Much of the NPD success literature, as we have seen, reinforces the association between understanding user needs and eventual new product success (Rothwell *et al.*, 1972, 1974; Maidique and Zirger, 1984). It follows, then, that at some point in the development process, customers' views on the product or service being developed should be sought and that, by dint of product use, knowledge and problems, customers will be an important potential source of ideas for future development. In the field of consumer goods, companies use this knowledge to locate gaps in the market which could be filled by new products. For example, the launch by Marks & Spencer into in-store cash machines from all the major UK high street banks is based on the inconvenience caused by the company's refusal to accept credit and debit cards (*Marketing*, 17 March 1994). The explosion in adult soft drinks results from the decline in alcohol consumption. Companies such as Coca-Cola, Pepsico, Perrier and Grand Metropolitan have introduced several products and product variants such as Aqua Libra, Fruitopia and diet colas developed to fill a gap for an adult alcohol-free cold drink. In Procter & Gamble, executives interview customers in grocery stores and some take time on the customer-services telephone service, to keep in touch with customer needs. A study commissioned by Carmaud Metalbox Closures in the market for dairy products has shown that UK shoppers would opt for glass packaging in most instances and are involved with dairy producers developing glass packs that can be reused as drinking glasses once the product has been consumed.

Research has shown that, in industrial markets, customers are a rich source of new product ideas. The seminal work of von Hippel (1978) summarized a number of previous studies in which significant percentages of new products came from customers. Boeing has included representatives from customer airlines in ideas for more fuel-efficient aircraft, while Hewlett-Packard involves customers in ideas for its laser printers (*Business Horizons*, 1992). Since then, further studies have confirmed the importance of customers in identifying ideas for new products. UB Networks Inc., Santa Clara, has instituted a customer involvement programme, now in its fourth year. Consisting of quarterly 'quality councils', the programme involves 10 to 15 vital customers from around the country, who discuss UB's plans for new products (*Industry Week*, 17 February 1997, p. 76).

Other companies combine traditional customer-analysis tools, such as user interviews, with more in-depth observation of how a customer actually uses a product. Such a company, Bose Corp, had used film to capture product usage. In one instance, the film captured a customer installing a new Bose ceiling speaker: on a ladder, holding the speaker in one hand, grasping around for tools with the other hand, while his mouth was full of screws and his eyes were blinking from ceiling-dust. The result of the film, watched by a design team, was a completely new mounting. Pavia (1991), in a sample of 118 high-technology companies, found that customers are an important source of new product ideas (Table 9.3).

In industrial markets where suppliers are in close contact with their customers, often through just-in-time delivery and materials requirements planning, there is frequent opportunity for discussing new products and how they might improve customer performance.

Of course, obtaining ideas from customers is not always appropriate, especially where customers are unable to think of new ways in which needs and desires might be satisfied. The often-cited example of the Sony Walkman, a huge success developed without direct reference to customers, stands as a testimony to the skills of researchers and

Table 9.3 ● Customer-related new product idea items[1]

Statement	Percentage of respondents who 'Agree' or 'Strongly Agree'
The following situation occurs in our firm: a customer states a need or a problem but does not have a particular solution in mind. Our firm finds a solution to the problem and sells the product to the customer	69%
Our new product ideas come from discussions with our customers	67%
The following situation occurs in our firm: a customer states a need or a problem along with a specific solution he has identified. Our firm then produces the 'solution' and sells the product to the customer	40%
Our firm maintains a database of potential products and their potential customers	38%
Our employees submit written reports when potential new products are suggested during client contacts	27%

[1] On a five-point Likert Scale – 5 means 'Strongly Agree' and 1 means 'Strongly Disagree'.
Source: Pavia (1991), p. 23.

designers whose acumen leads to the development of products with huge market appeal. This said, the Sony Corporation still deploys business teams studying markets in detail so that the information can be fed back into new product development. In addition, to match famous new product success stories there are also the failures, also developed without reference to customer needs, such as Sinclair's infamous C5, battery-operated automobile. Finally, user relevance *per se* is not enough to guarantee the success of a new product, since competitors will also develop such new products. It is important, therefore, to ensure that new product ideas have a competitive perspective, that is, a potential competitive advantage. Indeed, information for new product ideas often comes from competitors, a source which is discussed below.

Information from competitors

New product strategies serve the purpose of directing development activities in such a way as to capitalize on market opportunities. This necessitates a competitive perspective, since market needs may be currently or potentially served by competitors who will defend their positions. Therefore, identified opportunities should have explicit reference to the current or future presence of competitors, and companies must decide whether this competition can be successfully attacked. Such a perspective does not necessarily mean that a company must restrict itself to its current technologies, products and markets. A classic example of a successful competitive product development is that of Canon's entry into the copier market. Canon carried out a thorough analysis of the office equipment market in Europe and the US, and, based on their information, designed a range of products which were not only cheaper and more reliable than the competition, but simpler, too, to allow them to be distributed by a wide network of office equipment retailers. Their major competitors, Xerox, relied heavily on a direct sales force (Johne 1992). Thus, Canon's ideas during the development of their new range of products were inspired by the products and methods of their competitor as well as by the market. In the equally highly competitive leisure-transport markets, a careful audit of how competitors were dominating the sector allowed Land Rover to launch the 'Discovery'. In response to the launches of the Mitsubishi Shogun, the Daihatsu Fourtrak and the Toyota Landcruiser, to mention but a few, Land Rover began development work on their own mid-market four-wheel drive, aimed at the leisure market. Compared to the Japanese products, which research showed to be weak in terms of their interior comfort and fittings, as well as storage, the Discovery was developed to provide the comfort normally associated with a passenger car. Thus, analysis of the competitors, who had developed the market, helped to guide both the direction and the detail of a new product for Land Rover.

Underlying this approach, the debate about whether or not to take an 'innovator or follower' position rages. At the idea generation stage, such a debate is not directly relevant, since the leader–follower issue is strategic. In addition, even leaders cannot afford to ignore the benefits offered by competitors and so details about competitive offerings are an important source of ideas to be countenanced by a new product programme.

Specific techniques for gleaning information about competitive products are covered later in this chapter. Below, we turn to sources of technological information for new product ideas.

Information from the scientific/technological world

In Chapter 8, the need for companies to take cognizance of technological developments in their own and adjacent industries was introduced. This wider scanning of technology is fraught with difficulty, as examples in Chapter 8 have shown. However, faced with the need to bring forth new ideas for development, companies have a number of sources to which they might look, including:

● scientists and research institutes

● universities

● patents

● licensing

● government report/agencies

● trade associations

● technological consultants

● databanks.

The following examples show how external technology can be used to bolster product development.

The earlier example of Domino Printing Sciences is a UK success story built on an original technique developed by a US scientist. Although the application of the technique formed the basis of the company's success, the technological development originated elsewhere.

Specialised Laboratory Equipment (SLE), a small manufacturing company, turned to a development from within a medical school to revive its fortunes. The company manufactures electro-encephalograph (EEG) machines, used for measuring electrical impulses within the brain, and infant ventilators. The former products were inferior compared to newer technologies, and infant ventilator sales were affected by recession. However, the licensing of a new piece of technology enabled ventilators to be produced without a valve, delivering inspiratory gases at a higher rate. The company paid £20,000 for the licence and was required to pay a small royalty on every sale.

It is not only small companies, however, that look beyond their own immediate resources for new technologies. Ericson, the Swedish computing and telecommunications company, NCR Corporation and Merck Sharpe and Dohme have all made use of ideas from a small technological consultancy called the Technology Partnership. In addition to these sources, information for new product ideas may equally come from suppliers, or distributors and agents. Suppliers developing their own new products may produce ideas which can be incorporated into new products.

Channels of distribution and the services they offer are increasingly involved with manufacturers seeking to deliver total 'bundles of benefits'. For example, Commodore Business Machines delegated its repair and service to its delivery channel, Federal

Figure 9.2 ● Sources of information for new product ideas

Express. This kind of 'service innovation' requires close working with channel members to pinpoint the opportunities.

All sources of information, both external and internal, benefit from organization, not only to activate them in a systematic way, but also to guard against information over-load and to ensure a flow of information from which ideas can be developed. Figure 9.2 depicts the various sources of information discussed thus far.

The figure shows the potential for information overload and, if each source were to be activated successively, the process would be time-consuming, in an era where speed is an increasing component in new product success. Before proceeding, therefore, to the various techniques for activating the information sources, it is vital for companies to consider which of the sources are most salient for their needs.

The next section considers techniques for activating sources of information.

Techniques for activating sources of information

In many books and articles dealing with new product idea generation, it is the tech-niques which dominate. This is not surprising, given the number of techniques which exist. It is less clear, however, what proportion of these techniques are used in reality. A study of idea generation of 245 of the largest companies in the UK (Sowery, 1987) showed that the 10 most popular 'techniques' used were as follows:

  1. Competitors' visits

2. Store visits
3. Overseas store visits
4. Market analysis
5. Overseas trade magazines
6. Overseas sister company visits
7. Overseas exhibitions
8. Trade magazines
9. R&D department
10. Consumer group discussions.

A study of 118 high-technology US firms showed that informal discussions between personnel and inter-departmental meetings were vitally important to new product idea generation. Table 9.4 shows the results.

Results such as these would suggest that the wide variety of techniques available

Table 9.4 ● Importance of techniques for new product identification[1]

Technique	Percentage of respondents who rated technique vitally or quite important
Informal discussions between personnel	79%
Staff meetings which include both engineering and marketing/sales personnel to focus specifically on new products	63%
Attending trade shows and conferences	47%
Continuing education and training for employees	40%
An in-house database of customer contacts and potential new products	36%
The yearly strategic plan	36%
A person or group that is responsible for systematically scanning new technological developments in journals, trade publications, etc.	34%
Discussions with other firms in the industry	28%
Marketing research or industry surveys	17%
Obtaining licenses for new products	13%
Acquiring new firms or products	12%
Backwards engineering	12%

[1]On a five-point Likert Scale – 5 means 'Vitally Important' and 1 means 'Not Important'.
Source: Pavia (1991) p. 23.

tends not to be routinely adopted by management. In our discussion, therefore, we concentrate on the most commonly cited, grouping them as follows:

- techniques for activating *internal* sources only
- techniques for activating *both* internal and external sources
- techniques for activating external sources only.

Techniques for activating internal sources only

Job rotation

In an effort to encourage interdisciplinary communication, job rotation also benefits from encouraging a fresh approach. Either the system is fully flexible, with employees serving fixed periods of time in each department or section, or individuals are seconded to a development team for a specific period. The expectation is that, coming from a different perspective, individuals are not bound by the history, procedures or personalization of a given department.

Company suggestion schemes

If, as Majaro (1992) suggests, it takes 60 ideas to attain one successful innovation, then ideas are precious and companies should try to avoid the situation where ideas cannot get out. The aim of company suggestion schemes is to encourage people to come forward with their ideas, and therefore it is important that the scheme is actively communicated to employees, and that ideas, once received, are given due consideration. Sowery (1984) suggests six guidelines to ensure that schemes are seen to be fair (see Table 9.5).

Majaro (1992) cites 'poor promotion of the scheme' as one of seven reasons why company suggestion schemes do not appear to be effective. The other six reasons are shown in Table 9.6.

Company think tank

The philosophy behind the think tank is that intelligent people, working together in concentrated sessions, are more likely to develop creative solutions to problems facing

Table 9.5 ● Managing company suggestion scheme

1.	A special form could be made available at some central point, say Reception.
2.	Suggestions should go through one point of contact.
3.	An acknowledgment should be sent to the person submitting the idea.
4.	If the suggestion is not accepted, the reason should be given in writing directly to the person concerned. There is nothing worse for morale than a cold rejection slip.
5.	A scheme of awards should be clearly stated.
6.	Ideas should be reviewed by a committee and not by an individual if the scheme is to appear fair.

Table 9.6 ● Reasons for failure of company suggestion schemes and some ways of avoiding them

Reason for failure	Overcoming the reason
Lack of motivation	<ul><li>If employees are not motivated to be creative in a company which needs to be innovative, there is a serious value and cultural problem which needs to be tackled</li><li>Institute awards (not rewards) for creativity</li><li>Feed creativity into career development</li></ul>
Lack of feedback	<ul><li>Acknowledge all suggestions</li><li>Explain why ideas are accepted/rejected</li></ul>
Poor screening system	<ul><li>Criteria for acceptance or rejection of ideas should be clearly stated</li><li>The process and people involved in the choice should be known</li></ul>
Lack of tangible payoffs	<ul><li>Implement some suggestions regularly</li><li>Communicate the implementation</li></ul>
Negativity towards others' ideas	<ul><li>Word rejections carefully, so as not to make a general rejection (e.g. idea not compatible with company policy)</li></ul>
'Not invented here' syndrome	<ul><li>Avoid and reject negativity based on unfamiliarity or source of ideas</li></ul>

Source: Adapted from Majaro (1992).

the organization. Think tanks are generally, but not exclusively, composed of people from a managerial level. They are often used at a strategic level within companies, rather than for the purposes of generating new product ideas. At either level, a clearly defined set of objectives is vital to guide the selection of participants and to set their remits. The objectives must be framed in such a way as to be achievable; thus, in the context of idea generation, they may well be derived from the new product strategy statement. For an excellent, detailed review of how to manage a think tank, see Majaro (1992).

Invention groups

These are a less lofty alternative to think tanks, wherein a sample of employees are chosen from a cross-section of departments. Such a group may often work off-site for a number of days, with the specific remit of producing ideas for new products. The group is sent away to benefit from being released from day-to-day minutiae, which are often seen as counter-creative. Clearly, the interface between this type of group and a new products committee or department must be clearly thought out, to avoid conflict or duplication.

Techniques for activating internal and external sources

In this section, there are, potentially, scores of techniques; we concentrate on the most common, which fall into one of the following groups:

- brainstorming-type techniques
- product-centred techniques
- market-based techniques
- scenario analysis.

The techniques covered by each of these groups can be used with company employees (hence, internal), consumers, customers, distributors, exports, suppliers and so on (hence, external).

Brainstorming and brainstorming-type techniques

Brainstorming is a procedure whereby groups of individuals focus on an issue – idea generation – and use their brains to show the problem. It is a method used to foster intuitive thinking, where individuals are encouraged to use others' ideas to trigger and develop their own. Potentially, brainstorming can be used for a number of purposes; however, our concern is for its value in generating new product ideas. It is founded on a number of principles which are set to encourage creativity.

1. Deferral of judgment. The atmosphere to be encouraged in brainstorming is that of free-wheeling thoughts, where rejection of ideas is eschewed in favour of producing a large number of ideas, as quickly as possible.

2. Group idea building. As it is a technique based on intuition, associations of ideas are to be encouraged. This means that all the group members must be able and willing to listen to one another.

3. Multi-disciplinary composition. In order to encourage new perspectives and cross-fertilization of ideas, the group should be composed of individuals from several functions within the company. Where the group is composed of consumers, as well as or instead of employees, they should come from different consumer segments. Osborne (1963), who is recognized as the originator of the technique, suggests that a group should consist of a leader, an associate leader who performs the role of scribe, about five regular 'core' members and five guest members. Research has shown that four to seven members may achieve best results (Schlicksupp, 1977), but, as Majaro (1992) says, there is no magic number, and the leader should choose a group size that is comfortable to work with. A final point in relation to group composition relates to seniority: it is important not to include individuals ranked significantly 'higher' than other members, as this can hinder the latter's freedom to contribute, since an element of judgment may be inferred.

4. Quantity is the main aim. The more ideas produced, the greater the probability that a really original idea will emerge. This condition reinforces 'deferred judgment'. However, ideas are not described in detail at this stage.

5. Duration. There is no ideal time limit to be set. Sowery (1987) suggests that after the warm-up, the session should last between 20 and 45 minutes. Waddell (1990) suggests a ten-minute warm-up, followed by 30–35 minutes of discussion. Majaro (1992) suggests that if, after a warm-up of 20 minutes, and a further 20 minutes of brainstorming proper, fewer than 50 ideas have emerged, it is time to restart, beginning with a further warm-up.

Although concern has been expressed about the usefulness of the technique, where it has been deemed unsuccessful this is often due to a violation of one of the above principles, or because either the topic is inappropriate, or the leader does not prepare the session adequately.

Topics have to be well-defined and have to be focused on problems or opportunities which can be resolved or exploited in numerous ways. Typically, in brainstorming, the activity is focused on one question only. It is important, therefore, that this question is the right one, and that its wording is integrated in the same way by all participants. The question should not require expertise of a technical nature which is outside the experience of the group members.

In addition to classical brainstorming, there are a number of derivatives. These, taken from Geshka (1983), include:

1. Negative brainstorming. Carried out in two sessions, the first collects all the negative aspects of a new product idea or ideas and the second focuses on improvements to the weakest issues.

2. Brainwriting. Also based on association, participants do not communicate orally, but write their ideas down on paper, which is then circulated. The idea is to avoid the influence of dominant personalities in the group, but the technique may hinder the associative richness produced by verbal discussion.

3. Discussion 66. A relatively large group is divided into smaller teams of six people who brainstorm for six minutes, before the main group reassembles to present and discuss results. Again, this variant is used to reduce the influence of dominant personalities.

4. Method 635. Six persons brainstorm to produce three ideas in five minutes. The ideas are written down and passed to the next group, where association will be developed. This technique focuses discussion on a smaller number of ideas and maximizes variations on the basic themes.

5. Brainwriting pool. Participants write down four ideas on a sheet of paper which is placed in a central pool. They then pick from the pool, adding ideas to the bottom of the list until they run out of ideas, when they exchange sheets of paper. Other techniques which are based on this principle include 'card circulating' and the gallery method. In the former, each participant writes down one idea on a card and passes it on to his or her neighbour who can use it for further stimulation. With the latter method, it is the participants who walk from one card to the next.

6. Collective notebook method. A group of 8–10 participants are asked to put down ideas in a notebook, writing down at least one idea per day. After a week or so, notebooks are exchanged, allowing the associations to begin. This process continues for about four weeks.

Product-centred techniques

Like brainstorming, product-centred techniques may be used by people inside the company, or with groups of customers/consumers.

Attribute analysis

Attribute analysis covers a number of techniques whose objective is to evolve product improvements and line extensions. Their premise is simple: products are systems of attributes, including *features* which perform a series of *functions* which must deliver *benefits*. Any one, or any combination, might be altered to produce a revised product and a revised set of benefits. However, there is a danger that focusing on features alone will result in product differentiation which is not tailored to achieving a marketable improvement. If we take, for example, basic scissors, we can see the following features:

1. Two pieces of steel
2. A riveted joint in the centre
3. Loops in the steel at one end of each piece
4. Blades on the facing edges at the other end of each piece
5. Loops painted
6. One loop larger than the other.

Not all features have concomitant functions and benefits, for example the loops in the scissors are painted, which has no particular function but delivers an aesthetic benefit. The riveted joint, on the other hand, fixes the blades at such a position to allow a cutting action to take place, thus delivering both function and benefit. The various functions and benefits of each feature are listed in Table 9.7.

Any one of these attributes might be changed. For example, loops may be plastic-coated, for extra comfort. Most of the techniques described in this section deal with a mix of the attributes described above; the three principal ones are attribute listing, value analysis and morphological analysis.

1. *Attribute listing*, also called dimensional analysis, focuses on features, although, as has been noted above, benefits cannot be ignored if the resultant new product ideas are to be marketable. The technique is concerned with stripping down the basic

Table 9.7 ● Functions and benefits of each feature of scissors

	Feature	Function	Benefit
1.	Two pieces of steel	Handles to grasp Blades to cut	One-handed cutting
2.	A riveted joint in the centre	Allows blades to close and open	Cutting action performed
3.	Loops in the steel at one end of each piece of steel	Allow tool to be held	Comfort, ease of use, safety
4.	Blades on the facing edges at the other end of each piece of steel	Cutting	Cutting
5.	Loops painted	None	Aesthetic appeal
6.	One loop larger than the other	Allows grip of more than one finger	Comfort, ease of use

product to expose its constituent parts, whereupon changes to these parts are considered. As an example, we can take a basic product like a baby's feeding bottle, listing items like:

(a) a cylindrical plastic vessel

(b) vessel neck threaded

(c) a rubber teat, with a hole

(d) a plastic, circular, threaded cap

(e) a plastic disk

(f) a plastic, snap-on top.

To devise a new type of bottle, any one of these items might be changed. Attributes lead to questions, leading to ideas. Must the vessel be cylindrical? In fact, in the case of the shape, new forms have been introduced as easier to hold. Similarly, teats are also made from longer-lasting silicone. The overall shape of the bottle could be changed for easier cleaning. Thus the changes in features have some link to benefit, although changes to the basic features have been incorporated by some manufacturers. Newer ideas might be, for example: do the vessel neck and cap have to be threaded? Could the bottle be closed with a snap-on action?

2. *Value analysis*. Although primarily associated with cost reduction, this technique is a form of attribute listing which, by focusing on the cost of features, materials and so on, can help identify new or improved product ideas.

3. *Morphological analysis*. A third technique concerned with physical attributes. Again, it is based on listing attributes, and related benefits and situations describing customer use. These are then rearranged into different combinations. Data concerning benefits and customer use come from consumers, by means of research. A hypothe-

Table 9.8 ● Materials, shapes and locations of use

Handle material	Head material	Shape	Locations
Plastic	Plastic	Cylindrical	Home
Wood	Sponge	Pyramidal	Office
Minimum	Floss/tape	Collapsible	Travelling

tical example to illustrate this concerns oral hygiene. Table 9.8 shows the materials and shapes for equipment together with some hypothesized locations of use. From the matrix, we can pick out examples of existing products. For example, a plastic handle, a plastic head and a cylindrical shape for home use is the 'normal' style for a toothbrush. We can also generate new ideas: wooden, dental tape, collapsible, for travelling might prove a useful tool to encourage daily flossing of teeth. Although this example is based on a consumer product, the technique can equally be used by industrial goods companies. In fact, the technique originated in development work for what eventually became the jet engine (Zwicky, 1969).

Analogy

Just as morphological analysis juxtaposes attribution and features of use in unexpected ways, analogy can be used to see, more indirectly, unusual combinations of features, benefits, location of use and so on. Use of analogy is also related to brainstorming, in that it is a technique which is based on intuitive association. The derivation of the word is Greek, meaning joining together apparently unconnected elements. The technique is based on two parameters: making the strange familiar, and making the familiar strange. The result of this is to force solutions, since it is hypothesized that the mind will rearrange unfamiliar patterns into acceptable, more familiar ones. Sowery (1987) describes four analogies for making the familiar strange.

1. Personal analogy: personal identification with the elements of a problem and role playing release the individual from viewing the problem in terms of its previously analyzed elements. For instance the group might consider: 'What would I feel like if I were a closure on this wide-necked bottle?'.

2. Direct analogy: considering analogies in nature such as the human mouth or a clam to solve the problem of creating a new type of closure for a bottle. Biology in particular tends to be a rich source of relevant analogies.

3. Symbolic analogy: using recognized images, which might be aesthetically pleasing though technically impossible, to describe the problem, for instance perceiving the closure in terms of the door to Ali Baba's cave.

4. Fantasy analogy: wish fulfilment involving the best of all possible worlds, for instance imagining how in our wildest fantasies we might desire the closure to operate.

Sessions using analogies and synectics as a way of generating new ideas are organized in much the same way as brainstorming, lasting 45 to 60 minutes. Group members number five or six, with two leaders, one for administration and one for guiding the actual session. The analogies are proposed once the 'initial problem' is stated. Prince (1970) gives numerous examples of problems that might be dealt with.

Although the formalized technique may appear to be stretching the horizons of believability and pragmatism, it should be remembered that it intends to manage a phenomenon many would consider unmanageable: creativity. However, evidence that the human mind can and does operate on the level of analogy can be found in the example of Georges de Mestral, who found burdock seed heads sticking to his clothing. On closer examination, he discovered the seed heads contained tiny hooks which he used as the basic analogy to develop what we recognize today as Velcro.

Forced relationships

Zander and Ziegler described how the consideration of the relationship between normally unrelated products can help unlock chains and free associations which might lead to new product ideas. The combination of the unexpected may reveal new patterns worth exploring.

The array of potential product-centred techniques is vast, and their methodology for application is varied. Majaro (1992) provided an in-depth discussion of the details of morphological analysis. Further, there are several techniques associated with mapping products in relation to one another. However, as they usually require an amount of customer input and are concerned not with changing the mix of attributes within any one product, but rather with gauging the potential gaps in the product/market, they are dealt with below, under market-based techniques.

Market-based techniques

In this section we examine gap analysis, the repertory grid technique and the House of Quality. These approaches have a common goal when related to idea generation: they help build up a picture of the way in which products relate to one another, from a customer's point of view. They do exhibit differences which largely concern the way the data used to build the pictures is collected and analyzed. In addition, whilst the techniques reveal unfulfilled needs in a product-market category, thereby facilitating the task of idea generation, they can also be used further on in the NPD process, in particular at the concept development stage, to fine-tune the features and benefits of a proposed new product.

Gap analysis

Gap analysis encapsulates several techniques, including perceptual mapping, non-metric mapping and determinant mapping. These are introduced in this chapter as idea generation techniques, but, as with repertory grids and the House of Quality, because they focus on perceptions of product qualities and their match with market perceptions or needs, they can be reused at the concept development stage, when ideas are refined into more specific concepts. The underlying objective is to provide a 'map' of a product-market category, based on dimensions perceived to be of importance. These dimensions

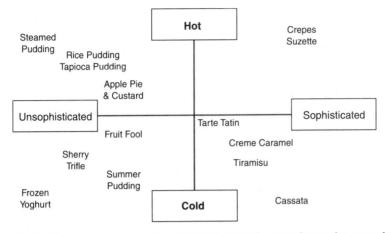

Figure 9.3 ● The dessert market (hypothetical – not based on real data)

are described on bipolar scales. Dimensions which might be relevant for the dessert market could be cold–hot, healthy–unhealthy, traditional–non-traditional. With *perceptual mapping* both buyers and users of a product describe their view of the attributes that products within a specific category may have. Thus, a total picture of the dessert market according to the customers can be created. Let us, for example, look at European desserts and map them according to a (hypothetical) view of the market along two dimensions shown in Figure 9.3: hot–cold and sophisticated–unsophisticated.

According to this map, there is a more obvious 'gap' in the market in the realm of hot, sophisticated desserts which might turn out to be worth exploiting. Moreover, with perceptual mapping, the dimensions used should be of importance to the customer. In other words, during the data collection exercise, the dimensions themselves should be derived from the respondents, prior to being used to rate the various products. This would seek to ensure that any gaps identified would be of importance to the customer. In order to identify those dimensions of importance, a qualitative stage of data gathering is required. Face-to-face, individual interviews, or focus groups interviews, where groups of six to eight individuals talk about product dimensions in relation to their experience and needs, are both excellent methods by which to unearth both individual and shared opinions. Once elicited, a second stage of measuring how different products rate on each dimension takes place. This will typically be carried out using structured interviewing (either face-to-face or via the telephone) or using a mail questionnaire. The emphasis on the second stage is on counting *how many* people feel *what degree* of agreement with the now pre-specified dimensions.

A number of key dimensions may have been identified at the first stage and measured at the second stage. It is possible to represent two or three dimensions on any one map, but how is the selection of dimensions to be presented on the map(s) carried out? Those thought to be most important in differentiating among products are of greatest use in identifying opportunities because they will reveal 'gaps' in attributes perceived by the market. Several methods are available to effect the identification of the key dimensions, once they have been 'measured', including managerial judgment, customer-sort, factor and cluster analysis. Detailed discussion of these techniques is beyond the scope of this book. Griffin (1989), however, compares and discusses the results of the first two.

Non-metric mapping

Non-metric mapping can be seen as an 'easier' version of perceptual mapping, where consumers rank products in a category according to preference, or the extent to which they find products similar. The rankings given are analyzed by customer, or by groups of customers, to produce a 'proximity matrix', showing how closely products lie in relation to one another, which can then be mapped. A hypothetical, non-matrix map of the soft drinks market is shown in Figure 9.4.

The managerial task is of labelling the axes. Here we see a hypothetical similarity between Aqua Vitae, a still 'health' drink, and Pepsi Max, a diet cola, with canned ice tea (Liptonice) being viewed as similar to regular colas. Clearly one dimension is not 'carbonation'. What might they be – newness on the market for the horizontal axis? Unlikely, with Liptonice being introduced in 1994. Looking at the vertical axis might be somewhat more straightforward. Perrier, San Pellegrino and fruited spring waters all appear in the upper quadrants, suggesting an association with the amount of flavouring. Deciding the parameters may be an intricate element in non-metric mapping, but the technique has two advantages over its cousin, perceptual mapping. First, it allows consumers to use the same type of criteria as they would when evaluating products for purchase, something they may not articulate accurately in the perceptual mapping procedure. Further, as similarities are often based on *preference*, it aims to identify gaps which, by definition, are most or least preferred. Determinant gap maps are typically prepared by managers using their ratings of *known* factors. These known factors must be both differentiating and important, criteria ideally established by previous market research. Two factors consumers used to discriminate mints are strength and crunchiness. The various mints available in the UK are shown in Figure 9.5.

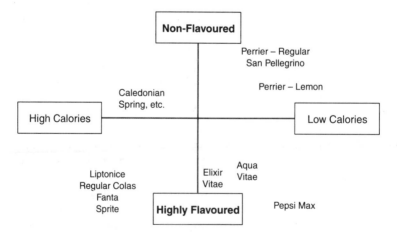

Figure 9.4 ● The soft drinks market

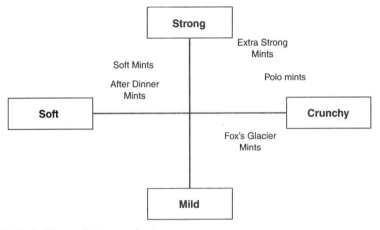

Figure 9.5 ● The mints market

Repertory grid technique

Although the repertory grid technique has a variety of applications in market research, its focus on similarities and dissimilarities among products allows the identification of 'gaps' in a given product-market category. Based on individual interviews, consumers are asked to evaluate brands in gaps of three, selecting two which are similar and one which is dissimilar. Explanations for similarities and dissimilarities are also elicited. This sequence is repeated until a complete list of brands within a product category are evaluated in triplet form. The explanation allows the analyst to derive 'constructs' which describe the way in which consumers relate to brands and evaluate them comparatively. Once all the relevant constructs have been described by consumers, a 'grid' can be constructed which represents their attitudes to the product category and which notes the ratings given to products according to those attitudes. When a number of grids are examined concurrently, common constructs emerge, expressed in the words used by the consumers, which can be used to depict the product-market, once again in map form.

Quality Function Deployment

The House of Quality, introduced in Chapter 7, describes a complete methodology for NPD, known as 'Quality Function Deployment' (QFD). Its underlying premise is that of linking the various functions in NPD via 'the voice of the customer'. It is comprised of four 'houses', the first being the most relevant for new product ideas, as it attempts to link customer needs to product attributes. Its linchpin, therefore, is the identification of customer needs, for which it uses several data collection methods, including in-depth personal interviews and group discussions. This process results in the articulation of between 200 and 400 needs, which are then categorized into primary and secondary needs. Primary needs describe the qualities sought by customers, whilst secondary needs describe attributes customers use to judge the qualities. At this level, attribute identification can be compared to that used in perceptual mapping. By way of an example, if the 'freshness' of a soft drink is a primary need, then associated secondary needs might be the colour, sweetness, bitterness and so on. Tertiary needs, which are also called operational, provide the type of detail needed by the development team to satisfy the secondary need. For example, the colour of the soft drink may be judged by transparency, the lack of 'fruit fibers' or effervescence. Once these needs have been categorized, they are ordered by level of importance to the customer.

The focus of gap analysis described above, as well as those in the House of Quality, are useful for identifying where gaps arise in the market, but are, at best, only weakly related to the strength of *demand* for products to fill the gap. Although non-metric mapping, when based on preference ranking, may indicate likely demand where gaps exist, the assumption is not explicitly examined by the technique. Further, if NPD were based exclusively on gaps in the *existing* product market, then firms would ignore newer technologies which might bring about new means of delivering satisfaction where there are currently no gaps. Not only does this force perceptual product modification, it opens companies to the risk of being superseded by others who do change the structure of the product-market via new technologies. The fundamental issue underlying this weakness is that of focusing on current solutions to current needs and not how those needs arise. The final set of techniques which may use the inputs of consumers and employees alike are scenario-based.

Scenario-based techniques

In this section, three variants are discussed: activity analysis, problem analysis and scenario analysis. *Activity analysis* involves a detailed examination of customer activity in a field of interest to a manufacturer. The activities analyzed may be quite specific, such as opening a packet of biscuits, or may be related to a wider 'set' of activities, such as gardening, or entertaining at home. In industrial markets examples of a specific task might be assessing warehouse storage or manoeuvring earth-moving equipment, while a wider set of activities might be 'office working' or installing heating, ventilation and air-conditioning (HEVAC) equipment. While the data might be collected by direct observation, video recording, self-completion diaries and interviewing may also be used.

Problem analysis is similar to activity analysis, but focuses exclusively on making an inventory of problems and analyzing them for solutions. Experienced customers are used to build a list of the problems experienced when using a particular product type, which are then ranked according to their severity. Again the methods for data collection are varied, including face-to-face interviews, direct observation, diaries, or setting up a user panel. Role play may also be useful, as in the case of the development of the wide-necked ketchup bottle. Users were asked to role-play the application of the condiment to a plate. The action that followed underlined how difficult consumers found getting 'just the right amount' onto the plate, as in anticipation of tasting their meal, complete with ketchup, they banged impatiently on the bottom of the bottle. The result – usually four times the amount of ketchup required – could be avoided by a wider-necked bottle. Both activity or problem analysis are locked into the present: they require analysis of current problems and current activities. This makes them vulnerable in the same way as gap analysis.

The next technique is *scenario analysis*, which tries to focus attention on the future, say 20 years ahead. For example, will the use of the private car be viewed in the anti-social terms of drink-driving or smoking cigarettes today? If so, what will the implications be for car, and other manufacturers? Will only 'clean' or 'green' cars be acceptable? Will there be a resurgence in efficient, reliable and comfortable public transport? Will this hasten the trend in 'teleworking' from home? Clearly visualizing scenarios does not directly produce a new product, but, by suspending the conditions of life, work, leisure and so forth that influence our behaviour and consumption *today*, it helps to identify the problems of tomorrow, which have to be solved.

Like others in this section, scenario-based techniques are used to activate sources of information which may reside in or outside a company. The last section in this chapter to deal with indicating sources of information for new product ideas describes the ways in which managers can integrate ideas from outside the company into the idea stage of the NPD process.

Techniques for activating external sources only

In this short section, we deal with supplier contact, the role of trade shows, and finally customer contact. As was outlined earlier in this chapter, there are several sources of information for new product ideas outside companies. In industrial markets, the most important of these is customers. The work of von Hippel (1978) and, more recently, Foxall (1988) gives evidence of the wealth of ideas residing in customers' factories and offices, ideas which are developed as much by customers as by manufacturers. How can ideas from customers be encouraged to emerge? Clearly, close customer contact is a prerequisite, which should not be confined to those solely involved in the purchase process. Taking a wider view of the customer, their own businesses, processes, systems and personnel can be a useful way of triggering new product ideas. This needs, however, to be done systematically, via visits which are focused in purpose.

As for customers, suppliers also have a role in the supply of ideas for new products. Bonaccorsi and Lipparini (1994) discuss the evolving nature of manufacturer–supplier levels throughout the whole NPD process, and identify that at idea generation both informal networking and direct formal requests for information will be deployed. Thus, the need to establish systematic links with customers is paralleled by the need to establish systematic links with suppliers.

Naturally, serendipitous developments may be brought by either to the attention of the development team, but the active pursuit of idea sources allows a company to gather more quickly a battery of new product ideas which can be screened for potential.

Attending trade shows and conferences is a fairly basic element in most companies' market intelligence. Although by the time a competitive new product is being shown officially, the trends and facts gleaned from attending such events, together with the opportunity to question the market and suppliers alike, make them a valuable source of information to support new product idea generation.

This section has shown the multitude of 'techniques' available for the activation of sources of new product ideas. They are varied in nature, from the informal visits described above, to complicated methodologies for researching customer need.

Table 9.9 ● Sources of new product ideas

Identification process	Internal sources of ideas	External sources of ideas
Formal	● R&D ● The strategic plan ● Organized creativity techniques like brainstorming	● Marketing research ● New product consultants ● Industry studies
Informal	● *Ad hoc* ideas from anywhere in the organization ● Ideas arising during day-to-day meetings and discussions	● Customer suggestions ● Casual conversations ● Response to competitors' products

Source: Pavia (1991).

However, there are several studies which show the extent to which these techniques are used by companies. McGuinness (1990) studied the new product idea activities of nine large industrial companies. A total of 34 'search processes' were examined, revealing that a majority of ideas were largely 'unplanned', that is, initiated by voluntary individual efforts, rather than by formal planning, echoing the earlier findings of Myers and Marquis (1969), Feldman and Page (1984) and More (1984). Pavia (1991), in discussing sources of information, gives evidence of the types of techniques used (see Table 9.9) and reported that the great majority of firms rely on informal processes to identify new products.

Finally, Sowery (1989) reports results from a survey of 95 UK companies, showing that the top ten techniques or sources considered to be most productive for ideas were

- marketing think tank
- marketing analysis
- customer group discussions
- consumer depth interviews
- R&D department
- competitors' products
- overseas sister company
- the advertising agency
- a supplier.

From this, albeit patchy, evidence, it is clear that from the array of sources and techniques, companies must, and do, actively choose those which best fit their markets, their competitive situation and their capabilities. This choice would aim to produce ideas which are creative, are produceable and which have market appeal. As has been suggested at several junctures in this chapter, and elsewhere in the book, there is a constant paradox between pursuing creativity and delivering a new product which meets market needs. This paradox requires active attention and demands a consistent approach to managing creativity. The management of creativity is the final section of this chapter.

Managing creativity

The underlying assumption of this book is that innovation is crucial to the survival of companies, that innovation is central to success. Innovation gives companies greater control over their commercial destinies because it allows them to lead the market and set the terms of trade. Although the term 'innovation' covers a plethora of associated concepts, any single innovation can be viewed as a result. It is the result of creativity, the physical expression of creativity. Figure 9.6 shows the relationship between creativity and innovation as clearly depicted by Majaro (1992).

While the success of the innovation, as we have said in Chapter 8, depends on the way in which it is developed and marketed, its existence is preceded by creativity. There are many definitions of creativity, of which Majaro's (1992) seems the most succinct: 'creativity is the thinking process that helps us to generate ideas'. If we accept the role of creativity as the originator of innovation, it is reasonable to ask whether it is possible or even desirable to manage creativity.

If the management of a thinking process is attempted, to what extent is it stifled? In the most familiar contexts, where creativity is associated with fine art, architecture, literature and music, the attempt to manage or control creativity would be expected to lead to its strangulation. Yet individuals and companies alike study how to be creative, the former equipping themselves with one of Edward de Bono's books on innovation, the latter joining the International Creative Forum to attend seminars and conferences on the subject. Managing creativity is about two key issues. First, creative individuals within organizations have to be nurtured. Organizations, however small, evolve ways of operating, which although necessary to co-ordinate and optimize activity may hinder the creative individuals and hamper their effectiveness. Second, the organization must be able to receive, disseminate and act upon the ideas of creative people, transforming them into eventual, successful innovations. Thus, creativity management happens at two levels: the individual and the organization. This is not to suggest that individuals

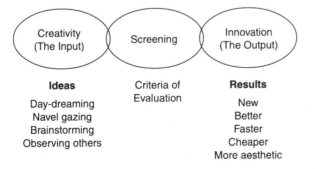

Figure 9.6 ● The relationship between creativity and innovation (*source*: Majaro, 1992, p. 7)

can be made creative if they are not essentially of this nature. Barriers, however, can be removed and the opportunity for them to produce can be given.

It is essential to identify creative individuals. Majaro (1992) believes that although stereotyping should be avoided, some traits are common among the creative.

1. Conceptual fluency: the ability to produce many ideas or solutions in a given situation.

2. Mental flexibility: also known as 'lateral thinking' – the ability to approach a problem from an entirely new angle.

3. Originality: usually evidenced by unusual answers to questions or atypical responses to problems.

4. Suspension of judgment: a willingness to defer judgment and express support for unusual ideas of others.

5. Impulse acceptance: a willingness to react impulsively to an idea.

6. Attitude to authority: greater willingness to challenge authority.

7. Tolerance: a higher threshold towards others' ideas, and fewer negative reactions such as 'that's not the way we do things here'.

Having summarized, very briefly, *some* of the characteristics which tend to be displayed by a creative person or persons, the next task is to facilitate their work.

There are five guidelines to managing creative individuals (Farnham, 1994):

1. *Accommodate*. Creative individuals may not conform to the 'norm'. Refusal to fill forms or pay attention to bureaucracy may have to be tolerated where the individuals are contributing creatively to the organization.

2. *Structure*. Creativity demands stimulation. In Bell Laboratories in the US, creative individuals are stimulated by office environments of their choice. At Hallmark, writers and artists are sent to new locations to observe and to be stimulated by their new surroundings.

3. *Recognize and reward*. Recognition for their work can be more important than financial reward, and commitment and resources devoted to the idea are more likely to encourage future creativity.

4. *Direct and give feedback*. Creative people should not be left in a vacuum. They should be given appropriate deadlines and constant interruptions should be avoided. A fruitful way of giving a context for the work of creative people is to put them into direct contact with customers. This method removes the dampening effect of an internal contact on the creative person.

5. *Protect*. Creative people may attract negative comments from others in the organization whose jobs, on the surface, seem a little less glamorous. Although it is important not to create a privileged elite, it is worth spending time on the interface between creative and other individuals.

Guidelines such as these are, by nature, generalist, whilst the subject of individual creativity has been much studied. However, they do imply changes to an organization, particularly to take account of recognized organizational barriers to creativity. These, taken from Majaro (1992) and Klein (1990), include the following.

Lack of organizational slack

The constant push to be 'lean and fit' can lead to a reduction in innovative capacity. Innovations, based on creativity, need time to be conceived, refined and produced. Whilst it is crucial to ensure that proper feedback and control mechanisms are in place, these should not be so tight as to reduce 'thinking' and, therefore, creativity time where it is required. Clearly, this is a question of finding an acceptable balance, but it is important to be cognizant of the possible squeeze on creativity.

Bureaucracy

The dictionary defines bureaucracy as a system where work is organized into divisions, in a hierarchy designed to carry it out efficiently. Although systems and procedures are usually installed in the belief that greater efficiency, productivity and control will ensue, bureaucracies often take on a life of their own which appears overly complicated, inhibiting flexibility in operation, and, more importantly, creativity. This is particularly true where *processes* and *procedures* are given greater importance than *outputs* or *results*.

Structure

This is a very large and complex issue, as we have discussed at length in Chapter 7. To recap briefly on structural issues and link these with creativity, it is flexible, decentralized, organic and non-hierarchical structures that seem to promote creativity.

Poor communication

As has been suggested elsewhere in the chapter, ideas abound in organizations. However, creativity may not result if the ideas cannot 'get out'. Individuals charged with the responsibility for being creative must know to whom their ideas should be transmitted for consideration, support and development. If the appropriate lines of communication are not made known – and visibly used – creativity will flow into a number of organizational rivulets and is unlikely to be retrieved.

'Imported talent' and 'not invented here'

It is tempting to think that only fresh blood can bring creativity to an organization. This view can be counter-productive because the implementation of creative ideas will still require the support of the 'traditional' personnel. If their expertise is not acknowledged and harnessed too, their levels of knowledge can be deployed to hamper the development of creative ideas into successful new products.

Tight financial control

Whilst financial control of the development process is of vital importance, it is important that in the early stages of the NPD process, where expenditure is low compared to the later stages, the scrutiny of accountants is not too close. Many companies operate by allocating a fixed amount to the first stages of idea generation, to allow the creative process to begin, relatively unfettered by accountants.

Overly large meetings

Although it might be tempting to think it important to put a number of creative people together, this rarely allows creative ideas to move forward. Managing creativity is central to the continued survival of companies and has been growing in importance, both as an academic discipline and as a focal point for company development. Japanese companies, in particular, have been taking steps to increase their capacity for creativity. Shiseido, Japan's largest manufacturer of cosmetics, has been taking steps to change the hierarchical structures, which, although useful and successful to date, are feared to be a constraining factor for future development. In a series of four seminars, managers are challenged to think laterally, creatively and introspectively about the role of the company in its industry. One such exercise involves observation of a goldfish, the analysis of its role in the world, its structure and behaviour and comparison with the company.

The question of managing creativity is vast, and a detailed discussion is beyond the scope of this book. However, although we have dealt with creativity as part of the 'idea generation' phase of new product development, creativity should be maintained throughout the process, right through and beyond the product launch.

Summary

This chapter has dealt with the first stage of the NPD process, that of managing ideas for new products. Idea management is viewed as two central tasks: locating sources of new ideas and activating those sources. The various sources of new product ideas, both internal and external to the company, and techniques for activating those sources are described. Several techniques may be used both inside and outside the company, that is, to encourage ideas from staff or from sources – usually the market – outside the company. These include the battery of 'idea generating techniques' widely referred to by the relevant literature: brainstorming, attribute analysis, forced relationships, gap analysis, repertory grids and scenario-based techniques. The final section of the chapter attempts to describe the wider context of idea management, that of managing creativity. This is important for many aspects of business, but has special relevance for the 'idea' stages of the NPD process.

QUESTIONS

1. What are the major internal sources of new product ideas available to a company?
2. What are the key external sources of new product ideas available to a company?
3. Contrast the major types of brainstorming-type techniques and say what must be done if they are to be fruitful.

4. What are the differences between attribute listing, value analysis and morphological analysis?

5. What are the differences between perceptual and non-metric mapping?

6. Construct a new map of the dessert market, using different descriptors of desserts and comment on the implications of this for new product developers.

Mini-case ● New Ideas in Consumer Durables

Harassed by the recent slump in sales, Johan Weber, the Market Research Director of Marlborough products, notified two groups of senior product and service managers that he would be conducting a brainstorming session to inject new life into the company's NPD. Johan had the full support and backing of the MD, Chris Gray, who counter-signed the memorandum requesting that the identified managers be in the Goil Room at 09.00 on their allocated days. The rest of the memo read as follows:

In two hours, we are going to try to generate about five or six concepts which might be taken forward for more research — both technical and market. We are going to use ways of triggering creativity. These will be changed frequently at first, until we settle into meaningful discussions. During the first half hour the rule is no judging what others have said, nothing negative or derisory can be said about anyone's views.

Scenario Visualising — Your Perfect Day In 5 Years' Time

Individually
Describe to the group 'your perfect day' either at work or at home, which must include a description of:

- telephone
- television
- electricity
- home appliances

Brainwriting — 5 minutes (a form of brainstorming)
On separate Post-Its, write down any ideas you have for new products within the perfect days you have discussed. Write clearly. Stick on wall.

Why can't we...
Now, we would like you to concentrate on what can't be done with the products and services SP provides at the moment. You may like to base your thoughts on either 'the perfect day' or your new ideas on the Post-Its. Or you can start this exercise afresh. We want as long

a list as possible of 'impossibilities'. Now, what needs to happen to make them possibilities?

Attribute Analysis
Once we have finished the why can't we, we will turn to the description of two products in detail.

Please make every effort to attend.

Every effort was made to attend. Over both days, 14 managers appeared at the Goil Suite, where they were introduced to two university researchers, Elena de Sanchez and Angela Prat. The two researchers' experience in facilitating idea generation was realized in the following report on the session.

Introduction to the report

This summary describes the key points of a brainstorming session aimed at generating and prioritizing new products in consumer durables. The group session lasted approximately three hours and took place in the Goil Suite at Marlborough's offices.

Scenario writing and analysis – the perfect day

The group spent the first 15 minutes writing down what they considered to be a perfect day. This could be at home or at work. Holidays were excluded and the only stipulation was that the perfect day would contain references to consumer durables. The scenario writing also helps, to some extent, disconnect busy people from their in-trays. The main points of the perfect days are summarized below.

1. Working at home. Wakes and activates by voice the stereo; takes a big bath, lots of hot water; fruit for breakfast; log in to computer; types report via voice; sends to office where report will be checked; video-conference meeting. Takes time out and does shopping from home on screen; puts on washing in 'intelligent machine'; leaves for lunch in electric car. After lunch amendments to report arrive via desk printer on fax modem. Finish report. End day with dinner for friends cooked by smart cooker; dishes, of course, done by intelligent dishwasher.

2. Saturday afternoon. Favourite football team has beaten major European team. Goes into office in electric car (no traffic on roads) to check progress on a huge contract with a major business customer.

3. At home, Saturday morning. Wakes up in technologically advanced bedroom where weather report can be accessed in order to check weather, plans activities to make the most of the weekend days. Take power shower, need to shop, done via computer/TV link; money automatically deducted from account. Wants to buy a new car. Checks bank balance via direct banking. Accesses agents' showrooms via IT/TV, books a couple of test drives this way. Goes to showrooms, picks best car, bills/finances all arranged automatically. Later, since weather was to be nice, takes new car for spin, has pub lunch and on the way home arranges, via mobile telecoms,

evening's entertainment. Gardening done for relaxation, with smart mower and music blaring. Takes a bath, orders taxi from online connection and books table for friends at favourite restaurant via online connection also. During meal, remembers TV programme needs to be taped, can do this remotely. Orders return taxi. Bills automatically deducted. Watches taped TV programme before retiring.

4. At work. Wakes up and programs shower and kettle to come on. Showers and break-fasts. Opens PC diary at table to check day's events, travels to work on public trans-port subsidized by a scheme which accrues credit points for having taken train instead of car. Walks a bit from station. Checks email in office, talks to colleagues via conference facility. No-hassle day ended by a meal in front of the digital TV, screening a premiere.

5. Weekend day. Kids wake after 8.30 am; makes hot breakfast, papers have arrived. Surfs net to arrange test drive for new car, checks bank account and listens to new albums via soundbites on computer. Checks XFile pages. Mid-morning goes out and thinks about a holiday, has lunch in pub or restaurant, goes for a city centre walk. Goes to record store to listen to more tracks, doesn't like them. Goes for test drive, picks kids up from various activities, goes home to play kids' games on CD. Evening, opens a good wine, goes to a concert, great seats at front, all ordered via IT/TV links during the day. After concert, meets friends in pub before going home.

6. A trouble-free day at work. Wakes up to a warm house, refreshing shower, early journey to work to miss the traffic. Day planned early; leaves for work and home in time for dinner. Free time after dinner with family, before retiring.

7. A trouble-free day at work. Wakes before the rest of the family, takes good shower, watches breakfast TV in peace without the family and gets out of the house before others are up. Telephone and computer are 'decommissioned', work for the day gets finished. Fewer meetings, less talking, more achieving. Finishes at a regular time, home at a regular time, finishes home decorating (outstanding for a year), goes for a swim.

8. A trouble-free day at work. Wakes with clear head since room air-conditioning has been optimized through the night; temperature controlled noiselessly, both provided by one company. Takes a power shower and close shave and goes to work on uncongested roads. Logs in to computer at work, checks year to date figures giving answers to questions about performance.

9. Working at home. Working at home to avoid travelling hassle. Wakes 7.30 (much later than if going to the office), using laptop contacts office and suppliers. Uses mobile phone connections. Automatic gadget makes cup of tea; checks business news via IT. Sets up appointments. Goes to business lunch with service supplier and makes other business visits; leaves last call at 5.30, home for 6 pm. Sets video to tape programmes, has microwave meal, watches video, goes to bed.

10 A weekend football victory. Finds that, against the odds, favourite team has won by a big margin. This victory was the subject of a bet, placed by email. Goes to pub to celebrate double victory.

11. A trouble-free day at work. Wakes; paper delivered with mail. Mail brings news of electricity offer – free electricity for the quarter as a promotion. Goes to work on traffic-free roads; meetings all cancelled for brainstorming session, which is very productive. Home early, a swim and a beer.

12. Working at home. Wakes to hot coffee; temperature controlled via voice-activated devices. Mail on PC system updated; checks weather using telemetry and radio systems; speaks to the office; books night out from anywhere.

13. Wakes at 8 am. Kids still asleep. Shower, shave and coffee. Arrives at work 9.30, no messages, no emails. Between 10 and 1 everyone agrees at all meetings; between 1 and 3, a business lunch, no messages in the afternoon. Goes to football match in the evening; team wins; comes home and watches highlights.

New product ideas

Against the background of these perfect days a wide variety of products were suggested:

Domestic electricity remote controls
Home management systems
Home and business security services
Electronic time manager and purse
Domestic/business answerphone/diverter
Car/home electronic interfaces
Home shopping on-line links
Holidays direct
Intelligent products
Intelligent home services
Links between telecom/durables products and retailers
Voice activated products
Transport timetable information
Domestic environmental control package (voice activation; simple control)
Educational products: early learning, distance learning, educational services
School–parent communications service
Telephone ordering
One payment on utilities and mortgage services
Green services – health and safety
Provide security – at home

Discussion questions

1. How effective do you think the brainstorming session has been and how would you improve it?

2. Can you make any further new product ideas from the scenarios?

3. Assess the usefulness of the new product ideas listed.

chapter 10

Screening new product ideas

LEARNING OBJECTIVES

This chapter is the first of those chapters which looks at how product development projects are evaluated. Its specific objectives are:

1. To define screening in its place in the NPD process.
2. To emphasize the importance of early screening.
3. To describe the mortality curve for new product ideas.
4. To discuss error and risk in screening.
5. To describe alternative types of screening procedure.
6. To put forward a new simplified screening procedure.

On completion of this chapter you will:

1. Understand the process of new product evaluation as one of continuous refinement.
2. Appreciate that the role of screening is as a 'first' evaluation.
3. Be able to articulate the limitations of screening.
4. Be conversant with the types of screen employed by industry.
5. Be able to design and implement a screening procedure commensurate with the strategic direction of a firm.

Introduction

Screening in new product development has a multitude of meanings. As will be explained, in this book it is viewed as the initial review of ideas emanating from the idea generation phase. At this stage, decisions regarding the precise forms of the product – the materials, production processes and so on – have not been taken, so the precise details of design, appeal, dimensions and comparability with other products on the market cannot be assessed. Despite these levels and dimensions of uncertainty, screening has been shown to be an important stage of the NPD process. This chapter reviews the reasons why screening is important and discusses how to evaluate risk in the context of the screening process. It then goes on to review types of screening as well as the criteria commonly employed by companies, before suggesting a simplified, prescriptive view of the screening process.

What is screening?
....

Screening is a term which applies to different concepts of evaluating new products, depending on which writer, researcher, consultant or company is using the term. These differences relate to the precise scheduling of the screening within the new product development process. Recalling the process represented by Booz, Allen and Hamilton, the 'screening' stage is the third step. However, from this third stage right through to the launch, the entire process is made up of development of the new product on the one hand, and the evaluation of each new development on the other, as shown in Figure 10.1. Therefore, screening or evaluation is a multi-staged activity, which uses a number of different techniques. These techniques depend largely on the amount of information which is available to evaluate – or screen. The confusion that arises regarding the meaning of 'screening' is exacerbated by the fact that there is no general agreement on the number of stages that comprise the new product development process. Perhaps a simpler way to provide a context for screening is to consider the conceptual and physical developments that a new product project undergoes on the way to full

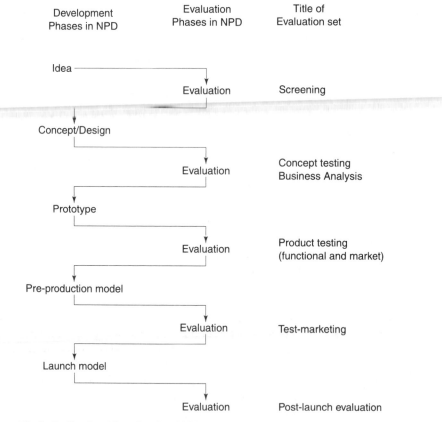

Figure 10.1 ● Evaluation in the NPD process

Table 10.1 ● Techniques associated with commercial evaluation sets

Evaluation set	Techniques
Screening	Informal, management-based
	Previous market analysis
	Checklists
	Drop/go analysis
	Strategic analysis
Concept testing	Marketing research: focus groups/depth interviews
	Beta-testing
	Perceptual mapping
	Conjoint analysis
	QFD techniques
	A-T-R model
Business analysis	Scoring models
	Break-even analysis
	Required rate of return
	Sensitivity testing

product launch. In Figure 10.1, we see the development stages, where an idea, a concept or a physical product is constructed, and the corresponding stage of evaluation. (Recall also, in Chapter 7, that these phases of evaluation are sometimes called reviews, or gates.)

Furthermore, since the NPD process itself is iterative, the discrete stages of evaluation implied by Figure 10.1 are misleading. In reality, each evaluation set includes techniques which may be repeated as alternative design concepts of product configuration are developed. Table 10.1 shows the techniques associated with each evaluation set.

In addition to these evaluation sets are concurrent technical development evaluation sets, which include assessment of design, production, and functional feasibility and specifications. In short, as well as market/commercial evaluation and re-evaluation, it is of critical importance to evaluate the function, form and production of the new product project. These parallel sets of evaluation are shown in Cooper's (1988) Stage Gate Model of the NPD process, Figure 10.2.

Cooper's model and others in the same mould show how each evaluation stage is really a combination of technical and commercial evaluation sets. Screening, as used in this book, is the first of a series of evaluations, beginning when the collection of new product ideas is complete. It follows, therefore, that this *initial* evaluation cannot be very sophisticated, as it is concerned with identifying ideas which can be developed into concepts and evaluated for their technical feasibility and market potential. Where other writers incorporate complex screening models, which require financial, technical and market data, they are implicitly, if not explicitly, relating to a stage much further down the development cycle. Screening, as defined above, is an initial assessment to weed out impractical ideas.

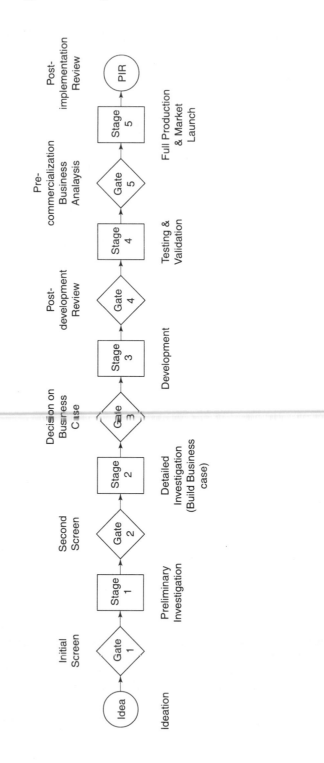

Figure 10.2 ● Cooper's Stage Gate Model (*source*: Cooper, 1988)

The importance of screening

Despite the caveats implied above, screening is an important stage in the NPD process. All estimation of future success or failure of a new product is fraught with inexactitude, often because data are unreliable or incomplete. This is particularly true of the screening stage, where, based on new product ideas, generated from the techniques and sources discussed in Chapter 9, an assessment of potential is made. At this stage, there are no precise product specifications, materials and costs may only be estimated, and market potential is a question of 'gut feel' rather than measurement. It is, therefore, tempting to think that the stage of screening is pretty useless. However, unless managers have unlimited resources, they are not going to devote them all to emergent new product ideas. Therefore, managers must find some ways of comparing one new product idea with another, in order to devote resources to those with the greatest apparent opportunity for return and to cut down expenditure on those projects with limited potential. The research by Booz, Allen and Hamilton in the early 1980s showed that companies which screened new product ideas had more successful new product launches and that these were less costly than for companies not employing a screening stage.

The decrease in costs that screening serves is based on two ideas introduced earlier: the idea mortality curve and the cumulative expenditures curve. We return to these briefly here.

The mortality curve

In Chapter 8, Figure 8.1 (p. 192) showed three different rates of kill for new product ideas. Curve A showed a slow kill rate, with many new product ideas being carried through generation and development stages, but being killed off before market launch. The implications of this are:

- wasted development and evaluation expenditure on ideas that would not be launched and which, therefore, would not generate return
- development resources being spread over a larger number of development projects, jeopardizing the resources and quality given to any one
- longer development times as effort is spread over a larger number of projects.

Although undesirable, these implications result from the desire to kill projects only when it becomes clear that their potential is too low for a full market launch. As discussed above, initial screening is inexact because the information that can be collected regarding market potential is inexact, based as it is on the assessment of an initial idea, whose form, specification and attractiveness are yet to be determined. By putting more ideas through the refining stages of concept development and testing, information regarding feasibility, market potential and so on becomes more reliable. The viability of this approach may be greater where costs of development are low, as in the case of services, where physical development is not as expensive or time-consuming.

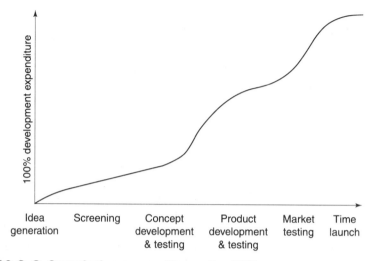

Figure 10.3 ● Cumulative expenditures for NPD

Curve B showed a faster kill rate, where many ideas are killed off early in their development cycle, before physical development takes place. The implications of this are:

● lower costs, as concept and product development occurs for a smaller number of products

● possible killing of products with potential due to insufficient development and testing.

The cost assumptions underlying the implications for these curves are associated with the notion of cumulative expenditures shown in Figure 10.3.

This average curve does not represent every industry. In some industries, where R&D costs are extremely high, the early expenditures are higher than would be suggested by the figure. Marketing costs may be comparatively low, for example in biotechnology, electronics and pharmaceuticals. On the other hand, in food processing, the largest percentage of development expenditure may not occur until fairly near market launch, where heavy promotion is needed to ensure distribution and awareness. Despite such sectoral variation, serious investment occurs when the prototypes or first samples are manufactured, because at that stage, investment is made in materials, tooling and subsequent testing. This can be exacerbated where frequent modification and redevelopment are required in the light of practical experience of manufacture and testing. It follows, therefore, that where evaluation and testing can be done relatively cheaply, i.e. before the physical development of a new product takes place, the overall development costs are likely to be lower. Further, if these development activities can take place for fewer ideas, based on rigorous screening, costs will be lower still, and accuracy of development and testing may be increased, as resources can be more sharply focused.

The influence of risk in screening

Ultimately, the stringency of the screen must depend on how managers view the risks. There are two basic types of error in screening which entail risks:

● killing off product ideas which may have potential
● developing product ideas which might fail.

The perceived seriousness of the risks of each type of error depends on the cumulative costs embedded in the development cycle of a given company and the extent to which the company can endure the result of the risks. The errors and their associated risks are shown in Table 10.2. Two correct decisions are possible – dropping a product that would fail and developing a product that would succeed. Clearly, the second of these is the more desirable. Equally, two wrong decisions are possible: dropping a product that would succeed and developing a product that would fail.

On the surface, it may seem that dropping a product that would succeed is the lesser of two evils, since although nothing has been gained, nothing has been lost. On the other hand, development of a product which fails not only wastes investment which will not yield any return, but it may also have both internal and external negative impacts, and the development may have eclipsed the opportunity to invest in a more successful project. However, only the managers of companies can assess this accurately for themselves, according to the competitive and technological climate of their industries and their current operating status. For example, in many high-technology industries, the option to drop a potential success is disastrous, as the pace of technology means that products in a current portfolio may become obsolete very quickly indeed. On the other hand, the development costs associated with the development of a new flavour of potato crisps for a company already established in the snack market are relatively low. In other words, the magnitude of the risk is situation-specific.

When Le Creuset launched its *casserole d'amour*, a heart-shaped pot, its marketing director was relatively unconcerned about reservations expressed since he believed its PR value alone would recover any tooling costs. The product has met with popularity, particularly in the Japanese market (Darwent, 1992). If Xerox had heeded the opinion

Table 10.2 ● Errors and risk in new product screening

| Eventual outcome | Screening decision | |
	Drop idea	Develop idea
New product success	Wrong decision – (A) ● lost revenue ● lost competitive standing	Correct decision
New product failure	Correct decision	Wrong decision – (B) ● lost investment ● opportunity cost ● lost market standing

of experts who had assessed the potential of photocopiers at around 1,000 machines per year, its current strengths might not have materialized. Similarly, Dr Louis Nisbet, founder of Xenova, a company focusing on the development of drugs from plants and micro-organisms, stated that

> 'We are dealing in breakthrough areas of medicine. By their very nature, you don't know whether these things are going to work. What we do know is that, if we can take them all the way down the track, we are dealing with products with potential market values of hundreds of millions a year.' (Darwent, 1992)

These examples show the importance of risk in relation to potential losses and potential gains. So how do firms manage these? The Eastman Chemical Co., for example, estimates growth prospects for R&D projects over 10–15 years, at different confidence levels. The company attempts not to stop uncertain projects, but to avoid wasting money blatantly. On the other hand Noranda Inc., a natural resource business based in Montreal, manages R&D by strict financial measures and attempts to apply a two-level rating system for both marketing and technical (*Industry Week*, 17 March 1997, p. 40). Risk is based on newness of technology and Noranda's familiarity with the technology, whereas marketing risk relates to timing to market and the level of resources required. Thus the level of investment can be matched with the assessment of risk in achieving ROI.

While the assessment of these continues at each stage of evaluation, it begins at the point where new product ideas are screened. As we have suggested, screening cannot be exact – it cannot give a definite picture of the potential of a new product idea. It must, however, be constructed in such a way as to give the best possible assessment of the likelihood of potential so that the decision can be made as to whether or not to take the idea onto the next stage of development and assessment. This suggests that its orientation must be strategic, rather than detailed. The next section examines the prerequisites of an effective screening system.

Effective screening

From the foregoing discussion, it is clear that a company's screening process must be constructed in the light of the risk faced by each type of error. If the 'go' error is fatal, the screening process must be more stringent; if the 'drop' error is fatal, the screening process must be less stringent. This over-arching evaluation should be made alongside a company's new product strategy. As will be recalled from Chapter 8, on new product strategy, companies should assess the direction of new product development based on a thorough evaluation of their strengths and weaknesses in the light of market, technological and competitive opportunities and threats. Thus, the new product strategy is articulated in terms of level of newness to be pursued, market(s) or market segments to be targeted, competition to be met or avoided, capabilities to be built on, financial investment and desired returns.

Each of these parameters – and any others – should be the focus of screening new product ideas. For example, taking 'capabilities to be built on', we can break this down further into its constituent elements such as production capability, technical capability,

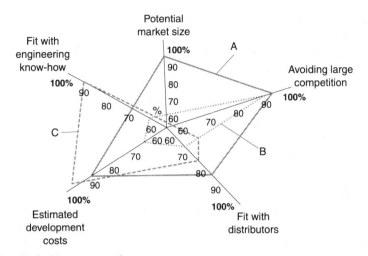

Figure 10.4 ● The screening map

marketing capability, and so on. Similarly with 'competition to be met or avoided', a new product idea might be assessed on whether it allows a company to avoid competition that is strong or, conversely, to challenge competition effectively. These elements can be considered separately, but ultimately it is the consideration of all the variables concurrently that gives the most complete picture of the relative advantages or disadvantages of a new product idea.

A methodology following these principles has been devised by a certain medium-sized manufacturer of axles to help them visualize the potential of new product ideas. Each area of strategic importance for new product development is used to assess new product ideas. These include potential market size, avoiding large competitors with a low cost-base, fit with current distribution channels, engineering know-how and estimated development costs. Elements within each of these categories are identified and used to assess the new product idea, and each category is then given a total weighting, expressed as a percentage. The final percentages are used to create a 'screen map' which allows, at a glance, to see the overall attractiveness of an idea. The map for a good idea looks like (A) in Figure 10.4, while that for a poor idea looks like (B) or (C).

Although the company would readily admit that the assessments are, at this early stage, subjective, the resultant map nevertheless allows managers to build a pattern which can be used to discuss and communicate screening decisions. Its value, therefore, is in focusing evaluation of a specific idea on a more strategically generated set of criteria that are wider than simply 'market potential', which although ultimately crucial is, at this stage, much harder to assess. In addition, the company insists on a map which has a regular form, on the basis that a 'miss' on any of the strategic criteria is not recoverable. For example, in the case of map C in Figure 10.4, the attractiveness of development costs scores highly, together with the project's fit with current engineering know-how: we have a development project that is relatively straightforward to deliver. On the other hand, the attractiveness of the market size and the project's ability to avoid large competitors score low, suggesting that a lot of marketing effort might be required in trying to compete in a small market.

These parameters at least give some guidelines for selecting projects to develop forward, and although based on initial managerial assessment, as suggested earlier, this stage of development does not usually provide the information upon which more 'objective' decisions might be made. Once a project passes on the strategic criteria, greater attention can be paid to development of the concept, which in turn allows more information to be subjected to marketing, production and technical scrutiny.

If, at this initial stage, screens are too rigid and detailed, they will tend to eliminate all new ideas. A more strategic approach allows the least appropriate ideas to be weeded out of the collection, in order to concentrate resources and effort on those with greater initial potential. Indeed, one of the main differences between practices studied by Booz, Allen and Hamilton in their studies of 1968 and 1982 was that the addition of a strategy stage allowed far more effective early screening, which was one of the factors leading to more successful new product outcomes (Booz, Allen and Hamilton, 1982). Effective screening involves tailoring the type of screen, and with this, the criteria used in the screen to evaluate products. Kucsmarski (1992) describes six types of screen which can be used as broad indications. These are examined below.

Types of screens

The six types of screen described by Kucsmarski (1992) are:

- growth role
- category
- strategic role
- new product type
- internal strength
- financial risk.

Each type is focused on a particular set of issues against which new product ideas might be evaluated, and each set, or the combination of sets would be selected according to a company's new product strategy.

Growth role screens can be used where the new product strategy stipulates a growth role for its new product development efforts. These screens demand of new product ideas that they:

- enter a new category of business that represents a 'net addition' to the company's portfolio
- expand a company's global market share within a product category
- deliver a price advantage which will allow the company to increase market share at the expense of the competition
- create a whole new category of product-market, strategical expanding sales.

Numerous examples of products which have been launched to promote growth on one or several of these issues exist. As mentioned in Chapter 9, Bird's Eye, part of Unilever, recently launched 'Baker's Bistro', a range of frozen savoury pastries, a category of product it did not previously compete in, despite its presence in the frozen food market. The launch of the new range was conceived to achieve growth since the demand for light and convenience meals is one of the fastest-growing sectors in food markets (*Marketing*, 17 March 1994, p. 5). On the other hand, Pillsbury's UK launch, in 1992, of the range of ready-to-cook pastries and bread, extended its market share in those products to a geographical area it had previously neglected. The way in which new product ideas might contribute to growth are varied, and not all methods entail equal risk. For example, Scottish and Newcastle Beverages' attempt to create a new product market from its development of 'fruit beer' is considerably more risky than the growth option pursued by Pillsbury, above, since the product concept of the former is newer.

Category screens can be used to encourage new product projects in categories where the capabilities of the company are most suited. For example, where a company has high costs, ideas falling into product-market categories of low value-added would be avoided. Equally, it is important that product-market categories are large enough and have lower levels of competitive industry. These screens demand that a new product idea targets a category which:

- has proven consumer attractiveness (in substantial numbers)
- is not dominated by one or two major players
- demonstrates growth potential
- has room for additional products which might offer benefits to the consumer or customer
- does not require marketing or other investment which the company cannot match easily.

This type of screen inevitably encourages a conservative approach to new product development, to minimize the size of the task and to maximize product synergy with existing strengths. However, it should be remembered that this type of screen might yield products which are imitated early, and while synergy was highlighted by Cooper's research work as a factor leading to success, this occurred only where the new product exhibited a definite advantage over the competition. In other words, there is no point in making an electro-mechanical radiator control system if it capitalizes on company strengths, for example, where customers prefer the electronic variety. The usefulness of the category screen is that it provides source guidelines for judging new areas (categories) to explore.

Strategic role screens are usually statements which define competitive, market and business requirements that new products will be expected to satisfy. These strategic roles can differ from industry to industry, and from company to company, but will flow directly from new product strategy. Issues relating to strategic role screens may demand that new product ideas:

- are technologically superior to products currently available
- capitalize on existing distribution and delivery systems
- are able to provide a foothold in product markets currently outside the company's sphere of activity

- allow the company to develop technical or marketing skills in a new sphere
- are aimed at growth markets
- will use up excess capacity.

This list is far from exhaustive. Companies' own lists would be derived from their overall and new product strategy.

Screens for new product types

Clearly, the screens used for 'modified' new products will be different from those used for 'radical' new products. As modified versions of products have associated products and markets from which adjacent information can be gleaned and extrapolated, it follows that the screen types used for 'modified' new products can be more stringent than those for 'radically' new products. In the latter case uncertainty levels regarding how to develop the physical product in the light of the current market trends (which may not yet exist) are much higher; so are levels of risk. This said, potential paybacks from radically new products tend to be higher than for modifications of older products, so it is important that screens take account of the balance between uncertainty, risk and reward. This would imply using a screen which varies the financial payback demand depending upon the level of newness implied by the new product idea. This suggests screening issues which classify ideas into:

- new to the world
- new to the market
- new to the company
- a new (additional) product line item

and which set criteria appropriate to the varying level of risk in each one.

Internal strength screens are usually set up to gauge the level of difficulty with which a new product idea can be developed, manufactured and sold. Kucsmarski (1992) makes the point that screens of this nature should not be used to *stop* a potential new product which falls foul of several criteria, but that this should cause reconsideration, at least. Internal strength screens raise issues which examine whether the idea:

- makes use of patented technology
- increases the use of an 'efficient manufacturing system'
- capitalizes on existing marketing and sales efforts
- exploits technological, engineering, design or marketing skills.

These issues seem similar to those raised by 'category screens', and inasmuch as the latter may focus on internal strengths that a new product idea in a specific category may exploit, the two are, indeed, similar. However, category screens also focus on the competitive position, and are attempting to 'screen out' whole categories of product-market which may be deemed inappropriate. On the other hand, internal strength screens will assess every idea against strengths – the more the idea builds on a strength, the better.

Financial screens are important, given that the objective of most NPD projects is to make money. However, as stated previously, it is often difficult to assess precisely how much money is likely to be made from a given idea, early on in the NPD process. Yet Kucsmarski (1992) reports financial screen usage criteria as revenue size, pre-tax profit contribution, ROI, payback period, gross margin and return on net assets. He goes on to say, however, that financial screens should be 'the final set of screens' which would be used *after* 'business analysis'. He is, therefore, extending the notion of screening further down the NPD process cycle.

Clearly, a comprehensive financial analysis must occur, and the earlier in the process the better, as unlikely candidates can be dropped from the development project. The suggestion that this can happen before the concept has been developed, with the necessary attention being given to both technical specification and market reaction to that specification, is rather optimistic. More likely at this stage is a general assessment of potential market size, growth rate and so on. Of course, it must be remembered that academic research looking at how companies screen new products and asking about financial criteria will get a response that they are important. It may not always be clear that researchers want to stick to a 'discrete' screening phase, which the practitioner does not even recognize!

To sum up thus far, it has been suggested that, despite the relative unreliability of the screening stage, it is an important step in the new product development process, if linked to strategy. This suggests that customizing screening to the strategic context of the firm is a sensible way to ensure effective screening. One study has looked into this, together with examining how companies actually *do* screen new products; the results are reported in the next section.

Screening: process and criteria

There are different recommended approaches to screening, many of which include the notion of a multi-staged process, which starts with broad project selection criteria, moving on to more sophisticated ratings of criteria. As explained above, it is likely that sophisticated scoring models are best suited to 'new' products which represent a minimal departure from current offerings, able to summarize the criteria that might be suggested for a two-staged screening process.

The way in which it is suggested that these criteria are measured varies. At the most qualitative level, all that may be required is a managerial evaluation of criteria. Even where such an evaluation is given numerically, as in the earlier example of the axle manufacturer, it is important to note that the numbers are a representation of judgment, and not 'hard fact'. At the most quantitative level, it is possible to have a project team score each new product idea and subject the average scores to a predetermined importance weighting. Shocker, Gensch and Simon (1969) suggested that, since criteria are interdependent (for example, potential market share and potential profitability), scores on these and other criteria should be subjected to statistical data reduction techniques that would eliminate interdependencies. However, as suggested above, and echoed by Davies and Pearson (1980), overly quantitative approaches do not necessarily work better, since they are based on the best available managerial judgment at the time.

Cooper and de Brentani (1984) has studied the use made of screening criteria, and the extent to which companies customized their screening processes. They found that four sets of criteria dominate the screening process: a project's expected financial potential (measured by expected market growth, sales growth, market share, profitability and likelihood of success); corporate synergy (the idea's fit with marketing, selling, distribution and managerial skills); technological and produc-tion fit (the idea's fit with current engineering, design and production resources and skills); and the potential for achieving a differential advantage (including issues like technological leadership and innovative application of technology). A further five sets of criteria were considered to be of secondary importance: the product's life expectancy; its ability to consolidate the current position; its ability to take the company into a new market; market size; and the international potential of the new product idea.

Neither the source nor the complexity of the funding required was considered to be of any importance, nor was the reserved objectivity of the potential customer base. Interestingly, although the researchers found some differences in screening behaviour among firms of different types, on the whole the similarities far outweighed the differences. In other words, the important sets of factors described above are common to a majority of companies. There is no explicit examination of whether or not different screening models used affect the outcome of the final new product project, but as screening is only one factor affecting the outcome of the process, establishing a connection would be very difficult.

Cooper (1985), on the other hand, used his findings regarding the characteristics of successful products to develop normative screening criteria. He found that two sets of characteristics – market and firm – described successful NPD, and suggested that selection of projects for development may be aided by using these characteristics as screening criteria. They are shown in Table 10.3.

Although these characteristics might well be used *throughout* the NPD process as benchmarks for success, key aspects such as 'product superiority' or 'economic advantage to the end user' will only be known once development is properly underway.

What are the implications of this research and discussion? Screening is a task hampered by paradox. The key to its success is to identify products with market potential, but this is difficult, if not impossible, due to lack of information. In view of this, screening in practice seems to centre on broad financial considerations and the extent of synergy a new product idea displays with regard to current skills and know-how. The

Table 10.3 ● Characteristics of successful projects

Market characteristics:	● high growth opportunities
	● low intensity of competition
	● product superiority
	● economic advantage to end users
Firm characteristics:	● synergy with corporate resource
	● synergy with technical resource
	● newness to the firm (negative)

problem with such an approach is that it may encourage low-risk development projects to dominate. What is required at this early first evaluation of the project is a more simplified view. Essentially, a number of key internal and external factors are central to the screening procedure. These include:

- technological feasibility
- demand/market need
- competition
- buyer behaviour
- channel behaviour
- corporate synergy
- product advantage
- marketability
- makeability.

Thus, the screening pattern being explored in this chapter is similar to that advocated by Wind (1982). The pattern is shown in Figure 10.5. At each stage of evaluation, the

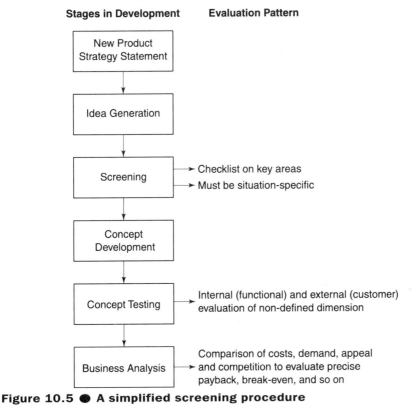

Figure 10.5 ● A simplified screening procedure

new product's evaluation is more complete and the evaluation may repeat several criteria, but becomes tighter, and is based to a greater extent on more reliable data.

Whilst more than one question may be needed to cover each area or issue, the question asked should be constructed with the objective of eliminating excessively impractical ideas. This said, the criteria should also be situation-specific, that is, derived from goals identified in either the corporate or the new product strategy. For example, if the new product strategy is principally concerned with maintaining market share or tackling a competitor, should return on investment be used as a screening criterion? Put simply, criteria in the screen must be related to the goal the company is seeking to achieve. More complex screening should take place at the next stage of the NPD process, concept development and testing, which is the subject of the next chapter. Concept development and testing, as we shall see, generates two vital pieces of information. First, a more complete picture of the product is developed, giving a better idea of costs. Second, since the product becomes developed in terms of shape, materials, design and cost, the customer can better evaluate its appeal.

Summary

This chapter focuses on the issues surrounding the first evaluative stage of the new product development process. It shows how there are different views towards the degree to which screening can and should be thorough, and links this to the question of risk and error. Whilst it is tempting to err on the side of caution by devising complex and demanding screens, the risk of only rarely introducing a new product, if at all, is nil. Several types of screen are discussed, followed by a discussion of what procedures and criteria are used in practice. Practice suggests that screening procedures may be overly complicated for the type and amount of information available at this early stage in the NPD process. Finally, a simplified prescription of screening is offered to take account of this comparative lack of information.

QUESTIONS

1. Explain the importance of the mortality curve as it relates to the role of screening.
2. How does screening relate to other stages of evaluation in new product development?
3. What are the limitations of screening?
4. Explain the major types of screen.
5. What is the relationship between a screening procedure and the strategic vision for NPD within the firm?
6. Design a screening procedure for the new product ideas described in the mini-case for Chapter 9.

Mini-case ● Hutchison Microtel

Introduction

In April 1994, Hutchison Microtel launched a new digital mobile phone service, under the radically different branding of Orange™. The service was identified as requiring mass market appeal and needed to be simple, friendly and approachable. Everything about the launch was big: the idea, the spend (£700m) and the design agency: Wolfe Olins. Its connotations were of warmth, reliability, non-threatening, embodying the 'personality' of the brand. Yet beneath the splash and innovation flair is a detailed and planned process designed to increase the number of successful new products, without jeopardizing innovation and creativity.

Screening new products at Hutchison Microtel

A recently instituted 'new products screening committee' (NPSC) oversees three types of evaluation: a 'sanity check' of the concept; an investigation of the feasibility of various alternatives; and, finally, a business case that is drawn up and evaluated. The new products steering committee comprises heads of marketing, engineering, customer service and regulatory functions. The basic sanity check attempts to assess the effort the new product will take to develop, the extent to which the idea fits with the business mission and the benefit customers are likely to derive. The basic purpose is to take off ideas which are unrealistic; at this stage the evaluation is rough enough to allow some product ideas in to the next stage of evaluation, although they entail much uncertainty regarding their potential. This is because the company seeks to be innovative and does not set too rigorous a screen at this stage, as some ideas with innovative potential could be prematurely cast aside. Information needed for the basic sanity check includes estimation of market size and market share of the major players, the potential number of subscribers, potential charges, and the operational and likely setup costs. However, of all the issues examined the most important at this stage are the extent to which the concept fits the organization's strategy and the cost/revenue indicators.

A basic case is made to the NPSC, presented by a 'sponsor'. If the NPSC accept the proposal as suitable for further development, a project manager will be assigned to take the ideas through to launch, and even through the life cycle of the eventual product. Of the concepts that come forward to the NPSC – on a two-page outline – a little over half go on to the next stage, where they are described in great detail, at the 'alternatives and feasibility' stage.

This stage sees the formation of a team, which tends to be 'as small as possible' to get the job done. There is always a marketing presence on the team. The objective of this stage is to take the major go/no go decision. This task requires detailed research on the market size, shares and usage rates among current users. In addition, qualitative primary research is often undertaken in order to draw up specifications on the appearance of products, features requirements, the positioning of the concept, the formats for billing and statements, and so on. On the internal side, information regarding the need for investment in hardware and infrastructure gives a clearer assessment of the likely costs than at the previous evaluation. After the new product idea has passed this stage, it goes on to be developed into a 'full business case', at which stage the final specifications are fixed. Not only does this relate to the physical specification, but also to the nature of the positioning, the competitive advantage and the all-important distribution, which are planned at this time. Much of this planning is based on the research and reports of the earlier screening stages at Hutchison Microtel, although final test markets are also used.

Discussion questions

1. How would you relate the new product evaluation system to the stages in the multiple convergent process, described in Chapter 7?

2. What are the advantages and disadvantages of HM's 'staged' approach?

This case was compiled from research data collected by the authors.

chapter 11

Concept development and testing

LEARNING OBJECTIVES

1. To position needs as the central issue in concept testing.
2. To explain the link between product characteristics and customer needs.
3. To describe the process of concept testing.
4. To outline the decisions managers need to make to design a concept test.
5. To discuss data collection methods for concept testing.

On completion of this chapter you will:

1. Understand more clearly the difference between screening ideas and testing concepts.
2. Appreciate the underlying relationships between the benefits customers seek from products and the characteristics that make up products.
3. Be able to describe the process of concept testing for new products.
4. Understand the array of concept testing techniques that may be employed by companies.
5. Appreciate the breadth of data collection methods for concept testing.
6. Be able to design a concept test for a particular new product.

Introduction

In Chapters 9 and 10, the focus of discussion related to how companies generate and screen ideas for further development. At the next stage, which this chapter examines, the screened ideas are developed into more fully specified concepts, which are evaluated for their appeal to the potential market segments for whom they are intended. Concept development and testing involves designing and presenting representations of the proposed new product to a sample of its intended customers. However, as has been discussed previously, these stages are by no means discrete, and much of what happens during concept development is conditioned by the nature of the idea generation and screening which has already taken place. The objective of concept development and testing is to estimate market reaction to a product idea before committing substantial funds to its physical development. In other words, this stage may be viewed as an extension of idea generation and screening, in that those ideas screened to be of potential value are developed and screened further in order to determine which idea specifications have greatest appeal to potential customers, in the light of competitive offerings. The more detailed the information gathered at this stage, the greater the chance of reducing total development costs, as alternative concepts can be derived and tested more cheaply than alternative, prototype, products. If a full commitment is made to market research at this stage, the prototypes developed will, in theory, more closely match customer needs and preferences, requiring fewer costly amendments later on.

The dual tasks of concept development and testing are intimately related. The first articulations of the new product concept will be derived from the activities carried during idea generation and screening, but these articulations can be reworked in the light of customer reaction, and retested, until an acceptable concept is modelled, which can be progressed to physical development. This 'in-stage' iteration is shown in Figure 11.1.

The concept testing cycle highlighted is repeated until the company identifies the concept which exhibits the acceptable level of appeal, both internally and externally.

The number of iterative cycles at this stage depends on the way in which the original ideas were generated and screened. For example, a very large number of ideas screened may still not have been subjected to any formal evaluation by the market, in which case there is greater scope for an initial concept formulation to be unsatisfactory as a number of versions for the target market may have to be drawn up. These initial formulations will have to be modified and retested. If, on the other hand, ideas are generated and screened on the basis of market research techniques such as perceptual maps, the

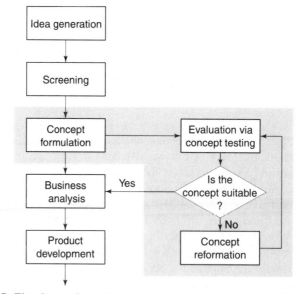

Figure 11.1 ● The iterations in concept development and testing

most appealing dimensions might well be present in the first concept formulations and fewer iterations are consequently required.

As was discussed in Chapter 10, there is a lack of consensus regarding the delineation of screening and concept testing in texts on NPD. In some cases, discussion of screening encompasses some of the concept testing techniques described in this chapter, depending on how lengthy and costly screening is presumed to be. For our purposes, concept development and testing is taken to begin with a vastly reduced number of ideas, that is after the initial evaluation or screening has taken place. The *actual* labels given to these stages are of less importance than the notion that as the NPD process unwinds, both the development of ideas and the dimensions which can be evaluated are more specific, therefore yielding greater amounts of increasingly reliable information from the market. Any confusion that arises in terminology is largely due to the fact that the 'stages' of NPD are not tidy, linear and discrete.

A final point of introduction is to emphasize the parallel strands of development and evaluation that run throughout the NPD process. This is shown in Figure 11.2, building on the ideas introduced in Chapter 10 (see Figure 10.1)

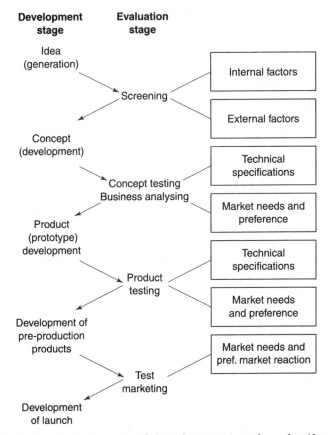

Figure 11.2 ● Parallel strands of development and evaluation

As before, each development stage feeds into an evaluation stage. These evaluation stages have dual purposes: evaluation of the technical aspects of the new product and its market appeal, based on market needs and preferences. This reinforces the ideas introduced in Chapter 10 (see Figure 10.2). As we have seen previously, market needs and preferences are germane to some methods used for idea generation and screening, which reinforces the idea that these early stages are closely linked, in both objective and method, as they are focused on evolving a concept attractive to the market, which can progress on to physical development and eventual market launch.

The remainder of this chapter is divided into three sections. The first looks at the various purposes of concept testing, the second deals with the managerial decisions to be made in developing concept tests, and the final section discusses the specific types of tests that might be used.

The purposes of concept testing

As explained above, concept testing has an overriding purpose: to estimate customer reaction to an idea before developing the physical product. However, at this stage in the development cycle, a number of supporting objectives are implied:

- To profile the market:
  - current buying pattern
  - existing segments
  - customers' view of the products available

  To assess likely purchase intention and position the product:
  - trial and repeat purchase
  - barriers to changing brands
- To make improvements to the new product concept:
  - overall product concept
  - features of the product concept.

Each of these different sets of objectives implies that different concept tests are appropriate, although the various ways in which data are collected may often permit several 'tests' or 'measures' to be made at once. The sets of objectives are linked, largely through the concepts of customer needs and preferences. These links are shown in Figure 11.3.

The centrality of needs

Figure 11.3 shows that while the three sets of objectives are themselves inter-related and interdependent, they are commonly informed by a thorough understanding of customer needs and preferences. Therefore, these necessarily form the core of all forms of concept testing. However, eliciting information regarding needs is not always straightforward, particularly if developers relate them to a new technology. The 'need' for compact discs was not apparent until laser technology was sufficiently developed to read digital imprints and amplify the music at a level of quality previously unknown. The need for personal stereo systems was not a recognizable need to the market before

Current buying patterns
Current views of current products
Existing customer segments

Customer needs and preferences

Attractiveness of overall concept
Attractiveness of concept features

Trial and report buying
Barriers to changing brands
Likely purchase intent

Figure 11.3 ● The purposes of concept testing

Sony designed, developed and launched the Walkman. There were, however, indications that the need for portable music existed, in the practice of carrying around radios and cassette-players. In other words, needs have varying levels of visibility. King (1987) categorizes needs into three types:

- *Basic needs* – those which a customer will assume the product satisfies. For example, a consumer assumes that a vacuum cleaner will clean carpets.
- *Articulated needs* – those which a consumer can express readily. These are often met by at least one current solution, or can be easily imagined as being met. For example, a consumer might imagine a vacuum cleaner that shampoos a carpet.
- *Exciting needs* – those that will delight and surprise a customer. These are usually not met by current products available and customers might find them difficult to articulate. For example, some customers might be excited by a vacuum cleaner that distributed anti-stain solution and fibre conditioner!

Any new project concept must tap into all levels of needs. The fulfilment of basic needs is, of course, a prerequisite; the satisfaction of articulated needs characterizes the basis upon which the intended new product might compete with others in the category; whilst addressing exciting needs provides a platform upon which to differentiate the new product and attract new customers. It should be remembered, however, that Baker's maxim 'the act of consumption changes the consumer' indicates the dynamism of the experience of needs. Once satisfied, needs migrate towards the 'basic' status.

In other words, a product concept which at the time of launch satisfied both basic and articulated needs will soon slip in status, to the part where it satisfies only basic needs. Examples of this can be found in passenger cars and personal computers alike. Concepts comprising features designed to reach articulated or even exciting needs, such as airbags and 'wysiwyg' screens, soon became viewed as 'standards'.

Concept testing is not always appropriate in every situation. For example, concepts expressing new art and entertainments are difficult to test, as the success or failure of the final result is difficult to determine, or indeed to re-create. Joseph Heller's Catch-22 was reputedly turned down by several publishers before being accepted and selling millions of copies worldwide. Conversely, the film 'The Great Waldo Pepper' had several tried and tested success ingredients: proven director, Hollywood star in the form of Robert Redford, for example. Commercially, it failed. A second category is where the concept is based on a new technology which the market does not understand and for which there are no reference points. Consumer acceptance of virtual-reality leisure products may fall into this category. A third category of concepts that is difficult to test reliably describes those expressing a new physical experience such as taste or smell.

Despite these exceptions, concept testing is widely accepted to be an important element in successful NPD. If concept testing is deemed worthwhile and procedures are aimed at all three sets of purposes, then the information collected, centred as it is on needs, will inform later stages in the NPD process, such as test marketing and launch. This is an important issue, as it shows how, relatively early on, information regarding eventual segmentation and positioning is being collected.

The next section describes the relationship between needs and product concepts that must be understood if the purposes of concept testing are to be achieved.

The relationship between needs and products

In Chapter 2, we reviewed formal definitions of a product, most of which agree that a product is the focus of an exchange process wherein customers exchange cash for satisfaction. In order to explicate the levels on which this satisfaction may or may not be delivered, Kotler (1989) used a 5-level product concept, comprising:

- Core benefit: the fundamental service or benefit being purchased.
- Generic product: the material properties which deliver the core benefit.
- Augmented product: the 'package' which includes additional services and benefits that distinguish the company's offering from competitors.
- Potential product: the augmentations and transformations that the product might endure in the future.

Viewed this way, a complete product *concept* would have to cover at least the first four of these levels. Even if each level were not to be individually subjected to concept tests, the internal picture is not complete without an indication of how the new product concept performs at this level. Recently, however, Saren and Tzokas (1994) have questioned the utility of this view of the product in a way which is particularly relevant for our discussion of the link between user needs and product concepts. The basic criticism is that conceptualization of the product such as Kotler's will attempt to define the product in isolation from the customer-supplier context:

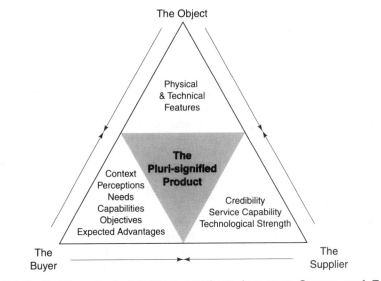

Figure 11.4 ● The pluri-signified product (*source*: Saren and Tzokas, 1994, p. 911)

'It regards the product as an autonomous unit which can be de-constructed and understood in its basic elements. But this is fundamentally wrong since the mere understanding of the existence of a product for consumption is realised, not by its material nature (which sometimes need not be there at all), but by its symbolic meaning that the society and individual consumers and producers have ascribed to it by means of culture, use or experience and their interaction with each other.' (Saren and Tzokas, 1994, p. 904).

Instead, the authors propose that a product is the outcome of a 'continuous tri-partite signification process' between buyers, suppliers and the object. This outcome – the pluri-signified product – is shown in Figure 11.4.

The significance of this alternative view is that it highlights the need for product developers to focus not only on needs and expectations but also on their underlying determination and on the relationship between the customer, the object and the supplier. This, it is argued, is of benefit to those engaged in new product development, as it introduces elements into concept testing which are usually ignored (company reputation, whether or not consumers usually buy the company's products) and over which the company has considerable control.

What is a new product concept?

A concept which can be subjected to testing is more than an idea, newly emerged. An example of this might be where an idea, from a food company, is to enter the 'health snack market', which is growing and for which there are documented consumer needs. This is still a vague idea, which must be turned into a more specific concept. There are several ways in which such a concept might be developed.

A health snack might take several forms: packet soups, vitality drink or a confectionery health bar, to name but three. These are still ideas. How could their potential be discussed – either internally or in the marketplace? First, there has to be some specification of the ingredients, in order for the company itself to assess the feasibility, likely competition and fit with strategy. Second, testing consumer need for an acceptance of a 'healthy snack soup' does not give them much idea of how this product might benefit them or how it might be different from other snack soups on the market. They might, however, indicate a 'trial' willingness, depending on their view and experience of the company concerned.

Concept tests are ultimately tests of perception, which are affected by influences such as past experience of a product or company, as well as the characteristics of any specific concept. Before going on to discuss the methods available for concept testing, however, it is important to define exactly what is being tested. As suggested above, it is difficult at this stage in the NPD process to test all the levels of a product concept, largely because they have not usually all been developed. For example, the 'augmented' product – the package of benefits including retailed services – may not be developed until a later stage in the product development cycle. Further, although research has shown that new products with potential longevity often have the seeds of the second generation within the conceptualization of the first, it is rarely a 'testuable' factor. In other words, the concept is a *promise* of the benefits which will be derived from certain product characteristics or attributes. These attributes are produced from the manipulation of certain material properties, either of which might be transformed by new or modified technology. These relationships may be described as the 'mechanics' of the new product concept, and are shown in Figure 11.5.

Why are these mechanics important, when the satisfaction of the need is the end result which is of interest to the customers? The answer is that rarely will customers be able to give an accurate assessment of their view of a new 'promise of benefits' unless they can compare it with *how* those benefits will deliver satisfaction. This allows them to make comparisons with current offerings, where they exist. For example, potential buyers of industrial heating and ventilation systems cannot readily and reliably evaluate the promise of 'greater comfort control, more cost savings' without an idea of at least

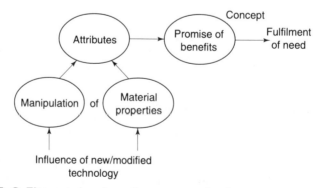

Figure 11.5 ● The mechanics of a new product concept

the attributes that will deliver the promise, and more usually a sketch of the material properties of the system, their functioning (manipulation) that will shape these attributes. In consumer durables, the benefit of dry as well as clean dishes from a dishwasher can only be evaluated, with some idea of the attributes which will accomplish the benefits. In this case the nature of the attribute would need to be explained in terms of materials, say a hot air blower. Finally, a promise of benefits may be evaluated if the attributes are amplified in terms of manipulation, rather than material properties. For example, a new process for freeze-drying coffee beans may be forwarded as producing stronger, but less bitter, coffee than others on the market. This is also a concept which might be tested.

A final example of a new concept is the Network Computer (NC), which might conceivably (if the concept is accepted by consumers) break the power of Microsoft and Intel in the PC market. One company pioneering NC technology is Oracle. The NC is a basic machine which has no hard drive or software storage space. It runs through the phone line and might eventually be as widespread as the phone, giving access to the Internet as well as basic computing applications that are used by the average person (*Marketing Week*, 13 December 1996, p. 20). An obvious benefit of the NC is the price, expected to be around £800, but what other benefits might it have to persuade consumers to change from the installed technological base, the PC?

These examples are driving towards the conclusion that a concept must be presented in such a way that the benefit, and one of the components of the potential product's attributes, must be apparent to the potential customer. Consider, for example, trying to have customers evaluate a 'new' concept such as a four-hour train journey from Edinburgh to the English side of the Channel Tunnel. While the benefit is clear, it is an idea which cannot be tested because the market would immediately ask questions about how this service might be accomplished. If their reactions to the idea were positive, but we added that the journey included a flight from London-City to the Tunnel, their reactions might change. In sum, a new product concept is not complete until it is articulated in terms of *both* attributes and benefits. Consumers can then evaluate whether they feel the benefits fulfil the need and whether the attributes deliver the promised benefits. This concept, however, is but a starting point. In order for concept testing to begin, a number of decisions must be made. These are the subject of the next section.

The process of concept testing

As outlined above, concept testing is a test of perception, and as such is influenced by all that influences perception, such as:

- Information given about the new product concept. The degree to which the concept is explained and linked to other product levels (for example the augmented product) will affect customer perceptions.

- Timing of the evaluation. The more time given to a customer to evaluate a concept influences the response. If only a short time is given, only first impressions will be forwarded.

- Context for the concept. The context for a product evaluation may be defined in many ways, *vis-à-vis* competition, place of consumption or use of the product, with reference to certain market segments and positioning.
- The nature of the product concept itself. This relates to the point where a product concept fits on the continuum between 'emotive' and 'functional'. In general, the more emotive a product concept, the more information is required to explain the concept. Of course, as has already been stated, highly emotive products such as perfume may not concept-test well or easily.

These overriding considerations influence the choices outlined below in dealing with the process of concept testing, which is generally made up of three phases: (1) definition of specific objectives; (2) types of concept presentation; (3) method for gathering data.

Defining objectives

The overall purpose of a concept test is likely to vary from one concept to another. Earlier, broad purposes of concept testing were introduced: to assess likely purchase intentions, to make improvements to the new product concept, and to profile the market. The relative importance of each purpose will influence the type of concept test carried out. Each is examined briefly below.

Assessment of purchase intent (PI)

It might be argued that this is the primary purpose of concept testing, so that those concepts with poor potential may be weeded out. All the techniques used are in some way related to key concepts in buyer behaviour generally and to those associated with the adoption of innovation. Both these subjects were covered in Chapter 4. The most common way to assess purchase intention is to provide a description of the product and ask respondents participating in the test to check the appropriate box, saying whether they:

☐ definitely would buy
☐ probably would buy
☐ might or might not buy
☐ probably would not buy
☐ definitely would not buy

It is usual to consider the 'top two boxes' responses in deciding the concept's potential. The percentage of respondents checking these can then be compared to any existing category norms. Alternatively, the percentage may be subjected to adjustments based on different levels of consumer awareness, distribution levels and other levels of promotional support. In either case, marketing managers must take a view on how likely the percentages are to be a realistic prediction of a real product launch. Many use past experience to adjust the percentage up or down. Research by Taylor, Houlahan and

Gabriel (1975) suggests that a concept should receive 80–90% of the responses in the 'top two boxes' to encourage further development work. Further, studies by Morrison (1979) and Kalwari and Silk (1982) suggest that purchase intention does correlate with actual purchases.

A vital consideration, particularly relevant in assessing market potential for fast-moving consumer goods, is to take account of 'repeat buying'. Clearly, high trial will not always be followed by levels of repeat buying which would realize potential.

Improving the product concept

Inherent to concept testing is concept development. Since respondents are asked to evaluate a concept, there is ample opportunity to adjust the details of the concept in order to pinpoint which concept has greatest appeal.

This development work may be carried out with respect to the overall product, in which case an indication of consumers' perceptions of a number of concept-specifics may be evaluated (Dolan, 1993):

- the concepts' uniqueness *vis-à-vis* other products available
- the concepts' believability
- the ability of concepts to solve a customer's problem
- inherent interest in the product concepts
- value for money.

These questions may be termed diagnostic. Moore (1982) defined diagnostic questions as those which shed light on reasons behind the intent-to-purchase questions, implying that diagnostic questioning tends to accompany intention-to-purchase questions. However, as one of the benefits of concept testing over product testing is the flexibility with which concepts can be altered and retested, diagnostic questions have a role in their own right in attaining the concept-to-market requirements.

In addition to diagnostic questions which elicit feedback regarding the entire concept, some may focus on specific attributes of the product concept. Again this may be investigated in relation to intention-to-purchase in a specific way, or to gauge preference among different attributes or the perceived importance of one attribute over another.

Market profiling

The third major purpose (objective) of concept testing is to assess the characteristics of likely buyers and non-buyers. At the most basic level, this will involve the collection of demographic information, but may extend to include information such as typical buying criteria, psychographic profiles, product usage patterns, and buying processes used. This kind of information helps to interpret analyses of the intention-to-purchase date, thereby leading to refinement of the concept under development and preliminary information for targeting, positioning, promoting and launching the product. Indeed Cooper (1993) contends that these decisions should not be left to the end of the development cycle.

It is important that the balance of these three possible objectives of concept testing is specified at the outset. Depending on these objectives – what the tests are to achieve – their nature will change. Diagnostic objectives may require both qualitative and quantitative tests to be carried out. The actual types of questions, whether focused on one concept or on more than one, whether the concept statements given to consumers include a 'positioning' signal, essentially flow from the objectives.

Initial choices

In addition to defining these broad objectives for the concept tests, the remit must be specified in relation to two important initial choices: points of comparison and target markets.

Points of comparison

Faced with a new product concept, a potential customer has to decide how to assess whether the attributes deliver the promised benefits. Those benefits must be set in the context intended by the developer. If, for example, we wish to test the concept of cheese-flavoured potato bites, customers must understand against *what* they are evaluating. A number of possibilities arise. First, it could be that no points of comparison are sought, that it is the intrinsic notion (core idea) of cheese plus potato in a bite size which needs to be evaluated. The danger with such an approach is that different customers *do* use competitive perspectives to make their evaluation. Some may have cheese-flavoured crisps in mind, others have 'take-away' finger foods such as chips or nachos, while still others may compare the concept with the huge variety of frozen potato variations available as a convenience meal complement. If the developer defines the cheese-flavoured potato bite as a new snack concept, then the points of comparison must encompass other snack opportunities. Failure to specify these points of comparison means that developers cannot understand what the concept is accepted (or rejected) as. This has implications, not only for the decision to continue or kill the development, but also for how the product is eventually positioned.

Target markets

The envisaged target market affects the marketing context into which the new product is placed. For example, cheese-flavoured potato bites may have several target audiences: children, food providers for children – itself a huge category which might be subdivided further, to include parents (working and non-working), nursery and infant schools, crèches – and snack-eating adults, who again might be subdivided into health-conscious and convenience-conscious. Each of these targets would require a slightly altered type of test, in search of what is rated and the points of comparison. Another issue relating to the target markets introduces the concept of 'expert consumers'. Faced with the criticism that 'confronted with a radically new technology, customers do not understand what needs the technology could satisfy' (Tauber, 1974, p. 22), some advocate the use of 'innovators' as the target market for concept tests (Ortt and Schoormans, 1993) or 'expert' consumers (Schoormans, Ortt and de Bont,

1995). This is paralleled in the industrial market by the work of von Hippel (1988) and Foxall (1988) who advocate the involvement of lead-users (experts) in new product development. The selection of the target segment does not happen once only throughout the NPD process. As we have seen in Chapter 8, the strategic context for NPD sets some broad parameters in which to consider target markets, whilst both idea generation and screening often involve research with a specific target market. Indeed, 'gaps in the market' necessarily define target (and non-target) segments. Further on in the NPD process, the stages of product testing and test marketing require further specification of target markets.

Once these broad issues have been delineated, the more specific but equally important issues of deciding on how to present the concept and collect the data are broached. The next section deals with the first of these.

Types of concept presentation

Once the basic research objectives have been set, the next step is to define what and how to present to customers. There are commonly six ways to present a concept to the market for evaluation.

A *verbal presentation* is the most basic type of representation. Verbal presentation generally gives an incomplete picture of the product concept (which may result in unreliable findings). Consider the following statement describing a 'smart radiator valve control':

> 'The new radiator valve control consists of a small (4 cm x 4 cm x 5 cm) cuboid, which is easily fitted to the existing valve by a simple screwing action. It has an attractive push button surface which controls the amount of heat generated by the radiator. The control is programmable by temperature, hour and day of the week, and can shut itself off when draughts (for example from open windows) are detected.'

A *black-and-white line drawing* can be used on its own (see Figure 11.6) or with accompanying text.

A *colour line drawing* can be used to portray more of the feel of the product (see Figure 11.7).

A *photograph* of a mock-up is normally used at the concept development phase. Also, where a 'new' product is introduced from a foreign market, photographs (or even product packs) may be available to evaluate the concept.

A *storyboard* is frequently used to evaluate advertising concepts. It allows a presentation of the product in the context for which it is designed.

A *mock-up* of the pack, shape or general form can be used – but at the concept stage this is not a 'working' mock-up. This type of representation gives a customer a better feel for the product he or she is being asked to evaluate.

Influences on the choice of presentation

There is no agreed 'best' way to represent a product for the evaluation of the basic concept. As we go through the six ways described above, the amount of information

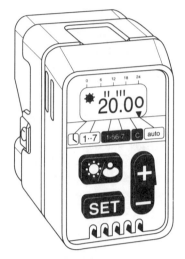

Figure 11.6 ● Electronic radiator controller (EHR)

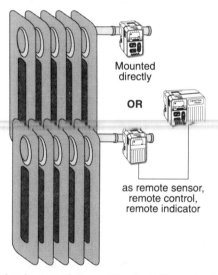

Mounted
directly

OR

as remote sensor,
remote control,
remote indicator

Figure 11.7 ● Positioning and mounting of the electronic radiator controller

increases. Thus, the more information is needed to convey to prospective consumers, the greater the value of using pictorial or mock-up representation, since more information can be understood visually than verbally. In addition, where a product is likely to be viewed from one angle only, a pictorial (or verbal) description will suffice. For example, a hob designed to be built-in is generally viewed and used from one position only, and might be readily represented by a picture. On the other hand, a free-standing cooker has several points from which it is viewed and used – the hob, the grill, the oven, and so on, and therefore it may be more comprehensively represented by a mock-up. A number of issues affect the choice of method of representation. These are dealt with below.

The product's frame of reference and product field.

The more familiar the concept, the easier it is to conceptualize what it is like. Product concepts are generally viewed in terms of what is already in the customer's mind – past experience of related brands and products. Therefore each product type is judged by a specific frame of reference which differs between product fields. Thus, the form of presentation must take the field frame of reference into account. Generally, the product field frame of reference depends on whether a product concept is familiar or unfamiliar. Where product concepts are unfamiliar, there tends to be a greater need for the amount of information given. An example of the effect of this can be seen with the hypothesized concept testing of mashed potato nests. Table 11.1 shows what consumers might think of various representations of the product in terms of its perceived size, its use and for whom it might be suitable.

The table shows how the opinions might alter, depending on the type of presentation. If a company launched the product on the strength of the information received after the third product concept test, the resultant sales might be very different from those achieved if the company carried on to the fifth product concept test. This example underlines the fact that concept tests are evaluating perception, and the potential role of the test itself in determining the reliability and/or validity of the data. It follows also that the actual product must, once developed, be in accordance with the concept presentation or a different market reaction might be obtained at a later stage in the NPD process. In most cases, however, only one or two presentation formats

Table 11.1 ● Concept test results for Bird's Eye Potato Nests

Presentation		Consumer evaluation of	
Format	Size	Use	Target market
1. Verbal	No clear indication	Snack →	Child
		Light meal →	Housewife
		Main meal →	Man
2. Black and white drawing and verbal description	Average	Snack →	Child
		Light meal →	Housewife
3. Colour drawing and verbal description	Average	Snack →	Child
		Light meal →	Housewife
4. Colour photograph showing product as part of a meal	Large	Main meal →	Child/housewife/man
5. Pack shot	Very small	Snack →	Child

will be chosen owing to cost constraints, so great care must be taken with the eventual choice.

Functionality of the product

A second factor influencing the product field frame of reference is where the product lies on the emotive–functional continuum mentioned earlier. In this case, the more emotive the product, the greater amount of information is required by customers attempting to evaluate it. This is because emotive products are sold more on image, connotation, personality and so on. It follows, therefore, that a low level of concept information will not adequately represent the 'attributes plus benefit' of the product. Consider, as an extreme example, the texts that go along with emotive products such as aftershave and perfume. The following are taken from descriptions of two major scents.

- Amirage de Givenchy: 'wonderfully feminine, lively and elegant, warm-hearted and generous, Amirage is an expression of intense happiness'.
- Jazz: 'Jazz starts with vibrating aromatic notes, moving onto a core of floral elegance over a base of wood, resinous warmth'.

For more functional products, the more information is given, the greater the amount of variation in customer/market responses. This happens because the descriptions may vary. For example, here are two statements about vinyl folders for loose-leaf student notepads:

- 'The folder is hard wearing, with a metal clip mechanism, and is expandable, holding up to one ream of A4 paper'.
- 'The folder comes in a variety of colours and laminated finishes, holds up to one ream of A4 paper and costs £1.50'.

The second description gives the person who is evaluating the product different information against which the evaluation can be made. This means the responses to the second description contain different variables that evaluators might choose to comment on. The decision regarding how much and what description to provide depends on the dimensions for which the developer would like to receive comment. The more variables, the greater the range of potential comments.

The amount of information given to evaluators in a concept test also depends on the purposes of the test, which may favour the use of a 'core idea' statement or a 'positioning concept' statement. The question of which of these approaches to adopt is debated. In favour of positioning concept statements are the following arguments:

- The assessors (respondents) relate the concept to current products more easily, resulting in a more lifelike assessment.
- Concept assessments are generally better, i.e. more favourable.

In favour of core statements are the following counter-arguments:

- The purpose of a concept test is to assess reactions, not persuade respondents.

- There is a need to elicit unbiased responses regarding the product, so there should be as little promotional appeal as possible.
- There is research showing how different copywriters' texts may affect concept score results (Haley and Gatty, 1971).

The evidence in favour of each approach suggests that neither is demonstrably better than the other. Moore (1982, p. 287) suggests that 'the amount of positioning and sell is a function of how great the benefit is, how well it is understood, how socially acceptable it is to admit a certain need and how emotional the need is. As a general rule, concept writers should use the minimum amount of sell required.'

Accuracy of information presented

The information should not be misleading. Accurate information is dependent upon the information presented to respondents in a concept test. This is particularly important with respect to size, colour and key features intended by the developer to differentiate the product from those of competitors. For example, information about a car's features must show, either by explanation or visually, whether or not the model includes an airbag, if this feature is an important aspect of the car's differentiation or positioning.

Comprehensiveness of information presented

Equally, the concept test must present all the relevant details. Respondents must be able to evaluate the concept against *all* the features of the product, not just the more attractive features. For example, the concept test for a jug kettle must describe not only its capacity and overall shape and dimensions, but all features, including whether or not there is a water-level indicator, an automatic switch-off mechanism, whether it is cordless and the location of the on-off button as any one of these might cause the reaction to the product to be negative.

Consistency of information presented

All the information has to be consistent. Any graphic representation should not conflict with verbal descriptions, or the validity and reliability of the evaluations will be rendered suspect due to an element of confusion. At best respondents might articulate any confusion; at worst they will tend to use one representation upon which to base their evaluations. The researchers will then not be able to know whether they are comparing reactions to the 'same' representation when interpreting the results of the concept test.

Time allocated to convey/understand information

The amount of time given to a respondent to assess the concept tends to increase the amount of criticism they will generate. Judgment must therefore be exercised when considering the time element. If the amount of time given for the concept test is too

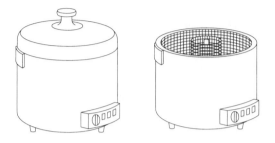

Spin fryer

- Fries food by circulating hot air and oil mist around food placed in basket.
- Requires only 2–3 oz. of oil.
- Cooks chicken 30% faster than deep fat frying with 20% less fat content.
- Controlled cooking process avoids burning or overcooking food.
- Can also be used as a steamer or slow cooker.

Figure 11.8 ● Concept test results for the spin-fryer. (Source: Page and Rosenbaum (1992))

short, then the overall reaction might be more positive than in a real purchase situation. A useful clue here is to consider the nature of purchases in the relevant product category. Low-involvement purchases which demand little effort in the purchase situation will need correspondingly less time in a concept test than products typically requiring a complicated search process.

There is relatively little evidence to shed light on which modes of presentation are used most frequently. In a recent study of one type of concept test, conjoint measurement, over 75% of studies used verbal descriptions (Wittink, Vriens and Burhenne, 1994). Studies by Page and Rosenbaum (1992) report that the Sunbeam Appliance Company has adopted a form of concept testing which combines freehand sketches and lists of three to five bullet points to describe the use of products, their features and benefits. This type of testing allows the company to evaluate a larger number of product concepts than by using either mock-ups or fully functional models, as it is much less expensive. An example of the type of concept card used is given in Figure 11.8, depicting a 'spin fryer'.

These procedures cost around £1,000 per concept tested, whereas testing consumer reactions even to mock-ups costs £3,000 for the mock-up alone. This said, the expenses of the company show that the concept tests are not sufficient, by themselves, to predict final market performance, since the way in which the final product is developed may change aspects of its appeal. Concept testing is not, therefore, a substitute for product testing, which is examined in Chapter 13, but is a way of further assessing potential before expensive physical development takes place.

The next section focuses on the choice of data collection techniques.

Research methods for concept testing

The research methods used for concept testing are numerous. Among the central issues are data collection methods, location of the research and question format.

Data collection methods

The methods for collecting the data may be qualitative or quantitative. Qualitative procedures such as in-depth interviewing of either individuals or groups of consumers are generally recognized to be of benefit, particularly for generating and refining concept statements, or indeed the concepts themselves. As with qualitative research in general, its intensive focus allows respondents the time and freedom to express likes, needs, preferences and opinions, without forcing a reply, as in quantitative methods. This, in turn, yields high levels of validity and delivers greater understanding to the developers in the dimensions along which eventual customers will judge their product. This is particularly relevant, since concepts are likely to be multi-attribute. The depth approach afforded by qualitative methods allows a fuller understanding of the relative appeal of these attributes as well as their collective contribution to the 'whole' concept. However, qualitative techniques require skilled fieldworkers and researchers (as do quantitative techniques, as discussed below) to avoid the pitfalls of leading consumers or misinterpreting their meaning. In addition, their intensiveness usually eclipses the possibility of carrying out research with large samples, which is problematic where the purpose of the tests is to generate representative estimations of market preferences and possible market shares.

Quantitative techniques, on the other hand, which cover survey techniques such as structured 'personal' interviewing mail and telephone surveys, are less intensive and can therefore be conducted on a much larger, random scale, with the resultant data being more easily generalizable. In reality, however, because concept testing is about assessing attitudes, perceptions, intentions and so forth, it is valuable for researchers to be able to explain issues and probe customers, so personal, structured interviewing is the most commonly used data collection method. Mail surveys in particular have a number of drawbacks: it is difficult to obtain full answers to any open-ended question regarding product dimensions; response rates to mail surveys are generally low, casting doubt on the representativeness of the responses obtained; respondents usually have no opportunity to ask questions about the concept; and, finally, the problem of the effects of question wording and question order on the responses given cannot be easily avoided. Telephone interviews suffer from limited opportunities to use any graphic representation, unless combined with mail contact, and the interview usually has to be kept rather short.

Research, however, by Jamieson and Bass (1989) showed that with multiple-wave telephoning, despite a reduction in numbers of respondents on each wave, the profile of respondents remained constant and the market share prediction levels were satisfactory. There is still, however, little evidence that concept testing is carried out via telephone interviews in Europe.

Location of tests

Given that the most common data collection method for concept testing tends to be the personal, structured interview, decisions regarding the location of such tests have to be made. The choice is usually made between carrying out the interviews at the respondent's home, or in a neutral location such as a shopping mall, a public thoroughfare, or a hotel seminar room.

Industrial companies may also execute concept tests at trade fairs or exhibitions, despite the drawback that competitors are present. Public places, such as the street, shopping malls or hotel seminar rooms (where people from the street may be invited), are usually varied to cover different times of the day as well as different days of the week, in order to generate samples that are as representative as possible.

Question format

In addition to decisions regarding the type of data collection strategy to be used, the types of question asked must be decided upon, in terms of their content and form. As discussed above, their precise content is in large measure dependent upon the objective of the concept test. Therefore, where the tests aim to identify the proportion of likely users, the questions will be different from where tests are focusing on diagnostic issues. The types of question that relate to different purposes will be returned to shortly. There is, however, an overriding choice governing the type of question. Specifically, developers must choose between *monadic* and *comparison* questions.

Monadic or comparison questions

Monadic questions are those which ask respondents about 'one' concept (hence monadic). If the concept testing phase as a whole is focused on several new concepts, then each one would be evaluated by one sample only, with comparisons being made after the data have been collected. No one respondent would be asked about more than one concept. Figure 11.9 shows how three new concepts might be tested using a monadic approach.

The three product concepts, A, B and C, are co-ordinated by three groups of respondents. These three groups, or samples, are matched. This means they are similar samples in forms of demographic characteristics, or indeed of characteristics which

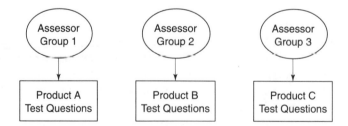

Figure 11.9 ● The monadic approach in concept testing

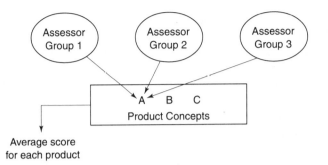

Figure 11.10 ● The comparative approach in concept testing

might be used to segment the market for the product, once launched. The groups of respondents are asked to rate the (one) product they are testing in terms of *overall* likes and dislikes, and in terms of likes and dislikes of specific attributes. These questions would satisfy the 'diagnostic' aims. For the purchase intention aims, each sample would be asked how likely they would be to purchase the product. The results from each group are then compared and inferences are drawn regarding which product concept has achieved highest acceptance.

The argument in favour of monadic testing posits that the test captures the reality of the purchase situation, since, faced with a choice of products, consumers compare products in their own minds. However, the disadvantage is that it is difficult to assess whether differences in scores for products are due to the fact that different people are testing them, rather than due to a consensus view that one product concept is better or worse than another. Using the *same* people to test different product concepts resolves this problem, and is called comparison or comparative testing.

In comparison testing, the same group of respondents is asked about two or more concepts. Several groups of respondents may be used in order to check the reliability of the results. Figure 11.10 depicts this approach.

One advantage of comparative testing is that since the same group of respondents is being used to test different new product concepts, the differences in average scores for each can be more reliably allocated to real perceived differences, rather than differences among the groups of assessors. In addition, some people favour comparative concept testing as they believe it reflects more accurately the purchase situation where a potential buyer assesses a new concept in relation to ones he or she already knows.

Question wording

Both the diagnostic and PI objectives can be pursued by both monadic and comparison questions. For purchase intention to be assessed monadically, the question wording might take the form of a checklist, as set out earlier under 'Assessment of purchase intent', or it might use a probability or point allocation question. A probability question for the spin fryer shown in Figure 11.8 might be: 'Please circle the number from 0 to 10 on the scale below which best indicates how likely you are to buy the product. If you would definitely not buy the spin-fryer, circle 0. If you would definitely buy it, circle 10. If your opinion is not definite, please indicate a number between 1 and 10 which indicates how likely you would be to buy, or not buy, the spin fryer.'

A point allocation system is suited to comparison tests. In this case, several concepts of the spin-fryer might be presented to respondents, along with other currently available deep-fryers. Then respondents may be given points, counters, or even fake money. The question posed to respondents might be: 'Based on the drawings and statements you have just seen, allocate these 10 counters across the brands in proportion to how likely you would be to purchase them.'

Concept A	Concept B	Brand C	Brand D

For diagnostic purposes, it will be recalled that a number of concept specifics may be evaluated, including uniqueness and believability, the concept's ability to solve a problem, inherent interest in the product concept, and value for money. Questions which might be used to elicit diagnostic information on these dimensions for a memo-pen might include:

Concept statement: 'The Memo-pen is a fully functioning ball-point pen with a built in tapeless voice recorder on to which up to 20 seconds of spoken notes, messages and aide-mémoires can be recorded' (Concept A)

Ability to solve a problem
How relevant is the concept described above in solving your personal organization needs?

Highly relevant					Not at all relevant

Believability
How believable is the claim that the Memo-pen can record 20 seconds of spoken notes without the use of a tape?

Completely believable					Not at all believable

Uniqueness
Check the box that most closely fits the description you just read:

An ordinary pen					A unique pen

Inherent interest
Please write, in the space provided, how interested you are in the concept of a pen which will record spoken memoranda.

_____

_____

_____

Or: please check the box that best describes how interested you are in the pen described above:

Extremely interested – it is a good idea							Not at all interested – it is a poor idea

Value for money
If the pen were offered to you at £29.99, how would you describe its value for money?

Good value for money							Poor value for money

These questions might also be modified to compare the Memo-pen with other concepts such as the Alarm-Clock Pen. In this case, a comparative question would include a second concept statement:

Concept statement: 'The Alarm-Clock Pen is a fully functioning ball-point pen with a built-in digital 24-hour clock and programmable alarm function' (Concept B)

The question regarding the comparative ability of the two concepts to solve a problem might read as follows:

How relevant is each concept described above in showing your personal organization needs? Indicate their relevance by writing A and B in the appropriate boxes.

Highly relevant						Not at all relevant

Finally, market profiling requires that a number of questions be included to allow developers to learn which groups of respondents like and dislike the concept. The questions will usually cover demographics and psychographics, as well as what products are usually bought and what the usual choice criteria are.

The above examples of the kind of questions used are intended only as *broad* suggestions. In fact, several techniques are commonly applied in concept testing, which are essentially specific combinations of purpose, objectives, approach (monadic vs. comparison), data collection technique, question wording and analysis. Three of these are the subject of the next and final section of the chapter: conjoint analysis, hybrid method and the 'House of Quality'.

Specific techniques for concept development and testing

This chapter has concentrated thus far on describing the purposes and decisions of concept testing in general. As explained above, some techniques described in 'idea generation' such as perceptual maps may have their uses also in designing and refining new product concepts.

Below we briefly discuss three more specific techniques associated with designing new products: conjoint analysis, hybrid conjoint analysis and the 'House of Quality'. As with other techniques described in previous chapters, there is no rule confining these only to the 'concept development and testing stage'. They may be usefully employed at earlier stages in developing and screening new product ideas, and adaptations may be of use in product testing. This largely depends on the type of new product process typically followed by a particular company and the type (newness) of the new product being developed. It is perfectly conceivable, for example, that the three techniques described below could be applied in product testing, where the 'new' product is a modification of, or an extension to, an existing product, since the physical presentation of different attributes would not be too costly. On the other hand, where innovations are more radical, the presentation of alternative designs and attributes is best kept to the 'concept' stage if costs are to be kept low.

Conjoint analysis

The key purpose of conjoint analysis is to evaluate how potential customers judge products in terms of their attributes and to examine the extent to which they might 'trade' one 'attribute' for another. The term covers a number of data collection and analytical techniques, which allow researchers to optimize the combination of product attributes in terms of the overall evaluations that potential customers make.

In order to explain how it works, we will use a much simplified example of a small manufacturer of decorative containers for food and beverages. One of their ranges uses wood veneers, which are fashioned into lightweight drums of a variety of sizes. Recently, the company wished to enter the market for speciality cheeses, a product category where packaging is an important indicator of quality. In order to design their product for this market, the company had two fundamental design decisions to make. The first related to the nature of the identification of the contents: labels or screen-printing. Screen-printing is more expensive. The second design decision related to the nature of the finish given to the wood, where three possibilities exist: natural, stained or lacquered. Thus, there are 3 x 2 = 6 combinations. In order to illustrate how conjoint analysis might provide insights into how these attributes might be combined, we can take the hypothetical individual rankings on each of the six combinations:

	Product identification	
Container finish	Labelled	Screen-printed
Natural	3	2
Stained	5	1
Lacquered	6	4

The preferred combination, therefore, from this individual is the screen-printed, stained container, while the least favoured combination is the lacquered, labelled container. These rankings are then assigned a utility value which, it is assumed, describes the perceived utility of the specific combinations, and from which the perceived utilities of each attribute can be deduced. Thus, the rankings of the overall product variations (in this case, six) allow the researchers to disaggregate the scores to derive the perceived utility of each attribute. (These utilities are also known as part worths.)

In assigning utilities, we can code the rankings so that the least attractive combination gets 0, and the most highly ranked gets 5:

	Product identification		
Container finish	Labelled	Screen-printed	
Natural	3	4	Average = 3.5
Stained	1	5	Average = 3
Lacquered	0	2	Average = 1
	Average = 1.3	Average = 3.7	

Since both product identification attributes are rated with each of the finish attributes, it is possible to use the average score of each attribute across the ratings as an indication of its 'utility' or 'part worth'. In this case, the individual's utility value for each attribute is as follows:

Identification: Label 1.3, Screen-printing 3.7

Container finish: Natural = 3.5, Stained = 3, Lacquered = 1

From this we can see that lacquer is the least favoured finish and that the preferred product identification method is screen-printing. However, were this individual typical of a market or market segment, the company might wish to know to what extent a lacquered finish might be acceptable along with a screen-printed product identification. Using the average utility scores we can estimate this. The decrease in utility value from having a lacquered finish is at least $3 - 1 = 2$. The increase in utility value from having screen-printed product identification is $3.7 - 1.3 = 2.4$, which is larger than the decrease in utility value perceived by the lacquered finish. Therefore, a trade-off might be possible.

The simplicity of this exercise is misleading. In reality, trade-off or conjoint analysis programmes are capable of handling far more levels of far more attributes of concepts. This can be done in one of two ways. The full-profile method may be used, where potential customers respond to complete descriptions (or full profiles) of the product. However, the term full-profile is rather misleading, since it is rarely possible to ask potential customers to rate all the possible combinations of attributes. Even if only four attributes were being addressed, where one attribute consists of two levels and the other three consist of three levels each, the number of combinations would be $2 \times 3 \times 3 \times 3 = 54$. If it were even possible to have respondents evaluate all 54, it

Table 11.2 ● Decision stages in conjoint analysis

Stage 1: Determine relevant attributes

↓

Stage 2: Choose stimulus representations (i.e. form of representation)

↓

Stage 3: Choose response type (i.e. rankings or ratings)

↓

Stage 4: Choose criterion (i.e. liking, preference, likelihood of purchase)

↓

Stage 5: Choose data analysis method

Source: Dolan (1993), p. 116

would be tedious in the extreme for them. It is more usual, therefore to use a subset of these concepts. This is called a fractional factorial design. It is still a 'full-profile method', because it is possible to contain all of the attributes in the study within the description.

The second method is called the paired comparison method, where respondents choose between two concepts, giving the one they prefer. Again, fractional factorial designs can be used, to avoid having to ask respondents to judge every possible combination of pairs. Whilst a detailed discussion of analytical methods for these techniques is beyond the scope of this book, a brief résumé of the decision steps in conjoint analysis is appropriate. Dolan (1993) presents a useful table of the decision stages in conjoint analysis, shown in Table 11.2.

For stages 1 and 2, the factors influencing the decision have already been discussed for concept testing in general. With respect to conjoint analysis in particular, it is important that all the salient attributes – those that might have an impact on the eventual decision to buy the product – are included. For stage 3, consideration must be given to the extent to which respondents can provide more reliable judgments by ranking preferences on attributes of alternative concepts, or by rating the alternatives independently in respect of the attributes. This relates back to the discussion regarding monadic and comparative tests and the degree to which a rating, on, say, 'liking' of an attribute can be made accurately without specific reference points being set by the researcher. Stage 4, deciding on the criterion, is related to the overall 'purpose' of the study, as discussed above, but carries the additional decision as to whether the criterion to be measured is 'preference' or 'purchase intention' (PI). The distinction is not a trivial one; while a respondent may *prefer* the aesthetic appeal of a Bang and Olufsen television, he may at the same time have no *intention to buy* one because of its price. Stage 5, choice of analytical method, is related to the chosen input data, as described above, and the purpose for which the data are intended. At the stage of concept evaluation, four purposes are implied for conjoint analysis: analysis of attributes, competitive analysis, market share prediction and market segmentation. It is not the intention of this section to describe in detail the analytical methods, which are discussed further in Dolan (1993), Urban and Hauser (1993) and Moore and Pessemier (1993).

The extent of usage of conjoint analysis has not been subject to investigation in Europe. However, Wittink and Cattin (1991) surveyed the use of the technique in over 1,000 projects during a five-year period from 1981 to 1985. Their findings showed that a majority of users were in consumer goods manufacturing. The most common purposes for which the technique was used included concept identification, competitive analysis, pricing, market segmentation and repositioning, and multiple purposes were used for studies.

The most common form of data collection was the personal interview, and the most common form of construction was 'full profile'. Both rating and ranking response scales were most typically used.

The decisions involved in conjoint studies affect the accuracy of results. One of the common criticisms of conjoint analysis in concept testing is that data might be somewhat artificial as they are typically gathered in isolation from existing products. This limits its use in market planning because it is unrelated to market structure (Acito and Hustad, 1981). In recognition of this, several proponents of a modified procedure called 'hybrid methods' have appeared (Green, 1984; Acito and Hustad, 1981). This is briefly described below.

Hybrid conjoint analysis

The hybrid procedure is intended to provide market share estimates for new and existing products, examining the impact of changes in product attributes, price and competitive reaction and taking into account 'subjective' factors such as manufacturer's reputation, reliability in delivery, and service levels given to customers. In addition, it is designed to anticipate the extent of brand substitution, also called cannibalization, since overall company revenues will not be enhanced if a new product's sales merely take the place of those provided by existing products. In order to deliver these insights, the procedure must not only specify the new product concept and select the experimental design, it must also define the set of relevant competing products. This involves, in the case of an entirely new product, finding which alternatives currently satisfy the needs the new product aims to satisfy.

In order to describe this in more detail, consider the example of two major manufacturers of industrial air cleaners. These products are usually ceiling-mounted. They draw in air, which is passed through a filter to remove dirt and dust particles, and the air is expelled once 'clean'. These products, when not used as part of an integrated air-conditioning system, are most suited for the 'Horeca' market (hotels, restaurants, cafés) across Europe. They tend not to be suited to offices or domestic use because of the rather noisy motor used to suck in and expel air. The manufacturers, whom we will call Atlas and Gaia (not their real names), each manufactures a 'standard' product, which has one power level (for air suction) and which costs around £3,000 to buy. Recently, Atlas introduced a reduced-noise version, which has reduced Gaia's market share. The reduced-noise version costs £3,500. Gaia, therefore, has been considering how to develop products which will strengthen their competitive position regarding this. Design engineers have found an alternative solution, which would increase the power levels, allowing greater volumes of air to be cleaned per hour, making the cleaner more effective. They have also identified ways of making the higher-power cleaner less noisy than the current standard cleaner they offer to the market. There are different cost implications for both options. Gaia must look at the impact of the new product on its other standard product as well as the potential impact on the competitor's products.

The procedure to examine these relationships begins with a description of all the potential and existing products. To begin with, there are two existing 'standard' products selling at £3,000. Second, there is Atlas' new product which exhibits the same power levels as the standard products, at a reduced level of noise. Its price is £3,500. The new concepts proposed by Gaia have either (1) increased power and reduced noise levels, costing £4,000, or (2) standard power and reduced noise levels, costing £3,500. Then respondents would be asked to rate their purchase intentions among existing products, as well as their preference based on different combinations of attributes of the concept. This allows the calculation of preference or PI weighting for attributes, which can be used to calculate potential market shares. These can then be compared with the PI on existing procedures to examine the effect of the new concept on Gaia's aim, and completing existing products.

This procedure entails different results than a conventional conjoint analysis. Specifically, its focus is not exclusively the trade-offs consumers or buyers will make between one attribute and another. It extends to consideration of the impact of the new product on other sales in the market. In addition, the results are not centred on an 'individual's' value system, but on an aggregate 'intention to buy' or preference indicators, which may be measured on a number of different scales, including ranking, rating and constant sum techniques.

As with standard, conjoint analysis, there is a limitation in respect of the number of features that may be tested. In addition, the customer assesses the product given the representations developed by the company. It follows, therefore, that highly abstract representations may lead to results which should be interpreted with caution.

The House of Quality (Quality Function Deployment, QFD)

The final technique considered is part of Quality Function Deployment (QFD) introduced in Chapter 7. The philosophy embedded in the 'House of Quality', which is the first series of steps in QFD, is the identification, structuring and prioritization of customer needs, allowing the early *development* of concepts to be need-focused, rather than attribute-focused, in the first instance. In Chapter 7, we briefly described how the 'House of Quality' is useful in identifying needs. It is important to realize that QFD is a holistic technique which does not benefit in practice from being 'split up'. However, its concurrent parts do fit well with various steps of the NPD process as it is commonly represented, and therefore it is the contribution on prioritizing needs that is related to concept development and testing. Prioritizing needs helps the developer to balance the cost of fulfilling the need with that of benefit to the customer. Griffin and Hauser (1993) describe the process of prioritizing needs as one of identifying the 'importance' of primary, secondary and tertiary needs as described in Chapter 7.

The first 'House of Quality' covers a number of market-based techniques which are traditionally spread across the early stages of the NPD process. The definition of importances is a prerequisite for design work, but ultimately it is the design team which identifies the product attributes which will fulfil those needs. The techniques for measuring importances are described below.

Needs can be prioritized using a number of methods, including direct rating scales, constant show scales and anchored scales. In Griffin and Hauser's (1993) comparison, each method yielded similar rank-ordering (importance) of needs. On the other hand, the technique of using 'frequency of mention' did not appear to be a good surrogate for importance. They also found that where the importance weights of attributes are *derived statistically* (called revealed techniques), there was little association of these with product preference or interest in the concept. In addition, they found that revealed estimates of importance did not have high face validity. In other words, revealed estimates did not make sense.

Summary

This chapter has introduced a number of issues concerned with the development and testing of new product concepts. It began with an explanation of where the stage 'fits' in the NPD process, and where overlaps and reiterations exist in relation to previous stages. Next, the various purposes of concept testing were explained, with emphasis on the centrality of customer needs and preferences to these purposes. The nature of a new product concept was defined and the process and decisions in designing a concept test were described. Finally, three more specific techniques associated with concept development and testing were introduced.

After the information is collected and analyzed, a major decision whether to continue with the development must be made, before making a commitment to full physical development of the product. The physical development of the product is a costly business, and, as mentioned previously in this book, the more 'up-front homework' that can be done the more efficient and effective the entire development will be.

The next chapter, therefore, details the kinds of financial decisions that must be made.

QUESTIONS

1. Describe the differences between testing concepts and screening ideas.
2. Examine the differences between product characteristics and customer needs.
3. Explain how the components of a product might or might satisfy customer needs.
4. Why are needs important in concept testing?
5. What are the different objectives that concept testing might meet?
6. Describe the factors that affect the choice of product presentation in a concept test.
7. Compare the data collection methods for concept testing.
8. What are the advantages and disadvantages of monadic and comparative testing?
9. Describe the concept of part-worths in conjoint analysis.
10. Do you consider QFD to be an improvement on other concept testing methods? Why or why not?

Mini-case ● A New Concept in Beer: Belhaven Best

Introduction

Belhaven is the oldest continually operated brewery in Scotland, indeed one of the oldest anywhere in Britain, tracing its history back to the year 1719. It remained a family-owned brewing and malting business until 1972, after which it suffered a number of changes of ownership until 1989 when it was sold to Control Securities and the present management team headed by Stuart Ross was appointed to run the business.

As a very small local and then regional brewer for almost 300 years, Belhaven's reputation and image was primarily as a cask-conditioned or real-ale brewer. However, the management team has, over the past five years, transformed this business beyond making beer primarily for a niche market, into a market-led company which is competing successfully with the giants of the brewing industry. This transformation has been brought about by the adoption of marketing principles to identify customer requirements, the development of new products to meet those requirements, the support of the products with imaginative promotion materials and the monitoring of customer care programmes to ensure that it was meeting customer needs effectively.

The success of adopting a marketing approach has been reflected in significant year on year increases in both turnover and profitability over the past four years.

The Scottish beer market: ripe for development

The Scottish beer market amounts to approximately 2.9m barrels of beer, of which 1.75m barrels is lager and 1.14m barrels is ale. The regional brewers have little chance to compete as serious players in the lager market which is dominated by national and international brands, and the heritage of regional brewers is vested in ale production. Real ale is an obvious target market for small brewers, but it accounts for only 4% of total sales.

It was apparent that small niche markets, both at home and abroad, for Belhaven's range of bottled beers and cask-conditioned ales would not be sufficient to sustain a brewery of Belhaven's size, then operating at less than 35% of capacity.

Ross's management team realized that if the company was to grow and prosper in the 1990s, Belhaven had to appeal to a wider sector of the drinking public by brewing and marketing beers more attuned to contemporary tastes. This means that Belhaven had to change its image from that of a rustic, regional brewer into a modern business which could profitably meet the identified needs of a more discriminating market. Belhaven had no future living solely on its past reputation, its heritage and its traditions.

It soon became apparent that Belhaven had to attack the keg ale sector that is dominated by Scottish Brewers (a division of Scottish and Newcastle plc) and Tennent Caledonian (a division of Bass plc) who between them have 80% of the free-trade market (that is, non-brewery-owned outlets where Belhaven could expect to compete). These market leaders have been building the awareness of their popular ales, such as Tartan Special, McEwans Export and Tennents Special, by heavy and very successful promotional campaigns for many years. Many attempts by both Scottish and English brewers, including giants of the brewing industry such as Whitbread, Courage and Watney Mann, to break this duopoly had resulted in abject failure. Many of the English predators had returned south of the border, tails between their legs, to think again.

In essence, the problem facing Belhaven, with very limited budgets, was how it could compete against the entrenched position of two much larger competitors, especially in the light of the long list of failures of pretenders to the throne of the duopoly. Plagiarizing the two major competitors was obviously not an option; a completely different marketing strategy was required.

Product development

Belhaven embarked upon a programme of consumer research in the summer of 1990. This indicated that a keg of beer with the following qualities would be successful:

- rich creamy head
- 'cling' down the glass
- low gas content – easy to quaff
- smooth texture
- thirst quenching.

Such a beer would be in stark contrast to the very cold, gassy, thinly headed beers that had become the norm in Scotland.

The brewers got to work on a programme of new product development, which produced a number of promising new formulations which were subjected to taste panel evaluation. However, the real breakthrough came when the concept of using a 'mixed gas' system of dispensing the beer was perfected. This technique gave the beer a very creamy taste with good 'cling' down the glass, which were exactly the characteristics identified by the research.

The beer was extensively test-marketed for a period of six months in the Scottish trade to see how it performed under various dispense conditions. A key component in the strategy of Belhaven senior management at this time was to considerably strengthen the resources allocated to brewing, processing and quality control. This involved a significant increase in overhead cost, but consistency of beer quality, taste and performance was by far the overriding priority.

During the test-market period a competition was run in a Sunday newspaper to 'name the beer' and this resulted in the adoption of the brand name of *Belhaven Best* which was seen to promote the new concept. Belhaven had achieved its objective of gaining product differentiation, by avoiding conventional terms such as Heavy, Special and 70/-.

A crucial question was how to position and present Best. Belhaven wished to portray a fresh and novel concept to reflect the pioneering qualities of the ale. By selecting a distinctive brass fount the desired positioning was attained, symbolizing the brand's modernity, quality and originality. No clip badge was used, to avoid consumers confusing Best as a cask ale. Best was to substitute sales of competitive products, not Belhaven's own extensive range of real ales.

Best was formally launched in April 1991. The strategy was to build distribution gradually. Sales intelligence indicated that outlets offering attainable access were golf, rugby and sports clubs, due to the absence of restrictive financial ties. The sales force were briefed to target specifically these accounts.

By 1992, Best had established a presence. To boost consumption further, a scratch card promotion was launched at point of sale. Scratch cards promote the dual benefits of trial and repeat custom. To support the brand still further, the range of point-of-sale material was extended to include bar towels, dripmats, ashtrays, shelf stickers and posters. At the end of 1992 a decision was made to switch promotional spend away from football sponsorship of Dundee United to advertising more capable of communicating a product message.

Various strategies were considered which would promote Best most effectively, and TV was chosen as maximizing impact and able to establish the beer as one to challenge the majors. The campaign, which was supported by extensive bus-advertising, positioned the brand using two key straplines – 'Belhaven Best The Cream of Scottish Beer' and 'Not as Smooth as Belhaven Best'. Three different TV executions were commissioned for screening over two separate bursts. There are two bus-side treatments which are being used in major conurbations throughout Central Scotland.

The 1993/94 campaign and burgeoning distribution of Belhaven Best has established it as a serious player in the Scottish beer market.

Post-launch appraisal

In addition the growth of Belhaven Best has had the effect of significantly reducing unit production costs and improving the sales mix in favour of own-produced brands against bought-in brands. This has resulted in substantial increases in both turnover and profitability over the past four years, despite the self-imposed price freezing during 1992/93 and the backcloth of an extremely difficult and depressed marketplace which has seen the profits of the national brewers tumble.

Proof that Belhaven had succeeded where others had failed – in the objective of breaking the stranglehold over the Scottish keg market held by the duopoly, through the creation of a new ale sector – lies in the fact that each of the giants, as well as quite a few others, have subsequently launched new beers to directly compete against Best.

The effect of the new management team's change of approach and the introduction of Belhaven Best has radically changed this. Many sales opportunities over the past 18 months have been triggered by consumer pressure on retailers to stock Best. Belhaven's emphasis has switched from wholesaling activities to brand-owning activities, a much securer foundation on which to build the future of any company.

Finally, the performance of the company in general, and Belhaven Best in particular, instilled sufficient confidence in venture capitalists and banks to support the management in the largest Scottish MBO of 1993 when the company was purchased from its ailing parent. With Belhaven firmly under independent Scottish control of its own destiny, the management team is fully committed to further expanding the business, well equipped with an exciting range of beers to meet *all* sectors of the market. The business is now well placed to build on the outstanding success of Belhaven Best – The Cream of Scottish Beer.

chapter 12

. . . .

Business analysis

LEARNING OBJECTIVES
. . . .

This chapter investigates various financial concepts and techniques needed in order to make one of the most important go–no go decisions throughout the NPD process. Its specific objectives are:

1. To introduce the content of a business analysis for new product development.
2. To explain how the business analysis draws on previous stages of the NPD process and how it feeds into and is fed by later stages in the process.
3. To introduce a basic financial summary for a new product.
4. To distinguish business analysis from new product investment analysis.
5. To point out the pitfalls of financial analysis for new products.
6. To describe empirically based methods of carrying out a business analysis.

On completion of this chapter you will:

1. Understand the key components of a business analysis for new product development.
2. Appreciate the extent to which business analysis for NPD depends on information collected at other stages of the process.
3. Be able to articulate the difference between business analysis and investment appraisal.
4. Be aware of the problems associated with business analysis techniques.
5. Know how to distinguish the basic financial analysis from the entire evaluation required to make the go–no go decision.
6. Be able to do the basic financial calculations for NPD.

Introduction
. . . .

In Chapter 11, we said that effectively from the 'third' stage, 'screening', right through to the launch the entire process is made up of the development of the process, on the one hand, and the evaluation of the development in terms of 'makeability' and 'customer appeal' on the other. This means that screening, or more generally evaluation, is a multi-staged activity which uses a number of techniques, depending largely on the amount of information available to evaluate. At the third stage, that of initial screening, the evaluation was concerned with identifying ideas which could be developed into concepts, which might then be evaluated for their technical feasibility and market potential. At the fourth stage, that of concept development and testing, the objective is to estimate market size and customer reaction to a new product concept before committing substantial funds to its physical development.

Information regarding the likely market profile, the desired new product attributes and estimates of purchase intent are collected during concept testing. This information can now be used to generate clear estimates about the likely product costs, production and design costs, market adoption, and hence, eventual profitability.

Recall also that in Chapter 11, we elaborated on the cumulative costs of the entire product development process, which move up sharply once the product starts to be developed physically. It is therefore vital that a rigorous go/no go decision, based on financial estimates, be made before the physical development begins. This is not to say that financial estimates will not continue to be made further down the development process. Indeed, in the next chapter, on new product testing, yet more data are collected regarding the reaction of the target market to the overall product or specific features; purchase intent is based on stronger evidence of what the product's benefits are than was available at the concept stage. Again this underlines the inherent difficulty in managing the NPD process and its uncertainties. Greatest uncertainty exists in the early stages of the process, making it desirable to assess whether there is a market for the proposed product and whether it has the necessary level of customer appeal. The new product, however, cannot be subjected to rigorous testing and appraisal because the design and characteristics are not formulated in these early stages and so cannot be put in front of the potential market. Nor are there any accurate estimations of the likely cost of the product against which the potential customer might assess the new product. Later in the development process, however, as designs materialize and costs become estimable, it becomes increasingly possible to assess the new product's appeal and therefore potential. By this time, of course, some investment will have been made. By the time the new product is nearing launch, more refinements on costing can also be entered into estimations of the eventual profit of the new product. What we refer to as business analysis, therefore, will be a recurrent feature of the new product process from after the concept tests, right through to post-launch evaluation.

What goes into a business analysis?

Business analysis is at its most basic a preliminary estimate of sales volumes and costs, based on data which should, by now, be more substantial than managerial hunches. Earlier evaluations may well rest on assumption of market growth rates, or the stage of the product category on its PLC, but now is the time to attempt to tie down specifics such as the production costs, unit costs and prices, overheads, the effect of the new product on existing products' sales, and to evaluate these in the light of likely revenues. Tying down these specifics is no easy task. First, the costs are not so simple to estimate since the development team is still basing its figures on a concept, not a physical product. Second, these figures might be constructed in a number of different ways, depending on various company policies, or arbitrary preferences of its financial advisers.

It is important to remember throughout this chapter that the business analysis for a new product draws very heavily on market research from previous activities throughout the development project. Equally, alterations will be made to the business analysis as a result of later activities, also based on market research. As in all instances of the use of market research data, their quality will affect the decisions taken. In business analysis for new products, market research data often form the basic inputs to the techniques. The results of the techniques are often numeric, which lends great 'factual' weight to their meaning. It is important to remember the adage 'garbage in, garbage out', and not rely purely on the import of numbers.

A three-staged approach to the explanation of financial analysis for new product decisions is taken. First, we review the basic financial concepts that underpin any projection of profits. Second, we explore a number of crucial techniques for analyzing the potential financial performance of a new product, which, we must remember, may not exist in a manufactured, physical form at the time of the financial assessment. Third, we introduce the specialist research-based techniques which have been developed to help decision makers in reaching a conclusion regarding whether or not to continue with the development of a specific new product.

Basic financial concepts

At its simplest, an analysis of the financial viability of a new product would need to give details of:

- unit sales (expected)
- revenues (net sales value)
- production costs (fixed and variable)
- direct marketing costs
- incremental profit (expected).

Each of these is briefly described in turn.

Unit sales

Throughout the new product development process, the team, or at least the team leader, will have had a focus on 'how many' of the products are likely to sell. As we have seen previously, several stages contribute to a company's understanding of potential unit sales. At the root of this estimation is the notion of market size, which features as an element of most stages of the new product process, from strategy formulation through to test marketing. In Chapter 8 on new product strategy, some of the methods for determining market size and potential were discussed. The chapter on screening discussed the six categories of screen, each making some reference to the likely market size, which include estimates of the total available market, once target segments, competitors' positions and the like have been taken into account. However, estimations of unit sales are ultimately made after some form of sales forecasting has taken place. The alternative forms of sales forecasting for new products are described in more detail later in the chapter.

Revenues (net sales value)

The generic definition of Net Sales Value is the total sales *after* standard trade discounts have been met. Clearly, estimation of NSV is a crucial element, although its calculation is not without some problems. In addition to the issue of forecasting unit sales, the intricacies of calculating NSV include (a) taking on board the customer mix for the new product, and the extent to which discounts are variable, and (b) allowing for target-based discounts, which are given to the distribution channel on the achievement of previously set sales targets. With (a), it should be remembered that different distributors may have negotiated different terms, or indeed various terms may exist depending on the sales promotion techniques to be used. As sales promotion (which includes introductory discounts) is a significant feature of the new product launch, the financial adjustments are likely to be important. Where discounts have been negotiated with distributors based on targets, NSV is fairly straightforward to pinpoint, since discounts rise according to volume sold and this kind of adjustment is fed into the analysis.

Fixed and variable costs

Production costs are usually assigned in a specific way by each firm and are made up of two types of cost: fixed and variable. Fixed costs are those incurred irrespective of any sales volume generated, until the point, of course, where new plant or equipment is needed to grow production and sales further. They can be very high for new products owing to special acquisitions needed for production. Also, they are generally high for capital goods such as manufacturing plant, robots or machine tooling which may be required to manufacture a new product. They should not, however, be confused with sunk development costs – those are incurred in the development to date and cannot be recovered even if, after the stage of business analysis, a decision is taken to abandon the development. So, for example, if one of the companies serving the markets for professional presentations with products such as slide carousels or overhead projectors wanted to add data projectors to their portfolio of presentation equipment, all the design and concept development work, the early market studies or customer feedback research, as well as the internal costs of estimating capital equipment required, fall into the category of sunk costs: they have no capital asset and no salvage value. The difficulty with sunk costs is that they do represent an investment which sometimes managers are reluctant to write off, where doubts regarding the success of the development are being expressed. There can be a tendency to 'throw good money after bad', which needs to be resisted. Variable costs are those costs which vary according to the quantity produced, including raw materials, direct labour, warehouse, storage and distribution. Per unit variable costs remain constant, despite increases or decreases in sales volume.

Direct marketing costs

Obviously these will be high for a new product launch *in relation to sales of the new product*. They include both above and below the line advertising, sales promotional material and other sales-related extraordinary items (such as a sales conference or meeting), to name but a few. If the projected life of the product is five years, it is wise to look at all costs over a five-year period, owing to fluctuations in costs that are normal with a new product launch.

Incremental profit

Once the previous information has been compiled, it is possible to have an estimate of the profit expected. Table 12.1 includes a simplified set of data inputs, whereas in most situations financial directors may insist on the addition of overheads and other expense items such as losses incurred through cannibalization. The revenues and costs should be plotted over a number of years – in the table we show five years.

So in the example, the incremental profit added by this new product is £250,000 in the second year, £600,000 in the third year, and so on. Although a simplified view of the analysis, it illustrates well several factors which are typical of financial issues in NPD. First, note the relationship between Net Sales Value and variable costs. Here, variable costs are shown to be half NSV, for purposes of clarity, but the important issue is that variable costs represent a constant proportion of sales, precisely because they do vary with the increases in sales volume. A second issue worth noting is the high fixed costs in the first few years of the product's life. Since fixed costs are 'written down' year by year, they become, over time, less important in the profit profile of the product. Looked at another way, the first few years of a product's profitability are bound to be affected by a 'disproportionately' high level of fixed costs. This is why a competent financial analysis must go further than the launch and immediate post-launch period if it is to serve as a useful decision aid. Third, marketing costs also follow a generalized pattern, based on some of the premises of the product life cycle. As a percentage of NSV, marketing costs are at their highest during the launch and post-launch stages. If such a cost can be borne, however, the long-term pay-offs in market awareness of the new product that translate into sales will stand a stronger chance of being realized, as shown in the example above. Finally, the losses in the early stages of a new product's life will be aggravated by corporation tax, as shown in Table 12.2.

Table 12.1 ● Basic financial summary for new product X (£000)

	Year 1	Year 2	Year 3	Year 4	Year 5
Net sales value	1,000	1,500	2,000	3,000	4,000
Fixed costs	1,000	200	50		
Variable costs	500	750	1,000	1,500	2,000
Marketing costs	200	300	350	300	300
Incremental profit	(700)	250	600	1,200	1,700
Cumulative profit contribution	(700)	(450)	150	1,350	3,050

[1]Brackets indicate losses.

Table 12.2 ● The influence of corporation tax (£000)

	Year 1	Year 2	Year 3	Year 4	Year 5	Year 6
Incremental profit	(700)	250	600	1,200	1,700	
Corporation tax (40%)	—	280	(100)	(240)	(480)	(680)
Total inflow	(250)	530	500	960	1,220	(680)
Cumulative inflow	(700)	(170)	330	1,290	2,510	1,830

The question for product development arising from this table is whether the company can sustain the pattern of losses, which must be funded from borrowings. These basic financial concepts form the background for financial analysis of new products. Despite plotting the basic costs and revenues over five years, it is important to realize that these analyses do not include all the costs which will be incurred to bring a new product to market and which embrace a wider view of the total investment required for the development project, which is now underway. Investment appraisal is a vast subject in its own right, beyond the scope of this chapter. That said, we highlight two related concepts: payback and discounted cash flow.

Payback

Payback is the period of time it takes for the revenues of an investment project to equal the expenditures on the project. It is seen as a rough indicator of the liquidity associated with a particular investment in a new product and *not* a measure of profitability. It can be used, therefore, as a rough screen to help decide where a company should place its investment in order to recoup it quickly. In NPD, where two possible projects are competing for funds, a hypothetical example might be where a British brewery known for bitter and mild beers wants to enhance its portfolio. The choice of new product investment, is, say, between developing a stout-type beer or a continental-style lager. The payback period would be analysed as follows:

	Stout-type beer	Continental-style lager
Development costs	£1,500,000	£2,000,000
Income Year 1	400,000	400,000
Income Year 2	500,000	500,000
Income Year 3	600,000	700,000
Income Year 4	450,000	800,000
Income Year 5	500,000	800,000

In this hypothetical example, the payback period for the stout project is at the end of three years, since the sum of the income for those three years is the same as the development cost of £1.5m. For the continental lager project, the payback period can be estimated as the first three years of operations (where the investment is not recouped) and the proportion of the fourth year during which the investment is matched by income. The proportion of the fourth year can be worked out as follows:

$$\frac{\text{Cost} - (\text{Year } 1 + \text{Year } 2 + \text{Year } 3 \text{ profits})}{\text{Year } 4 \text{ profits}} = \text{Portion of Year } 4$$

$$\frac{£2m - (£1,600,000)}{£800,000} = 0.5$$

So the payback period for the continental lager project is 3.5 years.

The concept of payback allows companies to make sense of some of the different outcomes of pursuing alternative new product projects. However, it does not consider the total profitability over the lives of the new products under consideration. For this, another concept, namely discounted cash flow (DCF), can be used.

Discounted cash flow (DCF)

DCF is based on year-by-year projection of cash flow, as explained above in the discussion of the 'payback' period. With DCF, however, the time value of money is recognized. What this means is that the investment under consideration represents an opportunity cost: an organization could invest in other ways which would bring in alternative returns or profits over a period of time. It is prudent, therefore, to measure any potential investment against a minimum return that investing alternatively might bring. In DCF, the cash flows calculated for each year are 'discounted' using the minimum acceptable or required rate of return in the company. The required rate of return is explained below.

The required rate of return

The required rate of return is, simply, the percentage return that management requires to make from its capital investment in the new product. It is, in effect, another 'cost line' on the simple projection of the new product's profit. Although the required rate of return is often a matter of degree in companies, set by the financial department, its level can make the difference between a new product proposal having a projected profit or a projected loss. In addition, the greater the perceived risk in the new product project, the higher the required rate of return. In short, this applies a 'risk penalty' or a hurdle, for high risk projects, increasing the 'costs' of the new product. Put simply, DCF takes into account the time value of money and the total profitability over the product's life.

With some of the basic financial concepts which are relevant for business analysis briefly explained, we now turn to some key techniques used in assessing potential new product performance.

Financial techniques for new product development

In this section, some of the issues involved in assembling the data for even the most basic financial analysis are briefly discussed. The first set of data is 'unit sales', which depends on various techniques of sales forecasting.

Sales forecasting

A host of techniques for sales forecasting in new products exist, but these generally fall into one of two categories: those undertaken *before* test marketing, and those undertaken *after* test marketing.

At the stage in the NPD process of carrying out the first financial analysis, the development team is very much pre-test marketing, and in many cases is pre-product testing. This means that 'sales forecasts' will be based on data collected during the screening and concept evaluation phases, namely, estimations of market size, market growth rate, market share of current product, market segments and any purchase intentions elicited in survey research. These estimations are not straightforward; each one has its difficulties and assumptions, many of which we have encountered in previous chapters. In addition, discussion of how certain developments evolved that appear in the press or in books do have the benefit of hindsight, when in reality no developers *know* with certainty that their product will be successful. For example, Virgin is about to launch a range of cosmetics products, with ambitious plans to open 100 stores over the next five years (*Marketing*, January 1997, p. 5). The market opportunity they have spotted is part of the £4.1bn market for cosmetics and toiletries, namely, 'brand aware, but not brand loyal females'. Hindsight allows us to see the success that has been achieved by The Body Shop and numerous articles have appeared analyzing the success of this venture, but at present no-one *knows* whether Virgin cosmetics will echo the success of The Body Shop. Inside companies, it is the judgments of managers, sales, and especially with industrial products, lead users, which shed light on likely sales volume. This is not to say that where market research does exist, it should be ignored. Brewco, a large Australian brewery, ignored several market reports when they developed and launched a lager for women; market research consistently showed that there was no niche market in lagers for women and the product failed.

Several market research companies now run computer simulations based on previous experience of new product launches in relevant industries, but these may require to be carried out after the product has been developed in order to get customer reactions, which means that the data are not necessarily available at the time of the business analysis. Here again we see the conundrum of product development where the information needed to make the correct early decisions is only available later in the process. This applies as much to potential cost information as it does to potential sales information.

A common model used to assess likely sales is the full awareness–trial–repeat model (A–T–R). A–T–R is based on the concept of the diffusion of innovation, and so models purchases as a function of buyers' *A*wareness of the new product, *T*rial of the new product and *R*epeat purchases. Its basic formula is that:

Sales volume = (Market size) × (% of market who are aware of the product)
× (% of those who try the product)
× (% of those who like the product to re-buy)
× (number of repeat purchases per year)
× (unit cost)

So if, for example, we take the launch of a low-calorie red wine in the UK, we might say:

Calorie-conscious red wine drinkers:	1.2m
% of those who became aware:	50%
% of those who try the product:	60%
% of those who will repeat:	40%
Average number of 'repeats' per annum:	30
Unit cost per bottle:	£2.00 (after trade margins)

Thus the annual sales forecast would be 1.2m × 0.5 × 0.6 × 0.4 × (30 × £2.00) = £8,640,000.

To take on board, however, some of the caveats issued earlier in this chapter, the reliability of a sales forecast of £8.64m would depend initially on an accurate estimation of the market size, which is far from straightforward. Furthermore, to gain accurate assessment of the potential trial and repeat, better data would be gathered after the product had been developed and subjected to taste tests by its target audience. It is important to remember the number of estimations this model entails, for numeric values are sometimes given more weight than 'ordinary' judgments. Some of this information can only be formalized after consumers have had the benefit of physically trying the product, i.e. after product development and testing. In addition, the model is subject to a number of potential modifications, including the availability of the product for purchase, which in this case would depend on the number of outlets that agreed to stock the product, the amount of competitive products already on the market and the likely reaction of competitors to the product. In addition, the type of new product would influence the initial trial figures, since a new type of wine does not entail as much risk, for example, as the purchase of a new car or hi-fi system.

Equally, the intangibility and inseparability of new services means that the new service cannot be tested in the way we apply the term to physical products. Either a new PEP is adopted or it is not. There are no ways in which to 'try it out' other than to adopt the product, therefore the task facing developers of new services needs special consideration in business analysis.

Sales forecasts are also available later again in the new product process, for example, after test markets have shown *actual* trial and repeat purchases. But, as already indicated, financial analysis is required before actual development begins and this gives rise to the following problems:

- Market research techniques designed to help forecast sales do not take into account that most people will say they'll try something once; this is even easier where the new product has to be described or depicted but not actually experienced.
- The description of the new product used in market research will affect the types of response (see Chapter 11, 'Influences on the choice of presentation').
- Forecasting is based on the extension of current trends; the more radical the new product idea, the more difficult it is to forecast sales, since there are no trends.
- Unanticipated changes in the marketing environment will alter the validity of a forecast.

Caveats such as these reduce the effectiveness of forecasting, upon which the calculations of potential profitability rely. A further influence on the actual sales volume achieved by a new product will be its price in the market, which is often not entirely under the control of management, where competitors use price as a powerful weapon to inhibit new product sales. It is vital, therefore, to know how small changes in price, or costs, which may be forced on the company from external sources, might affect product profitability. Examination of this is called sensitivity analysis.

Sensitivity analysis

Made much easier by simple spreadsheets, sensitivity analysis merely alters certain parts of the input data, in order to examine the effect these alterations might have on the new product's profitability. Let's go back to our earlier example of a low-calorie red wine in the UK, where we predicted through the A–T–R model that unit sales for Year 1 would be 4,320,000 bottles. The breakdown of this calculation is as follows:

Market segment total customers		1,200,000
% of those who became aware:	50%	600,000
% of those who try the product:	60%	360,000
% of those who will repeat:	40%	144,000
Average number of 'repeats' per annum:	30	
Number of bottles purchased in Year 1		4,320,000

As the unit cost per bottle (ex-factory price) was £2.00, the revenues for the first year were £8,640,000. The production and direct marketing costs are £4,984,000 and £200,000 respectively, giving a first-year incremental profit of £3,456,000.

Suppose in this example that the price to the consumer was £2.99 but previous experience suggested that competitors might react to the new product by lowering their price, forcing the developers also to lower prices by, say, 50p. The bottle price would then be £2.49. This would of course have a knock-on effect to the ex-factory price, which would have to preserve retail margins. The ex-factory price might have to be lowered to £1.50, giving a simplified analysis of incremental profit as:

	Year 1
Unit sales	4,320,000
Revenue @ £1.50	6,480,000
Production costs	4,984,000
Direct marketing costs	200,000
Incremental profit	1,296,000

This profit of £1,296,000 is considerably less than £3,456,000, but at least predicted volumes would be more likely to remain the same, and the wine (being a new selling proposition in the market) might have a better chance of becoming established in the longer term. Alternatively, the developing company might decide not to match a lower price, but spend more in distribution and advertising. The sensitivity analysis would make the necessary alterations:

	Year 1
Unit sales (expected to be lower)	2,880,000
Revenue (of £2.00 ex-factory per bottle)	5,760,000
Production costs (for lower volume)	3,456,000
Direct marketing costs (increased for more promotion)	300,000
Incremental profit	2,004,000

Almost any variable can be changed in this way, to examine the effect on the projected 'bottom line'. However, again it is prudent to caution against the apparent 'objectivity' of such techniques, since in the second case the change in demand – or sales figures – would be an estimate, at best suggested by purchase intent research.

The final element of cost not catered for in our simplified version of the new product financial analysis is cannibalization.

Cannibalization assessment

Cannibalization occurs where a new product competes with an existing product and a percentage of the new product's sales are taken from the existing product's sales. Four pieces of information are required for cannibalization assessment:

1. Unit selling price and variable costs for the existing product.
2. Unit selling price and variable costs for the new product.
3. Predictions of the amount of new product sales that would come from old product sales.
4. Forecasts of sales for the old product.

In order to illustrate this, let us take the example of a cheese producer who wishes to introduce a milder form of traditional cheddar cheese, since market research has shown declining numbers of consumers showing a preference for mature cheddar. Suppose that the finances of the new and old cheddar are:

	New cheddar	Old cheddar
Unit selling price	£1.50	£1.60
Unit variable cost	£0.80	£1.00
Unit contribution	£0.70	£0.60

From these data, every time a new cheddar block sells at the expense of an old one, the company will lose 10p. If the new cheddar is expected to sell two million units, and one million units were expected to be diverted from the old cheddar (which was itself expected to sell two million units also), what will the effect be on the overall contribution of this brand of cheddar?

First, as we have said, the 'brand' will lose 10p for each sale of the new product made at the expense of the old product. The total loss will be $1,000,000 \times £0.10 = £100,000$. The new cheese will sell a *further* 1,000,000 at a contribution of £0.70, generating £700,000. The net financial gain to the 'brand' is therefore $(£700,000 - £100,000) = £600,000$.

Thus far in our review of techniques we have been dealing with the sales (and by extension, profit) forecast and the specific techniques which are useful in determining how the forecasts might be affected, by competition either inside or outside the firm.

Break-even analysis

One of the key purposes of financial analysis is to give extra information to managers in order that they can decide (a) how much product to make and (b) how much to charge, so that the profit generated by the new product matches expectations. Break-even analysis is, in fact, a simple form of contribution analysis which pinpoints the volume (units) or sales turnover required to make neither losses nor profits. As before, the information required is as follows:

1. Variable costs per unit
2. Fixed costs
3. Selling price (proposed).

The formula for calculating break-even is:

$$\text{Number of units to break even} = \frac{\text{Total fixed costs}}{\text{Contribution per unit}}$$

Contribution per unit is unit selling price less unit variable cost. An example of this is given as follows. A small manufacturer of cosmetics has patented a formula for powdered skin cleanser. This will sell at £3 per pack. The variable costs are £1 per unit and the total fixed costs are £20,000. How many units need to be sold to break even?

$$\text{Number of units to break even} = \frac{20,000}{(3-1)} = \frac{20,000}{2}$$

$$= 10,000 \text{ units}$$

The break-even point can also be expressed in sales turnover needed to reach the point where costs match profits. To consider break-even point this way, the formula is changed:

$$\frac{\text{Total fixed costs}}{\text{Contribution margins}} = \text{Break-even turnover}$$

Here the margin is

$$\frac{£3-£1}{£3} = 66.6\%$$

Therefore, break-even turnover in this case is:

$$\frac{£20,000}{66.6\%} = £30,000$$

Note also that break-even analysis can also be subject to sensitivity analysis in order to examine the effect of different margins and volumes and selling price on break-even points.

Despite its widespread use, break-even analysis is limited because it does not look at what happens during the total life of the product. It does, however, provide a useful gauge for assessing the potential of a new product concept before major investments are made and it also gives an indication of the time horizon within which the development team has to work.

In considering both the broad financial concepts and those techniques especially useful for NPD, it is important to bear in mind that all are based on traditional accounting approaches to business. As with many spheres of business, it is often not the 'accounting numbers' that let projects down but a failure to consider so-called softer issues driving success and failure. Recently, for example, it has been noted that an unac-ceptably high proportion of mergers fail because of 'soft' factors such as trying to merge the cultures of organizations, rather than the hard factors, like merging the finances (*Marketing*, 23 January 1997, p. 20). Similarly, in new product business analysis, all the numerical techniques are only as good as the data upon which they are based. Among the major criticisms of traditional accounting techniques are that they encourage managers to be risk-averse, especially where internal rates of return are set in relation to the perceived magnitude of risk; they appear to produce 'hard' factual information upon which to base decisions, when the inputs to the calculations are as subjec-tive as any other form of managerial judgment; and they are a disincentive to managerial creativity through their demand for detailed information even at the earliest stages of a new product's development. Further, a host of internal issues such as the determination of the development team, the skill and expertise with the technology, and the enthusiasm of the sales force will contrive to help or hinder the development's potential for success. Indeed, any one of the success factors identified in Chapter 7 might be critical in assessing whether a concept should be taken forward for development. In view of this a number of techniques have evolved, among which NewProd^{TM} is widely used.

Specialist research-based techniques: the example of NewProd^{TM}

Much research has been devoted to the identification of factors in the new product process, leading to a number of decision support systems, among which NewProd is widely used. Others, such as ASSESSOR and SPRINTER, are also well known and used, but tend to be more appropriate at the later stages of a new product's development, since they are essentially pre-launch techniques. In this last section of the chapter, NewProd is explained, together with its implications for business analysis. NewProd is empirically derived, as distinct from an expert system, which is a set of decision rules agreed, as the name suggests, by experts. The NewProd system requires the team responsible for the *proposed* new product project to answer individually the 30 questions in Table 12.3.

For each question, a rating is sought, plus an evaluation of the assessor's confidence in his or her rating. The data are computer-analyzed to show major differences in the evaluator's opinions on the 30 questions. This allows a framework for discussion at a screening meeting, at the end of which the participants repeat the questionnaire. The second computer analysis collapses the 30 questions into the nine 'success factors' identified empirically as crucial to new product success, shown in Table 12.4.

On the basis of this analysis, the team can then decide:

- whether to go on to physical development
- how to deal with any weaknesses in the project specification
- how to handle broadly identified areas of uncertainty.

Actual results of this process have been analyzed by Cooper (1992), who has shown that in a sample of 179 new product projects, the NewProd system correctly identified 87.5% of eventual successes, but only 59.3% of failures. Procter & Gamble validated the system internally, finding that of the projects NewProd predicted to be successes, 80% succeeded in test markets and 60% were financial successes after the launch. Of those projects NewProd predicted to be failures, only 5% were financial successes after the launch.

As with all decision support systems, the output is only ever as good as the input. As we have noted, however, business analysis is supposed to take place before the physical development of the product, and so much of the so-called 'hard' financial 'data' are also based on judgment, experience and guesswork. Since NewProd tends to consider many qualitative characteristics of the proposed project, it is very suited to the pre-development evaluation.

Table 12.3 ● The NewProd questionnaire

Resources required

The first eight questions are designed to probe whether our company has the capabilities, talents, skills, resources, physical facilities and experience necessary to undertake the project, assuming that we were to move ahead with the project. The fact that these resources might otherwise be occupied at present is not relevant.

If certain facets of the project are to be carried out by others (e.g. subcontracted production or product design; distribution via middlemen; etc.), these available outside resources should be considered as available to the project. Be careful to be realistic about the availability and quality of these outside resources.

Remember – two answers per question: ● **a rating (0–10) of the resource adequacy;**
● **your confidence (0–10) in your rating.**

	Strongly disagree	Strongly agree	Confidence
1. Our company's financial resources are more than adequate for this project (10 = far more than adequate; 0 = far less)	0 1 2 3 4 5 6 7 8 9 10		_____
2. Our company's R&D skills and people are more than adequate for this project (10 = far more than adequate; 0 = far less)	0 1 2 3 4 5 6 7 8 9 10		_____
3. Our company's engineering skills and people are more than adequate for this project (10 = far more than adequate; 0 = far less)	0 1 2 3 4 5 6 7 8 9 10		_____
4. Our company's marketing research skills and people are more than adequate for this project (10 = far more than adequate; 0 = far less)	0 1 2 3 4 5 6 7 8 9 10		_____
5. Our company's management skills are more than adequate for this project (10 = far more than adequate; 0 = far less)	0 1 2 3 4 5 6 7 8 9 10		_____
6. Our company's production resources or skills are more than adequate for this project (10 = far more than adequate; 0 = far less)	0 1 2 3 4 5 6 7 8 9 10		_____
7. Our company's salesforce and/or distribution resources and skills are more than adequate for this project (10 = far more than adequate; 0 = far less)	0 1 2 3 4 5 6 7 8 9 10		_____
8. Our company's advertising and promotion resources and skills are more than adequate for this project (10 = far more than adequate; 0 = far less)	0 1 2 3 4 5 6 7 8 9 10		_____

Nature of project

These three questions provide some general descriptors of the product or project.

Here the terms 'market', 'customer' and 'competitor' must be defined. The market is defined both geographically and in terms of applications: think in terms of which users our product is targeted at, the target users, in order to define the 'market'. Competitive products are those products that these customers now use that our product is intended to replace.

	Strongly disagree	Strongly agree	Confidence
9. Our product is highly innovative – totally new to the market (10 = totally new; 0 = a direct copy)	0 1 2 3 4 5 6 7 8 9 10		_____
10. The product specifications – exactly what the product will be – are very clear (10 = very clearly defined; 0 = not defined at all)	0 1 2 3 4 5 6 7 8 9 10		_____
11. The technical aspects – exactly how the technical problems will be solved – are very clear (10 = very clear; 0 = not clear; not known)	0 1 2 3 4 5 6 7 8 9 10		_____

Newness to the company:

Is this a familiar project to our company or a totally new one to us? These next four questions probe how new or 'step out' the project and product are to our company. Again, be sure to define what you mean by 'market', 'customer' and 'competition' (see note before question 9 above).

	Strongly disagree	Strongly agree	Confidence
12. The potential customers for this product are totally new to our company (10 = totally new; 0 = our existing customers)	0 1 2 3 4 5 6 7 8 9 10		_____
13. The product class or type of product itself is totally new to our company (10 = totally new; 0 = existing product class for us)	0 1 2 3 4 5 6 7 8 9 10		_____
14. We have never made or sold products to satisfy this type of customer need or use before (10 = never; 0 = have done so, or are doing so now)	0 1 2 3 4 5 6 7 8 9 10		_____
15. The competitors we face in the market are totally new to our company (10 = totally new to us; 0 = competitors we have faced before)	0 1 2 3 4 5 6 7 8 9 10		_____

The final product

The next seven questions probe our product advantage. Be sure to think in terms of our product versus competitive products ... the products or solutions that the customer is now using to solve his/her problem.

	Strongly disagree	Strongly agree	Confidence
16. Compared to competitive products (or whatever the customer is now using), our product will offer a number of unique features, attributes or benefits to the customer (10 = many positive and unique features and benefits; 5 = same; 0 = fewer)	0 1 2 3 4 5 6 7 8 9 10		_____
17. Our product will be clearly superior to competing products in terms of meeting customer needs (10 = clearly superior; 5 = equal to; 0 = inferior to competitors)	0 1 2 3 4 5 6 7 8 9 10		_____
18. Our product will permit the customer to reduce his/her costs, when compared to what he/she is now using (10 = major reduction; 5 = same; 0 = higher costs)	0 1 2 3 4 5 6 7 8 9 10		_____
19. Our product will permit the customer to do a job or do something that he/she cannot do with what is now available on the market (10 = clearly yes; 5 = same; 0 = less so)	0 1 2 3 4 5 6 7 8 9 10		_____
20. Our product will be of higher quality – however quality is defined in this market – than competing products (10 = much higher quality; 5 = same; 0 = inferior to competitors)	0 1 2 3 4 5 6 7 8 9 10		_____
21. Our product will be priced considerably higher than competing products (10 = much higher; 5 = same; 0 = much lower)	0 1 2 3 4 5 6 7 8 9 10		_____
22. We will be first into the market with this type of product (10 = first in; 0 = one after many)	0 1 2 3 4 5 6 7 8 9 10		_____

Our market for this product

These last eight questions look at the nature of the marketplace. Again, be sure to define what you mean by 'market', 'customer' and 'competition' (see note before question 9 above).

	Strongly disagree	Strongly agree	Confidence
23. Potential customers have a great need for this class or type of product (10 = great need; 0 = no need)	0 1 2 3 4 5 6 7 8 9 10		_____
24. The dollar size of the market (either existing or potential market) for this product is large (10 = very large; 0 = very small)	0 1 2 3 4 5 6 7 8 9 10		_____

25. The market for this product is growing very quickly (10 = fast growth; 0 = no growth or negative growth)	0 1 2 3 4 5 6 7 8 9 10	_____
26. The market is characterized by intense price competition (10 = intense price competition; 0 = no price competition)	0 1 2 3 4 5 6 7 8 9 10	_____
27. There are many competitors in this market (10 = many; 0 = none)	0 1 2 3 4 5 6 7 8 9 10	_____
28. There is a strong dominant competitor – with a large market share – in this market (10 = dominant competitor; 0 = no dominant competitors)	0 1 2 3 4 5 6 7 8 9 10	_____
29. Potential customers are very satisfied with the products (competitors' products) they are currently using (10 = very satisfied; 0 = very dissatisfied)	0 1 2 3 4 5 6 7 8 9 10	_____
30. Users' needs change quickly in this market – a dynamic market situation (10 = change very quickly; 0 = stable needs, no change)	0 1 2 3 4 5 6 7 8 9 10	_____

Source: Cooper (1992).

Summary

This chapter began by situating financial or business analysis among the many iterations of product evaluation along the 'process' of new product development. Business analysis is a vital part of that process, and should be undertaken before any serious commitment is made to physical product development. That said, it is insufficient *alone* for making new product decisions for a number of reasons. First, the quality of input data needs to be checked. In nearly all the analyses, accuracy is jeopardized when sales forecasts are not reliable. Second, not all costs are included. Costs such as those 'invisible' demands like management's time are not entered into even the most detailed of balance sheets. Third, exogenous factors which affect sales forecasts are not always considered: seasonal fluctuations and retail practices may affect cash flow radically. Break-even volume must be evaluated alongside total market size, for if the former is 70% of the latter, its achievement will be possible only in very exceptional circumstances. A final word of warning regarding business analysis: new product development is often a long-term investment, where not only revenues but costs change over time. There is a need to consider 'cradle to grave costs' in order to evaluate a new product's full potential, but at present there is very little indication regarding the adoption of costing techniques which shed light on costs throughout the product life cycle. A study by Mahajan and Wind (1992) showed that four common 'methods' used for the 'go–no go' decision are attitude/usage studies, conjoint analysis and the PLC. Thus, there is a wide variation in the approaches taken.

Table 12.4 ● Nine underlying factors correlated with success

Factor number	Factor name and description	Regression coefficient
1	Product superiority/quality ... the competitive advantage the product has by virtue of features, benefits, quality, uniqueness, etc.	1.48
2	Economic advantage to the user ... the product's value for money for the customer	0.86
3	Overall company/project fit ... the product's synergy with the company – marketing, managerial, business fit	1.19
4	Technological compatibility ... the technological synergy with the company – R&D, engineering, production fit	0.23
5	Familiarity to the company ... how familiar or 'close to home' the project is to the company (as opposed to new or 'step out')	0.49
6	Market need, growth and size ... the magnitude of the market opportunity	0.70
7	Competitive situation ... how easy the market is to penetrate from a competitive standpoint (as opposed to a tough and competitive market)	0.25
8	Defined opportunity ... whether the product has a well defined category and established market (as opposed to a true innovation and new category of products)	0.30
9	Project definition ... how well defined the product and project are	0.23
	Constant	0.33

Notes:
Factors were identified via principal component analysis, varimax rotation, eigenvalues >1.0, SPSS routine; that is, the 30 variables were standardized, and then reduced to their underlying dimensions or orthogonal factors. The relationship between success/failure and these nine factors was determined via multiple regression analysis of factor scores, stepwise routine (the equation was significant at 0.001 level, factors at 0.05 level). The regression coefficients are shown in the right-hand column above.

In use with a new case, variables are first standardized and then reduced to the nine factors via the 30 × 9 factor score coefficient matrix (not shown here) to yield factor scores. The regression coefficients (above) are then multiplied by factor scores and summed to yield a product score and probability of success.

Source: Cooper (1992).

QUESTIONS

1. What are the main components of a business analysis for new products?

2. Discuss the role of payback and discounted cash flow in NPD.

3. What, if any, is the significance of sunk costs in business analysis for NPD?

4. What is the role of sales forecasting in business analysis?

5. What are the advantages and drawbacks of the A–T–R model?

6. What is the importance of cannibalization assessment?

7. What are the key limitations of break-even analysis?

8. Describe the advantages and disadvantages of using the NewProd questionnaire in business analysis for new product development.

Mini-case ● Fruit-Flavoured Lager

Introduction
A major division of a UK-based company with products and services spanning market sectors such as public houses, holiday and theme parks and brewing has been developing a new alcoholic drink aimed at women. The overall business is worth around £1bn with the beer product accounting for one quarter of this amount. The new product has been extensively tested as a concept, including positioning statements, name research, and research into the likely location of consumption. The target market is women in social classes C1 and C2, along with students.

Market background
The general strategic thrust of NPD tends to be for cost-reduction, but there is one NPD champion charged with the responsibility for developing first-to-market innovations. This new product champion has pioneered the new lager, based on brainstorming idea generation which focused on what consumers will want in 10 years' time. Ideas are screened in the first instance using managerial judgment and 'gut feel'. A ratio of ideas to launches of 100:1 is not uncommon. With the development of fruit-flavoured lager, all the usual concept development activities have been carried out. Consumer opinions of competitor products suggest a dissatisfaction in the target market with what is currently available. Demographic trends suggest equally that the C1 and C2 female segment (all ages) are consuming more alcohol and that this will continue in the future.

The facts and figures
The estimated market spend in these segments is around £18m annually and competing products include wine coolers and white ciders. Initial estimates of awareness after exposure to the product would be around 45%, with a further estimate of 50% trial. Repeat purchase estimates stand at 35%, with an average purchase frequency of 10 units per week. The investment cost estimates at present stand at £500,000, with initial fixed costs of £400,000, to be spread over four years. If development goes to plan, the target variable costs are £0.50 per unit. Direct marketing costs for the launch and immediate post-launch period are estimated to be £650,000.

Discussion questions
1. What do all these facts and figures mean?

2. How do they help or hinder the new product managers in making their decision?

3. How would you advise the company to proceed?

chapter 13

· ·

Product testing

LEARNING OBJECTIVES
· ·

1. To explain the overriding issues of concern in designing a product test: realism, sensitivity and validity.
2. To explore the different objectives of product tests.
3. To explain the key decisions managers must take to design a product test.
4. To discuss the key decisions managers must take to implement a product test.

On completion of this chapter you will:

1. Be able to discuss the importance of realism, sensitivity and validity in concept testing.
2. Understand the various objectives of concept testing.
3. Be able to take the necessary decisions to design and implement a concept test.
4. Appreciate the specific issues of Beta testing.

Introduction
· ·

Once the major 'go' decision has been taken, the actual product will be developed. Based on information collected previously, such as customer preferences, feasibility studies and cost analyses of alternative design, the team begins to work on making the product. As discussed previously, it is at this point that costs in the NPD process will begin to rise dramatically. The length of time devoted to the physical development of a new product will naturally depend on its complexity (Griffin, 1993). Once a first version, or prototype, has been achieved, however, it is essential to test whether it works in the way intended by earlier design specification. This requires functional testing and is long recognized as being at the very core of the NPD process. Before the product has been put together physically, its materials, the way in which they are combined and the resulting attributes were propositions. With the physical development, they become realities, which must undergo thorough testing to ensure the product has the attributes intended. In many cases, the functional tests are obvious. New drugs, for example, have to show that they work, without producing harmful side effects. New engine designs intended for better fuel efficiency must be shown to deliver a higher number of miles per litre. Low-noise passenger jets must be flown before their low-noise profiles can be verified. These tests, although essential, are incomplete. If we

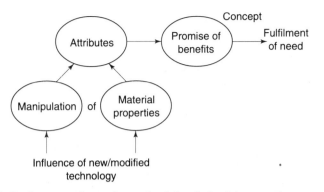

Figure 13.1 ● An overview of product test design queries

recall the figure representing the mechanics of a new product concept, the attributes proposed by the concept are expected to synthesize into a 'promise of benefits' which will address user needs (Figure 13.1).

Product testing must address not only whether the attributes have been physically delivered as intended, but also whether the same promise of benefits results from the collection of attributes. In other words, product testing must assess whether the new product does, in reality, deliver the benefits that were identified at the concept testing stage. In addition, it is necessary to check whether those benefits continue to fulfil a customer need. So product performance must be tested functionally (which is often carried out in-house) and with respect to the fulfilment of potential customers' expectations. Product testing covers both types of performance testing. In this chapter we are primarily concerned with the latter.

It may seem from previous chapters that, given the amount of market evaluation and positioning implicit in the process of identifying new ideas, screening them, designing and testing concepts and undertaking a complete business analysis, by this stage a product test would be all but superfluous. Indeed, the emphasis we have given to the need to get as much of the development project on the right track *before* physical development may confirm the view that product testing should be a rather perfunctory phase, if it takes place at all. While it is a stage of development which will definitely require resources, but which might not add much to what a development team already knows, it is nonetheless essential. The development of the Ford Mondeo was forced to change direction when it tested, in California, as a 'car of today, not the future' (Taylor, 1993). A good example of products which had defects revealed by product tests is that of a kitchen mixer which was made to be quiet, as indicated by concept tests, but which was considered to be 'underpowered' when switched on in product tests (Crawford, 1994). Examples such as these underline the need for testing the product in the market once physically developed, in such a way as to check that it has met market requirements previously outlined.

As the whole development process is one of increasing the amount of information available to inform decision-making, at the product testing stage, where customers can evaluate the real, not just the proposed, product, it follows that they can be presented with the fullest information thus far. Theoretically at least, this should enable them to give the most valid and reliable reaction to the new product thus far. From this perspective, product testing can be viewed as an activity which confirms the results of the positive concept test, if the product has been made in such a way as to fulfil its promise. In addition to performance testing in the market, the product may be tested alongside other elements of the eventual marketing mix: packaging, pricing and promotional message. These mix testing elements, however, are more comprehensively introduced at the stage of test marketing. This is discussed in Chapter 14.

This chapter explores the overriding concerns of product testing: realism, sensitivity and validity. It then discusses the major decisions managers need to take to carry out product testing. It finishes by presenting an overview of product test design choices and a discussion of product testing in industrial markets: Beta testing.

The purpose of product testing

The purpose of product testing is to reduce risks further in the decisions leading to the product launch. This is done by:

1. Examining the extent to which the new product fulfils the promises encapsulated in the concept statement.
2. Comparing the new product with its targeted competitive products.
3. Assessing how the product might be improved to conform better to buyer expectations.
4. Evaluating the effect of changes to the product (in content, materials, design, positioning or price) on customer preference levels.
5. Reassessing the purchase intent (PI) for the new product, given its actual (as opposed to concept) attributes.
6. Testing the proposed advertising, selling and packaging associated with the new product.

Many of these purposes are required for reformulations of current products, and it should be noted that advertising, packaging and product research are themselves complicated 'products' of the marketing research industry! As with concept testing, the required purpose of the product test will shape the nature of the test.

Within the context of new product development, however, there are factors against which the benefits of product testing must be traded. First, the incremental increase in knowledge gained by carrying out a product testing routine might not yield a sufficiently better decision that offsets the cost. Second, as time to market becomes an important competitive issue, delays to the new product development process can result in a company being 'leap frogged'. Third, in the case of radically new products, product testing needs to be accompanied by training, education and motivation of potential customers; this would make the task lengthy and expensive and would, therefore, duplicate the phase of test marketing. In addition, there are always examples of products which were successes without undergoing tests. For example, the 1993 launch of Caledonian Clear was not subject to tests; the product was launched directly at the 1993 International Food Exhibition. While these trade-offs are real, they do not eliminate the need for product testing. At this stage in the development cycle, the developers have no confirmed information that their proposed new product fits any potential user needs. If we recall that one of the most powerful and recurrent factors associated with new product success is 'a superior product meeting customer needs', we can see that the temptation to omit product testing should be resisted. Instead, the product testing must be quickly and effectively conducted, so that the final setup and tooling can go ahead for the first full production run of a new product that is compatible with user needs and competitively superior. In order to begin to consider how to conduct a product test, there are three issues which affect every stage of the process. Let's begin by looking at these.

The overriding concerns of product testing

The overall objective of product testing is assessing potential buyers' opinion of the actual products *vis-à-vis* competitive offerings. It is important, therefore, that the test is conducted in such a way as to provide potential buyers with a clear representation of the product which allows them to make comparisons in the same way as they would when faced with a choice in a buying situation. These conditions relate to realism, sensitivity and validity.

Realism

Realism refers to the extent to which the product test can portray the purchase, use or consumption of the product in such a way as to match its purchase, use or consumption in a natural or uncontrived situation. This means, for example, that vacuum cleaners should be product tested at home by consumers, that prepacked meals should be tested by consumers in their kitchens, and that a new model of car should be tested by members of the potential target market on the road. The choice, however, is often between a 'real' situation and one over which the researcher has more control and which affords greater experimental precision. For example, in a laboratory, potential consumers can try the vacuum cleaner on a variety of floor coverings which can be coated in a number of substances, allowing the researchers to develop a clear, controlled and precise picture of user preferences in different situations. Alternatively, where timing is important, it may be necessary to forego realism in order to make decisions quickly. For example, during the development of the Mondeo, Ford were faced with the decision to change fundamental elements of its suspension, engine mounts and exhaust system, owing to the introduction of the Nissan Primera, with its superior standards in handling and comfort. In order to decide whether to commit further resource, the product planning committee spent time driving the prototype and its competitors, including the Primera (Taylor, 1993).

Many decisions to be discussed in the next section have implications for realism, but key factors in the purpose of the test may require realism to be, at least partially, sacrificed. For example, in assessing how a product might be improved to conform better to buyer expectations, consideration must be given to the 'nature of the exposure'. This simply refers to whether the product is presented in its entirety (full benefit proposition), or whether only some elements are offered for evaluation. As well as saving money on a test of the full benefit proposition, elements can be tested individually and/ or in groups, reducing the time delays and furnishing crucial information on important product design decisions. For example, in testing a new aftershave, several elements might be evaluated separately: the perfume, the colour, the shape of the bottle. That way, corrections can be made to elements before they become subsumed by the whole product and their effect becomes difficult to test. Another purpose specified by the product test which affects realism is where the interest is in reassessing purchase intent. Here, the issue of the 'length of exposure' is important, since some products tends to be assessed, in reality, over time. Products such as shampoo or washing powder obviously require several 'testings', but even comestible consumer products and durables, such as hi-fi equipment or microwave ovens, may only receive a 'realistic' assessment if used more than once. Multiple exposure is both time-consuming and resource-intensive.

Sensitivity and validity

Sensitivity refers to the extent to which a product test enables consumers to identify differences between products, and furnishes the decision makers with a view of the new product's perceived uniqueness, a key ingredient in success. Although it is important for the new product to be positioned clearly against its competitors, there is a danger that the way in which the test might be designed will cause consumers to over-emphasize differences, thereby affecting the validity of the test. This would mean that by asking consumers to focus on differences between the new and other products, they can do so in a way which they would not in an 'unaffected' buying situation. This, in turn, would lead to positioning the product in a way which does not capture real consumer views on the differences in brands. On the other hand, a failure to pick up on the differences that consumers do perceive between the new and existing products not only reduces the opportunity for developing cogent positioning statements, it also increases the risk of launching a 'new and different' product which consumers do not recognize as being 'new and different'. In other words the claimed differentiating factors are not *valid* in the customer's eyes. Thus there is a tension between trying to achieve sensitivity and validity, in that an increase in one may be at the expense of the other.

As indicated above, many of the decisions to be made in designing a new product test directly impinge on realism, sensitivity and validity. These are discussed as appropriate in the next section.

Major decisions in constructing a product test

As with other stages in the NPD process, the product test encompasses a number of subsidiary decisions:

- Objective setting: what purposes will the test satisfy?
- Product-related decisions
- Sample selection
- Location of the product test

- Data collection method
- Measurement technique.

As alluded to above, these decisions have an impact on the over-riding factors of realism, sensitivity and validity. It is therefore crucial to design the tests used in product testing carefully, to ensure as far as possible that the information gathered will be of value to the decision makers, particularly in the light of the inevitable delays to the NPD process it causes and the increase in expenditure it incurs.

Objectives for product tests

Within the framework of the overall purposes of product testing, a number of specific objectives must be detailed in order to facilitate further design of the test. Objectives for product tests can be more specific than for concept testing, which is by nature more exploratory. Product testing objectives should be geared to providing information for specific decisions, which might fall into the following categories:

- To contribute to the positioning of the new product
- To contribute to the final selection of product features
- To contribute to market launch strategy.

Contributing to the positioning of the new product

Where the objective is to contribute to the positioning of the new product, a number of issues flow: the dimensions of the product which are subject to the test and the points of comparison. As described in Chapter 11, a new product concept covering the core, expected and augmented elements, is comprised of several dimensions. For example, new in-vehicle route-guiding systems for passenger cars are physically comprised of a touch-pad keyboard, a small screen, and a CD ROM containing a road map, perhaps amplified with 'busy centres' information. However, in deciding how these new products would be tested by consumers, the objective of supplying information for eventual product positioning would imply decision among which dimensions of the systems to test: screen clarity/size, ease of use of keyboard, positioning of screen and keyboard, price of the system and so on. In addition, the tests would have to be designed with specific reference points: other competing route-guiding systems or the methods currently used (lay-by and map!).

Contributing to the final selection of product features

Where the objective is to contribute to the final selection of product features, the following issues flow: the dimensional focus of assessment, whether to focus on discrimination or evaluation, and whether to choose a holistic or component approach.

The *focus of assessment* relates again to the choice of dimensions or what features to assess. For example, a company manufacturing route-guiding systems may need to decide between a 'qwerty' keyboard or a numeric one, in which case assessment by consumers would need to compare the two, especially in respect of how each affects intention to purchase (PI).

A product test concentrating on a customer's ability to *discriminate* with respect to the new product is one which assesses whether the customer thinks of the product as 'new'. In the case of the in-car route-guiding systems, which are not available in the UK as yet, there is probably little need for a test eliciting discrimination. On the other hand, there is still a need for the test to provide information on evaluation, which examines the question: given that the product is new, how well is it liked, and why? In Japan, where more than 500,000 cars currently have route-guiding systems on their dashboards, any individual company developing such a product would have to focus on discrimination as an objective of its product testing routine. This would obvious have implications for sensitivity and validity of the test.

The choice of a *holistic* approach is one which places value on the assessment of the entire system of route-guiding, rather than on aspects of it. It follows that such an approach assumes the component parts of the system to be, in themselves, satisfactory, and that it is the whole realization of the idea which requires to be tested. A component approach would follow the course mentioned above of examining 'partial-benefit propositions' in order to minimize risk, expenditure and time delays. The decision has a particular relevance for 'realism'.

Contributing to the market launch strategy

Where the objective is to contribute to the market launch, a number of issues relating to the extent of information collected must be resolved. This relates not only to the size and nature of the sample of potential customers, but also to whether, in addition to physical product testing, the associated question of advertising and package testing should be introduced at this stage. The issue of packaging is clearly more important where packaging is used, in addition to protection, for reinforcing the product's benefits and market position.

Several of the issues that are delineated by the nature of the objectives are tackled in their own right as decisions in the sections that follow. It should be remembered that the objectives of the test may, in fact, curtail the decisions made during the product testing phase.

Product-related decisions

There are three broad categories of decisions which are product related: the content and form of the presentation, the disclosure of identity (blind or branded), and the explanation and supervision of usage and consumption.

Content and form of presentation of test

The content and form of the presentation may vary. The first choice here relates to the number of product variants. Whether to present for testing the 'single best example' of a product under development or a variety of versions can be complex. The choice may

Table 13.1 ● Questions guiding product content and form

Question	Answer		Guide choice
Was the idea leading to the concept generated with the *active* participation of customers?	Yes No	→ →	Single best Variants
Was the screening stage stringent, resulting in a great reduction of possibilities?	Yes No	→ →	Variation Variants
Was extensive concept testing carried out?	Yes No	→ →	Single best Variants
Did the concept tests show clear preferences on key dimensions?	Yes No	→ →	Single best Variants
Is the manufacture of several product variants very expensive or time or resource intensive?	Yes No	→ →	Single best Variants
Is the target market well researched and understood?	Yes No	→ →	Single best Variants
Is the target market heterogeneous?	Yes No	→ →	Variants Single best
Is the target market's knowledge of the product *type* of a high level?	Yes No	→ →	Single best Variants

not in fact exist in situations where the prototype investment is such that only one variant of the product is prototyped. This is fairly rare, however, since even 'complicated' products may be developed in basic and value-added versions. The key to deciding which form(s) to present lies in the potential effects variants might have on the responses of potential customers. As with many of the stages in new product development, the conundrum is that knowledge of the potential effects cannot exist before the test takes place. It is therefore important to feed into the decision, market information from previous customer research. The questions listed in Table 13.1 should be used as a guide to the decision.

The weighting of each question will differ from company to company, and from project to project. Where the answers to questions produce a mixed view of the need to choose 'single best' or 'product variants', it should be remembered that building variants into the test results enriches information for the decision maker but is far more expensive and renders the test logistics and analyses more complex.

Blind or branded tests

The second element of choice relating to produce decisions is much debated, both within and outside the context of 'new' product testing: whether or not to use the product's brand name. The issue can be summarized as follows. Since consumers' reactions to products have as much to do with expectations and preconceived images, the sensory

Table 13.2 ● Preferences according to branding

	Formulation A over formulation B	Brand A over brand B	Formulation A (branded A) over formulation A (branded B)
Total sample	+ 12½%	+ 6%	− 2%
Exclusive users of A	+ 6%	+ 42%	+ 28%
Exclusive users of B	+ 22%	− 29%	− 22%
Users of A and B	+ 18%	+ 2%	− 12%
Users of neither	+ 8%	+ 2%	− 4%
% giving preference	(80%)	(83%)	(74%)

Source: Penny et al. (1972) p. 53.

reaction to a new product is passed through the filter of perception, which is informed by knowledge and experience of other products and competitors in the marketplace. In other words, the reaction to a new product may be enhanced or impaired, depending upon the 'stable' from which it is seen (or not seen) to come. Penny, Hunt and Twyman (1972), summarizing much of the previous literature, suggested that branded products are rated higher in tests than unbranded samples, but that there are exceptions in highly psychologically segmented markets, where branding might suggest a narrower appeal. They went on to show how two different brands of toothpaste were tested under three conditions: both blind, so that only the formulations were evaluated; branded correctly; and with one branded incorrectly and the other correctly. The results are shown in Table 13.2.

These results show that the 'blind' preference was for formulation A. Correct identification of the brands showed a majority of each user group favouring the brand they exclusively used. However, when comparing brand A with an incorrectly labelled brand B (which was in fact brand A) fewer users of A preferred brand A. In addition, exclusive users of B did not prefer A when it was compared to the *incorrectly labelled B*, whereas in blind tests, they did prefer A. These results show the influence of the blind product and 'brand' on preference estimates. The dilemma for a new product test is how the target customers' perception of the brands in the market will influence their answers. Of course, it can be argued that the influence of the brand in tests is of no greater importance than the influence of the brand on the shelves and that greater realism is achieved by using the brand name. Yet if the purpose of the new product test were to check the appeal of certain of its attributes, perhaps the 'noise' created by the brand – be it positive or negative – would not be useful. There is no correct answer to this issue. Ideally tastes could be done both branded and blind, as this would allow markets to understand the 'real' good points and develop launch strategies to so emphasize these in the light of the competitive perspective. A salutary warning, however, is in the now classic example of the development of New Coke. In blind tests, people tended to prefer Pepsi to Coke. Coca-Cola, therefore, developed New Coke, which was also preferred to 'old Coke'. However, when the New Coke was introduced onto the market, it met large-scale disapproval from Coke drinkers and the renamed 'Classic

Coke' was brought back. Given the resources spent on brand building, its effect cannot and should not be ignored.

Explanation and supervision of tests

The explanation and supervision of usage is the final issue in product-related decisions regarding product tests. Explanation of how to use a product can vary from virtually nothing to a full-scale set of instructions. Product complexity is an obvious factor governing this, as is the level of newness. Testing the appeal of programmable domestic appliances such as central heating controllers and video recorders may require patient explanation to testers to ensure that they can, in fact, reap the projected benefits. On the other hand, if explanations are required to be very copious, perhaps this would render a market success less likely. Again, the answer to this might be in repeat testing, where the first round, accompanied by exhaustive explanation, is followed by subsequent rounds that check on simplicity of use as well as the perceived benefits.

Supervision of usage is a related concept, which in many circumstances may be legally required, especially where user safety is implicated. However, as with explanation, it is desirable to allow consumers and customers to use the product as they see fit, even if 'normal' usage patterns do not concur with would-be manufacturer recommendations. While frequent breakdown due to wrong usage may not be, strictly speaking, the 'fault' of the developer, in marketing terms the breakdown will soon translate into a reputation which might impede new product success.

Sample selection

In deciding with whom the product tests should be executed, three issues are of importance: identification of 'testers', testing panels *vs.* ad hoc surveys, and sample size.

Identification of testers

Taking the first of these, the choice of testers, five potential user groups may be considered: experts, distributors, consumers or customers, employees, and development personnel. Some of these groups overlap. Development personnel are by definition employees, and are often expert. That said, they have different perspectives on the development. In the example of the development of the Mondeo referred to above, it was Ford's CEO, Harold Poling, and other top executives alongside members of the development team who were involved in test driving the Mondeo, particularly at difficult decision junctures. This kind of in-company expert testing is common in food processing, where company kitchens are used to try and taste new recipes. For products incorporated into other food products, such as yeast producers, there is a clear need to taste the effects of product variations on the taste of bread. This will often be carried out by in-house experts.

Some companies involve employees as representatives of the consumer marketplace. Linn Products, for example, a small manufacturer of highly specified hi-fi equipment, operates a 'small cottage' within its premises, where employees can listen to music on the latest equipment being produced. These initiatives are indeed useful sources of functional information, but are inevitably influenced by the fact that there is a connection between the 'user' and the company. In some instances this is desirable in itself, but in many it is vital to have an external opinion. Sometimes this is gleaned via external experts. The whisky industry, for example, relies on expert 'tasters' to inform the distilling and blending process. However, as with employees, there is no guarantee that their reaction bears any resemblance to that of the final target market. In the case of the whisky and, in addition, wine industries, tasters are an importance influence on market tastes, and are therefore vital. Similarly, distributors are a powerful influence on consumers' purchase habits, especially multiple retailers, since they account for such a large proportion of all FMCG sales. Caledonian Clear, launched at the 1993 International Food Exhibition, was met with enthusiastic responses from tasters at the stand, including the buying directors of Sainsbury, Tesco and Safeway! Similarly, the endorsement of consumer durables or industrial equipment by key distributors/retailers is vital for the product to be an eventual success.

The test groups mentioned thus far bring useful insights to the question of whether the developed product fulfils the promise intended. The real question, however, relates to what potential customers think. How do companies choose potential customers who can represent the likely reactions of the target market to the new product?

Panels or ad hoc surveys

Typically for consumer goods companies, testing is carried out either via a specifically designed, one-off research study, or by selecting consumers who are already 'signed-up' members of a panel and are regularly contacted to provide information regarding their needs, preferences and opinions of marketing activity in the widest sense. Such panels are usually accessed through a market research company; all the big ones recruit panels of consumers who may agree to be testers for new products. If this option is chosen, a key consideration is the extent to which these consumers do represent the opinions, expectations and behaviours of the market they are deemed to represent. Simply put, are consumers who sit on panels typical of all consumers, or is their willingness to provide information to market research companies something that sets them aside, in a way which might affect their view of a particular product? Once recruited on to a panel, the frequency with which they test various products will develop their critical abilities as well as their skill in completing questionnaires. The alternative, to design a specific study, for which a one-off (ad hoc) sample is selected, may compare the views of more 'ordinary' consumers, thus making the data more representative.

To date, there has been very little research into the different kinds of responses given by different types of sample. An exception is the previously-cited work of Penny, Hunt and Twyman, who monitored the levels of preference of panel and non-panel (i.e. freshly recruited) housewives for product attributes. Despite small, detailed differences, the groups' preferences did not vary significantly, leading to the conclusion that the amount of experience in testing of the panel members did not condition responses in any way that would affect business decisions. However, within the panel *vs.* ad hoc choice lies the issue of how to choose *which* testers, an issue related to the all-important question of market segmentation. Products designed with specific segments in mind should be tested by those segments. Equally, as we have seen in Chapter 3 some members of a population have a greater propensity to try, buy and adopt new products. Identifying those customers may be attempted in the ways used to segment markets more generally: using existing purchasing habits, using demographic variables, using psychographic variables, or in response to certain attributes of the product category under consideration, for example, sugar-free dilute-to-taste drinks. It should be emphasized, however, that segmentation decisions ought to have been made at an earlier stage, in order to define the product characteristics for the concept.

Sample size

The third and final consideration under target market is the sample size. Clearly the considerations vary, depending upon the identification of the testers: fewer experts are required than consumers. In addition, the purpose of the product test and the ensuing choice of data collection methods (qualitative or quantitative data collection techniques) have a direct bearing on sample sizes, since the objectives met via qualitative techniques typically require smaller samples than those of quantitative techniques.

For expert opinion a single-figure sample will suffice. In the case of employees, if firm size allows, the rule-of-thumb for sample size is 30. This is normally sufficient, particularly as employee tests should be more exploratory than the later consumer research. Where data collection methods are qualitative, three or four groups of 8–12 people, giving 30–40 personal depth interviews, will provide the diagnostic, positioning and preference information required to refine the new product. Once, however, product testing objectives are related to establishing purchase intent, and require a more quantitative approach, sample sizes will rarely fall below 100. Panel samples organized by major market research companies will commonly comprise 25,000, although not all will be contacted for any one test. With quantitative considerations in mind the key issue is related to sensitivity. The more a product test needs to establish the extent to which a target market understands, perceives and prefers the new product's differentiating qualities, the bigger the sample needs to be in order to avoid misinterpreting big differences in small samples.

Location of the product test

Broadly speaking, there are three choices with regard to the location of a product test: it may be carried out in a company's own laboratory, at a central location, or at a location of the product's use.

Own laboratory

The company's own laboratory may be used during the early iterations of product testing to establish employee, expert or even consumer preferences for certain features. Citibank Corp, for example, invite customers to use developing banking systems in their own premises to record the functionality and user-friendliness of their proposed systems. However, the obvious limitation of engaging consumers to attend is secondary to that of assessing to what extent the laboratory situation changes the responses of consumers since the product is not tested in real circumstances. Hence, while laboratory testing may improve the developer's control over sensitivity, an amount of realism may be lost.

Central location

Central locations include shopping malls, trade shows, retail outlets and hotel foyers. Consumers will be invited to test a product in much the same way as they might be invited to take part in a survey. This type of location is particularly suited to testing comestible products but is also used for specific forms of testing associated with new products such as pack and name testing. The advantages of central locations are related to the extent to which the test can be controlled. The use of the product can be held constant over the entire sample of testers. Alternatively, the reactions to different usage formats set by developers can be measured with greater control than out of sight of the developer. Thus, both laboratory and central locations may enhance the test's conformance to the requirement of sensitivity, but at the expense of reality.

Location of use

The final set of locations is related to the natural usage context of the product, and is typically in consumers' houses or workplaces. This choice is applicable in situations which require extended testing. Consumer durable products are an obvious example, since before reaching a conclusion regarding the usability, reliability and effectiveness of, say, a dishwasher or vacuum cleaner, it is wise to have them operated in a variety of circumstances as they would face once purchased. Penny, Hunt and Twyman (1972) carried out research into the extent to which consumers could identify preferences among soaps. They compared 'in-house' tests to 'instant', or in this case 'sniff', tests. They found that, for this type of product, the two methods yielded the same order of preference: an important finding, given that the cost of setting up the instant test is lower. However, in similar experiments with toothpaste, dishwashing liquids and foods, the results were less consistent between the two types of exposure. They conclude from these experiments that in-house tests are preferred for:

- products whose assessment must be made over a period of time
- products for which a heavy 'fatigue' element may be at play, or where people get used to (or bored with) a 'new' flavour
- products where consumer involvement at home is high, for example cake mixes
- products which tend to need usage instructions, which might be followed to a greater or lesser extent by individuals, for example contact lens cleaner.

Home or work locations tend to enhance the realism of the test, since products may be deployed in a wider or narrower field of activities than the manufacturer intended. Thus, the companies developing the products can detect where faults occur due to usage patterns they had wrongly predicted. Similarly, work locations are essential where companies 'customize' the product to their own precise requirements. On the negative side, the testers have far less control over home and work locations as tests, since customers will use the product in their own way and report back accordingly.

Decisions about location of the test are therefore related to several others: duration of the test, amount of control over usage, target market, expertise needed to use the product, sample size and purpose of the test. In reality these decisions are not taken one by one, but with reference to each issue simultaneously. Each of these is itself related to the next issue: the data collection method.

Data collection method

The decisions regarding data collection techniques in general have been introduced in Chapter 11 on concept testing. The basic characteristics of qualitative and quantitative options remain constant across all kinds of marketing research. In product testing, however, many situations will require face-to-face data collection methods. Mall/street intercept tests, hall tests and laboratory tests all require the presence of the tester, and usually the researcher, making it convenient to carry out face-to-face interviewing. In-house or work tests may either use face-to-face interview to assess the product's qualities, or testers can record their views on structured questionnaires. In the panel tests of soap formulation and margarine described by Penny, Hunt and Twyman (1972), 1,200 panel respondents were contacted after the product test via postal questionnaires or face-to-face interviews. The comparisons of the data collection methods suggested that where panel members were newly recruited, the subtle pressures of face-to-face interviewing were associated with a greater propensity to express preferences among product groups. These results are interesting because they show the interrelations between the data collection method and another vital consideration discussed above: expertise or experience of the testers.

A further choice is between group and individual data collection methods. Groups can be used more at the concept stage, where the emphasis can be firmly placed on gauging qualitative responses to the new product concept. As noted in Chapter 11, however, the most frequent data collection method is personal, structured interview. The product test, however, usually has a more fixed agenda in terms of the dimensions of what is being tested. Individual interviews tend to be used, therefore, to probe individual, uninfluenced (at least by other group methods) responses to these dimensions.

Measurement techniques and questions

The issues in measurement germane to product testing are similar to those outlined in Chapter 11, dealing with concept testing. The notion introduced earlier of monadic as against comparative tests re-emerges in decisions regarding how the responses to the product should be measured.

Monadic and comparative approaches in product testing

At this point, we can relate the monadic/comparative choice to the issues of realism, sensitivity and validity, the overriding concerns of product testing, in order to cast some light on how to make the choice. Table 13.3 give an overview of the impact of both types of testing measurement on three key areas.

Table 13.3 ● Impact of monadic and comparative approaches to product testing

	Monadic presentation	Comparative presentation
Realism	More like real life where products are usually used one at a time	Products are sometimes used in parallel or overlap in real life. If more appropriate, can always present the products one at a time
	Can be used realistically with an absolute rating (uninfluenced by other test products) which reflects marketplace performance. Can additionally ask for a comparative judgment against a known brand	Comparative judgment against another possibility sometimes corresponds to marketing decisions. Otherwise one of the test products can be one in the marketplace giving a known reference point for the test product. Ratings can always be asked additionally to ranking
Sensitivity	Sensitivity believed to be more like market sensitivity (i.e. more directly valid) and this is more useful for some marketing decisions	Sensitivity believed to be magnified and therefore more readily detectable with smaller samples (i.e. indirectly valid for some decisions)
Validity	On the *a priori* grounds of greater realism, assumed more like the marketplace in direction and extent of portraying product differences	Validity of size of differences questioned. Also, possible doubts as to whether direction of preferences could be distorted sometimes

Source: Adapted from Penny *et al.* (1972).

As has been stated throughout this chapter, choice of one option may necessitate the choice of another. For example, if the option of 'in-house' is chosen for a vacuum cleaner, then the choice of location is largely resolved to be 'in-house'. However, many combinations are possible, and indeed, product tests do take many different forms in practice.

The basic arguments that flow from this tabulation underline the importance of trade-off in realism and sensitivity. Where researchers are interested in finding the perceived differences among products, they run the risk that these differences, although identified, are neither important to the purchase nor considered outside the test environment. Validity of either approach of measurement is difficult to establish, since it relies on information about eventual launches with which to compare the product test results.

Scaling techniques in product testing

A second issue in measurement is the nature of the scales used. For a generalized discussion of scale usage, the reader should refer to a full-scale marketing/consumer research textbook. Five-point and seven-point scales are commonly used to fulfil the objectives outlined earlier in this chapter, all of which relate to the purchase intent and product diagnostics, in a similar fashion to the examples given with respect to concept tests. Indeed, we can use the earlier examples to illustrate the differences between the stages. The spin-fryer, introduced in Figure 11.8, once past the concept and business analysis stage would then be developed into a small batch of proto-types, which would be tested for functionality in-house. If this stage is successful, a pilot plant batch of product will be produced in order to identify and resolve prob-lems with producing the product. It is unwise to use these products for final customer-use tests because their production will vary in time, materials and amount of attention given from 'normal' production once it gets underway. A full production batch should be used for consumer tests. In this case, a consumer durable used for cooking would require in-house, extended testing (perhaps after a phase of controlled feature tests) in order to ensure that it receives the variety of treatments a typical family might expect to produce in their weekly menus. In other words, the developers need to ensure that consumers can achieve good results with battered, crumbed and uncoated food, with meats, fish, vegetables, cheeses or for whatever purpose the consumer would like to use the spin fryer. In this scenario, the questions regarding diagnostic analysis may take the forms shown in Table 13.4.

Any number of issues thought to have an impact on the appeal of the product may be 'tested'. Many of these will be derived from issues unearthed during the concept phase. In addition to diagnostics regarding specific features and benefits of the

---

Table 13.4 ● Diagnostic analysis questions for the spin-fryer

For each attribute below, please indicate your feelings about the spin-fryer:

Ease of use	☐ Extremely easy	☐	☐	☐	☐ Extremely difficult
Cooking time	☐ Food cooked quickly	☐	☐	☐	☐ Food cooked slowly
Crunchiness of cooked food	☐ Extremely crunchy	☐	☐	☐	☐ Soft
Oiliness of cooked food	☐ Extremely oily	☐	☐	☐	☐ Not at all oily
Ease of cleaning after use	☐ Extremely easy to clean	☐	☐	☐	☐ Extremely difficult to clean

spin-fryer, researchers will want to assess the overall attractiveness of the product. They might ask the following question:

Taking the spin-fryer's trial overall, how much did you like using the product?

1	2	3	4	5
Dislike strongly	Dislike a little	Neutral	Like a little	Like very much

Another strand of questioning (Table 13.5) may relate to the uses of the product, and its advantage over other methods of deep frying.

There is also the opportunity to ask some open-ended questions, in order to capture issues not revealed in the development and market testing process thus far:

What changes, if any, do you think would improve the product for you?

_____

_____

_____

At this stage in the development process, however, it is important to recognize that diagnostic questions are based on prior development work, and their emphasis is on confirming whether or not the product achieves what the results of concept tests suggested it should achieve. Similarly, if the result of research into purchase intent at the

Table 13.5 ● Product usage questions for the spin-fryer

Compared to your usual method of deep-frying, how well did the spin-fryer perform when cooking the following products?

	Cooked much better than my usual method	Cooked better than my usual method	About the same as my usual method	Cooked a little worse than my usual method	Cooked a lot worse than my usual method
Battered meat	☐	☐	☐	☐	☐
Breaded meat	☐	☐	☐	☐	☐
Uncoated meat	☐	☐	☐	☐	☐
Battered fish	☐	☐	☐	☐	☐
Breaded fish	☐	☐	☐	☐	☐
Uncoated fish	☐	☐	☐	☐	☐
Battered vegetables	☐	☐	☐	☐	☐
Breaded vegetables	☐	☐	☐	☐	☐
Uncoated vegetables	☐	☐	☐	☐	☐
Battered cheese	☐	☐	☐	☐	☐
Breaded cheese	☐	☐	☐	☐	☐
Uncoated cheese	☐	☐	☐	☐	☐

Table 13.6 ● Purchase intention for the spin-fryer

How likely are you to buy the product?

	Extremely likely	Quite likely	Neither likely nor unlikely	Not so likely	Extremely unlikely
At £29.99	☐	☐	☐	☐	☐
At £34.99	☐	☐	☐	☐	☐
At £39.99	☐	☐	☐	☐	☐
At £44.99	☐	☐	☐	☐	☐

concept test were positive, at the product test stage developers and researchers should be seeking confirmation of purchase intent figures. At this stage, purchase intent can be more firmly associated with price levels, as illustrated in Table 13.6.

Finally, the product test needs to measure some ways of classifying respondents. The usual marketing research variables will be asked, such as demographic, psychographic and socio-economic, but these will have informed the sample's selection.

Results of product testing

With this type of information collected, the developers should be in a position to know:

- whether or not the new product appeals to the target market
- whether or not the new product compares favourably with competitive or substantive offerings
- how the product might be improved
- the proportion of testers who have expressed purchase intention

In addition to testing the physical (core) product, this stage of the development cycle might be fruitfully used to test elements of the augmented product: packaging, research and name research, for example. Ford's Mondeo, as well as undergoing product tests described earlier in the chapter, undertook name research, a project which lasted six months. Whilst name research goes beyond its marketing implications to encompass important issues such as trademark searches and legal repercussions of names, the marketing implications are hugely important. Assuming that names cause neither offence nor hilarity, Hewitt (1994) recalls that Mitsubishi's 'Starion', the successor to the Colt, was hampered due to its apparently meaningless name. Although chosen to combined 'Star' and 'Orion', perhaps this is not obvious – or meaningful – to the target market. Similarly, Volkswagen's new 'Sharan' may have more connotations to the average UK driver as a girl's name than of its 'meaning': 'Car of Kings'.

Much of the above discussion of the process is based on product testing of consumer products of products. Before going on to discuss the issues involved in industrial product testing, it is useful to summarize the decisions involved in the process thus far, pointing out their interdependencies and summarizing some of the problem areas.

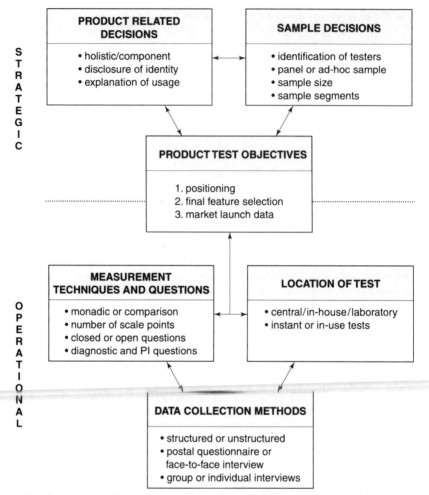

Figure 13.2 ● An overview of product test design choices

An overview of choices

As detailed in Figure 13.2, the choices in product test design relate to the objectives, which drive the strategic issues regarding the product and sample decisions. These, in turn, form the framework for the tactical decisions regarding test location, data collection methods and form of questions, although each of these must refer to the test's overall objectives. These cross-references, as we have seen, make product testing another complex phase in the development of new products. However, as noted above, the complexity sits on the basic choice to be made between realism and the level of control researchers might want to exert over the variables under observation. Table 13.7, therefore, summarizes the strategic and operational choices, outlining how the construction of the product test might change, depending on whether realism or control is the first priority.

Table 13.7 ● Realism *vs.* control in product test design for a spin-fryer

Strategic decision	Realism	Control
Product options		
Holistic *vs.* component	The whole product	Some features only: timer; switches; cleaning; temperature control
Identification disclosure	Branded supported by full product mix	Blind-products and marketing mix not identified
Exploration of usage	Normal, with usual instructions	Use controlled to suit test issues: how many times to be used, how often cleaned
Sample options		
Identification of testers	Customers, consumers	Customers, consumers, experts, employees
Panel or *ad hoc* sample	Evidence inconclusive	Random, consumer panel, experts
Sample size	Large	Large or small
Segments	All segments who will be targeted in launch	Certain segments who may have greater propensity to buy
Location options		
Central/laboratory/in-house/work	In-house/work	Central, laboratory
Instant or in-use	In-use	Instant
Data collection methods		
Postal or interviews	Postal	Interviews
Structured or unstructured	Unstructured	Structured
Group or individual	Group, individual	Individual
Measurement techniques and questions		
Monadic or comparative	Monadic	Comparative
Closed or open questions	Open	Closed

Product testing in industrial markets

This chapter has drawn on examples largely from manufactured consumer goods. What of product testing for earth-moving equipment, electronic hardware and software, electromechanical components, industrial bearings and machine tools? What are the specific problems of product testing in these fields? They derive from the fact that many industrial products are expensive to produce, are often customized, go through

a protracted and complicated buying process, and are sold to comparatively few customers. These factors, in turn, mean that:

- Buyers cannot decide on the merits and demerits of a new product quickly.
- There are not large numbers of potential testers, distinct from potential buyers.
- 'Testers' would still require to have the product adapted to their needs.
- Buyers are usually expert in the technology of the new product.

Because of these factors, industrial developers cannot afford, in either time or financial
terms, to produce 'test' offerings, install them or wait for a response on a large scale as
in the case of consumer products. Instead, industrial goods manufacturers may place
products in development with a selected handful of customers in order to monitor the
functioning, use and perceived benefit of the new product. This type of assessment is
known as Beta testing (where Alpha testing is that carried out by the developers themselves).

Beta testing is not new. In 1979, Cooper's seminal work into new product development processes showed that companies carrying out Beta tests were more successful
than those omitting a customer product test. Comparatively little research has been conducted on Beta site testing, a notable exception to this generality being the work of
Dolan (1993). While it is not intended to reiterate this analysis of over 20 Beta test
programmes in the US, below are summarized the main purposes of Beta tests, and
those factors which may affect the usefulness of Beta tests.

Purposes of the Beta test

The basic functions of a Beta test are similar to those of the 'regular' consumer test.
These are summarized as follows:

1. To check product functioning *in situ*.
2. To confirm selection of features, both core and optional.
3. To assess the accuracy and usefulness of support material.
4. To assess the level of training required.
5. To evaluate perceived strengths and weaknesses compared to those of competitors.
6. To promote sales with site chosen.
7. To use site as a demonstration example of product benefits.

As with product testing, despite the fact that function testing takes place at the developer's premises or using the developer's employees, there is little knowledge of how the
new product will be used by customers and the effect this might have on the functioning of the product. One example of a new product launch which went wrong involved
a UK company manufacturing cranes and lorry-loaded cranes which decided to extend
its range by introducing a lorry-loaded cement mixer. The design-base used was
French. There was no need for core testing because the product functioned in France.
Within months of the launch, the first customers were complaining of unreliability.
After investigation it was found that lorry drivers in the UK did not clear the cement

mixer funnel in the same way as French lorry drivers, causing the pouring mechanism to clog. A simple case of having only in-house tests resulted in massive redesign, maintenance and compensation costs.

As with consumer products, final design features must be chosen carefully, and customer input on those features that enhance the overall appeal of the product is desirable. Industrial products, however, often come with core (or basic) features as well as optional ones. It is important, therefore, that the Beta tests elicit the information necessary to make these decisions.

Support material is important in industrial products: technical, specifications, compatibility information, installation, working and maintenance instructions, service contact points. As in all documents intended to convey instruction, simplicity is not usually a strength. The accuracy, readability and comprehensibility has to be fully ensured before a full-scale launch. Linked with this is the question of training. Whilst developers may have a view as to the level of newness in the product and the level of necessary training this newness is likely to engender, it is again necessary to assess the specific training needs required in practice by a buying company to deploy the new product effectively.

The purposes of evaluating strengths and weaknesses compared to competitors are similar to those in consumer product testing which contribute to the positioning of the product.

Eventual sale of the product, once fully installed, adapted, refined and operational, is of course a goal of the process. This way, the developing company takes care of its relationship with the site company, forging closer collaborative links and benefiting from the concept of 'creeping commitment' (Robinson, Faris and Wind, 1967). Rabino and Moore (1989) take this one stage further by suggesting that the use of Beta tests often alerts customers' awareness to the forthcoming launch. This enhances recalled interest at the time of the launch proper.

Finally, a few studies also highlight the usefulness of Beta sites as demonstration sites. Easingwood and Beard (1989) propose that locating a well-known and reputable firm as a Beta test site enhances the legitimacy of a developer, particularly for very new and complex products.

Factors affecting the usefulness of Beta tests

An underlying threat to the usefulness of Beta tests is that given their considerable costs to manage, they are few in number, leading to potential problems over representatives. It is therefore important to supplement Beta testing with some comparative research with other potential buyers.

Beta test sites are a manifestation of the management of supplier–buyer relationships. In a normal 'transaction' the perceived benefits are more or less understood. In terms of relationship marketing, the 'promise' is given, and if the relationship is to be maintained, that promise will be fulfilled. With Beta tests, the promise is unclear, as is the expectation of benefits. This means the relationship might be damaged.

Confidentiality is an important issue in Beta testing if information is not to get into competitors' hands. Owing to the fast-moving nature of many technologies with input to industrial products, coupled with the large number of suppliers to Beta site companies, it is usually only a matter of time before the facts of a Beta test get out. This threat may be intensified by the fourth and final factor affecting the usefulness of Beta tests, namely the extent to which they lengthen the overall development cycle time. This in turn relates to the issue of *when* in the development cycle to send the product to the test site. While faults are easier to correct before the final design freeze, they are usually more numerous early on, and likely to cause the site company many problems.

Several of these factors can be contained, given adequate attention to the specification of goals for the Beta test, echoing the advice for general market testing of new products.

Summary

This chapter has described the issues, concepts and processes associated with new product testing. It starts by defining the 'position' of product tests in the overall process and goes on to outline the main purposes they serve. The overriding considerations of realism, sensitivity and validity are described as reference points for the subsequent decisions that must be made to conduct a product test.

The various options for product tests are described, making reference to empirical research. The chapter finishes with a discussion of the special problems in testing industrial products.

Once the tests are complete, and positive, the company is in a position to plan both commercial production and market launch. This is the subject of the next chapter.

QUESTIONS

1. Explain the concept of realism in product testing and say why it is important.
2. Explain the concept of sensitivity in product testing and discuss its value.
3. Explain the concept of validity in product testing.
4. What are the various purposes of product testing in NPD?
5. Outline the pros and cons of disclosing the identity of a product in product testing.
6. Explain the differences between the monadic and comparative approaches in product testing.
7. Outline the advantages of the various methods of data collection for product testing.

Mini-case ● Quorn TM

Introduction

In the early 1970s, Imperial Chemical Industries (ICI) and Rank Hovis McDougall (RHM) were involved in a joint venture programme to develop 'Quorn TM' – a synthetically produced, healthy alternative to meat. The decade of the 1980s saw opportunities to launch this new product against a background of emphasis on healthy living and a rapidly growing leisure service sector. The new product was not as successful as predicted.

The firm

The initial research was carried out jointly by ICI and RHM but in the experimental stage RHM sold its share to ICI who continued with the project. The association of a major chemical company in food production did not fit with the company's strategy and so the development was continued through acquisition of a subsidiary, Marlow Foods (whose sole venture would now be Quorn TM). Marlow Foods was initially a pilot plant set up in north-east England using existing ICI facilities.

ICI was restructured, with the demerger in 1992 of its Bioscience divisions, now called Zeneca plc. This demerger included Marlow Foods which is now part of the Specialities Chemicals Division which has a turnover of £500m and profits of £60m (1994). Marlow Foods continues to make a loss with projected break-even of its current production plants in the year 2000.

The industry

Zeneca plc is largely considered by the stock market as a pharmaceuticals company but it also includes agrochemical and specialities chemicals. However, its strength lies in its research and development, so it would describe itself as a bioscience company targeting its R&D, technological and marketing skills to develop new products that will solve scientific problems of their customers and consumers. It is the tenth largest pharmaceuticals company in the world with a global market share of approximately 2.5% overall.

The pharmaceuticals industry is highly fragmented with major competitors such as La Roche of Switzerland and Ciba-Geigy. Market leaders such as the newly formed Glaxo-Wellcome claim a 4.5% share of the global market. The industry is highly dependent on new product development and figures of 10% of profits retained for R&D are typical.

Zeneca is considered by the market to have a healthy new product pipeline with very few patents due to expire in the near future. The product life cycles tend to be in excess of 15 years; more typically they are 20–25 years owing to the regulatory issues associated with drug registration.

The development

Quorn TM is vegetable in origin, its source being *Fusarium graminearum*, a relative of the mushroom, naturally occurring in the soil. It was discovered by a German research scientist looking for a new form of protein. ICI had been doing similar research on a single-cell product for animal feed. The two ideas came to light through a patent search and a joint venture was set up.

Quorn TM is grown through a fermentation process. Glucose is added along with minerals and a small amount of egg white to form a 'pastry looking' substance which is then cooked and flavoured to form alternatives to meat dishes such as chicken, and beef. It is considered high in protein and healthy, with considerable versatility. Quorn TM was targeted as a direct substitute for skinless, boned chicken.

An initial pilot plant was set up using existing fermentation technology. Marlow Foods were bought over to cover as the packaging and distribution outlet. Supermarkets in south-east England (in particular Sainsbury) were approached by Marlow and asked if they could market the product using the retailer's own brand name. The south-east was chosen because it had the highest concentration of single, health-conscious consumers (mainly young female, age around 25 years) with high disposable incomes.

The result

The market impact of Quorn has been mixed. The original product was sold as QTI (Quorn The Ingredient) with various recipe cards. Separate seasonal recipe leaflets were also produced along with special recipe dishes for particular retailers. The deal Marlow Foods agreed with the supermarkets on localized distribution was proving difficult to control and very soon demand oustripped supply. Initial production was limited to the pilot plant and so ICI sanctioned expansion of two full production units in the UK and one in the USA. During the design and build phase of the main production plants, the European market was being seeded, with specially designed recipe dishes for particular countries.

In 1988 Sainsburys were using and advertising it as a meat substitute in pies. After the promising start, the company introduced Quorn TM as an ingredient in its own right; since 1990 chunks have been available in the London area. The product was targeted at 25–45-year-old women who were actively trying to cut down on meat consumption. In 1991 it had a repeat purchase rate of 70%. In 1992, Quorn was introduced in ready-meals such as Tesco's Kashmiri Korma; sales rose quickly and there are now 60 versions on sale.

In October 1993 it was becoming apparent that consumers in London, where the product was originally sold, were still confused about the product. It has no real features of its own but soaks up the flavours around it. The fact that it is an engineered food also worries people consciously trying to eat more healthily. According to a retail buyer, the product has a loyal band of followers, but most people see it as a bit faddish and aimed at vegetarians.

Quorn TM was deliberately sold chilled as opposed to frozen to emulate a Marks & Spencer style retailing which led to greater costs in storage and distribution. Vegetarians were initially targeted, but true 'vegans' were put off by the product because it contained egg white.

In 1994 it was decided to relaunch Quorn as a product in its own right, with work being done on the logo for Quorn and an ad campaign to position it as a mainstream healthy-eating food, rather than as a niche vegetarian food.

Discussion questions

1. Assess the positioning of Quorn as an alternative to chicken. What advantages and/or disadvantages does it have and what effect would these have on attaining the positioning?

2. Suggest how you might organize and conduct product tests to establish Quorn's optum 'positioning' in the market.

3. If the target segment were deemed to be 'healthy eaters', what implications might this have for distribution?

This case was compiled from data in public sources

part 3

Product
Management

chapter 14

· ·

Commercialization: test marketing and launching the new product

LEARNING OBJECTIVES

1. To define the objectives of test marketing.
2. To set out the basic steps involved in test marketing and suggest guidelines for effective implementation.
3. To identify limitations and pitfalls associated with test marketing.
4. To explain the importance of 'time to market'.
5. To review issues linked with the launch of new products.
6. To describe and explain the relevance of new products.
7. To introduce Rogers' five-point framework of product characteristics as a basis for assessing the likely reaction to new products.
8. To suggest criteria for identifying early adopters – individual and organizational.
9. To review the role and importance of communication in influencing the take-up of new products.

On completion of this chapter you will:

1. Understand the role and nature of test marketing.
2. Know how to set up an effective test marketing operation.
3. Be familiar with the advantages and disadvantages of test marketing.
4. Know why accelerating the new product development process (time to market) is vital to competitive success.
5. See the relevance of diffusion theory to the launching of new products.
6. Understand the importance of identifying potential early adopters of a new product and be familiar with factors involved in this process.
7. Recognize the importance of communication in introducing new product to the marketplace.

Introduction

In the Booz, Allen and Hamilton (BAH) model of new product development commercialization is seen as the final stage in the process. As we have stressed throughout our discussion, the normative theory as reflected in activity stage models of the BAH type will be essentially a convenient device for distinguishing the main activities or steps through which a new product will pass in the process from idea generation to market entry. These steps or stages provide the convergent points or critical path in our own model of multiple convergent processing. However, as this model and our description of it seek to emphasize, few new product projects proceed smoothly, the process may be terminated at any stage or, more likely, recycled as more and better information indicates a need for modifying the original idea. Further, rather than being a linear, sequential process, most new product development is circular in the sense that the launch of a product does not mark the end of the process but the beginning, as experience in the marketplace will invariably lead to further modification and improvement. Despite these observations it is still convenient to define a formal stage for the launch of the new product and this is usually designated 'commercialization'. It is this topic that we deal with in this chapter.

In earlier chapters we discussed the physical or objective testing of the product with representatives of the intended users. In this chapter we look at the pros and cons of test marketing in which one seeks to get a clearer understanding of the likely market reaction to the new product and its marketing mix through a small-scale trial in a sub-market believed to be representative of the larger regional or national market. Based on the findings of such testing and test marketing a final go/no go decision will be made, incorporating any modifications suggested by the testing. If this is the case then it is reasonable to expect that the full commercialization or launch phase will be a scaled-up version of the test market. On the other hand, we have seen that in an increasingly competitive marketplace, time to market has become a major issue and many new products will now move directly from the physical testing stage into the marketplace without benefit of the opportunities to test the marketing mix and the marketing plan on a small scale.

Following a brief review of time to market, we look at some of the general issues associated with launching a new product and then examine some of the key considerations for breaking into the market in some detail. Finally, we conclude with a detailed case history of the launch of an innovative new material – superplastic aluminium.

Test marketing

According to the normative theory of new product development, test marketing is a phase in the process which follows product development and testing and precedes launch and commercialization. As such, it is invariably a separate chapter in textbooks dealing with the subject and so it is here. However, as will become clear, the authors believe that the importance attached to the subject of test marketing is significantly greater than its practical use and application. Several reasons will be shown to account for this, amongst which the most important are:

- Test marketing as described in most texts is focused on the launch of major brands in FMCG markets. Despite the absolute importance of such launches, they constitute a minority of the instances when an organization is launching a new product or service into a marketplace.
- As a result of accelerating technological change and increased competition, time to market has become a critical success factor prompting many firms to avoid the loss of time implicit in a test marketing exercise.
- With improved understanding of markets, better marketing research and the benefits of information technology, together with a more professional approach to the NPD process itself, many innovators do not expect to acquire sufficient benefit from a test market to warrant the expense and delays involved.

However, in order to determine whether or not test marketing is either necessary or desirable one must first establish what are the perceived objectives or purposes of test marketing. Next, one should be familiar with the basic steps involved in conducting a test market, as well as have some understanding of the types of test marketing available. Given such an overview of the topic, it then becomes possible to determine the nature and importance of arguments for and against the practice of test marketing. We will address each of these topics in turn.

Objectives

There are two primary objectives of test marketing, which may be defined as mechanical and commercial. While the test marketer may have a stronger interest in one or other of these two objectives, most test markets will actually seek to satisfy both objectives.

The mechanical objective of test marketing can be defined as being 'to assess arrangements for handling and storing materials, producing and distributing the product in good condition, and monitoring a distributor/retailer performance'. In this sense the mechanical objective may be seen as a pilot run for production and distribution prior to gearing up for full-scale manufacturing and sales. Intuitively it would seem that whether one requires such a trial run depends very much upon the novelty of the product and/or market in terms of the innovator's past experience. If there is a high degree of novelty involved and the innovator's experience of producing or distributing the product/service in question is little or none, then a trial run would seem more necessary or beneficial than in cases where the firm is launching a brand extension into existing markets. Further, if a high degree of novelty is involved, the level of uncertainty as to how the product will perform in the distribution channels and in use will be much greater. Equally, because of this uncertainty, the likelihood of immediate competitive reaction is likely to be much lower as prospective competitors take a 'wait and see' approach.

The advantages of a large-scale pilot run or test market to help identify and eliminate problems of manufacture and distribution are obvious. With radically new products it is extremely difficult, if not impossible, to anticipate whether problems may arise. By launching the new product in a limited and controlled fashion one is better able to contain any problems that do arise and to rectify the faults, or even abort the project, before exposing oneself to the potential of a major loss. The case of the JCB 110 loader digger, discussed at length later, will illustrate this.

Clearly, when faced with a radically new product/market the logic of the product life cycle predicts that it will take time to both penetrate and develop this market. Under these circumstances a controlled rollout by the producer is a much more feasible strategic option than in the case where the new product or service is only marginally differentiated from other competitive offerings. In mature markets where consumer behaviour is well understood and market share, particularly of the major suppliers, is strongly established, the second, commercial objective of test marketing is more likely to prevail. Under these circumstances two major sub-objectives or purposes may be distinguished:

1. Providing forecasts of national sales
2. Evaluating the mix elements working together.

In turn, these two major sub-objectives provide the opportunity to:

1. Assess the speed of gaining distribution
2. Assess the speed of gaining trial
3. See how competition will react
4. Provide evidence for or against full launch
5. Enable the training of production, sales and distribution personnel
6. Provide proof of financial viability for investment.

In order to achieve these objectives it is necessary to consider the basic assumption of test marketing which is that one can find a representative sub-market or segment sufficiently similar in all its characteristics to the intended market; results may then be extrapolated to indicate what is likely to happen in the major market of which the test market is supposedly representative. If readers detect a note of scepticism in the foregoing comment, they are right to do so! As the discussion of buyer behaviour in Chapter 4 made clear, psychologists perceive each individual consumer as differing in some degree from every other. While sociologists argue that humans are gregarious and live in groups which influence their patterns of behaviour, the marketer's dilemma lies in detemining what degree of aggregation to use to establish the existence of a viable market segment.

As ACORN, MOSAIC and socio-demographic segmentation tools have demonstrated, people with similar buying behaviour patterns tend to live in similar types of accommodation. However, with many different categories of urban and rural housing to be accounted for, it is clear that one requires a fairly large geographical area to embrace them all. Clearly, the idea of a 'test town' is inadequate and one will usually need to consider at least the equivalent of a television region if one is to address a sample population representative of the national population.

In suggesting a television region as a basis for test marketing one is mindful that the television medium is a major one for promoting consumer goods. It follows that if one wishes to test the media which will be used in a national campaign one needs to include television, and the smallest scale on which one can do this is using a television region. Interestingly, independent television companies publish statistics to demonstrate that the population of the region covered by their broadcasts is representative of the country as a whole while, at the same time, claiming that the only way you can reach the distinctive population living within the area is by the use of their medium!

Because of the dominance of television many other media have now been modified so that their use can be contained to a television region in support of a TV campaign. As a consequence it is reasonable to claim that one can replicate a national marketing launch on a regional or test marketing scale in terms of the advertising, promotion and distribution elements of the marketing mix. It has to be appreciated, however, that a test market on this scale will still require a substantial investment and will quickly and visibly demonstrate to one's potential competitors the strategy and tactics one intends to use if it is intended to market the product or service on a national scale.

Much the same problems exist in other countries as described in the context of the United Kingdom. For example, recently a number of Scottish promotional agencies decided to test a campaign using the country of origin as an umbrella brand for a wide range of Scottish products. Recognition of many of the sub-brands was already well established in northern Italy and southern Germany, and the advertising agency involved was asked to cost a campaign to support a focused marketing effort in Munich and Milan. In order to target these two major shopping centres, it soon became clear that one would have to buy a media campaign covering most of northern Italy in order to target Milan and all of Bavaria to target Munich. The cost of such a campaign was more than £1.5m and far in excess of what the sponsors were willing to pay for a piece of essentially exploratory research.

What then does one hope to achieve from the execution of a test market? As suggested earlier, the test market offers the opportunity to evaluate the mix elements working together and should also enable the tester to forecast the likely volume of sales if the test area is expanded into a larger regional market. The elements of the marketing mix most subject to measurement are:

- packaging
- price
- merchandising
- distribution
- advertising
- sales promotion.

In seeking to assess the impact of each of these variables the tester will wish to measure three main kinds of reactions:

- consumer
- competitors
- the trade.

Some of the difficulties and complexities of making an objective evaluation are immediately apparent from the fact that we have mentioned at least six input variables about which we would like to make some predictions. Anyone familiar with the nature of experimental design will immediately appreciate that if one is seeking to measure the effect of varying an input variable, it is necessary to hold constant all the other input or independent variables in order to determine how a variation in the independent variable under consideration affects the dependent variable of consumer, competitor or trade reactions. Inevitably test marketers are unable to execute an experimental design of the kind which one would wish to conduct in a laboratory or, indeed, of the kind which one would normally use in developing the product itself. It follows that the use of a test market is essentially only viable to test the effectiveness of the chosen mix as a whole, albeit that one may desire some indication of the strengths or weaknesses of individual mix elements.

If, then, one is evaluating the reaction of the market to the new product or service with a given marketing mix, it seems that the major benefit to be derived will be in developing a forecast of likely volume if the product or service is sold into a larger market of which the test market is representative. Normally, a number of different measures will be used to develop a forecast of the total potential market.

In developing such a forecast most marketers tend to make implicit use of a hierarchy of effects model measuring first the number of people who are aware of a product, next the number who have tried it, and third, those who re-buy. Clearly these three measures are equivalent to awareness, interest and trial, and adoption. Ultimately, of course, it is only the last measure which is of any real use in forecasting total market potential. Textbooks and trade magazines contain many examples of products which have enjoyed an extremely successful initial launch but which have not resulted in a sufficient level of repeat sales to justify a national launch. At the same time there are also a number of examples of major companies which have launched a product unsuccessfully but have then learned sufficiently from that launch to redefine and relaunch the product successfully.

Quite often the reasons for the initial failure of a product are due to deep-seated emotional or motivational issues which are not readily determined in the somewhat artificial atmosphere of product testing and development. Ernest Dichter, the father of motivational research in marketing, is credited with a number of successful diagnoses of products which failed on launch but which were subsequently relaunched successfully. The introduction of instant coffee is probably the best-known case but cling film and 'non-scuff' floor polish are other well-known examples.

Basic steps

Essentially there are two types of test marketing – simulated and real. Much of the foregoing discussion has concentrated on the real test market in which the marketer replicates the strategy and tactics which they intend to use on a microcosm of the intended market. Because of the costs, and many difficulties involved in executing a real test market, many firms now limit their test market to some kind of simulation.

Most simulations contain six basic steps which may be summarized as:

1. Recruit subjects
2. Test attitudes and beliefs
3. Expose subjects to advertising stimuli
4. Subjects left to purchase
5. Subjects interviewed
6. Subjects may be post-contacted.

One of the favoured simulation techniques used by the manufacturers of FMCG is the use of a mobile shop containing an assortment of goods including those which are to be the subject of the test. The first step in the procedure is for the researcher to recruit 'shoppers' whose profile matches that of the intended target market. In order to produce a benchmark these shoppers are then asked to complete a number of attitudinal tests as well as provide information to establish their existing level of knowledge about other brands of products in the categories being tested. Having established a benchmark the subjects are then exposed to advertising stimuli which include the proposed advertising for the new product. The shoppers are then taken to the mobile shop, invited to select goods up to a particular value (their reward for participating in the simulation), and interviewed about their specific choices.

From a simulation of this kind one can obtain much valuable information concerning likely consumer response. However, it is obvious that the simulation is artificial when compared to the real world. For one thing, exposure to the advertising stimuli immediately precedes exposure to products available for purchase. In reality there is often a significant gap between exposure to advertising and exposure to the particular products advertised at the point of sale. Second, the range of products available for purchase is restricted and therefore does not reflect the purchasing situation experienced during a shopping expedition. Third, and most important, such simulation measures the willingness of a person to try a new product but it does not tell you anything about their likely future behaviour. It is for this reason that subjects may be post-contacted at a later date to see if they have in fact repeated their buying behaviour measured at the simulation.

With regard to the 'real' test market the three key issues to be addressed are the method to be followed, the location of the test market and the sample size. In the earlier discussion it was implied that all real test marketing was a full-scale test of all the major elements of the marketing mix which, inevitably, meant that one had to include running the intended advertising and promotional campaign. If one is prepared to relax this requirement, either completely or in part, then it becomes possible to execute a real test market on a much smaller scale. To test the packaging, price, merchandising and point of sale material a real test market could be limited to one or a very small number of outlets. By using local radio, newspapers, posters and cinema advertising, but excluding television, one could probably confine test marketing to one or a small number of towns, and this is a popular alternative followed by a number of firms.

The issue of an appropriate sample size to enable one to make reliable projections and extrapolations is more properly a subject for a textbook on marketing research. In addition to a detailed examination of sampling, most such textbooks also consider test marketing as a particular case and provide useful advice on the selection and implementation of a test marketing campaign.

Guidelines for effective test marketing

Irrespective of whether one is conducting a simulation exercise or a real test market, a number of guidelines have been suggested by A C Nielsen Co. (a major international research agency) for the conduct of an effective test market. These may be summarized in the following 20 steps:

1. Design the test to find an answer to a single major issue
2. Incorporate the test into an overall marketing plan
3. Set targets at the same level as national expectations
4. Be completely objective in evaluating results
5. Benefit from comparative testing where possible
6. Profit from professional advice
7. Select a representative area
8. Allow sufficient time to set up the test properly
9. Establish a test base against which to measure subsequent changes
10. Carefully analyze competitors' market shares
11. Welcome exposure to competitive retaliation during the test
12. Examine retailer co-operation and support
13. Examine repeat sales pattern
14. Co-ordinate advertising and promotion
15. Avoid using methods during the test which will not be repeated during the expansion period
16. Evaluate all possible factors which influence sales
17. Avoid interference with the test once it is launched
18. Adjust results to changes which may occur in the market prior to expansion or market launch
19. Allow sufficient time for the test to mature and for the results to be analyzed
20. Employ proper research procedures, and budget to allow sample size and design indicated by the test problem.

As noted, A C Nielsen Co. is a specialist marketing research agency heavily involved in test marketing on behalf of its numerous clients. As such its guidelines tend to amount to a counsel of perfection and may well be partially ignored or modified in the real-world situation. This is particularly true of guidelines 11, 16, 17 and 19, but despite these qualifications the checklist still provides best advice for those wishing to execute a test market.

Limitations

In appropriate circumstances test marketing can provide the marketer with valuable information and insights. However, as has been hinted at several places in this chapter, there are a number of specific limitations to the practice.

Inevitably, time and cost figure amongst the most important drawbacks of test marketing. Irrespective of whether the test market is simulated or real, one is bound to incur additional expenditure in setting up a test market operation. Against this, of course, must be offset the benefits of the improved information and insights one may obtain in the process. In the case of a large-scale real test market, the additional costs incurred may be negligible as one may consider it part of a regional rollout strategy whereby one builds up gradually towards full-scale manufacturing and national distribution and sales. Such a strategy is particularly appropriate under two sets of circumstances. First, if the new product (it can rarely be a service) is difficult to replicate and/ or enjoys some form of protection through patents, necessity for certification, government regulation, etc., then time to market and competitive reactions are less important. Second, and at the other end of the spectrum, if the new product or service is essentially a brand extension and the added value exists largely in the seller's existing customer franchise, it will be the effectiveness of the combination of packaging, price, distribution, advertising and promotion which will determine whether the new marketing mix is going to be effective in defending and possibly building market share. Clearly, if the new mix is not going to be effective in achieving either of the latter two objectives, it makes sense to find this out on the subset of the market rather than having a national launch which would result in a much greater loss from an ineffective marketing mix.

A third reason for not test marketing a product is that it is very easy for one's competitors to disrupt the test, so that the data obtained from it are unrepresentative of what would happen under 'normal' conditions. In the heavily contested markets for fast-moving consumer goods it is difficult, if not impossible, to disguise the fact that one is conducting a test market. Often the major companies' test marketing activities will be subject to reports in the trade press but, even if one can prevent such information leaking out, new activity in a market will soon be reported back through observation by one's competitors' sales forces. Feeding back information on competitor activity is a standard task of sales and merchandising forces and is used extensively in determining one's tactical response. For example, if one becomes aware of the fact that a competitor is conducting a test market one can easily disrupt this by offering point of sale incentives to purchase, couponing through direct mail or local media and stepping up local advertising activity. Because one is only having to counter the activity in a local test market one can probably bring to bear a disproportionate amount of resources, certainly greater than one could afford on a national scale, but the overall effect will be to compromise the test marketer's results and make any extrapolation of them dangerous.

We have already referred to a fourth limitation of test marketing which is that of finding a representative area which may be properly regarded as a microcosm of the intended full-scale market. This limitation is obviously more important when one is seeking to use the test market as a basis for forecasting sales and activity in the full market, but is less relevant when one is test marketing to gain operational experience.

Three other related limitations of test marketing are associated with the fact that a test is clearly not the 'real thing'. Test marketing tends to inculcate a 'hot house' approach in which the amount of effort devoted to the test is inevitably much greater than will be given to a product or market in a full-scale marketing operation. Setting up a test market invariably distracts operational marketing personnel such as salesmen and merchandisers from their main business, the neglect of which may have other undesirable knock-on effects. Another negative consequence is that too many tests may reduce morale as they will bring into question whether or not senior management knows what it is doing. In the research by Kheir El Din (1991) one of the significant findings was that Japanese managers have much greater confidence in their ability to identify customer needs and develop products to satisfy them than do their counterparts in many other national markets: little surprise, therefore, that few Japanese firms indulge in test marketing.

Added to the above limitations of test marketing there are a number of common pitfalls which may invalidate the activity. Leslie Rodger summarized these succinctly in his book *Marketing in a Competitive Economy* first published over 30 years ago, and they are reflected in the nine points set out in Table 14.1.

Rodger's listing of pitfalls is self evident and does not require any further explanation. It does, however, confirm the note of caution which has pervaded this chapter concerning the value of test marketing under prevailing competitive conditions. On balance there is much evidence to suggest that if one has executed the preceding steps of the new product development process effectively then the need for and benefits of test marketing are likely to be minimal. It is for this reason that many firms prefer to skip

Table 14.1 ● Common pitfalls of test marketing

1. Failure to decide what is to be tested. Each test should try to answer a major question, for example the most effective weight for advertising. Where one attempts to test several factors in a single test area, it is more difficult to identify the *real* causes of success or failure.

2. Failure to base the test-market plan on an overall national marketing plan which is both realistic and affordable.

3. Failure to make comparative tests.

4. Failure to establish benchmarks in the test area. Before any test begins it is necessary to establish individual and total sales and/or market penetration of competitive brands so that subsequent changes can then be compared and evaluated against this base.

5. Failure to select representative test areas.

6. Failure to adhere to the test-market plan.

7. Failure to consider and get objective and reliable data on all factors influencing sales results in the test area.

8. Failure to stay in the test market long enough to get a clear-cut stop or go decision.

9. Reading into test-market results more than is supportable by the objective facts.

Source: Rodger (1971).

formal test marketing of the kind described above and move straight in to the full commercialization of their new product or service.

Time to market

In recent years (since the mid-1980s) growing attention has been given to means of accelerating the development and launch of new products and reducing 'time to market', thereby securing a competitive advantage. As with most aspects of marketing practice this is not a new issue, and Robert Weigand crystallized many of the key issues in the *Journal of Marketing* as long ago as 1962. In an article entitled 'How extensive the planning and development program' he addressed the dilemma of cutting short the planning and development program and risking a serious mistake or fully evaluating all the elements of the marketing mix and risk losing a competitive advantage. As Weigand pointed out, the firm which is first to market with a new product with strong market appeal enjoys a significant and privileged advantage over later competitive offerings. Faced with a choice between too much and too little research and development, compromise is often inevitable. What is required is a clear understanding of the factors which bear most directly on the issue so that they may be fully evaluated in the specific context of each, often unique new product decision. Weigand suggested seven factors which merit consideration.

The first factor which Weigand isolated is the decision maker's own ability to identify and weigh the strategic variables which will have a major impact on the final outcome. It is important not only to isolate and weigh the strategic factors, but also to judge one's ability to evaluate them accurately, i.e. to determine how confident decision makers are in their ability 'to relate the facts of the situation to the consequences or risk involved'.

Of Weigand's remaining six factors, four relate to issues during development and two to the ability to take corrective action on or after the launch. In brief, the 'development' factors may be summarized as:

- The time length of a commitment
- Product line implications
- The need for secrecy
- The position of the competitors.

Obviously the longer the commitment, the more time and care should be taken in coming to a decision on that commitment. Similarly, if one has an established reputation for particular kinds of product, one has an opportunity to piggy-back new products on existing ones and benefit from their reputation. But the corollary is that a new product failure could seriously compromise an established product line.

Where a new product or service can be easily replicated, secrecy may be vital and extensive development and testing precluded. Conversely, a major technological breakthrough, especially if it has patent protection, offers much more opportunity for a deliberate and controlled development and testing sequence.

Given that NPD is invariably pursued to secure a competitive advantage, it follows that careful monitoring of competitors' activities is an essential part of one's own planning and development. Despite the benefits of being first to market there is also much evidence to commend the strategy of the 'fast second' where a firm monitors its main competitors' new products and market response to them and uses this knowledge to launch an improved variant of its own, more carefully targeted at the emerging market.

The two other factors which must influence the time and effort put into the original planning and development are what Weigand termed 'speed of feedback' and 'capacity to correct mistakes'. It is a well-known rule of consumer marketing that one never judges the success of a new product on its initial sales pattern. Given that marketing may be defined as 'selling goods that don't come back to people who do', it is the repeat purchase pattern which invariably determines success or failure. That said, quick feedback from the marketplace following launch can indicate whether things are going to plan or whether the product is meeting resistance and falling behind planned performance.

If the product launch does not go precisely to plan then the ability to put things right may well be crucial. When one is dealing with complex products it is often difficult to anticipate the kind of problems which will develop in use and the seller's ability to rectify problems and provide after-sales service can be crucial in ensuring that the product survives its introduction into the marketplace.

The launch of the JCB110 (Baker, 1983b) provides an excellent example of this. The UK firm of J C Bamford has a long tradition of innovation in the design and manufacture of earthmoving and related equipment. In the early 1970s it came up with a revolutionary new design for a shovel-loader with a capacity of 1 cubic metre. While the JCB incorporated a number of radical innovations, including hydrostatic transmission which eliminated the need for a conventional gearbox, one of the simplest but major changes was to relocate the engine.

Prior to the launch of the JCB110, conventional shovel-loaders had a cab with an engine and shovel in front. In order to counteract the weight of the loaded shovel, a counterweight had to be attached to the rear of the cab. In effect, this meant that the loader had to have sufficient power to move both the workload and its equivalent counterweight. Bamford's solution was to use the weight of the engine itself as the counterweight so that the configuration was engine/cab/shovel. Not only did this reduce overall weight and the power required, it meant that the operator, sitting immediately behind the shovel, had a much improved view of the working area.

The potential benefits were quickly appreciated and the new shovels were put into service. Within a short time, however, complaints began to come in about seized engines. An investigation soon established that this was due to the radiators on the engines becoming blocked because of the operator's habit of reversing from the workplace, often until they hit a bank of earth behind them. When the rear of the cab was protected by the counterweight this caused no problems but, with the engine relocated, it blocked the radiators and caused the overheating problem. Again, Bamford's solution was a simple one – they located the radiator on the side of the engine and this obviated the potential to block it by running into heaps of spoil. In this context, however, the important lesson was the company's ability to respond quickly to a problem and rectify it.

In some senses the JCB110 case may be regarded as a form of test marketing in that the company was able to identify design defects and product improvements only through experience in actual use. While it is possible that this could have been obtained through extended product testing, the benefits of being first to market with a revolutionary new design clearly outweighed this. Indeed, many regard the launch of the JCB110 as the development which established the firm as an international competitor in the global market for earth-moving equipment.

However, the JCB110 was a radical innovation and time to market is much more critical in markets subject to rapid technological change and intense competition. In the book describing the launch of IBM's AS/400 series in *The Silverlake Project* published in 1992 the authors advise 'Break time barriers by using parallel processing and getting it right first time. Everything these days has to be done in less time. In fact, time – getting to market first or fastest – has actually become as crucial as anything else in the race for competitiveness.' The MCP model of new product development developed by the authors addresses this issue directly and emphasizes the point that if product development is executed effectively time to market will be accelerated and test marketing, in the traditional sense, will be redundant.

Launching the new product

As discussed in the preceding sections, test marketing may provide valuable information about the launching of a new product. Indeed, under extreme circumstances a test market may suggest that the new product is unlikely to succeed and persuade the developer to abort the process at this point. In practice such no-go decisions are probably made less often than they should be as, inevitably, commitment to a new product increases the further one proceeds with the developmental process. Such a commitment is both financial and psychological. Of the two it is the psychological involvement which is probably the more difficult to overcome.

As we have seen earlier, the costs of new product development tend to increase, often exponentially, with each successive step in the process. It is for this reason that we have laid so much emphasis on the early stages of idea generation, concept testing and business analysis. While these phases may absorb considerable executive time, they rarely call for any significant capital investment of the kind which will become necessary as one moves into prototype development, physical testing and test marketing. Launching a product is another matter altogether. First, one must invest in the necessary plant and equipment to produce the product and then one must create a sufficient inventory to be able to respond to the initial demand stimulated by one's promotional and sales efforts. The amounts required will vary both absolutely and proportionately depending upon whether one is concerned with a product or a service, and the nature of the served market – business-to-business or ultimate consumer. As a broad generalization, the more tangible and complex the product, the greater is the investment required for manufacturing facilities, inventory, selling and after-sales service, and the less important are advertising and sales promotion. By contrast, with an intangible service, much greater emphasis will need to be placed upon advertising and sales promotion to create awareness, understanding and acceptance of the underlying concept as this cannot be inferred from the physical attributes of the product itself. Either way, the commitment to launch a new product will call for significant financial investment.

Later, we will examine in more detail some of the considerations to be taken into account when deciding whether or not to launch a new product. Here we only seek to make the point that, provided the decision-maker is familiar with and accepts the concept of sunk-cost, the launch decision needs to be made on the basis of the antici-pated revenues to be earned related to the total investment comprising both the sunk cost and the projected launch costs. To argue that one has invested substantial sums to develop an idea to the point where launch may be considered, and that one shouldn't 'throw this money away', is irrelevant. The guiding principle must always be not to throw good money after bad. In other words, if one cannot expect to recoup both the past and necessary future investment one should not proceed with any further invest-ment.

Of course, the problem with this advice is that one cannot predict the future – one can only form judgments about it. It is for this reason that we claimed that it is the psy-chological involvement with a new product which is more difficult to overcome. If the developer had perceived serious flaws in the product concept, or its development, they would have aborted the process much sooner. Now one is on the threshold of entering the market, the temptation to go forward becomes almost irresistible. After all, only the market can decide, so we will have to launch the product to find out! Just as it is usually impossible for the product champion to guarantee success, so it is equally impossible for any opponents to a product launch to prove it will lead to failure. Those in favour of going on will forecast a build-up of demand and margins that will ensure success; those against will do the opposite!

How then should we assess the likelihood of success or failure? Three basic steps are called for. First, we must revisit and review the assumptions which led us to believe there was a market opportunity in the first place. Second, we must confirm that the new product is capable of satisfying the market opportunity at an acceptable cost to the seller and price to the buyer. Third, we must plan and execute the launch effectively.

Elsewhere, we have cited the fact that the most frequently mentioned cause of new product failure is some variant or other of an inadequate understanding of the market. It is for this reason that the normative theory of new product development places so much emphasis upon research at every step in the developmental process. It has also been emphasized that research must be continuous throughout as few, if any, markets remain static for long. In highly competitive markets innovation and new product development are continuous, and there is no certainty that an opportunity identified at the start of one's own new product development will not have been pre-empted by someone else by the time one is ready to launch. Data of this kind may be secured using conventional market research procedures and there is nothing mystical about the process. The point to be stressed is that you need to check out your original assump-tions and make adjustments, if necessary, to allow for any changes that may have occurred.

The second step is also one of confirmation of earlier phases in the developmental process and calls for validation of the concept and product tests and the rerunning of the business analysis using the latest available information. It is here that some form of test marketing may be particularly helpful.

Provided these two sets of checks indicate a 'go' decision one must then set about devising a marketing plan to launch the product. Given that marketing mix decisions and the development of marketing plans are dealt with in considerable detail in most textbooks, discussion here will be focused on three issues which are of special significance to this phase of the NPD process:

1. Selection of launch strategy

2. Timing

3. Monitoring the launch.

Selecting a launch strategy

Four basic factors govern the selection of a launch strategy:

1. The degree of novelty embodied in the new product or service

2. The firm's existing familiarity with and position in the intended market

3. The current status of competition and the response anticipated to the launch of the new product

4. The resources available to the launch organization.

As a broad generalization, the greater the degree of novelty the less the threat of early competitor response and the higher the need for precise targeting of potential early adopters. Conversely, the less the degree of novelty the more important the manipulation of the other variables in the marketing mix – price, distribution, place and promotion.

Where a high degree of novelty is involved one may anticipate high levels of resistance to change and, usually, a slow build-up of demand over time as potential customers learn of the product's existence and switch to it from previously preferred products for which it is a substitute. A niche marketing strategy is likely to be most appropriate.

Where a low degree of novelty is involved the basic choice rests between a niche or a penetration strategy. Firms with limited resources will usually have no choice but to follow a niche strategy whereas larger and better endowed or established firms may choose either a saturation approach (penetration strategy) by launching in all segments and regions simultaneously or a segment by segment, market by market controlled 'rollout' (a variant of the niche strategy).

Breaking into the market

Market penetration

Earlier we saw that, as a new product proceeds through development towards market introduction, the investment involved accelerates rapidly, a trend which continues into

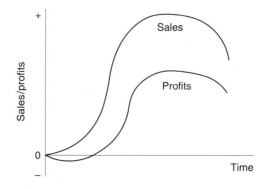

Figure 14.1 ● Sales and profits of a successful new product

the market launch phase. Indeed, with some consumer product innovations, the market-ing investment necessary to secure distribution and inform the public of the new pro-duct's availability may well exceed the costs of development. The phrase 'marketing investment' was used deliberately in the preceding sentence, for this is precisely what it is, despite many accountants' attempts to regard it as an operating expenditure and to set it against sales revenue on a period by period basis. Such a practice clearly will not help most new products to appear successful during their introductory phase and may well account for premature judgments of failure.

An obvious remedy is to educate accountants and senior management to regard launch expenditures as investment capital in precisely the same way as R&D costs and new production facilities, and to seek to recover these over a reasonable product life expectancy. Yet, even if one is successful in accomplishing it, it is a recognized fact that profits lag behind sales revenue so that the generalized profit expectation for a success-ful new product is as shown in Figure 14.1.

A major reason why profits lag behind sales is that costs fall with cumulative pro-duction as a result of experience effects. Originally the phenomenon was associated only with labour as a component of total cost and led to the use of the so-called 'learning curve' as a planning tool. However, in the 1960s the Boston Consulting Group (BCG) demonstrated that the same was true of total value-added costs and bought-in supplies, and described the relationship between costs and experience in terms of a curve. In simple terms, experience curves record the decline in costs to be anticipated with cumulative increases in output and are usually reported as a percen-tage for each doubling in output, for example an 85% experience curve means that every time output doubles costs decline to 85% of the earlier rate, or, put another way, there is a 15% decline in costs for every doubling in output. Other things being equal, such a cost saving goes straight to the bottom line of the profit-and-loss (P&L) account and, because of the relative ease of doubling up on sales when these are small, has a dramatic effect on profitability. It follows that, if the pioneer can expand his sales quickly enough, he will come to enjoy such a cost advantage that it will be impossible for his competitors to catch up with him – an enormous incentive for rapid market penetration.

The main sources of the experience effect are:

1. Labour efficiency arising from increased skill and from work specialization and method improvement associated with the division of labour.

2. The development of new production processes which become economic with large-scale output, such as automation, mass assembly and so on.

3. Increased capital efficiency – many process plants (e.g. steel mills) become more efficient with increased use and may achieve up to 50% more than their installed rating. (This increased efficiency is in addition to the scale effect, whereby doubling the size of a process plant like an oil refinery reduces unit cost by 25%.)

4. Purchasing economies for bulk orders. Such savings also go direct to the bottom line of the P&L account and may be very significant indeed, being directly proportionate to the percentage which materials represent in the cost of goods sold.

In addition to the cost benefits which flow from a rapid build-up of sales, one must also take into account the net present value of the cash flows associated with them, present money being literally worth more than an equivalent future amount as such income can be reinvested to generate further income.

Taken together, these are all very compelling reasons for wanting to get into the rapid growth phase of the product life cycle as quickly as possible. Furthermore, even if the product proves to be a failure, the earlier one becomes aware of this the better, for one can then minimize the losses incurred.

Diffusion theory and new product acceptance

At several points in the text so far we have referred to new products as 'innovations' and the process by which they spread through a body of users as 'diffusion'. This usage has been deliberate, for new products are but one category of innovation and there is a very extensive literature concerning innovation which goes far beyond the limited research that has been undertaken into innovation from a marketing perspective. At this juncture it will be helpful to consider this wider body of evidence in order to see if it can provide any pointers to the specific case in which we are interested: new products.

Earlier, when referring to the product life cycle, it was noted that the concept is firmly founded in the biological sciences and that there is a great deal of data to support the view that it is an accurate representation of the way in which products develop, prosper, mature, decline and die. Studies in the field of rural sociology confirm that new methods and techniques exhibit this pattern, as do studies in the field of education concerning the spread of ideas about curriculum development, new approaches to teaching and the like. In the realm of medicine, studies of the way in which new drugs are adopted by doctors exhibit the familiar S-shaped diffusion curve, as do a large number of individual studies of specific innovations in fields as diverse as man-made fibres, plastics, nuclear power, computers and numerically controlled machine tools. Taken together, these findings point inexorably to the existence of an underlying natural process.

Some of the implications of the PLC have already been touched on, particularly the importance of observing inflections in the curve which herald the need for modifications in the marketing mix and the overriding message of the inevitability of change which such curves convey. However, as noted in *Marketing New Industrial Products* (Baker, 1975), the significance of a consistent S-shaped diffusion curve is far greater in terms of its strategic implications than it is in terms of its tactical forecasting potential. This is so because such a curve stipulates that the speed of diffusion is a function of elapsed time from market introduction to first purchase. In other words, the critical determinant of innovational success/failure rests ultimately upon the time required to make an initial sale as the timing of all subsequent sales is functionally dependent upon this. The validity of this claim may be demonstrated.

Let it be assumed that:

(a) there are 100 potential adopters of an innovation;

(b) *a priori* there is an adoption sequence which will become clear *post facto* when one could identify the 100 adopters and number them sequentially from 1 to 100;

(c) the innovator uses a purely random approach when seeking to make an initial sale; and

(d) adoption by any given potential customer is dependent upon:
(i) time since introduction,
(ii) prior adoption by all those with lower adoption numbers,
(iii) contact with the innovator.

In other words, under these assumptions each potential user will only adopt after those preceding him in an *a priori* adoption sequence, i.e. 39 after 38, 38 after 37, and so on. Given these assumptions one could replicate the process by drawing from an urn containing 100 balls, one of which is numbered 1. Only when the '1' ball has been drawn will diffusion commence, which could be replicated experimentally by drawing from a second urn containing 99 balls one of which is numbered 2. Once the '2' ball has been drawn one proceeds to a third urn containing 98 balls, one of which is numbered 3, and so on to the 100th urn which contains only one ball.

Over an infinitely large number of drawings the law of large numbers dictates that the frequency with which the '1' ball is drawn first will be 1% of the time. By extension, if an innovator uses a purely random approach to contact 100 potential users of his innovation, the prior probability that he will contact the *post facto* first adopter first is 0.01. If one further assumes that the innovator can make only one call per day on potential users then one can predict that:

● The probability of calling on an adopter on day 1 is 0.01
● The probability of calling on an adopter by day 10 is 0.10
● The probability of calling on an adopter by day 50 is 0.50
● The probability of calling on an adopter by day 99 is 0.99.

Clearly, if there were some means of pre-identifying the first adopter it would enable one to reduce the elapsed time to first adoption in 99% of all cases where a purely random approach had previously been used, as one would go directly to the first

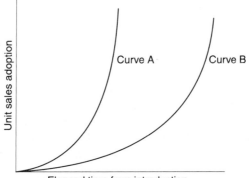

Curve A indicates exponential growth of sales if the first adoption
is secured twice as quickly as the first sale in case B

Figure 14.2 ● Graphical representation of the long-run impact of halving time to secure first adoption of an innovation

adopter on day 1. In turn, this would result in accelerated diffusion in a similar number of instances. The impact of only halving time to first adoption is readily apparent from Figure 14.2.

Patently, the above example is a gross simplification of a complex reality. Nonetheless we maintain that it is a reasonable representation of the *nature* of the process and the inferences which one may draw from it. Thus, although the number of potential users of an innovation may vary enormously, as may the number of sales calls the innovator can make per day, or the number necessary to secure an adoption, and so on, it is logically defensible to argue that certain prospective users will have a stronger incentive to adopt early. Hence, if one could identify in advance those potential users so predisposed, one could concentrate one's marketing efforts on this most receptive subsegment, thereby achieving initial sales more rapidly than would be the case if a random approach were followed which presumes that all prospective users are equally likely to adopt first.

In reality, of course, the assumption that all prospective users are equally likely to adopt is rarely applicable and most marketing plans are based upon some form of market subdivision or 'segmentation'. In essence, the concept of market segmentation rests upon recognition of a differentiated demand for a product, while its use as a marketing tool depends upon identification of the most appropriate variable or variables with which to subdivide total demand into economically viable segments. (In this context 'economically viable segment' may be interpreted as 'being of sufficient size to enable a marketer to earn an adequate profit by catering to the specific needs of its members'.) Thus, in practice, a major concern of the marketer when planning the introduction of a new product is determination of which segment has the strongest demand for the innovation and what are the most suitable policies for converting this demand into actual purchases.

It is difficult to assess just how effective such market segmentation strategies are but, as the incidence of new product failure cited in Chapter 5 clearly indicates, they meet with mixed success. In part, some failures are attributable to neglect of generally accepted marketing principles for which a remedy is immediately available. For the rest, however, it is reasonable to assume that there are many situations where a product is deemed to have failed because its sales have not achieved some pre-designated level after a given time which, in turn, is due to the marketing department having incorrectly identified the most receptive market segment. Therefore, reduction of new product failure is dependent upon improved identification of the most receptive market segment, and the most receptive individuals within that segment. While present segmentation techniques such as four-figure SIC analysis permit broad identification of the most likely segment, we need additional techniques to help us pinpoint specific prospects.

Identifying the early adopter

When the cumulative sales which give rise to an S-shaped curve are plotted in terms of actual sales per time period over the life of the product, the result is a normal distribution. For many years now researchers have used the parameters of such a distribution (the mean and standard deviation) as a useful basis for classifying adopters, as shown in Figure 14.3.

However, this classificatory system is probably too precise for our needs and is potentially confusing in that, strictly speaking, an innovator is someone who introduces a new product, not someone who is among the first to adopt it. Accordingly, we propose to use a simple three-way split into early adopters, followers and laggards without bothering to define what proportion of all adopters each represents. Clearly, our overriding objective is to see if we can find ways of distinguishing potential early users from followers and laggards.

According to our model of buying behaviour, two factors would seem to be critical in determining a potential purchaser's speed of reaction to a new product proposition: the characteristics of the new product itself and the way in which these characteristics are perceived by the potential user. As we saw earlier (p. 53), in the case of the former factor, Everett Rogers (1962) developed a very useful framework based upon an

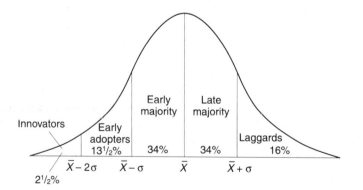

Figure 14.3 ● Adopter categories

exhaustive review of the available studies of innovation which classifies characteristics under five headings:

- Relative advantage
- Compatibility
- Complexity
- Divisibility
- Communicability.

The first characteristic, *relative advantage*, seeks to measure the economic benefit conferred upon or available to the adopter of an innovation adjusted to take cognizance of the adopter's present situation. Thus, for example, if a manufacturer has brought out three models of a machine, the first with a rated output of 1000 units per hour, the second with 1200 units per hour and the third with 1500 units per hour, then the introduction of model 3 offers a 50% improvement to owners of model 1, but only a 25% to owners of model 2. Clearly, the absolute performance is the same, but a 25% improvement may not offer a sufficient relative advantage for the model 2 owner to trade in or scrap his machine in favour of the new one, whereas 50% is a sufficient incentive for the model 1 owner to do so. Thus, a planned replacement policy related to the age of the existing stock of machines would suggest model 1 owners as better targets for the replacement than model 2 owners.

Compatibility and *complexity* are both dimensions of the degree of novelty associated with an innovation, but tend to be inversely related to each other. We have already touched on the nature of compatibility when discussing enabling conditions: the more compatible a new product is with the existing production system or way of doing things, the more likely it is to be readily accepted. Of course, beyond a certain point the new product may so resemble the existing product it seeks to replace that it is insufficiently distinguishable to prompt users to change. For example, a survey by McGraw-Hill indicated that many industrial purchasing agents were unwilling to switch from a currently satisfactory source of supply unless the change offered a saving equivalent to a reduction of 8–10% of the current price.

While complexity, defined as the degree of difficulty associated with full understanding of the application of an innovation, does not automatically increase with novelty, this is often the case. It certainly is true that the less compatible an innovation is with the existing way of doing things, the more complex it is likely to seem to be.

Divisibility is a measure of the extent to which it is possible to try an innovation before coming to a final adoption/rejection decision. It can have a significant influence upon attitudes towards a new product. Where there is a high degree of uncertainty about an innovation, and trial is possible only by firms or individuals for whom the economic risks are small, most potential users will prefer to wait and see. In other words, for them trial is vicarious and based upon the reactions of the early adopters. Two points are worth noting in this context.

First, it is an established fact that many early buyers in industrial markets are the largest firms in the industry. However, experience suggests that many large firms which buy during the launch phase do so only on a trial basis and without any commitment to large-scale or continued use. In some cases early trial may even be used as a delaying tactic, and it would be a mistake to concentrate all one's launch efforts on the biggest potential users. Equally, one should not ignore the opportunity to sell to 'trialists', for, in addition to generating much-needed revenue, they also provide feedback on problems which only become apparent when the new product is put into 'normal' use.

The second point to make is that sellers can do a great deal to minimize risk during the launch phase by providing a trial period or its equivalent. For example, one can supply goods on sale or return terms, provide additional guarantees to early adopters, or lease the product rather than sell it outright. Endorsement by an authority figure can also help to reduce risk.

The final characteristic, *communicability*, is heavily influenced by the preceding four factors, for it reflects the degree of difficulty associated with communicating the benefits of an innovation to prospective users, which, in turn, is a function of its relative advantage, its compatibility, complexity and divisibility. Communication is a vital activity throughout the new product purchase decision process, with impersonal or media communications being most important in creating initial awareness, both impersonal and personal sources influencing interest, personal sources becoming dominant as the buyer moves towards a decision, and impersonal sources assuming the primary role of reassurance after the decision has been made.

All five factors considered in the previous paragraphs can be measured objectively, but, as we have noted on a number of occasions, such objective measurement is of secondary importance. It is the way prospective users perceive and interpret the factors which is important. In turn, it would seem reasonable to infer that early adopters do perceive 'the facts' differently from followers and laggards – that is, the selling proposition must seem more attractive and/or less risky to them, and marketers have expended a great deal of effort in an attempt to determine what the distinguishing features are. In the following section, we review some of the findings of studies into correlates of individual innovativeness and then examine the case of the organizational buying unit.

Individual innovativeness

Research into the distinguishing characteristics of different categories of adopters is extensive and owes much to the pioneering work by rural sociologists into the diffusion of innovations through populations of farmers. These studies, using the adopter categories postulated in Figure 14.3, indicate significant differences: innovators are venturesome (willing to take risks), younger, wealthy, well informed about scientific developments in agriculture, of high social status and 'cosmopolitan' (i.e. worldly, looking beyond the local community). Innovators make greater use of impersonal sources of information and tend to interact more with other innovators. They also exercise some opinion leadership, in that others turn to them for advice. By contrast, the laggard is almost the direct opposite of the innovator. He or she is older, lowest in income and social status, resistant to change (tradition orientated), poorly informed and has little awareness of new developments. The laggard interacts most with other laggards and depends more upon them for information than upon external and impersonal sources.

Given distinctive personality profiles such as these, the marketer should have little difficulty in segmenting his or her potential market and in devising a marketing mix which enables selling-in efforts to be focused on the most receptive sub-group. The question is, do the findings concerning farmers apply equally to consumers in general? The short answer is 'yes' and 'no'.

Although dated now, one of the most comprehensive reviews of this issue is to be found in Thomas S. Robertson's *Innovative Behavior and Communications* (1971). In the first place, Robertson points to the difficulties in developing an innovator profile for new products in general as a consequence of the wide differences in the available studies of the issue – for example, lack of agreement upon what proportion of all adopters shall be considered innovators, concentration upon different factors in different studies and so forth – which collectively result in a lack of direct comparability between them. Robertson's review of the available studies led him to conclude that 'consistency of innovativeness cannot be expected across product categories, but can be expected within product categories and, sometimes, between related product categories.'

This conclusion accords well with the view expressed earlier concerning the possibility of deriving a highly specific model of buying behaviour applicable to all conceivable situations – one cannot do so. On the other hand, one can develop extended lists of factors or characteristics which are subsumed within the generalized summary variables in the general model. But which ones will be relevant in any given product market situation will be highly contingent upon the particularities and peculiarities of that situation, and underlines forcefully our claim that the practitioner's specialized experience and knowledge is necessary to make the model operational.

In the same way that marketing studies of individual innovativeness evolved from rural sociologists' studies of farmers, so research into industrial buying behaviour owes much to the work of economists. As one might expect, economists have tended to emphasize the objective and 'rational' dimensions but, as reported in *Marketing New Industrial Products* (Baker, 1975), these factors seem able to explain only about 50% of the variance in the speed with which firms adopt innovations. Thus Edward Mansfield (1968), one of the most prolific researchers in the field, finally concludes that:

> 'Perhaps these variables (profitability, liquidity and growth rate) are less important than other more elusive and essentially non-economic variables. The personality attributes, training and other characteristics of top and middle management may play a very important role in determining how quickly a firm introduces an innovation. The presence or absence of a few men in the right place who believe strongly in the value of a new technique may make a crucial difference.'

Other leading researchers, including Carter and Williams, Enos, Sutherland, Ray, and Nabseth and Ray, come to a very similar conclusion, and it was the consistency of these findings which led Baker to undertake the study reported in *Marketing New Industrial Products* (which contains an extended discussion of the issues touched on here), in which the primary focus is upon the nature and influence of managerial attitudes, or, as it is termed in the composite model, behavioural response. It so happens that there are two ways in which one can approach this problem. First, one can seek to document the internal decision process whereby the managers who comprise the internal decision-making unit (DMU) come to a conclusion on the adoption of innovations offered to it. Secondly, one can study populations of adopting firms and see if there are any features which distinguish between early and late adoption – effectively the approach used by the economists and followed by Baker.

While an understanding of the internal decision process is valuable, it has a fundamental weakness from the seller's point of view, namely, how do you come by this information? It is one thing for academics to persuade companies to allow them access to the firm so as to study the buying process at first hand, but it seems unlikely they would extend the same opportunity to a supplier, even supposing that the supplier had personnel qualified to conduct such a study and would find it cost-effective to do so. Furthermore, in the case of all innovations to be sold into a market new to the firm, the seller has by definition no prior knowledge of or contact with potential customers. It is for these reasons that we have preferred the second approach of trying to classify firms in terms of their potential innovativeness, in terms, in turn, of variables which are amenable to external observation, and regarding any 'inside information' as a bonus.

The critical assumption underlying this second approach is that one can treat the firm as a single decision-making unit which is sufficiently consistent in its response to enable one to predict its future behaviour on the basis of past decision and present structure and operating procedures. The theoretical basis for accepting this assumption is set out at length in *Marketing New Industrial Products* (Baker, 1975) and is founded on the observation that firms seem to develop an organizational 'climate' that shapes the behaviour of its members. In other words, firms seem to develop a corporate personality, and either individuals conform to this and are accepted by the organization – that is, are given a position of authority and responsibility – or they reject the organizational value system and are in turn rejected by the organization.

If this is so, then perhaps we can identify factors similar to those isolated in the studies of consumer innovativeness. In their study of 'The characteristics of technically progressive firms', Carter and Williams (1959) isolated 24 features as follows (the explanatory notes are a synthesis of their comments and our own):

1. *High quality of incoming communication.* The association of this characteristic with progressiveness is attributed to the fact that many new ideas are first aired in professional as opposed to trade journals. Thus the firm which subscribes to 'quality' journals is more likely to become aware of the existence of new ideas sooner after their evolution than is the firm which subscribes only to trade papers. A corollary of high standards of media intake is contact with scientists of high professional standing, that is, those whose research is most likely to be reported in the quality journal.

2. *A deliberate survey of potential ideas.* In the progressive firm, ideas, both internal and external, are subjected to a deliberate and regular review, 'in order that those offering the best promise of reward may be developed' (p. 179). Conversely, unprogressive firms are those which are wedded to traditional methods and ideas and feel that little improvement can be made in these methods (*cf.* the buggy whip firm in Levitt's 'Marketing myopia' (1960)).

3. *A willingness to share knowledge.* Carter and Williams' survey showed that progressive firms were 'astonishingly ready to throw open their factories to visits by competitors', while the unprogressive firm is usually secretive on technical matters. A firm's willingness to share its knowledge via access to its plant, the publication of papers, attendance at conferences and so forth, tends to increase with its technical achievements.

4. *A willingness to take new knowledge on licence and to enter joint ventures.* 'Progressive firms are willing to be adoptive when it is convenient – that is to say, to supplement their own research and development by buying knowledge from other firms' (p. 179). On the other hand, the unprogressive firm shrinks from association with another or others.

5. *A readiness to look outside the firm.* In devising their definition of progressiveness, Carter and Williams found that those firms which set their standards of performance in terms of the achievements of other firms were more progressive than those which did not seek to equal or better such standards of performance. (In establishing an appropriate 'yardstick', due notice must be taken of the firm's size. For example, large firms should seek to achieve the best standards on an international scale, while smaller firms might be considered equally progressive if they seek to equal or exceed the best national standards.)

6. *Effective internal communication and coordination.* In summary, this implies the presence in the progressive firm of the following:

    (a) Interdepartmental cooperation on new product development

    (b) Clear understanding of company objectives, related to individual and departmental authority and responsibility, to maximize effective coordination

    (c) Mechanisms for resolving differences in outlook between major business functions.

7. *High status of science and technology in the firm.* Although implicit in a number of other characteristics, its inclusion may be justified on the grounds that not only is more spent on research and development, thus accounting for the existence of larger staffs, but that higher status is accorded to personnel in this function *vis-à-vis* other functions.

8. *A consciousness of costs and profit in the research and development departments (if any).* This factor was found to be useful in distinguishing degrees of non-progressiveness among those firms with R&D departments, in that the most progressive firms were those which allocated funds on the basis of economic justification.

9. *Rapid replacement of machines.* 'Progressive firms replace machines earlier.'

10. *A sound policy of recruitment for management.* In progressive firms, there is a noticeable tendency to recruit better-educated and qualified personnel to fill management posts. Conversely, unprogressive firms prefer to recruit school-leavers and 'indoctrinate' them in the traditional mores and folkways.

11. *An ability to attract talented people.* Progressive firms wish not only to attract talented people but to provide appropriate inducements, for example, opportunity to work with others of high reputation in a given field, adequate facilities, and so on.

12. *A willingness to arrange for the effective training of staff.* While progressive firms actively encourage training at all levels, unprogressive firms tend to undertake the minimum necessary to satisfy their needs.

13. *Use of management techniques.* Progressive firms employ new managerial techniques while backward firms do not.

14. *Identifying the outcome of investment decisions.* The most progressive firms use formal methods for calculating the probable outcome of investment decisions; less progressive firms use a composite approach, based partly on formal analysis and partly on executive judgment, while the least progressive firms rely solely on judgmental processes.

15. *High quality in the chief executive(s).* 'The evidence strongly confirms the hypothesis that technically progressive firms are led by men [*sic*] of high general quality.'

16. *Adequate provision for intermediate managers.* After allowing for size differences, Carter and Williams found that the less progressive firms have fewer intermediate managers, with the consequence that senior management is heavily involved in day-to-day operations and so has less time to devote to the formulation of policy. By contrast, in the more progressive firms, the greater number of intermediate managers provided both a 'better ladder for promotion and a way of training for higher management'. (But consider the current trends to empowerment and downsizing.)

17. *Good quality in intermediate management.* The data collected by Carter and Williams indicated that it was the quality of middle management which differentiated between highly and moderately progressive firms whose senior executives were on a par with each other. Further, in the progressive firm the middle managers had a much better understanding of their area of responsibility and were able to initiate change, while in the unprogressive firm middle management tended to work to rule-of-thumb methods and were 'convinced of the eternal validity of the processes with which they are familiar'.

18. *An ability to bring the best out of managers.* In backward firms, it was found that junior managers were apt to be frustrated by their seniors' unwillingness to change, while in progressive firms junior managers were stimulated and encouraged to participate to the best of their abilities.

19. *Use of scientists and technologists on the board of directors.* This characteristic was not found to be 'a necessary condition of progressiveness, but it is a characteristic frequently found in progressive firms, and absent in unprogressive firms'.

20. *A readiness to look ahead.* Progressive firms exhibit a strong tendency to look ahead while backward firms are frequently immersed in the present.

21. *A high rate of expansion* (measured in terms of the rate of increase of assets). It is recognized that growth might be the result of past progressiveness or the spur to future progressiveness to capitalize on a favourable situation.

22. *Ingenuity in getting round material and equipment shortages.* The progressive firm takes a much more positive approach to overcoming shortages than its less progressive brethren, and will often develop substitutes of its own to meet essential needs.

23. *An effective selling policy.* Progressive firms can be identified by the fact that they devote equal time and effort to marketing their output in a seller's market, while backward firms tend to relax their efforts under such conditions.

24. *Good technical service to customers.* This characteristic is closely connected with the preceding factor.

While these factors apply to firms which are innovative in their own right, our own work into early adoption provides strong support for all these features, though once again it is important to point out that their relative importance is highly situation specific. It should also be appreciated that many of the characteristics are likely to be most apparent in firms which fit the customer-active model and take the initiative in stimulating other firms to innovate. (A recent study of Canadian manufacturing industry confirmed a strong association between the Carter and Williams factors and market leadership.)

However, for adoption and diffusion to occur one must first establish contact between the seller and the prospective buyer. In the next section we look briefly at the role of communication.

The role of communication

As noted earlier, communication has a vital role to play throughout the buying process, from the initial creation of awareness of a new product's existence right through to the reduction of uncertainty concerning the rightness of the decision once a purchase has been made.

Basically, communications fall into two categories – personal and impersonal – the use and importance of which vary according to the stage in the buying process which has been reached. As the term implies, personal communications involve direct person-to-person contact and may be buyer or seller initiated and formal or informal in nature. Sending a salesman to call on a potential customer is an example of a formal seller-initiated personal communication; asking a friend's opinion of Brand X an informal, buyer-initiated communication. By contrast, impersonal communication involves the use of one of the media – print, broadcast, Internet and so on – and is the major province of advertising, which has been defined as 'any paid form of non-personal presentation and promotion of ideas, goods or services by an identified sponsor'.

Non-personal media are usually most effective in establishing awareness and interest, while personal influence is necessary to move the members of an audience up the hierarchy of effects through desire to action. It has been found that personal influence is most effective in high-risk purchase situations, as, for example, where the buyer is expending relatively large amounts of money, purchases infrequently and is unfamiliar with the product(s) under consideration, while mass or impersonal communication is most effective in the case of familiar, frequently purchased items of low unit value.

However, while the emphasis may be on one or other sort of communication, it is usual to find both employed together and, even where this is not part of the seller's deliberate communication strategy, impersonal channels are almost invariably affected by the mediation of personal sources. This latter phenomenon is of particular importance to innovators and is usually referred to as the 'two-step flow of communication', a phrase coined by Lazarsfeld (1944) whose research into voters' information usage during the 1940 American presidential election led him to argue that the early view of communication as a direct one-way flow of effects from sender to receiver (a sort of stimulus–response model) was an inaccurate and misleading interpretation of reality.

According to the two-step model, mass media communications are picked up first by only a small proportion of the intended audience, who, in turn, pass on the message to other members of the audience. These intermediaries are designated *opinion leaders*, and it would seem that such persons get considerable personal satisfaction out of being regarded as knowledgeable or authoritative about the subject for which they are regarded as an opinion leader, this heightening their sensitivity to information. Accordingly, opinion leaders are most likely to be receptive to information regarding new products and processes, and a number of studies confirm this, a finding which offers considerable promise to the marketer of new products.

However, as Robertson (1971) notes, there are several deficiencies in the two-step model, and at least two basic difficulties associated with making it operational by marketers:

1. The identification of opinion leaders
2. The means by which to influence opinion leaders to promote the product.

Addressing this issue, he observes:

> 'Even if the two-step model accurately depicted reality, the difficulties of instituting marketing strategies in line with it would remain enormous. The first problem is how to single out opinion leaders who are found at all status levels and within all informal groups. This is compounded by the fact ... that within any given group, different opinion leaders are likely to exist for different product categories and interest areas. Furthermore, the individual is likely to belong to more than one group where consumer information may be transferred and where opinion leaders exist. Finally, if it were possible to identify opinion leaders, how could the marketer appeal to them so that they would promote his product?'

Despite the difficulties alluded to by Robertson, it is our belief that marketers can make use of the concept and should invest in identifying opinion leaders. Robertson's perception of the 'enormous' difficulties inherent in identifying opinion leaders stems from his desire to develop a simple but generalized model of communication flows applicable to all situations. This, in fact, is achieved, but in common with other marketing models – the PLC concept, the composite model of buyer behaviour – it would be unrealistic to expect the model to be specified in such detail that it would be immediately and directly applicable to all conceivable marketing situations. What is important is that the practitioner should appreciate the *implications* of the two-step model and set about identifying the opinion leaders in his own product-market situation, always assuming that the cost of so doing is justifiable by contrast with the alternative strategy, which is to broadcast information to the whole potential audience in the expectation that opinion leaders will then identify themselves. Thus, almost by definition, they will be the ones to receive the message and pass it on to their followers.

Furthermore, it is important to emphasize that the influence of word-of-mouth communication is equally as important in industrial markets as in consumer research. Research by John Czepiel (1979) convincingly demonstrates the need to take into account the social environment in which innovations diffuse through populations of adopters, for, as he comments, based on his studies of the steel and electrical utility industries:

> 'There exist regular, well defined, and socially meaningful communications networks linking technical decision-makers in competitive firms. These networks are used with some degree of frequency both for information acquisition and for validation and verification.
>
> The patterning of these communications networks seems to be related to the existence of shared or common interests and problems as evidenced by such factors as firm size or similarity in production and operations.'

In other words, opinion leadership operates in industrial markets and seems to be situation specific.

Devising a communication strategy

A basic and widely accepted model of the marketing communication process is that proposed by Shannon and Weaver (1962) containing five essential elements:

Who ...	*says what* ...	*how* ...	*to whom* ...
(Communicator)	(Message)	(Channels)	(Audience)

with what effect
(Feedback)

For successful communication to occur, Schramm (1955) argues that four basic conditions must be fulfilled, namely:

1. The message must be so designed and delivered as to gain the attention of the intended destination.

2. The message must employ signs which refer to experience common to source and destination, so as to 'get the meaning across'.

3. The message must arouse personality needs in the destination and suggest some ways to meet those needs.

4. The message must suggest a way to meet those needs which is appropriate to the group situation in which the destination finds himself at the time when he is moved to make the desired response.

If one is to satisfy these conditions, then it is clear that one must follow a marketing approach and start with the audience and its information needs, that is, with what they want to hear rather than what you want to tell them. Given an understanding of what the prospective customer is likely to be interested in, one can then devise a communication strategy in terms of the message(s) to be given to different media at different stages of the launch process and the balance between personal and impersonal approaches, that is, between advertising and personal selling.

Reprise
. . . .

In this chapter we started by reviewing some of the benefits which accrue from rapid market penetration in terms of the attraction of early cash flows and declining costs as the firm gains experience in making and marketing a new product. It was then proposed that consideration of the evidence from a number of other studies of the way in which innovations diffuse through a population of adopters might provide some pointers for improved performance.

The persistent and pervasive nature of S-shaped diffusion curves prompted the conclusion that the overall speed of diffusion is a function of elapsed time from market introduction to first purchase, which clearly puts a very high premium on being able to pre-identify good prospects early in the launch phase. Based on this observation, we then examined ways of identifying early adopters, first in terms of the characterstics of the new products and then in terms of the innovativeness of individuals and organizations.

A common thread throughout the consideration of correlates of innovativeness was the importance of communication, and the final section of the chapter dealt with some of the more salient aspects of the process.

Thus far we have been concerned primarily with establishing the critical importance of the launch phase through the examination of a wide body of evidence drawn from an extensive variety of sources. While we have argued that there are some consistent patterns which provide a useful conceptual framework for organizing one's thinking about market development, we have also had to acknowledge that marketing new products is highly situation specific. In *Market Development* Baker (1983b) reviewed a series of case histories of new product launches (both successful and unsuccessful) along very similar lines to Ray Corey's earlier *The Development of Markets for New Materials* (1956). Both these books, and numerous individual case histories which appear from time to time in both the academic and practitioner journals (e.g. *Long Range Planning*, *Journal of Product Innovation*, *Fortune*, *Business Week*, etc.), confirm that, given an intrinsically superior product or service, the difference between success and failure is very much a question of segmentation, targeting and positioning. First, one must segment the market in order to identify those potential users most likely to perceive benefits in switching to (adopting) the new product. Having identified the target segment, one must learn as much about it as one can in order to develop a profile of members of that segment (individuals or firms) so that one can develop an appropriate marketing plan for reaching them effectively (positioning).

Developing marketing plans is dealt with in considerable detail in most general marketing texts and will not be revisited here. To conclude this chapter we offer a case study of the launch of a new material – superplastic aluminium – which reinforces many of the points made above.

Case study: TI Superform – superplastic aluminium
. . . .

TI Superform is a wholly owned subsidary of Tube Investments and was set up in December 1973 to manufacture and market components made from superplastic aluminium with the brand name of 'Supral'.

Superplasticity is the property that allows certain metals and alloys to be extensively deformed under appropriate conditions. Although this phenomenon has been known to metallurgists since 1931, it has not been exploited until recent years. Much had been previously written about the mechanical properties in the superplastic state, but most of these alloys are commercially unattractive. Little, however, was known about the microstructural characteristics of materials which exhibit superplasticity.

In 1966 it became clear to physicists and metallurgists at the TI Research Laboratories at Hinxton Hall, near Cambridge, from reading published papers on the subject, that superplastic forming of complex components was feasible and that potentially this could be of some, though as yet unidentified, benefit to TI.

A basic research project was initiated in the same year to explore the production and development of the ultra fine-grained micro-structure that was known to be a prerequisite of superplastic behaviour. The eutectics of aluminium, copper and aluminium silicon formed the basis of this study.

This exploratory work lasted two years. It was then decided that further work could only be justified if the project's objectives were directed to more practical ends and a key meeting was held between the TI Research Laboratories and the British Aluminium Technological Centre at Chalfont Park in Buckinghamshire.

The single most important point to emerge from this meeting was the firm view held by British Aluminium that, to be of any commercial value, an alloy would have to contain a minimum of 90% aluminium for metallurgical reasons.

As a result, effort at the TI Research Laboratories was concentrated on high aluminium alloys. The significance of this is of great importance as it means that the research was aimed at making a conventional alloy superplastic metal and not, as most other research had done, taking a superplastic metal and trying to turn it into engineering material. After six months' work, sufficient progress had been made to warrant an intensive joint Tube Investments/British Aluminium research and development programme being initiated, and in 1967 the first provisional patent application for superplastic aluminium alloys was made. These materials were shown in tensile tests to be capable of elongations of over 1000% compared with 20–40% for normal alloys. The first forming rig had been developed by the Tube Investments Research Laboratories and was already in operation at Hinxton Hall. In March 1972, the first factory-produced sheet was available and formability trials were started, with engineering development becoming increasingly important as the project progressed.

Defining the market

As the properties and production costs of Supral became clearer, a marketing study was initiated to identify those applications where the new material would enjoy a competitive edge over existing materials. Based upon this analysis, certain key market segments were selected as holding the most promise for parts fabricated from Supral and became the focus for Superform's initial sales efforts.

Two years later (in 1976), TI Superform took stock of the situation with the assistance of TI Special Assignments (a parent company research group) by undertaking a detailed analysis of orders and enquiries received since starting operations, coupled with a thorough investigation of competitive processes for producing components in metal and plastics. This analysis largely confirmed the earlier work and permitted the development of a clearly stated product profile to be used in concentrating effort upon those applications where Supral was seen to have the greatest potential.

In essence, Supral offers significant benefits in the manufacture of complex shapes beyond the capabilities of rubber dye pressing, and in quantities below 10,000 off, where high tool costs would render multiple pressing or deep drawings of aluminium or steel uneconomic. Furthermore, while Supral is not competitive with plastics on price alone, there are many applications where the high temperature capability of aluminium makes its use preferable. It is also possible that, with escalating oil prices, aluminium could become directly competitive with plastics on price alone, which could give it a significant overall advantage.

Of course, Supral is not a perfect material, or at least not as yet, and components have to be designed to conform with its capability in terms of corner radii, draft angles, re-entrant features and so forth. However, Superform has developed considerable expertise in this area and this is available to customers, as is advice on finishing – indeed, many parts are available from Superform which can be incorporated directly into its customers' end products.

Augmenting the market

In the list of the basic performance and cost characteristics, Superform identified basic market sectors as follows:

1. Aerospace
2. Specialist vehicles
3. Commercial vehicles
4. Case shells
5. Electrical/instrument housing
6. Gaming/vending machine cases
7. Architectural panels
8. Others.

Some specific applications in the aerospace sector which build on Supral's ability to satisfy the need for complex shapes, high strength-to-weight ratio and low volume economy, are Martin Baker ejector seats; screening covers on missile guidance systems for BAC (tooling costs here were £350 compared with £5000 for plastic injection moulding); and covers for the Airbus undercarriage hydraulic system.

One of the most visible applications of Supral was the manufacture of the body panels on the Aston Martin Lagonda, where a crisp line was achieved with relatively shallow panels for a tooling cost of about £70,000. For matched dye pressing, the tooling cost would have been nearer £1.5 million.

Another highly visible application of Supral is in the cladding of the Sainsbury Visual Arts Centre at Norwich, where Supral has added a new dimension to aluminium forming in terms of depth of form, surface texture and complex shape. These features hold considerable promise for cladding and infill panels, for suspended ceilings and for doors.

Commercial vehicles are usually mass produced rather than in batches, and in numbers which make a high tooling cost acceptable. Accordingly, there is less potential for Supral here, although it is likely to be used for variations on the basic production models in terms of either appearance – for grills or cab panels, for example – or special features such as sumps.

Case shells for portable instrument housing – for example TC scanners, camera/attaché cases and electrical instrument housings – offer particularly suitable applications for Supral. The ability to produce deep, seam-free shapes with excellent heat dissipation and screening properties has proved of great benefit and resulted in a wide range of components and parts.

In gaming and vending machines there is a need for strength which is fully met by Supral, with the added advantage that low volume economy permits the frequent style changes necessary to stimulate sales to end-use customers.

Finally, 'others' embraces a wide variety of end uses, from luggage racks for British Rail to sumps and divider pans in bulk oxygen plants manufactured by Air Products Ltd.

However, this veritable wealth of market opportunities also constituted a significant danger which is common to many small companies starting up: spreading the available resources so thinly that they fail to make any significant impact on any given market segment. How then does one develop a policy for husbanding resources and putting them to most effective use?

Selling in

By 1977, the managing director of TI Superform, Iain Buchanan, was under some pressure to increase sales revenues as these were lagging behind the targets set for the company. Recognizing that surviving the introductory phase was critical, he decided to seek some external help and approached one of the authors for advice on ways to accelerate market penetration.

Preliminary discussions soon established that the parent company had established a linear sales forecast, so that while the sales of Supral were developing nicely in accordance with a classic product life cycle exponential curve, they were none-the-less seriously under-performing by comparison with target.

TI Superform's problem is one common to material suppliers and also to the manufacturers of components of sub-assemblies for incorporation in other finished products. In these situations, not only does the new product have to overcome the resistance to change which can be anticipated, but it will also usually require a change in the end product into which the innovation is to be incorporated. In the nature of things, manufacturers prefer to plan changes and are unlikely to initiate them in their own products solely because an alternative input becomes available. It follows that a direct cost comparison will not suffice, since it will not incorporate an adequate allowance for the unamortized capital costs associated with the current input, for the design costs and possible consequential costs of a design change to permit use of the new input, and certainly not for the perceived risk of changing to something new. In terms of the composite model of buyer behaviour, strong precipitating circumstances are absent and the seller may well have to search very hard to establish what these might be. To this end, a small survey was conducted of 20 firms; some had adopted Supral but others had rejected it.

The survey findings

Although some concern has been expressed about the proliferation of marketing research surveys and it is argued that many companies are becoming resistant to such investigations, we do not believe that this constraint applies to research into new product marketing. The reason for this opinion is that most firms have a direct interest in the subject matter and often regard interviews concerning particular new products to be of help in that they clarify many of the salient issues concerned with the adoption of a new product. Emphasis should also be given to the value of interviewing non-adopters, and in many cases their responses gave a much clearer indication of the missing elements in an effective marketing strategy whereas existing adopters merely confirmed that, in their case, one had got the mix right.

The more significant findings of our survey were:

1. Once awareness has been achieved (most often through trade press write-ups), a decision is taken on whether or not to evaluate the material. The main criteria considered are the potential technical and cost advantages of the material over alternative solutions to the same design problem, whether the material was being considered as a replacement for a part already being produced by another manufacturing route, or as a new part in a new, modified product. If no immediate application is discerned, information is 'filed'. Very few companies or individuals would seem to have efficient methods for recalling this information if suitable applications arise subsequently. The obvious implication is that the seller must continue to keep his product in front of prospective customers through publicity, advertising and personal selling.

2. If evaluation is undertaken, then the commitment of the supplier to helping the design engineer is of vital importance.

3. Several factors were considered by all companies in coming to an adoption/rejection decision, namely:

   (a) The likelihood of a design change or the introduction of a new product, where changes in tooling are required. The greater the likelihood of such change the greater the interest in Supral.

   (b) A requirement to produce a component with a deep drawn and/or complex shape.

(c) The batch size/tooling cost.

The first of these factors is clearly a precipitating circumstance and underlines the importance of trying to identify companies in the course of reviewing their own product mix.

4. In addition to the general factors, a number of situation specific factors were considered which tended to have a major influence on the final decision, viz.:

   (a) Potential users' own press shop/toolroom facilities. Where under-utilized capacity exists, manufacturers prefer to use their own facilities rather than buy in, even when buying in offers a saving on the individual piece price.

   (b) An integrated manufacturing process – the greater the integration, the greater the need for material *compatibility*. In other words, don't mix steel with aluminium or plastic if you can avoid it.

   (c) A reduction in hand finishing, i.e. ability to buy in a completed 'bolt-on' part will increase interest.

   (d) Prototype development: here the low tooling costs on small runs proved particularly attractive.

   (e) Single sourcing: a unique product is seen as more risky than one available from several competing sources.

5. Among the major barriers to adoption were included the following:

   (a) The product design or specifications were controlled by a non-UK holding company.

   (b) The company was using a performance specification to which all materials must conform, e.g. a British standard. The securing of a rating often takes a long time for a unique new material such as Supral, but the importance of such recognition cannot be over-emphasized.

   (c) The commitment to the known and existing technology, e.g. working in steel.

   (d) The costs of evaluating and testing the suitability of the new material in the context of the proposed user's product mix.

   (e) An existing commitment to suppliers through forward orders and/or investment in capital equipment.

   (f) Ineffective senior management unwilling to take risks and highly resistant to change.

6. Finally a number of particular incentives to early adoption were:

   (a) Operating in a market with frequent design changes.

   (b) The existence of formal value analysis programmes in user companies, which unfortunately does not seem to be very common in practice.

   (c) Familiarity with similar materials and/or manufacturing technology.

Armed with these insights, the company was able to focus its selling effort with greater precision than had been possible when it was faced with an embarrassing wealth of potential markets.

Summary

In the terms of our analytical framework, the TI Superform case provides compelling evidence of the need to extend conventional market research and market segmentation analysis so as to be able to rank order these segments in terms of their time to respond. The strength of the precipitating circumstances was key to the potential buyer's reaction, such that where manufacturers were actively considering a new design (Sainsbury Visual Arts Centre, Aston Martin car), then Supral was evaluated alongside other alternative materials and its superior techno-economic benefits led to purchase. Conversely, time spent in trying to persuade commercial vehicle manufacturers to use it for trim components was largely wasted as these parts represented a trivial part of the total design which had only recently been revised.

The case also provides evidence of the way in which the potential user's perception may be distorted both consciously (UK subsidiary of a US company with no latitude for change in its purchasing or manufacturing method) or semi-consciously (under-utilized capacity in alternative fabricating methods, lack of prior experience with fabricating or moulding).

Finally, the case demonstrated that the information needed to gain a better insight into the likely reactions of a completely new market (from the seller's point of view) faced with a radically different material is available if you ask.

(The research reported in this case history was first published in the October 1978 issue of *Marketing* magazine under the title 'TI Superform's academic launch' by Michael Baker and Stephen Parkinson. It is reproduced here by permission.)

QUESTIONS

1. What are the primary objectives of test marketing?
2. Discuss the pros and cons of 'real' versus simulated test marketing.
3. Summarize the major limitations of test marketing.
4. What is 'time to market'? Why has it become increasingly important to firms developing new products?
5. Review the factors to be taken into account when deciding whether or not to launch a new product.
6. Explain diffusion theory and suggest its implications for launching new products.
7. Selecting any new product with which you are familiar, show how Rogers' Five Factors might have been used to develop a launch strategy.
8. Why is it important to be able to pre-identify early adopters? How might you do this for a new consumer product? For a new industrial product?
9. What is the difference between personal and non-personal communication? What role do they have to play when launching new products?

Mini-case ● Persil Power

Introduction
In May 1994, Unilever launched the latest addition to its range of domestic laundry detergents. The development of Persil Power had taken over five years to complete and cost an estimated £200 million. The product launch was Unilever's largest for 15 years and was rushed ahead to beat Procter & Gamble's Ariel Future to market, in an attempt to regain leadership of the European detergent market from its US rival. The events of the following 10 months will make Persil Power one of the classic cases in new product development, but not in the way that Unilever had intended.

The firm
Unilever, the giant Anglo-Dutch food and detergents group, had a turnover of £30 billion in 1994, up 8% from the previous year. Operating profit was £2.58 billion (8.7% of turnover), also up by 8% from 1993. It employed 304,000 people around the world, with approximately a third of the total in Europe. The detergents part of the business includes fabric cleaning and conditioners, soaps and home cleaning products; the financial results of this part of the business over the last five years are summarized in Figures 14.4 and 14.5.

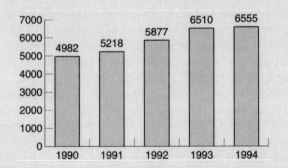

Figure 14.4 ● Unilever detergents business turnover (£ million)

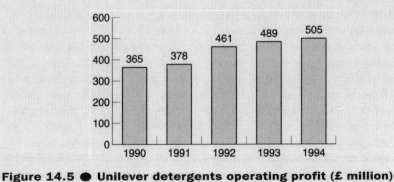

Figure 14.5 ● Unilever detergents operating profit (£ million)

The product was actually introduced by Lever Brothers, a subsidiary which represents one of Unilever's core businesses. Lever's turnover in 1993 was £670 million (£605 in 1992), with an operating profit of £32 million (–£11 million in 1992). Following poor results in 1992, the number of employees was reduced from 2180 to 1870. Persil was Lever's flagship brand, launched soon after the company's incorporation in 1937.

The industry

In the UK, the market for clothes washing detergents grew steadily from £650 million in 1989 to £886 million in 1994. After allowing for inflation, this represented a growth of 17% in real terms (because of the rise of concentrated products, volumes had actually decreased). The external factors driving the sales growth include the increasing trends in the household penetration of washing machines, the number of women in employment, and the number of single-person households.

Lever Brothers and Procter & Gamble (P & G) dominate the market by an overwhelming margin, representing a virtual duopoly of supply. Reckitt & Colman have entered the market, but only within the limited eco-friendly segment. Own-brand labels have found it difficult to penetrate the market against the power of long-established brand names.

Ten years ago, Lever Brothers had the largest UK market share of clothes washing detergents, but by 1992 it had fallen to 37% and by 1994 it was 34% (compared with a stable 53% for P & G). Lever had always been able to claim the largest single brand, Persil. However, even this was now only neck and neck with Ariel. P & G's overall market leadership was attributed to the significantly better performance of its secondary brands. In Europe as a whole, the overall detergent market was worth £6 billion, split 32% P & G, 26% Unilever and 13% others.

Although the industry in general can be considered as being in a long-term mature phase, the main feature between competing firms at present has been called 'innovation wars'. There is a strong focus on new product development by the main players; recent developments include moves towards liquid products, concentrated/micro products, 'biological' products, and those specifically for use at lower temperatures or with coloured clothes.

The development

The production technology of the clothes detergent industry is that of large-batch chemical manufacture, and has been in existence in its basic form since the first synthetic detergents were made in the 1930s. The traditional bleaching agent is hydrogen peroxide, which only starts to take effect at washing temperatures above 60°C. However, this basic detergent is gradually being phased out. Recent technical advances have been aimed at reducing the wash temperature to around 40°C to reduce water heating costs and damage to fabrics. In response to environmentalist pressures, the level of phosphates have been reduced, and the products have been made more concentrated to reduce packaging. Specialist formulae have been developed for delicate fabrics and for use with strong colours.

The main technical innovation in the formulation of Persil Power was the inclusion of a bleaching catalyst known as the Accelerator, which allowed the powder to function at lower temperatures. It belonged to a new family of organomanganese complexes called triazacyclononames, which was claimed could catalyze hydrogen peroxide bleaching at temperatures as low as 20°C and was 2–3 times more effective at removing stains at 40°C than the present generation of powders. It was intended as a substitute for existing Persil, with the advantage of shorter washing times and use at lower temperatures.

Lever's top management believed that in Persil Power's Accelerator they had a rare ingredient in the laundry market – a real product advantage. It had been successfully tested by thousands of consumers over a two-year period without any problems. However, it appears that the launch of the new product was rushed forward to pre-empt the expected launch of Ariel Future. It was intended to replace the existing Persil and also to regain some of the European market share lost to P & G in recent years. It was launched in May with a similar price and range of distribution channels as its predecessor. The typical triumphalism of the £26 million launch campaign emphasized its revolutionary new features and customer benefits as a new generation of washing powder, fully endorsed by the Good Housekeeping Institute.

The results

Events moved quickly in the months after launch. Within weeks, P & G's propaganda machine claimed that Persil Power could damage some coloured clothes under certain conditions and published the now infamous pictures of badly holed boxer shorts all over the tabloid press. Furthermore, they claimed that the revolutionary manganese compound stayed in the garments after washing, and was still active in subsequent washes made with conventional powders. There then followed an unprecedented and well-documented media battle with claim and counter-claim, each backed up by research findings.

Lever Brothers first denied the claims, but simultaneously reformulated and repackaged the product with the manganese content reduced by 90% and the conditions of use clarified. Then it admitted there may have been a problem, but continued with plans to introduce the original Accelerator into its Surf and Radion brands. The firm may be considered unlucky if, as claimed, the manganese catalyst only reacted with new dyes that were not used in the original tests, and even then only at high temperatures and after repeated use. However, the potential dangers of manganese in clothes detergents under certain conditions were already known by researchers. Legal action was initiated and then withdrawn. Even the reformulated product was shown to be harmful in extreme conditions. The Good Housekeeping Institute and other consumer associations withdrew their endorsements. Eventually, some of the major UK supermarkets including Safeway, Tesco and Sainsbury withdrew the product from their shelves. This was effectively the death knell for Persil Power. Lever Brothers launched its own competitor to Persil Power at the start of 1995, called New Generation Persil. It had originally been developed in parallel with Persil Power, but without the manganese Accelerator. It was launched following tests by six independent European research institutes. As far as Persil Power was concerned, the company had 'finally switched off its life support system. It may linger on for a few months as a speciality product but it is, for all practical purposes, dead'. Procter &

Gamble's response was to combine public relations with short, tactical advertising campaigns, in order to question the relative product advantage of Persil Power. They adopted what some commentators have called an 'uncharacteristic' open door policy to the press (*Marketing*, November 1994, p. 23) and they supplied the now-famous photographs of underwear allegedly shredded by Persil Power.

In the early stages after launch, consumers appeared to adopt Persil power very quickly, despite the soap wars ensuing in the media. Repeat purchases were reported to be running at 70% within the first two weeks. In the UK, Persil regained from Ariel the position of top brand with a market share of 30.2%. However, the figures eventually deteriorated as consumers became increasingly confused and lost confidence in the new product. After all the research and development costs and the £26 million launch budget, Lever's biggest brand was further behind than when it started.

Discussion questions

1. According to an executive of Unilever, the company launched a product with a defect they had not detected. What are the possible reasons for this?

2. How might Lever Brothers have tackled the launch differently, in order to influence results more positively?

3. Evaluate the role of competitive reaction to the launch and suggest a checklist for anticipating competitive response.

This case was compiled from material in public sources by Ian Park and the authors.

chapter 15

Managing growth

LEARNING OBJECTIVES

1. To introduce a typology of innovation.

2. To identify sources of resistance to new products and methods for overcoming them.

3. To emphasize the importance of differentiation in developing a new market.

4. To illustrate the nature of competition in the growth phase of market development.

On completion of this chapter you will:

1. Understand the factors which may delay or accelerate the take-up of new products.

2. Appreciate the importance of targeting the market segment with the strongest initial need for the new product.

3. Know the main sources of resistance to new products and ways of overcoming them.

4. Recognize the importance of maintaining differentiation throughout the growth phase to ward off competition.

Introduction

According to the classic product life cycle (PLC) concept, on first introduction new products will initially make slow progress in penetrating a market. However, if the new product can survive this introductory phase and establish itself in the market it can then look forward to a period of rapid growth – and increased competition.

In this chapter we look first at some of the factors which inhibit or slow the initial development of a new product and their implications for management. Next, we review the conditions which tend to initiate 'take-off' and the appropriate strategy and tactics to be used as new entrants seek to climb on the bandwagon and eliminate or erode the first mover's advantage.

Detailed discussion of the launch of the 16-bit PC and Computerized Tomography (the Body Scanner) illustrates the challenge of competitive reaction in the growth phase as well as tactics for dealing with this. In order to stay ahead the innovator must distinguish itself from a growing number of imitators, and the chapter concludes with a brief look at ways of sustaining differentiation in an increasingly competitive market.

Resistance to change

In the previous chapter we stressed the importance of segmentation, targeting and positioning in establishing which firms or individuals would be most likely to respond favourably to a new product on its first introduction to the marketplace. Based on the principle that there are no new needs, only new ways of satisfying them (*q.v.* 'Marketing myopia', Levitt, 1960), it follows that any new product will have to displace an existing product which satisfies the need and/or to increase the perceived benefit of satisfying the need such that persons or organizations which have not previously done so will be encouraged to enter the market. Examples of the latter would be making a cheap motor car, an easy to use computer, and so on.

As we have seen, the speed with which a new product penetrates a market will depend very much upon its relative advantage, compatibility, divisibility, communicability and (lack of) complexity. The more highly the new product scores on these attributes, the more quickly it is likely to be adopted, with the obvious caveat that if it is too similar to the existing means of satisfying a need, users may not be bothered to switch. Eric von Hippel of MIT offers a useful typology of innovation when he suggests three broad categories:

1. Known need
2. Customer active or need pull
3. Supplier active or technology push.

Observation and the limited evidence available (von Hippel located only eight studies of the customer active paradigm) suggest that this ordering reflects increasing resistance to change and, therefore, an increasing probability of failure due to delays in achieving an acceptable sales volume.

Known need innovations are instantly recognizable as 'just what I've always wanted'. ICI's synthetic pyrethroid insecticide Ambush fell exactly into this category in that it offered a whole cluster of desirable benefits – wide spectrum of activity, remarkable knock-down, a relatively fast good kill combined with very low mammalian toxicity and non-persistence in the environment. Undoubtedly, its very rapid market acceptance also owed much to careful pre-identification of the best target markets and imaginative marketing, but, fundamentally, its success may be ascribed to the best advice of all to an innovator – build a better product at an equivalent price, or an equivalent product at a lower price.

Needled woven polypropylene exhibited exactly the same instantaneous recognition when it was first offered to tufted carpet manufacturers, as it offered the opportunity to reduce the pile weight of the carpet without fear of the backing material 'grinning' through. The economies offered were significant and nearly every manufacturer with brands designed for the low price end of the market adopted the new material immediately.

Need pull innovations also encounter relatively little resistance for, by definition, they represent a response to a known and declared interest. Frequently, such innovations are the direct result of an approach by a user to a prospective supplier and are the outcome of joint development work. This is not to say that the innovator will not encounter any difficulties when they seek to offer the new product to a wider market, but it is usually much simpler to make adjustments to a product which exists and can be shown to work in analogous situations than is the case with a completely new and untried product. A recent example which came to our attention was the use of eddy current methods to detect cracks in fasteners used in aircraft construction. The innovator had developed a successful piece of equipment for the RAF under contract, but was surprised to find only limited interest from civil airlines when he tried to sell it to them. Analysis of this lack of interest made it clear that the main problem was that the innovator was seeking to 'push' his innovation on the civil airlines on the assumption that if it was good enough for the RAF it was good enough for them. In fact, it was too good and provided a level of performance far beyond that required, but at the sacrifice of speed which was seen as essential to keep planes in service. Once this fact became known it was a relatively simple modification to increase the speed of scan and desensitize the accuracy to an acceptable level.

Thus, it is with the third category – the supplier active or technology push innovation – that most difficulties are encountered, for in this case prospective customers have evinced no open or explicit interest in a new product. Such an approach is usually characterized as 'production orientated' and conforms with the stereotype of the lone inventor single-mindedly pursuing his goal oblivious to the world outside. While such an approach frequently does lead to the creation of products which are 'new' in the technical sense, the innovator then has to identify potential users whose needs match the benefits to be conferred from acquisition of the new product. There is much evidence to suggest that there the greatest potential for failure lies, due to a mismatch in the perception of supplier and user – the intervening variable to which reference was made earlier.

If prospective users are unaware of a need for an improved product to substitute for something in current consumption, then it seems reasonable to assume they are satisfied with the existing product. If we were to undertake a full appraisal of everything which might conceivably substitute for present behaviour, the information overload would become intolerable, but, fortunately, we have a defence mechanism of selective perception which suppresses or screens out irrelevant or redundant information. It follows that unless we can couch information about our new product in terms which are meaningful to prospective customers, they will never even be aware of it at the conscious level. Sophisticated marketers are very familiar with this possibility and devote considerable effort trying to pre-identify the most receptive market segment, i.e. the one with the least resistance to change. Surprisingly, they are often very poor at this and our research suggests that this is because they give too much weight to the most attractive segment in terms of potential sales volume rather than the segment with the most pressing need. On reflection, however, and with the benefit of a little hindsight, it is clear that the customers with the biggest potential need are likely to have the greatest commitment to the existing technology and, therefore, the greatest inertia to overcome to make a change. Three examples will help clarify this.

During the 1930s, Bakelite developed a process for the manufacture of continuous vinyl, suitable for smooth floor coverings. At the time Armstrong Cork and Congoleum

Nairn dominated the quality end of this market with linoleum, and it seemed logical for Bakelite to concentrate their sales efforts on these two companies. Three years later the outbreak of the Second World War diverted everyone's attention to other things but, despite expressing considerable interest, neither Armstrong nor Congoleum had sold a single yard of vinyl flooring. In 1947, Bakelite once again set out to try and sell the idea, but on this occasion they approached a small manufacturer of enamel-coated, felt-based products catering for the low price segment – Delaware Floor Products (DFP). Bakelite had to give DFP considerable technical assistance to get vinyl production started but within a year they had sold 0.76 million square yards. Table 15.1 shows their subsequent performance.

The linoleum manufacturers' reluctance to adopt vinyl can be attributed to the simple fact that it was a direct substitute for linoleum and possessed a number of advantages over the traditional material – which became patently obvious when customers were offered the choice. Thus, manufacturing vinyl, which requires a completely different production process, could only cannibalize existing sales and render current investment obsolete prematurely. Small wonder Bakelite's preferred customers proved so resistant to change!

Much the same problems faced the Aluminum Company of America (Alcoa) when they sought to interest van trailer builders in the merits of aluminium sheet over the traditional metal and wood methods of fabrication. As far as the van trailer manufacturers were concerned, using the new material would require them to change their fabricating equipment and learn new skills to produce a more expensive end product, an exercise which seemed pointless, since their customers appeared quite content with the existing product. It was only when Alcoa changed its marketing tactics and approached transport managers responsible for operating fleets of van trailers that the potential benefits were fully appreciated.

In the USA, road taxes are based on laden weight, such that the lower the vehicle weight the bigger the revenue-earning payload. A simple cost–benefit analysis quickly showed that by using aluminium the added cost of the new material would be amortized in 6–12 months, and thereafter would yield a continuous positive cash flow with the added benefit of very low maintenance costs compared with wood/steel construction. Faced with these potential benefits, the operators specified aluminium construction and provided sufficient leverage to overcome the builders' inertia.

Table 15.1 ● Growth in sales of vinyl flooring, 1948–52

Year	Number of producers	Millions of square yards	Factory value ($ million)
1948	6	4.48	5.80
1949	18	5.45	9.20
1950	19	8.97	12.56
1951	19	13.41	20.33
1952	26	29.52	34.40

When TI Superform introduced Superplastic aluminium to the UK market it had clearly identified the material's benefits *vis-à-vis* existing products such as die stamping, rubber moulding and GRP fabrication. Further, it had selected eight specific market segments which offered the greatest potential use of the material. But, as in the vinyl case, they had failed to determine who *within* each segment would have the most pressing need for an innovation, and so wasted considerable energy in approaching firms with only limited incentive to change, with the result that their subjective perception of the benefits was considerably less than that claimed by the innovator.

The question of how a new product can gain sufficient leverage to displace an existing product, and overcome the buyer's natural inertia, is dealt with at some length by Milind M. Lele in *Creating Strategic Leverage* (1992). The following section draws heavily on this source, especially Chapter 11, 'How successful new products capitalize on leverage'.

Leveraging new product growth

On introduction to a market a new product has to overcome at least three kinds of potential resistance before it is likely to 'take off' and grow rapidly. These may be characterized as technological, infrastructural and behavioural. Lele illustrates their effect by reference to the market for microwave ovens. The first designs of microwave ovens were introduced in 1957 but were large and expensive. The technology needed considerable refinement. Secondly, microwave cooking calls for special containers and most pre-prepared and convenience foods were not packed in the right materials. The infrastructure had to develop to make microwave meals available. Third, until more women began to enter the workforce there was an absence of a sufficiently powerful precipitating circumstance, convenience, to prompt the behavioural response. Lele describes this as the 'emerging' phase during which typically there may be many, often small, participants with a wide variety of products and marketing mixes largely due to the low resistance to entry. (As we shall see shortly, when describing the early marketing of body scanners, this is not always the case!)

In some senses we may regard the emergent or introductory phase as a period of trial and error which will lead to the evolution of a dominant design widely accepted by both producers and users. It is this dominant design which usually triggers the rapid growth phase and sees a switch in emphasis from product development to process innovation. Sellers and buyers are now agreed on the desirable attributes of the new product and competitive advantage resides in being able to produce and market the new product in the most efficient and effective way. During the growth phase Lele (p. 201) argues that 'the emphasis should be on identifying the most likely and profitable product/ market areas for introducing flankers, niche products, or complements'. To support this argument he uses the example of new product tactics in the 16-bit personal computer market over the period 1981–86.

In 1981, the year in which IBM launched its original PC, approximately 1.5 million PCs were in use. By 1986 this had grown to 25 million and annual sales were around 6 million units, a figure they had achieved in 1983, which Lele characterizes as the end of the growth phase. The original PC launched by IBM immediately became the dominant design and set the industry standard. It was followed by the PC-XT in 1983 and the PC-AT in 1984, which was to replace it, with the original PC being terminated in 1987. Only Apple, the previous industry leader, declined to change its basic architecture to copy that of IBM.

The PC-X7T and PC-AT are seen as flankers which were introduced by IBM to out-manoeuvre Zenith, Compaq and others who were making clones of the original PC. These latter companies established themselves as niche producers with Zenith targeting educational and government purchasers and Compaq emphasizing portables. Major complements for the PC which helped fuel its growth were hard disk drives, modems, applications software and other accessories, all of which were introduced during the period 1981–83.

In Lele's view IBM's product strategy in the growth and early maturity phases was 'virtually faultless'. By concentrating on flankers it maintained control over the market, as it did through using third-party providers to develop complementary products. It failed, however, in that it did not offer a lower priced product, either as a 'second brand' or as a private label, and so allowed the clones to enter and eventually dominate the market as it moved into maturity.

During the growth phase competitors may choose to follow one or other of three broad alternative strategies. They can attempt to develop a second standard, can adopt the first standard and compete head-on, or can identify potential niches and concentrate on getting into them first. Developing a second standard has major cost implications and, in effect, is equivalent to launching a new product which would have to survive launch and introduction while competing with the first standard in its rapid growth phase. Not exactly an easy or attractive proposition! Competing head-on also requires considerable resources but is often the approach taken by large firms pursuing the strategy of the fast second who delay entering the market until the onset of rapid growth indicates it is propitious for them to climb on the bandwagon. For smaller players this is not a viable alternative and most competitors will seek to develop specialist niches or complementary products and so ride on the coat-tails of the industry leader.

As Lele describes the developing PC market it is clear that the risks of developing a second standard are considerable. DEC, which enjoyed a high reputation for smaller computers, especially with engineers and scientists, sought to promote its 'Rainbow' design as a second standard. However, it entered the market 10 months behind IBM and failed to invest enough in its launch strategy. It failed to make any significant impact and quit the PC market. By contrast AT&T tried to position itself both as a second standard and as a credible alternative to IBM. Its UNIX PC and 6300 Plus failed to create a second standard and failed for the same reasons as DEC. With regard to its IBM-compatible machine, this would have been welcomed by resellers seeking to reduce their dependency on IBM. But by the time AT&T launched it, IBM was too well established to be displaced and Compaq had filled the compatible alternative slot. A third major player, Texas Instruments, also attempted to introduce its own design but quickly switched to an IBM compatible. Unfortunately for TI it failed to position itself as a credible alternative and, like AT&T, made no progress in the market.

By contrast both Zenith and Compaq succeeded because, as Lele points out, they

'(1) correctly identified the IBM PC as the dominant design;
(2) avoided competing head-on with IBM for the main market; and
(3) focused on identifying and occupying niche markets ahead of the competition.'

Apple's experience also illustrates the risks and rewards of new product development. Apple had been the dominant 8-bit computer but was displaced by IBM's 16-bit machine. Apple chose to develop an alternative standard but its first attempt, the Apple III, targeted at the corporate/office market, failed because of problems with reliability and a lack of software. Its next effort, the Lisa, introduced in March 1983, also failed and it was not until the launch of the Macintosh in January 1984 that Apple succeeded. To a large degree Apple's success may be attributed to its development of a specialist segment – the University Consortium – who adopted the machine in return for very substantial discounts. However, this tactic created a large installed base which attracted the development of complements, which in turn enhanced its commercial attractiveness and enabled it to attack the corporate and office markets in 1985 and 1986 as the IBM PC passed through maturity to decline.

Lele's analysis of development in the 16-bit personal computer market clearly illustrates the threats and opportunities faced by a company as its new product survives infancy and moves into rapid growth. Similar lessons are also apparent from the introduction of the body scanner described in the section which follows.

Computerized tomography (CT): the EMI scanner

The case of the EMI body scanner is a classic one in marketing history, an innovation which falls into the category of a 'known need' with the result that, on its introduction in 1972, it met with an immediate and enthusiastic response. However, despite the high-technology content of an innovation which must be considered 'radical' by anybody's standards and the early success enjoyed, in December 1979 EMI were forced to sell their interests in the product following a period of large and sustained losses.

Early days: the company and the product

At the beginning of the 1970s EMI Ltd was best known as a manufacturer of vinyl records and tapes and as the organization which introduced the Beatles to the world. Other interests of the EMI group included film studios, the ABC chain of cinemas, hotels and clubs, and a considerable electronics business. In all, the company employed 48,000 people in more than 30 countries.

While the entertainment side of EMI's activities was probably the best known, the company had an impressive record of innovation in the electronics sector and is credited with being the inventor of radar and the first firm to manufacture television sets commercially in the United Kingdom. The scanner, however, must be regarded as one of the company's most significant inventions, and it came at a period of flagging sales for its other lines. Thus, although EMI had little experience of medical equipment markets, they decided to develop and market the innovation themselves rather than seek to license or sell it through a joint-venture approach. As one of EMI's executives remarked at the time, 'We weren't exactly coming up with world beaters every day'.

The EMI scanner was invented by Godfrey Hounsfield while working in a rather different field, that of automatic electronic pattern recognition. Hounsfield's timing was perfect, for commercial computerized tomography only became feasible with the availability of massive and cheap computing power. In very simple terms, the computer is required to solve the complex algorithm calculations which reconstruct the X-ray information collected by the scanner's detectors and convert this into an electronic 3D picture that a doctor can examine on a TV monitor. An indication of the complexity of this algorithm program which is the heart of the scanner is that the original prototype required several hours of computer CPU time to produce a usable image. By the time that the first commercial scanner was introduced, improvements in the software and the available computing facilities had reduced this scan time to an order of minutes, and later systems could display a reconstructed picture within 20 seconds of scanning.

Computerized tomography had a remarkable impact on radiology. With its introduction radiologists could see details of the human body that had otherwise only been seen in practical anatomy classes or illustrated medical books. One of the most dramatic and significant uses of CT is in head scanning, where conventional X-rays were of little use unless special techniques were used. For example, angiography, the most commonly used technique, involved the injection of dyes into the cranial veins, which is both painful and dangerous to the patient, a mortality rate of 3% being cited. Further, given the complexity of the technique, it is necessary to hospitalize patients, and a successful analysis could not be guaranteed since some tumours are not blood absorbing and so could not be detected by this method.

The original EMI scanner was designed for analysis of the brain and was launched in the United States at the 1972 Annual Conference of the Radiological Society of North America (RSNA), held in Chicago in December. At this conference, papers describing Hounsfield's clinical results were supported by reports of trials of the prototype conducted by Dr Ambrose of the Atkinson Morley Hospital in London. The reaction was immediate and enthusiastic, and EMI was almost overwhelmed with the flood of orders which followed the conference.

They were quite unprepared for this reaction and had installed virtually no manufacturing capacity, so that the first production units supplied were little more than glorified versions of the prototype. Faced with an inability to meet orders, EMI adopted a skimming pricing policy, with a price almost four times higher than that of conventional X-ray equipment. In addition, they asked for a 30% down payment and were operating with a six months' delivery backlog.

Market development

Prior to the introduction of the EMI scanner, there had been little change in conventional X-ray equipment during the preceding 50 years. The introduction of the scanner coincided with another innovation in the field – ultrasound equipment – and the sales of conventional X-ray equipment declined dramatically as hospitals and other users turned to the more effective new products.

Table 15.2 ● CT competitors: market participants, 1973–76

Year	Head scanners	Body scanners
1973	EMI	
1974	EMI	Disco (ACTA scanner)
	Artronix	Ohio-Nuclear
	Siemens	
1975	EMI	EMI
	Artronix	Artronix
	Syntex	Syntex
	Neuroscan	Neuroscan
	General Electric	General Electric
	Siemens	Pfizer (ACYA scanner)
		Ohio-Nuclear
		Varian
		Picker
		Philips
1976	EMI	EMI
	Artronix	Artronix
	Syntex	Syntex
	Neuroscan	Neuroscan
	General Electriç	General Electriç
	Ohio-Nuclear	Ohio-Nuclear
	Siemens	Pfizer
		Varian
		Picker
		Philips
		American Science and Engineering
		Searle
		Compagnie Générale Radiographie (CGR) (France)
		Elseint (Israel)
		Hitachi (Japan)

Most of the traditional manufacturers of X-ray equipment were very large multinational corporations with extensive product portfolios. For these companies, X-ray equipment had been a cash cow product over many years. Faced with the threat of losing this attractive market and realizing that CT was a strategic product with respect to their product range in future sales, the equipment suppliers began to pour large sums of money into computerized tomography R&D. Within three years, 15 suppliers had joined the bandwagon and, as can be seen from Table 15.2, by 1975–76 were beginning to provide real competition to EMI.

In this initial period, EMI was reaping the monopoly profit which is the true reward of the innovator. By 1973–74, they had already capitalized their initial investment and declared a profit of £1.2 million on a turnover of £5 million. At this time, EMI's main problem was in creating sufficient capacity to satisfy the rapidly expanding demand. A second factory was soon acquired which doubled the capacity of the original manufacturing unit, but the overall rate of expansion was hindered by the lack of adequately qualified managers familiar with medical electronics. Despite these difficulties, sales in 1974–75 increased to £20.4 million with a profit of £9.2 million. In the following year, 1975–76, sales more than doubled to £42.1 million and profits increased to £12.5 million.

During the early period, EMI put considerable emphasis upon improving the basic product. The first production machines were relatively simple units capable only of taking brain scans. They were also slow, requiring five minutes to take a full scan, but were adequate for the purpose, since it is possible to keep a patient's head steady for this length of time by using a head brace. Nonetheless, work was done to speed up the operation of the system and more sophisticated computer software was written, reducing the processing time to one minute and with greatly improved resolution so that small objects within the picture could be examined and/or enlarged.

In March 1975, EMI announced the first 'true' body scanner. This machine had a bigger aperture, which made it possible to take a slice through the whole body of the patient. Scanning time had also been reduced dramatically to only 20 seconds, and in a clinical trial it was shown that such a speed made it possible to scan patients through the lungs or abdomen with less than 2.5% of the scans being spoiled as a result of patient movement. Although competitive machines were beginning to appear on the market at this time, they did not seem to be a threat as their scanning time was well in excess of one minute and the picture quality far inferior to that offered by the EMI machine.

First deliveries of the body scanner were made in 1976, at which time EMI clearly dominated the market. Within EMI, pressure was exerted upon EMI Medical for the company to stop further research and to treat the scanner as a cash cow. Scanner profits were reinvested in other parts of the group, it being assumed that the market lead, product excellence and monopoly situation through patent security would give more than adequate protection against possible competition. In the event, this assumption was badly misplaced for, in fact, the detail contained in the EMI patents became their Achilles heel, enabling potential competitors to copy the machine and launch their own CT scanner systems sooner than would otherwise have been possible. While such competitors probably anticipated that EMI would sue them for patent infringement, it was well known that a US court action would take years to bring to trial, by which time the competitors expected to be well into the business. Nevertheless, sales in 1976–77 more than doubled again to £93.2 million, although profits lagged behind at only £14.7 million.

During this period, EMI regarded marketing as unnecessary. Lack of capacity was seen as the most pressing problem, and salesmen performed a purely demonstration-and-order-taking function. After the creation of additional capacity, product improvement and after-sales service were seen as the next priorities.

With expensive clinical equipment like the body scanner, reliability is of paramount importance. To make the most efficient use of the machine, most scanners would have a patient schedule booked for several weeks in advance, so that if a machine failed, critically ill patients could lose their turn in the queue. Ideally, therefore, machines had to be repaired the same day, and this created enormous strains in the early market develop-ment period, as the machines were scattered widely around the globe and the service engineers were still familiarizing themselves with them.

EMI were successful in overcoming these problems, partly by improving machine reliability, partly by giving more effective training to their engineers, and partly by establishing an adequate network of spares depots. Service contracts were offered to customers after the initial 12-month warranty period expired, and although there were some complaints about the cost of these, by 1978 the service activity was approaching break-even and providing a high level of customer satisfaction.

Competitive reaction

The development of the body scanner took EMI into a completely new market: medical equipment. In terms of the product market matrix discussed by Baker (1983b) in *Market Development* (pp. 45–47), marketing the body scanner represented a diversifica-tion in which the company was unfamiliar with both the technology and the medical equipment market. As we have seen in the preceding pages, EMI were quick to build up expertise in the new technology and it was their lack of presence in the medical equipment market which was to prove their downfall when competitors began to intro-duce their own CT machines.

Much the most spirited reaction to EMI's entry into the medical equipment market came from such very large multinationals as General Electric in the United States, Siemens in Germany and Philips in the Netherlands, all of whom manufactured conven-tional X-ray equipment as part of a broadly based line of medical electronics.

Competitive reaction to EMI Medical came in three basic ways:

1. Price competition
2. Product differentiation
3. Emphasis upon the company's long-established medical equipment reputation.

Given that all the major competitors were far bigger than EMI, they could afford to compete on a price platform by selling their products as loss leaders, or at a low pene-tration price that would be raised later when the weaker companies had been eliminated from the market. Further, as we have seen, the EMI board was milking EMI Medical and diverting its profits into other areas of the group's activities. Lastly, EMI were unable to counter their competitors' claims to be long-established medical equipment suppliers with a broad product line, for EMI was a newcomer with a single product.

Despite its inability to compete on these two dimensions, EMI Medical sincerely believed that it did have the best product, but it would seem that, because of its lack of marketing expertise, it was unable to communicate this message effectively to its custo-mers.

EMI Medical's competitors set out to differentiate their products in terms of (a) reducing scan time, (b) increasing patient throughput and (c) improving image quality.

EMI argued against scan speed, claiming that 20 seconds was adequate and that any reduction would cause picture quality to suffer. Indeed, EMI's image quality was excel-lent and never really matched. Competitors promoted highly technical arguments of improved picture quality through increased matrix capability, which did influence some customers, but in effect was little more than a simple optical magnification of the TV monitor picture. At this early stage in the development of body scanners, few people understood the finer points. The image quality argument could therefore only be explained satisfactorily to the radiologist, and even then could be appreciated only if one made a comparative assessment of two different machines. Speed is an easier concept to grasp, and therefore more marketable as a product feature. 'People fell for the concept and believed that they needed a jet engine instead of a propeller-driven Avro', as an EMI Medical marketing director admitted in 1977. A scan speed difference between 20 and five seconds is actually insignificant during a half-hour patient study where some 20 scans are done and the rest of the time is spent on preparation of the patient and picture reconstruction time. However, the speed argument implied that overall patient throughput per day would be increased, thus making the machine more cost-effective. Initially, EMI ignored the competition, relying upon its claimed product superiority, but the pressure from the competition was inexorable; EMI began to offer more competitive terms. The 30% deposit was rarely asked for and some attempts were made to cut margins to meet competitors' prices. However, as noted, both Siemens and General Electric were marketing their products as loss leaders and, given their overall financial strength, there was no way in which EMI could match them on price.

Realizing that it faced some marketing problems, EMI Medical recruited a new director of marketing with expertise in the high-technology electronic products area. It was soon after this appointment that a decision was taken in 1976 to counter the criticisms that they had no real expertise with medical equipment in general. EMI decided to broaden its product portfolio through acquisition and to build an image as a medical diagnostic and therapy company. To broaden the diagnostic equipment range, the Edinburgh Nuclear Enterprise organization was acquired which manufactures medical ultrasound systems, while, on the therapy side, a Californian company making therapy planning systems and linear accelerators (machines using X-rays to burn out malignant cancer tissue) was acquired.

The third element of EMI's reaction to the competitive threat was to recognize the success achieved through the scan speed argument of their competitors.

EMI's existing machine was generally regarded as a second-generation piece of equipment, while the fast scanners offered by General Electric and Siemens, among others, were regarded as third-generation machines. To develop these third-generation scanners, EMI's competitors had had to undertake very considerable R&D programmes, and it soon became clear that if EMI was to fend off the competitive threat, it must achieve a quantum lead and develop a fifth-generation machine which would offer a fast scan speed yet not sacrifice image quality (the third-generation machine flaw) nor have a radiation dose as high as the fourth-generation machines which were just being introduced.

It was at this point that senior EMI Ltd management made a serious mistake, for they were convinced by the EMI Medical North American organization that the Americans were best placed to manage a crash programme which would enable them to offer the new fifth-generation machine within 12–18 months. In fact, the real CT expertise in EMI was to be found in the Central Research Laboratory. Here the original inventor, Hounsfield, was already well down the development path of a new fast scanner concept which he estimated would take two years to complete. This was considered to be too long in view of the US crash programme promise.

One of the major design problems with EMI's new scanner concept was that the company insisted that it would not sacrifice image quality for scan speed. This meant that the same amount of picture data would have to be fed into the processing computer during a three-second scan as had previously been handled during the 20-second scan of the second-generation machine.

At that time there were no mini-computers with sufficient processing capacity available on a commercial basis to handle this amount of data in the time required. Therefore EMI had to design its own special-purpose unit known as the Array Processor. Work on this had already started in the United Kingdom and responsibility for it was left with them. As a result, the R&D programme was being implemented by two separate teams nearly 3000 miles apart.

After two years, it was apparent that the US team was well behind schedule and floundering. Emergency action was taken with a team of some 50 UK engineers, including Godfrey Hounsfield, going to the Chicago base to help to complete the R&D programme. On arrival, the engineers were aghast at the lack of progress which had been made, and it took a year of intensive effort before the first prototype machine was ready for shipping.

Throughout the development programme, it had been assumed that the new scanner would be manufactured in America. In the event, it transpired that EMI had no real manufacturing expertise in America and all prior production had taken place in the United Kingdom.

Because of the R&D overrun, EMI Medical was beginning to suffer severe cash-flow problems and the parent company was unable to offer any assistance as its record business was going through a bad phase at the time. To make matters worse, the Americans had announced the intention of producing a fifth-generation machine as soon as the specification had been agreed, which had the immediate effect of killing off all orders for the existing second-generation machine. Although sales in non-US markets were maintained through clever relaunch marketing, the drain on cash created by the protracted R&D programme created intolerable losses, with the result that, by the end of 1979, although EMI Medical had finally succeeded in developing a technologically superior CT system, they had insufficient funds available to undertake full-scale manufacture or to mount an appropriate relaunch campaign. In December 1979, EMI Medical was taken over by the Thorn Group.

Two points are particularly worth emphasizing here. First, EMI lost their dominant position as inventors of a new technology because they declined to accept the importance of behavioural response (BR). Thus, EMI deemed speed of scan as irrelevant in the context of their machine performance *vis-à-vis* that of its competitors. Given that prospective buyers were using this as their basis for discriminating between what appeared to them to be very similar products, this was clearly a disastrous move and underlines yet again the need to put oneself in the customer's shoes.

Secondly, it is important to stress that, with a new technology, one must be prepared either to make a quick killing and get out or to reinvest the supernormal profits, which are the reward of being first to market, in further development to maintain one's initial lead. Once the market has shown its acceptance of and preference for the new product, the growth phase will commence and the innovator will have to maintain the initiative if it is to earn the just reward for its efforts. As the EMI case amply demonstrates, this calls for product improvement, aggressive marketing and the provision of effective after-sales service. It also calls for total commitment by top management and this EMI clearly did not provide.

Sustaining differentiation

The two case histories, describing the evolution of the 16-bit PC market and the body scanner, make it clear that a new product enjoys a competitive advantage because it is differentiated. It begins to lose this advantage as soon as similar or improved versions are introduced to the market by other firms. As we have seen earlier (Chapter 2), only two basic strategies are available – cost leadership and differentiation. We have also seen that cost leadership is a function of size and market share. EMI as a medium-sized firm was quite unable to cope with the predatory tactics of firms like GEC, Siemens and Philips with much greater resources to call on. It follows that for the great majority of innovators the only viable strategy is differentiation. With a new technology, further developments and improvements are possible, so product development remains a major source of differentiation during the growth phase, with the other elements of the marketing mix playing a supporting role. As we shall see in the next chapter, maturity sets in when further product improvements are no longer available and competition revolves entirely around manipulation of the price, place and promotional variables.

As Levitt pointed out in his famous article 'Exploit the product life cycle' (*Harvard Business Review*, Nov–Dec 1965): 'The ensuing fight [during the market growth phase] for the consumer's patronage poses to the originating producer an entirely new set of problems. Instead of seeking ways of getting consumers to *try the product*, the originator now faces the more compelling problem of getting them to *prefer his brand*' (p. 33). In part such preference will depend upon having a better, or equivalent product, when first mover advantages may lend added value, i.e. the company's name is most strongly associated with the new product. But, if the firm's product is seen as being of much of a muchness with all the new competitive offerings then price, promotion and distribution will assume increased importance in helping to differentiate the product.

There is considerable evidence to suggest that many innovators fail to reap the full reward of the growth phase. One reason for this is that the firm's own growth cycle may not reflect that of the industry as a whole. Indeed, the sudden upsurge in growth engendered by the rush of imitators seeking to cash in on the new market opportunity may stall the innovator's own growth curve. As Levitt (1965) comments, 'for the originating company its growth stage now becomes truncated. It has to share the boom with new competitors. Hence the potential rate of acceleration of its own take-off is diminished and, indeed, may actually fail to last as long as the industry's' (p. 86). It is for this reason that monitoring both the product and industry life cycles is so important in devising strategies to maintain the firm's competitive edge. As the kind of analysis described by Levitt makes clear, the impact of competition, which is a major driver of rapid growth, will have negative consequences for the originator, *unless* they heed the warnings of life cycle analysis and take deliberate steps to stay ahead of the game and control market growth.

A classic example of a firm doing this was Pilkington with the introduction of float glass. This process, patented by them, was a major technological breakthrough which offered a product far superior to that made by traditional methods. As a known need innovation with high relative advantage, high compatibility, low complexity (in use), high divisibility (buy a square metre or a square kilometre), and excellent communicability it was a sure-fire winner. Everyone wanted it. Clearly, there was no way Pilkington could cope with such a demand on a global scale. Equally clear was the fact that major competitors like St Gobain and Corning would do everything they could to replicate the process. Rather than encouraging a competitive response Pilkington defused it by offering licences to major producers in other countries and taking a royalty off every square metre sold.

Armed with the hindsight which product life cycle analysis offers, innovators can pre-plan their competitive moves so as to avoid being out-manoeuvred and overtaken by the competition. To quote Levitt again, 'advance planning should be directed at extending, or stretching out, the life of the product. It is this idea of *planning in advance* of the actual launching of a new product to take specific actions later in its life cycle – actions designed to sustain its growth and profitability – which appears to have great potential as an instrument of long-term product strategy' (p. 88).

Much of Levitt's analysis then focuses on extension or stretching strategies which mainly come into play when a product reaches maturity – the subject of the next chapter. However, bearing in mind the earlier comment that the onset of competition and rapid growth may truncate the originator's own growth cycle, it is quite likely that the originator will move into the mature phase of their product life cycle while the industry life cycle is still growing. This, too, may be a source of competitive advantage as the innovator may be able to consolidate their position by adopting extension strategies while the remaining competitors slug it out for a share of a market which still appears to be growing because of the aggressive competition.

Summary

During the rapid growth phase increasing numbers of customers will be seeking to secure a supply of the new product while growing numbers of suppliers will be scrambling to cater to them. Market leaders will attempt to stay ahead of the game through further improvements in the product (faster scan speeds for CT, more memory for PCs, etc.) while less innovative competitors seek to gain market share by discounting, offering lower prices for direct sale, and so on. Whatever the tactics, only those who succeed in distinguishing themselves from the mass can look forward to the onset of maturity with any equanimity.

QUESTIONS

1. Describe von Hippel's three broad categories of innovation. What use is this typology in developing a launch strategy?

2. What is resistance to change? How might you anticipate it? Overcome it? Illustrate your answer with specific examples.

3. Identify and describe three alternative growth phase strategies.

4. Why did EMI lose its pioneering advantage as the innovator that introduced the body-scanner? With the benefit of hindsight what would you have advised them to do differently?

5. What lessons does the PLC concept have for firms entering the growth phase?

Mini-case ● First Direct

Introduction

First Direct was launched in 1988 by Midland Bank, as a new concept in banking, where all banking transactions can be arranged by telephone, at any time of day or night, 365 days a year. It now has 500,000 ABC1 customers, but faces major competition now from all the major high-street banks: Bank of Scotland, Barclays and Building Societies. What factors will encourage or impede the future success of First Direct?

The firm

Set up as an offshoot of the Midland Bank, First Direct has revolutionized banking. It has spent millions on start-up and education of consumers on telephone banking, which is in development terms fairly easy to copy. Their unique selling proposition, the 'uncopiable' element in their operation, is claimed to be service, rather than the mechanics of a tele-phone banking operation. In order to deliver the service levels, First Direct seeks to build equality relationships with its customers. This entails equality relationships within the organization itself: common staff canteen, no parking privileges, no offices, for example. Employees are selected and trained to solve problems and make decisions and so have much more responsibility than the average retail bank teller. Service recovery, for making-good mistakes, is recognized to be an important ingredient in enhancing custo-mer loyalty, with staff being given their heads in deciding how best to compensate the customer for blunders made. Nearly one third of all customers come to First Direct as a result of 'word of mouth' and four out of ten applicants have to be turned away as they do not meet the criteria on credit.

First Direct has certainly made an impact with half a million customers and me-toos entering the market from other banks and building societies. The key question now is how to build the introductory success into a mainstream 'brand'.

The development

One of the major difficulties in building the brand has been the difficulty faced in predict-ing demand and therefore in setting up adequate systems to deal with heavy demand. In

1993, First Direct had to withdraw from a planned TV advertising campaign because the demand created by the press advertising and a mail shot had already stretched their ability to cope, with detrimental effects on the quality of service. Bank personnel have said that people's experience of buying over the telephone had developed very quickly in recent years. In contrast, competitive product launches have avoided the high-spend TV launch campaign in favour of direct mail campaigns and carefully controlled systems which can handle the demand generated. For example, Barclays' system can handle 20,000 new accounts per month and Barclays aims to have four million out of its seven million customers using telephone banking by the year 2000. First Direct is currently installing a second site which will allow it to handle more than 10,000 new accounts a month. In addition an integrated advertising campaign is planned to reinforce the brand's values: modern, striving, innovative. Approximately 50% of the marketing budget is still spent on customer education, but with a three-year gap in TV advertising, there is some question as to whether time has been lost in converting from education and awareness to building loyalty and reinforcement. The aim of First Direct, however, is to have one million customers by 2000, which would represent 20% of the dedicated telephone-banking market.

Discussion questions

1. If we treat this introductory phase as one of 'trial and error', whereby the dominant design will evolve, what do you consider to be the major lessons from which First Direct should learn?

2. During the growth phase, various market segments emerge. What would you consider the major segments for telephone banking and how should First Direct use this information?

3. Anticipate competitive strategies to gain a foothold in the market.

This case was compiled using research data from public sources.

chapter 16

· ·

Managing the mature product

LEARNING OBJECTIVES
· ·

1. To identify the nature and causes of maturity.

2. To describe four basic strategies appropriate to the management of mature products:

- an offensive or 'take-off' strategy
- a defensive strategy
- a recycle strategy
- a stretching and harvesting strategy.

On completion of this chapter you will:

1. Be familiar with the factors which characterize competition in the mature phase of the product life cycle.

2. Understand the strategies available for the successful management of mature products.

3. Appreciate the importance of relationship marketing in maintaining customer loyalty for mature products.

Introduction
· ·

In the preceding chapter it was pointed out that the onset of aggressive competition in the growth phase of a product life cycle may well lead to the beginning of premature maturity for the innovator who first introduced the new product to the marketplace. Thus, while industry sales continue to grow rapidly, the innovator's sales may plateau out and call for a quite different set of tactics from those appropriate in the growth phase. In this chapter we examine in some detail what factors result in the slowing down of the growth phase, the characteristics of maturity, and the options available to the product manager to exploit fully the opportunities available in the mature phase of product and market development.

Maturity – its nature and causes
· ·

As the market approaches saturation so the growth rate slows down until eventually it stabilizes at a sales level equivalent to the replacement rate together with any natural growth in market size due to increases in population. Usually this is the longest single phase of the life cycle and will normally be proportionate to the length of the gestation/

introduction phase. That this should be so is logical in that the very forces which accelerate or delay the acceptance of a new product invariably hasten or delay its decline. That said, it is also true that in the same way that medical science has been singularly successful in extending the mature phase of the human life cycle, so product managers have been particularly successful in prolonging the life of mature products. Indeed, it is this very success which has been cited by critics as a reason for dismissing the concept as not having any practical value. But, as we noted in Chapter 5, the classic PLC charts the progress of an innovation in the *absence* of managerial intervention. Our continued emphasis upon its utility means that by identifying the stage of the life cycle we can define the strategic options available to the product manager and so develop effective action plans. Further, by identifying the transition from one stage to the next we can judge when it will be beneficial to modify one strategy for another to take account of the changing conditions in the marketplace.

As growth slows and the product enters maturity, profit *margins* will begin to decline. (We emphasize margins because mature products usually make up the backbone of a company's product portfolio and are frequently the major source of cash to sustain current and future operations: hence, 'cash cow' in the BCG growth share matrix.) In *Marketing Strategy and Management* (Baker, 1992) seven reasons cited by Rogers (1962) are given for this decline in profit margins:

1. Increasing number of competitive products leading to over-capacity and intensive competition.
2. Market leaders under growing pressure from smaller companies.
3. Strong increase in R&D to find better versions of the product.
4. Cost economies used up.
5. Decline in product distinctiveness.
6. Dealer apathy and disenchantment with a product with declining sales.
7. Changing market composition where the loyalty of those first to adopt begins to waver.

Because of this profit erosion the industry tends to stabilize, with a set of well-entrenched competitors all seeking a competitive advantage, the absence of above-normal profits deterring any further new entrants. However, before examining the strategic options available to these entrenched competitors it will be useful to look more closely at the symptoms and causes of maturity, as summarized in Rogers' seven points.

The increasing number of competitive products leading to over-capacity and intensive competition is the natural reaction of suppliers in a market faced with slowing sales and a perceived limit to growth. As predicted in our life cycle model (Chapter 5), as a phenomenon approaches a limit to growth its behaviour becomes erratic ('hunting') as it seeks to avoid the limit or find a way around it. Once it is appreciated that the market is of a finite size, and approaching saturation, individual suppliers will recognize that further increases in their sales can only come from increased market share. While demand is growing rapidly all suppliers can benefit from this without worrying unduly about the sales of competitors – it is a win–win situation. But, when sales stabilize, the only route to continued growth is through aggressive competition for market share which, inevitably, is a win–lose situation. In these circumstances individual suppliers will resort to predatory tactics – product proliferation, discounting, own label manufacture, etc. – in an attempt to consolidate and protect their share'. Ironically, these tactics tend to accelerate maturity rather than stave it off.

The main reason why this should be so is that by concentrating on product, price and place, suppliers reduce their emphasis upon promotion. This is not to suggest that this reduction in promotional support is not justified, as it will usually be obvious that spending money to support new products will be more effective than seeking to prop up old ones. That said, the reduction in promotional support will often lead to a contraction in overall demand as the product loses the front-of-mind awareness, stimulated by advertising, so that usage will gradually decline. This phenomenon was quite marked in the market for FMCG in UK supermarkets during the late 1980s and early 1990s. As the major retailers increased the number of own brands, the branded-goods manufacturers' share of market declined. Faced with declining sales many manufacturers reduced their promotional spend and this was paralleled by a reduction in sales volume for the product category as a whole, i.e. consumers consumed less. This decline in volume sales impacted on the retailers' overall profitability with the result that many pegged the proportion of own label products so as not to discourage branded goods manufacturers from promoting the generic product – instant coffee, breakfast cereals, canned foods, etc. – through the medium of their own branded product – Nescafé, Kelloggs, Heinz, etc. In the case of Heinz it also prompted the company to use modern direct marketing methods to deliver promotional incentives direct to consumers, thereby encouraging them to 'pull' Heinz brands through the distribution channel.

Market saturation is not simply a case of having reached all potential consumers of the product in question. In reality sales will usually plateau before all potential users have tried the product. Drawing on the concept of adopter categories introduced in Chapter 4 (Figure 4.2), it is quite likely that by the time laggards are entering the market the innovators and early adopters will be becoming bored with the product and so consuming less of it, or even switching to other, possibly completely new products. This trend is likely to be accelerated by changes in the distribution channel as wholesalers and retailers become less willing to carry the product, as it offers them lower margins than other, newer products in the growth phase of their life cycle. Given that there is a limit to the amount of display space available in a retail outlet, most retailers will seek to carry that assortment of products which maximizes the return from the space available. Consequently, they will tend to reduce the space available to slow-moving products and those with low margins in favour of faster-moving products and those with higher margins.

Some years ago one of the authors (Baker, 1980) proposed a series of marketing maxims, one of which is that 'consumption is a function of availability'. Clearly, this is a truism but the implications are obvious. The bigger and more prominent the in-store display of a product the greater the likelihood that consumers will notice it and be prompted to buy. The obverse is equally true: as retailers reduce display space for mature brands so they are likely to hasten their decline. Further, the retailer is likely to use the evidence of declining sales to put pressure on the manufacturer to provide price incentives to boost its purchase, thereby reducing its profitability still further and encouraging the manufacturer to turn to other, more profitable products.

Despite the pressures on mature products described above, their classification as cash cows makes it clear that a mature product can be a considerable asset to the firm and an essential part of a balanced portfolio. It is for this reason that much thought and effort has been devoted to the management of mature products. Indeed, the discussion to be found in most marketing management textbooks implicitly assumes that one is dealing with such a product and focuses on how to manipulate the marketing mix to best advantage – it is the development and marketing of new products (usually the subject of a single chapter) that is regarded as the exceptional case. The effect of this concentration has been the prolonging of the mature stage of the PLC beyond what might be anticipated if events were allowed to take their normal course. In achieving this, four basic strategies are available to the marketing manager:

1. An offensive or 'take-off' strategy
2. A defensive strategy
3. A recycle strategy
4. A stretching and harvesting strategy.

In the following pages we look at each of these in more detail.

Offensive strategies

An offensive or 'take-off' strategy is, as the name implies, one designed to inject new life into a mature product. Here the objective is to try to initiate a new growth phase by pursuing one or other of the options implicit in the Johnson and Jones matrix. This is very similar to Ansoff's growth/vector matrix (Chapter 2). Both appeared within a few months of each other in the *Harvard Business Review* (May–June 1957 and Sept–Oct 1957 respectively) which suggests they were developed quite independently. The Johnson and Jones matrix is more complex than its Ansoff equivalent in that it is a 3 × 3 configuration compared to Ansoff's 2 × 2 and so offers five more options as illustrated in Figure 16.1.

The additional options available in the Johnson and Jones matrix arise from its use of an intermediate 'condition' (Improved Technology) between No Technological Change and New Technology, and of an intermediate market state (Strengthened Market) between No Market Change and New Market. If we discard the two options which call for a new technology (Replacement and Diversification) on the grounds that this is equivalent to developing another new product, we are left with six possible courses of action – Remerchandising, New Use, Reformulation, Improved Product, Market Extension and Product Line Extension. Depending on how they are pursued, these options may be considered offensive strategies, although under some circumstances they will be identified more readily with one of the other three strategies suggested earlier (defensive, recycle, harvest).

In 'Exploit the product life cycle' Levitt (1965) used the example of DuPont's development of nylon to illustrate four different approaches to increasing sales when initial

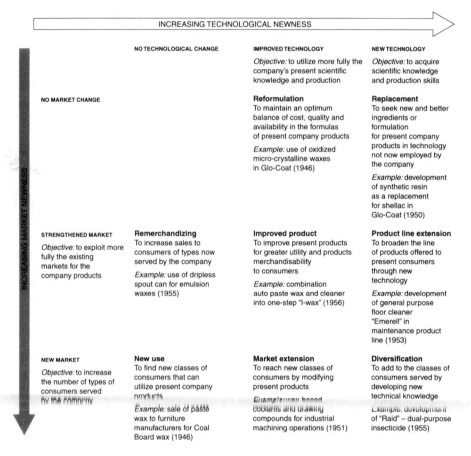

Figure 16.1 ● Classification of new products by product objective (*source*: Johnson and Jones, 1957)

uses of the material (dominated by hosiery) began to level off. Four distinct strategies were followed:

1. Promoting more frequent usage of the product among current users.
2. Developing more varied usage of the product among current users.
3. Creating new users for the product by expanding the market.
4. Finding new uses for the basic material.

Promoting more frequent usage equates with 'Remerchandising' in the Johnson and Jones matrix and poses an interesting dilemma for the marketing manager. Table 16.1 summarizes annual purchase concentration for 18 product categories and records the number of non-users and users, dividing the latter into two categories, heavy and light. Taking the first item, Lemon-Lime, as an example the table informs us that 42% of households do not consume this product. If we look at the 58% that do and simply

Table 16.1 ● Annual purchase concentration in 18 product categories

Product	Non-users (Households = 42%)	Light half 29%	Heavy half 29%
Lemon-lime	0 (Volume) ㉒	9% ㊴	91% ㊴
Colas	0 ㉘	10 ㊱	90 ㊱
Concentrated frozen orange juice	0 ㊾... ㊿	11 ⑳	89 ㉑
Bourbon	0 ㊾	11 ㉓	89 ㉓
Hair fixatives	0 ㊻	12 ⑯	88 ⑰
Beer	0 ㊻	12 ⑯	88 ⑰
Dog food	0 ㉒	13 ㉔	87 ㉔
Hair tonic	④ 0 ㊽	13	87 ㊽
Ready-to-eat cereals	0 ㊻	13 ⑯	87 ⑯
Canned hash	0 ㉗	14 ㊱	86 ㊲
Cake mixes	③ 0 ㊽	15	85 ㊾
Sausages	⑪ 0 ㊹	16	84 ㊺
Margarine	0 ㉞	17 ㉝	83 ㉝
Paper towels	⑥ 0 ㊼	17	83 ㊼
Bacon	⑱ 0 ㊶	18	82 ㊶
Shampoo	② 0 ㊾	19	81 ㊾
Soaps and detergents	② 0 ㊾	19	81 ㊾
Toilet tissue	0	26	74

Annual purchase concentration in 18 product categories

Source: Twedt (1964).

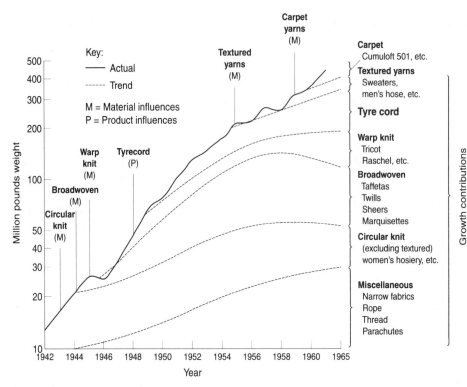

Figure 16.2 ● Innovation of new products postpones the time of total maturity – the nylon industry

divide them into two groups we see that the 'light half' only account for 9% of consumption while the 'heavy half' accounts for a staggering 91%. Very similar proportions apply to the other products listed and herein lies the dilemma – do we seek to persuade the heavy users to consume even more or do we persuade those who consume only small quantities to increase their usage?

In the nylon example DuPont could have tried to persuade light users – younger women and 'bobby soxers' – that more frequent use of stockings was a 'social necessity'. However, this was seen as being both difficult and expensive to execute, and the alternative of promoting more varied use by introducing multi-coloured and textured hosiery and emphasizing it as a fashion accessory (Reformulation?) was preferred. Much the same problems of increasing usage among light users were associated with converting non-users, i.e. you have to change people's behaviour. This problem is usually restricted to the served market and may be overcome by moving into new (geographical) markets which have previously not had access to the product – a clear case for exporting.

In the case of nylon and many other products the best opportunity is to find new uses for the existing product. Figure 16.2 illustrates clearly how DuPont extended nylon's life cycle by adapting the basic material to a series of new uses – tyre cord, textured yarns, carpet yarns, etc. As Levitt observed, if nylon's use had been confined to miscellaneous and circular knit applications its sales by weight would have levelled off at 50m pounds in 1962 when, in reality, total sales reached ten times that amount.

A classic case of extending the product life cycle through the discovery of new uses is that of Church & Dwight who, for over 50 years, have marketed Arm & Hammer baking soda. Back in the 1950s the company experienced falling sales as home baking declined under pressure from pre-packaged cake mixes and the like. Although Church & Dwight supplied baking soda in bulk to companies manufacturing such products, the margins on bulk sales were significantly less than on the branded product and the company initiated a programme to publicize other uses for their product. For example, $NaHCO_3$ absorbs food odours and it was promoted as a product to keep the larder or refrigerator fresh.

This strategy of refusing to regard the product as a commodity and positioning it as a speciality has earned handsome dividends for the company, particularly under its current CEO Dwight Church Minton, a fifth generation descendant of the founders, who took over in 1969. In a *Fortune* article (27 July 1992) Church & Dwight are reported to have tripled their sales and income over the past 10 years and now hold 60% of the world market against much larger competitors, including Rhone Poulenc and FMC Corp. This achievement has been secured largely by concentrating R&D efforts on process technology improvements, such as sorting the grains into uniform sizes, while listening to their customers for new ideas.

Back in the late 1960s when Minton took over, to quote the *Fortune* article, 'environmentally-conscious customers were starting to mix baking soda and soap in their washing machines to replace phosphate-rich detergents. Minton took the hint and introduced a phosphate-free and sodium-carbonate-rich detergent in 1970 that is now the company's largest-selling product'. On the same theme the company has launched a series of environmentally friendly consumer products during the 1980s including air fresheners, carpet deodorizers and toothpaste. Now the company is diversifying still further into industrial markets. Among these are the following:

> 'Armakleen, an industrial cleanser for printed circuit boards. The present cleansers of choice use chlorofluorocarbons, or CFCs, which scientists believe are depleting the ozone layer. Church & Dwight just introduced this product into a world market the company estimates to be as large as $1 billion a year.
>
> Armex, baking soda with other ingredients to blast walls and buildings. Because sandblasting can contribute to silicosis, a lung disease, its use is most strongly regulated in Europe. As a blasting agent, baking soda has a delicate touch. The crystals have sharp edges that wear down quickly, thus removing the paint and grime without eroding the underlying surface. (The Statue of Liberty was cleaned with the stuff in 1986.)
>
> Just plain baking soda. Church & Dwight is beginning to sell it as an additive to municipal water supplies. Experiments in Bennington, Vermont and Fitchburg, Massachusetts, show that it neutralises acids that can leach lead from old pipes and from solder.' (*Fortune*, 27 July 1992)

Similar examples are to be found in industrial markets. Aubrey Wilson has described how his company – Industrial Market Research – conducted surveys to establish possible new uses for existing products, often with dramatic results. For example, one client manufactured spring balances used on automated assembly lines so that when released the tool would spring clear of the work piece. When this market became saturated, market research suggested that the same principle could be adapted to abattoirs so that as butchered carcasses became lighter the spring extended to keep the carcass at a convenient height on the process line.

Where it is not possible to find new uses or new customers, reformulation can help extend the PLC almost indefinitely. As hinted when suggesting that coloured and patterned hosiery might be considered a reformulation, most cases involved changes in style and/or design without fundamentally changing the basic product. In an article in *The Sunday Times* (18 December 1994) Hugh Pearman provided an excellent example of reformulation when describing the evolution of the toaster to illustrate the role of design in prolonging the life of a product. As he explained:

> 'Toasters have been around as long as most people have had a domestic electricity supply, which is 80 years. The present generation is lined up on display in an electrical or department store near you. What does the act of choosing one say about our design awareness?
>
> All toasters are not exactly the same under the skin but they are as near the same as makes no difference. They are boxes which neatly grill the bread, waffles, Pop-Tarts, or whatever between little electric fires, and eject them just before they start to burn: an easy, well-proven technology, whether it is purely mechanical or microchip controlled. The last fundamental innovation in toaster design was in 1927, when the Sunbeam company of America marketed the first pop-up model. Since then, there has been little to do, design-wise, except to alter the styling according to the tastes of the times. That meant round and bulbous in the 1950s, square and angular in the 1960s, decorated in the 1970s, elongated in the 1980s, bulbous again in the 1990s.
>
> Designers try to give toasters the equivalent of sun-roof and anti-lock brakes – wider slots, double slots, "cool wall" designs and the like – but cannot get away from the fact that you need only two controls: a push down lever and a timer. Upgrades merely dress up a timeless concept and are anyway almost all adopted immediately by other manufacturers.'

The rest of Pearman's article contains a fascinating analysis of how different designs cater to different market segments, which reinforces the point that, while the product is functionally the same, it can be 'repackaged' into many different configurations to provide a competitive edge.

Extending the product life cycle

A particular benefit arising from an understanding of the implications of the 'normal' life cycle curve is that one can pre-plan courses of action in anticipation of evolutionary changes. This ability to anticipate is especially important when designing and launching a new product as it enables one to pre-plan competitive moves when the product reaches maturity by extending its life cycle. Levitt (1965) cites three benefits of such pre-planning:

1. It generates an active rather than reactive product policy.

2. It lays out a long-term plan designed to infuse new life into the product at the right time, with the right degree of care, and with the right amount of effort.

3. Perhaps the most important benefit of engaging in advance, pre-introduction planning for sales-extending, market-stretching activities later in the product's life is that this practice forces a company to adopt a wider view of the nature of the product it is dealing with.

Sony is a classic exponent of the product or brand extension strategy and can be seen to derive all three benefits cited by Levitt through its anticipatory product planning. As we noted in Chapter 15, and as was evidenced by the computerized tomography case study, even major technological breakthroughs can be easily copied. If patented then the patents themselves will often tell competitors all they need to know to make a 'me-too' product. If not patented then competitive benchmarking and the careful analysis of the new product will soon reveal most of its secrets to others. As a result it has been estimated that any major technological innovation is fully understood world-wide within 18 months of its appearance in the market. Once the principles of the Walkman or the camcorder became apparent the appearance of clones was not long delayed.

To counter these competitive threats Sony has used an extension strategy very effectively, mainly by introducing a constant stream of new products derived directly from the original product concept. In the case of the Walkman the sheer volume of new versions (over 150 in a period of 10 years during the 1980s) has ensured that Sony has covered every possible niche and microsegment and made it wholly uneconomic for any of its competitors, such as Aiwa or Sharp, to do the same. Similarly, Sony introduces a major new feature on its camcorders at approximately six-monthly intervals. In both cases the basic architecture of its products has remained constant, with each new product change being introduced in a planned succession to keep Sony a step ahead of its rivals.

Managing the relationship

While the essence of marketing has always been a mutually satisfying exchange relationship, the dominant paradigm for 30 years or more was that of marketing management and the manipulation of the marketing mix variables of product, price, place and promotion. This approach to marketing emerged in the 1950s with the writings of people like Keith, Levitt and McKitterick which marked the rediscovery of marketing as supply in the post-World War II period caught up and overtook demand in the USA. An emphasis upon production to increase supply, and sales to make it available, gave way to the more holistic marketing orientation which argued that success depended upon listening to the voice of the marketplace and then creating and supplying products which met customers' needs. With the benefit of hindsight, however, it has become apparent that the marketing management paradigm was concerned less with what suppliers did *for* their customers and more with what they did *to* them. The focus was too much upon the sale as a transaction which had to yield a profit rather than upon the sale as the basis for establishing an on-going relationship which would prove profitable to both parties on a long-term basis.

In the increasingly competitive 1980s, and especially in mature markets, it became obvious that customer retention was equally if not more important than customer creation. Given a saturated market everyone was somebody's customer and the only way you could grow your customer base was by winning new customers at your competitor's expense. It is also obvious that this is a zero-sum game on a grand scale. In fact it is even worse: it is a negative sum game for the simple reason that it costs more to create or win a customer than to keep one. Rule of thumb estimates confirm this in a number of ways.

One such estimate calculates that you will have to spend five times as much on marketing to win a customer as you need to spend to keep one happy. Another calculation indicates that if you could retain the 5% of your customer base which even successful firms tend to lose annually, you would improve your bottom line (profitability) between 25% and 80% depending upon the kind of business you're in. A third, well-known 'rule' is that most customers will not switch from their current supplier for less than a 10% improvement in value, whether this be a price discount or improved performance or some combination of these. Switching to a new supplier entails both risks and costs and it will have to be a very attractive offer that can overcome the inertia of resistance to change. In the growth phase it may be possible to afford the additional costs and inducements to secure customers; in the mature phase it rarely is!

A well-known definition of marketing is that it is 'selling goods that don't come back to people who do' – it is repeat purchase and maintenance of the relationship which is the key to long-run competitive advantage. It was this definition which F. Stewart De Bruicker and Gregory L. Summe probably had in mind when they wrote 'Make sure your customers keep coming back' *(Harvard Business Review,* Jan–Feb 1985). In this article the authors address the question of how the onset of maturity affects buyer–seller relationships and what steps sellers should take as buyers change from what they call inexperienced specialists to experienced specialists. With growing experience customer expectations change and four strategies are suggested for dealing with this:

1. Strengthening account management practices
2. Augmenting the product
3. Improving customer services
4. Lowering prices.

In the early stages of a product life cycle intending buyers, especially industrial ones, are heavily dependent upon sellers for advice on how to use a product and for after-sales service and support to get the maximum value from it. As the product matures it becomes more reliable and familiar and the buyer's dependency on the seller declines. As De Bruicker and Summe observe: 'As customers gain familiarity with a product they find a manufacturer's support programs to be of declining value. Their buying decisions become increasingly price-sensitive. They unbundle into components the products they once purchased as systems and open their doors to suppliers who sell on price and offer little in the way of product support. Even the most remote observer, once instructed can spot the pattern' (p. 93).

As noted earlier, an in-supplier always has a potential competitive advantage due to the perceived risks and costs of switching to another supplier. Rather the devil you know...! Indeed, research amongst consumers suggests that they will often stick with a known product and supplier through habit and inertia even when they gain no particularly strong benefit or satisfaction from the habit. Only if something occurs to create active dissatisfaction will the habitual buyer consider a change. Provided the in-supplier does not become complacent and continues to work at the relationship, using one or other of the four strategies cited earlier, they should be able to defend their position indefinitely.

The objective of account management is to try to maintain a multi-level relationship between seller and buyer and so keep purchasing decisions under review by general managers in senior positions. Such involvement helps prevent the product declining into commodity status when the purchasing manager (experienced specialist) will become the decision-maker and play one supplier off against another to secure the best price, delivery, and so on. In high-technology industries with rapid change and frequent new product development, multi-level relationships are easier to develop and sustain. In fact, under the customer-active paradigm of new product development suppliers are frequently members of their customers' own product development team and so enjoy a privileged status. The challenge is to ensure the continuation of these relationships into the mature phase.

The second strategy, product augmentation, is described in some detail by Levitt ('Marketing success through differentiation – of anything', *Harvard Business Review*, Jan–Feb 1980) and was touched on in Chapter 3. What constitutes product augmentation and added value may well vary from customer to customer, and the successful use of this approach will depend heavily on the seller's ability to diagnose just what will enable them to maintain a differential competitive advantage and so avoid the rigours of price competition.

Many years ago one of the authors was an industrial salesman selling a classic, undifferentiated product – tinplate. All suppliers made to precisely the same specification and, to add to the seller's problems, prices were regulated also. Because of the lack of differentiation between suppliers many customers had settled into a habit of placing their orders in proportion to the manufacturer's output, i.e. if you had 20% supply capacity you got 20% of the business. To break this impasse a differentiating factor had to be introduced and this was done successfully by carefully analyzing the customer's specifications. Over time, and through custom and practice, the customer, a tin-box manufacturer, had developed a very wide range of different containers to the extent that they ordered over 200 different sizes of tinplate. As the minimum order quantity was 8 tons – which makes a lot of tin boxes – the result was that they had a huge stock of tinplate each size of which was dedicated to the manufacture of a particular design. By analyzing the size of blanks required to make all these boxes it was discovered that they could be made with no extra waste out of just six standard sizes. Not only did this allow the buyer to greatly reduce their range of sizes, but standardization also allowed them to order larger quantities and qualify for significant volume discounts. The 'reward' was that the customer doubled his purchases and took two-thirds from the supplier of the 'augmented' product and only one-third from the rest.

The above example might also qualify as a customer service strategy which is the third approach suggested by De Bruicker and Summe. However, customer service is suggested as a particularly appropriate strategy for laggards who enter the market when the product is already mature. While the product may have been around for quite some time it is still new to the first-time buyer who may well have delayed entry because of 'techno-fear'. For such laggards distribution through non-specialist outlets which cater for novice buyers, customer training and education in how to use the product, and after-market support like IBM's Helpline will all add value for the new buyer.

Ultimately, however, the product will become so standardized and commonplace that price competition will become inevitable and some form of discount or financial incentive will be essential to maintain buyer loyalty. Perversely, however, too low a price may discourage buyers by increasing the buyer's perceived risk – 'if it's that cheap it can't be any good'. Such an attitude is often found in the case of suppliers who offer much lower prices than their competitors. For example, in the European car market cars made in Korea and Malaysia are offered at prices significantly below those asked for by Japanese and European manufacturers. In the UK virtually identical 1.6 litre, five-door saloon cars range from £8500 for a Proton (Malaysia) and £8750 for a Hyundai (Korea) to £13,000 for a Toyota (Japan) – a staggering 59% price premium for the latter which currently outsells its low-priced rivals by a factor of about 4:1. Part of the reason for the low level of support for Hyundai is that the general public do not regard Korea as sufficiently advanced to make a sophisticated product like a car – clearly untrue for the world's 12th largest trading nation – but this attitude is reinforced by the low price which is interpreted as an indicator of low quality (company research). In this case perhaps the best advice is to increase the price.

However, our emphasis on the importance of product strategy and management throughout this book has been that price competition can only be afforded by the few or be used as a short term tactical weapon. For the great majority of firms the objective is to avoid price competition through a differentiation strategy. Differentiation of anything – but especially the product! To conclude this chapter it will be useful to summarize the strategies available for mature businesses. In doing so we draw heavily on an article by Malcolm Schofield and David Arnold entitled 'Strategies for mature businesses' (*Long Range Planning*, Vol. 21, No. 5, 1988).

To begin with, Schofield and Arnold distinguish four phases to the mature phase of the life cycle – late growth, early maturity, mid-maturity and late maturity – and argue that 'the fundamental market conditions alter radically *during* the single phase of maturity, spanning the period from growth to decline' (p. 69).

It is in the late growth phase that price first begins to be used aggressively to stimulate demand and continues to be so until early maturity when the market is becoming saturated with little or no potential for any further growth. Once this state has been reached, price competition declines in importance and the tactics of account management, product augmentation and customer service described earlier take over. Air travel and package holidays are both cited as markets where demand stalled until significant price cuts got the market moving again. In both cases these are discretionary purchases where a stepped demand curve probably exists, i.e. instead of demand expanding smoothly in response to marginal reductions in price, demand will plateau and only begin to grow again given a major price decrease (Figure 16.3).

It is also in the late growth/early maturity phase that the larger competitors may seek

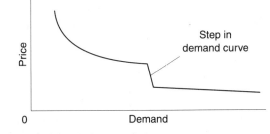

Figure 16.3 ● The stepped demand curve

to acheive a dominant market share and, through it, the cost leadership which will enable them to exercise a substantial degree of control over the mature market. In their attempts to win market share, price-cutting may well be used as a tactical weapon, but once the marginal suppliers have been eliminated prices may well revert to former levels.

While overall demand is stabilizing in the late growth/early maturity phase, important changes may be occurring within the market as different segments grow and decline. Careful monitoring is called for to identify hot spots where demand is still growing rapidly and care needs to be taken to avoid cold spots where demand may be collapsing rapidly. Schofield and Arnold cite specialist distribution, minicomputers, lager beers and fragrances as specific cases where certain segments have expanded dramatically but at the expense of other segments which have collapsed equally dramatically.

While early maturity is seen as the time to 'change habits and emphasis', middle maturity is the phase when 'customers come first'. In these markets customers are seen as 'increasingly more discerning, discriminating and less loyal' (p. 74).

Against this Schofield and Arnold (p. 74) identify a number of positive factors:

- *Price is not important to everyone* and probably not to the majority.
- *Industries that evolve gradually* offer time and space for careful strategy selection.
- *Sustainable real or perceived advantage* in either cost or performance will attract new business provided it is communicated effectively
- *Geographical niches are vulnerable*, and if attacked selectively and with perseverence, on the basis of customer needs, profitable business will accrue.
- *The market is stable*; any sense of instability probably points to a lack of clear and consistent strategy relative to compeition or trying to be all things to all people – the global mediocrity, which is the most common characteristic of the unsuccessful.
- *Matching capabilities and resources to particular market opportunities* is the underlying priority. As a rule of thumb, the more limited these are, the greater level of product/market concentration. The aim is to generate revenue through better margins and repeat orders rather than higher volume. Growth should then be achieved through existing product/market concentration, applying discipline to any unplanned and superficially attractive proliferation of activities.

● *Niches once secured require fewer resources to defend them* than they do to obtain them in the first instance. Attack strategies, therefore, rely heavily on good timing – when significant advantage rests with the predator.

Summary

As the market enters late maturity the choice is seen as resting between withdrawal and growth. In this stage the market is still very substantial and subject to little change. It offers little or no attraction for new entrants except for those with a radically new approach who may be prepared to attack the inertia and complacency of markets at this stage of their life cycle. Such attacks rarely come from within the industry. As we saw earlier, in the case of vinyl flooring this was a smooth floor covering much superior to linoleum which dominated the market. The major linoleum manufacturers were offered the opportunity to develop and launch vinyl but declined to do so – it could only cannibalize their existing product and make their current manufacturing resources obsolete. Only when vinyl was launched by a new entrant to the smooth floor-covering market did demand for linoleum begin to decline and linoleum manufacturers begin to switch into the new product. For the entrenched supplier in a market which is in late maturity, the best advice is probably to enjoy it while you can but to monitor competitive threats and be prepared to switch to new products once an irreversible decline sets in.

In offering this advice it is important to recognize that some firms can still make attractive profits in declining markets – a subject to which we return in the next chapter.

QUESTIONS

1. Discuss the factors which may lead to declining profit margins for mature products.
2. Explain the relevance and importance of the maxim that 'consumption is a function of availability' with particular reference to the marketing of mature products.
3. What basic strategies are available to the marketing manager for handling mature products?
4. Compare Ansoff's growth-vector matrix with the Johnson and Jones matrix. What additional advantages, if any, does the latter have when developing product strategies?
5. Suggest ways in which a manufacturer might successfully extend the mature product's life. Cite specific examples to illustrate your answer.
6. Why is developing relationships with customers so important to the long-term success of the seller?
7. Discuss Schofield and Arnold's (1988) view that the mature phase of the life cycle may be usefully broken down into four phases.

Introduction

In April 1993, Mars made the first significant change to its Milky Way brand. Worth £40m, it is the 'market leader' in the product category named 'children's filled bars', followed by brands such as Cadbury's Fudge (£15m), Chomp (£10m) and Curly Wurly (£5m). However, in the wider product category of 'children's chocolate confectionery' the market leader is Smarties, worth £45m. At the time of the relaunch, the company felt unhappy with its rate of sale and wanted customers to think afresh about the product.

The firm

In 1992, Mars merged its UK and European businesses, which managers feel is giving them the opportunity for cross-fertilization of ideas, learning from a wider experience, and thus a stronger competitive base. Recent changes, in addition to the relaunch of Marathon as Snickers, include the launch of Mars Ice Cream and increasing the Mars bar by 6%, making it 'smoother and creamier', resulting in an increase of 18% in sales. Several revamps of other big brands are planned, as the company actively manages some very mature products. The company's recent attention given to Milky Way is also a result, in part, of the merger.

The product

Milky Way is now 60 years old! It was launched originally in a red wrapper, essentially as a cheaper version of the Mars bar (the former cost one (old) penny, the latter cost two pence!). Its positioning as a 'light snack' was captured in the famous line 'the sweet you can eat between meals without ruining your appetite' and was consolidated in blue packaging, with white stars and 'Milky Way' written in white.

The relaunch aimed to repeat success in Germany, which was based on a new formula and which resulted in a doubling of sales in four years. A new white centre replaced the old chocolate-flavoured filling. The new centre contains 50% more milk, at a time when white chocolate is becoming more popular with children. The German formula has been adjusted for the UK by a 'creamier' chocolate coating.

Perhaps somewhat surprisingly, Mars uses its obvious outer-space association for the first time in advertising. The space setting has a clear link with the product and is thought to underline the property of 'lightness' which is central to the relaunch: 'So light it won't ruin your appetite'. This lightness was mirrored in the new packaging, which reversed the more traditional white-on-blue. The new, blue-on-white, had been used on the Milky Way Ice Cream, but was not thought to jeopardize its impact.

Advertising expenditure for the relaunch was set at £1.8m, which amounted to the usual annual budget. A further £1.8m would be budgeted for the rest of the year. The competitive reaction from big products such as Milky Bar (worth £28m), Milky Buttons (worth £13m) and Cadbury's Chocolate Buttons (worth £25m) was expected to be tough. Although the look, packaging and image of the new Milky Way is to give a feel of 'lightness', the new product is no lighter than before, but this dimension is expected to appeal to the core customer base: mothers with children. Research has shown that although mothers do buy for their children they eat a third of what they buy themselves.

Discussion questions

1. Of the four basic strategies discussed by Levitt (1965) and listed earlier in this chapter, which most closely applies to Milky Way, and why?

2. Of current buyers of Milky Way, do you think the advertising is directed at the light or heavy half? Which is more appropriate, and why?

3. In speculating about the success of new 'Milky Way' some commentators have pointed out that if Mars couldn't beat Smarties with M & Ms, they could not hope to do it with the relaunched Milky Way. Is this a reasonable view?

This case was compiled from public sources.

part 4

Product Elimination

chapter 17

· ·

Controlling the product line: an overview of the deletion decision

LEARNING OBJECTIVES
· ·

This chapter presents an overview of the decision process used to consider and implement the removal of a product from a company's portfolio. Its specific objectives are:

1. To introduce the importance of the deletion decision in product management.

2. To explain why, despite its importance, the decision may often be avoided.

3. To review and simplify the models of product deletion.

4. To distinguish the decision-reaching from the implementation stage.

5. To introduce the concept of product deletion triggers, which will influence the nature of the decision process.

6. To set a context for the next two chapters.

On completion of this chapter you will:

1. Be able to justify the importance of product deletion to the long-term health of a company.

2. Be able to explain the reasons why product deletion is an avoided activity.

3. Understand the major steps necessary to carry out product deletion.

4. Appreciate the range of reasons why products get deleted from a company's range.

Introduction
· ·

As introduced in Chapter 5 and mentioned again in the previous two chapters, the notion that 'every (declining) industry was once a growth industry' is a prompt to encourage critical review of a company's offerings at a given point in time, as continued success, expansion and growth *cannot* be guaranteed. Despite this apparent logic, it is understandable that people involved with the development, launch and success of products will tend to want to avoid the risk of repeating the whole process. In addition the phase of market saturation is, for those players left, a highly profitable one, and the temptation to stick with current products to mass markets is strong, as shown in Chapter 15. It is, however, crucial to the company to address these issues. Too often, the decision to delete a product from the range is one taken in crisis, without the time for adequate review and reflection, and usually without the ability or cash flow to fill the gap in the range with a new product (Avlonitis and James, 1982; Hart, 1988, 1991). Yet the importance of product deletion (also called elimination, pruning or obsoleting) has long been recognized by practitioners, as the following quote from Sir Adrian Cadbury (*The Sunday Times*, 14 April 1984) shows:

'If you put the same marketing effort behind a smaller range of lines, you can thus afford to give better value to the consumer and you can make up the same value over half the number of lines.'

Equally, the merging by Procter & Gamble of two of its brands, Clearasil and Biactol, has been explained by one of the company's spokeswomen (*Marketing*, 23 January 1997, p. 2):

'Given the size of the market and the brands, we decided it would be better to focus on our strengths.'

In fact what P& G meant is that in an attempt to win back market share from a major competitor, Smith Kline Beecham, the marketing expenditure could be put behind one major brand, rather than being split across two. However logical such a move may be, the decision to axe a product (or combine two into one) is not easy, nor are the implications trivial. In phasing out Biactol, for example, P & G are admitting defeat in their previous attempts to segment the spot-remedy market by gender. Biactol, introduced into the market in 1978, was designed to appeal to young men, while Clearasil, positioned in the female segment, was the market leader until the 1994 launch of SKB's Oxy range, which had a unisex appeal. The task in phasing out Biactol will be to convert male buyers to using Clearasil, which has been positioned as a more feminine product.

In product deletion the stakes are high and much previous investment in branding and positioning will have to be jettisoned. Little wonder that these decisions, despite their recognized importance, are often avoided by managers. In fact, the subject of product deletion is one facing neglect by managers and academic researchers alike, especially compared to new product development. The job of phasing out products whose competitive edge has blunted is certainly unglamorous, and in the cut-and-thrust world of brand management, such a task is probably unhelpful to career progression. That said, it is an important activity, since renewal of a company's product range requires not only the addition of new products, but also the removal of the old. This chapter will first reinforce the importance of the deletion decision, then review why the decision is often neglected; finally, it sets out a conceptual framework for considering the identification and deletion of products whose presence no longer delivers identifiable benefits to the company.

The importance of product deletion

Product deletion is important for a variety of reasons. The first relate to the way in which unproductive use is made of company finances.

A drain on finances

Given the finite financial resources of the company, those devoted to the weak product are less profitably invested than they might be if they were available to produce, promote and distribute either a new product or other existing products. The opportunity cost is therefore potentially enormous.

The expense of carrying a product which is weak, that is, one which is deteriorating in terms of profitability, sales volume or contribution to the objectives of the company, goes beyond production costs. No method of financial accounting can adequately report all indirect costs incurred by a weak product, which disappear in general 'overhead' classes in the accounts. Such costs include: (a) the costs of changeovers in the production lines for short runs; (b) handling costs for small orders; and (c) inventory carrying costs for slow-moving items. Having too many products increases the company's costs of doing business and having too few permits market opportunities to slip away and results in excess capacity. Both extremes are costly and affect profit adversely.

Marketing problems

Product overpopulation spreads a company's marketing resources too thinly. This in turn leads to further problems. Forecasting becomes more difficult and even the mechanics of product pricing become complex and time consuming. Also, the use of informative advertising as a means of persuasion, particularly by companies manufacturing shopping goods and industrial goods, may be difficult where an extensive product range is being promoted. Moreover, an excess of products in the line not only creates internal competition among the company's own products but also creates confusion in the minds of customers, since perceived differences among individual products usually diminish as more products are added to a given range. The announcement by Lever Brothers that they will cut the number of liquid sub-brands has been triggered by the perceived need to simplify the choices faced by customers (*Marketing*, 22 August 1996, p. 3).

Managerial problems

A weak product places a further burden on the company's facilities and management attention, which is disproportionate to its contribution. It may require excessive managerial effort with respect to pricing, sales, distribution and communication, and it may also require warehouse space, which is usually a premium resource for companies selling from stock.

A weak product is also damaging with respect to the future. Not only can it tarnish the company's image and promote dissatisfaction in the marketing channel, but the company may incur additional opportunity costs. By camouflaging the need for new product development and draining necessary resources, a weak product may delay the process of developing new products.

Planning and controlling a large number of products present serious problems. For instance, management must contend with co-ordinating shared parts and ingredients when planning production schedules, allocating production costs to products and purchasing additional production equipment. Also, as management attempts to spread its efforts over a wide and varied product mix, its ability to co-ordinate and control the portfolio is weakened. When a company has only a few products, its management can scrutinize and control each product's problems as they arise.

So, although the most obvious and accessible reason for the need to pay attention is to stop losses, as can be seen from the implications of proliferated product lines such as those detailed above, deletion needs to be considered for reasons other than simply stopping a cash drain from a company. By extension, the reasons for (or aims of) deletion are likely to be diverse. For example, a product could be removed from the product range with the aim of freeing resources to exploit new opportunities, or to simplify a company's product positioning or marketing communication strategy. Potentially, each of the implications of carrying extensive product lines gives rise to a different aim for deleting a product. These are shown in Table 17.1.

Despite these wide and varied aims for deletion, which might be used to actively manage and reward the decision, product management is often treated synonymously with new product development or product development only. Indeed, such a view is not surprising if we reconsider the evolution in marketing thinking from mass production to product differentiation, where management ideas became dominated by the need to offer a range of products commensurate with market forces. It follows that, in the progression from a single- to a multi-product organization, there arises a need for those organizations' managers to consider the possibility of withdrawing products that were not satisfying consumer demand. The evidence, however, suggests that product deletion is an activity which is often avoided by managers (Avlonitis, 1980; Gauthier, 1985; Hart, 1987). We now turn to the reasons why product deletion might have been neglected.

Table 17.1 ● A wider view of the potential aims of product deletion

Implications of carrying excess products	Aims of deletion
Excessive burden on company resources:	
● Physical	Create warehousing space for quick delivery of key lines
● Financial	Transfer promotional funds from several slow-moving lines to fewer, buoyant lines
● Managerial	Simplify product positioning
'Immeasurable Costs'	Streamline selling procedures, cut the costs of distributing small orders
Opportunity costs	Create physical, financial and managerial resources to exploit a new product opportunity
Resources are spread too thinly	Simplify production planning
Old products are damaging to market image	Initiate the development of new products

The reasons for the neglect of product deletion

'The whole subject of product elimination has been neglected by marketing managers and economists. The literature on product abandonment is very sparse and vaguely defined; no body of knowledge exists that can be referred to for guidance in this area. A comprehensive perspective cannot be obtained through a synthesis of the small amount of isolated data and bits and pieces of information lodged in many places.' (Berenson, 1963, p. 63).

More than 35 years have passed since Conrad Berenson made this observation about the state of the product deletion art. During this time articles, data and information concerning product deletion have accumulated, but the total pattern of normative advice to flow from these is still confused. Some research has indicated that it is a managerial decision which is often avoided, so the neglect that the decision has suffered in academic terms seems to be mirrored in the business community (Avlonitis, 1980; Hart, 1987).

Rational reasons for neglecting product deletion are as follows:

- Revitalization
- Product line scope
- Defrayal of overheads.

Less rational reasons include:

- Lack of appropriate financial data
- 'Ostrich attitudes'.

Revitalization

One rational reason for avoiding a deletion decision is that a situation may be 'saveable': a product could be revitalized in some way. If a product comes under the spotlight as a potential candidate for deletion, it may be for a number of reasons, the detail of which will be covered later in the chapter. The first course of action taken by managers will be to investigate the cause of the 'problem' and see if it can be solved. Take, for example, the body spray manufactured by Elida Fabergé, Impulse. The product was launched more than 20 years ago and, at the time, was an innovative concept: a perfumed deodorant. Recently, however, its sales began to fall drastically, as more competitors entered the market, which is principally made up of teenage females. In fact, the product was experiencing all the symptoms of maturity – even late maturity – that have been covered in Chapters 5 and 16. The decision was taken not to delete or replace the product, but to modernize it by making drastic changes to the marketing mix. This included extending the range and changing the promotional mix; 50% is now sold through direct marketing and much more attention is given to roadshows backed by the formation of a strategic alliance with *19* magazine, which previewed and promoted the events around the country. Thus a potential end-of-life product was successfully turned around: clearly, a better decision than replacement of the product, and a very rational reason for not deleting it. However, the story can be more easily relayed with the benefit of hindsight (*Marketing*, 9 January 1997, p. 22).

To take another example, one of the managers participating in Project Dropstrat, interviewed by the author (Hart, 1987) considered dropping a food product because, unlike its competitors, only one version was marketed. Most other companies offered a *range* of products, which made it easier for retailers to stock them. In the end, the way the product was assembled (the production line) was reorganized so that a variety of the products could be made, thus making them more competitive. These types of reasons are perfectly valid for not deleting a product.

Product line scope

Even when a remedy is either not possible or deemed by management to be not worth pursuing, a product might be retained for valid reasons which might have to do with evaluating the effect the deletion would have on the rest of the company's operation. For instance, the effect of deletion on the scope of the product line may be judged too severe where management values the concept of a full range; in these circumstances, management considers that the losses incurred by offering the product are less than those incurred by having a hole in the product line. Typically, market leaders carry a full range and to cut down is felt somehow to belittle their status.

Customer patronage may also encourage the retention of dubious products, particularly in the industrial market where customers often like to purchase materials from a single source.

Defrayal of overheads

Another reason a product may be retained is to assist the defrayal of overheads. Many of the costs of multi-product companies are shared among many products. Raw materials, product lines and labour may be interchangeable and shared between products. If one product is removed then the share of the burden is increased for the remaining products. This situation occurred in the confectionery industry, where several layered products were manufactured on the same production line. Layered chocolate confectionery includes Mars bars and Twix. One company manufactured three products all on the same line: Californian, a chewy bar aimed at children; Tropicale, a cherry and coconut mix aimed at the female 18–25 market; and Trophy, a fruit, nut and caramel bar aimed at men of 18–25. Although Tropicale and Trophy were not exceptionally big brands, they enjoyed steady sales and were profitable. Californian, however, aimed at a much more volatile market, was struggling. The problem facing the company was that the seemingly obvious course of action, namely cutting Californian from the portfolio, was not possible because the overhead of the production facility would fall on the other two products, reducing in turn their viability.

All of the above are of course good managerial reasons for not deleting a product, but there are also less rational reasons. These are described below.

Lack of appropriate financial data

Inadequate financial data available to judge whether or not a product should be continued in the portfolio leads to inactivity. This is because standard measures of profitability, the bottom line for making deletion decisions, are based on arbitrary methods of costing. For example, total absorption costing may yield a different profit figure from other costing methods. This can cause decision-makers to be unsure about whether to drop a product.

The more recent developments in management accounting, such as activity-based costing, target costing and product attribute costing, hold promise for making deletion decisions, but until now there is little evidence as to the extent to which these new techniques have been adopted by product and marketing managers who might be responsible for making the deletion decision. Further, deletion does little to affect the fixed costs associated with a product, particularly if those are shared with other products, nor does deletion typically affect the overheads of an organization, so it can be difficult to support the argument for deletion.

Another problem is that no costing method accounts for the intangible costs like production line changeovers and small-order handling that are associated with slow-moving lines. This does little to strengthen the resolve to get rid of them. It may seem ridiculous in the age of information technology that these would be reasons why deletion is avoided or delayed – but that is the reality for many firms.

Ostrich attitudes

A number of managerial attitudes are described as 'ostrich attitudes' for reasons that will become apparent. First, there is a general lack of management interest in deletion. This is because it is seen as a dull and boring task, especially when compared to the excitement of new product development. Also, it inevitably becomes linked with the notion of failure, and is not guided by any policy or objectives which could be used to gauge the outcome. Together these reasons are powerful disincentives to managers. Secondly, in looking at sales figures, it can be difficult to know what is a 'blip' in the figures and what is a trend. This, coupled with the fact that deletion is rarely governed by deadlines, serves to prolong the life of dubious products. Thirdly, there are often a whole collection of vested interests in the product, from product managers to salesmen (for whom it is another source of income, however small) to the MD, whose 'baby' it might have been in the first place.

So, it should be apparent by now that getting to grips with the decision to delete a product is far from straightforward. As mentioned earlier, contributions to improving the decision from the academic or consulting worlds have been few and far between, coming from fewer than 40 authors over a period of more than 20 years. Little wonder, then, that few guiding frameworks exist to channel thought and investigation to those areas of the subject which most need it. In the absence of an overall conceptual framework, writers and researchers have dealt with different aspects of the subject area, on different continents at different times, from different points of departure.

The next section summarizes some of the emergent themes and develops the structure for the remaining two chapters of the book.

The scope of the deletion decision
· ·

That a decision can be described as a series of sequential stages is not new (Cyert, Simon and Trow 1956; Mintzberg, Raisinghani and Theoret, 1976). While precise details of these stages can and do vary from decision to decision, perhaps the most common format begins with the recognition that a decision ought to be taken. A search for possible courses of action ensues, followed by an evaluation of these courses of action and choice of the most appropriate one. The final stage of the decision-implementing framework has also been applied, implicitly and explicitly, in the work dealing with product elimination decision-making. However, no consensus exists as to what the entire product elimination decision-making process embraces, nor do all authors deal with all stages, and even the terms used to describe the stages differ. In this respect, description of product deletion will be very different from description of new product development. However, it is possible to discern some consistency among writers in relation to the following description of the stages in the decision-making process.

As early as 1964, Alexander's model of what he calls 'product elimination' showed a three-stage process (see Figure 17.1). Alexander recommends that a periodic screening procedure should be established to scrutinize products against the following criteria: sales trends, price trend, profit trend, introduction of a new product, product effectiveness and amount of executive time soaked up by the product. The next stage is analysis and decision making, where the author outlines the 'critical' factors by regrouping them into five categories: profits, financial considerations, employee relations, marketing, and other possibilities. The third stage is the deletion of the product, and here the opportunities and threats presented by the implementation of the decision to drop a product are considered.

Kotler (1965) endorses Alexander's view of the elimination process as multi-staged and sequential, comprising recognition, evaluation and decision-making and implementation stages. He forwards a two-phased procedure to deal with the decision: a 'creation stage' and an 'operational stage' which has six steps (see Figure 17.2).

The creation stage has a double purpose: assignment of responsibilities among members of the review committee and the development by this committee of a product

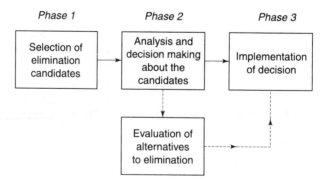

Figure 17.1 ● Schematic overview of Alexander's model (*source*: Alexander, 1964)

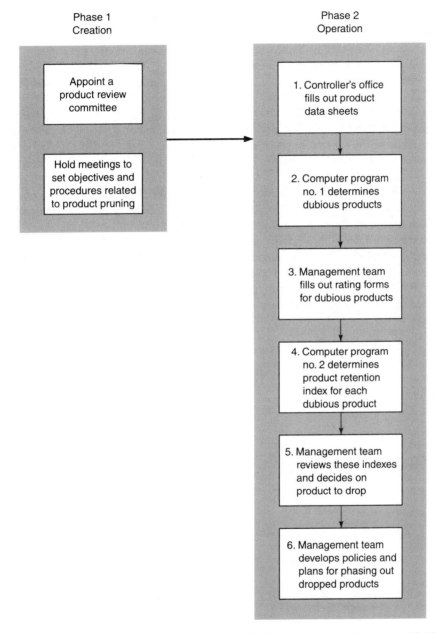

Figure 17.2 ● Schematic overview of Kotler's model (*source*: Kotler, 1965)

control system comprising criteria and procedures that will be used to evaluate products.

The operational stage is divided into six steps and should be effected annually. Much of the detail of these steps builds on Alexander's work. A third writer, Avlonitis (1980), proposed a comprehensive overview of the product elimination process, based on both previous writing and an empirical study of industrial goods firms. In his overview, stages already described by Alexander and Kotler are repeated, such as 'audit (review) of the product line', 'diagnosis', 'decision-making' and 'implementation'. In addition, he shows some of the subroutines within each stage as well as the possible impact of organizational factors and the information-gathering procedures on the whole process.

This brief summary of seminal work, together with research in a cross-section of British manufacturing goods, helped develop a conceptual framework for understanding and examining product deletion decisions and was used to inform a study by Hart (1987). The resulting model of the product deletion decision is shown in Figure 17.3.

Basically, this model builds on the simplified view of Kotler, that product deletion consists of two major stages: a decision-reaching stage and a decision-implementation stage. Both stages consist of sub-decisions, which are covered in the next two chapters. In addition to a number of refinements, this model differs from the early work more radically in its identification of a set of 'triggers' for deletion which may occur indepen-

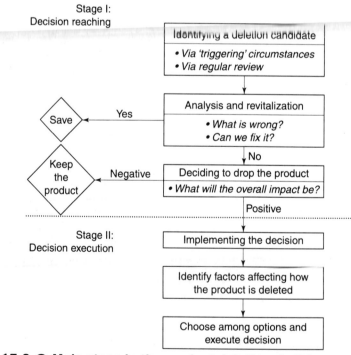

Figure 17.3 ● Main steps in the product deletion decision

dently of the type of systematic product performance reviews suggested. These are shown in Figure 17.3 as part of the routine of 'identifying a deletion candidate'.[1]

Triggers in product deletion

The 17 triggers can be grouped into four categories and are described below using examples from the study. First are those historically associated with deletion: poor performance. This, however, has several variants, which may or may not coincide.

Poor performance triggers

Decline in market potential

This is the classic product management situation where a market has moved on to new pastures. One manufacturer of instant foods and beverages dropped an instant-soup product after many years because they finally became convinced that the market had no interest in it and that the quest for sales in that product category was futile. Another company, which manufactured domestic heating equipment, dropped one of its products after identifying a decline in the market for solid fuel, the market for which the product was uniquely designed. The Marketing Manager explained that, although they could have carried it on, it would have quickly become a liability.

Poor sales performance despite a generally viable market

A large manufacturer of chocolate and sugar confectionery eliminated a fudge, biscuit and fruit bar simply because sales had fallen below acceptable levels. The product was run out over one year. There is, however, another permutation of the 'poor sales' category of precipitating circumstances: the failure of a relatively new product. The point at which management should give up on sluggish new products is possibly more difficult to ascertain than in the case of products which have reached the maturity stage of their life cycle. For this reason, a certain amount of doubt regarding the correct course of action seems to remain.

Poor profit performance

A large manufacturer of conversions of paper and board deleted a product whose cost base was increasing, but whose profitability could not be maintained because higher prices were denied by the company's competitive position. In fact, an attempt was made to hold profit levels steady by increasing the price, but this only led to lower sales volumes, smaller batches and increased costs.

Poor product quality

The Marketing Director of a small company manufacturing cakes and biscuits claimed that where they were dubious about product quality they would take a product out of the range. Of course, it must be stated that few, if any, 'bad quality' products are immensely successful, yet the awareness is there to delete any product not properly reflecting the quality standard of the brand name. The Product Manager of a large company manufacturing fiber optic connectors dropped a product that was low in quality and specification, and which, correspondingly, was manufactured on old production lines and therefore suffered from high manufacturing cost variances. The decision was taken to transfer the resources (people and space) to better projects.

Strategic triggers

A second set of triggers relate to strategic decisions taken by managers.

Resources required elsewhere

With small companies in particular, a low-volume product may be dropped in order to create the 'slack' necessary to develop and launch a new product.

Development of an active variety reduction (rationalization) programme

A manufacturer of automotive components had developed an active policy to reduce the variety of different parts held in stock. Over the years, a phenomenal number of different parts had accumulated in the warehouses, since, for every new model or limited edition brought out by the car manufacturers, a new or modified component had been fitted. Reducing the variety was tackled in two ways. Firstly, they evaluated the breadth of components, appraising the functional differentiation among similar parts. Where a component part could be used satisfactorily in more than one vehicle, the slow-moving, superfluous part numbers were eliminated. Secondly, where customers were insistent upon supplies of a specific part number, a minimum quantity had to be ordered.

Poor fit with strategic plans and company capabilities

The General Manager of a large manufacturer of instant foods and beverages developed strategic plans for factory rationalization and changes that had resulted in the elimination of some products. Another company, manufacturers of large domestic appliances, had at one time diversified into smaller home appliances, such as irons and kettles. Management had, however, discontinued these lines, as its lack of experience in both manufacturing and marketing these products appeared to blunt their competitive edge.

Rationalization due to mergers and acquisitions

This was a common issue in the 1980s. A medium-sized company in the carpet industry took over another manufacturing outfit of similar proportions. As a result, the company had two sets of product lines containing similar products manufactured and marketed to the same market segments. They set about rationalizing these two sets of product lines into one logical and attractive mix of products.

Poor fit with company image

A large manufacturer of electronic testing equipment replaced a product which had been in the catalogue for eight years – somewhat long for the electronics industry. When the initial concern was raised, it was largely because the product did not reflect the up-to-date, pioneering image the company sought to foster. It should be said, however, that for management the final trigger came when the competition launched a new product. Another example, this time in the Cola industry, is the decision (not yet taken) to drop the 'Diet' tag for Pepsi. This potential move had been considered as part of the overall 'Blue relaunch' of the brand in 1996 (*Marketing*, 30 January 1997, p. 1).

Parent company decisions and policies

A manufacturer of automotive components was instructed to cease production by its parent company who wanted to move all production of the particular product to one European location, in Spain.

The development of a new product

This is a classic deletion trigger: the new product simply replaces the old. Hart's (1987) study showed this might occur as a direct or indirect replacement. The direct replacement is the obvious situation of a new, improved or second generation of a product taking the place of the previous version. However, in launching a new range of products, companies do decide to remove other products from a different range, in order to keep the overall portfolio manageable.

Operational triggers

In contrast to the strategic triggers listed above, a number take place resulting from an unforeseen change in operational matters.

Problems associated with raw materials and parts

The increase in price of a component or ingredient, such as flavouring, may cause the complete withdrawal of a product. Of course, the flexibility to do this is dependent upon the characteristics of the market. In general terms, companies serving large markets can choose this route more easily than where there is a small and finite number of buyers.

Operational problems

In some instances, the elimination of certain products in a company's range would eradicate several operational problems, such as storage and logistics. However, the lack of appropriate financial data and the prospect of a loss in turnover often militate against deletion. For example, one small company manufacturing cakes and biscuits distributed its products mainly through the multiple retail chains. The common struggle for all manufacturers selling to the consumer through the multiples is the struggle for shelf space. The amount of shelf space allocated to a manufacturer is a crucial determinant of sales volume, all other things being equal. Another important factor is the presentation of the product mix on the shelf. Often, before introducing a new product, a company has to drop an existing product, in order to maintain an appropriate balance on the supermarket shelf. Simply put, there is not enough space to carry ever-increasing amounts of new product. Operationally, one might have to be dropped.

External triggers

A further four triggers are external to the firm.

Competitive activity

The competitive entry of a new product may cause incumbent manufacturers to consider deletion. This is particularly so where competition has the edge on costs. While there is little new in the proposition, the point with regard to deletion is that products retaining adequate profits may be forced out of the market. While it is necessary to avoid such situations, and indeed, product management is about avoiding them by keeping ahead of the competitive game, the fact is that deletions do occur for this reason. In fact, Hart's (1987) study showed that this was the sixth most important reason for deletion, out of seventeen!

Third-party decisions

Distributors or retailers, in deciding to de-list a product, present an important trigger in the decision to delete.

Another facet of third-party decisions might again stem from the struggle for shelf space for consumer goods. Major multiple chains set themselves a 'minimum standard' of sales which products must achieve to be allowed shelf space. This is a precarious position for smaller companies who do not often have the position to bargain, as do companies such as Unilever or Procter & Gamble.

Government policies and regulations

This situation highlights government's idiosyncratic effect on product policy. One company distilling alcoholic beverages operated internationally, when the United Kingdom joined the EEC. The management was forced to comply with Article 86 of the Treaty of Rome, which seeks to establish the free flow of goods among member states. Under the article, the company was accused of operating a two-tier price system, and took the decision to eliminate the product from the UK. The alternative course of action was to modify the price. However, the consequences that this entailed for their product positioning policy and pricing would have resulted not only in operational problems with respect to the financial structure of the company, but also in marketing problems, as the differentiation between the company's products would have been reduced, causing confusion and even cannibalization.

A change in exchange rates

A manufacturer of wood- and metal-cutting saw blades exported a product to the former West Germany. The value of sterling increased, effectively increasing the price of the product to the West Germans. The company knew that if they did not subsidize the selling price they would have to cease producing the product as the customer would refuse to buy at the increased price. So, while technically leaving the decision to the customer by increasing the price, the company eliminated the product and lost business worth £250,000.

Overlap and combination of triggers

While these triggers show that the 'poor sales' scenario is not the only reason companies consider getting rid of products, there is considerable overlap among them. A close look at one elimination decision exemplifies this. A company manufactured rolls of flexible tubing, such as silicon tubing which is used in the automotive and aircraft industries and is subjected to very high and very low temperatures. Production started to report problems in manufacturing the ducting to a consistently high standard, which meant that the quality of the product could not be guaranteed to a market where quality is crucial. The company was unable to ascertain the reason for this problem, although it believes the problem originated in a change in the quality of the silicon rubber used to manufacture the product. In such an instance, three precipitating circumstances overlap: 'operational problems', 'problems associated with raw materials and parts', and 'poor product quality'. The silicon ducting was eventually replaced by another product. Another, more common overlap is encountered with regard to new product development. While the development of a new product often leads to the deletion of an existing one (the scenario most commonly inferred by the academic world), it is often the detection of a weak existing product which leads to the development of a new one.

In addition to overlap, the factors are often combined, that is more than one precipitating circumstance may work in concert, triggering the decision to eliminate a product. For example, a large manufacturer of wood-free paper produced a product which experienced rather stagnant sales. In healthier economic times, this would not have posed a problem, but a recent managerial decree had emphasized the need to increase market share as the only way to meet strategic objectives in a mature, static market. The decision was taken to reposition several related brands with the resultant elimination of the brand in question.

The importance of the triggers is in their contribution to our understanding of the numerous circumstances which cause a product to be considered for deletion. This in turn has implications for the way in which a decision is reached and implemented, which will be dealt with in the next two chapters of the book.

Summary

··

This chapter has sought to introduce the concept of product deletion as one which should be actively managed as part of overall product management. In contrast, it is an activity which is often avoided by managers and has also been neglected in the research and consulting world. A number of reasons why proper attention should be given to deletion have been described, together with the explanations for its general neglect. Of course, there can be good reasons to avoid deleting a product, especially where its fortunes can be turned round, or where its existence makes other, successful products viable. It is important, however, that it is not just left alone because it is a difficult decision or because the appropriate data to answer questions are not readily available.

This chapter briefly reviewed some of the seminal articles on product deletion before presenting a model of the decision which is used to structure the next two chapters of the book. Specifically, the model has two major stages, a decision-reaching stage and a decision-implementing stage. Both are affected by the variety of triggers which have been discussed, showing that 'poor product performance' is not the only reason to consider removing a product from the line.

The next chapter further explores the decision-reaching stages of the product deletion decision.

QUESTIONS

1. Why is product deletion important to the health of a company?

2. Explain the reasons why deletion is often a neglected activity.

3. Describe the main stages in the product deletion decision.

4. Examine the effects of product proliferation on a company.

5. Compare and contrast the various reasons why products are deleted.

Mini-case ● Ellipse

Dumbraid plc is a large manufacturer of paper and board products and a niche player in a global, highly competitive market. As part of its quarterly review of product performance, business managers had noticed stagnant sales with one of the ranges – Ellipse. The brand was a range of coloured boards weighing 160–300 g/m^2. The market for these types of products is highly diverse, comprising office stationery, speciality printers, and publishers of all kinds. At the time it came under scrutiny its annual sales volume was 2m tonnes. It accounted for about 5% of branded products' volume for the company, which amounted to about 1% of total company sales volume. The capacity required to manufacture it was similarly around 1% of total, although it was a strong contributor to the profitability of the machine that made it and around 100 people were employed directly in the use of that machine. If it were to be deleted, there was no replacement, so a lot of production jobs and capacity were at risk. It was generally agreed that although sales had been static, no-one had tried to do anything with it. Its contribution to profit was strong and it was holding market share, so there was no necessity to do anything with the product.

In comparative terms, the product still performed poorly in the light of other products. Despite the target markets being of central importance to Dumbraid, it held only 15% of the market share of its nearest market rival, whereas in other product categories Dumbraid had 150% of the share of the nearest competitor.

On closer scrutiny, the product was found to have several weaknesses. First, the quality of the product was unreliable. Several complaints had been received from customers that its stiffness was below an acceptable standard. Second, its positioning, both internally and externally, was unclear. Externally it had little to offer over competitive products; internally it sat uneasily in the portfolio; nominally it was targeted at the business stationery market (where the company already had other product ranges), but its actual appeal was limited to six large printing companies. In the latter market, however, the competition had better products, so a simple 'rebranding' exercise was not considered to be an effective move.

The choices open to Dumbraid were:

1. Redevelop and relaunch Ellipse.

2. Develop a new 'board' product and replace Ellipse.

3. Integrate Ellipse as the 'board' end of a high quality printer paper range called Revolver.

4. Do nothing.

Discussion questions

1. What are the risks associated with each of these options?

2. What information is required to choose among the options?

Note

1. In Avlonitis' earlier study, he identified a number of circumstances drawing attention to products as potential candidates for elimination. This study, as well as those by Salerno (1983) and Gauthier (1985), began to question the earlier assumptions embedded in the work of Alexander and Kotler, that all decisions to drop a product are based on unsatisfactory sales and profits. In addition, the studies by Avlonitis, Salerno and Gauthier also showed that not all 'weak' or 'mature' products are suitable for withdrawal and that not all withdrawal candidates are weak or mature products. Furthermore, at the beginning of the chapter, the proposition that product deletion is merely a corollary of new product development was forwarded as a reason for its comparative neglect in research.

chapter 18

· ·

Reaching the decision to delete a product

LEARNING OBJECTIVES
· ·

1. To review the decision criteria used to identify candidates for product deletion.

2. To explain the decision criteria used to analyze, and if possible revitalize, the deletion candidate.

3. To describe the criteria used to evaluate deletion candidates which cannot be revitalized.

4. To explain the interconnection among stages.

5. To explain the situational factors affecting those stages.

On completion of this chapter you will:

1. Understand how deletion candidates come to the attention of management.

2. Be able to explain how the deletion candidates can be analyzed and revitalized.

3. Understand how the analysis depends on how the deletion candidate came to light.

4. Appreciate the importance and complexities of the evaluation stage.

5. Be able to design a procedure to analyze and evaluate a deletion candidate.

6. Know how these stages of the decision are affected by situational factors surrounding the product.

Introduction
· ·

As was outlined at the beginning of Chapter 17, deletion is not a decision reached easily. It involves a good deal of information, analysis and evaluation. This chapter focuses on the stages of deliberation that are needed to reach the decision to drop (or retain) a product which is no longer contributing in a satisfactory way to the company's or the market's needs. It begins by discussing how companies identify deletion candidates, goes on to review the factors used to analyze the situation and, if possible, correct any problems., and finally discusses the issues pertaining to the retain/drop decision.

Identification of deletion candidates

The first stage in the deletion process involves the identification of products whose performance requires further analysis, with a view to considering whether or not the product should be retained in the range. As already noted in Chapter 17, the triggers relate to a variety of circumstances which may be outside managerial control. As we have seen, a candidate for product deletion may be identified in one of the following ways:

● When a crisis presents itself to management requiring immediate attention

● When formulation of strategic plans reveals a product ill-suited to strategic objectives

● When an opportunity is spotted for enhancing company performance

● When a product falls below a level of performance acceptable to management.

Each of these four situations would be alerted to management in a different way. For example, where a crisis arises, there is little need to address actively the question of identifying elimination candidates. If a third party changes the specification of a product, or decides not to purchase at all, it will inform the manufacturing company of its intentions. Similarly, where the parent group board takes a decision that affects the product line of a subsidiary, the subsidiary will be notified by headquarters. A sudden change in exchange rates will make itself felt in the company with heavy exporting commitments.

If these and other 'crisis' situations present themselves, the affected company does not need to do anything actively to recognize such deletion candidates. However, other situations may well originate within the company, and a number of factors may be used to indicate their incidence. The normative view presents such factors as 'review criteria' – criteria used to review or audit the performance of products. Prescriptive models also suggest the extensive use of minimum standards of performance and product objectives to detect any product elimination candidates.

Minimum standards and product goals

A study of 31 companies' deletion practices by one of the authors (Hart, 1987) suggests that deletion does not always occur. While a company may have weekly or monthly targets for each product, if several lines are trading below the target figure, then the potential revenue cost of deleting each one can amount to substantial sums. Instead, the firms can, and often do, learn to live below target levels, or, as in the case of a company manufacturing printed circuit boards quoted below, find another way of handling the problem:

'We have a minimum market share for our major lines – but we keep it open so that we can react quickly. There's a good example of flexible circuits which we took a decision to come out of. After making that decision we reversed it. When we pulled out, four companies made the product. We had the lowest share so we decided to abandon it. However, subsequently we combined the product with another manufacturer's component to add value to both products, and split the profit.'

Table 18.1 ● Product goals and objectives from a study of 31 companies

Total number of companies with product objectives	25
Number of companies with*	
Sales volume (unit of £) objective	20
Market share objective	8
Profit (contribution) objective	14
Number of companies with no product objectives	6

*Several companies had more than one product objective.
Source: Hart (1987).

The normative literature (and logic) suggests there is a difference between a minimum standard and a product goal/objective. A product's deviation from its targets might not warrant further investigation, as it can be due to temporary circumstances: out of stocks, market fluctuations, competitive activity. A *minimum standard* should be set at a level which reflects an excessive deviation from expectation and which cannot be altered or excused by subjective argument. In Hart's study referred to above, several companies that claimed to have 'minimum standards' did not, upon further examination, distinguish between a minimum standard of performance and a sales objective. Instead, goals and minimum standards are often blurred; they fall into the following categories of product objectives: sales volume, market share, and profit. The frequencies of use of these categories by the companies in Hart's study are shown in Table 18.1.

Of the six companies that did not have objectives, three concentrated on minimum standards as a 'warning signal' and the other three were somewhat different. One company was small and tended not to set product objectives of any kind, sticking to overall budget figures. Most of their turnover came from servicing one very large customer. The other companies set minimum profit standards or profit objectives at the company level, which, if not attained, would trigger an analysis to find the culprit product(s). Three of these six companies did not engage in strategic planning, which might also explain their apparent lack of product goals.

In many cases objectives may be set not by individual product but rather by product group or category. Alternatively, slightly different parameters for setting targets, including 'waste limits' and 'inventory holding', are used to help track operating problems and slow-moving items respectively.

The cause of a product's departure from plan may be known to be of a temporary nature, caused by any number of operational hiccups or market changes: temporarily 'out of stock' due to production or distribution problems, competitive promotional activity, or political events. Refinements such as these are not present in the 'normative view' but are real measures used by companies to keep track of product performance. The next section examines in greater detail the 'review criteria' such as these, as well as others that have been found to be of use to companies in identifying potential candidates for product deletion.

Review criteria

The point introduced above is that review criteria often go beyond the parameters of 'product performance', reflecting the fact that 'control meetings' are more than marketing or product-related meetings. The breadth of the following 15 criteria shows the scope of managerial control activity used in the real world. Table 18.2 lists the criteria typically used.

Sales-related criteria

Past sales volume may refer to the past week, month, six-month period or year, depending on the occasion of the review. The figures may be collected via the ordering or invoicing systems which are typically computerized and can be broken down by product category, product range, or even individual items.

A product's share of the company's sales allows its sales performance to be comparatively reviewed. Many firms will construct 'company league tables' or 'ranking lists', which are used to discuss options for product range changes.

Future sales volume also incorporates the dimension of time, helping management to extend the horizon of the immediate review, which might encourage proactive rather than reactive decisions.

Table 18.2 ● Review criteria for identifying deletion candidates

Sales-related criteria
- Past sales volume
- The product's percentage of overall company sales
- Future sales volume

Market-related criteria
- Market growth
- Market share
- The stage of the product on its PLC curve
- Customer acceptance of the product
- Competitive activity in the marketplace

Profit-related criteria
- The product's profit contribution
- Price trends
- Sales generated versus resources used in generating sales

Operating criteria
- Stock inventory levels
- Service levels
- Batch sizes
- Operational problems

Market-related criteria

Market share is another comparative measure of sales volume, comparing the company's unit sales or revenue with that of its competitors. Market growth introduces a future perspective into product and company appraisals. A product performing poorly in a market which is growing slowly or where growth has stopped is, in effect, the classic 'dog' referred to in Chapter 6.

A product's position on its life cycle curve is used by companies to indicate both the likely growth in sales and changes in *relative* product quality, especially where life cycles tend to be five years or less. However, given the criticism levelled at the PLC with regard to the extent to which a product's stage can be identified, this is likely to be a secondary rather than a primary measure.

Customer acceptance examines not so much the absolute quality and performance of a product (if such a thing exists), but rather the customer's opinion of the product's quality and performance. This is important as a measure of likely future sales, but requires active customer monitoring and incorporating their views into routine evaluation.

Competitive activity, when reviewed, can help position the company's efforts in the marketplace and help to gain an overall view of strengths and weaknesses.

Profit-related criteria

Profit margin/contribution refers to any number of profit ratios: return on investment, return on assets employed, marginal contribution, marketing contribution, gross and net margins. The figures used are often derived from the computerized ordering and invoice systems mentioned above and can be broken down in a similar fashion to sales volume figures.

Price trends can be used to gauge a market's potential in relation to a company's capabilities. They also help monitor *profit* trends, as an increase or decrease in price may increase or decrease profit accordingly.

Sales versus resources utilized is a way of considering sales volume which allows management to assess the value of effort required to generate a specified sales figure. The Marketing Director of a large producer of confectionery explains:

> 'Even though some products may be earning money it's just not worth our while keeping them on – in salesmen's time. . . . When it becomes clear that a brand is not worth the time and effort to sell, we drop it.'

Operating criteria

Stock levels are used by management to indicate both sales and profit levels. The Marketing Manager of a medium-sized company manufacturing carpets explains:

> 'We've got to look at stock turnover in relation to profits: a range has got to move at a certain level or we get liquidity problems.'

Service levels or the 'time required to meet demand' is another measure of the effort needed to generate a specified level of sales. The Logistics Manager of a company producing reprographic equipment and supplies explains:

> '70 per cent of our products are fast-moving, can be produced and shipped in large volumes and we can therefore guarantee delivery within 24 hours. 25 per cent of our products move at an average speed and don't present major problems. But with 5 per cent of our products that move slowly, we try to manufacture in economic batches – meaning we can't always deliver quickly, as we wait for a sufficient quantity to manufacture. This means that competition can move in, in which case we lose money. But if we hold stock, we'll still lose money.'

Actual versus projected production loading allows managers to monitor the sizes of batches. Variances in batch sizes can often alert management to the unsatisfactory performance of a product and will also increase overall running costs.

Operational problems such as high warranty costs or a large number of service calls can often alert managers to poor product quality. Production problems such as large variances in materials usage may be of such proportions in themselves as to warrant immediate attention and changes to the product line. The Marketing Director of a large manufacturer of paper in the author's study comments:

> '... a basic objective is to run our machines fully and we always need to achieve an output level of so much. We have a standard for this and we know how much paper we should get off the machine, and how much raw materials we should use. We can therefore evaluate the "actual" against the standard.'

Summary of review criteria

The breadth of these 15 criteria should not suggest that each is used independently of the others. Several measure a similar dimension, in a more or less sophisticated way. They also imply the involvement in the deletion decision of more than one function or department; product deletion is by no means the sole responsibility of marketing. In fact, it is often those in inventory or production that become acutely aware of the nuisance factors associated with under-performing product lines, as stocks of raw materials, parts or ingredients pile up ready for manufacturing. As well as sales and marketing functions, production, inventory, logistics and services functions are all necessary to furnish the information required. Although this suggests that information will be gathered and analyzed systematically in order to promote efficiency in identifying weak products, such a view is naive. Relevant information often resides within functions without being introduced to those involved in making the deletion decision, contributing to the avoidance of the decision altogether.

Once a candidate comes to the attention of those charged with the responsibility of containing the product range, there has to be some analysis of what to do next. Attention is now turned to this phase. It consists of two separate tasks: discussion of what has happened to create the situation and consideration of appropriate corrective action, or revitalization.

The diagnostic routine: analysis and revitalization

The very title of this routine implies that something is wrong. A 'problem' has to exist before it can be diagnosed. It follows then, given the extensive set of circumstances that may cause a product to be dropped (Hart, 1988), that not all elimination candidates have to be diagnosed, since not all are 'problem' products. For example, where a product is dropped to free resources for other opportunities, it is unlikely that the management of a company will spend time diagnosing the problem. A small manufacturer of fresh and frozen foods replaced a traditional product with a modern one to free the disproportionate space used by the traditional product. The analysis undertaken centred on the likely reaction of the grocery retailers, rather than on why the situation came about in the first place. Similarly, when a new product is developed to replace an existing one, little time is wasted on how competitive the old product is, and energies are transferred to executing a well-planned and smooth changeover. It should therefore be remembered that this stage of the decision is almost exclusively reserved for products that are performing poorly. The next section looks in greater detail at the analysis of poorly performing products.

Analysis of deletion candidates

The form the analysis takes is largely dependent on what is initially perceived to be wrong with the product. The next two paragraphs examine what analyses are undertaken when profits shrink or when sales fall. These analyses are summarized in Table 18.3.

When profits shrink...

When profits fall, attention may be turned to either or both sides of the profit equation: costs incurred and prices charged. Several cost-related issues frequently require inspection. The first of these is the cost of ingredients or parts which can fluctuate due to increased supplier charges, changes in the exchange rates or short supply of raw materials. A second cost-related issue is the efficiency of manufacture lines. This issue goes beyond the question of batch sizes, embracing important issues such as breakdowns, stoppages or the manufacturing process itself. Fluctuations in these areas add to costs, insidiously eating away at profit margins. On occasion the reasons may not require specific diagnostic attention, as in the case of a customer going into liquidation.

A further cost-related issue which might explain a fall in profits is a variance in materials usage. The cost of a product is usually preset on the basis of a standard mix of parts or ingredients. Should practice deviate from this standard, then profits will deviate accordingly. High raw material or parts stock may also account for diminishing profits and can be investigated when a dip in profits is detected. Side two of the profit equation – price – is also subject to investigation. A major concern to companies is the extent to which profits might be restored by price increases without being harmful to volume. A final area of analysis relevant to a decline in profits is the mix of sales across the product range. The profit margin for a product is often set in relation to its

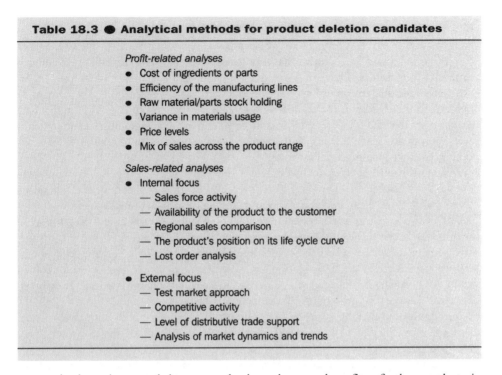

Table 18.3 ● Analytical methods for product deletion candidates

Profit-related analyses
- Cost of ingredients or parts
- Efficiency of the manufacturing lines
- Raw material/parts stock holding
- Variance in materials usage
- Price levels
- Mix of sales across the product range

Sales-related analyses
- Internal focus
  — Sales force activity
  — Availability of the product to the customer
  — Regional sales comparison
  — The product's position on its life cycle curve
  — Lost order analysis

- External focus
  — Test market approach
  — Competitive activity
  — Level of distributive trade support
  — Analysis of market dynamics and trends

expected sales volume *and* the expected sales volume and profits of other products in the company's range (e.g. loss leader). Should the balance of sales alter, then profit may alter accordingly. A decline in overall profitability can be traced to a change in the mix of products sold.

When sales volume falls . . .

Where a drop in sales is giving cause for concern, companies are faced with a multitude of possible explanations which could be explored. Several of these are internally focused. First, sales force activity is sometimes examined, on two counts. The actual performance of a salesperson might reveal a disenchantment interfering with sales performance, or the performance of the sales force as a whole might reveal underlying problems regarding the products they are trying to sell.

The availability of the product to the customer needs to be checked to ensure that a dip in sales volume is not merely the result of 'out of stocks'. Stock has to be checked throughout the chain of distribution. If a drop in sales has been detected, a further way to pinpoint the cause is to carry out a regional analysis. Such a procedure, comparing sales in various regions served by the company, enables management to locate the root of the problem.

A fourth issue taken into consideration following a decline in sales volume is the age of the product, or its position on the product life cycle curve. This issue is most relevant where products experience short life cycles, due to either changing fashions or speedy rates of technological innovation. The relative age of the product can be used to indicate the corrective possibilities open to the company. A fifth type of analysis is really an amalgamation of several analyses: lost order analysis. This analysis attempts to diagnose why a specific order or contract has not been won by systematically examining a number of key factors. Depending on the company and the nature of its operations, such factors include customer expectations, standards and specifications, the company's approach to the customer, the competition in general, their product services and prices, the company that did win the order and its competitive advantage. Such an approach is most appropriate when dealing with one or two big orders or contracts for a small number of large prospective customers. However, in the consumer field there is an equivalent all-round analysis to investigate a drop in sales: the test market approach, described in Chapter 14. This diagnosis involves adjusting elements of the marketing mix to isolate those elements which appear to influence the sales rate.

A number of analysis issues concentrate fully on the less controllable forces at play in the distributive chain and in the marketplace. For example, investigating current competitive activity can reveal a source of sales loss. Again, competitive activity need not be formally addressed in an investigation, as a competitive promotion or new product would not normally be detected *after* a decline in sales, but *before*. The level of distributive trade support is important to companies who rely on middlemen to sell the product to the end user. It is especially important to consumer goods companies, where distributive pricing has to be checked along with the amount of shelf or floor space given to a product.

An analysis of market dynamics and trends often shows up structural reasons for a product's poor performance, as does an examination of market or customer acceptance of a product which attempts to isolate those features of the product which prevent a customer or market segment from buying the product.

As was previously mentioned, the diagnosis need not always be formally initiated. This might be because the root of the problem is obvious without looking any further, or because management perceives the problem to be short-term. In a similar vein, a problem perceived to be ephemeral may only receive cursory managerial attention. Once the diagnosis has been carried out, the next step is to consider whether the problem can be alleviated, managed or even reversed. Recently, *The Independent* newspaper diagnosed its falling circulation (55% in the past seven years) to poor positioning, the resource-hungry launch of *The Independent on Sunday* and several changes in ownership, all leading to a weak brand image. In addition, the major competitors turned to price-cutting and promotional offers. The efforts to revitalize the paper include advertising, aggressive promotions and the rebirth of its launch slogan, 'It is . . . Are you?'. This has been accompanied by changes to the paper itself (*Marketing*, 30 January 1997, p. 10). This is one way in which the fortunes of a failing product might be turned round.

But not all candidates for deletion will be reprieved. Research also suggests that where a product has become an elimination candidate because of external forces (government policy, parent company decisions), or an active variety reduction policy, or because resources are required for other endeavours, little is done to revitalize product performance. A manufacturer of office equipment and supplies was instructed by its parent group to drop a product which was deemed incompatible with company policy. On receiving instructions, the management in Britain attended to matters of stock and to informing customers before phasing out the product. Where products are being rationalized or reduced in variety, there is little evidence of any corrective action being initiated, as the object of the exercise is to reduce the amount of duplication and proliferation of products, not to restore them to previous levels of success. In other circumstances, the product will be considered for revitalization, the various methods for which are discussed below.

Revitalization of deletion candidates

For convenience, the methods of revitalization can be organized under the *aide-mémoire* of the 4Ps. These are shown in Table 18.4.

Price-related methods

One of the most frequently cited responses to ailing product performance is to decrease price. As this phase of the decision-making process is directly dependent upon the specific circumstances of the product under consideration, the tactic is adopted either to meet a competitive price promotion or to attempt to resuscitate sales in the longer term. Decreasing the price of a product is also used to run down finished stocks of a product which is being replaced by a new one. There are problems in using price as a tool. First, price cuts decrease profits and can encourage the competition to follow suit, leaving lowered profits without a competitive advantage. Second, cutting price on some of the company's brands can stimulate 'cannibalization'. In some situations, price cuts do not actually *increase* sales of a product, they merely change the date of purchase. Cuts can also undermine the confidence of the distribution.

Price decreases mean that the company accepts lower margins. However, this is not suitable in all circumstances. Another popular method of revitalization is a cost reduc-tion which can be undertaken, either to prepare for a price cut without a loss

---

Table 18.4 ● Methods of revitalization

Price-related methods
- Decrease price
- Increase price
- Production efficiency improvements
- Cost reduction

Product-related methods
- Product modification
- Quality improvements
- Product range extension
- Product range reduction
- Extension of warranties
- Packaging changes

Promotion-related methods
- Increase sales force efforts
- Increase sales promotion
- Increase advertising

Distribution-related methods
- Distribution improvements
- Change channels of distribution

Marketing-strategy methods
- Extend product to new markets
- Withdraw product from some markets
- Factor or source

in profits or to increase the profit margin on a product. A cost reduction is achieved in a number of ways: altering the mix of parts or ingredients in the product, altering the source or quality of parts or ingredients, reducing the numbers of parts or components, reinvesting in more productive plant or withdrawing promotional support.

Production efficiency improvements may reduce costs. Where demand justifies it, production batch sizes are increased to achieve lower unit costs which are passed on to customers by a price reduction.

While a price increase can often increase the speed of an ailing product's demise, this is not always the case. Where declining markets are involved, companies may increase the price of products to increase the yield of the products in those markets.

Product-related methods

Rather than a short-term approach, some companies, where appropriate, might try product modification as a way of altering the sales or profit trends of a particular product. This differs from 'cost reduction' in that it represents an attempt to add value or variety to the product, which, although it *can* result in a lower price, is not done specifically to achieve a lower price. Not unrelated to 'product modification' are packaging changes which can be used either to reduce the cost, without actually impinging on *product* quality, or to alter the image of the product in the mind of the customer, or to differentiate it from competitive products. Obviously, the more packaging used to market a product, the greater the options are, and generally this option is confined to consumer goods companies. A branch of 'product modification' important enough to warrant separate treatment is quality improvements, which are considered where quality was known to be inferior and unsatisfactory. An alternative way of enhancing product quality is the extension of warranties and guarantees.

Two further product-related options for revitalizing products are product range extension and product range reduction. The former option allows the company to compete with a wider choice of products for potential customers, with little physical or functional difference among the products: an altered feature or form perhaps, or trimming, or a slightly cheaper version. Product range reduction can help the problems of managing extended product ranges, eliminating the disproportionately high costs of manufacturing and stocking slow-moving items. Where customers can be persuaded to purchase alternative items from the range, batches of such items could also be produced, reducing unit costs further.

Promotion-related methods

In contrast to stimulating demand for ailing products through product and price alterations, companies encourage increased effort by the sales force, greater use of print-media advertising and more sales promotion as tried and tested means of encouraging sales.

An increase in effort by the sales force can be achieved through higher incentives, sales competitions, or a period of retraining to establish the 'selling proposition' of the product in question in the salespeople's minds. However, despite the popularity of this corrective measure it can be somewhat short-term in its approach, especially if incentives are part of a larger promotional deal. Also reserved for short-term use was an increase in sales promotion. This means attending trade shows, increasing and revamping sales brochures and literature as well as incentives for the distributive trade. Increased advertising is also used to mobilize customers' support, although it can be no more than a short-term answer, especially where mature products are concerned.

Distribution-related methods

The first is distribution improvements, attempts to improve the display or shelf space given to a product by the distributive trade. Hart (1987) describes how a number of companies underlined the importance of shelf space to the sales of their products. As the retail multiples become bigger and account for a larger share of consumer purchase, and companies' allocation of shelf space becomes more and more centralized, it becomes as crucial to negotiate the 'number of facings' given to a product as it was to negotiate entry to the store itself. Accordingly an increase in shelf space can greatly enhance sales of the product. The second option is to change channels of distribution and is only feasible where a few key wholesalers and retailers do not account for a large proportion of sales.

Marketing-strategy methods

Finally, some methods of 'revitalizing' amount to a wider view of the marketing strategy of the firm. First, decisions may be taken to extend the product to new markets to enhance sales performance. A similar option in this connection is for the company to export the product, thereby increasing its sales base. Another method reverses the procedure: market concentration involves withdrawing a product from those markets or segments where its performance is sluggish. Finally, a company may decide that factoring or sourcing, which amounts to a psychological elimination of the product, is an effective method of keeping the products on the books for customers who depend on it. Deciding to buy the product in rather than making it, or to source it, allows a company to market the product without having the production headaches that accompany a product in decline.

Despite this wide range of possibilities for revitalizing the product deletion candidate, managers often find that there is no obvious way to renew a product's sales, even for a short while. At this point, or having attempted (and failed) to revitalize the product, the decision to delete it can no longer be postponed. The next paragraph describes the major factors that managers consider at this point.

Evaluation of deletion candidates: deciding to drop the product

When a product has been revitalized without much success, or when management believes that no corrective action is feasible, or judges that the product's circumstances do not justify improvement or investment, the next stage is to evaluate whether elimination of the product is an appropriate course of action. Despite the neat and objective solutions forwarded by some of the theoretical contributions to the literature (Alexander, 1964; Kotler, 1965; Hamelman and Mazze, 1972), empirical work (Avlonitis,

1984; Gauthier, 1985; Hart, 1990) would suggest that the evaluation stage is the most perplexing of the entire product elimination process. It is at this stage that a decision must finally be taken, with or without adequate knowledge, and usually complicated by uncertainty and risk. The words of the Marketing Manager of a small company manufacturing carpets summarize the dilemma of the evaluation stage:

> 'If we've got a product not selling particularly well, we'd try a special promotion. If that isn't successful we've really got to analyse whether we've got a long-term future with the product. If we reduce the sales budget, we then have to consider if we still need full-time working – we can't just go on producing something that's not selling. So there comes a point where we've got to bite the bullet.'

Research has shown a wide variety of factors, both internal and external, to be relevant to this evaluation, which are listed in Table 18.5.

Internal evaluation factors

Internal factors include those which focus managerial attention on what might happen to resources in the event of a deletion as well as the direct financial implications of such a decision.

Table 18.5 ● Factors used to evaluate whether a deletion candidate should be retained

Internal evaluation factors

1. Resource-related:
   - Availability of a new product
   - Effect of the elimination on recovery of overheads
   - Reallocation of resources to other opportunities
   - Effect of the deletion on fixed capital (i.e. plant and equipment)
   - Interchangeability (communization) of parts, materials or packing
   - Effect of the deletion on capacity utilization
   - Reallocation of executive and selling time
   - Effect of the deletion on working capital (e.g. stock)
   - Effect of the deletion on employment prospects of the workforce

2. Finance-related:
   - Effect of the deletion on total company sales volume
   - Effect of the deletion on sales and profitability of other products in the range
   - Product's contribution to a profit centre (e.g. branch, factory, depot)

External evaluation factors

- Product's market potential
- Effect of the deletion on distribution (e.g. loss of shelf space)
- Effect of the deletion on 'full-range' policy
- Existence of substitutes to satisfy the customer
- Effect of the deletion on company image
- Competitive reaction to the withdrawal
- Customer relations

The effect of the deletion on the recovery of overheads

Even the slowest-selling lines often contribute to overhead recovery, and in removing one product, its contribution would have to be absorbed by the remainder of the product range. This, in turn, means that often there is no net advantage in dropping the product, and that there may even be a net loss, as explained by the Commercial Director of a large company manufacturing dairy produce:

> 'We try to analyse the effect of elimination on profitability through our marginal costing system. We'll sometimes produce a product at a loss, knowing that if we take that product out of the production profile, the cost will go on to another.'

The effect of the deletion on sales and profits of other products

The profitability of other products can be affected by the elimination of one product from the range, as described above. In addition, where there is a degree of complementarity among the company's products, the removal of a product has to be considered in the light of its commercial association with any other product in the range.

The effect of the deletion on total sales

The prospect of a shortfall in sales volume may inhibit management from going ahead with the decision to drop a product. While normative arguments in favour of product elimination cite greater efficiency, productivity, perhaps even higher profits, as examples of the benefits to be gained, in reality there is often a pressing need to achieve volume targets, particularly where performance of individuals is measured in this way.

The product's contribution to a profit centre

A product can gain management's attention because of its poor performance in relation to other products in the range. Yet, its particular manufacturing or marketing circumstances may make it vital to a part of the company's operation. The Commercial Director of the company manufacturing dairy products explains how a regional operation may depend on a product which appears 'weak' on a national comparison:

> 'The 80/20 principle is interesting because if you look at national sales figures you might find one product right down at the bottom which turns about £100,000 in a company, with a turnover of over seven million. When you look more closely though, it's £100,000 in one depot or factory and it's often fantastic business for them.'

The 'financial implications' focus managerial attention on the effect a product deletion will have on the company's ability to generate *income*. However, the reverse side of the profit coin is also affected by the decision to delete a product, namely, the resources used to create products which generate income. Five evaluation factors relate to the implications for resources that dropping a product may entail. They are described in turn.

The effect of the deletion on working capital

Raw materials, parts and ingredients that go to produce a product, as well as finished stocks, are affected by the decision to drop a product. Essentially, there are two choices: either drop the product and write off the losses, or defer the elimination until the working capital involved in the product is finished, or reduced to an acceptable level for disposal. Research in this field suggests that the existence of working capital did not so much influence the decision whether to drop a product, as when to drop it (Hart, 1987).

Communization of parts, ingredients or raw materials

Where the elimination candidate shares either raw materials or parts used in the manufacture of another product, the need to drop is often reduced, since the disadvantages in holding stock for the elimination candidate are eclipsed by the fact that the stock will be held for other purposes. Indeed, this factor is not only related to 'the effect of the elimination on working capital', but also to 'the effect of the elimination on sales and profits of other products', as the cost base of two products manufactured from similar components will also be affected.

The effect of the deletion on fixed capital

Where capital equipment is used exclusively to produce a product which is being considered for elimination, that equipment has to be redeployed, written off or sold. The specific circumstances of the company may well prohibit any of those options, leaving management in a position where it 'might as well' continue with the product. As with shared working capital, where two products share plant or machinery, the proposed deletion of one product may adversely affect the other. A large confectionery company in the UK has experienced problems in this regard because one manufacturing line was dedicated to three distinct brands. One brand had already been dropped due to sluggish sales, but they could not drop a second candidate, as this would precipitate the withdrawal of the third, relatively successful line. The effect of deleting a product, leaving machines and buildings under-utilized, is even more severe in times of recession, where firms are operating below capacity.

The effect of the deletion on capacity utilization

While this is related to the issue discussed above, where a company is working below capacity, the normal benefits of dropping a product (cost saving, reallocation of resources) are unlikely to be felt. This is because there is no overload in any part of the operation which would benefit from redeployment and few cost savings can be made on idle plant. Thus, the incentive to drop a product is vastly reduced.

The effect of the deletion on employment prospects for the workforce

Dropping a product often entails a good deal of disruption for the company's employees, which can serve to discourage product withdrawal.

The availability of a new product

The nine internal evaluation factors discussed so far postulate on the commercial and operational context of the firm where a 'gap' might be left due to the proposed elimination. These issues are often less important where a substitution or new product is envisaged. For example, an important evaluation factor is the effect of an elimination on the recovery of overheads. However, the defrayal of overheads can be sustained at previous levels where a replacement product is available. In studies, companies with various product ranges have been shown to defer the deletion of a weak product until a replacement is necessary, as they would have too little to sell in the interim.

The availability of a new product tends to dissipate, to some extent, the concern for recovery of overheads, sales and profits of other products in the company's range, maintenance of overall volume, fixed and working capital, capacity utilization and so on, since a new product would fill the gap left by the deleted product. Complete relief from such concerns would depend on how well the new product performed.

Opportunity cost factors

The final internal factors relate to the opportunity cost of supporting an elimination candidate in the range. Specifically, the reallocation of resources and sales or executive time are important criteria for evaluating elimination candidates. Where resources or executive personnel can be transferred, the decision to eliminate is made more easily, as the potential benefits of deletion are more obvious to everyone concerned. This said, although theoretically and logically sound, the argument can be difficult to quantify or prove in practice (Hart, 1987).

The foregoing discussion highlights the fact that the 12 internal evaluation factors listed in Table 18.5 are interrelated. A reduced product range affects both sides of the profit equation – income generated and costs incurred. Lost revenue and profit is rarely complemented by a corresponding drop in manufacturing and marketing expenditure. These sensitive issues are further complicated by insufficient information about the cost structure of the entire range, which in turn perpetuates faith in volume as a solution to business problems. The most certain route for a deletion to take is through product replacement. By assuming the cost burden of the deleted product, the replacement alleviates, to some extent, managerial concern for the company's cost structure. It also presents a clear opportunity to which resources and executive time may be reallocated. These are, however, somewhat introspective concerns.

The remaining (external) evaluation factors are used by management to gauge the impact that a proposed deletion will have on the marketplace.

External evaluation factors

The effect of the deletion on customer/trade relations

This factor is deemed important for various reasons. First, a marginal product may well support business with a customer placing valuable orders that the company does not want to lose. Second, a customer may be dependent upon a marginal product, which creates a complication when the product becomes a candidate for eliminator. In most cases, it is important to reduce the inconvenience caused to customers; often this is done by granting the condemned product a stay of execution. Third, even where products are replaced by new ones, the views and needs of customers and the trade may be accommodated, for example in scheduling decisions.

Existence of substitutes to satisfy the customer

Even when management has decided to forego sales of its own products with a customer, it may be reluctant to finalize the decision, where no other substitute product is available in the market.

The effect of the deletion on 'full range' policy

If a company is serious about serving the needs of a market, then it should carry a wide selection of related products. For example, major companies in the home laundry business need to sell washing machines and dryers, so theoretically, at least, they would accept a less profitable situation on tumble dryers than on another product range that stood on its own, because of the need for tumble dryers as part of the home laundry range.

Hart (1987) reports numerous examples of this – the cake range of a national bakery being incomplete without Swiss Rolls and the carpet manufacturers who must have a red carpet in their range.

The effect of the deletion on distribution

The increasing competition for space in the supermarket is a major preoccupation of manufacturing companies, which, if serious about reaching the majority of consumers, have to be listed by the major multiples. Once listed, maintaining shelf space is of major concern, as it is indirectly related to sales turnover. The General Manager of a large company manufacturing instant foods and beverages highlighted these concerns, relating them to the product deletion decision.

The question of the implications for the company's shelf space is also linked to an issue mentioned earlier, namely loss of overall sales volume. If a company withdraws a product, and shelf space diminishes accordingly, a loss in overall sales volume will ensue.

The product's market potential

One of the most powerful evaluation factors is the market potential that management believes the product has. Indeed, the dairy company mentioned earlier kept a low-volume product in the market for 20 years, such was its commitment to the product-market and its belief that the product had potential. Exactly what engenders this commitment is situation-specific. Hart (1987) cites examples such as belief in market growth potential, competitive positioning in a smaller market or the need to maintain a presence in a particular sector.

The competitive reaction to withdrawal

Even when a product is performing poorly, the prospect of competitive products taking over seems to hinder the decision. In accounting for this reluctance, respondents have expressed an unwillingness to open a gap in the market which might be filled – perhaps more successfully by competitive products.

The effect of the deletion on company image

A company's market position is usually related not only to the total package it offers the customer, but also to the customer's perception of that package. Also, where a company's identity is typified by a product or product ranges, the emphasis tends to be towards development and replacement. This said, such 'typical' products are also usually central to the financial health of the company. One can hardly imagine Hoover deleting the upright vacuum cleaner from their product portfolio!

There is a huge breadth and complexity of issues that concern managers faced with the choice between dropping or retaining an elimination candidate. Not all factors, however, are equally important, nor do all of them have to be considered on every occasion. The number and nature of factors evaluated and the extent of the evaluation are subject to many influences which are touched on in the next paragraph. In addition, research shows little evidence to suggest a formalized evaluation procedure of the type expounded by normative theory (Hart 1987). Hart reports no tabulations, weightings or ratings of factors, no index of product desirability produced to aid the decision. This stage is characterized by a lack of knowledge and information and the subsequent reliance on managerial experience and judgment, which tends to suggest that a set of unwritten factors is evaluated, depending upon the specifics of the case at hand.

Summary

Many analytical, revitalization and evaluation factors are considered in concert. Consider, for example, the range problems facing a small manufacturer of fresh and frozen foods. The company produces 40 major ranges, with as many as six variants on each range. The smallest variants in each range are slow moving, less profitable than the fast-selling products, but not unprofitable. The company feels that its success lies partly in the breadth of the range of high quality foods, but also has ascertained that its slow-moving lines are perceived as being rather expensive. Costs are difficult to reduce further. The Marketing Director is convinced of the fact that as numbers of products increase arithmetically their associated problems increase geometrically, not only on the production line but also in the warehouse, in despatch vans and even in selling and pricing. Yet, a number of seemingly interrelated evaluation factors stop the MD from deleting products: loss of shelf space, loss of volume, competitive pressure.

The structure of the market where the company operates and the nature of its marketing operation are such that the maintenance of sales volume is related, as explained above, to the maintenance of shelf space, which in turn becomes vulnerable if the competitors have more products available to encroach upon the space. Thus, the three factors act synergetically to impose a set of constraints on the company more powerful than they might appear individually. Similarly, the 'recovery of overheads' and 'profitability of other products in the range' figure jointly, since the removal of a product which might adversely affect overhead recovery might well adversely affect the profits of the remaining products. Thus, right from the initial analyses of why lines are slow-moving, through the realization that little can be done to solve the problems, the potential to delete the product is slim. These decision-reaching stages are inter-related and complex.

This chapter has described this process in detail and has explained a complicated set of inter-related stages in the decision to delete a product. The final decision requires finely tuned judgment based on the fullest availability of the facts. There seems to be, as discussed at the beginning of this chapter, a reluctance to grasp the nettle, and considering the breadth of the impact a deletion may have, this is hardly surprising.

The next chapter describes the steps involved in implementing the decision, once taken.

QUESTIONS

1. Explain how deletion candidates come to the attention of managers.
2. What is the role of minimum standards in the recognition of deletion candidates?
3. What are the main ways to analyze a product suffering from shrinking profits?
4. What are the main ways to revitalize a product suffering from low sales volume?
5. What are the main reasons for keeping a failing product in the range?

Mini-case ● Hebden plc

Introduction

Hebden plc is a Strategic Business Unit within a large food processing firm, which bakes two broad ranges (or brands) of cakes. One brand, the Hebden Bakery, includes whole sponge cakes, whole and small swiss rolls, small fancy cakes, and sponge slabs. The second brand, 'Ma Hebden's', includes large tarts, small tarts, large and small fruit pies and fruit fingers. The first range of cakes and sponges is the older of the two brands. It enjoys healthy market share, but demand is decreasing for sponge-type cakes and the baking facility is inefficient. In the 'tarts and pies' market, Ma Hebden is not so well established, but the range of tarts and pies sell steadily and, importantly, profitably.

In the bakery business single items are constantly being deleted from the range. For example, 'white chocolate swiss rolls' have recently been replaced by milk and dark chocolate swiss rolls. There is no implication for capital equipment with such a switch, as it continues to be used. Similarly, in tarts and pies, products can be dropped quite easily, either by changing the ingredients, such as pie fillings, or by increasing volume production on mainstream items, such as apple pie.

Recently, however, problems have arisen in the chocolate sponge-cake sector, where production inefficiencies are causing product quality to vary and profit levels to fluctuate. In addition, the 'dry' sponge cake sector is coming under increasing competitive pressure from the frozen chocolate cake sector and is deemed now to be in long-term decline.

Deletion proposal

Jack Hebden, who started the company 40 years ago, is still on the Board as the firm's MD, but at a recent meeting the case for deleting the chocolate sponge cake range was put by the financial director.

Reasons forwarded to support the case for deletion were:

- Decrease in profit from the production line of five percentage points in two years.
- Downward trend over five years in sales volume (although in 1996/97 sales had increased).
- The sales turnover of £750,000 represented less than 10% of the company's sales.
- Competitor activity in the frozen chocolate market was eroding sales. Also in the non-frozen sector, research showed their products to be less well received by customers.
- Market perception of the product was low in product tests.
- A deletion would create slack with which to develop new products for the next century.

Against this case, however, Jack Hebden cited the following problems:

- Any substantial baker must be seen to have a chocolate sponge.
- Supermarket shelf space would be lost if the product were deleted, leaving a gap for competitors.
- Profitability of the remaining products would fall as extra overheads would be allocated to them.
- There were no substitutes at present.
- Deletion will adversely affect the company's image, with both the grocery trade and the consumer.
- Deletion would have a detrimental affect on morale.

As a result of the discussion, a full analysis was required in order to take a decision at the next Board meeting.

Discussion questions

1. What information would the 'full analysis' require and how would this information be retrieved?

2. Evaluate the case 'for' and 'against' the deletion. What is your preferred course of action, and why?

chapter 19

Implementing the deletion decision

LEARNING OBJECTIVES

1. To review strategies used to implement deletion.

2. To review factors influencing choice of method of implementation.

3. To establish that implementing the decision is not a simple issue.

On completion of this chapter you will:

1. Understand the alternative ways to implement the decision to delete a product.

2. Be able to choose between the alternatives depending on the situation facing a product.

3. Appreciate the factors that influence the timing and method of the deletion implementation.

Introduction

The final chapter in this section deals with the way in which the decision to delete a product from the range might be implemented. Perhaps because this stage of the process is readily identified, partly because it involves doing rather than intellectualizing, relatively few authors have set out to tackle the problems and issues facing managers actively involved in the mechanics of deleting a product from its range. It is generally assumed that once the decision to delete a product has been made, the steps necessary to implement the decision are straightforward and can go ahead without delay or complication. This is not entirely the case. It is clear that a number of different methods of deleting a product exist, and that the choice of methods depends on a number of factors. The methods are referred to as 'implementation strategies' and the factors as 'implementation factors'. They are the subject of this penultimate chapter of the book.

How deletion decisions are implemented

Research has shown that there are five alternative methods of deleting the product: drop immediately, phase out immediately, run out, sell out, and drop from the standard

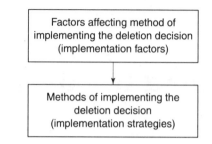

Figure 19.1 ● The implementation stage of the deletion decision

range – retaining the capacity. A number of factors influence managers' choices regarding which of the strategies is best suited to implement a specific decision, including whether or not there is a replacement waiting to be launched. This is depicted in Figure 19.1.

To understand this final stage of the deletion decision, it is important to understand both sets of issues. First, the actual strategies are described; second, the influencing factors are explained.

The implementation strategies

Drop immediately

Dropping immediately, rather evidently, is the fastest possible route to implementing a deletion. This involves immediately notifying the work force, the sales force and customers that the product is now no longer available and carries with it the need to write off stocks of raw materials and finished goods. It is, in fact, comparatively rarely used as it requires virtually no complicating factors to be present. Research suggests that only companies in the fast-moving consumer goods (FMCG) industry claim this as an option, since ingredients, pack stocks, manufacturing lines and workers can be interchangeable and resources can be used elsewhere. So, for example, where particular pack sizes or variations in flavour are being deleted, the manufacturing lines, the ingredients and personnel are transferred to the production of other items in the range. Where complicating factors arise, such as orders waiting for delivery, a high level of non-transferable stocks and dependent customers, this option only rarely makes business sense. If stocks of raw materials or finished goods were present, then another implementation option might be more appropriate. These and other factors are discussed later in the chapter. Where ramifications are few, fast-moving consumer goods companies can, where they want, drop products immediately. Where a decision is taken to delete a product of which there are stocks of finished goods, the 'drop immediately' option is favoured, with the last of the line being sold off as a promoted offer.

More often, however, the decision is taken to cease production, but wind down more slowly the selling of the product. This option for implementation is discussed next.

Phase out immediately

This implementation strategy differs from 'drop immediately' in that it allows for the run-down of finished goods and raw materials, parts or ingredients, and allows the option of satisfying orders received up until the decision day. In practice, research suggests this as the most favoured option among companies in all industries. As well as satisfying orders already placed, the simple matter of giving customers notice of withdrawal means that the product will be phased out immediately rather than simply dropped. The factors that impinge upon 'fixing a date' are examined later in the chapter. With the 'phase out immediately' option, a date is indeed fixed, which is not always the case with the third implementation option, namely 'run out'.

Run out (harvest/milk)

The run-out (also called harvesting or milking) strategy is mostly applicable to products which have enjoyed some success as fully mature products. It is rarely used with the 'failed new product'. In early normative writing on the implementation of a deletion decision, a run-out strategy implied changing the product's marketing strategy until a final date, in order to maximize profits (Talley, 1964; Weller, 1969). More recently, however, Avlonitis (1983) found that companies in the engineering sector can and do run out a product without significantly altering its market strategy. In Hart's (1987) study, a run-out strategy was also used with and without an alteration to a product's marketing strategy across all the major sections of manufacturing industry. In some situations products are maintained at a very low level – a typical, classic harvest strategy: no investment, no advertising, but continuation of production of a limited number of different versions and models of a product range, which command a good price from customers from which extra profits accrue. The end of the PLC profit curve, then, looks slightly different from the classical representation. This is shown in Figure 19.2.

The intention with this strategy is to reap as much benefit (in profit) as possible, before the product's sales become so low as to threaten its unit contribution. In other situations companies might delete outlying sizes and versions of a declining product before increasing the price on the remaining offerings. In this case, the pruning of the

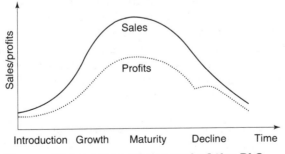

Figure 19.2 ● The profit increase of the end of the PLC

range is an attempt to improve overall sales volume by concentrating production on fewer lines. The success of this implementation strategy depends on having a core of committed customers who prefer the 'old' product to the new and alternative ones on the market. Even with this situation, however, the improvement in sales is likely to be only a temporary fluctuation, and the downward sales trend is usually expected to continue. The final effect of raising the price of the product is a usually more speedy if profitable demise (Hart, 1987). Further reasons for adopting a run-out strategy include keeping a presence in the market while a new product is being developed, allowing wholesalers or retailers to run down their stocks of a deletion candidate, and allowing customers to find alternative sources of supply.

So far, the options for implementing the deletion have really concentrated on timing. The next two procedures are more innovative ways in which managers deal with the difficulties that deletion presents to customers, suppliers and others who might depend on the deletion candidate.

Sell out

This option has a number of variants. The first is where the manufacturer sells finished stock to a dealer or another company in one batch, allowing them to maintain the product on the market for as long as stocks last. This option means foregoing the better margins that would be derived from selling directly to customers, but has the benefit of removing the manufacturer in time from the point where the product actually becomes unavailable. A second variation is where the manufacture of some deletion candidates is switched to another of the international parent group's subsidiaries. The advantage of this approach is that the company is immediately freed from the operation of making and selling the product, but dependent customers and suppliers are not left unsupported immediately. The third, more drastic variant on this theme is to sell the production capacity on to another company.

Drop the product from the standard range and re-introduce as a 'special'

The fifth and final implementation strategy was first described by Avlonitis (1983). This occurs where a company will manufacture a negotiated batch, provided the customer can wait and is willing to pay for a minimum batch quantity. The logic of this strategy is that customers dependent on the product are not left in any difficulty and the company can still make a profit from a product which is unprofitable if still produced and sold as part of 'normal' operations. Although this has traditionally been viewed as an option only in industrial markets, W H Smith recently used a similar tactic in de-listing its ostensibly pornographic titles. Instead of dropping them completely, desperate customers may still order titles like *Penthouse*, *Playboy*, *For Women*, *Mayfair* and *Video and Satellite World* (*Marketing Week*, 14 February 1997, p. 7).

Table 19.1 ● Use of various methods of deletion implementation

Strategy	Mean score[1]
Run out	3.5
Phase out immediately	2.9
Drop from the standard range	2.8
Drop immediately	2.2
Sell out	1.7

[1]Measured on a five-point scale where 1 = not at all frequently and 5 = very frequently.
Source: Hart (1987).

These five options, then, show that there are numerous considerations to be made before a product is actually put to bed. Over the years, there has been some debate in academic circles as to the most commonly used methods of deletion. Avlonitis (1983) contrasted his findings with those of Rothe (1971) and Eckels (1970), both of whom indicated that 'drop immediately' was the preferred implementation strategy. In the engineering sector Avlonitis did not find this to be a viable option and forwarded explanations which are based on the operating differences between consumer and industrial goods companies. Specifically, the differences are in the provision of spare parts, the existence of substitutes on the market and amounts of investment costs. Hart's (1987) research, which covered both industrial and consumer companies goods, suggested that 'drop immediately' is only an option for consumer goods companies in the sample, with the additional observation that by no means was it their *preferred* method. Indeed, of the 50 specific deletions she studied, only eight were dropped immediately. The most frequently cited option was 'phase out immediately' across *all* industry categories, while the run-out option was more frequently mentioned in industrial companies. This would suggest that where spare parts need to be provided, or fewer substitute products exist, or the unit value of and investment in a product is very high, the deletion time is longer. In a survey of 166 product deletions, Hart (1990) found that the run-out strategy was most frequently used, while 'sell out' was least frequently used. These findings are shown in Table 19.1.

Having looked at the number of ways to implement a deletion decision, attention is now turned to the major factors which influence the choice. These factors are called implementation factors.

The implementation factors

Implementation factors and strategies are so interrelated that it is difficult to deal with them separately. Indeed, it was suggested that one of the major differences between 'drop immediately' and 'phase out immediately' is really a question of the amount of stock on hand. Stock on hand is an example of what we refer to as an 'implementation factor'. Its effect is explained below, together with that of other implementation factors.

Stock on hand

Although a company may decide to drop a product, this does not mean that there are no remaining stocks associated with the product. Supplies of parts and ingredients as well as finished products all represent money and a decision has to be made regarding the implications on that money of dropping the product. Where raw material stocks are interchangeable, they can be transferred to another product, or to the (new) replacement product, if one exists. In dealing with stocks of raw materials, parts or ingredients, two options exist. Either management resolves to make more of the product to use up inventory, or it has to write it off. First, managers must establish the amount of stock in or awaiting production; usually, with ranges that are not selling, there is a lot of finished stock. Thus the estimation of pre-production stock will give an indication of how much longer the company has to go before all such stock is used up. It is rare also that all the pre-production stocks for a product are held in even quantities, so there may be enough stock of one of the ingredients or parts, but far less of another. In this case, additional costs incurred in either buying or making some of the parts in order to use up stocks of the other parts must be assessed.

Estimations of stocks of finished goods will be made in order to determine how long the market could be supplied with the deletion candidate. Again, managers must decide whether it is better to write off stocks of finished goods rather than sell them over a period of time. Here, in addition to financial implications of writing off the stock, are the marketing implications of either deleting a product forthwith or knowingly selling a product whose future is curtailed. Where finished stocks are available, these can, after a certain date, be sold off in a final promotion, with the proviso that selling off a discontinued product should not affect the sales of the replacement, or any other product in the range. In Hart's (1987) study, firms had fairly clear policy guidelines for stock write-offs. Up to a certain amount of write-off the decision could be made by middle managers, but higher levels of write-offs had to be sanctioned by top marketing and financial managers.

Residual demand

This factor is an important influence on the timing of a deletion. Where it is a consideration, a deletion is often postponed so that a certain amount of product can be produced for important customers still requiring it. Alternatively, assessment of the strength of the residual demand may encourage those strategies which increase profitability at the end of the PLC. Where a product is to be replaced, residual demand is thought to be satisfied by the availability of the new product. Specific strategies for replacement timing are dealt with later in the chapter.

The effect of the deletion on middlemen and customers

While the potential nuisances caused to middlemen and customers are reviewed at the evaluation stage, minimizing the nuisance has to be handled at the implementation stage, which affects the timing. At the most extreme, this can involve indeterminately deferring the deletion until agreement can be reached. Given the importance of key customers in business to business markets, this is a vital ingredient in a successful, long-term relationship. However, in many cases customers and middlemen receive notice of the company's intention to delete a range of products. Many companies are at pains to manage the communication process carefully, through their local sales contact. It helps the implementation to decentralize the announcement, rather than an order appearing from headquarters. It is important to tell the customer in advance of the discontinuation and ask them for documentary evidence of their requirement to balance the stocks.

The notification of customers/middlemen is a complicated issue. Pre-notification of the company's intentions may have an adverse affect on sales of the product. It may be important to distinguish between large and small customers to avoid upsetting key accounts. On the other hand, telling customers in advance may inevitably provoke an argument, particularly if the deletion is likely to affect their operation substantially. One approach to this problem may be to differentiate between crucial and less crucial customers, but this involves confidentiality agreements to ensure that plans are known only to those customers the company wishes to inform. Hart's (1987) study showed that companies deleting products always run the risk of provoking arguments with pre-notification. Another solution, where a replacement product is planned, involves the smooth management of scheduling the deletion with the availability of the new product, which is discussed below.

In FMCG companies, however, where products are stocked by the retail trade, this issue of 'inconveniencing' the channel of distribution is much less problematic. Due to the intense competition for shelf space and the sophisticated methods of tracking product sales volumes, it is more likely that the retailer will delete the product for the manufacturer than the other way round.

The availability of a new product

Where companies plan to replace the deletion candidate with a new product, the availability of the new product and the timing of its launch are instrumental to the deletion schedule. The availability of a new product is of major concern when scheduling withdrawal of products. The timetabling of the new product launch is itself influenced by the stock availability of the old one. It is important not to allow a 'gap' between the old and new product to occur, a subject covered by Saunders and Jobber (1988).

In their research, these authors reported that the most common replacement strategy was to use 'parallel marketing', a period of time which lasted, in the sample of companies they researched, between one month and longer than one year! Most often, the reason behind this approach was the existence of finished stock of the old product.

In a more recent study (Saunders and Jobber, 1994), they shared a range of 'phasing strategies', together with examples, which are reproduced in Figure 19.3.

Where a new product is an improvement on the old, there can be resistance. One method of overcoming resistance to new products involves a change in pricing strategy, to make the new product compare attractively with the old, or, as is more usual, to concentrate on the benefits offered by the new one. In short, there are two distinct changes in pricing strategy associated with the phase-in/phase-out operation. The first is a

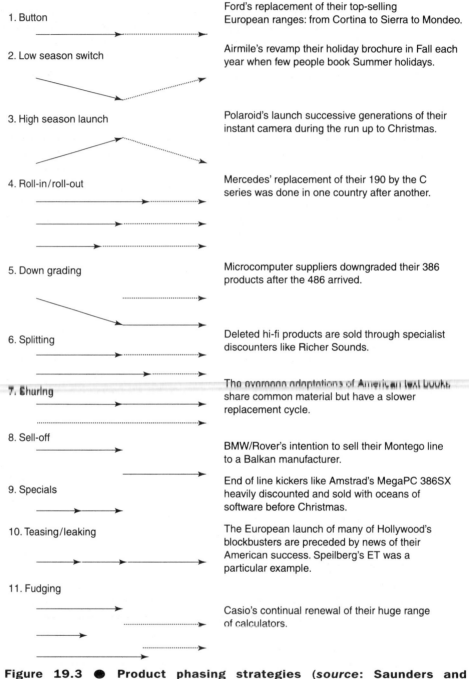

1. Button

Ford's replacement of their top-selling European ranges: from Cortina to Sierra to Mondeo.

2. Low season switch

Airmile's revamp their holiday brochure in Fall each year when few people book Summer holidays.

3. High season launch

Polaroid's launch successive generations of their instant camera during the run up to Christmas.

4. Roll-in/roll-out

Mercedes' replacement of their 190 by the C series was done in one country after another.

5. Down grading

Microcomputer suppliers downgraded their 386 products after the 486 arrived.

6. Splitting

Deleted hi-fi products are sold through specialist discounters like Richer Sounds.

7. Sharing

The overseas adaptations of American text books share common material but have a slower replacement cycle.

8. Sell-off

BMW/Rover's intention to sell their Montego line to a Balkan manufacturer.

9. Specials

End of line kickers like Amstrad's MegaPC 386SX heavily discounted and sold with oceans of software before Christmas.

10. Teasing/leaking

The European launch of many of Hollywood's blockbusters are preceded by news of their American success. Speilberg's ET was a particular example.

11. Fudging

Casio's continual renewal of their huge range of calculators.

Figure 19.3 ● Product phasing strategies (*source*: Saunders and Jobber, 1994, p. 437)

decrease in the price of the old product, to empty warehouses and the distribution chain of finished goods. This is used where it is felt necessary not to have both old and new products on the market simultaneously. The second is an increase in price, not only to profit from the declining product where people insisted on buying it, but also to help the launch of the new product through diminishing the price difference.

Seasonality

Where products are subject to seasonal fluctuations in volume, it is often easier to eliminate them during the low-volume season. Seasonality is an important implementation factor. Manufacturers of hot beverages will eliminate a product during the summer, as 'tea is more easily disposed of in the summer'. Alternatively, companies may wait for a commercial 'event' which makes it easier to drop the product in question – the publication of a new price list, for example. It should be mentioned, however, that seasonality factors also influence the timing of the introduction of a new or replacement product and, thereby, the deletion also.

The salvage value of machinery and equipment

Disposing of plant and machinery as painlessly as possible, by either selling or reusing it, is a major consideration which impinges upon the scheduling of a withdrawal. This factor is important to companies that, through shedding a product-line, shed an entire manufacturing unit as well. Time may be needed to sell off the constituent parts of the manufacturing facility, during which managers have to decide whether to keep the facility working.

Time required to shift resources

This implementation factor differs from the previous one in that a decision *has* been taken to reallocate certain resources and the time delay merely represents the logistics of the changeover. Obviously the time required to transfer resources is affected by matters already discussed, such as the amount of spare parts or finished stocks as well as the time needed to prepare for the manufacture of the product to which the resources will be transferred.

The status of replacement parts

The manufacture of components for future service and replacement is an influence on the timing of a deletion. Estimating future replacement demand is handled in two ways: asking customers about their likely future requirements, and historical service and breakdown reports. Many companies have a 'parts policy', where they guarantee to provide for a number of years after the discontinuation.

Finally, it is interesting to muse over the entire implementation process which combines the factors and strategies, to see how the companies arrive at their choice of implementation. In Hart's (1987) study half of the sample companies constructed a plan to guide them through the pitfalls of dropping the product. In some cases, such plans were quite extensive, with the rationale for the deletion committed to paper. In contrast to previous stages in the decision, where virtually no written guidelines are used, the implementation stage stands out as being structured and ordered in most cases.

As previously stated, the implementation stage is the least well documented of all the stages in the deletion process. This said, more has been written about the 'factors' than the strategies. Going back 30 years, the need for considering 'the status of replacement parts', 'stock' and 'holdover (residual) demand' were identified (Alexander, 1964; Kotler, 1965). More recently, research studies have uncovered the breadth of factors which impinge upon the choice of implementation strategy. More specifically, Avlonitis (1983) found that 'holdover (residual) demand', 'stock on hand', 'replacement parts', 'effect on middlemen/customers' and 'replacement product development' affected the timing of the decision.

The nature of the implementation factors that prevailed in Hart's (1990) study seemed in some cases to vary, depending on the industry. The status of replacement parts was not considered by any companies manufacturing fast-moving consumer goods, since, as might well be expected, the need to hold replacement stock does not exist. 'Residual demand' was again of less concern to FMCG companies, as was 'new product availability'.

Overall, the most important factor influencing the timing is 'stock on hand' and the least important is 'salvage value of plant'. Their relative importance is shown in Table 19.2.

The specific method chosen to implement a deletion decision, then, depends on a number of internal and external factors, specific to each case. Unlike previous stages in the deletion decision, Hart (1987) found that written guidelines existed in many companies, including simple checklists and sophisticated flow diagrams. However, the study also showed that despite the existence of these guidelines products which had been consigned to the implementation stage of the deletion processes were still waiting to be deleted, sometimes years later.

Table 19.2 ● Relative importance of implementation factors

Implementation factor	Mean score[1]
Stock on hand	3.6
Residual demand	3.1
Effect on middlemen and customers	3.0
Availability of a replacement	3.0
Status of replacement parts	2.1
Time required to shift resources	2.1
Seasonal issues	1.7
Salvage value of plant	1.7

[1]Measured as in Table 19.1.
Source: Hart (1987).

Summary

This chapter has reviewed how companies go about implementing a decision to delete a product, once the deletion has been decided. Although analysis and delay are easily understood in the earlier phases, further delays at the stage of implementation are, on the face of it, more difficult to explain. The discussion in this chapter, however, has shown that even once the decision to delete has been taken firmly, there remain a number of issues which may cause further delay. These issues may relate to customers, to resources and to suppliers, and are therefore important. However, the evidence available suggests that the whole implementation phase is not typically characterized by detailed plans and procedures. This is in stark contrast to the implementation of new product decisions – the launch – where the implications for the company may be more apparent and immediate. While it might be overly mechanistic to call for a full plan similar to those used for product launch, if the decision has been taken after full consideration, it is in the interests of the company, its suppliers and customers to plan the execution of the deletion in a more explicit way.

QUESTIONS

1. Explain why 'drop immediately' is an option preferred in Fast Moving Consumer Goods.

2. What is the difference between phase-out immediately and phase-out slowly?

3. What customer-related factors might legitimately delay the deletion of a product?

4. How might the interests of a supplier affect the method and/or timing of a decision?

5 What are the various options available for phasing out an old product in favour of its replacement?

Mini-case ● Link Europe PLC

In July 1997, Keith Ray has to begin to write a plan for the replacement of two products in the category for which he is responsible. This task provides several difficulties, and as a relatively new appointee, he is unsure how to deal with the problem. Formerly, Keith Ray was a top salesman of these products in the UK, but was promoted to the position of market manager for the product category for the whole of Western Europe.

The problem in hand is how to co-ordinate the phase-in/phase-out of old and new products. The products in question are ceiling-mounted electronic air cleaners, known as 'Indoor Air Quality' (AIQ) products. The G77 model is the larger of the two units and is suited for cleaning air spaces of between 200 and 450 square metres. The smaller G78 is suitable for spaces of between 100 and 250 square metres. The new products were considered to improve upon quality and reliability. However, these new products will not be available from the R&D department until January 1997, which is halfway through the 1996/97 season. This implies certain delete/launch problems. Specifically, any new product to be introduced into this market should be timed for September. This is to allow distributors time to order products for the beginning of the season, from October–November to March–April. In the current instance, if distributors are to have the product in January 1997, then the sales managers need to have *committed* orders by June or July at the latest, because production batches will only be run to sufficient orders, and this requires a lead time of between 18 and 24 weeks. Clearly, if distributors are encouraged to place orders for a new product, they are unlikely to place orders for the old one for the first half of the season, leaving Link with a considerable gap in their early-season sales, a gap which may well be filled by competitors' products. A further problem is that the major competitor is expected to launch a new product range into this market in August 1997. The second major competitor is expected to launch its new products in November 1997.

Keith's job is now to decide on when and how to launch the new products, and if, when and how to delete the old products. In particular, he has to consider whether or not to launch the product at the annual exhibition of air cleaning and conditioning products in Paris, in September 1997, even if the products are not ready for delivery then.

Link Europe – the company

There are three major divisions in the company: computer products, industrial components and residential products. The indoor air cleaners belong to the residential division along with domestic heating equipment and components, and comfort control systems and controls. Various factories exist throughout Europe; the indoor air cleaners are manufactured at the Welsh plant.

The sales and marketing for all the residential products is headed by Ms Françoise Lefèvre, who is located at European HQ in Amsterdam. Reporting to her are 10 sales affiliates, each with an affiliate manager and an Indoor Air Quality (IAQ) sales manager. Keith, although located in Wales at the plant, also reports to Françoise, and is responsible for decisions involving the Indoor Air Quality (IAQ) products.

Products

The basic function of the products in this category is to draw dirty air into the unit by means of an electric fan, and by passing it through an ionizer, remove its impurities.

The features of Link's products are:

- washable air cleaning cells
- simple installation
- remote control operation (optional extra)
- low voltage (for easy wiring)
- infrared transmitter (optional extra)
- adjustments for speed and efficiency
- variable airflow controls.

Not all these features are unique to Link. The benefits of using these products are:

- lower heating costs (windows don't have to be open for 'fresh air')

- redecoration is needed less frequently
- improvement in the quality of air for employees and customers alike.

Markets

The markets for these products are still in a relatively early stage of development. Potentially, any buildings where people gather and cause the air to become polluted are potential customers for indoor air quality products. The main end-user sectors at the moment are hotels, cafés and restaurants (HORECA). A particularly strong sector in the UK is defined as public houses. These products could be used in hospitals, dental surgeries, hairdressers and offices (particularly those open to the public). Link has collected virtually no information on either the size of these segments or their willingness to buy such products. The direct customers, the distributors, stock air cleaning equipment, water coolers and air movement equipment. The last two are not manufactured by Link, but are included in the range of the main competitor, Eurostyle plc.

Link executives estimate their share of the European market to be around 26%, while Eurostyle's is thought to be around 18%. The next largest competitor is thought to account for around 14%, while the remaining market is shared among seven or eight smaller players.

Link's prices are between 35% and 40% more expensive than those of its two nearest competitors. The G77 sells at around £450 to distributors, while the G78 sells at around £350. Distributors will add around 40% (35%–50%) to their buying price for the end user. The new product price has not yet been finalized, but the objective of the development exercise was not so much to reduce the distributor's buying price as to increase the manufacturing margins and deliver a better product for the same price.

Demand for these products is highly seasonal with sales peaking in January–February. March sales figures are comparable to those of December.

Competition

The major competitor, Eurostyle, is a Belgian company, which, as well as making and marketing direct copies of the G77 and G78, also makes and markets a number of related models: a wall-mounted version, and desk-top ionizers, for example. Their principal strength is in Belgium and France. Information regarding their new product is scant, but one of Link's Belgian distributors has spoken to the product managers, Ms Shelagh Sproule, and information to hand suggests that while their new products improve upon the reliability of Link's current range, there is little in the way of any basic engineering modifications, although the outer shells have certainly been made more aesthetically pleasing. Their new products are expected to be launched in August 1996. In preparation for their new product launch, Eurostyle are running down stocks of their old products and, in so doing, have left themselves short of stocks, particularly with their distributors. Link sales managers have been quick to take maximum advantage from this. Early signs that Link salespeople have been able to read suggest that their distributors are happier with the new product, and that Eurostyle's strategy is to concentrate entirely on the new range. The second major competitor, Cleanair plc, also manufactures and markets a couple of copies of the G77 and G78, as well as a series of smaller versions (wall, desk and free-standing models). Cleanair is based in Italy and operates on a pan-European basis.

Both these companies' existing products are generally reckoned to be poorer in quality than Link's products. In particular, options such as the infrared control and variable speed settings are not available. This said, in some circles the greater noise level of the G77 and G78 – which is due to superior power – has been mistaken for inferior quality.

Distribution

The products are sold to the end user through distributors who are not *uniquely* involved with Link's products. The distributors themselves tend not to hold large stocks, but Link will run batches to meet a number of 'committed' orders. At the beginning of the season, however, distributors will usually carry more stocks.

Where distributors decide to change from one supplier to another, it is generally for a whole season.

Promotion in the industry

Promotion is generally directed at the distributors in this industry. These take the form of volume discounts, or offering the service of free installation for the end user. Recently Link has been experimenting with tear-off coupons in hotel and catering trade magazines in the UK, featuring the distributors' names. Little is known of competitive promotion, other than offering volume discounts.

Some joint advertising, mail shots and exhibition attendance is supported 50-60 by Link and major distributors.

Product development

Link's venture into the European market for air cleaners started off on the wrong footing. Product quality was spotty, and compared to the competition there has been a consistent lack of variation in models and sizes which could help expand the customer base. The existing products are therefore to be replaced for a number of internal and market reasons. Internally, they are not efficient to produce. Manufacturing costs are unacceptably high, production technology is outdated and the resultant product is expensive with low margins. In addition, the company felt that the products suffered from quality problems and this has been substantiated by conversion with both key affiliates and distributors throughout Europe. The new products have an identical function to the old products, and very similar format. Production technology is improved, resulting in zero defect production. (By zero defects, Link means that no complaints would come back from the market via the customary product trouble report.) The products are quieter and more reliable in use. Due to the low level of penetration of this market, the company hopes to use the new products as tools for expanding the market. This will involve a campaign to generate high awareness of the benefits the product can bring. The new products are to be positioned as the only (or best) electronic air cleaners.

With the replacement of the two basic units, management hopes to lay the strong foundation for a slow expansion of the number of products and the ensuing expansion of the customer base. The existing products did the job of getting the company into the market, but will not serve as core, state-of-the-art products that provide a springboard for other products in the family.

Managerial commitment to the new products is strong. Central management supports the initiative, although levels of support are not uniform throughout all European countries. In general, however, the decision to revamp the product range represents a new commitment to the product category, witnessed by the commitment of financial resources to the project, together with the appointment of Keith, the market manager and Shelagh, the product manager.

Deletion/replacement issues

Now Keith Ray has to decide on the next step. The new product will not be available until January 1997, leaving only four months of the season in which to maximize launch efforts. Delaying the launch date until the following September is a high-risk strategy, given the intentions of the two major competitors. Postponing the Link launch gives competitors a 12 to 18 month start with their new product. However a January launch carries with it certain important implications which need to be considered. The implications are derived from both internal and external factors.

External implications

1. It is understood that IAQ sales managers need to have committed orders for the new product by July/August at the latest, if the first production batches are to be ready for the launch date.

2. If distributors are encouraged to place orders for the new range during the summer months, they are unlikely to want to continue to place orders for the old range to meet the first half season sales. This could potentially create a gap in the market that could be filled by competitors' improved ranges, resulting in a loss in market share for Link. (This is happening to Eurostyle in April 1995, prior to their August launch.)

3. Alternatively, it is likely to be a difficult selling proposition to secure commitment for a new product halfway through the season.

4. The launch of the new product is planned to be pan-European, a substantial operation. Disposal of the old range has the potential to divert managerial attention from this major – and important – task.

5. There are undoubtedly European distributors who are significantly more important to Link in this market than others. Their support and goodwill will be vital to the success of the new product.

6. Such forecasts that are currently available for 1996 show an increase in sales that does not take into consideration the fact that 1997 sales will come from the new range. It is reasonable to assume, therefore, that once figures take new developments into account, sales targets for the new ranges will exceed current forecasts. Again, this emphasizes the importance of a strong and successful launch.

7. The affiliate managers and IAQ sales managers must be encouraged to sell the new

product actively to distributors. Apart from the opportunity for increasing sales, the affiliates are not *obliged* to sell the new range.

This means, in turn, that the objectives and strategy for the smooth phase-in of the new range must be made apparent and attractive to them. The initial briefing date is set for early September.

Internal implications

1. Spare parts for the old product have to be available for five years after the deletion date. Their production has to be planned for – and executed – before or soon after the deletion.

2. Components and parts are not common between old and new ranges, which might have eased the complexities of service and maintenance on the old range.

3. The manufacturing/assembly lines that will be used for the new range are not entirely compatible with those for the old range, so there is limited opportunity for running the product simultaneously through the phase-in/phase-out period. That said, discussions to date suggest that this is not entirely impossible.

4. Provision of stocks at the factory is not encouraged at the end of the financial year, in December. However, the importance of this venture, together with the need to preserve some continuity, might allow an exception to be made on this occasion.

Given the foregoing analysis, it is vital that the implementation of the replacement be planned. The key issues are:

- The need to secure the affiliates' enthusiasm for and commitment to the new product range
- The need to secure forward orders from the distributors for the new range
- The need to preserve existing market share for the first half of the 1996/97 season, i.e. maximize continuity
- The need to minimize factory disruption during the phase-in/phase-out period.

Discussion questions

1. What are the advantages and disadvantages of pre-empting the competitive product launch, due in November 1996?

2. What options are available to Link in order to maximize the impact of the new product launch?

3. What factors should Link take into consideration in order to phase the withdrawal of the old products?

The information for this case was provided from private sources. Names are changed to preserve confidentiality.

chapter 20

Reprise

Introduction

There is an old maxim that says that teachers should first tell their students what they are going to tell them, then tell them, and finally tell them what they have told them. This final chapter is designed to meet the third of these requirements by providing a short résumé of some of the key features of the book. Its purpose is both to remind you of the concepts, ideas and information contained in the book and to reinforce what we consider are some of the key points you should have taken from your studies.

Before looking at the content of the individual chapters it will be useful to remind ourselves of the *perspective* as set out in Chapter 1. Our *objective* in writing the book was to offer a holistic discussion and explanation of product strategy and management (PSM). This objective was based on our view that whereas the product (or service) is central to the whole process of exchange, in recent years its importance has tended to be diluted by an emphasis on other elements of the marketing mix. Thus, in most marketing texts the 'product' is regarded as only one of the four P's or elements which go to make up the marketing mix and frequently the space given to it is less than that given to selling and promotion. Even in those books which do deal with product strategy and management in any detail, the emphasis tends to be largely on the process of new product development with little attention given to any other aspects. In the real world it is the day-to-day management of the product through its life cycle which is likely to be the primary concern of an organization.

In our view, product strategy lies at the very heart of the firm's overall strategy and must occupy a dominant, if not *the* dominant position in the firm's thoughts and actions. As such, knowledge and understanding of the nature and practice of product strategy and management is a necessary element in the development and formation of the professional manager. Indeed, issues related to product strategy and management are among the few which are common to the curricula of both engineers and business students. Similarly, the manufacture and sale of specific products is the usual training ground for new entrants to industry so that an understanding of PSM provides an invaluable foundation on which to build. This book was developed specifically to meet this need.

Structure

While we have taken a holistic view of product strategy and management, the subject falls naturally into four major parts which may be identified as:

1. The theoretical foundations.

2. New product development.

3. Product management.

4. Product elimination.

Part 1, The Theoretical Foundations, comprises five chapters which define, describe and analyze some of the main theoretical and practical considerations which underpin the practice of product management.

Part 2, New Product Development (NPD), contains seven chapters dealing with different aspects of the process by which ideas and market opportunities are brought together so as to enable new companies to enter or create markets and established companies to protect and enhance their competitive position. In this part, in common with numerous other books which concentrate solely on NPD, we trace the development of the new product from the original idea through to its launch into the marketplace. We regard the process of new product development as a period of *gestation* which precedes the life history of the product as conceptualized in the product life cycle (PLC). Conventionally, the PLC is seen as having four basic phases – introduction, growth, maturity and decline. It is the management of products or services through these life cycle phases that is central to all major marketing textbooks. However, as we have noted, the role of the product is often taken for granted with the emphasis given to other factors. In our experience, too, more emphasis tends to be given to the positive, early stages of the product life cycle than to those associated with decline and elimination. Given, as the PLC concept suggests, that the distribution of sales over a product's life involves the parameters of a normal distribution, it is clear that as much of a product's life is spent declining as it is in growing. On these grounds we have chosen to structure our discussion of product management into two main parts.

Part 3, Product Management, deals with commercialization, the management of growth and maturity; while Part 4, Product Elimination, deals with managing decline and the making and implementation of deletion decisions. We regard this as a distinctive feature of the book as it recognizes that declining products tend to have received little attention hitherto when it is clear that successful withdrawal strategies have a great deal to offer to the firm's overall success. The key features of the chapters which make up these four major parts may be summarized as follows.

Part 1 – The theoretical foundations

Chapter 2 – Competition and product strategy

A major objective of this chapter was to explain and justify our claim that product strategy and management lie at the very heart of business strategy and are critical to survival and competitive success.

To begin with, we reviewed the forces which have led to the emergence of global competition. Throughout recorded history the major challenge facing humankind has been an excess of demand over supply. To address this problem task specialization is an essential first step towards increased productivity. However, task specialization can only succeed given the existence of exchange and the market. Initially, exchange is local in character but becomes increasingly international as countries pursue the benefits associated with exploiting their comparative advantages.

Paradoxically, early efforts to increase supply through specialization and exchange resulted in increased demand due to exponential population growth based on improved standards of living. Inevitably, the emphasis has been on increasing production still further. It is only in this century that accelerating technological change has so enhanced productivity and output that supply has begun to catch up with demand. With the stabilization of population growth in the more advanced and affluent economies the balance of power between producer and consumer has moved increasingly in favour of the consumer. The result has been an enormous increase in competition domestically, nationally and internationally between producers, with the product/service as the focal point of this competition.

Competition as we know it today is the consequence of centuries of evolutionary change. The central theme of this book is that such evolutionary change proceeds in cycles, each of which is initiated by the introduction of an innovation or new product believed to offer greater benefits to users compared with the existing product which it seeks to replace. In essence, innovation is a process of substitution. To begin with, innovations make slow progress as most consumers buy from habit and are the victims of inertia. For them change represents risk. However, if an innovation does offer real benefits, people will switch to it in increased numbers, resulting in rapid growth until all persons with the need which the innovation satisfies have converted to it. This state of saturation or maturity will prevail until the next cycle of innovation occurs when sales of the new product will erode those of the existing product, leading to decline and eventual withdrawal. It is this cycle of change, central to the concept of a product life cycle, which provides structure for the book as a whole.

In competitive markets suppliers struggle or compete with one another for the customer's patronage. Invariably customers will act in pursuit of their own self-interest and so will buy from the supplier who offers them the best value for money. In devising a competitive product strategy two basic options exist – *cost leadership* and *differentiation*. Where the consumer is unable to distinguish between the offerings of competing suppliers then clearly they will prefer the one that offers the lowest price (cost leadership). Given that cost leadership is strongly associated with economies of scope and scale (especially in marketing) the inevitable consequence is that in undifferentiated markets the largest firms will always displace the small ones. To avoid this threat to their survival smaller firms must differentiate their product so that in the perception of the consumer it is seen to offer values not present in the undifferentiated product. The majority of smaller producers can only survive through such a strategy of differentiation whereby customers will be willing to pay higher prices for what they see as additional benefits. Innovation or new product development is seen as central to this process and accounts for the product or service being regarded as at the very heart of every successful competitive strategy.

Chapter 3 – The product in theory and practice

The key message contained in Chapter 2 is that competition is based on perceived differences between the offerings of competing suppliers. In Chapter 3 we looked at some of the foundations of the basis of these perceived differences which determine consumer demand. To begin with, we looked at a number of different kinds of demand – effective, latent and potential – and the factors which shape and influence these differences. All demand rests on the existence of a felt need. The stronger the need the more likely the individual or organization is to try to satisfy it. To satisfy a need the product or service must possess some minimal set of criteria or characteristics. It is these characteristics of the product which define the nature of the industry and so enable firms to identify their immediate competitors and devise strategies for out-manoeuvring and outperforming them. It follows that the classification of products is an essential first step in determining the nature of direct competition.

Classifying products inevitably raises the question as to whether physical and tangible objects can be regarded and dealt with in the same way as intangible services. A discussion of the features which are claimed to differentiate between products and services led us to the conclusion that, while there may be some important differences in degree, there are no important differences in kind. Most products and services contain elements of the other – air travel and banking (services) depend upon a very large array of physical objects for their delivery. Conversely, in the market for physical products such as earth-moving equipment or instant coffee, customers would not consider buying unless the product met those characteristics which defined the essence of the product itself. Inevitably, many physical products are essentially undifferentiated and the only way in which their producers may compete effectively is through the addition of service elements which add value to the basic product configuration.

Given that objective differences are easy to define and benchmark they are necessary but not sufficient conditions for effective competition. In today's increasingly competitive marketplaces, where objective advantages are easily eroded and imitated, service and reputation (branding) have assumed an increasingly important role in determining competitive outcomes. Clearly, it is vital that the producer should be able to find out what these subjective needs and characteristics are. In order to do so they need to understand the process by which intending buyers evaluate competitive offerings and the process followed in choosing between them. This was the subject of the next chapter.

Chapter 4 – Buyer behaviour

This chapter was based on the proposition that while products or services are the embodiment of all of the firm's inputs, which may be immensely important in determining the nature and characteristics of that product or service, in the final analysis success will be determined entirely by customers' buying behaviour. Accordingly, Chapter 4 looked first at some of the better known and accepted models of buyer behaviour. Consideration of these models led to three broad conclusions. First, a decision to buy is usually the outcome of a sequential process. Second, while some models claim to represent industrial or organizational buying behaviour and others deal with consumer behaviour, we do not find this distinction to be helpful. In fact, such a distinction may be positively harmful, for it can lead sellers to underestimate the ultimate consumer's ability to make judgments based on objective criteria, while in the case of industrial purchase decisions, undue emphasis upon 'the facts' can lead to a neglect of the subjective dimensions which are often critical when the buyer is seeking to choose between two or more evenly matched alternatives. Third, the models describe what we subsequently identified as a 'new buy' situation. In such circumstances the buyer will invest proportionately greater effort in identifying possible alternatives and evaluating them before coming to a decision. Once a buyer has been through the process for the first time they may well omit several of the stages so that repurchase becomes a habit or form of learned behaviour. Changing this learned behaviour is invariably more difficult than reinforcing it.

Discussion of models of buying behaviour also led to recognition of the importance of perception in influencing final choice decisions. To accommodate the influence of this intervening factor we proposed a simple composite model in which the phenomenon of selective perception was seen to determine what information is consciously attended to in the first place and also the interpretation which is placed upon that information. In accordance with rational principles buyers then seek to differentiate between closely competing alternatives on the basis of their performance characteristics and the cost benefits associated with acquiring them. Because performance characteristics and price are readily observed and quantified, competition results in the existence of products or service providers who are seen as close substitutes for one another. In order to distinguish between them our model proposes that the decision-maker will have to have further recourse to their selective perception and personal preferences to find a basis for preferring one supplier over another. This we identified as *behavioural response*.

Another important concept introduced into the chapter was that of perceived risk. Essentially, the more uncertainty that is associated with the purchase and the greater the extent of the potential loss if the decision proves to be a bad one, the higher the degree of perceived risk. The idea of perceived risk is also associated with that of involvement, with a distinction being made between high involvement and low involvement purchases. With high involvement purchases, such as the purchase of a piece of industrial equipment or a consumer durable, the intending buyer is likely to spend more time and give more effort to each of the stages in the buying process. Conversely, where the perceived risk is low – usually because the price is low – intending buyers will frequently purchase the product with little or no formal evaluation at all. Such behaviour, where one acts without much prior formal thought, usually occurs when the unit cost is very low and the claimed benefits are very much a matter of personal taste. One can only decide whether one likes a new food or beverage product through direct experience. As the cost of trial is usually very low one will purchase such a low involvement product without the need to form any formal attitude towards it prior to purchase.

Similarly, in cases which we identified as 'modified re-buys' and 'straight re-buys' little or no prior evaluation precedes purchase. From these observations we conclude that the launch of new products is intrinsically more complex and risky than when one is encouraging buyers to repeat purchase products with which they are already familiar. It was also recognized that some buyers are more risk averse or resistant to change than others, from which it follows that a sound understanding of buyer behaviour is an essential prerequisite for successful marketing. This proposition was then exemplified by an extended case study of the launch of aluminium sleeve bearings by the Aluminum Company of America.

Chapter 5 – The product life cycle in theory and practice

In this chapter we defined the product life cycle as 'a generalized model of the sales trend for a product class or category over a period of time, and of reflected changes in competitive behaviour'. Our earlier discussion of economic growth and development (Chapter 2) had underlined its evolutionary nature, and it was for this reason that we decided to adopt the PLC concept as the organizing principle for the book as a whole. In doing so we were conscious that the PLC, both concept and theory, had been widely challenged by many and rejected by some. Accordingly, our objectives in Chapter 5 were to define precisely what we understand to be the PLC concept, explain its use as an analytical framework, review and respond to criticisms, and suggest how the PLC may be operationalized and put into practice.

To begin with, we described the basic model of the PLC and its four stages of *introduction*, *growth*, *maturity* and *decline* which are analogous to the phases of the biological life cycle from which the concept is derived. We then suggested it would be helpful to 'stretch' the four-stage model to include an initial phase of *gestation*, a period of *saturation* between maturity and decline, and a final phase of *elimination* to mark the withdrawal of a product from the market. Each of these seven phases was then described in some detail.

From our discussion we concluded that the PLC reflects an inevitable cycle of change and the substitution of new ways of doing things for old. This perspective suggests that the PLC is essentially an analytical and planning tool. It is not a technique for forecasting. Most criticisms which have been levelled against the PLC have been on the grounds that it lacks the predictive utility necessary for a forecasting device. As we saw, this is unsurprising in that the same generalized biological life cycle, consisting of the various stages identified, may be used to describe the phases through which any living organism will pass without being able necessarily to tell you how long any of these phases are likely to last.

Our support for the PLC rests on the view that it defines the underlying process of growth and decay and so permits the isolation and possible use of factors which may accelerate or slow down different phases of the process. In other words, it provides us with a diagnostic and analytical framework that offers the opportunity to influence the cycle through managerial intervention.

While some critics of the concept have rejected it on the grounds that it ignores the possibility of managerial intervention, we believe that its real value lies in just that – the recognition that without mediation the process will proceed inexorably to an inevitable conclusion. Accordingly, we gave some attention to ways in which it is possible to operationalize the PLC so that it may be used in practice, as well as discussing possible deviant cases which do not conform with the general theory and so call for alternative treatments.

Chapter 6 – Product portfolios

This chapter started by recognizing that most textbooks describing normative theory take the perspective of the large multidivisional and multinational corporations. The reality is that most firms (more than 90%) employ less than 200 persons and operate on a quite different scale. Perhaps the greatest threat to small companies is that they are too dependent upon a single product and so may be faced with extinction if an improved product is brought to the marketplace which serves the same end-user needs. If follows that even the smallest company needs to pay careful attention to the creation of a *portfolio* of products to ensure its continued survival.

The desirability of a portfolio or range of different products is implicit in the concept of the product life cycle which emphasizes that, ultimately, all products and the technologies which underlie them will change. Analysis also indicates that as products proceed through their life cycle they encounter quite different market responses which in turn call for quite different marketing strategies. Initially, the future of new products is almost always uncertain as they seek to displace the established and accepted market favourites. Most potential competitors will prefer to sit on the fence and wait and see what happens to the pioneer. If it appears to be succeeding and generating increased demand, others will seek to exploit this growth opportunity and climb on the bandwagon. As we saw in Chapter 5, rapid growth is as much a consequence of changes on the supply side as on the demand side as firms jockey for position. The onset of maturity leads to a shaking out of the competition and much more stable market conditions under which the survivors are likely to cash in on their early investments. Inevitably the cycle begins to repeat itself, and as new products begin to win market share from old so sales of the old product go into decline.

It was in diagnosing the consequences of change through the product life cycle that the Boston Consulting Group came up with its concept of the product portfolio or 'Boston Box'. In identifying the differing market conditions and the threats and opportunities associated with them as the product moves through its life cycle, the key message to be taken from the BCG analysis is the need to have a number of products with each of them preferably at a different and complementary stage of its life cycle.

Like the PLC the Boston Box or growth–share matrix derived from it has been subjected to considerable criticism. We believe that it is both valuable and important because:

1. It reinforces the inevitability of change implicit in the PLC concepts.

2. It underlines the importance of having a portfolio of products at different stages of development.

3. It requires formal consideration of the competition and their relative standing.

4. It is intuitively appealing and simple to implement conceptually despite some of the difficulties of operationalizing it in practice.

Similar benefits were also seen to attach to other analytical frameworks, and Shell's directional policy matrix was described in some detail to reinforce this point.

Part 2 – new product development

Chapter 7 – The importance, nature and management of the new product development process

This chapter was the first in Part 2 in which we moved from the theoretical foundations into a detailed consideration of the manner in which new products are conceived, developed and brought to the marketplace.

The first part of the chapter outlined a number of new product development (NPD) models which have been identified through observation of actual practice. At least five different approaches can be identified, each of which seeks to provide a template or map that can be used to describe and guide the activities necessary to bring a new product from an idea or opportunity through to a successful market launch. These models were described and reviewed to assess their usefulness as a managerial action guide.

However, the management of the NPD process involves more than simply the number and sequencing of its activities so the second part of this chapter looked at other research findings to establish what other factors may have an impact upon the success or failure of the process. Based on content analysis, several key themes were identified as being crucial to success in new product development. These key themes – process, organizational structure, people, strategy, information and management – were analysed in some detail in order to draw some conclusions about their implications for managing the actual process. This topic comprised the third section of the chapter. In this we highlighted two recent attempts to remodel the process in such a way as to incorporate the lessons of research into success and failure. The first of these two attempts, the multiple convergent process model, is a normative model developed by the authors from their own experience, while the second, the quality function deployment model, was developed by engineers.

Both of these models recognize the need to have inputs from many different functions in a company, from manufacturing to R & D, marketing to purchasing, engineering to customers. Since the integration of these points must be managed, the chapter concluded by discussing some of the key structures used to organize NPD activities.

Chapter 8 – New product strategy

Chapter 8 picked up the themes discussed earlier in Chapters 2 and 6 that were concerned with the need for an overall strategy and the importance of product development within such a strategy. Similarly, in the previous chapter, the benefits of articulating a new product strategy were clearly linked directly to several of the critical success factors associated with NPD. Perhaps the single most compelling piece of evidence of the importance of having a formal new product strategy is to be seen in the findings of the two studies conducted by Booz, Allen and Hamilton in 1968 and 1980. In the 1968 study it was shown that it required 58 new product ideas to produce a single successful new product. Their second study revealed that this ratio had been reduced to 7:1, the only significant difference being the creation of a preliminary stage concerned with the formulation of explicit new product strategies which identified the strategic business requirements which new products should satisfy.

On the grounds that product strategy is concerned with the interaction between technologies and markets, it follows that new product strategy requires a sound understanding of both technological and market *newness*. These were considered in some detail, first separately and then together. Depending upon the degree of novelty to be addressed in terms of both market and technology, it is possible to suggest the magnitude of the endeavour and risk as well as the organizational issues which may be implied.

Chapter 9 – Idea management for new product development

In Booz, Allen and Hamilton's original conceptualization of the new product development process idea generation was the first stage. As we saw in the previous chapter, this activity will be both better structured and more focused given the existence of an explicit product strategy. It was for this reason that we entitled the chapter Idea Management rather than Idea Generation. In our view, the distinction is not trivial in the sense that the vast majority of ideas already exist and do not have to be conjured out of thin air by some such process as brainstorming. Our viewpoint is that if the ideas already exist then the challenge is to manage them. This chapter was about managing new ideas and involved two central themes: locating sources of new ideas and activating those sources.

Against this background the first part of the chapter was concerned with practical advice on identifying both external and internal sources of ideas and the steps necessary to activate these to produce a stream of new product ideas capable of future development. Numerous techniques are available for activating sources of information and it is the description of these which tends to dominate many other books on the subject. Our own review concentrated mainly on techniques for activating internal sources, as research has shown that these tend to be the most important sources of ideas. However, many of these internal ideas are stimulated by external events, particularly environmental and competitor analysis, so some consideration was given to external sources also. Overall, our analysis suggested that there is a constant paradox between pursuing creativity and delivering a new product which meets market needs. This paradox requires active attention and demands a consistent approach to managing creativity, which was the subject of the final part of this chapter.

Chapter 10 – Screening new product ideas

In this chapter we looked first at the reasons why screening is important and discussed the evaluation of risk in the context of the screening process. To begin with, it was stressed that given the iterative nature of the NPD process, 'screening' occurs at a number of stages but, as used in this book, screening is seen as the first of a series of evaluations, beginning when the collection of new product ideas is complete. In other words, we use 'screening' to describe the initial evaluation which is concerned primarily with identifying ideas which can be developed into concepts that may then be evaluated for their technical feasibility and market potential. Screening, as we describe it, is simply an initial assessment to weed out impractical ideas. It is most effectively executed where an explicit new product strategy is in place.

When screening new products two errors are to be avoided. First, one should not eliminate ideas which, if developed, would have been successful. Conversely, one should not continue to develop ideas that subsequently fail. While this may seem to be a 'blinding glimpse of the obvious' it highlights the importance of setting appropriate criteria in accordance with the degree of risk seen as acceptable within the product strategy. However, in contrast to other treatments of screening, it is contended that detailed, numerical approaches are inappropriate at this early stage in the process, where the information available is somewhat sketchy. A number of different approaches are discussed and we concluded that customizing screening to the strategic context of the firm is a sensible way to ensure effective screening.

Chapter 11 – Concept development and testing

This chapter focused on how ideas which have passed the screening stage are developed into more fully specified concepts which may be more fully evaluated in terms of their appeal to the potential market segments for which they are intended.

Concept development and testing is very much an iterative process. The first articulations of a new product concept are likely to be little more than an elaboration of the screened idea. Given the reactions of intended customers to this basic idea it may be further refined and focused before being subjected to further testing. While a number of different objectives may be explored in concept testing, the primary purpose remains to establish customer needs and preferences. At the early iterations, techniques such as perceptual mapping contribute to the initial concept positioning, whereas later iterations of concept testing involve research methods which assess purchase intent as well as the customers' preferred 'bundle of attributes'. Several techniques are discussed in detail, covering those applying to early and later iterations of concept testing.

Chapter 12 – Business analysis

Given the success of a concept test in terms of intending customers' likely reactions, the objective of this step in the NPD process is to estimate the costs and likely revenues from further development. Given that the concept test should have established the likely market profile, desired new product attributes, estimates of purchase intent and an estimate of market size, the information may be used to generate clear estimates about the likely product costs, production and design costs, market response and potential profitability.

To this end Chapter 12 identified the key components of a business analysis and the sources of information to be used. Inevitably, difficulties will be encountered in coming up with accurate estimates, but a review of Cooper's (1992) NewProd system indicated that a structured analysis was particularly successful in predicting successes although less so in terms of failures.

Chapter 13 – Product testing

Given a *go* decision from the business analysis the first priority is to develop a prototype to see whether this will work in the way intended by the design specification. Functional testing of this kind is at the very core of the NPD process. Once a working prototype has been developed then this must be product tested to ensure that it delivers the benefits identified at the concept testing stage. The emphasis in Chapter 13 was on this latter form of testing. The concepts of realism, sensitivity and validity were seen as being of primary importance in devising a product test and these were discussed in some detail. The techniques used for product testing are central to market research and have been subject to much evaluation as to their effectiveness.

Various techniques for product tests were described, making reference to the extensive body of empirical research. Finally, we looked at some special problems which may be encountered in testing industrial products.

Part 3 – product management

Chapter 14 – Commercialization: Test marketing and launching the new product

The chapter opened with a review of the advantages and disadvantages of test marketing through which one seeks to get a clearer understanding of likely market reaction to the new product and its marketing mix through a small-scale trial in a sub-market believed to be representative of the larger regional or national market.

While test marketing of this kind is frequently regarded as common practice in today's increasingly competitive marketplace, time to market has become a major issue and many new products move directly from the physical testing stage into the marketplace without benefit of the opportunities to test the marketing mix and the marketing plan on a small scale.

A discussion of time to market highlighted the importance of speeding up the development process. Equally important, however, is the launch itself and the achievement of rapid market penetration. It was concluded that rapid market penetration is highly correlated with being able to pre-identify good prospects early in the launch phase. Based on this observation, we then examined ways of identifying early adopters, first in terms of the new product's characteristics and then in terms of the innovativeness of individuals and organizations. Effective communication was seen to be key to the whole process and we reviewed some of the more salient aspects of effective communication.

Based upon a large number of case studies of new product launches it was concluded that given an intrinsically superior product or service, the difference between success and failure is very much a question of segmentation, targeting and positioning. A detailed study of the launch of Superplastic Aluminium shows clearly that a superior product is insufficient in itself to guarantee market success. Effective marketing planning and management is equally important.

Chapter 15 – Managing growth

This chapter looked first at some of the factors which inhibit or slow the initial development of a new product and their implications for management. To begin with, we identified sources of resistance to new products and then discussed methods of overcoming these. Particular emphasis was given to the importance of differentiation in order to persuade potential customers of the benefits to be gained by switching to or adopting the new product. In turn, this reinforced the point made in the previous chapter concerning the importance of targeting the market segments with the strongest potential need for the new product.

We argued that in some senses one may regard the emergent or introductory phase following the launch as a period of trial and error which will lead to the evolution of a design widely accepted by both producers and users. Given the pressures to bring products to market quickly it would seem that many producers, particularly the Japanese, take this approach. In any event, it is the emergence of a dominant design marking the end of the introductory phase and usually triggering rapid growth that sees a switch in emphasis from product development to process innovation.

Three broad alternative growth phase strategies were identified. One can adopt the first standard and compete head-on with the pioneer; one can attempt to develop a second standard, or one may identify potential niches and concentrate on getting into them first. Examples of all three strategies were described.

During the rapid growth phase increasing numbers of customers will be seeking to secure a supply of the new product while growing numbers of suppliers will be scrambling to cater to them. Market leaders will attempt to stay ahead of the game through further improvements in the product, while less innovative competitors seek to gain market share by discounting, offering lower prices for direct sale, and so on.

Chapter 16 – Managing the mature product

Inevitably the market for a new product will become saturated once every person with a need for it has decided to adopt it. As growth slows and the PLC moves into its mature phase there is usually a shake-out of the weaker competitors as the stronger ones consolidate their market position and share. As sales stabilize the only route to continued growth is through aggressive competition for market share, which results in a win–lose situation quite different from the win–win conditions of rapid growth. While margins may be better during the growth phase once a product enters maturity, more stable market shares and reduced marketing expenditures result in substantial positive cash flows – hence the Cash Cow. It is for this reason that much thought and effort has been devoted to the management of mature products. Indeed, the discussion to be found in most marketing management textbooks implicitly assumes that one is dealing with such a product and focuses on how to manipulate the marketing mix to best advantage. The effect of this concentration has been the prolonging of the mature stage of the PLC through the use of one or more of four basic strategies:

1. An offensive or take-off strategy.
2. A defensive strategy.
3. A recycling strategy.
4. A stretching and harvesting strategy.

Each of these was considered in some detail.

During the mature phase, with little or no potential for creating new customers, the importance of customer retention through relationship marketing becomes paramount. Active account management, product augmentation, enhanced services and better value for money through lower prices are also strategies which may be used to maintain and strengthen relationships.

Part 4 – product elimination

Chapter 17 – Controlling the product line: An overview of the deletion decision

This chapter was the first of three dealing with the decline phase of the product life cycle. In the authors' experience insufficient attention has been given to this less glamorous phase of product management than it deserves. Given that, by definition, 50% of a product's life cycle is spent in decline this is more than surprising. It was for this reason that we decided to treat product elimination as equally as important as product development and devote a complete part of the book to it.

To begin with, Chapter 17 examined the importance of the deletion decision in some detail, together with some of the reasons why such decisions are often avoided by management. Next, we explored some of the partial models that have been developed to deal with this phase of the life cycle as background to the development of our own model of the deletion decision. In addition to a number of refinements compared with earlier models, Hart's model differs from early work more radically in its identification of a set of 'triggers' for deletion which may occur independently of the type of systematic product performance reviews suggested in other models.

Chapter 18 – Reaching the decision to delete a product

This chapter picked up the theme introduced in the previous chapter in which candidates for product deletion were seen as being identifiable in one of the following ways:

1. When a crisis presents itself to management requiring immediate attention.
2. When formulation of strategic plans reveals a product ill suited to strategic objectives.
3. When an opportunity is spotted for enhancing company performance.
4. When a product falls below a level of performance acceptable to management.

Each of these four situations suggests a different context and therefore different criteria for analysis, evaluation and decision. These were discussed in some detail as a basis for explaining how deletion candidates can be analyzed and possibly revitalized. The chapter considers the ways in which deletion candidates are identified by managers, using a number of 'review criteria'. It then describes how such candidates are analyzed, to determine why they have become deletion candidates and whether they have the potential to be revitalized. Finally, where it is deemed that the product cannot be revitalized, 15 'evaluation factors' are described, which are used to determine whether the product should in fact be dropped, given the impact of its deletion on the company as a whole.

Chapter 19 – Implementing the deletion decision

Because implementation involves doing rather than intellectualizing, relatively few authors have set out to tackle the problems and issues facing managers actively involved in the mechanics of deleting a product from its range. Chapter 19 sets out to address this issue and recognizes that there are a number of different methods of deleting a product: drop immediately, phase out immediately, run out, sell out, or drop from the standard range while retaining the capacity. Each of these was discussed in turn.

Consideration of the alternatives available prompted a discussion of the major factors which influence the decision-maker's choice – the 'implementation' factors.

In conclusion, we suggest that planning the deletion decision deserves as much care and attention as does the development and launch of new products. And so we have come full circle. Having identified why the product or service is at the very heart of the exchange process, the raison d'être of the company's existence and the essential source of customer satisfaction, we have traced the product through its life cycle. From recognition of the need for product strategy to guide and give direction to the firm's future survival we have explored in detail the processes of new product development, product management, and the usually neglected field of product elimination. In doing so we believe we have achieved the objective we set ourselves of a holistic treatment of product strategy and management. We hope you agree!

Bibliography

Acito, F. and Hustad, T.P. (1981) Industrial product concept testing. *Industrial Marketing Management*, **10**: 157–64.

Alexander, R.S. (1964) The death and burial of 'sick' products. *Journal of Marketing*, **28,** April.

Allen, T.J. (1985) *Managing the Flow of Technology*. Cambridge, MA: MIT Press.

Ansoff, H.I. (1957) Strategies for diversification. *Harvard Business Review*, Sept–Oct.

Ansoff, H.I. (1965) *Corporate Strategy*. New York: McGraw-Hill. (1968: Harmondsworth: Pelican).

Artingstall, R. (1980) New product development. Supplement to MRS *Newsletter*, no. 168, March.

Avlonitis, G.J. (1980) An exploratory investigation of the product elimination decision-making process in the UK engineering industry. Unpublished PhD thesis, University of Strathclyde.

Avlonitis, G.J. (1983) Product elimination: decision and strategies. *Industrial Marketing Management*, **12**.

Avlonitis, G.J. (1984) Industrial product elimination: major factors to consider. *Industrial Marketing Management*, **13**, May.

Avlonitis, G.J. (1985) Revitalising weak industrial products. *Industrial Marketing Management*, **14**, May.

Avlonitis, G.J. and James, B.G. (1982) Some dangerous axioms of product elimination decision-making. *European Journal of Marketing*, **16** (1).

Baker, M.J. (1975) *Marketing New Industrial Products*. London: Macmillan.

Baker, M.J. (1980) Maxims for marketing in the eighties. *Advertising*, **66**, Winter.

Baker, M.J. (1983a) *Marketing, Theory and Practice*. London: Macmillan.

Baker, M.J. (1983b) *Market Development*. Harmondsworth: Penguin.

Baker, M.J. (1991) *Research for Marketing*. London: Macmillan.

Baker, M.J. (1992) *Marketing Strategy and Management*, 2nd edn. Basingstoke: Macmillan.

Baker, M.J. (1993) *The Marketing Book*. Oxford: Butterworth-Heinemann.

Baker, M.J. (1996) *Marketing: An Introductory Text*, 6th edn. Basingstoke: Macmillan.

Baker, M.J. and Hart, S.J. (1989) *Marketing and Competitive Success*. London: Philip Allan.

Baker, M.J. and Parkinson, S.T. (1978) TI Superform's academic launch. *Marketing*, October.

Becker, S. and Whistler, T.L. (1967) The innovative organisation: a selective view of current theory and research. *Journal of Business*, **40** (4): 462–9.

Bentley, K. (1990) A discussion of the link between one organisation's style and structure and its connection with its market. *Journal of Product Innovation Management*, **7** (1): 19–34.

Berenson, C. (1963) Pruning the product line. *Business Horizons*, **6**, Summer: 63–70.

Berenson, C. (1967) The purchasing executives' adaptation to the product life cycle. *Journal of Purchasing*, **3**, May.

Biemans, W.G. (1992) *Managing Innovation within Networks*. London: Routledge.

Bonaccorsi, A. and Lipparini, A. (1994) Strategic partnerships in new product development: an Italian case study. *Journal of Product Innovation Management*, **11** (2): 134–45.

Bonnet, D.C.L. (1986) Nature of the R&D/marketing co-operation in the design of technologically advanced new industrial products. *R&D Management*, **16** (2).

Booz, Allen and Hamilton (1968) *Management of New Products*. New York: Booz, Allen and Hamilton.

Booz, Allen and Hamilton (1982) *New Products Management for the 1980s*. New York: Booz, Allen and Hamilton.

Boston Consulting Group (1968) *Perspectives on Experience*. Boston, MA: Boston Consulting Group, Inc.

Brand, G.T. (1972) *The Industrial Buying Decision*. London: Cassell Associated Business Programmes.

Brockoff, K. and Chakaborti, A.K. (1988) R&D/marketing linkage and innovation strategy: some West German experience. *IEEE Transactions on Engineering Management*, **35** (3) (August): 167–74.

Brown, S.L. and Eisenhardt, K.M. (1995) Product development: past research, present findings and future directions. *Academy of Management Review*, **2**: 343–78.

Bruce, M. (1992) The black box of design management. Marketing Working Paper Series, UMIST, Manchester.

Bucklin, L.P. (1963) Retail strategy and the classification of consumer goods. *Journal of Marketing*, **23** (January): 50–5.

Bucklin, L.P. (1968) The locus of channel control. *Proceedings of the Fall 1968 Conference of the AMA*, 142–7.

Bucklin, L.P. (1973) A theory of channel control. *Journal of Marketing*, **37** (January): 39–47.

Buckner, H. (1967) *How British Industry Buys*. London: Hutchinson.

Burns, T. and Stalker, G.M. (1961) *The Management of Innovation*. London: Tavistock.

Buzzell, R.D. (1966) Competitive behavior and product life cycles *Proceedings of the 1966 World Congress*, Chicago: American Marketing Association, p. 50.

Buzzell, R.D. and Gale, B.T. (1987) *The PIMS Principles: Linking Strategy to Performance*. London: Collier Macmillan.

Carter, C.F. and Williams, B.R. (1959) The characteristics of technically progressive firms. *Journal of Industrial Economics*, March.

Clausing, D.P. (1986) *QFD Phase II: Parts Deployment*. Dearborn, MI: American Supplier Institute.

Club of Rome (1972) *The Limits to Growth*.

Cook, L.G. and Morrison, W.A. (1961) *The Origins of Innovation*. Report 61-GP-214, June, General Electric Co., Research Information Section, New York.

Cook, V. and Polli, R. (1969) Validity of the product life cycle. *Journal of Business of the University of Chicago*, **42**, October.

Cooper, R.G. (1979) The dimensions of industrial new product success and failure. *Journal of Marketing*, **43** (1): 93–103.

Cooper, R.G. (1980) How to identify potential new product winners. *Research Management*, September.

Cooper, R.G. (1982) New product success in industrial firms. *Industrial Marketing Management*, **11** (3): 215–23.

Cooper, R.G. (1984) The strategy performance link in product innovation. *R&D Management*, **14** (4): 247–67.

Cooper, R.G. (1985) Selecting winning new product projects: using the NewProd system. *Journal of Product Innovation Management*, **2** (1): 34–44.

Cooper, R.G. (1987) Defining the new product strategy. *IEEE Transactions on Engineering Management*, **EM-34** (3): 184–93.

Cooper, R.G. (1988) The new product process: a decision guide for management. *Journal of Marketing Management*, **3** (3): 238–55.

Cooper, R.G. (1992) The NewProd system: the industry experience. *Journal of Product Innovation Management*, **9**: 113–27.

Cooper, R.G. (1993) *Winning at New Products: Accelerating the Process from Idea to Launch*. Cambridge, MA: Addison-Wesley.

Cooper, R.G. and de Brentani, U. (1984) Criteria for screening new industrial products. *Industrial Marketing Management*.

Cooper, R.G. and Kleinschmidt, E.J. (1986) An investigation into the new product development process: steps, deficiencies and impact. *Journal of Product Innovation Management*, **3** (1): 71–85.

Cooper, R.G. and Kleinschmidt, E.J. (1987) New products: what separates winners from losers? *Journal of Product Innovation Management*, **4**.

Cooper, R.G. and Kleinschmidt, E.J. (1990) New product success factors: a comparison of 'kills' versus successes and failures. *R&D Management*, **20** (1): 169–84.

Cooper, R.G. and Kleinschmidt, E.J. (1991) The impact of product innovativeness on performance. *Journal of Product Innovation Management*, **8** (4): 240–51.

Cooper, R.G. and Kleinschmidt, E.J. (1994) Determinants of timeliness in product development. *Journal of Product Innovation Management*, **11** (5): 381–96.

Copeland, M.T. (1923) Relation of consumers' buying habits to marketing methods. *Harvard Business Review*, **1** (April): 282–9.

Cordero, R. (1991) Managing for speed to avoid product obsolescence: a survey of techniques. *Journal of Product Innovation Management*, **8** (4): 283–94.

Corey, E.R. (1956) *The Development of Markets for New Materials*. Boston: Harvard University Press.

Cox, W. E. (1967) Product life cycles as marketing models. *Journal of Business*, **40** (4), October.

Craig, A. and Hart, S. (1992) Where to now in new product development research? *European Journal of Marketing*, **26** (11): 3–49.

Crawford, C.M. (1984) Protocol: a new tool for product innovation. *Journal of Product Innovation Management*, **2**: 85–91.

Crawford, C.M. (1994) *New Product Management*, 3rd edn. Homewood, IL: Irwin.

Cyert, R.M., Simon, H.A. and Trow, D.B. (1956) Observation of a business decision. *Journal of Business*: 237–48.

Czepiel, J.A. (1979) Communications networks and innovation in industrial communities. In Baker, M.J. (ed.), *Industrial Innovation*. London: Macmillan.

Darwent, C. (1992) The king of cookware. *Management Today*, December: 55–6.

Datamonitor (1994)

Davies, G.B. and Pearson, A.W. (1980) The application of some group problem-solving approaches to project selection in research and development. *IEEE Transactions on Engineering Management*, EM-27 (3).

Davis, J.S. (1988) New product success and failure: three case studies. *Industrial Marketing Management*, **17** (2) (May): 103–9.

Day, G.S. (1977) Diagnosing the product portfolio. *Journal of Marketing*, April.

Day, G.S. (1981) The product life cycle: analysis and applications issues. *Journal of Marketing*, **45** (Fall): 60–7.

de Brentani, U. (1986) Do firms need a custom-designed new product screening model? *Journal of Product Innovation Management*, **3** (2): 108–19.

de Brentani, U. (1989) Success and failure in new industrial services. *Journal of Product Innovation Management*, **6** (4): 239–58.

De Bruicker, F.S. and Summe, G.L. (1985) Make sure your customers keep coming back. *Harvard Business Review*, Jan–Feb.

DeLozier, M.W. (1976) *The Marketing Communications Process*. New York: McGraw-Hill.

de Meyer, A. (1985) The flow of technological innovation in an R&D department. *Research Policy*, **14**: 315–28.

Deschamps, J.-P. and Nayak, P.R. (1993) Lesson from product juggernauts. *Prism*, Second Quarter.

Dhalla, N.K. and Yuspeh, S. (1976) Forget the product life cycle. *Harvard Business Review*, Jan–Feb.

Dolan, R.J. (ed.) (1993) *Managing the New Product Development Process*. Reading, MA: Addison-Wesley.

Dougherty, D. (1992) A practice centred model of organisational renewal through product innovation. *Strategic Management Journal*, **13**: 77–92.

Doyle, P. (1976) The realities of the product life cycle. *Quarterly Review of Marketing*, Summer: 1–6.

Doyle, P. (1992a) Branding. In Baker, M.J. (ed.), *The Marketing Book*, 2nd edn, Chapter 18. Oxford: Butterworth-Heinemann.

Doyle, P. (1992b) What are the excellent companies? *Journal of Marketing Management*, **8** (2), April.

Doyle, P. (1995) Product life cycle management. In Baker, M.J. (ed.), *The Companion Encyclopedia of Marketing*, Chapter 28. London: Routledge.

Drucker, P. (1954) *The Practice of Management*. New York: Harper and Row.

Drucker, P. (1963) Managing for business effectiveness. *Harvard Business Review*, **42**, May–June.

Dumaine, B. (1991) Earning more by moving faster. *Fortune*, 7 (October): 89–90.

Dwyer, L. and Mellor, R. (1990) Organisational environment, new product process activities and project outcomes. *Journal of Product Innovation Management*, **8** (1): 39–48.

Easingwood, C. and Beard, C. (1989) High technology launch strategies in the UK. *Marketing Management*, **18**: 125–38.

Eckels, R.W. (1970) Product line deletion and simplification. *Business Horizons*, October.

Engel, J.F., Kollat, D.T. and Blackwell, R.D. (1968) *Consumer Behaviour*, Chapter 3. New York: Holt, Rinehart and Winston.

Evans, C. (1979) *The Mighty Micro*. London: Victor Gollancz.

Evans, J.R. and Berman, B. (1982) *Marketing*. New York: Macmillan.

Evans, S. (1990) Implementation framework for integrated design teams. *Journal of Engineering Design*, **1** (4): 355–63.

Farnham, A. (1994) How to nurture creative sparks. *Fortune*, 10 January.

Feldman, L.P. and Page, A.L. (1984) Principles versus practice in product planning. *Journal of Product Innovation*.

Foxall, G. (1988) The theory and practice of user-initiated innovation. *Journal of Marketing Management*, **4** (2): 230–48.

Gabb, A. (1991) How the discovery took off. *Management Today*, October: 64–8.

Gabor, A. and Granger, C.W.J. (1973) A systematic approach to effective pricing. In Rodger, L.W., *Marketing Concept and Strategies in the Next Decade*. New York: John Wiley.

Galbraith, J.K. (1958) *The Affluent Society*. Harmondsworth: Penguin.

Galbraith, J.K. (1974) *The New Industrial State*. London: Penguin.

Gauthier, J.P. (1985) The product elimination process in French manufacturing companies: a theoretical and empirical analysis. Unpublished MSc thesis, University of Strathclyde.

Gehani, R.R. (1992) Concurrent product development for fast-track corporations. *Long Range Planning*, **25** (6): 40–7.

Geshka, H. (1983) Creativity techniques in product planning and development: a view from West Germany. *R&D Management*, **13** (3): 169–83.

Goltz, G.E. (1986) A guide to development. *R&D Management*, **16**: 243–9.

Green, P.E. (1984) Hybrid models for conjoint analysis: an expository review. *Journal of Marketing Research*, **21** (May): 155–69.

Griffin, A. (1989) Functionally integrated new product development. Unpublished PhD thesis, Sloan School of Management, MIT, Cambridge, MA.

Griffin, A. (1992) Evaluating development processes: QFD as an example. *Journal of Product Innovation Management*, **9** (3).

Griffin, A. (1993) Metrics for measuring product development cycle time. *Journal of Product Innovation Management*, **10** (2): 112–25.

Griffin, A. and Hauser, J.R.L. (1993) The voice of the customer. *Marketing Science*, **12** (1): 1–27.

Gupta, A.K. and Wilemon, D. (1988) The credibility/co-operation connection at the R&D/marketing interface. *Journal of Product Innovation Management*, **5** (1): 20–31.

Gupta, A.K. and Wilemon, D. (1990) Improving R&D/Marketing relations: R&D's perspective. *R&D Management*, **20** (4): 277–90.

Gupta, A.K., Raj, S.P. and Wilemon, D. (1986) A model for studying R&D/Marketing interface in the product innovation process. *Journal of Marketing*, April: 7–17.

Haley, R.L. and Gatty, R. (1971) The trouble with concept testing. *Journal of Market Research*, **8** (May): 230–2.

Hamelman, H.P. and Mazze, E.M. (1972) Improving product abandonment decisions. *Journal of Marketing*, **36**, April.

Harris, J, Shaw, R and Summers, W (1984) 'The strategic management of technology in Lam, R. (ed.) *Competitive Strategic Management*, Englewood Cliffs, NJ: Prentice Hall, pp. 530–55.

Hart, S.J. (1987) An exploratory investigation of the product elimination decision in British manufacturing industry. Unpublished PhD thesis, University of Strathclyde.

Hart, S.J. (1988) The causes of product deletion in British manufacturing companies. *Journal of Marketing Management*, **3** (3).

Hart, S.J. (1990) The evaluation of product deletion candidates. Working Paper 90/6, Department of Marketing, University of Strathclyde.

Hart, S.J. (1991) The managerial setting of the product deletion decision. *Irish Marketing Review*, **5** (3): 41–54.

Hart, S.J. and Service, L.M. (1988) The effects of managerial attitudes to design on company performance. *Journal of Marketing Management*, **4** (2): 217–29.

Hart, S.J., Tzokas, N. and Saren, M.A.J. (1997) The effectiveness of marketing information in enhancing new product success rates. *Academy of Marketing Conference*, Manchester, July: 431–54.

Hastorf, A.H. and Cantril, H. (1954) They saw a game: a case history. *Journal of Abnormal and Social Psychology*, **49**: 129–34.

Hauser, G.L., Urban, J.R. and Roberts, J.H. (1990) Forecasting of new automobiles. *Management Science*, **8**: 401–21.

Hauser, J.R. and Clausing, D.P. (1988) The house of quality. *Harvard Business Review*, **66** (3), May–June: 63–73.

Hayes, R.H. and Abernathy, W.J. (1980) Managing our way to economic decline. *Harvard Business Review*, July–August.

Hegarty, H.W. and Hoffman, R.C. (1990) Product/market innovations: a study of top management involvement among four cultures. *Journal of Product Innovation Management*, 7 (2): 186–99.

Henderson, B. (1968) *Perspectives on Experience*. Boston Consulting Group, Boston, MA.

Henderson, B. (1983) The anatomy of competition. *Journal of Marketing*, **47** (2), Spring.

Henderson, B. (1989) The origin of strategy. *Harvard Business Review*, Nov–Dec.

Hewitt, M. (1994) A car by any other name. *Marketing*, 13 October: 15.

Hill, P. (1988) The market research contribution to new product failure and success. *Journal of Marketing Management*, **3** (3): 269–77.

Hill, R. and Hillier, T. (1977) *Organizational Buying Behaviour*. London: Macmillan.

Hirschmann, W.B. (1964) Profit from the learning curve. *Harvard Business Review*, Jan–Feb: 125–39.

Inwood, D. and Hammond, J. (1993) *Product Development: an Integrated Approach*. London: Kogan Page.

Jamieson, L.F. and Bass, F.M. (1989) Adjusting stated intentions measures to predict the trial purchase of new products: a comparison of methods. *Journal of Marketing Research*, **26** (August): 336–46.

Johne, F.A. (1992) How to pick a winning product. *Management Today*, February.

Johne, F.A. and Snelson, P.A. (1988) Success factors in product innovation: a selective review of the literature. *Journal of Product Innovation Management*, **5** (2): 114–28.

Johne, F.A. and Snelson, P.A. (1989) Product development approaches in established firms. *Industrial Marketing Management*, **18** (2): 113–24.

Johnson, S.C. and Jones, C. (1957) How to organize for new products. *Harvard Business Review*, **35** (3), May–June: 49–62.

Kalwari, M.U. and Silk, A.J. (1982) On the reliability and predictive validity of purchase intention measures. *Marketing Science*, **1** (Summer): 243–86.

Kheir El Din, A. (1991) Unpublished doctoral dissertation, University of Strathclyde.

King, R. (1987) *Better Designs in Half the Time: Implementing Quality Function Deployment (QFD) in America*, Lawrence, MA: GOAL.

Klein, A.R. (1990) Organisational barriers to creativity … and how to knock them down. *Journal of Consumer Marketing*, **7** (1): 65–6.

Kline, C.H. (1955) The strategy of product policy. *Harvard Business Review*, July–August: 91–100.

Kortge, D.G. and Okonkwo, P.A. (1989) Simultaneous new product development: reducing the new product failure rate. *Industrial Marketing Management*, **18**: 301–6.

Kotler, P. (1965) Phasing out weak products. *Harvard Business Review*, **43**, March–April.

Kotler, P. (1967) *Marketing Management, Analysis, Planning and Control*. Englewood Cliffs, NJ: Prentice-Hall.

Kotler, P. (1980) *Principles of Marketing*. Englewood Cliffs, NJ: Prentice-Hall.

Kotler, P. (1989) *Marketing Management: Analysis, Planning, Implementation and Control*, 6th edn (8th edn, 1994). Englewood Cliffs, NJ: Prentice-Hall.

Kruse and Berry (1997), Management Today, April, pp. 28–32.

Kucsmarski, T.D. (1992) Screening potential new products. *Planning Review*, July–August: 24–31.

Landor Associates (1990) *The Landor Image Power Survey*. London: Landor Associates.

Larson, C. (1988) Team tactics can cut development costs. *Journal of Business Strategy*, **9** (5): 22–5.

Larson, E.W. and Gobeli, D.H. (1989) Significance of project management structure on development success. *IEEE Transactions on Engineering Management*, **EM-36** (2).

Lavidge, R.J. and Steiner, G.A. (1961) A model for predictive measurements of advertising effectiveness. *Journal of Marketing*, **25**, October.

Lawrence, P.R. and Lorsch, J.W. (1967) *Organization and Environment*. Homewood, IL: Irwin,

Lazarsfeld, P.F. (1944) *The People's Choice*. Sloan and Pearce.

Lele, M.M. (1992) *Creating Strategic Leverage*. Chichester: John Wiley.

Levitt, T. (1960) Marketing myopia. *Harvard Business Review*, July–August.

Levitt, T. (1965) Exploit the product life cycle. *Harvard Business Review*, Nov–Dec.

Levitt, T. (1976a) The industrialization of service. *Harvard Business Review*, Sept–Oct.

Levitt, T. (1976b) *The Marketing Imagination*. New York: Free Press.

Levitt, T. (1980) Marketing success through differentiation – of anything. *Harvard Business Review*, Jan–Feb.

Levitt, T. (1983) *The Marketing Imagination*. London: Collier Macmillan.

Link, P.L. (1987) Keys to new product success and failure. *Industrial Marketing Management*, **16**: 109–18.

Little, B. (1970) Characterising the new product for better evaluation and planning. Working Paper No. 21, University of Western Ontario, London, Ontario, Canada, July.

Lowe, A. and Hunter, R.B. (1991) The role of design and marketing management in the culture of innovation. *European Marketing Academy Conference Proceedings*.

Lucas, G. and Bush, A.J. (1988) The marketing/R&D interface: do personality factors have an impact? *Journal of Product Innovation Management*, **5** (4): 257–68.

MacKenzie, G.F. (1971) On marketing's missing link – the product life cycle concept. *Industrial Marketing*, April.

Mahajan, V. and Wind, J. (1992) New product models: practice, shortcomings and desired improvements. *Journal of Product Innovation Management*, **9** (2): 128–39.

Maidique, M.A. and Zirger, B.J. (1984) A study of success and failure in product innovation: the case of the US electronics industry. *IEEE Transactions on Engineering Management*, **EM-31** (4): 192–203.

Maidique, M.A. and Zirger, B.J. (1985) The new product learning cycle. Research Report Series, Innovation and Entrepreneurship Institute, School of Business Administration, University of Miami, Coral Gables, FL, 407–31.

Majaro, S. (1992) *Managing Ideas for Profit: the Creative Gap*. London and New York: McGraw-Hill.

Mansfield, E. (1968) *The Economics of Technological Change*. New York: W.W. Norton.

Maslow, A. (1943) A theory of human motivation. *Psychological Review*, **50**.

Mathur, S. (1992) Talking straight about competitive strategy. *Journal of Marketing Management*, **8**.

McDonough, E.F. III (1986) Matching management control systems to product strategies. *R&D Management*, **16** (2): 141–9.

McDonough, E.F. III and Leifer, R.P. (1986) Effective control of new product projects: the integration of organization, culture and project leadership. *Journal of Product Innovation Management*, **3** (3): 149–57.

McGuinness, N. (1990) New product idea activities in large technology based firms. *Journal of Product Innovation Management*, 7(2): 173.

Meadows, D. *et al.* (1972) *The Limits to Growth*. London: Earth Island.

Mintzberg, H., Raisinghani, D. and Theoret, A. (1976) The structure of 'unstructured' decision processes. *Administrative Science Quarterly*, **21** (June): 246–75.

Moenaert, R.K. and Souder, W.E. (1990) An information transfer model for integrating marketing and R&D personnel in new product development projects. *Journal of Product Innovation Management*, 7 (2): 91–107.

Moenaert, R.K., Souder, W.E., de Meyer, A. and Deschoolmeester, D. (1994) R&D/marketing integration mechanisms, communication flows and innovation success. *Journal of Product Innovation Management*, **11** (1): 31–45.

Moore, W.L. (1982) Concept testing. *Journal of Business Research*, **10**: 279–94.

Moore, W.L. and Pessemier, E.A. (1993) *Product Planning and Management*. New York: McGraw-Hill.

More, R.A. (1984) Perspective: barriers to innovation: intraorganisational dislocations. *Journal of Product Innovation Management*, **2** (3): 205.

Morgan, G. (1983) *Beyond Method Strategies for Social Research*. Beverly Hills, CA, and London: Sage.

Morgan, G. (1986) *Images of Organization*. Beverly Hills, CA: Sage.

Morita, A., Reingold, H. and Shimomura, I. (1987) *Made in Japan*. London: Penguin.

Morrison, D. (1979) Purchase intentions and purchase behaviour. *Journal of Marketing*, Spring: 65–74.

Murrin, T.J. (1990) Design for manufacturing: an imperative for U.S. global competitiveness. *Design Management Journal*, **1** (2): 37–41.

Myers, S. and Marquis, D.G. (1969) Successful industrial innovations: a study of factors underlying innovation in selected firms. National Science Foundation, Washington, DC.

National Industrial Conference Board (1964) Why new products fail. *The Conference Board Record*, NICB, New York.

Nauman, E. and Shannon, P. (1992) What is customer-driven marketing? *Business Horizons*, Nov–Dec: 44–52.

Nicholas (1994) Guinness plans world NPD push. *Marketing*, 13 October: 4.

Olsen, Walker, and Ruekert (1995) Organizing for effective new product development: the moderating influence of product innovativeness. *Journal of Marketing*, **59**: 48–62.

Ortt, R.J. and Schoormans, P.L. (1993) Consumer research in the development process of a major innovation. *Consumer Research and Innovation*, **35** (4): 375–89.

Osborne, A.F. (1963) *Applied Imagination*, 3rd edn. New York: Charles Scribner's Sons,

Packard, V. (1957) *Hidden Persuaders*. London, Longmans Green.

Packard, V. (1961) *The Waste Makers*. London: Longmans Green.

Page, A.L. (1993) Assessing new product development practices and performance: establishing crucial norms. *Journal of Product Innovation Management*, **10** (4): 273–90.

Page, A.L. and Rosenbaum, H.F. (1992) Developing an effective concept testing program for consumer durables. *Journal of Product Innovation Management*, **9** (4): 267–77.

Pascale, R.T. (1993) The perspectives on strategy: the real story behind Honda's success. *California Management Review*, **26** (3): 47–72.

Pavia, T. (1991) New product development in high tech firms. *Journal of Product Innovation Management*, **8** (1).

Penny, J.C., Hunt, I.M. and Twyman, W.A. (1972) Product testing methodology in relation to marketing problems – a review. *Journal of the Market Research Society*, **4**: 50–63.

Peters, T. (1987) *Thriving on Chaos*. London: Macmillan.

Peters, T. and Waterman, R. (1982) *In Search of Excellence*. New York: Harper and Row.

Pinto, M.B. and Pinto, J.K. (1990) Project team communication and cross-functional co-operation in New Program Development. *Journal of Product Innovation Management*, 7 (4): 200–12.

Polli, R. and Cook, V. (1969) Validity of the product life cycle. *Journal of Business*, **42** (4) (October): 385–400.

Porter, M. (1979) How competitive forces shape strategy. *Harvard Business Review*, March–April: 141.

Porter, M. (1980) *Competitive Strategy: Techniques for Analyzing Industries and Competitors*. New York: Free Press.

Porter, M. (1985) *Competitive Advantage*. New York: Free Press.

Porter, M. (1990) *The Competitive Advantage of Nations*. London: Macmillan.

Prince, G.M. (1970) *The Practice of Creativity: a Manual for Group Problem Solving*. London: Harper and Row.

Rabino, S. and Moore, T.E. (1989) Managing new product announcements in the computer industry. *Industrial Marketing Management*, **18** (1): 35–43.

Raiffa, H. (1968) *Decision Analysis*. Reading, MA: Addison-Wesley.

Ramanujam, V. and Mensch, G.O. (1985) Improving the strategy-innovation link. *Journal of Product Innovation Management*, **2** (4): 213–23.

Rapaport, C. (1984) Breathing life into new products. *Financial Times*.

Roberts, E.B. and Fusfield, A.R. (1991) Staffing the innovative technology based organisation. *Sloan Management Review*, **22** (Spring): 19–34.

Roberts, R.W. and Burke, J.E. (1974) Six new products – what made them successful? *Research Management*, May: 21–4.

Robertson, T.S. (1970) *Consumer Behavior*. Glenview, IL: Scott Foresman.

Robertson, T.S. (1971) *Innovative Behavior and Communications*. New York: Holt, Rinehart and Winston.

Robinson, P.J., Faris, C.W. and Wind, Y. (1967) *Industrial Buying and Creative Marketing*. Boston, MA: Allyn & Bacon, and the Marketing Science Institute.

Rochford, L. and Rudelius, W. (1992) How involving more functional areas within a firm affects the new product process. *Journal of Product Innovation Management*, **9** (4): 287–99.

Rodger, L.W. (1971) *Marketing in a Competitive Economy*, 3rd edn. London: Cassell.

Rogers, E.M. (1962) *Diffusion of Innovations* (3rd edn 1983, 4th edn 1995). New York: Free Press.

Rogers, E.M. (1983) *Communications of Innovation*.

Rogers, E.M. and Shoemaker, F.M. (1971) *The Communications of Innovation*.

Ronkainen, I.A. (1985) Criteria changes across product development stages. *Industrial Marketing Management*, **14**: 171–8.

Rothe, J.T. (1971) The product elimination decision. *MSU Business Topics*, **18** (Autumn): 45–52.

Rothwell, R. (1977) The characteristics of successful innovators and technically progressive firms (with some comments on innovation research). *R&D Management*, 7 (3): 191–206.

Rothwell, R. *et al.* (1972) Factors for success in industrial innovations. Project SAPPHO – A comparative study of success and failure in industrial innovation, Science Policy Research Unit, University of Sussex, Brighton, UK.

Rothwell, R. *et al.* (1974) SAPPHO updated – Project SAPPHO phase II. *Research Policy*, **3**: 258–79.

Rothwell, R. and Gardiner, P. (1988) Re-innovation and robust designs. *Journal of Marketing Management*, **3** (3): 373.

Rothwell, R. and Whiston, T.G. (1990) Design, innovation and corporate integration. *R&D Management*, **20** (3).

Rothwell, R., Gardiner, P. and Schott, K. (1983) *Design and the Economy*. London: The Design Council.

Rubenstein, A.H., Chakrabarti, A.K., O'Keefe, R.D., Souder, W.E. and Young, H.C. (1976) Factors influencing innovation success at the project level. *Research Management*, **3**: 15–20.

Salerno, F. (1983) Processus et compartements d'abandon de produit: analyse et implications. Thèse de Doctorat *D'Art et Science de Gestian*, Université de Lille, March.

Saren, M.A. (1984) A classification and review of models of the intra-firm innovation process. *R&D Management*, **14** (1): 11–24.

Saren, M.A.J. and Tzokas, N. (1994) *Proceedings of the Annual Conference of the European Marketing Academy*.

Saunders, J. and Jobber, D. (1988) An exploratory study of the management of product replacement. *Journal of Marketing Management*, **3** (3): 344–51.

Saunders, J. and Jobber, D. (1994) Product replacement: strategies for simultaneous product deletion and launch. *Journal of Product Innovation Management*, **11**: 437.

Scheuing, E.E. (1974) *New Product Management*. Hinsdale, IL: Dryden Press.

Schlaifer, R. (1969) *Analysis of Decisions under Uncertainty*. New York: McGraw-Hill.

Schlicksupp, H. (1977) Idea generation for industrial firms – report on an international investigation. *R&D Management*, **8**: ????.

Schnaars, S.P. (1989) Where forecasters go wrong. *Across the Board*, December: 38–45.

Schnaars, S.P. (1991) *Marketing Strategy*. New York: Free Press.

Schofield, M. and Arnold, D. (1988) Strategies for mature businesses. *Long Range Planning*, **21** (5).

Schon, D.A. (1967) *Technology and Change*. Oxford: Pergamon.

Schoormans, J.P.L., Ortt, R.J. and de Bont, C.J.P.M. (1995) Enhancing concept test validity by using expert consumers. *Journal of Product Innovation Management*, **12**: 153–62.

Schramm, W. (1955) *The Process and Effects of Mass Communications*. Urbana, IL: University of Illinois Press.

Schumpeter, J.A. (1934) *Theory of Economic Development*. Harvard, MA: Harvard Economic Studies Series.

Senge, P. (1990) *The Fifth Discipline*. New York: Doubleday.

Shannon, C. and Weaver, W. (1962) *The Mathematical Theory of Communication*. Urbana, IL: University of Illinois Press.

Shapiro, B.P. and Jackson, B.B. (1978) Industrial pricing to meet customer needs. *Harvard Business Review*, Nov–Dec.

Shell (1975) *The Directional Policy Matrix: a New Aid to Corporate Planning*. Shell International Chemical Co.

Shocker, A.D. and Hall, W.A. (1986) Premarket models: a critical evaluation. *Journal of Product Innovation Management*, **3** (2): 86–107.

Shocker, A.D., Gensch, D. and Simon, L. (1969) Toward the improvement of new product search and screening. *Proceedings of the Fall Conference, American Marketing Association*: 168–75.

Shostack, G.L. (1977) Breaking free from product marketing. *Journal of Marketing*, **41** (2): 73–80.

Shostack, G.L. (1982) How to design a service. *European Journal of Marketing*, **16** (1): 49–63.

Shostack, G.L. (1984) Designing services that deliver. *Harvard Business Review*, Jan–Feb: 133–9.

Smallwood, J.E. (1973) The product life cycle: a key to strategic market planning. *MSU Business Topics*, Winter: 35.

Smith, A. (1776) *The Wealth of Nations* (ed. Skinner, A., 1970). Harmondsworth: Pelican.

Souder, W.E. (1988) Managing relations between R&D and marketing in new product development projects. *Journal of Product Innovation Management*, **5** (1): 6–19.

Sowery, J.T. (1984) Idea generation, the sourcing of ideas for new products in consumer markets. Unpublished PhD thesis, University of Strathclyde.

Sowery, J.T. (1987) *The Generation of Ideas for New Products*. London: Kogan Page.

Sowery, J.T. (1989) Idea generation: identifying the most useful techniques. *European Journal of Marketing*, **24** (5): 20–9.

Staudt, T.A. (1954) Program for product diversification. *Harvard Business Review*, **32** (6), Nov–Dec.

Stoll, H.W. (1986) Design for manufacture: an overview. *Applied Mechanics Review*, **39** (9): 1356–64.

Stone, M. (1976) *Product Planning*. London: Macmillan.

Strong, E.K. (1912) The effect of length of series upon recognition. *Psychological Review*, **19** (January): 44–7.

Strong, E.K. (1925) *The Psychology of Selling*. New York: McGraw-Hill.

Takeuchi, H. and Nonaka, I. (1986) The new new product development game. *Harvard Business Review*, Jan–Feb: 137–46.

Talley, W.J. (1964) Profiting from the declining product. *Business Horizons*, 7 (Spring): 14–18.

Taninecz, G. (1996) What went wrong? *Industry Week*, 16 December: 45–50.

Tauber, E.M. (1974) How market research discourages major innovations. *Business Horizons*, **17**: 22–6.

Taylor, A. (1993) Ford's $6 billion baby. *Fortune*, 28 June: 72–5.

Taylor, J.W., Houlahan, J.R. and Gabriel, A.C. (1975) The purchase intent question in New Product Development: a field test. *Journal of Marketing*, **39** (January): 90–2.

Tellis, G. (1981) An evolutionary approach to growth theory. *Journal of Marketing*, **45** (Fall): 125–32.

Thamhain, H.J. (1990) Managing technologically innovative team efforts towards new product success. *Journal of Product Innovation Management*, 7 (1): 5–18.

Thomas, M.J. (1994) Product development and management. In Baker, M.J. (ed.), *The Marketing Book*, 3rd edn. Oxford: Butterworth-Heinemann.

Trygg, L. (1992) Simultaneous engineering: a movement or an activity of the few. Paper presented at the EISAM Conference on International Product Development – New Approaches to Development and Engineering, Brussels, May.

Twedt, B. (1964) How important to marketing strategy is the 'heavy user'? *Journal of Marketing*, January.

Twiss, B. (ed.) (1987) *Managing Technological Innovation*, 3rd edn. London: Longman.

Tzokas, N. and Saren, M. (1991) Innovation diffusion: the emerging role of suppliers versus the traditional dominance of buyers. *Journal of Marketing Management*, **8** (1): 69–79.

Urban, G.L. and Hauser, J.H. (1993) *Design and Marketing of New Products*, 2nd edn. Englewood Cliffs, NJ: Prentice Hall.

Utterback, M. (1971) The process of technological innovation within the firm. *Academy of Management Journal*, March: 75–88.

UK Select Committee on Science and Technology (1995) *Innovation in Manufacturing Industry*. London, HMSO.

von Hippel, E. (1978) Successful industrial products from customer ideas. *Journal of Marketing*, January: 39–49.

von Hippel, E. (1979) A customer-active paradigm for industrial product idea generation. In Baker, M.J. (ed.), *Industrial Innovation*. London: Macmillan.

von Hippel, E. (1988) *The Sources of Innovation*. New York: Oxford University Press.

Voss, C.A. (1985) Determinants of success in the development of applications software. *Journal of Product Innovation Management*, **2** (2): 122–9.

Waddell, F. (1990) Effective brainstorming. *Manage*, 4–9.

Wasson, C.R. (1968) How predictable are fashion and other product life cycles? *Journal of Marketing*, **32**, July.

Wasson, C.R. (1974) *Dynamic Competitive Strategy and Product Life Cycles*. St Charles, IL: Challenge Books.

Webster, F.E. Jr (1992) The changing role of marketing in the corporation. *Journal of Marketing*, **56**: 1–17.

Weigand, R.E. (1962) How extensive the planning and development program? *Journal of Marketing*, **26**.

Weigand, R.E. (1968) Why studying the purchasing agent is not enough. *Journal of Marketing*, **32**, January.

Weller, D.G. (1969) Run-out strategy – profits from the failing product. *Marketing Forum*, Nov–Dec.

Wensley, R. (1981) Strategic marketing: betas, boxes or basics. *Journal of Marketing*.

Wheelwright, S.C. and Clark, K.B. (1992) Competing through development capability in a manufacturing based organisation. *Business Horizons*, July–August: 29–43.

Wheelwright, S. and Madrikatis, S. (1985) *Forecasting Methods for Management*. New York: John Wiley.

Wind, J. and Mahajan, V. (1987) Marketing hype: a new perspective for new product research and introduction. *Journal of Product Innovation Management*, **4** (1): 43–9.

Willigan, G.E. (1992) Harvard Business Review, July–Aug: 91–101.

Wind, Y.J. (1982) *Product Policy: Concepts, Methods and Strategy*. Reading, MA: Addison-Wesley.

Winzar, H. (1992) Product classifications and marketing strategy. *Journal of Marketing Management*, **8**: 259–68.

Wittink, D.R. and Cattin, P. (1991) Commercial use of conjoint analysis: an update. *Journal of Marketing*, **53** (July): 91–6.

Wittink, D.R., Vriens, M. and Burhenne, W. (1994) Commercial use of conjoint analysis in Europe: results and critical reflection. *International Journal of Research in Marketing*, **11**: 41–52.

Wong, V., Saunders, J. and Doyle, P. (1992) A comparative study of British, US and Japanese marketing strategies. *Journal of International Business Studies*, October.

Wong, Y. (1964) Critical path analysis for new product planning. *Journal of Marketing*, October.

Wood, L. (1990) The end of the product life cycle. *Journal of Marketing Management*, **6** (2), Autumn.

Workman, J.P. (1993) Marketing's limited role in new product development in one computer system firm. *Journal of Marketing Research*, **30** (November): 405–21.

Zwicky, F. (1969) *Discovery Invention, Research through Morphological Approach*. New York: Mac-Millan.

Index

Note: Page reference in *italics* refer to Figures; those in **bold** refer to Tables

Resources
Newspapers.
Nexis UK

Discover for
journal articles

1. Stationery